Course   **BUS 204**

STONEHILL COLLEGE

BUSINESS ADMINISTRATION

http://create.mheducation.com

ISBN-10: 1308606648   ISBN-13: 9781308606644

Contents

Credits

CHAPTER 1

Managerial Accounting: An Overview

Managerial Accounting: It's More Than Just Crunching Numbers

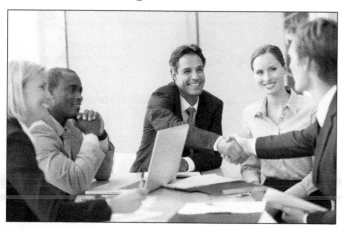

"Creating value through values" is the credo of today's management accountant. It means that management accountants should maintain an unwavering commitment to ethical values while using their knowledge and skills to influence decisions that create value for organizational stakeholders. These skills include managing risks and implementing strategy through planning, budgeting and forecasting, and decision support. Management accountants are strategic business partners who understand the financial and operational sides of the business. They not only report and analyze financial measures, but also nonfinancial measures of process performance and corporate social performance. Think of these responsibilities as profits (financial statements), process (customer focus and satisfaction), people (employee learning and satisfaction), and planet (environmental stewardship). ■

Source: Conversation with Jeff Thomson, president and CEO of the Institute of Management Accountants.

2

Chapter 1

This chapter explains why managerial accounting is important to the future careers of all business students. It begins by answering two questions: (1) What is managerial accounting? and (2) Why does managerial accounting matter to your career? It concludes by discussing six topics—ethics, strategic management, enterprise risk management, corporate social responsibility, process management, and leadership—that define the business context for applying the quantitative aspects of managerial accounting.

What Is Managerial Accounting?

Many students enrolled in this course will have recently completed an introductory *financial accounting* course. **Financial accounting** is concerned with reporting financial information to external parties, such as stockholders, creditors, and regulators. **Managerial accounting** is concerned with providing information to managers for use within the organization. Exhibit 1–1 summarizes seven key differences between financial and managerial accounting. It recognizes that the fundamental difference between

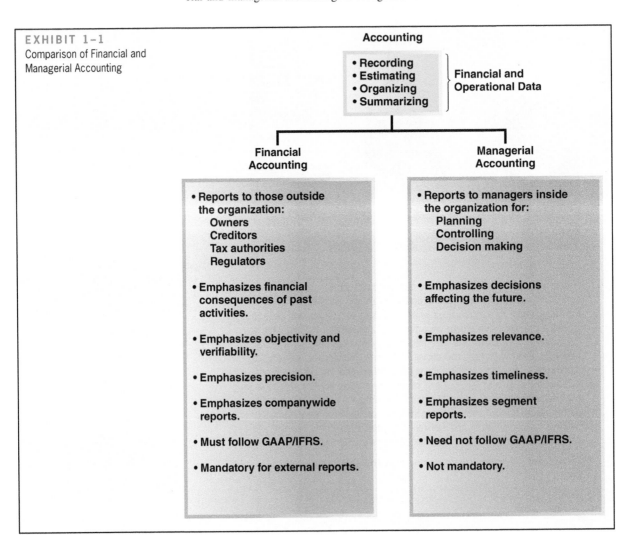

EXHIBIT 1–1
Comparison of Financial and Managerial Accounting

Accounting

- **Recording**
- **Estimating**
- **Organizing**
- **Summarizing**

Financial and Operational Data

Financial Accounting

- Reports to those outside the organization:
  Owners
  Creditors
  Tax authorities
  Regulators

- Emphasizes financial consequences of past activities.

- Emphasizes objectivity and verifiability.

- Emphasizes precision.

- Emphasizes companywide reports.

- Must follow GAAP/IFRS.

- Mandatory for external reports.

Managerial Accounting

- Reports to managers inside the organization for:
  Planning
  Controlling
  Decision making

- Emphasizes decisions affecting the future.

- Emphasizes relevance.

- Emphasizes timeliness.

- Emphasizes segment reports.

- Need not follow GAAP/IFRS.

- Not mandatory.

financial and managerial accounting is that financial accounting serves the needs of those *outside* the organization, whereas managerial accounting serves the needs of managers employed *inside* the organization. Because of this fundamental difference in users, financial accounting emphasizes the financial consequences of past activities, objectivity and verifiability, precision, and companywide performance, whereas managerial accounting emphasizes decisions affecting the future, relevance, timeliness, and *segment* performance. A **segment** is a part or activity of an organization about which managers would like cost, revenue, or profit data. Examples of business segments include product lines, customer groups (segmented by age, ethnicity, gender, volume of purchases, etc.), geographic territories, divisions, plants, and departments. Finally, financial accounting is mandatory for external reports and it needs to comply with rules, such as generally accepted accounting principles (GAAP) and international financial reporting standards (IFRS), whereas managerial accounting is not mandatory and it does not need to comply with externally imposed rules.

As mentioned in Exhibit 1–1, managerial accounting helps managers perform three vital activities—*planning, controlling,* and *decision making.* **Planning** involves establishing goals and specifying how to achieve them. **Controlling** involves gathering feedback to ensure that the plan is being properly executed or modified as circumstances change. **Decision making** involves selecting a course of action from competing alternatives. Now let's take a closer look at these three pillars of managerial accounting.

Planning

Assume that you work for Procter & Gamble (P&G) and that you are in charge of the company's campus recruiting for all undergraduate business majors. In this example, your planning process would begin by establishing a goal such as: our goal is to recruit the "best and brightest" college graduates. The next stage of the planning process would require specifying how to achieve this goal by answering numerous questions such as:

- How many students do we need to hire in total and from each major?
- What schools do we plan to include in our recruiting efforts?
- Which of our employees will be involved in each school's recruiting activities?
- When will we conduct our interviews?
- How will we compare students to one another to decide who will be extended job offers?
- What salary will we offer our new hires? Will the salaries differ by major?
- How much money can we spend on our recruiting efforts?

As you can see, there are many questions that need to be answered as part of the planning process. Plans are often accompanied by a *budget.* A **budget** is a detailed plan for the future that is usually expressed in formal quantitative terms. As the head of recruiting at P&G, your budget would include two key components. First, you would have to work with other senior managers inside the company to establish a budgeted amount of total salaries that can be offered to all new hires. Second, you would have to create a budget that quantifies how much you intend to spend on your campus recruiting activities.

Controlling

Once you established and started implementing P&G's recruiting plan, you would transition to the control process. This process would involve gathering, evaluating, and responding to feedback to ensure that this year's recruiting process meets expectations. It would also include evaluating the feedback in search of ways to run a more effective recruiting campaign next year. The control process would involve answering questions such as:

- Did we succeed in hiring the planned number of students within each major and at each school?
- Did we lose too many exceptional candidates to competitors?

4   Chapter 1

- Did each of our employees involved in the recruiting process perform satisfactorily?
- Is our method of comparing students to one another working?
- Did the on-campus and office interviews run smoothly?
- Did we stay within our budget in terms of total salary commitments to new hires?
- Did we stay within our budget regarding spending on recruiting activities?

As you can see, there are many questions that need to be answered as part of the control process. When answering these questions your goal would be to go beyond simple yes or no answers in search of the underlying reasons why performance exceeded or failed to meet expectations. Part of the control process includes preparing *performance reports*. A **performance report** compares budgeted data to actual data in an effort to identify and learn from excellent performance and to identify and eliminate sources of unsatisfactory performance. Performance reports can also be used as one of many inputs to help evaluate and reward employees.

Although this example focused on P&G's campus recruiting efforts, we could have described how planning enables FedEx to deliver packages across the globe overnight, or how it helped Apple develop and market the iPad. We could have discussed how the control process helps Pfizer, Eli Lilly, and Abbott Laboratories ensure that their pharmaceutical drugs are produced in conformance with rigorous quality standards, or how Kroger relies on the control process to keep its grocery shelves stocked. We also could have looked at planning and control failures such as BP's massive oil spill in the Gulf of Mexico. In short, all managers (and that probably includes you someday) perform planning and controlling activities.

Decision Making

Perhaps the most basic managerial skill is the ability to make intelligent, data-driven decisions. Broadly speaking, many of those decisions revolve around the following three questions. *What* should we be selling? *Who* should we be serving? *How* should we execute? Exhibit 1–2 provides examples of decisions pertaining to each of these three categories.

The left-hand column of Exhibit 1–2 suggests that every company must make decisions related to the products and services that it sells. For example, each year Procter & Gamble must decide how to allocate its marketing budget across 25 brands that each generates over $1 billion in sales as well as other brands that have promising growth potential. Mattel must decide what new toys to introduce to the market. Southwest Airlines must decide what ticket prices to establish for each of its

---

EXHIBIT 1–2
Examples of Decisions

What should we be selling?	Who should we be serving?	How should we execute?
What products and services should be the focus of our marketing efforts?	Who should be the focus of our marketing efforts?	How should we supply our parts and services?
What new products and services should we offer?	Who should we start serving?	How should we expand our capacity?
What prices should we charge for our products and services?	Who should pay price premiums or receive price discounts?	How should we reduce our capacity?
What products and services should we discontinue?	Who should we stop serving?	How should we improve our efficiency and effectiveness?

thousands of flights per day. General Motors must decide whether to discontinue certain models of automobiles.

The middle column of Exhibit 1–2 indicates that all companies must make decisions related to the customers that they serve. For example, Sears must decide how to allocate its marketing budget between products that tend to appeal to male versus female customers. FedEx must decide whether to expand its services into new markets across the globe. Hewlett-Packard must decide what price discounts to offer corporate clients that purchase large volumes of its products. A bank must decide whether to discontinue customers that may be unprofitable.

The right-hand column of Exhibit 1–2 shows that companies also make decisions related to how they execute. For example, Boeing must decide whether to rely on outside vendors such as Goodrich, Saab, and Rolls-Royce to manufacture many of the parts used to make its airplanes. Cintas must decide whether to expand its laundering and cleaning capacity in a given geographic region by adding square footage to an existing facility or by constructing an entirely new facility. In an economic downturn, a manufacturer might have to decide whether to eliminate one 8-hour shift at three plants or to close one plant. Finally, all companies have to decide among competing improvement opportunities. For example, a company may have to decide whether to implement a new software system, to upgrade a piece of equipment, or to provide extra training to its employees.

This portion of the chapter has explained that the three pillars of managerial accounting are planning, controlling, and decision making. This book helps prepare you to become an effective manager by explaining how to make intelligent data-driven decisions, how to create financial plans for the future, and how to continually make progress toward achieving goals by obtaining, evaluating, and responding to feedback.

Why Does Managerial Accounting Matter to Your Career?

Many students feel anxious about choosing a major because they are unsure if it will provide a fulfilling career. To reduce these anxieties, we recommend deemphasizing what you cannot control about the future; instead focusing on what you can control right now. More specifically, concentrate on answering the following question: What can you do now to prepare for success in an unknown future career? The best answer is to learn skills that will make it easier for you to adapt to an uncertain future. You need to become adaptable!

Whether you end up working in the United States or abroad, for a large corporation, a small entrepreneurial company, a nonprofit organization, or a governmental entity, you'll need to know how to plan for the future, how to make progress toward achieving goals, and how to make intelligent decisions. In other words, managerial accounting skills are useful in just about any career, organization, and industry. If you commit energy to this course, you'll be making a smart investment in your future—even though you cannot clearly envision it. Next, we will elaborate on this point by explaining how managerial accounting relates to the future careers of business majors and accounting majors.

Business Majors

Exhibit 1–3 provides examples of how planning, controlling, and decision making affect three majors other than accounting—marketing, supply chain management, and human resource management.

The left-hand column of Exhibit 1–3 describes some planning, controlling, and decision-making applications in the marketing profession. For example, marketing managers make planning decisions related to allocating advertising dollars across various communication mediums and to staffing new sales territories. From a control standpoint, they may closely track sales data to see if a budgeted price cut is generating an

EXHIBIT 1-3
Relating Managerial Accounting
to Three Business Majors

	Marketing	Supply Chain Management	Human Resource Management
Planning	How much should we budget for TV, print, and Internet advertising?	How many units should we plan to produce next period?	How much should we plan to spend for occupational safety training?
	How many salespeople should we plan to hire to serve a new territory?	How much should we budget for next period's utility expense?	How much should we plan to spend on employee recruitment advertising?
Controlling	Is the budgeted price cut increasing unit sales as expected?	Did we spend more or less than expected for the units we actually produced?	Is our employee retention rate exceeding our goals?
	Are we accumulating too much inventory during the holiday shopping season?	Are we achieving our goal of reducing the number of defective units produced?	Are we meeting our goal of completing timely performance appraisals?
Decision Making	Should we sell our services as one bundle or sell them separately?	Should we transfer production of a component part to an overseas supplier?	Should we hire an on-site medical staff to lower our health care costs?
	Should we sell directly to customers or use a distributor?	Should we redesign our manufacturing process to lower inventory levels?	Should we hire temporary workers or full-time employees?

anticipated increase in unit sales, or they may study inventory levels during the holiday shopping season so that they can adjust prices as needed to optimize sales. Marketing managers also make many important decisions such as whether to bundle services together and sell them for one price or to sell each service separately. They may also decide whether to sell products directly to the customer or to sell to a distributor, who then sells to the end consumer.

The middle column of Exhibit 1-3 states that supply chain managers have to plan how many units to produce to satisfy anticipated customer demand. They also need to budget for operating expenses such as utilities, supplies, and labor costs. In terms of control, they monitor actual spending relative to the budget, and closely watch operational measures such as the number of defects produced relative to the plan. Supply chain managers make numerous decisions, such as deciding whether to transfer production of a component part to an overseas supplier. They also decide whether to invest in redesigning a manufacturing process to reduce inventory levels.

The right-hand column of Exhibit 1-3 explains how human resource managers make a variety of planning decisions, such as budgeting how much to spend on occupational safety training and employee recruitment advertising. They monitor feedback related to numerous management concerns, such as employee retention rates and the timely completion of employee performance appraisals. They also help make many important decisions such as whether to hire on-site medical staff in an effort to lower health care costs, and whether to hire temporary workers or full-time employees in an uncertain economy.

For brevity, Exhibit 1–3 does not include all business majors, such as finance, management information systems, and economics. Can you explain how planning, controlling, and decision-making activities would relate to these majors?

Accounting Majors

Many accounting graduates begin their careers working for public accounting firms that provide a variety of valuable services for their clients. Some of these graduates will build successful and fulfilling careers in the public accounting industry; however, most will leave public accounting at some point to work in other organizations. In fact, the Institute of Management Accountants (IMA) estimates that more than 80% of professional accountants in the United States work in nonpublic accounting environments (www.imanet.org/about_ima/our_mission.aspx).

The public accounting profession has a strong financial accounting orientation. Its most important function is to protect investors and other external parties by assuring them that companies are reporting historical financial results that comply with applicable accounting rules. Managerial accountants also have strong financial accounting skills. For example, they play an important role in helping their organizations design and maintain financial reporting systems that generate reliable financial disclosures. However, the primary role of managerial accountants is to partner with their co-workers within the organization to improve performance.

Given the 80% figure mentioned above, if you are an accounting major there is a very high likelihood that your future will involve working for a nonpublic accounting employer. Your employer will expect you to have strong financial accounting skills, but more importantly, it will expect you to help improve organizational performance by applying the planning, controlling, and decision-making skills that are the foundation of managerial accounting.

A NETWORKING OPPORTUNITY

The Institute of Management Accountants (IMA) is a network of more than 60,000 accounting and finance professionals from over 120 countries. Every year the IMA hosts a student leadership conference that attracts 300 students from over 50 colleges and universities. Guest speakers at past conferences have discussed topics such as leadership, advice for a successful career, how to market yourself in a difficult economy, and excelling in today's multigenerational workforce. One student who attended the conference said, "I liked that I was able to interact with professionals who are in fields that could be potential career paths for me." For more information on this worthwhile networking opportunity, contact the IMA at the phone number and website shown below.

Source: Conversation with Jodi Ryan, the Institute of Management Accountants' Director, Education/Corporate Partnerships. (201) 474-1556 or visit its website at www.imanet.org.

Professional Certification—A Smart Investment If you plan to become an accounting major, the Certified Management Accountant (CMA) designation is a globally respected credential (sponsored by the IMA) that will increase your credibility, upward mobility, and compensation. Exhibit 1–4 summarizes the topics covered in the two-part CMA exam. For brevity, we are not going to define all the terms included in this exhibit. Its purpose is simply to emphasize that the CMA exam focuses on the planning, controlling, and decision-making skills that are critically important to nonpublic accounting employers. The CMA's internal management orientation is a complement to the highly respected Certified Public Accountant (CPA) exam that focuses on rule-based compliance—assurance standards, financial accounting standards, business law, and the tax code. Information about becoming a CMA is available on the IMA's website (www.imanet.org) or by calling 1-800-638-4427.

EXHIBIT 1–4
CMA Exam Content
Specifications

Part 1   *Financial Planning, Performance, and Control*
           Planning, budgeting, and forecasting
           Performance management
           Cost management
           Internal controls
           Professional ethics

Part 2   *Financial Decision Making*
           Financial statement analysis
           Corporate finance
           Decision analysis and risk management
           Investment decisions
           Professional ethics

IN BUSINESS

HOW'S THE PAY?

The Institute of Management Accountants has created the following table that allows individuals to estimate what their salary would be as a management accountant.

			Your Calculation
Start with this base amount		$75,807	$75,807
If you are top-level management	ADD	$28,000	
OR, if you are entry-level management	SUBTRACT	$25,995	
Number of years in the field ____	TIMES	$700	
If you have an advanced degree	ADD	$13,873	
If you hold the CMA	ADD	$11,126	
If you hold the CPA	ADD	$10,193	
Your estimated salary level			_____

For example, if you make it to top-level management in 10 years, have an advanced degree and a CMA, your estimated salary would be $135,806 [$75,807 + $28,000 + (10 × 700) + $13,873 + $11,126].

Source: Lee Schiffel, David L. Schroeder, and Kenneth A. Smith, "IMA 2011 Salary Survey," *Strategic Finance* June 2012, pp. 29–47.

Managerial Accounting: Beyond the Numbers

Exhibit 1–5 summarizes how each chapter of the book teaches measurement skills that managers use on the job every day. For example, Chapter 8 teaches you the measurement skills that managers use to answer the question—how should I create a financial plan for next year? Chapters 9 and 10 teach you the measurement skills that managers use to answer the question—how well am I performing relative to my plan? Chapter 7 teaches you measurement skills related to product, service, and customer profitability. However, it is vitally important that you also understand managerial accounting involves more than just "crunching numbers." To be successful, managers must complement their measurement skills with six business management perspectives that "go beyond the numbers" to enable intelligent planning, control, and decision making.

Chapter Number	The Key Question from a Manager's Perspective
Chapter 2	What cost classifications do I use for different management purposes?
Chapters 3 & 4	What is the value of our ending inventory and cost of goods sold for external reporting purposes?
Chapter 5	How will my profits change if I change my selling price, sales volume, or costs?
Chapter 6	How should the income statement be presented?
Chapter 7	How profitable is each of our products, services, and customers?
Chapter 8	How should I create a financial plan for next year?
Chapters 9 & 10	How well am I performing relative to my plan?
Chapter 11	What performance measures should we monitor to ensure that we achieve our strategic goals?
Chapter 12	How do I quantify the profit impact of pursuing one course of action versus another?
Chapter 13	How do I make long-term capital investment decisions?
Chapter 14	What cash inflows and outflows explain the change in our cash balance?
Chapter 15	How can we analyze our financial statements to better understand our performance?

EXHIBIT 1–5
Measurement Skills:
A Manager's Perspective

An Ethics Perspective

Ethical behavior is the lubricant that keeps the economy running. Without that lubricant, the economy would operate much less efficiently—less would be available to consumers, quality would be lower, and prices would be higher. In other words, without fundamental trust in the integrity of business, the economy would operate much less efficiently. Thus, for the good of everyone—including profit-making companies—it is vitally important that business be conducted within an ethical framework that builds and sustains trust.

Code of Conduct for Management Accountants The Institute of Management Accountants (IMA) of the United States has adopted an ethical code called the *Statement of Ethical Professional Practice* that describes in some detail the ethical responsibilities of management accountants. Even though the standards were developed specifically for management accountants, they have much broader application. The standards consist of two parts that are presented in full in Exhibit 1–6 (page 10). The first part provides general guidelines for ethical behavior. In a nutshell, a management accountant has ethical responsibilities in four broad areas: first, to maintain a high level of professional competence; second, to treat sensitive matters with confidentiality; third, to maintain personal integrity; and fourth, to disclose information in a credible fashion. The second part of the standards specifies what should be done if an individual finds evidence of ethical misconduct.

The ethical standards provide sound, practical advice for management accountants and managers. Most of the rules in the ethical standards are motivated by a very practical consideration—if these rules were not generally followed in business, then

---

EXHIBIT 1–6
IMA Statement of Ethical Professional Practice

Members of IMA shall behave ethically. A commitment to ethical professional practice includes: overarching principles that express our values, and standards that guide our conduct.

PRINCIPLES

IMA's overarching ethical principles include: Honesty, Fairness, Objectivity, and Responsibility. Members shall act in accordance with these principles and shall encourage others within their organizations to adhere to them.

STANDARDS

A member's failure to comply with the following standards may result in disciplinary action.

I. COMPETENCE

Each member has a responsibility to:
1. Maintain an appropriate level of professional expertise by continually developing knowledge and skills.
2. Perform professional duties in accordance with relevant laws, regulations, and technical standards.
3. Provide decision support information and recommendations that are accurate, clear, concise, and timely.
4. Recognize and communicate professional limitations or other constraints that would preclude responsible judgment or successful performance of an activity.

II. CONFIDENTIALITY

Each member has a responsibility to:
1. Keep information confidential except when disclosure is authorized or legally required.
2. Inform all relevant parties regarding appropriate use of confidential information. Monitor subordinates' activities to ensure compliance.
3. Refrain from using confidential information for unethical or illegal advantage.

III. INTEGRITY

Each member has a responsibility to:
1. Mitigate actual conflicts of interest. Regularly communicate with business associates to avoid apparent conflicts of interest. Advise all parties of any potential conflicts.
2. Refrain from engaging in any conduct that would prejudice carrying out duties ethically.
3. Abstain from engaging in or supporting any activity that might discredit the profession.

IV. CREDIBILITY

Each member has a responsibility to:
1. Communicate information fairly and objectively.
2. Disclose all relevant information that could reasonably be expected to influence an intended user's understanding of the reports, analyses, or recommendations.
3. Disclose delays or deficiencies in information, timeliness, processing, or internal controls in conformance with organization policy and/or applicable law.

RESOLUTION OF ETHICAL CONFLICT

In applying the Standards of Ethical Professional Practice, you may encounter problems identifying unethical behavior or resolving an ethical conflict. When faced with ethical issues, you should follow your organization's established policies on the resolution of such conflict. If these policies do not resolve the ethical conflict, you should consider the following courses of action:
1. Discuss the issue with your immediate supervisor except when it appears that the supervisor is involved. In that case, present the issue to the next level. If you cannot achieve a satisfactory resolution, submit the issue to the next management level. If your immediate superior is the chief executive officer or equivalent, the acceptable reviewing authority may be a group such as the audit committee, executive committee, board of directors, board of trustees, or owners. Contact with levels above the immediate superior should be initiated only with your superior's knowledge, assuming he or she is not involved. Communication of such problems to authorities or individuals not employed or engaged by the organization is not considered appropriate, unless you believe there is a clear violation of the law.
2. Clarify relevant ethical issues by initiating a confidential discussion with an IMA Ethics Counselor or other impartial advisor to obtain a better understanding of possible courses of action.
3. Consult your own attorney as to legal obligations and rights concerning the ethical conflict.

TOYOTA ENCOUNTERS MAJOR PROBLEMS

When Toyota Motor Corporation failed to meet its profit targets, the company set an aggressive goal of reducing the cost of its auto parts by 30%. The quality and safety of the company's automobiles eventually suffered mightily resulting in recalls, litigation, incentive campaigns, and marketing efforts that analysts estimate will cost the company more than $5 billion. The car maker's president, Akio Toyoda, blamed his company's massive quality lapses on an excessive focus on profits and market share. Similarly, Jim Press, Toyota's former top U.S. executive, said the problems were caused by "financially-oriented pirates who didn't have the character to maintain a customer-first focus."

Sources: Yoshio Takahashi, "Toyota Accelerates Its Cost-Cutting Efforts," *The Wall Street Journal,* December 23, 2009, p. B4; Mariko Sanchanta and Yoshio Takahashi, "Toyota's Recall May Top $5 Billion," *The Wall Street Journal,* March 10, 2010, p. B2; and Norihiko Shirouzu, "Toyoda Rues Excessive Profit Focus," *The Wall Street Journal,* March 2, 2010, p. B3.

the economy and all of us would suffer. Consider the following specific examples of the consequences of not abiding by the standards:

- Suppose employees could not be trusted with confidential information. Then top managers would be reluctant to distribute such information within the company and, as a result, decisions would be based on incomplete information and operations would deteriorate.
- Suppose employees accepted bribes from suppliers. Then contracts would tend to go to the suppliers who pay the highest bribes rather than to the most competent suppliers. Would you like to fly in aircraft whose wings were made by the subcontractor who paid the highest bribe? Would you fly as often? What would happen to the airline industry if its safety record deteriorated due to shoddy workmanship on contracted parts and subassemblies?
- Suppose the presidents of companies routinely lied in their annual reports and financial statements. If investors could not rely on the basic integrity of a company's financial statements, they would have little basis for making informed decisions. Suspecting the worst, rational investors would pay less for securities issued by companies and may not be willing to invest at all. As a consequence, companies would have less money for productive investments—leading to slower economic growth, fewer goods and services, and higher prices.

Not only is ethical behavior the lubricant for our economy, it is the foundation of managerial accounting. The numbers that managers rely on for planning, control, and decision making are meaningless unless they have been competently, objectively, and honestly gathered, analyzed, and reported. As your career unfolds, you will inevitably face decisions with ethical implications. Before making such decisions, consider performing the following steps. First, define your alternative courses of action. Second, identify all of the parties that will be affected by your decision. Third, define how each course of action will favorably or unfavorably impact each affected party. Once you have a complete understanding of the decision context, seek guidance from external sources such as the IMA Statement of Ethical Professional Practice, the IMA Ethics Helpline at (800) 245-1383, or a trusted confidant. Before executing your decision ask yourself one final question—would I be comfortable disclosing my chosen course of action on the front page of *The Wall Street Journal*?

A Strategic Management Perspective

Companies do not succeed by sheer luck; instead, they need to develop a *strategy* that defines how they intend to succeed in the marketplace. A **strategy** is a "game plan" that enables a company to attract customers by distinguishing itself from competitors. The focal

12   Chapter 1

point of a company's strategy should be its target customers. A company can only succeed if it creates a reason for its target customers to choose it over a competitor. These reasons, or what are more formally called *customer value propositions,* are the essence of strategy.

Customer value propositions tend to fall into three broad categories—*customer intimacy, operational excellence,* and *product leadership.* Companies that adopt a *customer intimacy* strategy are in essence saying to their customers, "You should choose us because we can customize our products and services to meet your individual needs better than our competitors." Ritz-Carlton, Nordstrom, and Virtuoso (a premium service travel agency) rely primarily on a customer intimacy value proposition for their success. Companies that pursue the second customer value proposition, called *operational excellence,* are saying to their target customers, "You should choose us because we deliver products and services faster, more conveniently, and at a lower price than our competitors." Southwest Airlines, Walmart, and Google are examples of companies that succeed first and foremost because of their operational excellence. Companies pursuing the third customer value proposition, called *product leadership,* are saying to their target customers, "You should choose us because we offer higher quality products than our competitors." Apple, Cisco Systems, and W.L. Gore (the creator of GORE-TEX® fabrics) are examples of companies that succeed because of their product leadership.[1]

The plans managers set forth, the variables they seek to control, and the decisions they make are all influenced by their company's strategy. For example, Walmart would not make plans to build ultra-expensive clothing boutiques because these plans would conflict with the company's strategy of operational excellence and "everyday low prices." Apple would not seek to control its operations by selecting performance measures that focus solely on cost-cutting because those measures would conflict with its product leadership customer value proposition. Finally, it is unlikely that Rolex would decide to implement drastic price reductions for its watches even if a financial analysis indicated that establishing a lower price might boost short-run profits. Rolex would oppose this course of action because it would diminish the luxury brand that forms the foundation of the company's product leadership customer value proposition.

IN BUSINESS

A FOUR-YEAR WAITING LIST AT VANILLA BICYCLES

Sacha White started Vanilla Bicycles in Portland, Oregon, in 2001. After eight years in business, he had a four-year backlog of customer orders. He limits his annual production to 40–50 bikes per year that sell for an average of $7,000 each. He uses a silver alloy that costs 20 times as much as brass (which is the industry standard) to join titanium tubes together to form a bike frame. White spends three hours taking a buyer's measurements to determine the exact dimensions of the bike frame. He has resisted expanding production because it would undermine his strategy based on product leadership and customer intimacy. As White said, "If I ended up sacrificing what made Vanilla special just to make more bikes, that wouldn't be worth it to me."

Source: Christopher Steiner, "Heaven on Wheels," *Forbes,* April 13, 2009, p. 75.

An Enterprise Risk Management Perspective

Every strategy, plan, and decision involves risks. **Enterprise risk management** is a process used by a company to identify those risks and develop responses to them that enable it to be reasonably assured of meeting its goals. The left-hand column of Exhibit 1–7 provides 12 examples of the types of business risks that companies face. They range from risks that relate to the weather to risks associated with computer hackers, complying

---

[1] These three customer value propositions were defined by Michael Treacy and Fred Wiersema in "Customer Intimacy and Other Value Disciplines," *Harvard Business Review,* Volume 71 Issue 1, pp. 84–93.

Managerial Accounting: An Overview 13

Examples of Business Risks	Examples of Controls to Reduce Business Risks
• Intellectual assets being stolen from computer files	• Create firewalls that prohibit computer hackers from corrupting or stealing intellectual property
• Products harming customers	• Develop a formal and rigorous new product testing program
• Losing market share due to the unforeseen actions of competitors	• Develop an approach for legally gathering information about competitors' plans and practices
• Poor weather conditions shutting down operations	• Develop contingency plans for overcoming weather-related disruptions
• A website malfunctioning	• Thoroughly test the website before going "live" on the Internet
• A supplier strike halting the flow of raw materials	• Establish a relationship with two companies capable of providing needed raw materials
• A poorly designed incentive compensation system causing employees to make bad decisions	• Create a balanced set of performance measures that motivates the desired behavior
• Financial statements inaccurately reporting the value of inventory	• Count the physical inventory on hand to make sure that it agrees with the accounting records
• An employee stealing assets	• Segregate duties so that the same employee does not have physical custody of an asset and the responsibility of accounting for it
• An employee accessing unauthorized information	• Create password-protected barriers that prohibit employees from obtaining information not needed to do their jobs
• Inaccurate budget estimates causing excessive or insufficient production	• Implement a rigorous budget review process
• Failing to comply with equal employment opportunity laws	• Create a report that tracks key metrics related to compliance with the laws

EXHIBIT 1–7
Identifying and Controlling
Business Risks

with the law, employee theft, and products harming customers. The right-hand column of Exhibit 1–7 provides an example of a control that could be implemented to help reduce each of the risks mentioned in the left-hand column of the exhibit.[2] Although these types of controls cannot completely eliminate risks, they enable companies to proactively manage their risks rather than passively reacting to unfortunate events that have already occurred.

In managerial accounting, companies use controls to reduce the risk that their plans will not be achieved. For example, if a company plans to build a new manufacturing facility within a predefined budget and time frame, it will establish and monitor control measures to ensure that the project is concluded on time and within the budget. Risk management is also a critically important aspect of decision making. For example, when a company quantifies the labor cost savings that it can realize by sending jobs overseas, it should complement its financial analysis with a prudent assessment of the accompanying

---

[2] Besides using controls to reduce risks, companies can also chose other risk responses, such as accepting or avoiding a risk.

IN BUSINESS

MANAGING THE RISK OF A POWER OUTAGE

Between January and April of 2010, the United States had 35 major power outages. For business owners, these power outages can be costly. For example, a New York night club called the Smoke Jazz and Supper Club lost an estimated $1,500 in revenue when a power outage shut down its on-line reservation system for one night. George Pauli, the owner of Great Embroidery LLC in Mesa, Arizona, estimates that his company has an average of six power outages every year. Since Pauli's sewing machines cannot resume exactly where they leave off when abruptly shut down, each power outage costs him $120 in lost inventory. Pauli decided to buy $700 worth of batteries to keep his sewing machines running during power outages. The batteries paid for themselves in less than one year.

Source: Sarah E. Needleman, "Lights Out Means Lost Sales," *The Wall Street Journal*, July 22, 2010, p. B8.

risks. Will the overseas manufacturer use child labor? Will the product's quality decline, thereby leading to more warranty repairs, customer complaints, and lawsuits? Will the elapsed time from customer order to delivery dramatically increase? Will terminating domestic employees diminish morale within the company and harm perceptions within the community? These are the types of risks that managers should incorporate into their decision-making processes.

A Corporate Social Responsibility Perspective

Companies are responsible for creating strategies that produce financial results that satisfy stockholders. However, they also have a *corporate social responsibility* to serve other stakeholders—such as customers, employees, suppliers, communities, and environmental and human rights advocates—whose interests are tied to the company's performance. **Corporate social responsibility** (CSR) is a concept whereby organizations consider the needs of all stakeholders when making decisions. CSR extends beyond legal compliance to include voluntary actions that satisfy stakeholder expectations. Numerous companies, such as Procter & Gamble, 3M, Eli Lilly and Company, Starbucks, Microsoft, Genentech, Johnson & Johnson, Baxter International, Abbott Laboratories, KPMG, PNC Bank, Deloitte, Southwest Airlines, and Caterpillar, prominently describe their corporate social performance on their websites.

Exhibit 1–8 presents examples of corporate social responsibilities that are of interest to six stakeholder groups.[3] If a company fails to meet the needs of these six stakeholder groups it can adversely affect its financial performance. For example, if a company pollutes the environment or fails to provide safe and humane working conditions for its employees, the negative publicity from environmental and human rights activists could cause the company's customers to defect and its "best and brightest" job candidates to apply elsewhere—both of which are likely to eventually harm financial performance. This explains why in managerial accounting a manager must establish plans, implement controls, and make decisions that consider impacts on all stakeholders.

A Process Management Perspective

Most companies organize themselves by functional departments, such as the Marketing Department, the Research and Development Department, and the Accounting Department. These departments tend to have a clearly defined "chain of command" that specifies superior and subordinate relationships. However, effective managers understand that *business processes,* more so than functional departments, serve the needs of a company's

---

[3] Many of the examples in Exhibit 1–8 were drawn from Terry Leap and Misty L. Loughry, "The Stakeholder-Friendly Firm," *Business Horizons*, March/April 2004, pp. 27–32.

Companies should provide *customers* with:	Companies and their suppliers should provide *employees* with:	EXHIBIT 1–8

Companies should provide *customers* with:
- Safe, high-quality products that are fairly priced.
- Competent, courteous, and rapid delivery of products and services.
- Full disclosure of product-related risks.
- Easy-to-use information systems for shopping and tracking orders.

Companies should provide *suppliers* with:
- Fair contract terms and prompt payments.
- Reasonable time to prepare orders.
- Hassle-free acceptance of timely and complete deliveries.
- Cooperative rather than unilateral actions.

Companies should provide *stockholders* with:
- Competent management.
- Easy access to complete and accurate financial information.
- Full disclosure of enterprise risks.
- Honest answers to knowledgeable questions.

Companies and their suppliers should provide *employees* with:
- Safe and humane working conditions.
- Nondiscriminatory treatment and the right to organize and file grievances.
- Fair compensation.
- Opportunities for training, promotion, and personal development.

Companies should provide *communities* with:
- Payment of fair taxes.
- Honest information about plans such as plant closings.
- Resources that support charities, schools, and civic activities.
- Reasonable access to media sources.

Companies should provide *environmental and human rights advocates* with:
- Greenhouse gas emissions data.
- Recycling and resource conservation data.
- Child labor transparency.
- Full disclosure of suppliers located in developing countries.

EXHIBIT 1–8
Examples of Corporate Social Responsibilities

GREENPEACE LEVERAGES THE POWER OF SOCIAL MEDIA

When Nestlé purchased palm oil from an Indonesian supplier to manufacture Kit-Kat candy bars Greenpeace International used social media to express its disapproval. Greenpeace claimed that the Indonesian company destroyed rainforest to create its palm oil plantation; therefore, Nestlé's actions were contributing to global warming and endangering orangutans. Greenpeace posted YouTube videos, added comments to Nestlé's Facebook page, and sent Twitter Tweets to communicate its message to supporters. At one point, the number of fans on Nestlé's Facebook page grew to 95,000, most of them being protesters. Nestlé terminated its relationship with the supplier, which provided 1.25% of Nestlé's palm oil needs. A Nestlé spokesperson says the difficulty in responding to social media is to "show that we are listening, which we obviously are, while not getting involved in a shouting match."

Source: Emily Steel, "Nestlé Takes a Beating on Social-Media Sites," *The Wall Street Journal*, March 29, 2010, p. B5.

most important stakeholders—its customers. A **business process** is a series of steps that are followed in order to carry out some task in a business. These steps often span departmental boundaries, thereby requiring managers to cooperate across functional departments. The term *value chain* is often used to describe how an organization's functional departments interact with one another to form business processes. A **value chain**, as shown in Exhibit 1–9, consists of the major business functions that add value to a company's products and services.

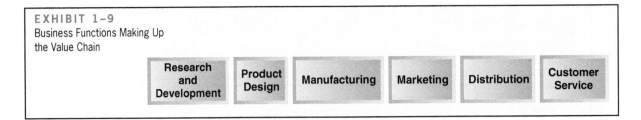

EXHIBIT 1–9
Business Functions Making Up
the Value Chain

Research and Development	Product Design	Manufacturing	Marketing	Distribution	Customer Service

Managers need to understand the value chain to be effective in terms of planning, control, and decision making. For example, if a company's engineers plan to design a new product, they must communicate with the Manufacturing Department to ensure that the product can actually be produced, the Marketing Department to ensure that customers will buy the product, the Distribution Department to ensure that large volumes of the product can be cost-effectively transported to customers, and the Accounting Department to ensure that the product will increase profits. From a control and decision-making standpoint, managers also need to focus on process excellence instead of functional performance. For example, if the Purchasing Department focuses solely on minimizing the cost of purchased materials, this narrowly focused attempt at cost reduction may lead to greater scrap and rework in the Manufacturing Department, more complaints in the Customer Service Department, and greater challenges in the Marketing Department because dissatisfied customers are turning their attention to competitors.

Managers frequently use a process management method known as *lean thinking,* or what is called *Lean Production* in the manufacturing sector. **Lean Production** is a management approach that organizes resources such as people and machines around the flow of business processes and that only produces units in response to customer orders. It is often called *just-in-time* production (or *JIT*) because products are only manufactured in response to customer orders and they are completed just-in-time to be shipped to customers. Lean thinking differs from traditional manufacturing methods, which organize work departmentally and encourage departments to maximize their output even if it exceeds customer demand and bloats inventories. Because lean thinking only allows production in response to customer orders, the number of units produced tends to equal the number of units sold, thereby resulting in minimal inventory. The lean approach also results in fewer defects, less wasted effort, and quicker customer response times than traditional production methods.

IN BUSINESS

LOUIS VUITTON IMPLEMENTS LEAN PRODUCTION

Louis Vuitton, headquartered in Paris, France, used lean production to increase its manufacturing capacity without having to build a new factory. It created U-shaped work arrangements for teams of 10 workers, thereby freeing up 10% more floor space in its factories. The company was able to hire 300 more workers without adding any square footage. Louis Vuitton also uses robots and computer programs to reduce wasted leather and the time needed to perform certain tasks.

Source: Christina Passariello, "At Vuitton, Growth in Small Batches," *The Wall Street Journal,* June 27, 2011, pp. B1 and B10.

A Leadership Perspective

An organization's employees bring diverse needs, beliefs, and goals to the workplace. Therefore, an important role for organizational leaders is to unite the behaviors of their fellow employees around two common themes—pursuing strategic goals and making optimal decisions. To fulfill this responsibility, leaders need to understand how *intrinsic motivation, extrinsic incentives,* and *cognitive bias* influence human behavior.

Intrinsic Motivation   Intrinsic motivation refers to motivation that comes from within us. Stop for a moment and identify the greatest accomplishment of your life. Then ask yourself what motivated you to achieve this goal? In all likelihood, you achieved it because you wanted to, not because someone forced you to do it. In other words, you were intrinsically motivated. Similarly, an organization is more likely to prosper when its employees are intrinsically motivated to pursue its interests. A leader, who employees perceive as *credible* and *respectful* of their value to the organization, can increase the extent to which those employees are intrinsically motivated to pursue strategic goals. As your career evolves, to be perceived as a credible leader you'll need to possess three attributes—technical competence (that spans the value chain), personal integrity (in terms of work ethic and honesty), and strong communication skills (including oral presentation skills and writing skills). To be perceived as a leader who is respectful of your co-workers' value to the organization, you'll need to possess three more attributes—strong mentoring skills (to help others realize their potential), strong listening skills (to learn from your co-workers and be responsive to their needs), and personal humility (in terms of deferring recognition to all employees who contribute to the organization's success). If you possess these six traits, then you'll have the potential to become a leader who inspires others to readily and energetically channel their efforts toward achieving organizational goals.

Extrinsic Incentives   Many organizations use *extrinsic incentives* to highlight important goals and to motivate employees to achieve them. For example, assume a company establishes the goal of reducing the time needed to perform a task by 20%. In addition, assume the company agrees to pay bonus compensation to its employees if they achieve the goal within three months. In this example, the company is using a type of extrinsic incentive known as a bonus to highlight a particular goal and to presumably motivate employees to achieve it.

While proponents of extrinsic incentives rightly assert that these types of rewards can have a powerful influence on employee behavior, many critics warn that they can also produce dysfunctional consequences. For example, suppose the employees mentioned above earned their bonuses by achieving the 20% time reduction goal within three months. However, let's also assume that during those three months the quality of the employees' output plummeted, thereby causing a spike in the company's repair costs, product returns, and customer defections. In this instance, did the extrinsic incentive work properly? The answer is yes and no. The bonus system did motivate employees to attain the time reduction goal; however, it also had the unintended consequences of causing employees to neglect product quality, thereby increasing repair costs, product returns, and customer defections. In other words, what may have seemed like a well-intended extrinsic incentive actually produced dysfunctional results for the company. This example highlights an important leadership challenge that you are likely to face someday—designing financial compensation systems that fairly reward employees for their efforts without inadvertently creating extrinsic incentives that motivate them to take actions that harm the company.

Cognitive Bias   Leaders need to be aware that all people (including themselves) possess *cognitive biases,* or distorted thought processes, that can adversely affect planning, controlling, and decision making. To illustrate how cognitive bias works, let's consider the scenario of a television "infomercial" where someone is selling a product with a proclaimed value of $200 for $19.99 if viewers call within the next 30 minutes. Why do you think the seller claims that the product has a $200 value? The seller is relying on a cognitive bias called *anchoring bias* in an effort to convince viewers that a $180 discount is simply too good to pass up. The "anchor" is the false assertion that the product is actually worth $200. If viewers erroneously attach credibility to this contrived piece of information, their distorted analysis of the situation may cause them to spend $19.99 on an item whose true economic value is much less than that amount.

While cognitive biases cannot be eliminated, effective leaders should take two steps to reduce their negative impacts. First, they should acknowledge their own susceptibility to cognitive bias. For example, a leader's judgment might be clouded by optimism bias (being overly optimistic in assessing the likelihood of future outcomes) or self-enhancement bias (overestimating ones strengths and underestimating ones weaknesses relative to others). Second, they should acknowledge the presence of cognitive bias in others and introduce techniques to minimize their adverse consequences. For example, to reduce the risks of confirmation bias (a bias where people pay greater attention to information that confirms their preconceived notions, while devaluing information that contradicts them) or groupthink bias (a bias where some group members support a course of action solely because other group members do), a leader may routinely appoint independent teams of employees to assess the credibility of recommendations set forth by other individuals and groups.

Summary

This chapter defined managerial accounting and explained why it is relevant to business and accounting majors. It also discussed six topics—ethics, strategic management, enterprise risk management, corporate social responsibility, process management, and leadership—that define the context for applying the quantitative aspects of managerial accounting. The most important goal of this chapter was to help you understand that managerial accounting matters to your future career regardless of your major. Accounting is the language of business and you'll need to speak it to communicate effectively with and influence fellow managers.

Glossary

Budget A detailed plan for the future that is usually expressed in formal quantitative terms. (p. 3)

Business process A series of steps that are followed in order to carry out some task in a business. (p. 15)

Controlling The process of gathering feedback to ensure that a plan is being properly executed or modified as circumstances change. (p. 3)

Corporate social responsibility A concept whereby organizations consider the needs of all stakeholders when making decisions. (p. 14)

Decision making Selecting a course of action from competing alternatives. (p. 3)

Enterprise risk management A process used by a company to identify its risks and develop responses to them that enable it to be reasonably assured of meeting its goals. (p. 12)

Financial accounting The phase of accounting that is concerned with reporting historical financial information to external parties, such as stockholders, creditors, and regulators. (p. 2)

Lean Production A management approach that organizes resources such as people and machines around the flow of business processes and that only produces units in response to customer orders. (p. 16)

Managerial accounting The phase of accounting that is concerned with providing information to managers for use within the organization. (p. 2)

Performance report A report that compares budgeted data to actual data to highlight instances of excellent and unsatisfactory performance. (p. 4)

Planning The process of establishing goals and specifying how to achieve them. (p. 3)

Segment A part or activity of an organization about which managers would like cost, revenue, or profit data. (p. 3)

Strategy A company's "game plan" for attracting customers by distinguishing itself from competitors. (p. 11)

Value chain The major business functions that add value to a company's products and services, such as research and development, product design, manufacturing, marketing, distribution, and customer service. (p. 15)

Questions

1–1 How does managerial accounting differ from financial accounting?

1–2 Pick any major television network and describe some planning and control activities that its managers would engage in.

1–3 If you had to decide whether to continue making a component part or to begin buying the part from an overseas supplier, what quantitative and qualitative factors would influence your decision?

1–4 Why do companies prepare budgets?

1–5 Why is managerial accounting relevant to business majors and their future careers?

1–6 Why is managerial accounting relevant to accounting majors and their future careers?

1–7 Pick any large company and describe its strategy using the framework in the chapter.

1–8 Why do management accountants need to understand their company's strategy?

1–9 Pick any large company and describe three risks that it faces and how it responds to those risks.

1–10 Provide three examples of how a company's risks can influence its planning, controlling, and decision-making activities.

1–11 Pick any large company and explain three ways that it could segment its companywide performance.

1–12 Locate the website of any company that publishes a corporate social responsibility report (also referred to as a sustainability report). Describe three nonfinancial performance measures included in the report. Why do you think the company publishes this report?

1–13 Why do companies that implement Lean Production tend to have minimal inventories?

1–14 Why are leadership skills important to managers?

1–15 Why is ethical behavior important to business?

Multiple-choice questions are provided on the text website at www.mhhe.com/garrison15e.

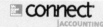 Exercises

For this chapter, LearnSmart and Interactive Presentations are available with McGraw-Hill's Connect® Accounting.

EXERCISE 1–1 Planning and Control

Many companies use budgets for three purposes. First, they use them to plan how to deploy resources to best serve customers. Second, they use them to establish challenging goals, or stretch targets, to motivate employees to strive for exceptional results. Third, they use them to evaluate and reward employees.

Assume that you are a sales manager working with your boss to create a sales budget for next year. Once the sales budget is established, it will influence how other departments within the company plan to deploy their resources. For example, the manufacturing manager will plan to produce enough units to meet budgeted unit sales. The sales budget will also be instrumental in determining your pay raise, potential for promotion, and bonus. If actual sales exceed the sales budget, it bodes well for your career. If actual sales are less than budgeted sales, it will diminish your financial compensation and potential for promotion.

Required:

1. Do you think it would be appropriate for your boss to establish the sales budget without any input from you? Why?

2. Do you think the company would be comfortable with allowing you to establish the sales budget without any input from your boss? Why?

3. Assume the company uses its sales budget for only one purpose—planning to deploy resources in a manner that best serves customers. What thoughts would influence your estimate of future sales as well as your boss's estimate of future sales?

4. Assume the company uses its sales budget for only one purpose—motivating employees to strive for exceptional results. What thoughts would influence your estimate of future sales as well as your boss's estimate of future sales?

5. Assume the company uses its sales budget for only one purpose—to determine your pay raise, potential for promotion, and bonus. What thoughts would influence your estimate of future sales as well as your boss's estimate of future sales?

6. Assume the sales budget is used for all three purposes described in questions 3–5. Describe any conflicts or complications that might arise when using the sales budget for these three purposes.

Chapter 1

EXERCISE 1–2 Controlling

Assume that you work for an airline unloading luggage from airplanes. Your boss has said that, on average, each airplane contains 100 pieces of luggage. Furthermore, your boss has stated that you should be able to unload 100 pieces of luggage from an airplane in 10 minutes. Today an airplane arrived with 150 pieces of luggage and you unloaded all of it in 13 minutes. After finishing with the 150 pieces of luggage, your boss yelled at you for exceeding the 10 minute allowance for unloading luggage from an airplane.

Required:
How would you feel about being yelled at for taking 13 minutes to unload 150 pieces of luggage? How does this scenario relate to the larger issue of how companies design control systems?

EXERCISE 1–3 Decision Making

Exhibit 1–2 (see page 4) includes 12 questions related to 12 types of decisions that companies often face. In the chapter, these 12 decisions were discussed within the context of for-profit companies; however, they are also readily applicable to nonprofit organizations. To illustrate this point, assume that you are a senior leader, such as a president, provost, or dean, in a university setting.

Required:
For each of the 12 decisions in Exhibit 1–2, provide an example of how that type of decision might be applicable to a university setting.

EXERCISE 1–4 Ethics and the Manager

Richmond, Inc., operates a chain of 44 department stores. Two years ago, the board of directors of Richmond approved a large-scale remodeling of its stores to attract a more upscale clientele.

Before finalizing these plans, two stores were remodeled as a test. Linda Perlman, assistant controller, was asked to oversee the financial reporting for these test stores, and she and other management personnel were offered bonuses based on the sales growth and profitability of these stores. While completing the financial reports, Perlman discovered a sizable inventory of outdated goods that should have been discounted for sale or returned to the manufacturer. She discussed the situation with her management colleagues; the consensus was to ignore reporting this inventory as obsolete because reporting it would diminish the financial results and their bonuses.

Required:
1. According to the IMA's Statement of Ethical Professional Practice, would it be ethical for Perlman *not* to report the inventory as obsolete?
2. Would it be easy for Perlman to take the ethical action in this situation?

(CMA, adapted)

EXERCISE 1–5 Strategy

The table below contains the names of six companies.

Required:
For each company, categorize its strategy as being focused on customer intimacy, operational excellence, or product leadership. If you wish to improve your understanding of each company's customer value proposition before completing the exercise, review its most recent annual report. To obtain electronic access to this information, perform an Internet search on each company's name followed by the words "annual report."

	Company	Strategy
1.	Deere	?
2.	FedEx	?
3.	State Farm Insurance	?
4.	BMW	?
5.	Amazon.com	?
6.	Charles Schwab	?

EXERCISE 1–6 Enterprise Risk Management

The table below refers to seven industries.

Required:
For each industry, identify one important risk faced by the companies that compete within that industry. Also, describe one control that companies could use to reduce the risk that you have identified.

Industry	Type of Risk	Control to Reduce the Risk
1. Airlines (e.g., Delta Airlines)		
2. Pharmaceutical drugs (e.g., Merck)		
3. Package delivery (e.g., United Parcel Service) . . .		
4. Banking (e.g., Bank of America)		
5. Oil & gas (e.g., Exxon Mobil)		
6. E-commerce (e.g., eBay)		
7. Automotive (e.g., Toyota)		

EXERCISE 1–7 Ethics in Business

Consumers and attorney generals in more than 40 states accused a prominent nationwide chain of auto repair shops of misleading customers and selling them unnecessary parts and services, from brake jobs to front-end alignments. Lynn Sharpe Paine reported the situation as follows in "Managing for Organizational Integrity," *Harvard Business Review,* Volume 72 Issue 3:

> In the face of declining revenues, shrinking market share, and an increasingly competitive market . . . management attempted to spur performance of its auto centers. . . . The automotive service advisers were given product-specific sales quotas—sell so many springs, shock absorbers, alignments, or brake jobs per shift—and paid a commission based on sales. . . . [F]ailure to meet quotas could lead to a transfer or a reduction in work hours. Some employees spoke of the "pressure, pressure, pressure" to bring in sales.
>
> This pressure-cooker atmosphere created conditions under which employees felt that the only way to satisfy top management was by selling products and services to customers that they didn't really need.

Suppose all automotive repair businesses routinely followed the practice of attempting to sell customers unnecessary parts and services.

Required:
1. How would this behavior affect customers? How might customers attempt to protect themselves against this behavior?
2. How would this behavior probably affect profits and employment in the automotive service industry?

EXERCISE 1–8 Cognitive Bias

In the 1970s, one million college-bound students were surveyed and asked to compare themselves to their peers. Some of the key findings of the survey were as follows:
a. 70% of the students rated themselves as above average in leadership ability, while only 2% rated themselves as below average in this regard.
b. With respect to athletic skills, 60% of the students rated their skills as above the median and only 6% of students rated themselves as below the median.
c. 60% of the students rated themselves in the top 10% in terms of their ability to get along with others, while 25% of the students felt that they were in the top 1% in terms of this interpersonal skill.

Required:
What type of cognitive bias reveals itself in the data mentioned above? How might this cognitive bias adversely influence a manager's planning, controlling, and decision-making activities? What steps could managers take to reduce the possibility that this cognitive bias would adversely influence their actions?

Source: Dan Lovallo and Daniel Kahneman, "Delusions of Success: How Optimism Undermines Executives' Decisions," *Harvard Business Review,* July 2003, pp. 56–63.

EXERCISE 1–9 Ethics and Decision Making

Assume that you are the chairman of the Department of Accountancy at Mountain State University. One of the accounting professors in your department, Dr. Candler, has been consistently and uniformly regarded by students as an awful teacher for more than 10 years. Other accounting professors within your department have observed Dr. Candler's classroom teaching and they concur that his teaching skills are very poor. However, Dr. Candler was granted tenure 12 years ago, thereby ensuring him life-long job security at Mountain State University.

Much to your surprise, today you received a phone from an accounting professor at Oregon Coastal University. During this phone call you are informed that Oregon Coastal University is on the verge of making a job offer to Dr. Candler. However, before extending the job offer, the faculty at Oregon Coastal wants your input regarding Dr. Candler's teaching effectiveness while at Mountain State University.

Required:
How would you respond to the professor from Oregon Coastal University? What would you say about Dr. Candler's teaching ability? Would you describe your answer to this inquiry as being ethical? Why?

EXERCISE 1-10 Corporate Social Responsbility
In his book *Capitalism and Freedom,* economist Milton Friedman wrote on page 133: "There is one and only one social responsibility of business—to use its resources and engage in activities designed to increase its profits so long as it . . . engages in open and free competition, without deception or fraud."

Required:
Explain why you agree or disagree with this quote.

EXERCISE 1-11 Intrinsic Motivation and Extrinsic Incentives
In a *Harvard Business Review* article titled "Why Incentive Plans Cannot Work," (Volume 71, Issue 5) author Alfie Kohn wrote: "Research suggests that, by and large, rewards succeed at securing one thing only: temporary compliance. When it comes to producing lasting change in attitudes and behavior, however, rewards, like punishment, are strikingly ineffective. Once the rewards run out, people revert to their old behaviors. . . . Incentives, a version of what psychologists call extrinsic motivators, do not alter the attitudes that underlie our behaviors. They do not create an enduring *commitment* to any value or action. Rather, incentives merely—and temporarily—change what we do."

Required:
1. Do you agree with this quote? Why?
2. As a manager, how would you seek to motivate your employees?
3. As a manager, would you use financial incentives to compensate your employees? If so, what would be the keys to using them effectively? If not, then how would you compensate your employees?

EXERCISE 1-12 Cognitive Bias and Decision Making
During World War II, the U.S. military was studying its combat-tested fighter planes to determine the parts of the plane that were most vulnerable to enemy fire. The purpose of the study was to identify the most vulnerable sections of each plane and then take steps to reinforce those sections to improve pilot safety and airplane durability. The data gathered by the U.S. military showed that certain sections of its combat-tested fighter planes were consistently hit more often with enemy fire than other sections of the plane.

Required:
1. Would you recommend reinforcing the sections of the plane that were hit most often by enemy fire, or would you reinforce the sections that were hit less frequently by enemy fire? Why?
2. Do you think cognitive bias had the potential to influence the U.S. military's decision-making process with respect to reinforcing its fighter planes?

Source: Jerker Denrell, "Selection Bias and the Perils of Benchmarking," *Harvard Business Review,* Volume 83, Issue 4, pp. 114–119.

EXERCISE 1-13 Ethics and Decision Making
Assume that you just completed a December weekend vacation to a casino within the United States. During your trip you won $10,000 gambling. When the casino exchanged your chips for cash they did not record any personal information, such as your driver's license number or social security number. Four months later while preparing your tax returns for the prior year, you stop to contemplate the fact that the Internal Revenue Service requires taxpayers to report all gambling winnings on Form 1040.

Required:
Would you report your gambling winnings to the Internal Revenue Service so that you could pay federal income taxes on those winnings? Do you believe that your actions are ethical? Why?

Appendix 1A: Corporate Governance

Effective *corporate governance* enhances stockholders' confidence that a company is being run in their best interests rather than in the interests of top managers. **Corporate governance** is the system by which a company is directed and controlled. If properly implemented, the corporate governance system should provide incentives for the board of directors and top management to pursue objectives that are in the interests of the company's owners and it should provide for effective monitoring of performance.[1]

Unfortunately, history has repeatedly shown that unscrupulous top managers, if unchecked, can exploit their power to defraud stockholders. This unpleasant reality became all too clear in 2001 when the fall of Enron kicked off a wave of corporate scandals. These scandals were characterized by financial reporting fraud and misuse of corporate funds at the very highest levels—including CEOs and CFOs. While this was disturbing in itself, it also indicated that the institutions intended to prevent such abuses weren't working, thus raising fundamental questions about the adequacy of the existing corporate governance system. In an attempt to respond to these concerns, the U.S. Congress passed the most important reform of corporate governance in many decades—*The Sarbanes-Oxley Act of 2002.*

The Sarbanes-Oxley Act of 2002

The **Sarbanes-Oxley Act of 2002** was intended to protect the interests of those who invest in publicly traded companies by improving the reliability and accuracy of corporate financial reports and disclosures. We would like to highlight six key aspects of the legislation.[2]

First, the Act requires that both the CEO and CFO certify in writing that their company's financial statements and accompanying disclosures fairly represent the results of operations—with possible jail time if a CEO or CFO certifies results that they know are false. This creates very powerful incentives for the CEO and CFO to ensure that the financial statements contain no misrepresentations.

Second, the Act established the Public Company Accounting Oversight Board to provide additional oversight over the audit profession. The Act authorizes the Board to conduct investigations, to take disciplinary actions against audit firms, and to enact various standards and rules concerning the preparation of audit reports.

Third, the Act places the power to hire, compensate, and terminate the public accounting firm that audits a company's financial reports in the hands of the audit committee of the board of directors. Previously, management often had the power to hire and fire its auditors. Furthermore, the Act specifies that all members of the audit committee must be independent, meaning that they do not have an affiliation with the company they are overseeing, nor do they receive any consulting or advisory compensation from the company.

Fourth, the Act places important restrictions on audit firms. Historically, public accounting firms earned a large part of their profits by providing consulting services to the companies that they audited. This provided the appearance of a lack of independence because a client that was dissatisfied with an auditor's stance on an accounting issue might threaten to stop using the auditor as a consultant. To avoid this possible conflict of interests, the Act prohibits a public accounting firm from providing a wide variety of nonauditing services to an audit client.

Fifth, the Act requires that a company's annual report contain an *internal control report.* Internal controls are put in place by management to provide assurance to investors that financial disclosures are reliable. The report must state that it is management's

---

[1] This definition of corporate governance was adapted from the 2004 report titled OECD Principles of Corporate Governance published by the Organization for Economic Co-Operation and Development.

[2] A summary of the Sarbanes-Oxley Act of 2002 can be obtained at www.soxlaw.com.

responsibility to establish and maintain adequate internal controls and it must contain an assessment by management of the effectiveness of its internal control structure. The internal control report is accompanied by an opinion from the company's audit firm as to whether management has maintained effective internal control over its financial reporting process.

Finally, the Act establishes severe penalties of as many as 20 years in prison for altering or destroying any documents that may eventually be used in an official proceeding and as many as 10 years in prison for managers who retaliate against a so-called whistle-blower who goes outside the chain of command to report misconduct. Collectively, these six aspects of the Sarbanes-Oxley Act of 2002 were intended to help reduce the incidence of fraudulent financial reporting.

Internal Control—A Closer Look

Internal control is an important concept for all managers to understand and, although you may not be aware of it, it also plays an important role in your personal life. **Internal control** is a process designed to provide reasonable assurance that objectives are being achieved. For example, one objective for your personal life is to live to a ripe old age. Unfortunately, there are risks that we all encounter that may prohibit us from achieving this objective. For example, we may die prematurely due to a heart attack, a car accident, or a house fire. To reduce the risk of these unfortunate events occurring, we implement controls in our lives. We may exercise regularly and make nutritional food choices to reduce the likelihood of a heart attack. We always wear seat belts and instruct our friends to prohibit us from drinking alcohol and driving a vehicle to reduce the risk of a fatal car crash. We install fire detectors in our homes to reduce the risk of a fatal fire. In short, internal controls are an integral part of our daily lives.

A company uses internal controls to provide reasonable assurance that its financial reports are reliable.[3] Its financial statements may contain intentional or unintentional errors for three reasons. First, the statements may erroneously exclude some transactions. For example, the income statement may fail to include legitimate expenses. Second, the statements may improperly include some transactions. For example, the income statement may include sales revenue that was not earned during the current period. Third, the statements may include transactions that have been recorded erroneously. For example, an expense or sales transaction may be recorded at the wrong amount.

Exhibit 1A–1 describes seven types of internal controls that companies use to reduce the risk that these types of errors will occur. Each item in the exhibit is labeled as a *preventive control* and/or a *detective control*. A **preventive control** deters undesirable events from occurring. A **detective control** detects undesirable events that have already occurred. Requiring authorizations for certain types of transactions is a preventive control. For example, companies frequently require that a specific senior manager sign all checks above a particular dollar amount to reduce the risk of an inappropriate cash disbursement. Reconciliations are a detective control. If you have ever compared a bank statement to your checkbook to resolve any discrepancies, then you have performed a type of reconciliation known as a bank reconciliation. This is a detective control because you are seeking to identify any mistakes already made by the bank or existing mistakes in your own records.

Segregation of duties is a preventive control that separates responsibilities for authorizing transactions, recording transactions, and maintaining custody of the related assets. For example, the same employee should not have the ability to authorize inventory purchases, account for those purchases, and manage the inventory storeroom. Physical safeguards prevent unauthorized employees from having access to assets such as inventories and computer equipment. Performance reviews are a detective control performed

---

[3] Companies also use internal controls to achieve efficient and effective operations and to ensure compliance with applicable laws and regulations.

Type of Control	Classification	Description	
Authorizations	Preventive	Requiring management to formally approve certain types of transactions.	**EXHIBIT 1A–1** Types of Internal Controls for Financial Reporting
Reconciliations	Detective	Relating data sets to one another to identify and resolve discrepancies.	
Segregation of duties	Preventive	Separating responsibilities related to authorizing transactions, recording transactions, and maintaining custody of the related assets.	
Physical safeguards	Preventive	Using cameras, locks, and physical barriers to protect assets.	
Performance reviews	Detective	Comparing actual performance to various benchmarks to identify unexpected results.	
Maintaining records	Detective	Maintaining written and/or electronic evidence to support transactions.	
Information systems security	Preventive/Detective	Using controls such as passwords and access logs to ensure appropriate data restrictions.	

by employees in supervisory positions to ensure that actual results are reasonable when compared to relevant benchmarks. If actual results unexpectedly deviate from expectations, then it triggers further analysis to determine the root cause of the deviation. Companies maintain records to provide evidence that supports each transaction. For example, companies use serially numbered checks so that they can readily track all of their cash disbursements. Finally, companies use passwords (a preventive control) and access logs (a detective control) to restrict electronic data access as appropriate.

It is important to understand that internal controls cannot guarantee that objectives will be achieved. For example, a person can regularly exercise and eat healthy foods, but this does not guarantee that they will live to a certain age. Similarly, an effective internal control system can provide reasonable assurance that financial statement disclosures are reliable, but it cannot offer guarantees because even a well-designed internal control system can break down. Furthermore, two or more employees may collude to circumvent the control system. Finally, a company's senior leaders may manipulate financial results by intentionally overriding prescribed policies and procedures. This reality highlights the importance of having senior leaders (including the chief executive officer, the chief financial officer, and the audit committee of the board of directors) who value the importance of effective internal controls and are committed to creating an ethical "tone at the top" of the organization.

Glossary

Corporate governance The system by which a company is directed and controlled. (p. 23)

Detective control A control that detects undesirable events that have already occurred. (p. 24)

Internal control A process designed to provide reasonable assurance that objectives are being achieved. (p. 24)

Preventive control A control that deters undesirable events from occurring. (p. 24)

Sarbanes-Oxley Act of 2002 A law intended to protect the interests of those who invest in publicly traded companies by improving the reliability and accuracy of corporate financial reports and disclosures. (p. 23)

Questions

1A–1   Imagine that you are the head coach of a college sports team. One of your most important objectives is to win as many games as possible. Describe some controls that you would implement to help achieve the objective of winning as many games as possible.

1A–2   Perhaps your most important post-graduation objective is to get a job. Describe some control activities that you would pursue to help achieve this objective.

1A–3   Describe some controls that parents use to keep their homes safe for themselves and their children.

1A–4   Many retail companies experience customer and employee theft (or what is referred to as shrinkage) that equals 1%–2% of their total sales. For a company such as Walmart, this seemingly small percentage of total sales translates to billions of dollars. What types of internal controls might Walmart use to reduce its shrinkage?

1A–5   If you were a restaurant owner, what internal controls would you implement to help maintain control of your cash?

1A–6   As a form of internal control, what documents would you review prior to paying an invoice received from a supplier?

1A–7   What internal controls would you implement to help maintain control of your credit sales and accounts receivable?

1A–8   Why do companies take a physical count of their inventory on hand at least once per year?

1A–9   Why do companies use sequential prenumbering for documents such as checks, sales invoices, and purchase orders?

1A–10 How can an annual budget function as a form of internal control?

CHAPTER 2

Managerial Accounting and Cost Concepts

BUSINESS FOCUS

Lowering Healthcare Costs and Improving Patient Care

Providence Regional Medical Center's (PRMC) "single stay" ward is lowering healthcare costs and increasing patient satisfaction. Rather than transporting post-surgical patients to stationary equipment throughout the hospital, a "single stay" ward brings all required equipment to stationary patients. For example, "after heart surgery, cardiac patients remain in one room throughout their recovery, only the gear and staff are in motion. As the patient's condition stabilizes, the beeping machines of intensive care are removed and physical therapy equipment is added." The results of this shift in orientation have been impressive. Patient satisfaction scores have skyrocketed and the average length of a patient's stay in the hospital has declined by more than a day. ■

Source: Catherine Arnst, "Radical Surgery," Bloomberg Businessweek, January 18, 2010, pp. 40–45.

LEARNING OBJECTIVES

After studying Chapter 2, you should be able to:

LO2–1 Understand cost classifications used for assigning costs to cost objects: direct costs and indirect costs.

LO2–2 Identify and give examples of each of the three basic manufacturing cost categories.

LO2–3 Understand cost classifications used to prepare financial statements: product costs and period costs.

LO2–4 Understand cost classifications used to predict cost behavior: variable costs, fixed costs, and mixed costs.

LO2–5 Analyze a mixed cost using a scattergraph plot and the high-low method.

LO2–6 Prepare income statements for a merchandising company using the traditional and contribution formats.

LO2–7 Understand cost classifications used in making decisions: differential costs, opportunity costs, and sunk costs.

LO2–8 (Appendix 2A) Analyze a mixed cost using a scattergraph plot and the least-squares regression method.

LO2–9 (Appendix 2B) Identify the four types of quality costs and explain how they interact.

LO2–10 (Appendix 2B) Prepare and interpret a quality cost report.

This chapter explains that in managerial accounting the term *cost* is used in many different ways. The reason is that there are many types of costs, and these costs are classified differently according to the immediate needs of management. For example, managers may want cost data to prepare external financial reports, to prepare planning budgets, or to make decisions. Each different use of cost data demands a different classification and definition of costs. For example, the preparation of external financial reports requires the use of historical cost data, whereas decision making may require predictions about future costs. This notion of *different costs for different purposes* is a critically important aspect of managerial accounting.

Exhibit 2–1 summarizes the cost classifications that will be defined in this chapter, namely cost classifications (1) for assigning costs to cost objects, (2) for manufacturing companies, (3) for preparing financial statements, (4) for predicting cost behavior, and (5) for making decisions. As we begin defining the cost terminology related to each of these cost classifications, please refer back to this exhibit to help improve your understanding of the overall organization of the chapter.

Cost Classifications for Assigning Costs to Cost Objects

LO2–1

Understand cost classifications used for assigning costs to cost objects: direct costs and indirect costs.

Costs are assigned to cost objects for a variety of purposes including pricing, preparing profitability studies, and controlling spending. A **cost object** is anything for which cost data are desired—including products, customers, jobs, and organizational subunits. For purposes of assigning costs to cost objects, costs are classified as either *direct* or *indirect*.

Direct Cost

A **direct cost** is a cost that can be easily and conveniently traced to a specified cost object. For example, if **Reebok** is assigning costs to its various regional and national sales offices, then the salary of the sales manager in its Tokyo office would be a direct

EXHIBIT 2–1
Summary of Cost Classifications

Purpose of Cost Classification	Cost Classifications
Assigning costs to cost objects	• Direct cost (can be easily traced) • Indirect cost (cannot be easily traced)

Accounting for costs in manufacturing companies	• Manufacturing costs
	  • Direct materials
	  • Direct labor
	  • Manufacturing overhead
	• Nonmanufacturing costs
	  • Selling costs
	  • Administrative costs

Preparing financial statements	• Product costs (inventoriable) • Period costs (expensed)
Predicting cost behavior in response to changes in activity	• Variable cost (proportional to activity) • Fixed cost (constant in total) • Mixed cost (has variable and fixed elements)
Making decisions	• Differential cost (differs between alternatives) • Sunk cost (should be ignored) • Opportunity cost (foregone benefit)

cost of that office. If a printing company made 10,000 brochures for a specific customer, then the cost of the paper used to make the brochures would be a direct cost of that customer.

Indirect Cost

An **indirect cost** is a cost that cannot be easily and conveniently traced to a specified cost object. For example, a Campbell Soup factory may produce dozens of varieties of canned soups. The factory manager's salary would be an indirect cost of a particular variety such as chicken noodle soup. The reason is that the factory manager's salary is incurred as a consequence of running the entire factory—it is not incurred to produce any one soup variety. *To be traced to a cost object such as a particular product, the cost must be caused by the cost object.* The factory manager's salary is called a *common cost* of producing the various products of the factory. A **common cost** is a cost that is incurred to support a number of cost objects but cannot be traced to them individually. A common cost is a type of indirect cost.

A particular cost may be direct or indirect, depending on the cost object. While the Campbell Soup factory manager's salary is an *indirect* cost of manufacturing chicken noodle soup, it is a *direct* cost of the manufacturing division. In the first case, the cost object is chicken noodle soup. In the second case, the cost object is the entire manufacturing division.

Cost Classifications for Manufacturing Companies

Manufacturing companies such as Texas Instruments, Ford, and DuPont separate their costs into two broad categories—manufacturing and nonmanufacturing costs.

Manufacturing Costs

Most manufacturing companies further separate their manufacturing costs into two direct cost categories, direct materials and direct labor, and one indirect cost category, manufacturing overhead. A discussion of each of these categories follows.

LO2–2
Identify and give examples of each of the three basic manufacturing cost categories.

Direct Materials The materials that go into the final product are called **raw materials**. This term is somewhat misleading because it seems to imply unprocessed natural resources like wood pulp or iron ore. Actually, raw materials refer to any materials that are used in the final product; and the finished product of one company can become the raw materials of another company. For example, the plastics produced by Du Pont are a raw material used by Hewlett-Packard in its personal computers.

Raw materials may include both *direct* and *indirect materials*. **Direct materials** are those materials that become an integral part of the finished product and whose costs can be conveniently traced to the finished product. This would include, for example, the seats that Airbus purchases from subcontractors to install in its commercial aircraft and the electronic components that Apple uses in its iPhones.

Sometimes it isn't worth the effort to trace the costs of relatively insignificant materials to end products. Such minor items would include the solder used to make electrical connections in a Sony HDTV or the glue used to assemble an Ethan Allen chair. Materials such as solder and glue are called **indirect materials** and are included as part of manufacturing overhead, which is discussed shortly.

Direct Labor   **Direct labor** consists of labor costs that can be easily (i.e., physically and conveniently) traced to individual units of product. Direct labor is sometimes called *touch labor* because direct labor workers typically touch the product while it is being made. Examples of direct labor include assembly-line workers at Toyota, carpenters

FOOD PRICES HIT RECORD HIGHS FOR RESTAURANTS

Direct material costs are critically important to restaurants and fast-food chains. In recent years, some food costs have spiked to record highs. For example, unexpected freezing temperatures in the southwestern portion of the United States caused the cost of lettuce to increase 290%. Similarly, the costs of green peppers, tomatoes, and cucumbers jumped 145%, 85%, and 30%, respectively. A large chain such as Subway can withstand these price increases better than smaller competitors because of its buying power and long-term contracts.

Source: Anne VanderMey, "Food For Thought," *Fortune*, May 9, 2011, p. 12.

at the home builder KB Home, and electricians who install equipment on aircraft at Bombardier Learjet.

Labor costs that cannot be physically traced to particular products, or that can be traced only at great cost and inconvenience, are termed **indirect labor**. Just like indirect materials, indirect labor is treated as part of manufacturing overhead. Indirect labor includes the labor costs of janitors, supervisors, materials handlers, and night security guards. Although the efforts of these workers are essential, it would be either impractical or impossible to accurately trace their costs to specific units of product. Hence, such labor costs are treated as indirect labor.

Manufacturing Overhead   **Manufacturing overhead**, the third manufacturing cost category, includes all manufacturing costs except direct materials and direct labor. Manufacturing overhead includes items such as indirect materials; indirect labor; maintenance and repairs on production equipment; and heat and light, property taxes, depreciation, and insurance on manufacturing facilities. A company also incurs costs for heat and light, property taxes, insurance, depreciation, and so forth, associated with its selling and administrative functions, but these costs are not included as part of manufacturing overhead. Only those costs associated with *operating the factory* are included in manufacturing overhead.

Various names are used for manufacturing overhead, such as *indirect manufacturing cost, factory overhead,* and *factory burden.* All of these terms are synonyms for *manufacturing overhead.*

Nonmanufacturing Costs

Nonmanufacturing costs are often divided into two categories: (1) *selling costs* and (2) *administrative costs.* **Selling costs** include all costs that are incurred to secure customer orders and get the finished product to the customer. These costs are sometimes called *order-getting* and *order-filling costs.* Examples of selling costs include advertising, shipping, sales travel, sales commissions, sales salaries, and costs of finished goods warehouses. Selling costs can be either direct or indirect costs. For example, the cost of an advertising campaign dedicated to one specific product is a direct cost of that product, whereas the salary of a marketing manager who oversees numerous products is an indirect cost with respect to individual products.

Administrative costs include all costs associated with the *general management* of an organization rather than with manufacturing or selling. Examples of administrative costs include executive compensation, general accounting, secretarial, public relations, and similar costs involved in the overall, general administration of the organization *as a whole.* Administrative costs can be either direct or indirect costs. For example, the salary of an accounting manager in charge of accounts receivable collections in the East region is a direct cost of that region, whereas the salary of a chief financial officer who oversees all of a company's regions is an indirect cost with respect to individual regions.

Nonmanufacturing costs are also often called selling, general, and administrative (SG&A) costs or just selling and administrative costs.

Cost Classifications for Preparing Financial Statements

When preparing a balance sheet and an income statement, companies need to classify their costs as *product costs* or *period costs*. To understand the difference between product costs and period costs, we must first discuss the matching principle from financial accounting.

Generally, costs are recognized as expenses on the income statement in the period that benefits from the cost. For example, if a company pays for liability insurance in advance for two years, the entire amount is not considered an expense of the year in which the payment is made. Instead, one-half of the cost would be recognized as an expense each year. The reason is that both years—not just the first year—benefit from the insurance payment. The unexpensed portion of the insurance payment is carried on the balance sheet as an asset called prepaid insurance.

The *matching principle* is based on the *accrual* concept that *costs incurred to generate a particular revenue should be recognized as expenses in the same period that the revenue is recognized.* This means that if a cost is incurred to acquire or make something that will eventually be sold, then the cost should be recognized as an expense only when the sale takes place—that is, when the benefit occurs. Such costs are called *product costs.*

LO2–3
Understand cost classifications used to prepare financial statements: product costs and period costs.

Product Costs

For financial accounting purposes, **product costs** include all costs involved in acquiring or making a product. In the case of manufactured goods, these costs consist of direct materials, direct labor, and manufacturing overhead.[1] Product costs "attach" to units of product as the goods are purchased or manufactured, and they remain attached as the goods go into inventory awaiting sale. Product costs are initially assigned to an inventory account on the balance sheet. When the goods are sold, the costs are released from inventory as expenses (typically called cost of goods sold) and matched against sales revenue on the income statement. Because product costs are initially assigned to inventories, they are also known as **inventoriable costs**.

We want to emphasize that product costs are not necessarily recorded as expenses on the income statement in the period in which they are incurred. Rather, as explained above, they are recorded as expenses in the period in which the related products *are sold*.

Period Costs

Period costs are all the costs that are not product costs. *All selling and administrative expenses are treated as period costs.* For example, sales commissions, advertising, executive salaries, public relations, and the rental costs of administrative offices are all period costs. Period costs are not included as part of the cost of either purchased or manufactured goods; instead, period costs are expensed on the income statement in the period in which they are incurred using the usual rules of accrual accounting. Keep in mind that the period in which a cost is incurred is not necessarily the period in which cash changes hands. For example, as discussed earlier, the costs of liability insurance are spread across the periods that benefit from the insurance—regardless of the period in which the insurance premium is paid.

---

[1] For internal management purposes, product costs may exclude some manufacturing costs. For example, see Appendix 3A and the discussion in Chapter 6.

Chapter 2

Prime Cost and Conversion Cost

Two more cost categories are often used in discussions of manufacturing costs—*prime cost* and *conversion cost*. **Prime cost** is the sum of direct materials cost and direct labor cost. **Conversion cost** is the sum of direct labor cost and manufacturing overhead cost. The term *conversion cost* is used to describe direct labor and manufacturing overhead because these costs are incurred to convert materials into the finished product.

To improve your understanding of these definitions, consider the following scenario: A company has reported the following costs and expenses for the most recent month:

Direct materials	$69,000
Direct labor	$35,000
Manufacturing overhead	$14,000
Selling expenses	$29,000
Administrative expenses	$50,000

These costs and expenses can be categorized in a number of ways, including product costs, period costs, conversion costs, and prime costs:

$$\text{Product cost} = \text{Direct materials} + \text{Direct labor} + \text{Manufacturing overhead}$$
$$= \$69,000 + \$35,000 + \$14,000$$
$$= \$118,000$$

$$\text{Period cost} = \text{Selling expenses} + \text{Administrative expenses}$$
$$= \$29,000 + \$50,000$$
$$= \$79,000$$

$$\text{Conversion cost} = \text{Direct labor} + \text{Manufacturing overhead}$$
$$= \$35,000 + \$14,000$$
$$= \$49,000$$

$$\text{Prime cost} = \text{Direct materials} + \text{Direct labor}$$
$$= \$69,000 + \$35,000$$
$$= \$104,000$$

IN BUSINESS

WALMART LOOKS TO REDUCE ITS SHIPPING COSTS

Walmart hopes to lower its shipping costs, thereby enabling it to reduce its "everyday low prices." In years past, suppliers would ship their merchandise to Walmart's distribution centers, and then Walmart would use its own fleet of trucks to ship goods from its distribution centers to its retail store locations. However, now Walmart wants to assume control of transporting merchandise from its suppliers' manufacturing facilities to its distribution centers. Walmart believes it can lower these shipping costs by carrying more merchandise per truck and by taking advantage of volume purchase price discounts for fuel. In exchange for assuming these shipping responsibilities, Walmart is seeking price reductions from suppliers that it can pass along, at least in part, to its customers.

Source: Chris Burritt, Carol Wolf, and Matthew Boyle, "Why Wal-Mart Wants to Take the Driver's Seat," *Bloomberg Businessweek*, May 31–June 6, 2010, pp. 17–18.

Cost Classifications for Predicting Cost Behavior

It is often necessary to predict how a certain cost will behave in response to a change in activity. For example, a manager at Under Armour may want to estimate the impact a 5 percent increase in sales would have on the company's total direct materials cost. **Cost behavior** refers to how a cost reacts to changes in the level of activity. As the activity level rises and falls, a particular cost may rise and fall as well—or it may remain constant. For planning purposes, a manager must be able to anticipate which of these will happen; and if a cost can be expected to change, the manager must be able to estimate how much it will change. To help make such distinctions, costs are often categorized as *variable, fixed,* or *mixed*. The relative proportion of each type of cost in an organization is known as its **cost structure**. For example, an organization might have many fixed costs but few variable or mixed costs. Alternatively, it might have many variable costs but few fixed or mixed costs.

LO2–4
Understand cost classifications used to predict cost behavior: variable costs, fixed costs, and mixed costs.

Variable Cost

A **variable cost** varies, in total, in direct proportion to changes in the level of activity. Common examples of variable costs include cost of goods sold for a merchandising company, direct materials, direct labor, variable elements of manufacturing overhead, such as indirect materials, supplies, and power, and variable elements of selling and administrative expenses, such as commissions and shipping costs.[2]

For a cost to be variable, it must be variable *with respect to something*. That "something" is its *activity base*. An **activity base** is a measure of whatever causes the incurrence of a variable cost. An activity base is sometimes referred to as a *cost driver*. Some of the most common activity bases are direct labor-hours, machine-hours, units produced, and units sold. Other examples of activity bases (cost drivers) include the number of miles driven by salespersons, the number of pounds of laundry cleaned by a hotel, the number of calls handled by technical support staff at a software company, and the number of beds occupied in a hospital. *While there are many activity bases within organizations, throughout this textbook, unless stated otherwise, you should assume that the activity base under consideration is the total volume of goods and services provided by the organization. We will specify the activity base only when it is something other than total output.*

To provide an example of a variable cost, consider Nooksack Expeditions, a small company that provides daylong whitewater rafting excursions on rivers in the North

IN BUSINESS

COST DRIVERS IN THE ELECTRONICS INDUSTRY

Accenture Ltd. estimates that the U.S. electronics industry spends $13.8 billion annually to rebox, restock, and resell returned products. Conventional wisdom is that customers only return products when they are defective, but the data show that this explanation only accounts for 5% of customer returns. The biggest cost drivers that cause product returns are that customers often inadvertently buy the wrong products and that they cannot understand how to use the products that they have purchased. Television manufacturer Vizio Inc. has started including more information on its packaging to help customers avoid buying the wrong product. Seagate Technologies is replacing thick instruction manuals with simpler guides that make it easier for customers to begin using their products.

Source: Christopher Lawton, "The War on Returns," *The Wall Street Journal*, May 8, 2008, pp. D1 and D6.

---

[2] Direct labor costs often can be fixed instead of variable for a variety of reasons. For example, in some countries, such as France, Germany, and Japan, labor regulations and cultural norms may limit management's ability to adjust the labor force in response to changes in activity. In this textbook, always assume that direct labor is a variable cost unless you are explicitly told otherwise.

FOOD COSTS AT A LUXURY HOTEL

The Sporthotel Theresa (http://www.theresa.at/), owned and operated by the Egger family, is a four star hotel located in Zell im Zillertal, Austria. The hotel features access to hiking, skiing, biking, and other activities in the Ziller alps as well as its own fitness facility and spa.

Three full meals a day are included in the hotel room charge. Breakfast and lunch are served buffet-style while dinner is a more formal affair with as many as six courses. The chef, Stefan Egger, believes that food costs are roughly proportional to the number of guests staying at the hotel; that is, they are a variable cost. He must order food from suppliers two or three days in advance, but he adjusts his purchases to the number of guests who are currently staying at the hotel and their consumption patterns. In addition, guests make their selections from the dinner menu early in the day, which helps Stefan plan which foodstuffs will be required for dinner. Consequently, he is able to prepare just enough food so that all guests are satisfied and yet waste is held to a minimum.

Source: Conversation with Stefan Egger, chef at the Sporthotel Theresa.

Cascade Mountains. The company provides all of the necessary equipment and experienced guides, and it serves gourmet meals to its guests. The meals are purchased from a caterer for $30 a person for a daylong excursion. The behavior of this variable cost, on both a per unit and a total basis, is shown below:

Number of Guests	Cost of Meals per Guest	Total Cost of Meals
250	$30	$7,500
500	$30	$15,000
750	$30	$22,500
1,000	$30	$30,000

While total variable costs change as the activity level changes, it is important to note that a variable cost is constant if expressed on a *per unit* basis. For example, the per unit cost of the meals remains constant at $30 even though the total cost of the meals increases and decreases with activity. The graph on the left-hand side of Exhibit 2–2 illustrates that the total variable cost rises and falls as the activity level rises and falls. At an activity level of 250 guests, the total meal cost is $7,500. At an activity level of 1,000 guests, the total meal cost rises to $30,000.

Fixed Cost

A **fixed cost** is a cost that remains constant, in total, regardless of changes in the level of activity. Examples of fixed costs include straight-line depreciation, insurance, property taxes, rent, supervisory salaries, administrative salaries, and advertising. Unlike variable costs, fixed costs are not affected by changes in activity. Consequently, as the activity level rises and falls, total fixed costs remain constant unless influenced by some outside force, such as a landlord increasing your monthly rental expense. To continue the Nooksack Expeditions example, assume the company rents a building for $500 per month to store its equipment. The total amount of rent paid is the same regardless of the number of guests the company takes on its expeditions during any given month. The concept of a fixed cost is shown graphically on the right-hand side of Exhibit 2–2.

Because total fixed costs remain constant for large variations in the level of activity, the average fixed cost *per unit* becomes progressively smaller as the level of activity increases. If Nooksack Expeditions has only 250 guests in a month, the $500 fixed rental cost would amount to an average of $2 per guest. If there are 1,000 guests, the fixed rental cost would average only 50 cents per guest. The table below illustrates

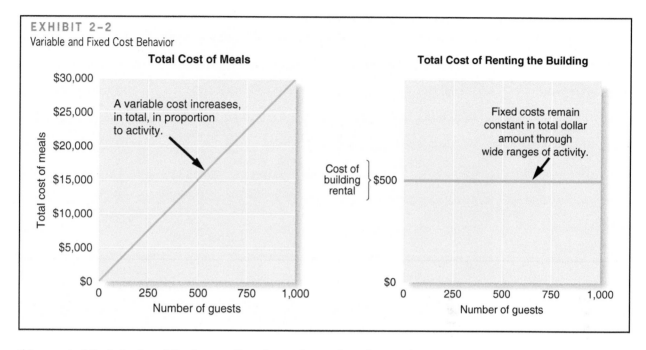

EXHIBIT 2–2
Variable and Fixed Cost Behavior

this aspect of the behavior of fixed costs. Note that as the number of guests increase, the average fixed cost per guest drops.

Monthly Rental Cost	Number of Guests	Average Cost per Guest
$500	250	$2.00
$500	500	$1.00
$500	750	$0.67
$500	1,000	$0.50

As a general rule, *we caution against expressing fixed costs on an average per unit basis in internal reports because it creates the false impression that fixed costs are like variable costs and that total fixed costs actually change as the level of activity changes.*

For planning purposes, fixed costs can be viewed as either *committed* or *discretionary*. **Committed fixed costs** represent organizational investments with a *multiyear* planning horizon that can't be significantly reduced even for short periods of time without making fundamental changes. Examples include investments in facilities and equipment, as well as real estate taxes, insurance expenses, and salaries of top management. Even if operations are interrupted or cut back, committed fixed costs remain largely unchanged in the short term because the costs of restoring them later are likely to be far greater than any short-run savings that might be realized. **Discretionary fixed costs** (often referred to as *managed fixed costs*) usually arise from *annual* decisions by management to spend on certain fixed cost items. Examples of discretionary fixed costs include advertising, research, public relations, management development programs, and internships for students. Discretionary fixed costs can be cut for short periods of time with minimal damage to the long-run goals of the organization.

The Linearity Assumption and the Relevant Range

Management accountants ordinarily assume that costs are strictly linear; that is, the relation between cost on the one hand and activity on the other can be represented by a straight line. Economists point out that many costs are actually curvilinear; that is, the relation between cost and activity is a curve. Nevertheless, even if a cost is not strictly

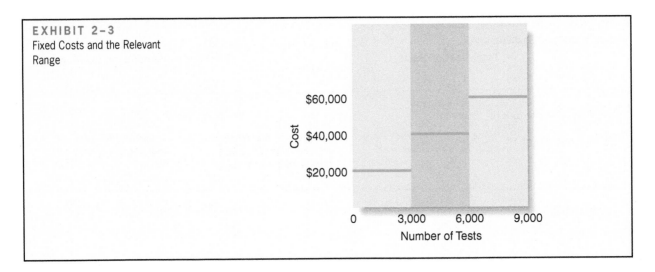

EXHIBIT 2–3
Fixed Costs and the Relevant
Range

linear, it can be approximated within a narrow band of activity known as the *relevant range* by a straight line. The **relevant range** is the range of activity within which the assumption that cost behavior is strictly linear is reasonably valid. Outside of the relevant range, a fixed cost may no longer be strictly fixed or a variable cost may not be strictly variable. Managers should always keep in mind that assumptions made about cost behavior may be invalid if activity falls outside of the relevant range.

The concept of the relevant range is important in understanding fixed costs. For example, suppose the Mayo Clinic rents a machine for $20,000 per month that tests blood samples for the presence of leukemia cells. Furthermore, suppose that the capacity of the leukemia diagnostic machine is 3,000 tests per month. The assumption that the rent for the diagnostic machine is $20,000 per month is only valid within the relevant range of 0 to 3,000 tests per month. If the Mayo Clinic needed to test 5,000 blood samples per month, then it would need to rent another machine for an additional $20,000 per month. It would be difficult to rent half of a diagnostic machine; therefore, the step pattern depicted in Exhibit 2–3 is typical for such costs. This exhibit shows that the fixed rental expense is $20,000 for a relevant range of 0 to 3,000 tests. The fixed rental expense increases to $40,000 within the relevant range of 3,001 to 6,000 tests. The rental expense increases in discrete steps or increments of 3,000 tests, rather than increasing in a linear fashion per test.

This step-oriented cost behavior pattern can also be used to describe other costs, such as some labor costs. For example, salaried employee expenses can be characterized using a step pattern. Salaried employees are paid a fixed amount, such as $40,000 per year, for providing the capacity to work a prespecified amount of time, such as 40 hours per week for 50 weeks a year (= 2,000 hours per year). In this example, the total salaried employee expense is $40,000 within a relevant range of 0 to 2,000 hours of work. The total salaried employee expense increases to $80,000 (or two employees) if the organization's work requirements expand to a relevant range of 2,001 to 4,000 hours of work. Cost behavior patterns such as salaried employees are often called *step-variable costs*. Step-variable costs can often be adjusted quickly as conditions change. Furthermore, the width of the steps for step-variable costs is generally so narrow that these costs can be treated essentially as variable costs for most purposes. The width of the steps for fixed costs, on the other hand, is so wide that these costs should be treated as entirely fixed within the relevant range.

Exhibit 2–4 summarizes four key concepts related to variable and fixed costs. Study it carefully before reading further.

Managerial Accounting and Cost Concepts

37

	Behavior of the Cost (within the relevant range)		EXHIBIT 2–4
Cost	In Total	Per Unit	Summary of Variable and Fixed Cost Behavior
Variable cost	Total variable cost increases and decreases in proportion to changes in the activity level.	Variable cost per unit remains constant.	
Fixed cost	Total fixed cost is not affected by changes in the activity level within the relevant range.	Fixed cost per unit decreases as the activity level rises and increases as the activity level falls.	

HOW MANY GUIDES?

Majestic Ocean Kayaking, of Ucluelet, British Columbia, is owned and operated by Tracy Morben-Eeftink. The company offers a number of guided kayaking excursions ranging from three-hour tours of the Ucluelet harbor to six-day kayaking and camping trips in Clayoquot Sound. One of the company's excursions is a four-day kayaking and camping trip to The Broken Group Islands in the Pacific Rim National Park. Special regulations apply to trips in the park—including a requirement that one certified guide must be assigned for every five guests or fraction thereof. For example, a trip with 12 guests must have at least three certified guides. Guides are not salaried and are paid on a per-day basis. Therefore, the cost to the company of the guides for a trip is a step-variable cost rather than a fixed cost or a strictly variable cost. One guide is needed for 1 to 5 guests, two guides for 6 to 10 guests, three guides for 11 to 15 guests, and so on.

Sources: Tracy Morben-Eeftink, owner, Majestic Ocean Kayaking. For more information about the company, see www.oceankayaking.com.

Mixed Costs

A **mixed cost** contains both variable and fixed cost elements. Mixed costs are also known as semivariable costs. To continue the Nooksack Expeditions example, the company incurs a mixed cost called fees paid to the state. It includes a license fee of $25,000 per year plus $3 per rafting party paid to the state's Department of Natural Resources. If the company runs 1,000 rafting parties this year, then the total fees paid to the state would be $28,000, made up of $25,000 in fixed cost plus $3,000 in variable cost. Exhibit 2–5 depicts the behavior of this mixed cost.

Even if Nooksack fails to attract any customers, the company will still have to pay the license fee of $25,000. This is why the cost line in Exhibit 2–5 intersects the vertical cost axis at the $25,000 point. For each rafting party the company organizes, the total cost of the state fees will increase by $3. Therefore, the total cost line slopes upward as the variable cost of $3 per party is added to the fixed cost of $25,000 per year.

Because the mixed cost in Exhibit 2–5 is represented by a straight line, the following equation for a straight line can be used to express the relationship between a mixed cost and the level of activity:

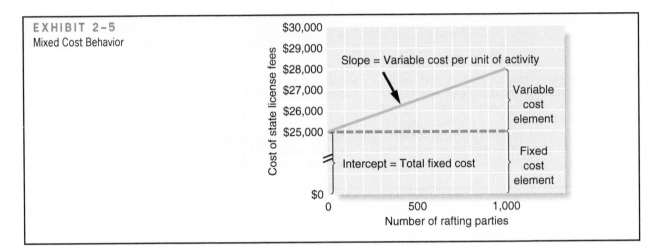

EXHIBIT 2–5
Mixed Cost Behavior

$$Y = a + bX$$

In this equation,

Y = The total mixed cost

a = The total fixed cost (the vertical intercept of the line)

b = The variable cost per unit of activity (the slope of the line)

X = The level of activity

Because the variable cost per unit equals the slope of the straight line, the steeper the slope, the higher the variable cost per unit.

In the case of the state fees paid by Nooksack Expeditions, the equation is written as follows:

$$Y = \$25,000 + \$3.00X$$

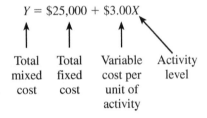

| Total mixed cost | Total fixed cost | Variable cost per unit of activity | Activity level |

This equation makes it easy to calculate the total mixed cost for any level of activity within the relevant range. For example, suppose that the company expects to organize 800 rafting parties in the next year. The total state fees would be calculated as follows:

$$Y = \$25,000 + (\$3.00 \text{ per rafting party} \times 800 \text{ rafting parties})$$

$$= \$27,400$$

The Analysis of Mixed Costs

Mixed costs are very common. For example, the overall cost of providing X-ray services to patients at the **Harvard Medical School Hospital** is a mixed cost. The costs of equipment depreciation and radiologists' and technicians' salaries are fixed, but the costs of X-ray film, power, and supplies are variable. At **Southwest Airlines**, maintenance costs are a mixed cost. The company incurs fixed costs for renting maintenance facilities and for keeping skilled mechanics on the payroll, but the costs of replacement parts, lubricating oils, tires, and so forth, are variable with respect to how often and how far the company's aircraft are flown.

The fixed portion of a mixed cost represents the minimum cost of having a service *ready and available* for use. The variable portion represents the cost incurred for *actual consumption* of the service, thus it varies in proportion to the amount of service actually consumed.

Managers can use a variety of methods to estimate the fixed and variable components of a mixed cost such as *account analysis,* the *engineering approach,* the *high-low method,* and *least-squares regression analysis.* In **account analysis**, an account is classified as either variable or fixed based on the analyst's prior knowledge of how the cost in the account behaves. For example, direct materials would be classified as variable and a building lease cost would be classified as fixed because of the nature of those costs. The **engineering approach** to cost analysis involves a detailed analysis of what cost behavior should be, based on an industrial engineer's evaluation of the production methods to be used, the materials specifications, labor requirements, equipment usage, production efficiency, power consumption, and so on.

The high-low and least-squares regression methods estimate the fixed and variable elements of a mixed cost by analyzing past records of cost and activity data. We will use an example from Brentline Hospital to illustrate the high-low method calculations and to compare the resulting high-low method cost estimates to those obtained using least-squares regression. Appendix 2A demonstrates how to use Microsoft Excel to perform least-squares regression computations.

Diagnosing Cost Behavior with a Scattergraph Plot

Assume that Brentline Hospital is interested in predicting future monthly maintenance costs for budgeting purposes. The senior management team believes that maintenance cost is a mixed cost and that the variable portion of this cost is driven by the number of patient-days. Each day a patient is in the hospital counts as one patient-day. The hospital's chief financial officer gathered the following data for the most recent seven-month period:

LO2–5

Analyze a mixed cost using a scattergraph plot and the high-low method.

Month	Activity Level: Patient-Days	Maintenance Cost Incurred
January	5,600	$7,900
February	7,100	$8,500
March	5,000	$7,400
April	6,500	$8,200
May	7,300	$9,100
June	8,000	$9,800
July	6,200	$7,800

The first step in applying the high-low method or the least-squares regression method is to diagnose cost behavior with a scattergraph plot. The scattergraph plot of maintenance costs versus patient-days at Brentline Hospital is shown in Exhibit 2–6. Two things should be noted about this scattergraph:

1. The total maintenance cost, *Y,* is plotted on the vertical axis. Cost is known as the **dependent variable** because the amount of cost incurred during a period depends on the level of activity for the period. (That is, as the level of activity increases, total cost will also ordinarily increase.)

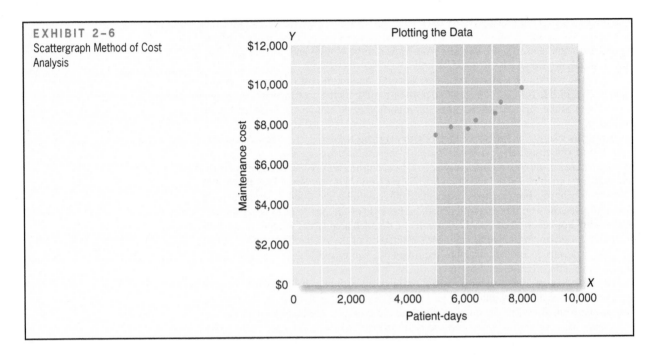

EXHIBIT 2–6
Scattergraph Method of Cost
Analysis

2. The activity, X (patient-days in this case), is plotted on the horizontal axis. Activity is known as the **independent variable** because it causes variations in the cost.

From the scattergraph plot, it is evident that maintenance costs do increase with the number of patient-days in an approximately *linear* fashion. In other words, the points lie more or less along a straight line that slopes upward and to the right. Cost behavior is considered **linear** whenever a straight line is a reasonable approximation for the relation between cost and activity.

Plotting the data on a scattergraph is an essential diagnostic step that should be performed before performing the high-low method or least-squares regression calculations. If the scattergraph plot reveals linear cost behavior, then it makes sense to perform the high-low or least-squares regression calculations to separate the mixed cost into its variable and fixed components. If the scattergraph plot does not depict linear cost behavior, then it makes no sense to proceed any further in analyzing the data.

The High-Low Method

Assuming that the scattergraph plot indicates a linear relation between cost and activity, the fixed and variable cost elements of a mixed cost can be estimated using the *high-low method* or the *least-squares regression method*. The high-low method is based on the rise-over-run formula for the slope of a straight line. As previously discussed, if the relation between cost and activity can be represented by a straight line, then the slope of the straight line is equal to the variable cost per unit of activity. Consequently, the following formula can be used to estimate the variable cost:

$$\text{Variable cost} = \text{Slope of the line} = \frac{\text{Rise}}{\text{Run}} = \frac{Y_2 - Y_1}{X_2 - X_1}$$

To analyze mixed costs with the **high-low method**, begin by identifying the period with the lowest level of activity and the period with the highest level of activity. The period with the lowest activity is selected as the first point in the above formula and the period with the highest activity is selected as the second point. Consequently, the formula becomes:

$$\text{Variable cost} = \frac{Y_2 - Y_1}{X_2 - X_1} = \frac{\text{Cost at the high activity level} - \text{Cost at the low activity level}}{\text{High activity level} - \text{Low activity level}}$$

or

$$\text{Variable cost} = \frac{\text{Change in cost}}{\text{Change in activity}}$$

Therefore, when the high-low method is used, the variable cost is estimated by dividing the difference in cost between the high and low levels of activity by the change in activity between those two points.

To return to the Brentline Hospital example, using the high-low method, we first identify the periods with the highest and lowest *activity*—in this case, June and March. We then use the activity and cost data from these two periods to estimate the variable cost component as follows:

	Patient-Days	Maintenance Cost Incurred
High activity level (June)	8,000	$9,800
Low activity level (March)	5,000	7,400
Change	3,000	$2,400

$$\text{Variable cost} = \frac{\text{Change in cost}}{\text{Change in activity}} = \frac{\$2,400}{3,000 \text{ patient-days}} = \$0.80 \text{ per patient-day}$$

Having determined that the variable maintenance cost is 80 cents per patient-day, we can now determine the amount of fixed cost. This is done by taking the total cost at *either* the high or the low activity level and deducting the variable cost element. In the computation below, total cost at the high activity level is used in computing the fixed cost element:

$$\text{Fixed cost element} = \text{Total cost} - \text{Variable cost element}$$

$$= \$9,800 - (\$0.80 \text{ per patient-day} \times 8,000 \text{ patient-days})$$

$$= \$3,400$$

Both the variable and fixed cost elements have now been isolated. The cost of maintenance can be expressed as $3,400 per month plus 80 cents per patient-day or as:

$$Y = \$3,400 + \$0.80X$$

$$\uparrow \qquad\qquad \uparrow$$

Total maintenance cost   Total patient-days

The data used in this illustration are shown graphically in Exhibit 2–7. Notice that a straight line has been drawn through the points corresponding to the low and high levels of activity. In essence, that is what the high-low method does—it draws a straight line through those two points.

Sometimes the high and low levels of activity don't coincide with the high and low amounts of cost. For example, the period that has the highest level of activity may not

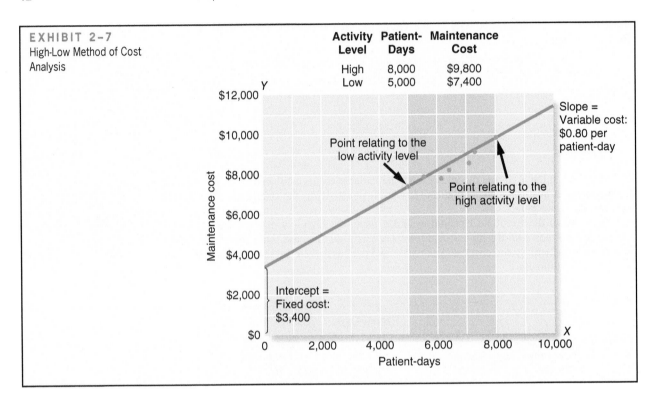

EXHIBIT 2–7
High-Low Method of Cost
Analysis

Activity Level	Patient-Days	Maintenance Cost
High	8,000	$9,800
Low	5,000	$7,400

have the highest amount of cost. Nevertheless, the costs at the highest and lowest levels of *activity* are always used to analyze a mixed cost under the high-low method. The reason is that the analyst would like to use data that reflect the greatest possible variation in activity.

The high-low method is very simple to apply, but it suffers from a major (and sometimes critical) defect—it utilizes only two data points. Generally, two data points are not enough to produce accurate results. Additionally, the periods with the highest and lowest activity tend to be unusual. A cost formula that is estimated solely using data from these unusual periods may misrepresent the true cost behavior during normal periods. Such a distortion is evident in Exhibit 2–7. The straight line should probably be shifted down somewhat so that it is closer to more of the data points. For these reasons, least-squares regression will generally be more accurate than the high-low method.

The Least-Squares Regression Method

The **least-squares regression method**, unlike the high-low method, uses all of the data to separate a mixed cost into its fixed and variable components. A *regression line* of the form $Y = a + bX$ is fitted to the data, where a represents the total fixed cost and b represents the variable cost per unit of activity. The basic idea underlying the least-squares regression method is illustrated in Exhibit 2–8 using hypothetical data points. Notice from the exhibit that the deviations from the plotted points to the regression line are measured vertically on the graph. These vertical deviations are called the regression errors. There is nothing mysterious about the least-squares regression method. It simply computes the regression line that minimizes the sum of these squared errors. The formulas that accomplish this are fairly complex and involve numerous calculations, but the principle is simple.

Managerial Accounting and Cost Concepts

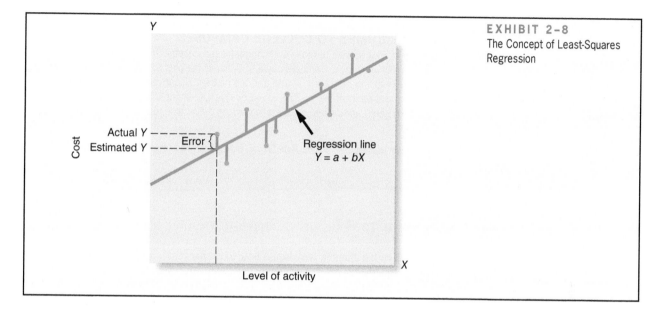

EXHIBIT 2–8
The Concept of Least-Squares Regression

Fortunately, computers are adept at carrying out the computations required by the least-squares regression formulas. The data—the observed values of X and Y—are entered into the computer, and software does the rest. In the case of the Brentline Hospital maintenance cost data, a statistical software package on a personal computer can calculate the following least-squares regression estimates of the total fixed cost (a) and the variable cost per unit of activity (b):

$$a = \$3{,}431$$

$$b = \$0.759$$

Therefore, using the least-squares regression method, the fixed element of the maintenance cost is $3,431 per month and the variable portion is 75.9 cents per patient-day.

In terms of the linear equation $Y = a + bX$, the cost formula can be written as

$$Y = \$3{,}431 + \$0.759X$$

where activity (X) is expressed in patient-days.

Appendix 2A discusses how to use Microsoft Excel to perform least-squares regression calculations. For now, you only need to understand that least-squares regression analysis generally provides more accurate cost estimates than the high-low method because, rather than relying on just two data points, it uses all of the data points to fit a line that minimizes the sum of the squared errors. The table below compares Brentline Hospital's cost estimates using the high-low method and the least-squares regression method:

	High-Low Method	Least-Squares Regression Method
Variable cost estimate per patient-day	$0.800	$0.759
Fixed cost estimate per month	$3,400	$3,431

When Brentline uses the least-squares regression method to create a straight line that minimizes the sum of the squared errors, it results in estimated fixed costs that are $31 higher than the amount derived using the high-low method. It also decreases the slope of the straight line resulting in a lower variable cost estimate of $0.759 per patient-day rather than $0.80 per patient-day as derived using the high-low method.

THE ZIPCAR COMES TO COLLEGE CAMPUSES

Zipcar is a car sharing service based in Cambridge, Massachusetts. The company serves 13 cities and 120 university campuses. Members pay a $50 annual fee plus $7 an hour to rent a car. They can use their iPhones to rent a car, locate it in the nearest Zipcar parking lot, unlock it using an access code, and drive it off the lot. This mixed cost arrangement is attractive to customers who need a car infrequently and wish to avoid the large cash outlay that comes with buying or leasing a vehicle.

Source: Jefferson Graham, "An iPhone Gets Zipcar Drivers on Their Way," *USA Today*, September 30, 2009, p. 3B.

Traditional and Contribution Format Income Statements

LO2–6

Prepare income statements for a merchandising company using the traditional and contribution formats.

In this section of the chapter, we discuss how to prepare traditional and contribution format income statements for a merchandising company.[3] Merchandising companies do not manufacture the products that they sell to customers. For example, Lowe's and Home Depot are merchandising companies because they buy finished products from manufacturers and then resell them to end consumers.

The Traditional Format Income Statement

Traditional income statements are prepared primarily for external reporting purposes. The left-hand side of Exhibit 2–9 shows a traditional income statement format for merchandising companies. This type of income statement organizes costs into two categories—cost of goods sold and selling and administrative expenses. Sales minus cost of goods sold equals the *gross margin*. The gross margin minus selling and administrative expenses equals net operating income.

The cost of goods sold reports the *product costs* attached to the merchandise sold during the period. The selling and administrative expenses report all *period costs* that have been expensed as incurred. The cost of goods sold for a merchandising company

---

EXHIBIT 2–9

Comparing Traditional and Contribution Format Income Statements for Merchandising Companies (all numbers are given)

Traditional Format		Contribution Format		
Sales	$12,000	Sales		$12,000
Cost of goods sold*	6,000	Variable expenses:		
Gross margin	6,000	Cost of goods sold	$6,000	
Selling and administrative expenses:		Variable selling	600	
Selling	$3,100	Variable administrative	400	7,000
Administrative	1,900 5,000	Contribution margin		5,000
Net operating income	$ 1,000	Fixed expenses:		
		Fixed selling	2,500	
		Fixed administrative	1,500	4,000
		Net operating income		$ 1,000

*For a manufacturing company, the cost of goods sold would include some variable costs, such as direct materials, direct labor, and variable overhead, and some fixed costs, such as fixed manufacturing overhead. Income statement formats for manufacturing companies will be explored in greater detail in a subsequent chapter.

---

[3] Subsequent chapters compare the income statement formats for manufacturing companies.

can be computed directly by multiplying the number of units sold by their unit cost or indirectly using the equation below:

$$\text{Cost of goods sold} = \text{Beginning merchandise inventory} + \text{Purchases} - \text{Ending merchandise inventory}$$

For example, let's assume that the company depicted in Exhibit 2–9 purchased $3,000 of merchandise inventory during the period and had beginning and ending merchandise inventory balances of $7,000 and $4,000, respectively. The equation above could be used to compute the cost of goods sold as follows:

$$\begin{aligned}
\text{Cost of goods sold} &= \text{Beginning merchandise inventory} + \text{Purchases} - \text{Ending merchandise inventory} \\
&= \$7,000 + \$3,000 - \$4,000 \\
&= \$6,000
\end{aligned}$$

Although the traditional income statement is useful for external reporting purposes, it has serious limitations when used for internal purposes. It does not distinguish between fixed and variable costs. For example, under the heading "Selling and administrative expenses," both variable administrative costs ($400) and fixed administrative costs ($1,500) are lumped together ($1,900). Internally, managers need cost data organized by cost behavior to aid in planning, controlling, and decision making. The contribution format income statement has been developed in response to these needs.

The Contribution Format Income Statement

The crucial distinction between fixed and variable costs is at the heart of the **contribution approach** to constructing income statements. The unique thing about the contribution approach is that it provides managers with an income statement that clearly distinguishes between fixed and variable costs and therefore aids planning, controlling, and decision making. The right-hand side of Exhibit 2–9 shows a contribution format income statement for merchandising companies.

The contribution approach separates costs into fixed and variable categories, first deducting variable expenses from sales to obtain the *contribution margin.* For a merchandising company, cost of goods sold is a variable cost that gets included in the "Variable expenses" portion of the contribution format income statement. The **contribution margin** is the amount remaining from sales revenues after variable expenses have been deducted. This amount *contributes* toward covering fixed expenses and then toward profits for the period.

The contribution format income statement is used as an internal planning and decision-making tool. Its emphasis on cost behavior aids cost-volume-profit analysis (such as we shall be doing in a subsequent chapter), management performance appraisals, and budgeting. Moreover, the contribution approach helps managers organize data pertinent to numerous decisions such as product-line analysis, pricing, use of scarce resources, and make or buy analysis. All of these topics are covered in later chapters.

Cost Classifications for Decision Making

Costs are an important feature of many business decisions. In making decisions, it is essential to have a firm grasp of the concepts *differential cost, opportunity cost,* and *sunk cost.*

LO2–7
Understand cost classifications used in making decisions: differential costs, opportunity costs, and sunk costs.

Differential Cost and Revenue

Decisions involve choosing between alternatives. In business decisions, each alternative will have costs and benefits that must be compared to the costs and benefits of the other available alternatives. A difference in costs between any two alternatives is known as a

Chapter 2

differential cost. A difference in revenues (usually just sales) between any two alternatives is known as **differential revenue**.

A differential cost is also known as an **incremental cost**, although technically an incremental cost should refer only to an increase in cost from one alternative to another; decreases in cost should be referred to as *decremental costs*. Differential cost is a broader term, encompassing both cost increases (incremental costs) and cost decreases (decremental costs) between alternatives.

The accountant's differential cost concept can be compared to the economist's marginal cost concept. In speaking of changes in cost and revenue, the economist uses the terms *marginal cost* and *marginal revenue*. The revenue that can be obtained from selling one more unit of product is called marginal revenue, and the cost involved in producing one more unit of product is called marginal cost. The economist's marginal concept is basically the same as the accountant's differential concept applied to a single unit of output.

Differential costs can be either fixed or variable. To illustrate, assume that Natural Cosmetics, Inc., is thinking about changing its marketing method from distribution through retailers to distribution by a network of neighborhood sales representatives. Present costs and revenues are compared to projected costs and revenues in the following table:

	Retailer Distribution (present)	Sales Representatives (proposed)	Differential Costs and Revenues
Sales (Variable)	$700,000	$800,000	$100,000
Cost of goods sold (Variable)	350,000	400,000	50,000
Advertising (Fixed)	80,000	45,000	(35,000)
Commissions (Variable)	0	40,000	40,000
Warehouse depreciation (Fixed)	50,000	80,000	30,000
Other expenses (Fixed)	60,000	60,000	0
Total expenses	540,000	625,000	85,000
Net operating income	$160,000	$175,000	$ 15,000

According to the above analysis, the differential revenue is $100,000 and the differential costs total $85,000, leaving a positive differential net operating income of $15,000 in favor of using sales representatives.

In general, only the differences between alternatives are relevant in decisions. Those items that are the same under all alternatives and that are not affected by the decision can be ignored. For example, in the Natural Cosmetics, Inc., example above, the "Other expenses" category, which is $60,000 under both alternatives, can be ignored because it has no effect on the decision. If it were removed from the calculations, the sales representatives would still be preferred by $15,000. This is an extremely important principle in management accounting that we will revisit in later chapters.

Opportunity Cost and Sunk Cost

Opportunity cost is the potential benefit that is given up when one alternative is selected over another. For example, assume that you have a part-time job while attending college that pays $200 per week. If you spend one week at the beach during spring break without pay, then the $200 in lost wages would be an opportunity cost of taking the week off to be at the beach. Opportunity costs are not usually found in accounting records, but they are costs that must be explicitly considered in every decision a manager makes. Virtually every alternative involves an opportunity cost.

A **sunk cost** is a cost *that has already been incurred* and that cannot be changed by any decision made now or in the future. Because sunk costs cannot be changed by any decision, they are not differential costs. And because only differential costs are relevant in a decision, sunk costs should always be ignored.

To illustrate a sunk cost, assume that a company paid $50,000 several years ago for a special-purpose machine. The machine was used to make a product that is now obsolete and is no longer being sold. Even though in hindsight purchasing the machine may have been unwise, the $50,000 cost has already been incurred and cannot be undone. And it would be folly to continue making the obsolete product in a misguided attempt to "recover" the original cost of the machine. In short, the $50,000 originally paid for the machine is a sunk cost that should be ignored in current decisions.

Summary

In this chapter, we have discussed ways in which managers classify costs. How the costs will be used—for assigning costs to cost objects, preparing external reports, predicting cost behavior, or decision making—will dictate how the costs are classified.

For purposes of assigning costs to cost objects such as products or departments, costs are classified as direct or indirect. Direct costs can be conveniently traced to cost objects. Indirect costs cannot be conveniently traced to cost objects.

For external reporting purposes, costs are classified as either product costs or period costs. Product costs are assigned to inventories and are considered assets until the products are sold. At the point of sale, product costs become cost of goods sold on the income statement. In contrast, period costs are taken directly to the income statement as expenses in the period in which they are incurred.

For purposes of predicting how costs will react to changes in activity, costs are classified into three categories—variable, fixed, and mixed. Variable costs, in total, are strictly proportional to activity. The variable cost per unit is constant. Fixed costs, in total, remain the same as the activity level changes within the relevant range. The average fixed cost per unit decreases as the activity level increases. Mixed costs consist of variable and fixed elements and can be expressed in equation form as $Y = a + bX$, where X is the activity, Y is the total cost, a is the fixed cost element, and b is the variable cost per unit of activity.

If the relation between cost and activity appears to be linear based on a scattergraph plot, then the variable and fixed components of a mixed cost can be estimated using the high-low method, which implicitly draws a straight line through the points of lowest activity and highest activity, or the least-squares regression method, which uses all of the data points to compute a regression line that minimizes the sum of the squares errors.

The traditional income statement format is used primarily for external reporting purposes. It organizes costs using product and period cost classifications. The contribution format income statement aids decision making because it organizes costs using variable and fixed cost classifications.

For purposes of making decisions, the concepts of differential cost and revenue, opportunity cost, and sunk cost are vitally important. Differential costs and revenues are the costs and revenues that differ between alternatives. Opportunity cost is the benefit that is forgone when one alternative is selected over another. Sunk cost is a cost that occurred in the past and cannot be altered. Differential costs and opportunity costs should be carefully considered in decisions. Sunk costs are always irrelevant in decisions and should be ignored.

Review Problem 1: Cost Terms

Many new cost terms have been introduced in this chapter. It will take you some time to learn what each term means and how to properly classify costs in an organization. Consider the following example: Porter Company manufactures furniture, including tables. Selected costs are given below:

1. The tables are made of wood that costs $100 per table.
2. The tables are assembled by workers, at a wage cost of $40 per table.
3. Workers assembling the tables are supervised by a factory supervisor who is paid $38,000 per year.
4. Electrical costs are $2 per machine-hour. Four machine-hours are required to produce a table.
5. The depreciation on the machines used to make the tables totals $10,000 per year. The machines have no resale value and do not wear out through use.
6. The salary of the president of the company is $100,000 per year.
7. The company spends $250,000 per year to advertise its products.
8. Salespersons are paid a commission of $30 for each table sold.
9. Instead of producing the tables, the company could rent its factory space for $50,000 per year.

Required:

Classify these costs according to the various cost terms used in the chapter. *Carefully study the classification of each cost.* If you don't understand why a particular cost is classified the way it is, reread the section of the chapter discussing the particular cost term. The terms *variable cost* and *fixed cost* refer to how costs behave with respect to the number of tables produced in a year.

Solution to Review Problem 1

	Variable Cost	Fixed Cost	Period (Selling and Administrative) Cost	Direct Materials	Direct Labor	Manufacturing Overhead	Sunk Cost	Opportunity Cost
1. Wood used in a table ($100 per table)	X			X				
2. Labor cost to assemble a table ($40 per table)	X				X			
3. Salary of the factory supervisor ($38,000 per year)		X				X		
4. Cost of electricity to produce tables ($2 per machine-hour)	X					X		
5. Depreciation of machines used to produce tables ($10,000 per year)		X				X	X*	
6. Salary of the company president ($100,000 per year)		X	X					
7. Advertising expense ($250,000 per year)		X	X					
8. Commissions paid to salespersons ($30 per table sold)	X		X					
9. Rental income forgone on factory space								X†

*This is a sunk cost because the outlay for the equipment was made in a previous period.
†This is an opportunity cost because it represents the potential benefit that is lost or sacrificed as a result of using the factory space to produce tables. Opportunity cost is a special category of cost that is not ordinarily recorded in an organization's accounting records. To avoid possible confusion with other costs, we will not attempt to classify this cost in any other way except as an opportunity cost.

Review Problem 2: High-Low Method

The administrator of Azalea Hills Hospital would like a cost formula linking the administrative costs involved in admitting patients to the number of patients admitted during a month. The Admitting Department's costs and the number of patients admitted during the immediately preceding eight months are given in the following table:

Month	Number of Patients Admitted	Admitting Department Costs
May	1,800	$14,700
June	1,900	$15,200
July	1,700	$13,700
August	1,600	$14,000
September	1,500	$14,300
October	1,300	$13,100
November	1,100	$12,800
December	1,500	$14,600

Required:
1. Use the high-low method to estimate the fixed and variable components of admitting costs.
2. Express the fixed and variable components of admitting costs as a cost formula in the form $Y = a + bX$.

Solution to Review Problem 2

1. The first step in the high-low method is to identify the periods of the lowest and highest activity. Those periods are November (1,100 patients admitted) and June (1,900 patients admitted).

   The second step is to compute the variable cost per unit using those two data points:

Month	Number of Patients Admitted	Admitting Department Costs
High activity level (June)	1,900	$15,200
Low activity level (November)	1,100	12,800
Change	800	$ 2,400

$$\text{Variable cost} = \frac{\text{Change in cost}}{\text{Change in activity}} = \frac{\$2,400}{800 \text{ patients admitted}} = \$3 \text{ per patient admitted}$$

   The third step is to compute the fixed cost element by deducting the variable cost element from the total cost at either the high or low activity. In the computation below, the high point of activity is used:

   Fixed cost element = Total cost − Variable cost element

   = $15,200 − ($3 per patient admitted × 1,900 patients admitted)

   = $9,500

2. The cost formula is $Y = \$9,500 + \$3X$.

Glossary

Account analysis A method for analyzing cost behavior in which an account is classified as either variable or fixed based on the analyst's prior knowledge of how the cost in the account behaves. (p. 39)

Activity base A measure of whatever causes the incurrence of a variable cost. For example, the total cost of X-ray film in a hospital will increase as the number of X-rays taken increases. Therefore, the number of X-rays is the activity base that explains the total cost of X-ray film. (p. 33)

Chapter 2

Administrative costs All executive, organizational, and clerical costs associated with the general management of an organization rather than with manufacturing or selling. (p. 30)

Committed fixed costs Investments in facilities, equipment, and basic organizational structure that can't be significantly reduced even for short periods of time without making fundamental changes. (p. 35)

Common cost A cost that is incurred to support a number of cost objects but that cannot be traced to them individually. For example, the wage cost of the pilot of a 747 airliner is a common cost of all of the passengers on the aircraft. Without the pilot, there would be no flight and no passengers. But no part of the pilot's wage is caused by any one passenger taking the flight. (p. 29)

Contribution approach An income statement format that organizes costs by their behavior. Costs are separated into variable and fixed categories rather than being separated into product and period costs for external reporting purposes. (p. 45)

Contribution margin The amount remaining from sales revenues after all variable expenses have been deducted. (p. 45)

Conversion cost Direct labor cost plus manufacturing overhead cost. (p. 32)

Cost behavior The way in which a cost reacts to changes in the level of activity. (p. 33)

Cost object Anything for which cost data are desired. Examples of cost objects are products, customers, jobs, and parts of the organization such as departments or divisions. (p. 28)

Cost structure The relative proportion of fixed, variable, and mixed costs in an organization. (p. 33)

Dependent variable A variable that responds to some causal factor; total cost is the dependent variable, as represented by the letter Y, in the equation $Y = a + bX$. (p. 39)

Differential cost A difference in cost between two alternatives. Also see *Incremental cost*. (p. 46)

Differential revenue The difference in revenue between two alternatives. (p. 46)

Direct cost A cost that can be easily and conveniently traced to a specified cost object. (p. 28)

Direct labor Factory labor costs that can be easily traced to individual units of product. Also called *touch labor*. (p. 29)

Direct materials Materials that become an integral part of a finished product and whose costs can be conveniently traced to it. (p. 29)

Discretionary fixed costs Those fixed costs that arise from annual decisions by management to spend on certain fixed cost items, such as advertising and research. (p. 35)

Engineering approach A detailed analysis of cost behavior based on an industrial engineer's evaluation of the inputs that are required to carry out a particular activity and of the prices of those inputs. (p. 39)

Fixed cost A cost that remains constant, in total, regardless of changes in the level of activity within the relevant range. If a fixed cost is expressed on a per unit basis, it varies inversely with the level of activity. (p. 34)

High-low method A method of separating a mixed cost into its fixed and variable elements by analyzing the change in cost between the high and low activity levels. (p. 40)

Incremental cost An increase in cost between two alternatives. Also see *Differential cost*. (p. 46)

Independent variable A variable that acts as a causal factor; activity is the independent variable, as represented by the letter X, in the equation $Y = a + bX$. (p. 40)

Indirect cost A cost that cannot be easily and conveniently traced to a specified cost object. (p. 29)

Indirect labor The labor costs of janitors, supervisors, materials handlers, and other factory workers that cannot be conveniently traced to particular products. (p. 30)

Indirect materials Small items of material such as glue and nails that may be an integral part of a finished product, but whose costs cannot be easily or conveniently traced to it. (p. 29)

Inventoriable costs Synonym for product costs. (p. 31)

Least-squares regression method A method of separating a mixed cost into its fixed and variable elements by fitting a regression line that minimizes the sum of the squared errors. (p. 42)

Linear cost behavior Cost behavior is said to be linear whenever a straight line is a reasonable approximation for the relation between cost and activity. (p. 40)

Manufacturing overhead All manufacturing costs except direct materials and direct labor. (p. 30)

Mixed cost A cost that contains both variable and fixed cost elements. (p. 37)

Opportunity cost The potential benefit that is given up when one alternative is selected over another. (p. 46)

Period costs Costs that are taken directly to the income statement as expenses in the period in which they are incurred or accrued. (p. 31)

Prime cost Direct materials cost plus direct labor cost. (p. 32)

Product costs All costs that are involved in acquiring or making a product. In the case of manufactured goods, these costs consist of direct materials, direct labor, and manufacturing overhead. Also see *Inventoriable costs.* (p. 31)

Raw materials Any materials that go into the final product. (p. 29)

Relevant range The range of activity within which assumptions about variable and fixed cost behavior are valid. (p. 36)

Selling costs All costs that are incurred to secure customer orders and get the finished product or service into the hands of the customer. (p. 30)

Sunk cost A cost that has already been incurred and that cannot be changed by any decision made now or in the future. (p. 46)

Variable cost A cost that varies, in total, in direct proportion to changes in the level of activity. A variable cost is constant per unit. (p. 33)

Questions

2–1 What are the three major elements of product costs in a manufacturing company?

2–2 Define the following: (*a*) direct materials, (*b*) indirect materials, (*c*) direct labor, (*d*) indirect labor, and (*e*) manufacturing overhead.

2–3 Explain the difference between a product cost and a period cost.

2–4 Distinguish between (*a*) a variable cost, (*b*) a fixed cost, and (*c*) a mixed cost.

2–5 What effect does an increase in volume have on—
  a. Unit fixed costs?
  b. Unit variable costs?
  c. Total fixed costs?
  d. Total variable costs?

2–6 Define the following terms: (*a*) cost behavior and (*b*) relevant range.

2–7 What is meant by an *activity base* when dealing with variable costs? Give several examples of activity bases.

2–8 Managers often assume a strictly linear relationship between cost and volume. How can this practice be defended in light of the fact that many costs are curvilinear?

2–9 Distinguish between discretionary fixed costs and committed fixed costs.

2–10 Does the concept of the relevant range apply to fixed costs? Explain.

2–11 What is the major disadvantage of the high-low method?

2–12 Give the general formula for a mixed cost. Which term represents the variable cost? The fixed cost?

2–13 What is meant by the term *least-squares regression?*

2–14 What is the difference between a contribution format income statement and a traditional format income statement?

2–15 What is the contribution margin?

2–16 Define the following terms: differential cost, opportunity cost, and sunk cost.

2–17 Only variable costs can be differential costs. Do you agree? Explain.

Multiple-choice questions are provided on the text website at www.mhhe.com/garrison15e.

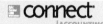 **Applying Excel**

Available with McGraw-Hill's *Connect*® Accounting.

The Excel worksheet form that appears on the next page is to be used to recreate Exhibit 2–9 on page 44. Download the workbook containing this form from the Online Learning Center at www.mhhe.com/garrison15e. *On the website you will also receive instructions about how to use this worksheet form.*   **LO2–6**

	A	B	C	D
1	Chapter 2: Applying Excel			
2				
3	Data			
4	Sales	$12,000		
5	Variable costs:			
6	Cost of goods sold	$6,000		
7	Variable selling	$600		
8	Variable administrative	$400		
9	Fixed costs:			
10	Fixed selling	$2,500		
11	Fixed administrative	$1,500		
12				
13	Enter a formula into each of the cells marked with a ? below			
14	Exhibit 2-9			
15				
16	Traditional Format Income Statement			
17	Sales		?	
18	Cost of goods sold		?	
19	Gross margin		?	
20	Selling and administrative expenses:			
21	Selling	?		
22	Administrative	?	?	
23	Net operating income		?	
24				
25	Contribution Format Income Statement			
26	Sales		?	
27	Variable expenses:			
28	Cost of goods sold	?		
29	Variable selling	?		
30	Variable administration	?	?	
31	Contribution margin		?	
32	Fixed expenses:			
33	Fixed selling	?		
34	Fixed administrative	?	?	
35	Net operating income		?	
36				

⊩ ◀ ▶ ▶⊩   Chapter 2 Form   Filled in Chapter 2 Fo ◀

Required:

1. Check your worksheet by changing the variable selling cost in the Data area to $900, keeping all of the other data the same as in Exhibit 2–9. If your worksheet is operating properly, the net operating income under the traditional format income statement and under the contribution format income statement should now be $700 and the contribution margin should now be $4,700. If you do not get these answers, find the errors in your worksheet and correct them.

   How much is the gross margin? Did it change? Why or why not?

2. Suppose that sales are 10% higher as shown below:

Sales	$13,200
Variable costs:	
Cost of goods sold	$6,600
Variable selling	$990
Variable administrative	$440
Fixed costs:	
Fixed selling	$2,500
Fixed administrative	$1,500

Enter this new data into your worksheet. Make sure that you change all of the data that are different—not just the sales. Print or copy the income statements from your worksheet.

What happened to the variable costs and to the fixed costs when sales increased by 10%? Why? Did the contribution margin increase by 10%? Why or why not? Did the net operating income increase by 10%? Why or why not?

Managerial Accounting and Cost Concepts   **53**

 The Foundational 15

Available with McGraw-Hill's *Connect® Accounting.*

Martinez Company's relevant range of production is 7,500 units to 12,500 units. When it produces and sells 10,000 units, its unit costs are as follows:

LO2–1, LO2–2, LO2–3,
LO2–4, LO2–6, LO2–7

	Amount Per Unit
Direct materials	$6.00
Direct labor	$3.50
Variable manufacturing overhead	$1.50
Fixed manufacturing overhead	$4.00
Fixed selling expense	$3.00
Fixed administrative expense	$2.00
Sales commissions	$1.00
Variable administrative expense	$0.50

Required:

1. For financial accounting purposes, what is the total amount of product costs incurred to make 10,000 units?
2. For financial accounting purposes, what is the total amount of period costs incurred to sell 10,000 units?
3. If 8,000 units are sold, what is the variable cost per unit sold?
4. If 12,500 units are sold, what is the variable cost per unit sold?
5. If 8,000 units are sold, what is the total amount of variable costs related to the units sold?
6. If 12,500 units are sold, what is the total amount of variable costs related to the units sold?
7. If 8,000 units are produced, what is the average fixed manufacturing cost per unit produced?
8. If 12,500 units are produced, what is the average fixed manufacturing cost per unit produced?
9. If 8,000 units are produced, what is the total amount of fixed manufacturing cost incurred to support this level of production?
10. If 12,500 units are produced, what is the total amount of fixed manufacturing cost incurred to support this level of production?
11. If 8,000 units are produced, what is the total amount of manufacturing overhead cost incurred to support this level of production? What is this total amount expressed on a per unit basis?
12. If 12,500 units are produced, what is the total amount of manufacturing overhead cost incurred to support this level of production? What is this total amount expressed on a per unit basis?
13. If the selling price is $22 per unit, what is the contribution margin per unit sold?
14. If 11,000 units are produced, what are the total amounts of direct and indirect manufacturing costs incurred to support this level of production?
15. What total incremental cost will Martinez incur if it increases production from 10,000 to 10,001 units?

 Exercises

All applicable exercises are available with McGraw-Hill's *Connect® Accounting.*

EXERCISE 2–1 Identifying Direct and Indirect Costs [LO2–1]
Northwest Hospital is a full-service hospital that provides everything from major surgery and emergency room care to outpatient clinics.

Required:
For each cost incurred at Northwest Hospital, indicate whether it would most likely be a direct cost or an indirect cost of the specified cost object by placing an X in the appropriate column.

Cost	Cost Object	Direct Cost	Indirect Cost
Ex. Catered food served to patients	A particular patient	X	
1. The wages of pediatric nurses	The pediatric department		
2. Prescription drugs	A particular patient		
3. Heating the hospital	The pediatric department		
4. The salary of the head of pediatrics	The pediatric department		
5. The salary of the head of pediatrics	A particular pediatric patient		
6. Hospital chaplain's salary	A particular patient		
7. Lab tests by outside contractor	A particular patient		
8. Lab tests by outside contractor	A particular department		

EXERCISE 2–2 Classifying Manufacturing Costs [LO2–2]

The PC Works assembles custom computers from components supplied by various manufacturers. The company is very small and its assembly shop and retail sales store are housed in a single facility in a Redmond, Washington, industrial park. Listed below are some of the costs that are incurred at the company.

Required:

For each cost, indicate whether it would most likely be classified as direct labor, direct materials, manufacturing overhead, selling, or an administrative cost.

1. The cost of a hard drive installed in a computer.
2. The cost of advertising in the *Puget Sound Computer User* newspaper.
3. The wages of employees who assemble computers from components.
4. Sales commissions paid to the company's salespeople.
5. The wages of the assembly shop's supervisor.
6. The wages of the company's accountant.
7. Depreciation on equipment used to test assembled computers before release to customers.
8. Rent on the facility in the industrial park.

EXERCISE 2–3 Classification of Costs as Product or Period Cost [LO2–3]

Suppose that you have been given a summer job as an intern at Issac Aircams, a company that manufactures sophisticated spy cameras for remote-controlled military reconnaissance aircraft. The company, which is privately owned, has approached a bank for a loan to help it finance its growth. The bank requires financial statements before approving such a loan. You have been asked to help prepare the financial statements and were given the following list of costs:

1. Depreciation on salespersons' cars.
2. Rent on equipment used in the factory.
3. Lubricants used for machine maintenance.
4. Salaries of personnel who work in the finished goods warehouse.
5. Soap and paper towels used by factory workers at the end of a shift.
6. Factory supervisors' salaries.
7. Heat, water, and power consumed in the factory.
8. Materials used for boxing products for shipment overseas. (Units are not normally boxed.)
9. Advertising costs.
10. Workers' compensation insurance for factory employees.
11. Depreciation on chairs and tables in the factory lunchroom.
12. The wages of the receptionist in the administrative offices.
13. Cost of leasing the corporate jet used by the company's executives.
14. The cost of renting rooms at a Florida resort for the annual sales conference.
15. The cost of packaging the company's product.

Required:

Classify the above costs as either product costs or period costs for the purpose of preparing the financial statements for the bank.

EXERCISE 2–4 Fixed and Variable Cost Behavior [LO2–4]

Espresso Express operates a number of espresso coffee stands in busy suburban malls. The fixed weekly expense of a coffee stand is $1,200 and the variable cost per cup of coffee served is $0.22.

Required:

1. Fill in the following table with your estimates of total costs and cost per cup of coffee at the indicated levels of activity for a coffee stand. Round off the cost of a cup of coffee to the nearest tenth of a cent.

	Cups of Coffee Served in a Week		
	2,000	2,100	2,200
Fixed cost	?	?	?
Variable cost	?	?	?
Total cost	?	?	?
Average cost per cup of coffee served	?	?	?

2. Does the average cost per cup of coffee served increase, decrease, or remain the same as the number of cups of coffee served in a week increases? Explain.

EXERCISE 2–5 High-Low Method [LO2–5]

The Cheyenne Hotel in Big Sky, Montana, has accumulated records of the total electrical costs of the hotel and the number of occupancy-days over the last year. An occupancy-day represents a room rented out for one day. The hotel's business is highly seasonal, with peaks occurring during the ski season and in the summer.

Month	Occupancy-Days	Electrical Costs
January	1,736	$4,127
February	1,904	$4,207
March	2,356	$5,083
April	960	$2,857
May	360	$1,871
June	744	$2,696
July	2,108	$4,670
August	2,406	$5,148
September	840	$2,691
October	124	$1,588
November	720	$2,454
December	1,364	$3,529

Required:

1. Using the high-low method, estimate the fixed cost of electricity per month and the variable cost of electricity per occupancy-day. Round off the fixed cost to the nearest whole dollar and the variable cost to the nearest whole cent.
2. What other factors other than occupancy-days are likely to affect the variation in electrical costs from month to month?

EXERCISE 2–6 Traditional and Contribution Format Income Statements [LO2–6]

Cherokee Inc. is a merchandiser that provided the following information:

	Amount
Number of units sold	20,000
Selling price per unit	$30
Variable selling expense per unit	$4
Variable administrative expense per unit	$2
Total fixed selling expense	$40,000
Total fixed administrative expense	$30,000
Beginning merchandise inventory	$24,000
Ending merchandise inventory	$44,000
Merchandise purchases	$180,000

56

Chapter 2

Required:
1. Prepare a traditional income statement.
2. Prepare a contribution format income statement.

EXERCISE 2–7 Differential, Opportunity, and Sunk Costs [LO2–7]
Northwest Hospital is a full-service hospital that provides everything from major surgery and emergency room care to outpatient clinics. The hospital's Radiology Department is considering replacing an old inefficient X-ray machine with a state-of-the-art digital X-ray machine. The new machine would provide higher quality X-rays in less time and at a lower cost per X-ray. It would also require less power and would use a color laser printer to produce easily readable X-ray images. Instead of investing the funds in the new X-ray machine, the Laboratory Department is lobbying the hospital's management to buy a new DNA analyzer.

Required:
For each of the items below, indicate by placing an *X* in the appropriate column whether it should be considered a differential cost, an opportunity cost, or a sunk cost in the decision to replace the old X-ray machine with a new machine. If none of the categories apply for a particular item, leave all columns blank.

Item	Differential Cost	Opportunity Cost	Sunk Cost
Ex. Cost of X-ray film used in the old machine	X		
1. Cost of the old X-ray machine			
2. The salary of the head of the Radiology Department			
3. The salary of the head of the Pediatrics Department			
4. Cost of the new color laser printer			
5. Rent on the space occupied by Radiology			
6. The cost of maintaining the old machine			
7. Benefits from a new DNA analyzer			
8. Cost of electricity to run the X-ray machines			

EXERCISE 2–8 Cost Behavior; High-Low Method [LO2–4, LO2–5]
Hoi Chong Transport, Ltd., operates a fleet of delivery trucks in Singapore. The company has determined that if a truck is driven 105,000 kilometers during a year, the average operating cost is 11.4 cents per kilometer. If a truck is driven only 70,000 kilometers during a year, the average operating cost increases to 13.4 cents per kilometer.

Required:
1. Using the high-low method, estimate the variable and fixed cost elements of the annual cost of the truck operation.
2. Express the variable and fixed costs in the form $Y = a + bX$.
3. If a truck were driven 80,000 kilometers during a year, what total cost would you expect to be incurred?

EXERCISE 2–9 Cost Terminology for Manufacturers [LO2–2, LO2–3]
Arden Company reported the following costs and expenses for the most recent month:

Direct materials	$80,000
Direct labor	$42,000
Manufacturing overhead	$19,000
Selling expenses	$22,000
Administrative expenses	$35,000

Required:
1. What is the total amount of product costs?
2. What is the total amount of period costs?
3. What is the total amount of conversion costs?
4. What is the total amount of prime costs?

EXERCISE 2–10 Cost Behavior; Contribution Format Income Statement [LO2–4, LO2–6]
Harris Company manufactures and sells a single product. A partially completed schedule of the company's total and per unit costs over the relevant range of 30,000 to 50,000 units produced and sold annually is given below:

	Units Produced and Sold		
	30,000	40,000	50,000
Total costs:			
Variable costs	$180,000	?	?
Fixed costs	300,000	?	?
Total costs	$480,000	?	?
Cost per unit:			
Variable cost	?	?	?
Fixed cost	?	?	?
Total cost per unit	?	?	?

Required:
1. Complete the schedule of the company's total and unit costs above.
2. Assume that the company produces and sells 45,000 units during the year at a selling price of $16 per unit. Prepare a contribution format income statement for the year.

EXERCISE 2–11 High-Low Method; Scattergraph Analysis [LO2–4, LO2–5]
The following data relating to units shipped and total shipping expense have been assembled by Archer Company, a wholesaler of large, custom-built air-conditioning units for commercial buildings:

Month	Units Shipped	Total Shipping Expense
January	3	$1,800
February	6	$2,300
March	4	$1,700
April	5	$2,000
May	7	$2,300
June	8	$2,700
July	2	$1,200

Required:
1. Prepare a scattergraph using the data given above. Plot cost on the vertical axis and activity on the horizontal axis. Is there an approximately linear relationship between shipping expense and the number of units shipped?
2. Using the high-low method, estimate the cost formula for shipping expense. Draw a straight line through the high and low data points shown in the scattergraph that you prepared in requirement 1. Make sure your line intersects the Y axis.
3. Comment on the accuracy of your high-low estimates assuming a least-squares regression analysis estimated the total fixed costs to be $910.71 per month and the variable cost to be $217.86 per unit. How would the straight line that you drew in requirement 2 differ from a straight line that minimizes the sum of the squared errors?
4. What factors, other than the number of units shipped, are likely to affect the company's shipping expense? Explain.

EXERCISE 2–12 Cost Classification [LO2–2, LO2–3, LO2–4, LO2–7]
Wollogong Group Ltd. of New South Wales, Australia, acquired its factory building about 10 years ago. For several years, the company has rented out a small annex attached to the rear of the building. The company has received a rental income of $30,000 per year on this space. The renter's lease will expire soon, and rather than renewing the lease, the company has decided to use the space itself to manufacture a new product.

Direct materials cost for the new product will total $80 per unit. To have a place to store finished units of product, the company will rent a small warehouse nearby. The rental cost will be $500 per month. In addition, the company must rent equipment for use in producing the new product; the rental cost will be $4,000 per month. Workers will be hired to manufacture the new product, with direct labor cost amounting to $60 per unit. The space in the annex will continue to be depreciated on a straight-line basis, as in prior years. This depreciation is $8,000 per year.

Advertising costs for the new product will total $50,000 per year. A supervisor will be hired to oversee production; her salary will be $1,500 per month. Electricity for operating machines will be $1.20 per unit. Costs of shipping the new product to customers will be $9 per unit.

Chapter 2

To provide funds to purchase materials, meet payrolls, and so forth, the company will have to liquidate some temporary investments. These investments are presently yielding a return of about $3,000 per year.

Required:
Prepare an answer sheet with the following column headings:

Name of the Cost	Variable Cost	Fixed Cost	Product Cost			Period (Selling and Administrative) Cost	Opportunity Cost	Sunk Cost
			Direct Materials	Direct Labor	Manufacturing Overhead			

List the different costs associated with the new product decision down the extreme left column (under Name of the Cost). Then place an *X* under each heading that helps to describe the type of cost involved. There may be *X*'s under several column headings for a single cost. (For example, a cost may be a fixed cost, a period cost, and a sunk cost; you would place an *X* under each of these column headings opposite the cost.)

EXERCISE 2–13 Traditional and Contribution Format Income Statements [LO2–6]
The Alpine House, Inc., is a large retailer of snow skis. The company assembled the information shown below for the quarter ended March 31:

	Amount
Total sales revenue	$150,000
Selling price per pair of skis	$750
Variable selling expense per pair of skis	$50
Variable administrative expense per pair of skis	$10
Total fixed selling expense	$20,000
Total fixed administrative expense	$20,000
Beginning merchandise inventory	$30,000
Ending merchandise inventory	$40,000
Merchandise purchases	$100,000

Required:
1. Prepare a traditional income statement for the quarter ended March 31.
2. Prepare a contribution format income statement for the quarter ended March 31.
3. What was the contribution toward fixed expenses and profits for each pair of skis sold during the quarter? (State this figure in a single dollar amount per pair of skis.)

EXERCISE 2–14 High-Low Method; Predicting Cost [LO2–4, LO2–5]
The Lakeshore Hotel's guest-days of occupancy and custodial supplies expense over the last seven months were:

Month	Guest-Days of Occupancy	Custodial Supplies Expense
March	4,000	$7,500
April	6,500	$8,250
May	8,000	$10,500
June	10,500	$12,000
July	12,000	$13,500
August	9,000	$10,750
September	7,500	$9,750

Guest-days is a measure of the overall activity at the hotel. For example, a guest who stays at the hotel for three days is counted as three guest-days.

Required:
1. Using the high-low method, estimate a cost formula for custodial supplies expense.
2. Using the cost formula you derived above, what amount of custodial supplies expense would you expect to be incurred at an occupancy level of 11,000 guest-days?
3. Prepare a scattergraph using the data given above. Plot custodial supplies expense on the vertical axis and the number of guest-days occupied on the horizontal axis. Draw a straight line

through the two data points that correspond to the high and low levels of activity. Make sure your line intersects the *Y*-axis.

4.   Comment on the accuracy of your high-low estimates assuming a least-squares regression analysis estimated the total fixed costs to be $3,973.10 per month and the variable cost to be $0.77 per guest-day. How would the straight line that you drew in requirement 3 differ from a straight line that minimizes the sum of the squared errors?

5.   Using the least-squares regression estimates given in requirement 4, what custodial supplies expense would you expect to be incurred at an occupancy level of 11,000 guest-days?

EXERCISE 2–15 Classification of Costs as Variable or Fixed and as Product or Period [LO2–3, LO2–4]

Below are listed various costs that are found in organizations.

1.   Hamburger buns in a Wendy's outlet.
2.   Advertising by a dental office.
3.   Apples processed and canned by Del Monte.
4.   Shipping canned apples from a Del Monte plant to customers.
5.   Insurance on a Bausch & Lomb factory producing contact lenses.
6.   Insurance on IBM's corporate headquarters.
7.   Salary of a supervisor overseeing production of printers at Hewlett-Packard.
8.   Commissions paid to automobile salespersons.
9.   Depreciation of factory lunchroom facilities at a General Electric plant.
10.   Steering wheels installed in BMWs.

Required:

Classify each cost as being either variable or fixed with respect to the number of units produced and sold. Also classify each cost as either a selling and administrative cost or a product cost. Prepare your answer sheet as shown below. Place an *X* in the appropriate columns to show the proper classification of each cost.

	Cost Behavior		Period (Selling and Administrative) Cost	Product Cost
Cost Item	Variable	Fixed		

 Problems

All applicable problems are available with McGraw-Hill's *Connect® Accounting*.

PROBLEM 2–16 Cost Behavior; High-Low Method; Contribution Format Income Statement [LO2–4, LO2–5, LO2–6]

Morrisey & Brown, Ltd., of Sydney is a merchandising company that is the sole distributor of a product that is increasing in popularity among Australian consumers. The company's income statements for the three most recent months follow:

Morrisey & Brown, Ltd. Income Statements For the Three Months Ended September 30			
	July	August	September
Sales in units	4,000	4,500	5,000
Sales	$400,000	$450,000	$500,000
Cost of goods sold	240,000	270,000	300,000
Gross margin	160,000	180,000	200,000
Selling and administrative expenses:			
Advertising expense	21,000	21,000	21,000
Shipping expense	34,000	36,000	38,000
Salaries and commissions	78,000	84,000	90,000
Insurance expense	6,000	6,000	6,000
Depreciation expense	15,000	15,000	15,000
Total selling and administrative expenses	154,000	162,000	170,000
Net operating income	$ 6,000	$ 18,000	$ 30,000

Required:
1. Identify each of the company's expenses (including cost of goods sold) as either variable, fixed, or mixed.
2. Using the high-low method, separate each mixed expense into variable and fixed elements. State the cost formula for each mixed expense.
3. Redo the company's income statement at the 5,000-unit level of activity using the contribution format.

PROBLEM 2–17 High-Low Method; Predicting Cost [LO2–4, LO2–5]
Sawaya Co., Ltd., of Japan is a manufacturing company whose total factory overhead costs fluctuate considerably from year to year according to increases and decreases in the number of direct labor-hours worked in the factory. Total factory overhead costs at high and low levels of activity for recent years are given below:

	Level of Activity	
	Low	High
Direct labor-hours	50,000	75,000
Total factory overhead costs	$14,250,000	$17,625,000

The factory overhead costs above consist of indirect materials, rent, and maintenance. The company has analyzed these costs at the 50,000-hour level of activity as follows:

Indirect materials (variable)	$ 5,000,000
Rent (fixed)	6,000,000
Maintenance (mixed)	3,250,000
Total factory overhead costs	$14,250,000

To have data available for planning, the company wants to break down the maintenance cost into its variable and fixed cost elements.

Required:
1. Estimate how much of the $17,625,000 factory overhead cost at the high level of activity consists of maintenance cost. (*Hint:* To do this, it may be helpful to first determine how much of the $17,625,000 consists of indirect materials and rent. Think about the behavior of variable and fixed costs!)
2. Using the high-low method, estimate a cost formula for maintenance.
3. What total factory overhead costs would you expect the company to incur at an operating level of 70,000 direct labor-hours?

PROBLEM 2–18 Variable and Fixed Costs; Subtleties of Direct and Indirect Costs [LO2–1, LO2–4]
Madison Seniors Care Center is a nonprofit organization that provides a variety of health services to the elderly. The center is organized into a number of departments, one of which is the Meals-On-Wheels program that delivers hot meals to seniors in their homes on a daily basis. Below are listed a number of costs of the center and the Meals-On-Wheels program.
example The cost of groceries used in meal preparation.
  a. The cost of leasing the Meals-On-Wheels van.
  b. The cost of incidental supplies such as salt, pepper, napkins, and so on.
  c. The cost of gasoline consumed by the Meals-On-Wheels van.
  d. The rent on the facility that houses Madison Seniors Care Center, including the Meals-On-Wheels program.
  e. The salary of the part-time manager of the Meals-On-Wheels program.
  f. Depreciation on the kitchen equipment used in the Meals-On-Wheels program.
  g. The hourly wages of the caregiver who drives the van and delivers the meals.
  h. The costs of complying with health safety regulations in the kitchen.
  i. The costs of mailing letters soliciting donations to the Meals-On-Wheels program.

Required:
For each cost listed above, indicate whether it is a direct or indirect cost of the Meals-On-Wheels program, whether it is a direct or indirect cost of particular seniors served by the program, and

whether it is variable or fixed with respect to the number of seniors served. Use the form below for your answer.

Item	Description	Direct or Indirect Cost of the Meals-on-Wheels Program		Direct or Indirect Cost of Particular Seniors Served by the Meals-on-Wheels Program		Variable or Fixed with Respect to the Number of Seniors Served by the Meals-on-Wheels Program	
		Direct	Indirect	Direct	Indirect	Variable	Fixed
Example	The cost of groceries used in meal preparation...	X		X		X	

PROBLEM 2–19 Contribution Format versus Traditional Income Statement [LO2–6]

Marwick's Pianos, Inc., purchases pianos from a large manufacturer and sells them at the retail level. The pianos cost, on the average, $2,450 each from the manufacturer. Marwick's Pianos, Inc., sells the pianos to its customers at an average price of $3,125 each. The selling and administrative costs that the company incurs in a typical month are presented below:

Costs	Cost Formula
Selling:	
Advertising	$700 per month
Sales salaries and commissions	$950 per month, plus 8% of sales
Delivery of pianos to customers	$30 per piano sold
Utilities	$350 per month
Depreciation of sales facilities	$800 per month
Administrative:	
Executive salaries	$2,500 per month
Insurance	$400 per month
Clerical	$1,000 per month, plus $20 per piano sold
Depreciation of office equipment	$300 per month

During August, Marwick's Pianos, Inc., sold and delivered 40 pianos.

Required:
1. Prepare an income statement for Marwick's Pianos, Inc., for August. Use the traditional format, with costs organized by function.
2. Redo (1) above, this time using the contribution format, with costs organized by behavior. Show costs and revenues on both a total and a per unit basis down through contribution margin.
3. Refer to the income statement you prepared in (2) above. Why might it be misleading to show the fixed costs on a per unit basis?

PROBLEM 2–20 High-Low Method; Predicting Cost [LO2–4, LO2–5]

Nova Company's total overhead cost at various levels of activity are presented below:

Month	Machine-Hours	Total Overhead Cost
April	70,000	$198,000
May	60,000	$174,000
June	80,000	$222,000
July	90,000	$246,000

62   Chapter 2

Assume that the total overhead cost above consists of utilities, supervisory salaries, and maintenance. The breakdown of these costs at the 60,000 machine-hour level of activity is:

Utilities (variable)	$ 48,000
Supervisory salaries (fixed) ...	21,000
Maintenance (mixed)	105,000
Total overhead cost	$174,000

Nova Company's management wants to break down the maintenance cost into its variable and fixed cost elements.

Required:
1. Estimate how much of the $246,000 of overhead cost in July was maintenance cost. (*Hint:* to do this, it may be helpful to first determine how much of the $246,000 consisted of utilities and supervisory salaries. Think about the behavior of variable and fixed costs!)
2. Using the high-low method, estimate a cost formula for maintenance.
3. Express the company's *total* overhead cost in the linear equation form $Y = a + bX$.
4. What *total* overhead cost would you expect to be incurred at an activity level of 75,000 machine-hours?

PROBLEM 2–21 Cost Classification [LO2–1, LO2–3, LO2–4]
Listed below are costs found in various organizations.
1. Property taxes, factory.
2. Boxes used for packaging detergent produced by the company.
3. Salespersons' commissions.
4. Supervisor's salary, factory.
5. Depreciation, executive autos.
6. Wages of workers assembling computers.
7. Insurance, finished goods warehouses.
8. Lubricants for production equipment.
9. Advertising costs.
10. Microchips used in producing calculators.
11. Shipping costs on merchandise sold.
12. Magazine subscriptions, factory lunchroom.
13. Thread in a garment factory.
14. Billing costs.
15. Executive life insurance.
16. Ink used in textbook production.
17. Fringe benefits, assembly-line workers.
18. Yarn used in sweater production.
19. Wages of receptionist, executive offices.

Required:
Prepare an answer sheet with column headings as shown below. For each cost item, indicate whether it would be variable or fixed with respect to the number of units produced and sold; and then whether it would be a selling cost, an administrative cost, or a manufacturing cost. If it is a manufacturing cost, indicate whether it would typically be treated as a direct cost or an indirect cost with respect to units of product. Three sample answers are provided for illustration.

Cost Item	Variable or Fixed	Selling Cost	Administrative Cost	Manufacturing (Product) Cost	
				Direct	Indirect
Direct labor	V			X	
Executive salaries	F		X		
Factory rent	F				X

PROBLEM 2–22 High-Low and Scattergraph Analysis [LO2–4, LO2–5]

Pleasant View Hospital of British Columbia has just hired a new chief administrator who is anxious to employ sound management and planning techniques in the business affairs of the hospital. Accordingly, she has directed her assistant to summarize the cost structure of the various departments so that data will be available for planning purposes.

The assistant is unsure how to classify the utilities costs in the Radiology Department because these costs do not exhibit either strictly variable or fixed cost behavior. Utilities costs are very high in the department due to a CAT scanner that draws a large amount of power and is kept running at all times. The scanner can't be turned off due to the long warm-up period required for its use. When the scanner is used to scan a patient, it consumes an additional burst of power. The assistant has accumulated the following data on utilities costs and use of the scanner since the first of the year.

Month	Number of Scans	Utilities Cost
January	60	$2,200
February	70	$2,600
March	90	$2,900
April	120	$3,300
May	100	$3,000
June	130	$3,600
July	150	$4,000
August	140	$3,600
September	110	$3,100
October	80	$2,500

The chief administrator has informed her assistant that the utilities cost is probably a mixed cost that will have to be broken down into its variable and fixed cost elements by use of a scattergraph. The assistant feels, however, that if an analysis of this type is necessary, then the high-low method should be used, since it is easier and quicker. The controller has suggested that there may be a better approach.

Required:

1. Using the high-low method, estimate a cost formula for utilities. Express the formula in the form $Y = a + bX$. (The variable rate should be stated in terms of cost per scan.)
2. Prepare a scattergraph by plotting the number of scans and utility cost on a graph. Draw a straight line though the two data points that correspond to the high and low levels of activity. Make sure your line intersects the Y-axis.
3. Comment on the accuracy of your high-low estimates assuming a least-squares regression analysis estimated the total fixed costs to be $1,170.90 per month and the variable cost to be $18.18 per scan. How would the straight line that you drew in requirement 2 differ from a straight line that minimizes the sum of the squared errors?

PROBLEM 2–23 High-Low Method; Contribution Format Income Statement [LO2–5, LO2–6]

Milden Company has an exclusive franchise to purchase a product from the manufacturer and distribute it on the retail level. As an aid in planning, the company has decided to start using a contribution format income statement. To have data to prepare such a statement, the company has analyzed its expenses and has developed the following cost formulas:

Cost	Cost Formula
Cost of good sold	$35 per unit sold
Advertising expense	$210,000 per quarter
Sales commissions	6% of sales
Shipping expense	?
Administrative salaries	$145,000 per quarter
Insurance expense	$9,000 per quarter
Depreciation expense	$76,000 per quarter

Chapter 2

Management has concluded that shipping expense is a mixed cost, containing both variable and fixed cost elements. Units sold and the related shipping expense over the last eight quarters follow:

Quarter	Units Sold	Shipping Expense
Year 1:		
First	10,000	$119,000
Second	16,000	$175,000
Third	18,000	$190,000
Fourth	15,000	$164,000
Year 2:		
First	11,000	$130,000
Second	17,000	$185,000
Third	20,000	$210,000
Fourth	13,000	$147,000

Milden Company's president would like a cost formula derived for shipping expense so that a budgeted contribution format income statement can be prepared for the next quarter.

Required:
1. Using the high-low method, estimate a cost formula for shipping expense.
2. In the first quarter of Year 3, the company plans to sell 12,000 units at a selling price of $100 per unit. Prepare a contribution format income statement for the quarter.

PROBLEM 2–24 Ethics and the Manager [LO2–3]
M. K. Gallant is president of Kranbrack Corporation, a company whose stock is traded on a national exchange. In a meeting with investment analysts at the beginning of the year, Gallant had predicted that the company's earnings would grow by 20% this year. Unfortunately, sales have been less than expected for the year, and Gallant concluded within two weeks of the end of the fiscal year that it would be impossible to ultimately report an increase in earnings as large as predicted unless some drastic action was taken. Accordingly, Gallant has ordered that wherever possible, expenditures should be postponed to the new year—including canceling or postponing orders with suppliers, delaying planned maintenance and training, and cutting back on end-of-year advertising and travel. Additionally, Gallant ordered the company's controller to carefully scrutinize all costs that are currently classified as period costs and reclassify as many as possible as product costs. The company is expected to have substantial inventories at the end of the year.

Required:
1. Why would reclassifying period costs as product costs increase this period's reported earnings?
2. Do you believe Gallant's actions are ethical? Why or why not?

PROBLEM 2–25 Cost Classification and Cost Behavior [LO2–1, LO2–2, LO2–3, LO2–4]
The Dorilane Company specializes in producing a set of wood patio furniture consisting of a table and four chairs. The set enjoys great popularity, and the company has ample orders to keep production going at its full capacity of 2,000 sets per year. Annual cost data at full capacity follow:

Direct labor	$118,000
Advertising	$50,000
Factory supervision	$40,000
Property taxes, factory building	$3,500
Sales commissions	$80,000
Insurance, factory	$2,500
Depreciation, administrative office equipment	$4,000
Lease cost, factory equipment	$12,000
Indirect materials, factory	$6,000
Depreciation, factory building	$10,000
Administrative office supplies (billing)	$3,000
Administrative office salaries	$60,000
Direct materials used (wood, bolts, etc.)	$94,000
Utilities, factory	$20,000

Required:

1. Prepare an answer sheet with the column headings shown below. Enter each cost item on your answer sheet, placing the dollar amount under the appropriate headings. As examples, this has been done already for the first two items in the list above. Note that each cost item is classified in two ways: first, as variable or fixed with respect to the number of units produced and sold; and second, as a selling and administrative cost or a product cost. (If the item is a product cost, it should also be classified as either direct or indirect as shown.)

Cost Item	Cost Behavior		Period (Selling or Administrative) Cost	Product Cost	
	Variable	Fixed		Direct	Indirect*
Direct labor	$118,000			$118,000	
Advertising		$50,000	$50,000		

*To units of product.

2. Total the dollar amounts in each of the columns in (1) above. Compute the average product cost of one patio set.
3. Assume that production drops to only 1,000 sets annually. Would you expect the average product cost per set to increase, decrease, or remain unchanged? Explain. No computations are necessary.
4. Refer to the original data. The president's brother-in-law has considered making himself a patio set and has priced the necessary materials at a building supply store. The brother-in-law has asked the president if he could purchase a patio set from the Dorilane Company "at cost," and the president agreed to let him do so.
    a. Would you expect any disagreement between the two men over the price the brother-in-law should pay? Explain. What price does the president probably have in mind? The brother-in-law?
    b. Because the company is operating at full capacity, what cost term used in the chapter might be justification for the president to charge the full, regular price to the brother-in-law and still be selling "at cost"?

 Cases

All applicable cases are available with McGraw-Hill's *Connect® Accounting.*

CASE 2–26 Mixed Cost Analysis and the Relevant Range [LO2–4, LO2–5]

The Ramon Company is a manufacturer that is interested in developing a cost formula to estimate the fixed and variable components of its monthly manufacturing overhead costs. The company wishes to use machine-hours as its measure of activity and has gathered the data below for this year and last year:

Month	Last Year		This Year	
	Machine-Hours	Overhead Costs	Machine-Hours	Overhead Costs
January	21,000	$84,000	21,000	$86,000
February	25,000	$99,000	24,000	$93,000
March	22,000	$89,500	23,000	$93,000
April	23,000	$90,000	22,000	$87,000
May	20,500	$81,500	20,000	$80,000
June	19,000	$75,500	18,000	$76,500
July	14,000	$70,500	12,000	$67,500
August	10,000	$64,500	13,000	$71,000
September	12,000	$69,000	15,000	$73,500
October	17,000	$75,000	17,000	$72,500
November	16,000	$71,500	15,000	$71,000
December	19,000	$78,000	18,000	$75,000

Chapter 2

The company leases all of its manufacturing equipment. The lease arrangement calls for a flat monthly fee up to 19,500 machine-hours. If the machine-hours used exceeds 19,500, then the fee becomes strictly variable with respect to the total number of machine-hours consumed during the month. Lease expense is a major element of overhead cost.

Required:
1. Using the high-low method, estimate a manufacturing overhead cost formula.
2. Prepare a scattergraph using all of the data for the two-year period. Fit a straight line or lines to the plotted points using a ruler. Describe the cost behavior pattern revealed by your scattergraph plot.
3. Assume a least-squares regression analysis using all of the given data points estimated the total fixed costs to be $40,102 and the variable costs to be $2.13 per machine-hour. Do you have any concerns about the accuracy of the high-low estimates that you have computed or the least-squares regression estimates that have been provided?
4. Assume that the company consumes 22,500 machine-hours during a month. Using the high-low method, estimate the total overhead cost that would be incurred at this level of activity. Be sure to consider only the data points contained in the relevant range of activity when performing your computations.
5. Comment on the accuracy of your high-low estimates assuming a least-squares regression analysis using only the data points in the relevant range of activity estimated the total fixed costs to be $10,090 and the variable costs to be $3.53 per machine-hour.

CASE 2–27 Scattergraph Analysis; Selection of an Activity Base [LO2–5]
Angora Wraps of Pendleton, Oregon, makes fine sweaters out of pure angora wool. The business is seasonal, with the largest demand during the fall, the winter, and Christmas holidays. The company must increase production each summer to meet estimated demand.

The company has been analyzing its costs to determine which costs are fixed and variable for planning purposes. Below are data for the company's activity and direct labor costs over the last year.

Month	Thousands of Units Produced	Number of Paid Days	Direct Labor Cost
January	98	20	$14,162
February	76	20	$12,994
March	75	21	$15,184
April	80	22	$15,038
May	85	22	$15,768
June	102	21	$15,330
July	52	19	$13,724
August	136	21	$14,162
September	138	22	$15,476
October	132	23	$15,476
November	86	18	$12,972
December	56	21	$14,074

The number of workdays varies from month to month due to the number of weekdays, holidays, and days of vacation in the month. The paid days include paid vacations (in July) and paid holidays (in November and December). The number of units produced in a month varies depending on demand and the number of workdays in the month.

The company has eight workers who are classified as direct labor.

Required:
1. Plot the direct labor cost and units produced on a scattergraph. (Place cost on the vertical axis and units produced on the horizontal axis.)
2. Plot the direct labor cost and number of paid days on a scattergraph. (Place cost on the vertical axis and the number of paid days on the horizontal axis.)
3. Which measure of activity—number of units produced or paid days—should be used as the activity base for explaining direct labor cost? Explain.

Appendix 2A: Least-Squares Regression Computations

The least-squares regression method for estimating a linear relationship is based on the equation for a straight line:

$$Y = a + bX$$

LO2–8

Analyze a mixed cost using a scattergraph plot and the least-squares regression method.

As explained in the chapter, least-squares regression selects the values for the intercept a and the slope b that minimize the sum of the squared errors. The following formulas, which are derived in statistics and calculus texts, accomplish that objective:

$$b = \frac{n(\Sigma XY) - (\Sigma X)(\Sigma Y)}{n(\Sigma X^2) - (\Sigma X)^2}$$

$$a = \frac{(\Sigma Y) - b(\Sigma X)}{n}$$

where:

X = The level of activity (independent variable)
Y = The total mixed cost (dependent variable)
a = The total fixed cost (the vertical intercept of the line)
b = The variable cost per unit of activity (the slope of the line)
n = Number of observations
Σ = Sum across all n observations

Manually performing the calculations required by the formulas is tedious at best. Fortunately, Microsoft® Excel can be used to estimate the intercept (fixed cost) and slope (variable cost per unit) that minimize the sum of the squared errors. Excel also provides a statistic called the R^2, which is a measure of "goodness of fit." The R^2 tells us the percentage of the variation in the dependent variable (cost) that is explained by variation in the independent variable (activity). The R^2 varies from 0% to 100%, and the higher the percentage, the better. You should always plot the data in a scattergraph, but it is particularly important to check the data visually when the R^2 is low. A quick look at the scattergraph can reveal that there is little relation between the cost and the activity or that the relation is something other than a simple straight line. In such cases, additional analysis would be required.

To illustrate how Excel can be used to prepare a scattergraph plot and to calculate the intercept a, the slope b, and the R^2, we will use the Brentline Hospital data for patient-days and maintenance costs on page 39 (which is recreated in Exhibit 2A–1).[1]

To prepare a scattergraph plot, begin by highlighting the data in cells B4 through C10. From the Charts group within the Insert tab, select the "Scatter" subgroup and then click on the choice that has no lines connecting the data points. This should produce a scattergraph plot similar to the one shown in Exhibit 2A–2. Notice that the number of patient-days is plotted on the X-axis and the maintenance costs are plotted on the Y-axis.[2] The data is approximately linear, so it makes sense to proceed with estimating a regression equation that minimizes the sum of the squared errors.

---

[1] The authors wish to thank Don Schwartz, Professor of Accounting at National University, for providing suggestions that were instrumental in creating this appendix.

[2] To insert labels for the X-axis and Y-axis, go to the Layout tab in Excel. Then, within the Labels group, select Axis Titles.

EXHIBIT 2A-1
The Least-Squares Regression
Worksheet for Brentline Hospital

	A	B	C
1		Patient	Maintenance
2		Days	Cost
3	*Month*	*X*	*Y*
4	January	5,600	$ 7,900
5	February	7,100	$ 8,500
6	March	5,000	$ 7,400
7	April	6,500	$ 8,200
8	May	7,300	$ 9,100
9	June	8,000	$ 9,800
10	July	6,200	$ 7,800
11			

|◄ ◄ ► ►| Least-squares regression

To determine the intercept a, the slope b, and the R^2, begin by right clicking on any data point in the scattergraph plot and selecting "Add Trendline." This should produce the screen that is shown in Exhibit 2A–3. Notice that under "Trend/Regression Type" you should select "Linear." Similarly, under "Trendline Name" you should select "Automatic." Next to the word "Backward" you should input the lowest value for the independent variable, which in this example is 5000 patient-days. Taking this particular step instructs Excel to extend your fitted line until it intersects the Y-axis. Finally, you should check the two boxes at the bottom of Exhibit 2A–3 that say "Display Equation on chart" and "Display R-squared value on chart."

Once you have established these settings, then click "Close." As shown in Exhibit 2A–4, this will automatically insert a line within the scattergraph plot that minimizes the sum of the squared errors. It will also cause the estimated least-squares regression equation and R^2 to be inserted into your scattergraph plot. Instead of depicting the results using the form $Y = a + bX$, Excel uses an equivalent form of the equation depicted as $Y = bX + a$. In other words, Excel reverses the two terms shown to the right of the equals sign. So, in Exhibit 2A–4, Excel shows a least-squares regression equation of $y = 0.7589x + 3{,}430.9$. The slope b in this equation of $0.7589 represents the estimated variable maintenance cost per patient-day. The intercept a in this equation of $3,430.90 (or approximately $3,431) represents the estimated fixed monthly maintenance cost. Note that the R^2 is approximately 0.90, which is quite good and indicates that 90% of the variation in maintenance costs is explained by the variation in patient-days.

EXHIBIT 2A-2
A Scattergraph Plot for
Brentline Hospital

EXHIBIT 2A-3
Trendline Options in Microsoft Excel

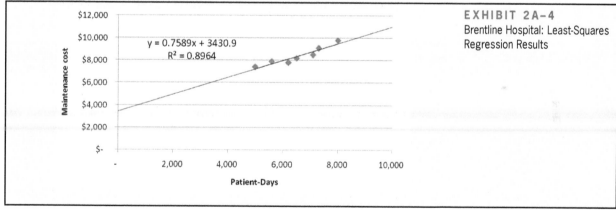

$y = 0.7589x + 3430.9$
$R^2 = 0.8964$

EXHIBIT 2A-4
Brentline Hospital: Least-Squares Regression Results

Glossary (Appendix 2A)

R^2 A measure of goodness of fit in least-squares regression analysis. It is the percentage of the variation in the dependent variable that is explained by variation in the independent variable. (p. 67)

 Appendix 2A Exercises and Problems

All applicable exercises and problems are available with McGraw-Hill's Connect® Accounting.

EXERCISE 2A-1 Least-Squares Regression [LO2–8]

Bargain Rental Car offers rental cars in an off-airport location near a major tourist destination in California. Management would like to better understand the behavior of the company's costs. One of those costs is the cost of washing cars. The company operates its own car wash

Chapter 2

facility in which each rental car that is returned is thoroughly cleaned before being released for rental to another customer. Management believes that the costs of operating the car wash should be related to the number of rental returns. Accordingly, the following data have been compiled:

Month	Rental Returns	Car Wash Costs
January	2,380	$10,825
February	2,421	$11,865
March	2,586	$11,332
April	2,725	$12,422
May	2,968	$13,850
June	3,281	$14,419
July	3,353	$14,935
August	3,489	$15,738
September	3,057	$13,563
October	2,876	$11,889
November	2,735	$12,683
December	2,983	$13,796

Required:
1. Prepare a scattergraph plot. (Place car wash costs on the vertical axis and rental returns on the horizontal axis.)
2. Using least-squares regression, estimate the fixed cost and variable cost elements of monthly car wash costs. The fixed cost element should be estimated to the nearest dollar and the variable cost element to the nearest cent.

EXERCISE 2A–2 Least-Squares Regression [LO2–4, LO2–8]
George Caloz & Frères, located in Grenchen, Switzerland, makes prestige high-end custom watches in small lots. One of the company's products, a platinum diving watch, goes through an etching process. The company has observed etching costs as follows over the last six weeks:

Week	Units	Total Etching Cost
1	4	$ 18
2	3	17
3	8	25
4	6	20
5	7	24
6	2	16
	30	$120

For planning purposes, management would like to know the amount of variable etching cost per unit and the total fixed etching cost per week.

Required:
1. Prepare a scattergraph plot. (Place etching costs on the vertical axis and units on the horizontal axis.)
2. Using the least-squares regression method, estimate the variable and fixed elements of etching cost. Express these estimates in the form $Y = a + bX$.
3. If the company processes five units next week, what would be the expected total etching cost?

PROBLEM 2A–3 Least-Squares Regression; Scattergraph; Comparison of Activity Bases [LO2–4, LO2–8]
The Hard Rock Mining Company is developing cost formulas for management planning and decision-making purposes. The company's cost analyst has concluded that utilities cost is a mixed cost, and he is attempting to find a base with which the cost might be closely correlated. The controller has suggested that tons mined might be a good base to use in developing a cost formula. The

production superintendent disagrees; she thinks that direct labor-hours would be a better base. The cost analyst has decided to try both bases and has assembled the following information:

Quarter	Tons Mined	Direct Labor-Hours	Utilities Cost
Year 1:			
First	15,000	5,000	$50,000
Second	11,000	3,000	$45,000
Third	21,000	4,000	$60,000
Fourth	12,000	6,000	$75,000
Year 2:			
First	18,000	10,000	$100,000
Second	25,000	9,000	$105,000
Third	30,000	8,000	$85,000
Fourth	28,000	11,000	$120,000

Required:
1. Using tons mined as the independent variable, prepare a scattergraph that plots tons mined on the horizontal axis and utilities cost on the vertical axis. Determine a cost formula for utilities cost using least-squares regression. Express this cost formula in the form $Y = a + bX$.
2. Using direct labor-hours as the independent variable, prepare a scattergraph that plots direct labor-hours on the horizontal axis and utilities cost on the vertical axis. Determine a cost formula for utilities cost using least-squares regression. Express this cost formula in the form $Y = a + bX$.
3. Would you recommend that the company use tons mined or direct labor-hours as a base for planning utilities cost?

PROBLEM 2A–4 Least-Squares Regression Method; Scattergraph; Cost Behavior [LO2–4, LO2–8]
Professor John Morton has just been appointed chairperson of the Finance Department at Westland University. In reviewing the department's cost records, Professor Morton has found the following total cost associated with Finance 101 over the last several terms:

Term	Number of Sections Offered	Total Cost
Fall, last year	4	$10,000
Winter, last year	6	$14,000
Summer, last year	2	$7,000
Fall, this year	5	$13,000
Winter, this year	3	$9,500

Professor Morton knows that there are some variable costs, such as amounts paid to graduate assistants, associated with the course. He would like to have the variable and fixed costs separated for planning purposes.

Required:
1. Prepare a scattergraph plot. (Place total cost on the vertical axis and number of sections offered on the horizontal axis.)
2. Using the least-squares regression method, estimate the variable cost per section and the total fixed cost per term for Finance 101. Express these estimates in the linear equation form $Y = a + bX$.
3. Assume that because of the small number of sections offered during the Winter Term this year, Professor Morton will have to offer eight sections of Finance 101 during the Fall Term. Compute the expected total cost for Finance 101. Can you see any problem with using the cost formula from (2) above to derive this total cost figure? Explain.

CASE 2A–5 Analysis of Mixed Costs in a Pricing Decision [LO2–4, LO2–8]
Maria Chavez owns a catering company that serves food and beverages at parties and business functions. Chavez's business is seasonal, with a heavy schedule during the summer months and holidays and a lighter schedule at other times.

One of the major events Chavez's customers request is a cocktail party. She offers a standard cocktail party and has estimated the cost per guest as follows:

Food and beverages	$15.00
Labor (0.5 hrs. @ $10.00/hr.)	5.00
Overhead (0.5 hrs. @ $13.98/hr.)	6.99
Total cost per guest	$26.99

The standard cocktail party lasts three hours and Chavez hires one worker for every six guests, so that works out to one-half hour of labor per guest. These workers are hired only as needed and are paid only for the hours they actually work.

When bidding on cocktail parties, Chavez adds a 15% markup to yield a price of about $31 per guest. She is confident about her estimates of the costs of food and beverages and labor but is not as comfortable with the estimate of overhead cost. The $13.98 overhead cost per labor-hour was determined by dividing total overhead expenses for the last 12 months by total labor-hours for the same period. Monthly data concerning overhead costs and labor-hours follow:

Month	Labor-Hours	Overhead Expenses
January	2,500	$ 55,000
February	2,800	59,000
March	3,000	60,000
April	4,200	64,000
May	4,500	67,000
June	5,500	71,000
July	6,500	74,000
August	7,500	77,000
September	7,000	75,000
October	4,500	68,000
November	3,100	62,000
December	6,500	73,000
Total	57,600	$805,000

Chavez has received a request to bid on a 180-guest fund-raising cocktail party to be given next month by an important local charity. (The party would last the usual three hours.) She would like to win this contract because the guest list for this charity event includes many prominent individuals that she would like to land as future clients. Maria is confident that these potential customers would be favorably impressed by her company's services at the charity event.

Required:
1. Prepare a scattergraph plot that puts labor-hours on the X-axis and overhead expenses on the Y-axis. What insights are revealed by your scattergraph?
2. Use the least-squares regression method to estimate the fixed and variable components of overhead expenses. Express these estimates in the form $Y = a + bX$.
3. Estimate the contribution to profit of a standard 180-guest cocktail party if Chavez charges her usual price of $31 per guest. (In other words, by how much would her overall profit increase?)
4. How low could Chavez bid for the charity event in terms of a price per guest and still not lose money on the event itself?
5. The individual who is organizing the charity's fund-raising event has indicated that he has already received a bid under $30 from another catering company. Do you think Chavez should bid below her normal $31 per guest price for the charity event? Why or why not?

(CMA, adapted)

Appendix 2B: Cost of Quality

A company may have a product with a high-quality design that uses high-quality components, but if the product is poorly assembled or has other defects, the company will have high warranty repair costs and dissatisfied customers. People who are dissatisfied with a product are unlikely to buy the product again. They often tell others about their bad experiences. This is the worst possible sort of advertising. To prevent such problems, companies expend a great deal of effort to reduce defects. The objective is to have high *quality of conformance.*

Quality of Conformance

A product that meets or exceeds its design specifications and is free of defects that mar its appearance or degrade its performance is said to have high **quality of conformance**. Note that if an economy car is free of defects, it can have a quality of conformance that is just as high as a defect-free luxury car. The purchasers of economy cars cannot expect their cars to be as opulently equipped as luxury cars, but they can and do expect them to be free of defects.

Preventing, detecting, and dealing with defects causes costs that are called *quality costs* or the *cost of quality.* The use of the term *quality cost* is confusing to some people. It does not refer to costs such as using a higher-grade leather to make a wallet or using 14K gold instead of gold-plating in jewelry. Instead, the term **quality cost** refers to all of the costs that are incurred to prevent defects or that result from defects in products.

Quality costs can be broken down into four broad groups. Two of these groups—known as *prevention costs* and *appraisal costs*—are incurred in an effort to keep defective products from falling into the hands of customers. The other two groups of costs—known as *internal failure costs* and *external failure costs*—are incurred because defects occur despite efforts to prevent them. Examples of specific costs involved in each of these four groups are given in Exhibit 2B–1.

LO2–9
Identify the four types of quality costs and explain how they interact.

Several things should be noted about the quality costs shown in the exhibit. First, quality costs don't relate to just manufacturing; rather, they relate to all the activities in a company from initial research and development (R&D) through customer service. Second, the number of costs associated with quality is very large; total quality cost can be very high unless management gives this area special attention. Finally, the costs in the four groupings are quite different. We will now look at each of these groupings more closely.

Prevention Costs

Generally, the most effective way to manage quality costs is to avoid having defects in the first place. It is much less costly to prevent a problem from ever happening than it is to find and correct the problem after it has occurred. **Prevention costs** support activities whose purpose is to reduce the number of defects.

Note from Exhibit 2B–1 that prevention costs include activities relating to quality circles and statistical process control. **Quality circles** consist of small groups of employees that meet on a regular basis to discuss ways to improve quality. Both management and workers are included in these circles. Quality circles are widely used and can be found in manufacturing companies, utilities, health care organizations, banks, and many other organizations.

Statistical process control is a technique that is used to detect whether a process is in or out of control. An out-of-control process results in defective units and may be caused by a miscalibrated machine or some other factor. In statistical process control, workers use charts to monitor the quality of units that pass through their workstations. With these charts, workers can quickly spot processes that are out of control and that are creating defects. Problems can be immediately corrected and further defects prevented rather than waiting for an inspector to catch the defects later.

Note also from the list of prevention costs in Exhibit 2B–1 that some companies provide technical support to their suppliers as a way of preventing defects. Particularly

EXHIBIT 2B-1
Typical Quality Costs

Prevention Costs	Internal Failure Costs
Systems development	Net cost of scrap
Quality engineering	Net cost of spoilage
Quality training	Rework labor and overhead
Quality circles	Reinspection of reworked products
Statistical process control activities	Retesting of reworked products
Supervision of prevention activities	Downtime caused by quality problems
Quality data gathering, analysis, and reporting	Disposal of defective products
Quality improvement projects	Analysis of the cause of defects in production
Technical support provided to suppliers	Re-entering data because of keying errors
Audits of the effectiveness of the quality system	Debugging software errors

Appraisal Costs	External Failure Costs
Test and inspection of incoming materials	Cost of field servicing and handling complaints
Test and inspection of in-process goods	Warranty repairs and replacements
Final product testing and inspection	Repairs and replacements beyond the warranty period
Supplies used in testing and inspection	Product recalls
Supervision of testing and inspection activities	Liability arising from defective products
Depreciation of test equipment	Returns and allowances arising from quality problems
Maintenance of test equipment	Lost sales arising from a reputation for poor quality
Plant utilities in the inspection area	
Field testing and appraisal at customer site	

in just-in-time (JIT) systems, such support to suppliers is vital. In a JIT system, parts are delivered from suppliers just in time and in just the correct quantity to fill customer orders. There are no parts stockpiles. If a defective part is received from a supplier, the part cannot be used and the order for the ultimate customer cannot be filled on time. Hence, every part received from a supplier must be free of defects. Consequently, companies that use JIT often require that their suppliers use sophisticated quality control programs such as statistical process control and that their suppliers certify that they will deliver parts and materials that are free of defects.

Appraisal Costs

Any defective parts and products should be caught as early as possible in the production process. **Appraisal costs**, which are sometimes called *inspection costs*, are incurred to identify defective products *before* the products are shipped to customers. Unfortunately, performing appraisal activities doesn't keep defects from happening again, and most managers now realize that maintaining an army of inspectors is a costly (and ineffective) approach to quality control. Therefore, employees are increasingly being asked to be responsible for their own quality control. This approach, along with designing products to be easy to manufacture properly, allows quality to be built into products rather than relying on inspection to get the defects out.

Internal Failure Costs

Failure costs are incurred when a product fails to conform to its design specifications. Failure costs can be either internal or external. **Internal failure costs** result from identifying defects before they are shipped to customers. These costs include scrap, rejected products, reworking of defective units, and downtime caused by quality problems. In some companies, as little as 10% of the company's products make it through the production process without rework of some kind. Of course, the more effective a company's appraisal activities, the greater the chance of catching defects internally and the greater the level of internal failure costs. This is the price that is paid to avoid incurring external failure costs, which can be devastating.

External Failure Costs

External failure costs result when a defective product is delivered to a customer. As shown in Exhibit 2B–1, external failure costs include warranty repairs and replacements, product recalls, liability arising from legal action against a company, and lost sales arising from a reputation for poor quality. Such costs can decimate profits.

In the past, some managers have taken the attitude, "Let's go ahead and ship everything to customers, and we'll take care of any problems under the warranty." This attitude generally results in high external failure costs, customer ill will, and declining market share and profits.

Distribution of Quality Costs

Quality costs for some companies range between 10% and 20% of total sales, whereas experts say that these costs should be more in the 2% to 4% range. How does a company reduce its total quality cost? The answer lies in how the quality costs are distributed. Refer to the graph in Exhibit 2B–2, which shows total quality costs as a function of the quality of conformance.

The graph shows that when the quality of conformance is low, total quality cost is high and that most of this cost consists of costs of internal and external failure. A low quality of conformance means that a high percentage of units are defective and hence the company has high failure costs. However, as a company spends more and more on prevention and appraisal, the percentage of defective units drops. This results in lower internal and external failure costs. Ordinarily, total quality cost drops rapidly as the quality of conformance increases. Thus, a company can reduce its total quality cost by focusing its efforts on prevention and appraisal. The cost savings from reduced defects usually swamp the costs of the additional prevention and appraisal efforts.

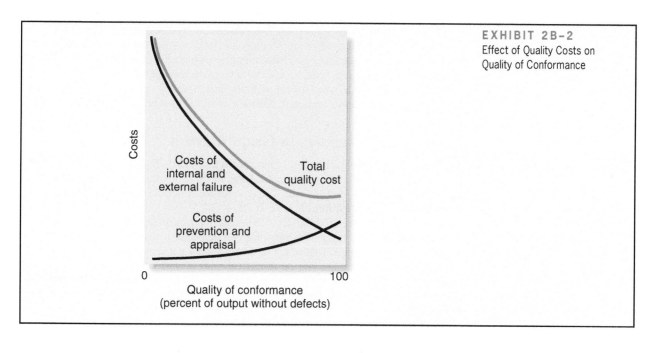

EXHIBIT 2B-2
Effect of Quality Costs on
Quality of Conformance

The graph in Exhibit 2B–2 has been drawn so that the total quality cost is minimized when the quality of conformance is less than 100%. However, some experts contend that the total quality cost is not minimized until the quality of conformance is 100% and there are no defects. Indeed, many companies have found that the total quality costs seem to keep dropping even when the quality of conformance approaches 100% and defect rates get as low as 1 in a million units. Others argue that total quality cost eventually increases as the quality of conformance increases. However, in most companies this does not seem to happen until the quality of conformance is very close to 100% and defect rates are very close to zero.

As a company's quality program becomes more refined and as its failure costs begin to fall, prevention activities usually become more effective than appraisal activities. Appraisal can only find defects, whereas prevention can eliminate them. The best way to prevent defects from happening is to design processes that reduce the likelihood of defects and to continually monitor processes using statistical process control methods.

Quality Cost Reports

LO2–10
Prepare and interpret a quality cost report.

As an initial step in quality improvement programs, companies often construct a *quality cost report* that provides an estimate of the financial consequences of the company's current level of defects. A **quality cost report** details the prevention costs, appraisal costs, and costs of internal and external failures that arise from the company's current quality control efforts. Managers are often shocked by the magnitude of these costs. A typical quality cost report is shown in Exhibit 2B–3.

Several things should be noted from the data in the exhibit. First, Ventura Company's quality costs are poorly distributed in both years, with most of the costs due to either internal failure or external failure. The external failure costs are particularly high in Year 1 in comparison to other costs.

Second, note that the company increased its spending on prevention and appraisal activities in Year 2. As a result, internal failure costs went up in that year (from $2 million in Year 1 to $3 million in Year 2), but external failure costs dropped sharply (from $5.15 million in Year 1 to only $2 million in Year 2). Because of the increase in appraisal activity in Year 2, more defects were caught inside the company before they were shipped to customers. This resulted in more cost for scrap, rework, and so forth, but saved huge amounts in warranty repairs, warranty replacements, and other external failure costs.

Third, note that as a result of greater emphasis on prevention and appraisal, *total* quality cost decreased in Year 2. As continued emphasis is placed on prevention and appraisal in future years, total quality cost should continue to decrease. That is, future increases in prevention and appraisal costs should be more than offset by decreases in failure costs. Moreover, appraisal costs should also decrease as more effort is placed into prevention.

Quality Cost Reports in Graphic Form

As a supplement to the quality cost report shown in Exhibit 2B–3, companies frequently prepare quality cost information in graphic form. Graphic presentations include pie charts, bar graphs, trend lines, and so forth. The data for Ventura Company from Exhibit 2B–3 are presented in bar graph form in Exhibit 2B–4.

The first bar graph in Exhibit 2B–4 is scaled in terms of dollars of quality cost, and the second is scaled in terms of quality cost as a percentage of sales. In both graphs, the data are "stacked" upward. That is, appraisal costs are stacked on top of prevention costs, internal failure costs are stacked on top of the sum of prevention costs plus appraisal costs, and so forth. The percentage figures in the second graph show that total quality cost equals 18% of sales in Year 1 and 15% of sales in Year 2, the same as reported earlier in Exhibit 2B–3.

EXHIBIT 2B–3
Quality Cost Report

Ventura Company
Quality Cost Report
For Years 1 and 2

	Year 1		Year 2	
	Amount	Percent*	Amount	Percent*
Prevention costs:				
Systems development	$ 270,000	0.54%	$ 400,000	0.80%
Quality training	130,000	0.26%	210,000	0.42%
Supervision of prevention activities	40,000	0.08%	70,000	0.14%
Quality improvement projects	210,000	0.42%	320,000	0.64%
Total prevention cost	650,000	1.30%	1,000,000	2.00%
Appraisal costs:				
Inspection	560,000	1.12%	600,000	1.20%
Reliability testing	420,000	0.84%	580,000	1.16%
Supervision of testing and inspection	80,000	0.16%	120,000	0.24%
Depreciation of test equipment	140,000	0.28%	200,000	0.40%
Total appraisal cost	1,200,000	2.40%	1,500,000	3.00%
Internal failure costs:				
Net cost of scrap	750,000	1.50%	900,000	1.80%
Rework labor and overhead	810,000	1.62%	1,430,000	2.86%
Downtime due to defects in quality	100,000	0.20%	170,000	0.34%
Disposal of defective products	340,000	0.68%	500,000	1.00%
Total internal failure cost	2,000,000	4.00%	3,000,000	6.00%
External failure costs:				
Warranty repairs	900,000	1.80%	400,000	0.80%
Warranty replacements	2,300,000	4.60%	870,000	1.74%
Allowances	630,000	1.26%	130,000	0.26%
Cost of field servicing	1,320,000	2.64%	600,000	1.20%
Total external failure cost	5,150,000	10.30%	2,000,000	4.00%
Total quality cost	$9,000,000	18.00%	$7,500,000	15.00%

*As a percentage of total sales. In each year, sales totaled $50,000,000.

Data in graphic form help managers to see trends more clearly and to see the magnitude of the various costs in relation to each other. Such graphs are easily prepared using computer graphics and spreadsheet applications.

Uses of Quality Cost Information

A quality cost report has several uses. First, quality cost information helps managers see the financial significance of defects. Managers usually are not aware of the magnitude of their quality costs because these costs cut across departmental lines and are not normally tracked and accumulated by the cost system. Thus, when first presented with a quality cost report, managers often are surprised by the amount of cost attributable to poor quality.

Second, quality cost information helps managers identify the relative importance of the quality problems faced by their companies. For example, the quality cost report may show that scrap is a major quality problem or that the company is incurring huge warranty costs. With this information, managers have a better idea of where to focus their efforts.

Third, quality cost information helps managers see whether their quality costs are poorly distributed. In general, quality costs should be distributed more toward prevention and appraisal activities and less toward failures.

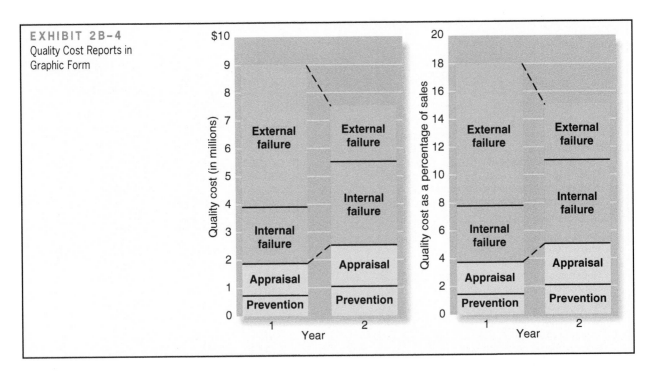

EXHIBIT 2B-4
Quality Cost Reports in Graphic Form

Counterbalancing these uses, three limitations of quality cost information should be recognized. First, simply measuring and reporting quality costs does not solve quality problems. Problems can be solved only by taking action. Second, results usually lag behind quality improvement programs. Initially, total quality cost may even increase as quality control systems are designed and installed. Decreases in quality costs may not begin to occur until the quality program has been in effect for some time. And third, the most important quality cost, lost sales arising from customer ill will, is usually omitted from the quality cost report because it is difficult to estimate.

Typically, during the initial years of a quality improvement program, the benefits of compiling a quality cost report outweigh the costs and limitations of the reports. As managers gain experience in balancing prevention and appraisal activities, the need for quality cost reports often diminishes.

International Aspects of Quality

Many of the tools used in quality management today were developed in Japan after World War II. In statistical process control, Japanese companies borrowed heavily from the work of W. Edwards Deming. However, Japanese companies are largely responsible for quality circles, JIT, the idea that quality is everyone's responsibility, and the emphasis on prevention rather than on inspection.

In the 1980s, quality reemerged as a pivotal factor in the market. Many companies now find that it is impossible to effectively compete without a very strong quality program in place. This is particularly true of companies that wish to compete in the European market.

The ISO 9000 Standards

The International Organization for Standardization (ISO), based in Geneva, Switzerland, has established quality control guidelines known as the **ISO 9000 standards**. Many companies and organizations in Europe will buy only from ISO 9000-certified suppliers. This means that the suppliers must demonstrate to a certifying agency that:

1. A quality control system is in use, and the system clearly defines an expected level of quality.
2. The system is fully operational and is backed up with detailed documentation of quality control procedures.
3. The intended level of quality is being achieved on a sustained, consistent basis.

The key to receiving certification under the ISO 9000 standards is documentation. It's one thing for a company to say that it has a quality control system in operation, but it's quite a different thing to be able to document the steps in that system. Under ISO 9000, this documentation must be so detailed and precise that if all the employees in a company were suddenly replaced, the new employees could use the documentation to make the product exactly as it was made by the old employees. Even companies with good quality control systems find that it takes up to two years of painstaking work to develop this detailed documentation. But companies often find that compiling this documentation results in improvements in their quality systems.

The ISO 9000 standards have become an international measure of quality. Although the standards were developed to control the quality of goods sold in European countries, they have become widely accepted elsewhere as well. Companies in the United States that export to Europe often expect their own suppliers to comply with ISO 9000 standards because these exporters must document the quality of the materials going into their products as part of their own ISO 9000 certification.

The ISO program for certification of quality management programs is not limited to manufacturing companies. The American Institute of Certified Public Accountants was the first professional membership organization in the United States to win recognition under an ISO certification program.

Summary (Appendix 2B)

Defects cause costs, which can be classified into prevention costs, appraisal costs, internal failure costs, and external failure costs. Prevention costs are incurred to keep defects from happening. Appraisal costs are incurred to ensure that defective products, once made, are not shipped to customers. Internal failure costs are incurred as a consequence of detecting defective products before they are shipped to customers. External failure costs are the consequences (in terms of repairs, servicing, and lost future business) of delivering defective products to customers. Most experts agree that management effort should be focused on preventing defects. Small investments in prevention can lead to dramatic reductions in appraisal costs and costs of internal and external failure.

Quality costs are summarized on a quality cost report. This report shows the types of quality costs being incurred and their significance and trends. The report helps managers understand the importance of quality costs, spot problem areas, and assess the way in which the quality costs are distributed.

Glossary (Appendix 2B)

Appraisal costs Costs that are incurred to identify defective products before the products are shipped to customers. (p. 74)

External failure costs Costs that are incurred when a product or service that is defective is delivered to a customer. (p. 75)

Internal failure costs Costs that are incurred as a result of identifying defective products before they are shipped to customers. (p. 74)

ISO 9000 standards Quality control requirements issued by the International Organization for Standardization that relate to products sold in European countries. (p. 78)

Prevention costs Costs that are incurred to keep defects from occurring. (p. 73)

Quality circles Small groups of employees that meet on a regular basis to discuss ways of improving quality. (p. 73)

Quality cost Costs that are incurred to prevent defective products from falling into the hands of customers or that are incurred as a result of defective units. (p. 73)

Quality cost report A report that details prevention costs, appraisal costs, and the costs of internal and external failures. (p. 76)

Quality of conformance The degree to which a product or service meets or exceeds its design specifications and is free of defects or other problems that mar its appearance or degrade its performance. (p. 73)

Statistical process control A charting technique used to monitor the quality of work being done in a workstation for the purpose of immediately correcting any problems. (p. 73)

Appendix 2B Exercises and Problems   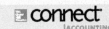 |ACCOUNTING

All applicable exercises and problems are available with McGraw-Hill's *Connect*® *Accounting*.

EXERCISE 2B–1 Cost of Quality Terms [LO2–9]

A number of terms relating to the cost of quality and quality management are listed below:

Appraisal costs	Quality circles
Quality cost report	Prevention costs
Quality of conformance	External failure costs
Internal failure costs	Quality costs

Required:

Choose the term or terms that most appropriately complete the following statements. The terms can be used more than once and a blank can hold more than one word.

1. A product that has a high rate of defects is said to have a low _____.
2. All of the costs associated with preventing and dealing with defects once they occur are known as _____.
3. In many companies, small groups of employees, known as _____, meet on a regular basis to discuss ways to improve quality.
4. A company incurs _____ and _____ in an effort to keep defects from occurring.
5. A company incurs _____ and _____ because defects have occurred.
6. Of the four groups of costs associated with quality of conformance, _____ are generally the most damaging to a company.
7. Inspection, testing, and other costs incurred to keep defective products from being shipped to customers are known as _____.
8. _____ are incurred in an effort to eliminate poor product design, defective manufacturing practices, and the providing of substandard service.
9. The costs relating to defects, rejected products, and downtime caused by quality problems are known as _____.
10. When a product that is defective in some way is delivered to a customer, _____ are incurred.
11. Over time a company's total quality costs should decrease if it redistributes its quality costs by placing its greatest emphasis on _____ and _____.
12. One way to ensure that management is aware of the costs associated with quality is to summarize such costs on a _____.

EXERCISE 2B–2 Classification of Quality Costs [LO2–9]

A number of activities that are a part of a company's quality control system are listed below:

a.	Product testing.	f.	Cost of field servicing.
b.	Product recalls.	g.	Inspection of goods.
c.	Rework labor and overhead.	h.	Quality engineering.
d.	Quality circles.	i.	Warranty repairs.
e.	Downtime caused by defects.	j.	Statistical process control.

k. Net cost of scrap.
l. Depreciation of test equipment.
m. Returns and allowances arising from poor quality.
n. Disposal of defective products.

o. Technical support to suppliers.
p. Systems development.
q. Warranty replacements.
r. Field testing at customer site.
s. Product design.

Required:
1. Classify the costs associated with each of these activities into one of the following categories: prevention cost, appraisal cost, internal failure cost, or external failure cost.
2. Which of the four types of costs in (1) above are incurred in an effort to keep poor quality of conformance from occurring? Which of the four types of costs in (1) above are incurred because poor quality of conformance has occurred?

PROBLEM 2B–3 Analyzing a Quality Cost Report [LO2–10]

Mercury, Inc., produces cell phones at its plant in Texas. In recent years, the company's market share has been eroded by stiff competition from overseas. Price and product quality are the two key areas in which companies compete in this market.

A year ago, the company's cell phones had been ranked low in product quality in a consumer survey. Shocked by this result, Jorge Gomez, Mercury's president, initiated a crash effort to improve product quality. Gomez set up a task force to implement a formal quality improvement program. Included on this task force were representatives from the Engineering, Marketing, Customer Service, Production, and Accounting departments. The broad representation was needed because Gomez believed that this was a companywide program and that all employees should share the responsibility for its success.

After the first meeting of the task force, Holly Elsoe, manager of the Marketing Department, asked John Tran, production manager, what he thought of the proposed program. Tran replied, "I have reservations. Quality is too abstract to be attaching costs to it and then to be holding you and me responsible for cost improvements. I like to work with goals that I can see and count! I'm nervous about having my annual bonus based on a decrease in quality costs; there are too many variables that we have no control over."

Mercury's quality improvement program has now been in operation for one year. The company's most recent quality cost report is shown below.

Mercury, Inc. Quality Cost Report (in thousands)	Last Year	This Year
Prevention costs:		
Machine maintenance	$ 70	$ 120
Training suppliers	0	10
Quality circles	0	20
Total prevention costs	70	150
Appraisal costs:		
Incoming inspection	20	40
Final testing	80	90
Total appraisal costs	100	130
Internal failure costs:		
Rework	50	130
Scrap	40	70
Total internal failure costs ...	90	200
External failure costs:		
Warranty repairs	90	30
Customer returns	320	80
Total external failure costs ..	410	110
Total quality cost	$ 670	$ 590
Total production cost	$4,200	$4,800

82

Chapter 2

As they were reviewing the report, Elsoe asked Tran what he now thought of the quality improvement program. Tran replied. "I'm relieved that the new quality improvement program hasn't hurt our bonuses, but the program has increased the workload in the Production Department. It is true that customer returns are way down, but the cell phones that were returned by customers to retail outlets were rarely sent back to us for rework."

Required:
1. Expand the company's quality cost report by showing the costs in both years as percentages of both total production cost and total quality cost. Carry all computations to one decimal place. By analyzing the report, determine if Mercury, Inc.'s quality improvement program has been successful. *List specific evidence to support your answer.*
2. Do you expect the improvement program as it progresses to continue to increase the workload in the Production Department?
3. Jorge Gomez believed that the quality improvement program was essential and that Mercury, Inc., could no longer afford to ignore the importance of product quality. Discuss how Mercury, Inc., could measure the cost of *not* implementing the quality improvement program.

(CMA, adapted)

PROBLEM 2B–4 Quality Cost Report [LO2–9, LO2–10]
In response to intensive foreign competition, the management of Florex Company has attempted over the past year to improve the quality of its products. A statistical process control system has been installed and other steps have been taken to decrease the amount of warranty and other field costs, which have been trending upward over the past several years. Costs relating to quality and quality control over the last two years are given below:

	Costs (in thousands)	
	Last Year	This Year
Inspection	$750	$900
Quality engineering	$420	$570
Depreciation of test equipment	$210	$240
Rework labor	$1,050	$1,500
Statistical process control	$0	$180
Cost of field servicing	$1,200	$900
Supplies used in testing	$30	$60
Systems development	$480	$750
Warranty repairs	$3,600	$1,050
Net cost of scrap	$630	$1,125
Product testing	$810	$1,200
Product recalls	$2,100	$750
Disposal of defective products	$720	$975

Sales have been flat over the past few years, at $75,000,000 per year. A great deal of money has been spent in the effort to upgrade quality, and management is anxious to see whether or not the effort has been effective.

Required:
1. Prepare a quality cost report that contains data for both this year and last year. Carry percentage computations to two decimal places.
2. Prepare a bar graph showing the distribution of the various quality costs by category.
3. Prepare a written evaluation to accompany the reports you have prepared in (1) and (2) above. This evaluation should discuss the distribution of quality costs in the company, changes in this distribution that you see taking place, the reasons for changes in costs in the various categories, and any other information that would be of value to management.

CHAPTER 3

Job-Order Costing

University Tees: Serving Over 150 Campuses Nationwide

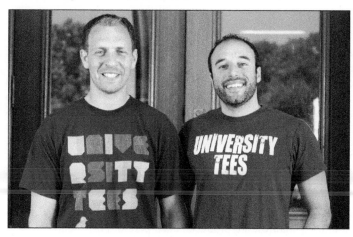

University Tees was founded in 2003 by two Miami University college students to provide screen-printing, embroidery, and promotional products for fraternities, sororities, and student organizations. Today, the company, which is headquartered in Cleveland, Ohio, employs as many as four Campus Managers on each of over 150 college campuses across America.

Accurately calculating the cost of each potential customer order is critically important to University Tees because the company needs to be sure that the sales price exceeds the cost associated with satisfying the order. The costs include the cost of the blank T-shirts themselves, printing costs (which vary depending on the quantity of shirts produced and the number of colors per shirt), screen costs (which also vary depending on the number of colors included in a design), shipping costs, and the artwork needed to create a design. The company also takes into account its competitors' pricing strategies when developing its own prices.

Given its success on college campuses, University Tees has introduced a sister company called On Point Promos to serve for-profit companies and nonprofit organizations. ■

Source: Conversation with Joe Haddad, cofounder of University Tees.

LEARNING OBJECTIVES

After studying Chapter 3, you should be able to:

LO3–1 Compute a predetermined overhead rate.

LO3–2 Apply overhead cost to jobs using a predetermined overhead rate.

LO3–3 Compute the total cost and average cost per unit of a job.

LO3–4 Understand the flow of costs in a job-order costing system and prepare appropriate journal entries to record costs.

LO3–5 Use T-accounts to show the flow of costs in a job-order costing system.

LO3–6 Prepare schedules of cost of goods manufactured and cost of goods sold and an income statement.

LO3–7 Compute underapplied or overapplied overhead cost and prepare the journal entry to close the balance in Manufacturing Overhead to the appropriate accounts.

LO3–8 *(Appendix 3A) Use activity-based absorption costing to compute unit product costs.*

LO3–9 *(Appendix 3B) Understand the implications of basing the predetermined overhead rate on activity at capacity rather than on estimated activity for the period.*

Understanding how products and services are costed is vital to managers because the way in which these costs are determined can have a substantial impact on reported profits, as well as on key management decisions.

A managerial costing system should provide cost data to help managers plan, control, and make decisions. Nevertheless, external financial reporting and tax reporting requirements often heavily influence how costs are accumulated and summarized on managerial reports. This is true of product costing. In this chapter we use *absorption costing* to determine product costs. In **absorption costing**, all manufacturing costs, both fixed and variable, are assigned to units of product—units are said to *fully absorb manufacturing costs.*

Most countries—including the United States—require some form of absorption costing for both external financial reports and for tax reports. In addition, the vast majority of companies throughout the world also use absorption costing in their management reports. Because absorption costing is the most common approach to product costing throughout the world, we discuss it first and then discuss the alternatives in subsequent chapters.

Job-Order Costing—An Overview

Under absorption costing, product costs include all manufacturing costs. Some manufacturing costs, such as direct materials, can be directly traced to particular products. For example, the cost of the airbags installed in a Toyota Camry can be easily traced to that particular auto. But what about manufacturing costs like factory rent? Such costs do not change from month to month, whereas the number and variety of products made in the factory may vary dramatically from one month to the next. Because these costs remain unchanged from month to month regardless of what products are made, they are clearly not caused by—and cannot be directly traced to—any particular product. Therefore, these types of costs are assigned to products and services by averaging across time and across products. The type of production process influences how this averaging is done.

Job-order costing is used in situations where many *different* products, each with individual and unique features, are produced each period. For example, a Levi Strauss clothing factory would typically make many different types of jeans for both men and women during a month. A particular order might consist of 1,000 boot-cut men's blue denim jeans, style number A312. This order of 1,000 jeans is called a *job.* In a job-order costing system, costs are traced and allocated to jobs and then the costs of the job are divided by the number of units in the job to arrive at an average cost per unit.

Other examples of situations where job-order costing would be used include large-scale construction projects managed by Bechtel International, commercial aircraft produced by Boeing, greeting cards designed and printed by Hallmark, and airline meals prepared by LSG SkyChefs. All of these examples are characterized by diverse outputs. Each Bechtel project is unique and different from every other—the company may be simultaneously constructing a dam in Nigeria and a bridge in Indonesia. Likewise, each airline orders a different type of meal from LSG SkyChefs' catering service.

Job-order costing is also used extensively in service industries. For example, hospitals, law firms, movie studios, accounting firms, advertising agencies, and repair shops all use a variation of job-order costing to accumulate costs. Although the detailed example of job-order costing provided in the following section deals with a manufacturing company, the same basic concepts and procedures are used by many service organizations.

IS THIS REALLY A JOB?

VBT Bicycling Vacations of Bristol, Vermont, offers deluxe bicycling vacations in the United States, Canada, Europe, and other locations throughout the world. For example, the company offers a 10-day tour of the Puglia region of Italy—the "heel of the boot." The tour price includes international airfare, 10 nights of lodging, most meals, use of a bicycle, and ground transportation as needed. Each tour is led by at least two local tour leaders, one of whom rides with the guests along the tour route. The other tour leader drives a "sag wagon" that carries extra water, snacks, and bicycle repair equipment and is available for a shuttle back to the hotel or up a hill. The sag wagon also transports guests' luggage from one hotel to another.

Each specific tour can be considered a job. For example, Giuliano Astore and Debora Trippetti, two natives of Puglia, led a VBT tour with 17 guests over 10 days in late April. At the end of the tour, Giuliano submitted a report, a sort of job cost sheet, to VBT headquarters. This report detailed the on the ground expenses incurred for this specific tour, including fuel and operating costs for the van, lodging costs for the guests, the costs of meals provided to guests, the costs of snacks, the cost of hiring additional ground transportation as needed, and the wages of the tour leaders. In addition to these costs, some costs are paid directly by VBT in Vermont to vendors. The total cost incurred for the tour is then compared to the total revenue collected from guests to determine the gross profit for the tour.

Sources: Giuliano Astore and Gregg Marston, President, VBT Bicycling Vacations. For more information about VBT, see www.vbt.com.

Job-Order Costing—An Example

To introduce job-order costing, we will follow a specific job as it progresses through the manufacturing process. This job consists of two experimental couplings that Yost Precision Machining has agreed to produce for Loops Unlimited, a manufacturer of roller coasters. Couplings connect the cars on the roller coaster and are a critical component in the performance and safety of the ride. Before we begin our discussion, recall from the previous chapter that companies generally classify manufacturing costs into three broad categories: (1) direct materials, (2) direct labor, and (3) manufacturing overhead. As we study the operation of a job-order costing system, we will see how each of these three types of costs is recorded and accumulated.

Yost Precision Machining is a small company in Michigan that specializes in fabricating precision metal parts that are used in a variety of applications ranging from deep-sea exploration vehicles to the inertial triggers in automobile air bags. The company's top managers gather every morning at 8:00 A.M. in the company's conference room for the daily planning meeting. Attending the meeting this morning are: Jean Yost, the company's president; David Cheung, the marketing manager; Debbie Turner, the production manager; and Marc White, the company controller. The president opened the meeting:

MANAGERIAL ACCOUNTING IN ACTION
THE ISSUE

Jean: The production schedule indicates we'll be starting Job 2B47 today. Isn't that the special order for experimental couplings, David?

David: That's right. That's the order from Loops Unlimited for two couplings for their new roller coaster ride for Magic Mountain.

Debbie: Why only two couplings? Don't they need a coupling for every car?

David: Yes. But this is a completely new roller coaster. The cars will go faster and will be subjected to more twists, turns, drops, and loops than on any other existing roller coaster. To hold up under these stresses, Loops Unlimited's engineers completely redesigned the cars and couplings. They want us to make just two of these new couplings for testing purposes. If the design works, then we'll have the inside track on the order to supply couplings for the whole ride.

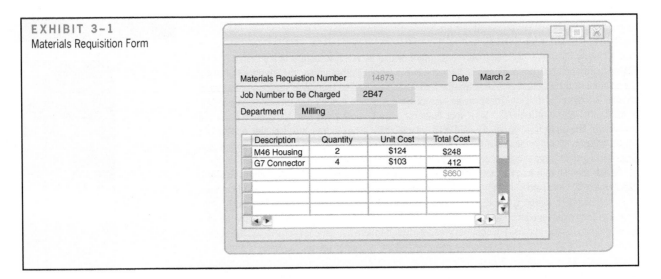

EXHIBIT 3–1
Materials Requisition Form

Jean: We agreed to take on this initial order at our cost just to get our foot in the door. Marc, will there be any problem documenting our cost so we can get paid?

Marc: No problem. The contract with Loops stipulates that they will pay us an amount equal to our cost of goods sold. With our job-order costing system, I can tell you the cost on the day the job is completed.

Jean: Good. Is there anything else we should discuss about this job at this time? No? Well then let's move on to the next item of business.

Measuring Direct Materials Cost

The blueprints submitted by Loops Unlimited indicate that each experimental coupling will require three parts that are classified as direct materials: two G7 Connectors and one M46 Housing. Since each coupling requires two connectors and one housing, the production of two couplings requires four connectors and two housings. This is a custom product that is being made for the first time, but if this were one of the company's standard products, it would have an established *bill of materials*. A **bill of materials** is a document that lists the type and quantity of each type of direct material needed to complete a unit of product.

When an agreement has been reached with the customer concerning the quantities, prices, and shipment date for the order, a *production order* is issued. The Production Department then prepares a *materials requisition form* similar to the form in Exhibit 3–1. The **materials requisition form** is a document that specifies the type and quantity of materials to be drawn from the storeroom and identifies the job that will be charged for the cost of the materials. The form is used to control the flow of materials into production and also for making entries in the accounting records.

The Yost Precision Machining materials requisition form in Exhibit 3–1 shows that the company's Milling Department has requisitioned two M46 Housings and four G7 Connectors for the Loops Unlimited job, which has been designated as Job 2B47.

Job Cost Sheet

After a production order has been issued, the Accounting Department's job-order costing software system automatically generates a *job cost sheet* like the one presented in Exhibit 3–2. A **job cost sheet** records the materials, labor, and manufacturing overhead costs charged to that job.

IN BUSINESS

SUPPLY AND DEMAND INFLUENCE LUMBER PRICES

When the housing market crumbled between 2005 and 2009, lumber mills responded by slashing output by 45%. However, in 2010 many home builders decided to expand speculative construction on the belief that an expiring federal tax credit would entice more customers to purchase new homes. The result of plummeting supply coupled with an uptick in demand was predictable—the price of lumber spiked to $279 per thousand board feet, thereby adding about $1,000 to the price of a typical new home. Pulte Homes told investors that it would attempt to offset the increase in direct materials cost by reducing its labor costs.

Home builders use job-order costing systems to accumulate the costs incurred to build each new home. When materials and labor costs fluctuate, job-order costing systems can measure these impacts on each customer's new home construction costs.

Source: Liam Pleven and Lester Aldrich, "Builders Nailed by Lumber Prices," *The Wall Street Journal*, February 16, 2010, pp. C1 and C4.

After direct materials are issued, the cost of these materials are automatically recorded on the job cost sheet. Note from Exhibit 3–2, for example, that the $660 cost for direct materials shown earlier on the materials requisition form has been charged to Job 2B47 on its job cost sheet. The requisition number 14873 from the materials requisition form appears on the job cost sheet to make it easier to identify the source document for the direct materials charge.

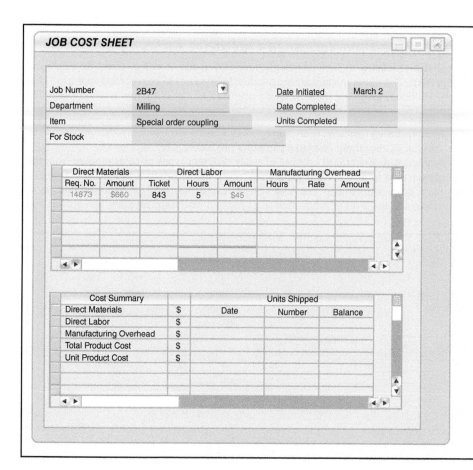

EXHIBIT 3–2
Job Cost Sheet

Measuring Direct Labor Cost

Direct labor consists of labor charges that are easily traced to a particular job. Labor charges that cannot be easily traced directly to any job are treated as part of manufacturing overhead. As discussed in the previous chapter, this latter category of labor costs is called *indirect labor* and includes tasks such as maintenance, supervision, and cleanup.

Most companies rely on computerized systems to maintain employee *time tickets*. A completed **time ticket** is an hour-by-hour summary of the employee's activities throughout the day. One computerized approach to creating time tickets uses bar codes to capture data. Each employee and each job has a unique bar code. When beginning work on a job, the employee scans three bar codes using a handheld device much like the bar code readers at grocery store checkout stands. The first bar code indicates that a job is being started; the second is the unique bar code on the employee's identity badge; and the third is the unique bar code of the job itself. This information is fed automatically via an electronic network to a computer that notes the time and records all of the data. When the task is completed, the employee scans a bar code indicating the task is complete, the bar code on his or her identity badge, and the bar code attached to the job. This information is relayed to the computer that again notes the time, and a time ticket, such as the one shown in Exhibit 3–3, is automatically prepared. Because all of the source data is already in computer files, the labor costs can be automatically posted to job cost sheets. For example, Exhibit 3–3 shows $45 of direct labor cost related to Job 2B47. This amount is automatically posted to the job cost sheet shown in Exhibit 3–2. The time ticket in Exhibit 3–3 also shows $9 of indirect labor costs related to performing maintenance. This cost is treated as part of manufacturing overhead and does not get posted on a job cost sheet.

LO3–1
Compute a predetermined overhead rate.

Computing Predetermined Overhead Rates

Recall that product costs include manufacturing overhead as well as direct materials and direct labor. Therefore, manufacturing overhead also needs to be recorded on the job cost sheet. However, assigning manufacturing overhead to a specific job involves some difficulties. There are three reasons for this:

1. Manufacturing overhead is an *indirect cost.* This means that it is either impossible or difficult to trace these costs to a particular product or job.
2. Manufacturing overhead consists of many different types of costs ranging from the grease used in machines to the annual salary of the production manager. Some of these costs are variable overhead costs because they vary in direct proportion to changes in the level of production (e.g., indirect materials, supplies, and power) and

EXHIBIT 3–3
Employee Time Ticket

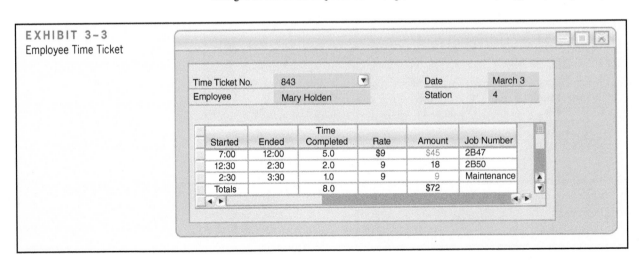

	Started	Ended	Time Completed	Rate	Amount	Job Number
	7:00	12:00	5.0	$9	$45	2B47
	12:30	2:30	2.0	9	18	2B50
	2:30	3:30	1.0	9	9	Maintenance
	Totals		8.0		$72	

Time Ticket No. 843   Date March 3
Employee Mary Holden   Station 4

some are fixed overhead costs because they remain constant as the level of production fluctuates (e.g., heat and light, property taxes, and insurance).

3. Because of the fixed costs in manufacturing overhead, total manufacturing overhead costs tend to remain relatively constant from one period to the next even though the number of units produced can fluctuate widely. Consequently, the average cost per unit will vary from one period to the next.

Given these problems, allocation is used to assign overhead costs to products. Allocation is accomplished by selecting an *allocation base* that is common to all of the company's products and services. An **allocation base** is a measure such as direct labor-hours (DLH) or machine-hours (MH) that is used to assign overhead costs to products and services. The most widely used allocation bases in manufacturing are direct labor-hours, direct labor cost, machine-hours, and (where a company has only a single product) units of product.

Manufacturing overhead is commonly assigned to products using *a predetermined overhead rate*. The **predetermined overhead rate** is computed by dividing the total estimated manufacturing overhead cost for the period by the estimated total amount of the allocation base as follows:

$$\text{Predetermined overhead rate} = \frac{\text{Estimated total manufacturing overhead cost}}{\text{Estimated total amount of the allocation base}}$$

The predetermined overhead rate is computed before the period begins using a four-step process. The first step is to estimate the total amount of the allocation base (the denominator) that will be required for next period's estimated level of production. The second step is to estimate the total fixed manufacturing overhead cost for the coming period and the variable manufacturing overhead cost per unit of the allocation base. The third step is to use the cost formula shown below to estimate the total manufacturing overhead cost (the numerator) for the coming period:

$$Y = a + bX$$

where,

Y = The estimated total manufacturing overhead cost
a = The estimated total fixed manufacturing overhead cost
b = The estimated variable manufacturing overhead cost per unit of the allocation base
X = The estimated total amount of the allocation base

The fourth step is to compute the predetermined overhead rate. Notice, the estimated amount of the allocation base is determined before estimating the total manufacturing overhead cost. This needs to be done because total manufacturing overhead cost includes variable overhead costs that depend on the amount of the allocation base.

Applying Manufacturing Overhead

To repeat, the predetermined overhead rate is computed *before* the period begins. The predetermined overhead rate is then used to apply overhead cost to jobs throughout the period. The process of assigning overhead cost to jobs is called **overhead application**. The formula for determining the amount of overhead cost to apply to a particular job is:

LO3–2
Apply overhead cost to jobs using a predetermined overhead rate.

$$\text{Overhead applied to a particular job} = \text{Predetermined overhead rate} \times \text{Amount of the allocation base incurred by the job}$$

For example, if the predetermined overhead rate is $8 per direct labor-hour, then $8 of overhead cost is *applied* to a job for each direct labor-hour incurred on the job. When the allocation base is direct labor-hours, the formula becomes:

$$\text{Overhead applied to a particular job} = \text{Predetermined overhead rate} \times \text{Actual direct labor-hours charged to the job}$$

Chapter 3

Manufacturing Overhead—A Closer Look

To illustrate the steps involved in computing and using a predetermined overhead rate, let's return to Yost Precision Machining and make the following assumptions. In step one, the company estimated that 40,000 direct labor-hours would be required to support the production planned for the year. In step two, it estimated $220,000 of total fixed manufacturing overhead cost for the coming year and $2.50 of variable manufacturing overhead cost per direct labor-hour. Given these assumptions, in step three the company used the cost formula shown below to estimate its total manufacturing overhead cost for the year:

$$Y = a + bX$$

$$Y = \$220,000 + (\$2.50 \text{ per direct labor-hour} \times 40,000 \text{ direct labor-hours})$$

$$Y = \$220,000 + \$100,000$$

$$Y = \$320,000$$

In step four, Yost Precision Machining computed its predetermined overhead rate for the year of $8 per direct labor-hour as shown below:

$$\text{Predetermined overhead rate} = \frac{\text{Estimated total manufacturing overhead cost}}{\text{Estimated total amount of the allocation base}}$$

$$= \frac{\$320,000}{40,000 \text{ direct labor-hours}}$$

$$= \$8 \text{ per direct labor-hour}$$

The job cost sheet in Exhibit 3–4 indicates that 27 direct labor-hours (i.e., DLHs) were charged to Job 2B47. Therefore, a total of $216 of manufacturing overhead cost would be applied to the job:

$$\begin{array}{l} \text{Overhead applied to} \\ \text{Job 2B47} \end{array} = \begin{array}{l} \text{Predetermined} \\ \text{overhead rate} \end{array} \times \begin{array}{l} \text{Actual direct labor-hours} \\ \text{charged to Job 2B47} \end{array}$$

$$= \$8 \text{ per DLH} \times 27 \text{ DLHs}$$

$$= \$216 \text{ of overhead applied to Job 2B47}$$

This amount of overhead has been entered on the job cost sheet in Exhibit 3–4. Note that this is *not* the actual amount of overhead caused by the job. Actual overhead costs are *not* assigned to jobs—if that could be done, the costs would be direct costs, not overhead. The overhead assigned to the job is simply a share of the total overhead that was estimated at the beginning of the year. A **normal cost system**, which we have been describing, applies overhead to jobs by multiplying a predetermined overhead rate by the actual amount of the allocation base incurred by the jobs.

The Need for a Predetermined Rate

Instead of using a predetermined rate based on estimates, why not base the overhead rate on the *actual* total manufacturing overhead cost and the *actual* total amount of the allocation base incurred on a monthly, quarterly, or annual basis? If an actual rate is computed monthly or quarterly, seasonal factors in overhead costs or in the allocation base can produce fluctuations in the overhead rate. For example, the costs of heating and cooling a factory in Illinois will be highest in the winter and summer months and lowest in the spring and fall. If the overhead rate is recomputed at the end of each month or each quarter based on actual costs and activity, the overhead rate would go up in the winter and summer and down in the spring and fall. As a result, two identical jobs, one completed in the winter and one completed in the spring, would be assigned different manufacturing overhead costs. Many managers believe that such fluctuations in product costs serve

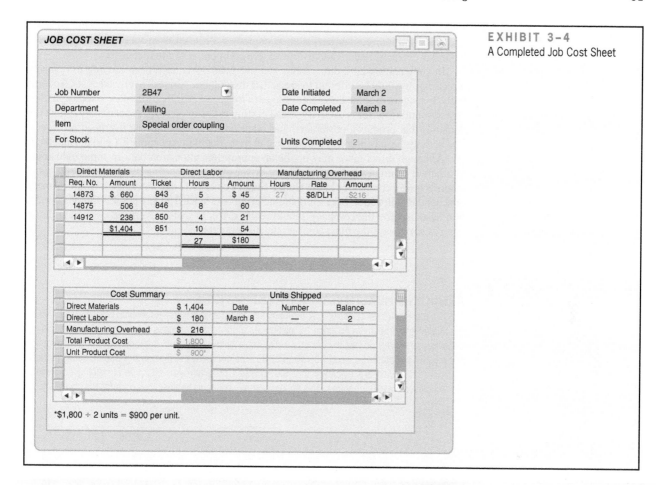

EXHIBIT 3–4
A Completed Job Cost Sheet

no useful purpose. To avoid such fluctuations, actual overhead rates could be computed on an annual or less-frequent basis. However, if the overhead rate is computed annually based on the actual costs and activity for the year, the manufacturing overhead assigned to any particular job would not be known until the end of the year. For example, the cost of Job 2B47 at Yost Precision Machining would not be known until the end of the year, even though the job will be completed and shipped to the customer in March. For these reasons, most companies use predetermined overhead rates rather than actual overhead rates in their cost accounting systems.

Choice of an Allocation Base for Overhead Cost

Ideally, the allocation base in the predetermined overhead rate should *drive* the overhead cost. A **cost driver** is a factor, such as machine-hours, beds occupied, computer time, or flight-hours, that causes overhead costs. If the base in the predetermined overhead rate does not "drive" overhead costs, product costs will be distorted. For example, if direct labor-hours is used to allocate overhead, but in reality overhead has little to do with direct labor-hours, then products with high direct labor-hour requirements will be overcosted.

Most companies use direct labor-hours or direct labor cost as the allocation base for manufacturing overhead. In the past, direct labor accounted for up to 60% of the cost of many products, with overhead cost making up only a portion of the remainder. This situation has changed for two reasons. First, sophisticated automated equipment has taken over functions that used to be performed by direct labor workers. Because the costs of acquiring and maintaining such equipment are classified as overhead, this increases overhead while decreasing direct labor. Second, products are becoming more sophisticated and complex and are changed more frequently. This increases the need for highly skilled indirect workers such as engineers. As a result of these two trends, direct labor has decreased relative to overhead as a component of product costs.

In companies where direct labor and overhead costs have been moving in opposite directions, it would be difficult to argue that direct labor "drives" overhead costs. Accordingly, managers in some companies use *activity-based costing* principles to redesign their cost accounting systems. Activity-based costing is designed to more accurately reflect the demands that products, customers, and other cost objects make on overhead resources. The activity-based approach is discussed in more detail in Appendix 3A and in Chapter 7.

Although direct labor may not be an appropriate allocation base in some industries, in others it continues to be a significant driver of manufacturing overhead. Indeed, most manufacturing companies in the United States continue to use direct labor as the primary or secondary allocation base for manufacturing overhead. The key point is that the allocation base used by the company should really drive, or cause, overhead costs, and direct labor is not always the most appropriate allocation base.

IN BUSINESS

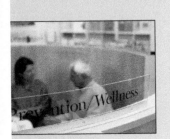

REDUCING HEALTH-DAMAGING BEHAVIORS

Cianbro is an industrial construction company headquartered in Pittsfield, Maine, whose goal is "To be the healthiest company in America." It introduced a corporate wellness program to attack employee behaviors that drive up health-care costs. The table below summarizes the number of employees in five health risk categories as of 2003 and 2005. The decreases in the number of employees in these high-risk categories are evidence that the wellness program was effective in helping employees make positive lifestyle changes. This should result in reduced health-care costs for the company.

Health Risk Category	Number of Employees		
	January 2003	March 2005	Decrease
Obesity	432	353	79
High cholesterol	637	515	122
Tobacco use	384	274	110
Inactivity	354	254	100
High blood pressure	139	91	48

Source: Cianbro, WELCOA's *Absolute Advantage* Magazine, 2006.

LO3–3

Compute the total cost and average cost per unit of a job.

Computation of Unit Costs

With the application of Yost Precision Machining's $216 of manufacturing overhead to the job cost sheet in Exhibit 3–4, the job cost sheet is complete except for two final steps. First, the totals for direct materials, direct labor, and manufacturing overhead are transferred to the Cost Summary section of the job cost sheet and added together to obtain the total cost for the job.[1] Then the total product cost ($1,800) is divided by the number of units (2) to obtain the unit product cost ($900). This unit product cost information is used for valuing unsold units in ending inventory and for determining cost of goods sold. As indicated earlier, *this unit product cost is an average cost and should not be interpreted as the cost that would actually be incurred if another unit were produced.* The incremental cost of an additional unit is something less than the average unit cost of $900 because much of the actual overhead costs would not change if another unit were produced.

---

[1] Notice, we are assuming that Job 2B47 required direct materials and direct labor beyond the charges shown in Exhibits 3–1 and 3–3.

In the 8:00 A.M. daily planning meeting on March 9, Jean Yost, the president of Yost Precision Machining, once again drew attention to Job 2B47, the experimental couplings:

MANAGERIAL ACCOUNTING IN ACTION
THE WRAP-UP

Jean: I see Job 2B47 is completed. Let's get those couplings shipped immediately to Loops Unlimited so they can get their testing program under way. Marc, how much are we going to bill Loops for those two units?

Marc: Because we agreed to sell the experimental couplings at cost, we will be charging Loops Unlimited just $900 a unit.

Jean: Fine. Let's hope the couplings work out and we make some money on the big order later.

YOST
Precision Machining

IN BUSINESS

ONE-OF-A-KIND MASTERPIECE

In a true job-order costing environment, every job is unique. For example, Purdey manufactures 80–90 shotguns per year with each gun being a specially commissioned one-of-a-kind masterpiece. The prices start at $110,000 because every detail is custom built, engraved, assembled, and polished by a skilled craftsman. The hand engraving can take months to complete and may add as much as $100,000 to the price. The guns are designed to shoot perfectly straight and their value increases over time even with heavy use. One Purdey gun collector said "when I shoot my Purdeys I feel like an orchestra conductor waving my baton."

Source: Eric Arnold, "Aim High," *Forbes*, December 28, 2009, p. 86.

Job-Order Costing—The Flow of Costs

We are now ready to discuss the flow of costs through a job-order costing system. Exhibit 3–5 provides a conceptual overview of these cost flows. It highlights the fact that *product costs* flow through inventories on the balance sheet and then on to cost of goods sold in the income statement. More specifically, raw materials purchases are recorded in the *Raw Materials* inventory account. **Raw materials** include any materials that go into the final product. When raw materials are used in production, their costs are transferred to the *Work in Process* inventory account as direct materials.[2] **Work in process** consists of units of product that are only partially complete and will require further work before they are ready for sale to the customer. Notice that direct labor costs are added directly to Work in Process—they do not flow through Raw Materials inventory. Manufacturing overhead costs are applied to Work in Process by multiplying the predetermined overhead rate by the actual quantity of the allocation base consumed by each job.[3] When goods are completed, their costs are transferred from Work in Process to *Finished Goods*. **Finished goods** consist of completed units of product that have not yet been sold to customers. The amount transferred from Work in Process to Finished Goods is referred to as the *cost of goods manufactured*. The **cost of goods manufactured** includes the manufacturing costs associated with the goods that were finished during the period. As goods are sold, their costs are transferred from Finished Goods to Cost of Goods Sold. At this point, the various costs required to make the product are finally recorded as an expense. Until that point, these costs are in inventory accounts on the balance sheet. Period costs (or selling and administrative expenses) do not flow through inventories on the balance sheet. They are recorded as expenses on the income statement in the period incurred.

LO3–4
Understand the flow of costs in a job-order costing system and prepare appropriate journal entries to record costs.

---

[2] Indirect material costs are accounted for as part of manufacturing overhead.

[3] For simplicity, Exhibit 3–5 assumes that Cost of Goods Sold does not need to be adjusted as discussed later in the chapter.

EXHIBIT 3–5
Cost Flows and Classifications in a Manufacturing Company

To illustrate the cost flows through a company's general ledger, we will consider a single month's activity at Ruger Corporation, a producer of gold and silver commemorative medallions. Ruger Corporation has two jobs in process during April, the first month of its fiscal year. Job A, a special minting of 1,000 gold medallions commemorating the invention of motion pictures, was started during March. By the end of March, $30,000 in manufacturing costs had been recorded for the job. Job B, an order for 10,000 silver medallions commemorating the fall of the Berlin Wall, was started in April.

The Purchase and Issue of Materials

On April 1, Ruger Corporation had $7,000 in raw materials on hand. During the month, the company purchased on account an additional $60,000 in raw materials. The purchase is recorded in journal entry (1) below:

(1)

Raw Materials	60,000	
Accounts Payable		60,000

Remember that Raw Materials is an asset account. Thus, when raw materials are purchased, they are initially recorded as an asset—not as an expense.

Issue of Direct and Indirect Materials   During April, $52,000 in raw materials were requisitioned from the storeroom for use in production. These raw materials included $50,000 of direct and $2,000 of indirect materials. Entry (2) records issuing the materials to the production departments.

(2)

Work in Process	50,000	
Manufacturing Overhead	2,000	
Raw Materials		52,000

The materials charged to Work in Process represent direct materials for specific jobs. These costs are also recorded on the appropriate job cost sheets. This point is illustrated in Exhibit 3–6, where $28,000 of the $50,000 in direct materials is charged to Job A's cost sheet and the remaining $22,000 is charged to Job B's cost sheet. (In this example, all data are presented in summary form and the job cost sheet is abbreviated.)

The $2,000 charged to Manufacturing Overhead in entry (2) represents indirect materials. Observe that the Manufacturing Overhead account is separate from the Work in Process account. The purpose of the Manufacturing Overhead account is to accumulate all manufacturing overhead costs as they are incurred during a period.

Before leaving Exhibit 3–6, we need to point out one additional thing. Notice from the exhibit that the job cost sheet for Job A contains a beginning balance of $30,000. We stated earlier that this balance represents the cost of work done during March that has been carried forward to April. Also note that the Work in Process account contains the same $30,000 balance. Thus, the Work in Process account summarizes all of the costs appearing on the job cost sheets of the jobs that are in process. Job A was the only job in process at the beginning of April, so the beginning balance in the Work in Process account equals Job A's beginning balance of $30,000.

Labor Cost

In April, the employee time tickets included $60,000 recorded for direct labor and $15,000 for indirect labor. The following entry summarizes these costs:

(3)

Work in Process	60,000	
Manufacturing Overhead	15,000	
Salaries and Wages Payable		75,000

Only the direct labor cost of $60,000 is added to the Work in Process account. At the same time that direct labor costs are added to Work in Process, they are also added to the individual job cost sheets, as shown in Exhibit 3–7. During April, $40,000 of direct labor cost was charged to Job A and the remaining $20,000 was charged to Job B.

The labor costs charged to Manufacturing Overhead ($15,000) represent the indirect labor costs of the period, such as supervision, janitorial work, and maintenance.

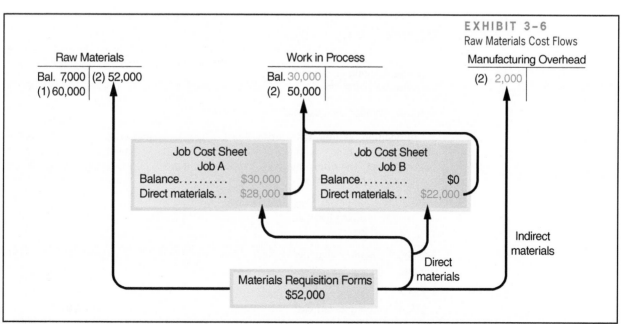

EXHIBIT 3–6
Raw Materials Cost Flows

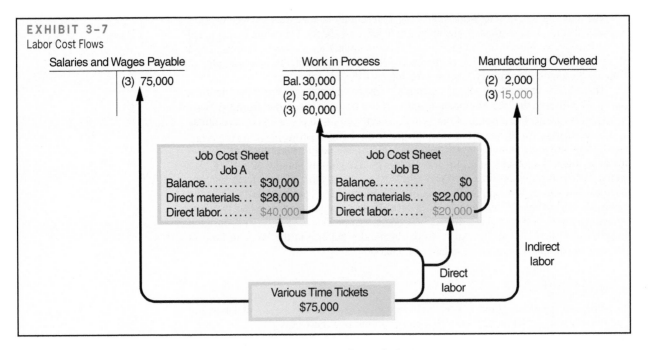

EXHIBIT 3–7
Labor Cost Flows

Manufacturing Overhead Costs

Recall that all manufacturing costs other than direct materials and direct labor are classified as manufacturing overhead costs. These costs are entered directly into the Manufacturing Overhead account as they are incurred. To illustrate, assume that Ruger Corporation incurred the following general factory costs during April:

Utilities (heat, water, and power)	$21,000
Rent on factory equipment	16,000
Miscellaneous factory overhead costs	3,000
Total	$40,000

The following entry records the incurrence of these costs:

(4)

Manufacturing Overhead	40,000	
Accounts Payable*		40,000

*Accounts such as Cash may also be credited

In addition, assume that during April, Ruger Corporation recognized $13,000 in accrued property taxes and that $7,000 in prepaid insurance expired on factory buildings and equipment. The following entry records these items:

(5)

Manufacturing Overhead	20,000	
Property Taxes Payable		13,000
Prepaid Insurance		7,000

Finally, assume that the company recognized $18,000 in depreciation on factory equipment during April. The following entry records the accrual of this depreciation:

(6)

Manufacturing Overhead	18,000	
Accumulated Depreciation		18,000

In short, all actual manufacturing overhead costs are debited to the Manufacturing Overhead account as they are incurred.

Applying Manufacturing Overhead

Because actual manufacturing costs are charged to the Manufacturing Overhead control account rather than to Work in Process, how are manufacturing overhead costs assigned to Work in Process? The answer is, by means of the predetermined overhead rate. Recall from our discussion earlier in the chapter that a predetermined overhead rate is established at the beginning of each year. The rate is calculated by dividing the estimated total manufacturing overhead cost for the year by the estimated total amount of the allocation base (measured in machine-hours, direct labor-hours, or some other base). The predetermined overhead rate is then used to apply overhead costs to jobs. For example, if machine-hours is the allocation base, overhead cost is applied to each job by multiplying the predetermined overhead rate by the number of machine-hours charged to the job.

To illustrate, assume that Ruger Corporation's predetermined overhead rate is $6 per machine-hour. Also assume that during April, 10,000 machine-hours were worked on Job A and 5,000 machine-hours were worked on Job B (a total of 15,000 machine-hours). Thus, $90,000 in overhead cost ($6 per machine-hour $\times$ 15,000 machine-hours = $90,000) would be applied to Work in Process. The following entry records the application of Manufacturing Overhead to Work in Process:

(7)

Work in Process	90,000	
Manufacturing Overhead		90,000

The flow of costs through the Manufacturing Overhead account is shown in Exhibit 3–8. The actual overhead costs on the debit side in the Manufacturing Overhead account in Exhibit 3–8 are the costs that were added to the account in entries (2)–(6). Observe that recording these actual overhead costs [entries (2)–(6)] and the application of overhead to Work in Process [entry (7)] represent two separate and entirely distinct processes.

The Concept of a Clearing Account　The Manufacturing Overhead account operates as a clearing account. As we have noted, actual factory overhead costs are debited to the account as they are incurred throughout the year. When a job is completed (or at the end of an accounting period), overhead cost is applied to the job using the predetermined overhead rate, and Work in Process is debited and Manufacturing Overhead is credited. This sequence of events is illustrated below:

**Manufacturing Overhead
(a clearing account)**

Actual overhead costs are charged to this account as they are incurred throughout the period.	Overhead is applied to Work in Process using the predetermined overhead rate.

As we emphasized earlier, the predetermined overhead rate is based entirely on estimates of what the level of activity and overhead costs are *expected* to be, and it is established before the year begins. As a result, the overhead cost applied during a year will almost certainly turn out to be more or less than the actual overhead cost incurred. For example, notice from Exhibit 3–8 that Ruger Corporation's actual overhead costs for the period are $5,000 greater than the overhead cost that has been applied to Work in Process, resulting in a $5,000 debit balance in the Manufacturing Overhead account. We will reserve discussion of what to do with this $5,000 balance until later in the chapter.

For the moment, we can conclude from Exhibit 3–8 that the cost of a completed job consists of the actual direct materials cost of the job, the actual direct labor cost of the job, and the manufacturing overhead cost *applied* to the job. Pay particular attention to the following subtle but important point: *Actual overhead costs are not charged to jobs;*

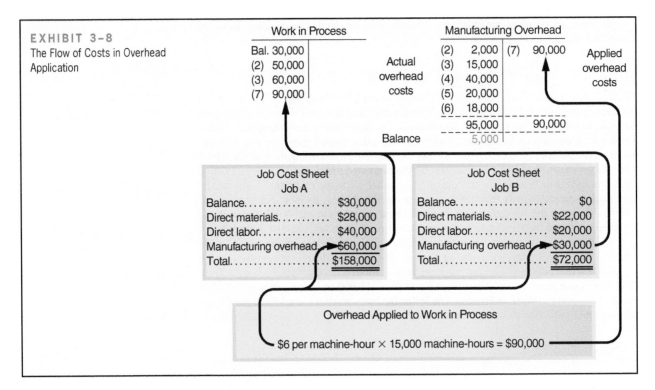

EXHIBIT 3–8
The Flow of Costs in Overhead Application

actual overhead costs do not appear on the job cost sheet nor do they appear in the Work in Process account. Only the applied overhead cost, based on the predetermined overhead rate, appears on the job cost sheet and in the Work in Process account.

Nonmanufacturing Costs

In addition to manufacturing costs, companies also incur selling and administrative costs. These costs should be treated as period expenses and charged directly to the income statement. *Nonmanufacturing costs should not go into the Manufacturing Overhead account.* To illustrate the correct treatment of nonmanufacturing costs, assume that Ruger Corporation incurred $30,000 in selling and administrative salary costs during April. The following entry summarizes the accrual of those salaries:

(8)

Salaries Expense	30,000	
Salaries and Wages Payable		30,000

Assume that depreciation on office equipment during April was $7,000. The entry is as follows:

(9)

Depreciation Expense	7,000	
Accumulated Depreciation		7,000

Pay particular attention to the difference between this entry and entry (6) where we recorded depreciation on factory equipment. In journal entry (6), depreciation on factory equipment was debited to Manufacturing Overhead and is therefore a product cost. In journal entry (9) above, depreciation on office equipment is debited to Depreciation Expense. Depreciation on office equipment is a period expense rather than a product cost.

Finally, assume that advertising was $42,000 and that other selling and administrative expenses in April totaled $8,000. The following entry records these items:

(10)

Advertising Expense	42,000	
Other Selling and Administrative Expense	8,000	
Accounts Payable*		50,000

———

*Other accounts, such as Cash may be credited.

The amounts in entries (8) through (10) are recorded directly into expense accounts—they have no effect on product costs. The same will be true of any other selling and administrative expenses incurred during April, including sales commissions, depreciation on sales equipment, rent on office facilities, insurance on office facilities, and related costs.

Cost of Goods Manufactured

When a job has been completed, the finished output is transferred from the production departments to the finished goods warehouse. By this time, the accounting department will have charged the job with direct materials and direct labor cost, and manufacturing overhead will have been applied using the predetermined overhead rate. A transfer of costs is made within the costing system that *parallels* the physical transfer of goods to the finished goods warehouse. The costs of the completed job are transferred out of the Work in Process account and into the Finished Goods account. The sum of all amounts transferred between these two accounts represents the cost of goods manufactured for the period.

In the case of Ruger Corporation, assume that Job A was completed during April. The following entry transfers the cost of Job A from Work in Process to Finished Goods:

(11)

| Finished Goods .... | 158,000 | |
| Work in Process .... | | 158,000 |

The $158,000 represents the completed cost of Job A, as shown on the job cost sheet in Exhibit 3–8. Because Job A was the only job completed during April, the $158,000 also represents the cost of goods manufactured for the month.

Job B was not completed by the end of the month, so its cost will remain in the Work in Process account and carry over to the next month. If a balance sheet is prepared at the end of April, the cost accumulated thus far on Job B will appear as the asset "Work in Process inventory."

Cost of Goods Sold

As finished goods are shipped to customers, their accumulated costs are transferred from the Finished Goods account to the Cost of Goods Sold account. If an entire job is shipped at one time, then the entire cost appearing on the job cost sheet is transferred to the Cost of Goods Sold account. In most cases, however, only a portion of the units involved in a particular job will be immediately sold. In these situations, the unit product cost must be used to determine how much product cost should be removed from Finished Goods and charged to Cost of Goods Sold.

For Ruger Corporation, we will assume 750 of the 1,000 gold medallions in Job A were shipped to customers by the end of the month for total sales revenue of $225,000. Because 1,000 units were produced and the total cost of the job from the job cost sheet was $158,000, the unit product cost was $158. The following journal entries would record the sale (all sales were on account):

(12)

| Accounts Receivable .... | 225,000 | |
| Sales .... | | 225,000 |

(13)

Cost of Goods Sold	118,500	
Finished Goods		118,500
(750 units × $158 per unit = $118,500)		

LO3–5
Use T-accounts to show the
flow of costs in a job-order
costing system.

Entry (13) completes the flow of costs through the job-order costing system. To pull the entire Ruger Corporation example together, journal entries (1) through (13) are summarized in Exhibit 3–9. The flow of costs through the accounts is presented in T-account form in Exhibit 3–10.

EXHIBIT 3–9
Summary of Journal Entries—
Ruger Corporation

(1)

| Raw Materials | 60,000 | |
| Accounts Payable | | 60,000 |

(2)

Work in Process	50,000	
Manufacturing Overhead	2,000	
Raw Materials		52,000

(3)

Work in Process	60,000	
Manufacturing Overhead	15,000	
Salaries and Wages Payable		75,000

(4)

| Manufacturing Overhead | 40,000 | |
| Accounts Payable | | 40,000 |

(5)

Manufacturing Overhead	20,000	
Property Taxes Payable		13,000
Prepaid Insurance		7,000

(6)

| Manufacturing Overhead | 18,000 | |
| Accumulated Depreciation | | 18,000 |

(7)

| Work in Process | 90,000 | |
| Manufacturing Overhead | | 90,000 |

(8)

| Salaries Expense | 30,000 | |
| Salaries and Wages Payable | | 30,000 |

(9)

| Depreciation Expense | 7,000 | |
| Accumulated Depreciation | | 7,000 |

(10)

Advertising Expense	42,000	
Other Selling and Administrative Expense	8,000	
Accounts Payable		50,000

(11)

| Finished Goods | 158,000 | |
| Work in Process | | 158,000 |

(12)

| Accounts Receivable | 225,000 | |
| Sales | | 225,000 |

(13)

| Cost of Goods Sold | 118,500 | |
| Finished Goods | | 118,500 |

EXHIBIT 3–10
Summary of Cost Flows—Ruger Corporation

Accounts Receivable		
Bal. XX		
(12) 225,000		

Prepaid Insurance		
Bal. XX		
	(5)	7,000

Raw Materials		
Bal. 7,000	(2)	52,000
(1) 60,000		
Bal. 15,000		

Work in Process		
Bal. 30,000	(11)	158,000
(2) 50,000		
(3) 60,000		
(7) 90,000		
Bal. 72,000		

Finished Goods		
Bal. 10,000	(13)	118,500
(11) 158,000		
Bal. 49,500		

Accumulated Depreciation		
	Bal.	XX
	(6)	18,000
	(9)	7,000

Manufacturing Overhead		
(2) 2,000	(7)	90,000
(3) 15,000		
(4) 40,000		
(5) 20,000		
(6) 18,000		
95,000		90,000
Bal. 5,000		

Accounts Payable		
	Bal.	XX
	(1)	60,000
	(4)	40,000
	(10)	50,000

Salaries and Wages Payable		
	Bal.	XX
	(3)	75,000
	(8)	30,000

Property Taxes Payable		
	Bal.	XX
	(5)	13,000

Sales		
	(12)	225,000

Cost of Goods Sold		
(13) 118,500		

Salaries Expense		
(8) 30,000		

Depreciation Expense		
(9) 7,000		

Advertising Expense		
(10) 42,000		

Other Selling and Administrative Expense		
(10) 8,000		

Explanation of entries:
(1) Raw materials purchased.
(2) Direct and indirect materials issued into production.
(3) Direct and indirect factory labor cost incurred.
(4) Utilities and other factory costs incurred.
(5) Property taxes and insurance incurred on the factory.
(6) Depreciation recorded on factory assets.
(7) Overhead cost applied to Work in Process.
(8) Administrative salaries expense incurred.
(9) Depreciation recorded on office equipment.
(10) Advertising and other selling and administrative expense incurred.
(11) Cost of goods manufactured transferred to finished goods.
(12) Sale of Job A recorded.
(13) Cost of goods sold recorded for Job A.

Schedules of Cost of Goods Manufactured and Cost of Goods Sold

LO3–6

Prepare schedules of cost of goods manufactured and cost of goods sold and an income statement.

This section uses the Ruger Corporation example to explain how to prepare schedules of cost of goods manufactured and cost of goods sold as well as an income statement. The **schedule of cost of goods manufactured** contains three elements of product costs—direct materials, direct labor, and manufacturing overhead—and it summarizes the portions of those costs that remain in ending Work in Process inventory and that are transferred out of Work in Process into Finished Goods. The **schedule of cost of goods sold** also contains three elements of product costs—direct materials, direct labor, and manufacturing overhead—and it summarizes the portions of those costs that remain in ending Finished Goods inventory and that are transferred out of Finished Goods into Cost of Goods Sold.

Exhibit 3–11 presents Ruger Corporation's schedules of cost of goods manufactured and cost of goods sold. We want to draw your attention to three equations that are embedded within the schedule of cost of goods manufactured. First, the *raw materials used in production* are computed using the following equation:

$$\text{Raw materials used in production} = \text{Beginning raw materials inventory} + \text{Purchases of raw materials} - \text{Ending raw materials inventory}$$

For Ruger Corporation, the beginning raw materials inventory of $7,000 plus the purchases of raw materials of $60,000 minus the ending raw materials inventory of $15,000

EXHIBIT 3–11
Schedules of Cost of Goods Manufactured and Cost of Goods Sold

Cost of Goods Manufactured

Direct materials:		
Beginning raw materials inventory	$ 7,000	
Add: Purchases of raw materials	60,000	
Total raw materials available	67,000	
Deduct: Ending raw materials inventory	15,000	
Raw materials used in production	52,000	
Deduct: Indirect materials included in manufacturing overhead	2,000	$ 50,000
Direct labor		60,000
Manufacturing overhead applied to work in process		90,000
Total manufacturing costs		200,000
Add: Beginning work in process inventory		30,000
		230,000
Deduct: Ending work in process inventory		72,000
Cost of goods manufactured		$158,000

Cost of Goods Sold

Beginning finished goods inventory	$ 10,000
Add: Cost of goods manufactured	158,000
Cost of goods available for sale	168,000
Deduct: Ending finished goods inventory	49,500
Unadjusted cost of goods sold	118,500
Add: Underapplied overhead	5,000
Adjusted cost of goods sold	$123,500

*Note that the underapplied overhead is added to cost of goods sold. If overhead were overapplied, it would be deducted from cost of goods sold.

equals the raw materials used in production of $52,000. Second, the *total manufacturing costs* are computed using the following equation:

$$\begin{array}{c} \text{Total} \\ \text{manufacturing} \\ \text{costs} \end{array} = \text{Direct materials} + \text{Direct labor} + \begin{array}{c} \text{Manufacturing} \\ \text{overhead applied to} \\ \text{work in process} \end{array}$$

For Ruger Corporation, the direct materials of $50,000 plus the direct labor of $60,000 plus the manufacturing overhead applied to work in process of $90,000 equals the total manufacturing costs of $200,000. Notice, the direct materials used in production ($50,000) is included in total manufacturing costs instead of raw materials purchases ($60,000). The direct materials used in production will usually differ from the amount of raw material purchases when the raw materials inventory balance changes or indirect materials are withdrawn from raw materials inventory. You should also make a note that *this equation includes manufacturing overhead applied to work in process rather than actual manufacturing overhead costs*. For Ruger Corporation, its manufacturing overhead applied to work in process of $90,000 is computed by multiplying the predetermined overhead rate of $6 per machine-hour by the actual amount of the allocation base recorded on all jobs, or 15,000 machine-hours. *The actual manufacturing overhead costs incurred during the period are not added to the Work in Process account.*

The third equation included in the schedule of cost of goods manufactured relates to computing the cost of goods manufactured:

$$\begin{array}{c} \text{Cost of goods} \\ \text{manufactured} \end{array} = \begin{array}{c} \text{Total} \\ \text{manufacturing costs} \end{array} + \begin{array}{c} \text{Beginning work in} \\ \text{process inventory} \end{array} - \begin{array}{c} \text{Ending work in} \\ \text{process inventory} \end{array}$$

For Ruger, the total manufacturing costs of $200,000 plus the beginning work in process inventory of $30,000 minus the ending work in process inventory of $72,000 equals the cost of goods manufactured of $158,000. The cost of goods manufactured represents the cost of the goods completed during the period and transferred from Work in Process to Finished Goods.

The schedule of cost of goods sold shown in Exhibit 3–11 relies on the following equation to compute the unadjusted cost of goods sold:

$$\begin{array}{c} \text{Unadjusted cost} \\ \text{of goods sold} \end{array} = \begin{array}{c} \text{Beginning finished} \\ \text{goods inventory} \end{array} + \begin{array}{c} \text{Cost of goods} \\ \text{manufactured} \end{array} - \begin{array}{c} \text{Ending finished} \\ \text{goods inventory} \end{array}$$

The beginning finished goods inventory ($10,000) plus the cost of goods manufactured ($158,000) equals the cost of goods available for sale ($168,000). The cost of goods available for sale ($168,000) minus the ending finished goods inventory ($49,500) equals the unadjusted cost of goods sold ($118,500). Finally, the unadjusted cost of goods sold ($118,500) plus the underapplied overhead ($5,000) equals adjusted cost of goods sold ($123,500). The next section of the chapter takes a closer look at why cost of goods sold needs to be adjusted for the amount of underapplied or overapplied overhead.

Exhibit 3–12 presents Ruger Corporation's income statement for April. Observe that the cost of goods sold on this statement is carried over from Exhibit 3–11. The selling and administrative expenses (which total $87,000) did not flow through the schedules of cost of goods manufactured and cost of goods sold. Journal entries 8–10 (pages 98–99) show that these items were immediately debited to expense accounts rather than being debited to inventory accounts.

EXHIBIT 3–12
Income Statement

Ruger Corporation Income Statement For the Month Ending April 30		
Sales		$225,000
Cost of goods sold ($118,500 + $5,000)		123,500
Gross margin		101,500
Selling and administrative expenses:		
Salaries expense	$30,000	
Depreciation expense	7,000	
Advertising expense	42,000	
Other expense	8,000	87,000
Net operating income		$ 14,500

Underapplied and Overapplied Overhead—A Closer Look

LO3–7
Compute underapplied or overapplied overhead cost and prepare the journal entry to close the balance in Manufacturing Overhead to the appropriate accounts.

This section explains how to compute underapplied and overapplied overhead and how to dispose of any balance remaining in the Manufacturing Overhead account at the end of a period.

Computing Underapplied and Overapplied Overhead

Because the predetermined overhead rate is established before the period begins and is based entirely on estimated data, the overhead cost applied to Work in Process will generally differ from the amount of overhead cost actually incurred. In the case of Ruger Corporation, for example, the predetermined overhead rate of $6 per hour was used to apply $90,000 of overhead cost to Work in Process, whereas actual overhead costs for April proved to be $95,000 (see Exhibit 3–8). The difference between the overhead cost applied to Work in Process and the actual overhead costs of a period is called either **underapplied** or **overapplied overhead**. For Ruger Corporation, overhead was underapplied by $5,000 because the applied cost ($90,000) was $5,000 less than the actual cost ($95,000). If the situation had been reversed and the company had applied $95,000 in overhead cost to Work in Process while incurring actual overhead costs of only $90,000, then the overhead would have been overapplied.

What is the cause of underapplied or overapplied overhead? Basically, the method of applying overhead to jobs using a predetermined overhead rate assumes that actual overhead costs will be proportional to the actual amount of the allocation base incurred during the period. If, for example, the predetermined overhead rate is $6 per machine-hour, then it is assumed that actual overhead costs incurred will be $6 for every machine-hour that is actually worked. There are at least two reasons why this may not be true. First, much of the overhead often consists of fixed costs that do not change as the number of machine-hours incurred goes up or down. Second, spending on overhead items may or may not be under control. If individuals who are responsible for overhead costs do a good job, those costs should be less than were expected at the beginning of the period. If they do a poor job, those costs will be more than expected.

To illustrate these concepts, suppose that two companies—Turbo Crafters and Black & Howell—have prepared the following estimated data for the coming year:

	Turbo Crafters	Black & Howell
Allocation base	Machine-hours	Direct materials cost
Estimated manufacturing overhead cost (a)	$300,000	$120,000
Estimated total amount of the allocation base (b)	75,000 machine-hours	$80,000 direct materials cost
Predetermined overhead rate (a) ÷ (b)	$4 per machine-hour	150% of direct materials cost

Note that when the allocation base is dollars (such as direct materials cost in the case of Black & Howell) the predetermined overhead rate is expressed as a percentage of the allocation base. When dollars are divided by dollars, the result is a percentage.

Now assume that because of unexpected changes in overhead spending and in demand for the companies' products, the *actual* overhead cost and the actual activity recorded during the year in each company are as follows:

	Turbo Crafters	Black & Howell
Actual manufacturing overhead cost	$290,000	$130,000
Actual total amount of the allocation base	68,000 machine-hours	$90,000 direct materials cost

For each company, note that the actual data for both cost and the allocation base differ from the estimates used in computing the predetermined overhead rate. This results in underapplied and overapplied overhead as follows:

	Turbo Crafters	Black & Howell
Actual manufacturing overhead cost	$290,000	$130,000
Manufacturing overhead cost applied to Work in Process during the year:		
Predetermined overhead rate (a)	$4 per machine-hour	150% of direct materials cost
Actual total amount of the allocation base (b)	68,000 machine-hours	$90,000 direct materials cost
Manufacturing overhead applied (a) × (b)	$272,000	$135,000
Underapplied (overapplied) manufacturing overhead	$18,000	$(5,000)

For Turbo Crafters, the amount of overhead cost applied to Work in Process ($272,000) is less than the actual overhead cost for the year ($290,000). Therefore, overhead is underapplied.

For Black & Howell, the amount of overhead cost applied to Work in Process ($135,000) is greater than the actual overhead cost for the year ($130,000), so overhead is overapplied.

A summary of these concepts is presented in Exhibit 3–13.

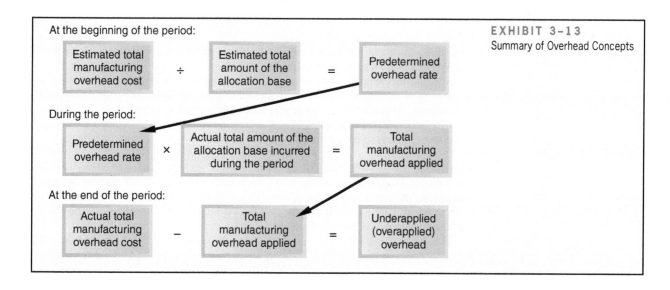

EXHIBIT 3-13
Summary of Overhead Concepts

Chapter 3

Disposition of Underapplied or Overapplied Overhead Balances

If we return to the Ruger Corporation example and look at the Manufacturing Overhead T-account in Exhibit 3–10, you will see that there is a debit balance of $5,000. Remember that debit entries to the account represent actual overhead costs incurred, whereas credit entries represent overhead costs applied to jobs. In this case, the actual overhead costs incurred exceeded the overhead costs applied to jobs by $5,000—hence, the debit balance of $5,000. This may sound familiar. We just discussed in the previous section the fact that the overhead costs incurred ($95,000) exceeded the overhead costs applied ($90,000), and that the difference is called underapplied overhead. These are just two ways of looking at the same thing. If there is a *debit* balance in the Manufacturing Overhead account of X dollars, then the overhead is *underapplied* by X dollars. On the other hand, if there is a *credit* balance in the Manufacturing Overhead account of Y dollars, then the overhead is *overapplied* by Y dollars. What do we do with the balance in the Manufacturing Overhead account at the end of the accounting period?

The underapplied or overapplied balance remaining in the Manufacturing Overhead account at the end of a period is treated in one of two ways:

1. Closed out to Cost of Goods Sold.
2. Allocated among the Work in Process, Finished Goods, and Cost of Goods Sold accounts in proportion to the overhead applied during the current period in ending balances.

Closed Out to Cost of Goods Sold   Closing out the balance in Manufacturing Overhead to Cost of Goods Sold is simpler than the allocation method. In the Ruger Corporation example, the entry to close the $5,000 of underapplied overhead to Cost of Goods Sold is:

(14)

Cost of Goods Sold	5,000	
Manufacturing Overhead		5,000

Note that because the Manufacturing Overhead account has a debit balance, Manufacturing Overhead must be credited to close out the account. This has the effect of increasing Cost of Goods Sold for April to $123,500:

Unadjusted cost of goods sold [from entry (13)]	$118,500
Add underapplied overhead [from entry (14)]	5,000
Adjusted cost of goods sold	$123,500

After this adjustment has been made, Ruger Corporation's income statement for April will appear as shown earlier in Exhibit 3–12.

Note that this adjustment makes sense. The unadjusted cost of goods sold is based on the amount of manufacturing overhead applied to jobs, not the manufacturing overhead costs actually incurred. Because overhead was underapplied, not enough cost was applied to jobs. Hence, the cost of goods sold was understated. Adding the underapplied overhead to the cost of goods sold corrects this understatement.

Allocated between Accounts   Allocation of underapplied or overapplied overhead between Work in Process, Finished Goods, and Cost of Goods Sold is more accurate than closing the entire balance into Cost of Goods Sold. This allocation assigns overhead costs to where they would have gone had the estimates included in the predetermined overhead rate matched the actual amounts.

Had Ruger Corporation chosen to allocate the underapplied overhead among the inventory accounts and Cost of Goods Sold, it would first be necessary to determine the amount of overhead that had been applied during April to each of the accounts. The computations would have been as follows:

Overhead applied in work in process inventory, April 30 (Job B) . . .	$30,000	33.33%
Overhead applied in finished goods inventory, April 30		
Job A: ($60,000/1,000 units = $60 per unit) × 250 units	15,000	16.67%
Overhead applied in cost of goods sold, April		
Job A: ($60,000/1,000 units = $60 per unit) × 750 units	45,000	50.00%
Total overhead applied	$90,000	100.00%

Based on the above percentages, the underapplied overhead (i.e., the debit balance in Manufacturing Overhead) would be allocated as shown in the following journal entry:

Work in Process (33.33% × $5,000)	1,666.50	
Finished Goods (16.67% × $5,000)	833.50	
Cost of Goods Sold (50.00% × $5,000)	2,500.00	
Manufacturing Overhead		5,000.00

Note that the first step in the allocation process was to determine the amount of overhead applied in each of the accounts. For Finished Goods, for example, the total amount of overhead applied to Job A, $60,000, was divided by the total number of units in Job A, 1,000 units, to arrive at the average overhead applied of $60 per unit. Because 250 units from Job A were still in ending finished goods inventory, the amount of overhead applied in the Finished Goods Inventory account was $60 per unit multiplied by 250 units or $15,000 in total.

    If overhead had been overapplied, the entry above would have been just the reverse, because a credit balance would have existed in the Manufacturing Overhead account.

Which Method Should Be Used for Disposing of Underapplied or Overapplied Overhead?

The allocation method is generally considered more accurate than simply closing out the underapplied or overapplied overhead to Cost of Goods Sold. However, the allocation method is more complex. We will always specify which method you are to use in problem assignments.

A General Model of Product Cost Flows

Exhibit 3–14 presents a T-account model of the flow of costs in a product costing system. This model can be very helpful in understanding how production costs flow through a costing system and finally end up as Cost of Goods Sold on the income statement.

Multiple Predetermined Overhead Rates

Our discussion in this chapter has assumed that there is a single predetermined overhead rate for an entire factory called a **plantwide overhead rate**. This is a fairly common practice—particularly in smaller companies. But in larger companies, *multiple predetermined overhead rates* are often used. In a **multiple predetermined overhead rate** system each production department may have its own predetermined overhead rate. Such a system, while more complex, is more accurate because it can reflect differences across departments in how overhead costs are incurred. For example, in departments that are relatively labor intensive overhead might be allocated based on direct labor-hours and in departments that are relatively machine intensive overhead might be allocated based on machine-hours. When multiple predetermined overhead rates are used, overhead is applied in each department according to its own overhead rate as jobs proceed through the department.

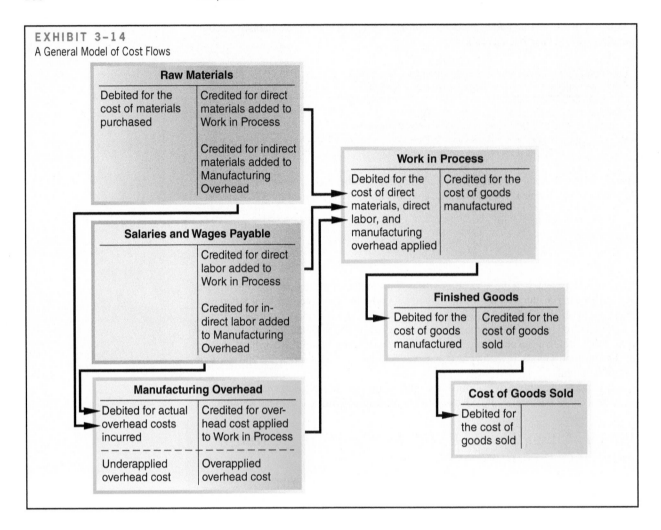

EXHIBIT 3–14
A General Model of Cost Flows

Job-Order Costing in Service Companies

Job-order costing is used in service organizations such as law firms, movie studios, hospitals, and repair shops, as well as in manufacturing companies. In a law firm, for example, each client is a "job," and the costs of that job are accumulated day by day on a job cost sheet as the client's case is handled by the firm. Legal forms and similar inputs represent the direct materials for the job; the time expended by attorneys is like direct labor; and the costs of secretaries and legal aids, rent, depreciation, and so forth, represent the overhead.

In a movie studio such as **Columbia Pictures**, each film produced by the studio is a "job," and costs of direct materials (costumes, props, film, etc.) and direct labor (actors, directors, and extras) are charged to each film's job cost sheet. A share of the studio's overhead costs, such as utilities, depreciation of equipment, wages of maintenance workers, and so forth, is also charged to each film.

In sum, job-order costing is a versatile and widely used costing method that may be encountered in virtually any organization that provides diverse products or services.

COMPUTING JOB COSTS AT FAST WRAP

In 2007, Michael Enos founded Fast Wrap, a company that shrink-wraps everything from jet skis and recreation vehicles (RVs) to entire buildings. Today, the company has 64 locations across America and generates more than $6 million in annual sales. The company's revenues far exceed its direct materials and direct labor costs. For example, Fast Wrap charges customers $400 to wrap a 20-foot boat that requires $25 worth of plastic and $30 worth of labor. Larger jobs are even more profitable. For example, Fast Wrap signed a $250,000 contract to shrink-wrap a 244,000-square-foot hospital under construction in Fontana, California. The materials and labor for this job cost Fast Wrap $44,000.

Source: Susan Adams, "It's a Wrap," *Forbes*, March 15, 2010, pp. 36–38.

Summary

Job-order costing is used in situations where the organization offers many different products or services, such as in furniture manufacturing, hospitals, and legal firms. Materials requisition forms and labor time tickets are used to assign direct materials and direct labor costs to jobs in a job-order costing system. Manufacturing overhead costs are assigned to jobs using a predetermined overhead rate. All of the costs are recorded on a job cost sheet. The predetermined overhead rate is determined before the period begins by dividing the estimated total manufacturing overhead cost for the period by the estimated total amount of the allocation base for the period. The most frequently used allocation bases are direct labor-hours and machine-hours. Overhead is applied to jobs by multiplying the predetermined overhead rate by the actual amount of the allocation base recorded for the job.

Because the predetermined overhead rate is based on estimates, the actual overhead cost incurred during a period may be more or less than the amount of overhead cost applied to production. Such a difference is referred to as underapplied or overapplied overhead. The underapplied or overapplied overhead for a period can be either closed out to Cost of Goods Sold or allocated between Work in Process, Finished Goods, and Cost of Goods Sold. When overhead is underapplied, manufacturing overhead costs have been understated and therefore inventories and/or expenses must be adjusted upwards. When overhead is overapplied, manufacturing overhead costs have been overstated and therefore inventories and/or expenses must be adjusted downwards.

Review Problem: Job-Order Costing

Hogle Corporation is a manufacturer that uses job-order costing. On January 1, the beginning of its fiscal year, the company's inventory balances were as follows:

Raw materials	$20,000
Work in process	$15,000
Finished goods	$30,000

The company applies overhead cost to jobs on the basis of machine-hours worked. For the current year, the company's predetermined overhead rate was based on a cost formula that estimated $450,000 of total manufacturing overhead for an estimated activity level of 75,000 machine-hours. The following transactions were recorded for the year:

a. Raw materials were purchased on account, $410,000.

b. Raw materials were requisitioned for use in production, $380,000 ($360,000 direct materials and $20,000 indirect materials).

c. The following costs were accrued for employee services: direct labor, $75,000; indirect labor, $110,000; sales commissions, $90,000; and administrative salaries, $200,000.

d. Sales travel costs were $17,000.

e. Utility costs in the factory were $43,000.

f. Advertising costs were $180,000.
g. Depreciation was recorded for the year, $350,000 (80% relates to factory operations, and 20% relates to selling and administrative activities).
h. Insurance expired during the year, $10,000 (70% relates to factory operations, and the remaining 30% relates to selling and administrative activities).
i. Manufacturing overhead was applied to production. Due to greater than expected demand for its products, the company worked 80,000 machine-hours on all jobs during the year.
j. Goods costing $900,000 to manufacture according to their job cost sheets were completed during the year.
k. Goods were sold on account to customers during the year for a total of $1,500,000. The goods cost $870,000 to manufacture according to their job cost sheets.

Required:
1. Prepare journal entries to record the preceding transactions.
2. Post the entries in (1) above to T-accounts (don't forget to enter the beginning balances in the inventory accounts).
3. Is Manufacturing Overhead underapplied or overapplied for the year? Prepare a journal entry to close any balance in the Manufacturing Overhead account to Cost of Goods Sold. Do not allocate the balance between ending inventories and Cost of Goods Sold.
4. Prepare an income statement for the year.

Solution to Review Problem

1. a. Raw Materials 410,000
        Accounts Payable 410,000
    b. Work in Process 360,000
        Manufacturing Overhead 20,000
        Raw Materials 380,000
    c. Work in Process 75,000
        Manufacturing Overhead 110,000
        Sales Commissions Expense 90,000
        Administrative Salaries Expense 200,000
        Salaries and Wages Payable 475,000
    d. Sales Travel Expense 17,000
        Accounts Payable 17,000
    e. Manufacturing Overhead 43,000
        Accounts Payable 43,000
    f. Advertising Expense 180,000
        Accounts Payable 180,000
    g. Manufacturing Overhead 280,000
        Depreciation Expense 70,000
        Accumulated Depreciation 350,000
    h. Manufacturing Overhead 7,000
        Insurance Expense 3,000
        Prepaid Insurance 10,000
    i. The predetermined overhead rate for the year is computed as follows:

$$\text{Predetermined overhead rate} = \frac{\text{Estimated total manufacturing overhead cost}}{\text{Estimated total amount of the allocation base}}$$

$$= \frac{\$450,000}{75,000 \text{ machine-hours}}$$

$$= \$6 \text{ per machine-hour}$$

Based on the 80,000 machine-hours actually worked during the year, the company applied $480,000 in overhead cost to production: $6 per machine-hour × 80,000 machine-hours = $480,000. The following entry records this application of overhead cost:

        Work in Process 480,000
        Manufacturing Overhead 480,000
    j. Finished Goods 900,000
        Work in Process 900,000
    k. Accounts Receivable 1,500,000
        Sales 1,500,000
        Cost of Goods Sold 870,000
        Finished Goods 870,000

2.

Accounts Receivable	
(k) 1,500,000	

Prepaid Insurance	
	(h) 10,000

Raw Materials	
Bal. 20,000	(b) 380,000
(a) 410,000	
Bal. 50,000	

Work in Process	
Bal. 15,000	(j) 900,000
(b) 360,000	
(c) 75,000	
(i) 480,000	
Bal. 30,000	

Finished Goods	
Bal. 30,000	(k) 870,000
(j) 900,000	
Bal. 60,000	

Manufacturing Overhead	
(b) 20,000	(i) 480,000
(c) 110,000	
(e) 43,000	
(g) 280,000	
(h) 7,000	
460,000	480,000
	Bal. 20,000

Accumulated Depreciation	
	(g) 350,000

Accounts Payable	
	(a) 410,000
	(d) 17,000
	(e) 43,000
	(f) 180,000

Salaries and Wages Payable	
	(c) 475,000

Sales	
	(k) 1,500,000

Cost of Goods Sold	
(k) 870,000	

Sales Commissions Expense	
(c) 90,000	

Administrative Salaries Expense	
(c) 200,000	

Sales Travel Expense	
(d) 17,000	

Advertising Expense	
(f) 180,000	

Depreciation Expense	
(g) 70,000	

Insurance Expense	
(h) 3,000	

3. Manufacturing overhead is overapplied for the year. The entry to close it out to Cost of Goods Sold is as follows:

Manufacturing Overhead	20,000	
Cost of Goods Sold.		20,000

4.

Hogle Corporation
Income Statement
For the Year Ended December 31

Sales		$1,500,000
Cost of goods sold ($870,000 − $20,000)		850,000
Gross margin		650,000
Selling and administrative expenses:		
Sales commissions expense	$ 90,000	
Administrative salaries expense	200,000	
Sales travel expense	17,000	
Advertising expense	180,000	
Depreciation expense	70,000	
Insurance expense	3,000	560,000
Net operating income		$ 90,000

Glossary

Absorption costing A costing method that includes all manufacturing costs—direct materials, direct labor, and both variable and fixed manufacturing overhead—in the cost of a product. (p. 84)

Allocation base A measure of activity such as direct labor-hours or machine-hours that is used to assign costs to cost objects. (p. 89)

Bill of materials A document that shows the quantity of each type of direct material required to make a product. (p. 86)

Cost driver A factor, such as machine-hours, beds occupied, computer time, or flight-hours, that causes overhead costs. (p. 91)

Cost of goods manufactured The manufacturing costs associated with the goods that were finished during the period. (p. 93)

Finished goods Units of product that have been completed but not yet sold to customers. (p. 93)

Job cost sheet A form that records the materials, labor, and manufacturing overhead costs charged to a job. (p. 86)

Job-order costing A costing system used in situations where many different products, jobs, or services are produced each period. (p. 84)

Materials requisition form A document that specifies the type and quantity of materials to be drawn from the storeroom and that identifies the job that will be charged for the cost of those materials. (p. 86)

Multiple predetermined overhead rates A costing system with multiple overhead cost pools and a different predetermined overhead rate for each cost pool, rather than a single predetermined overhead rate for the entire company. Each production department may be treated as a separate overhead cost pool. (p. 107)

Normal cost system A costing system in which overhead costs are applied to a job by multiplying a predetermined overhead rate by the actual amount of the allocation base incurred by the job. (p. 90)

Overapplied overhead A credit balance in the Manufacturing Overhead account that occurs when the amount of overhead cost applied to Work in Process exceeds the amount of overhead cost actually incurred during a period. (p. 104)

Overhead application The process of charging manufacturing overhead cost to job cost sheets and to the Work in Process account. (p. 89)

Plantwide overhead rate A single predetermined overhead rate that is used throughout a plant. (p. 107)

Predetermined overhead rate A rate used to charge manufacturing overhead cost to jobs that is established in advance for each period. It is computed by dividing the estimated total manufacturing overhead cost for the period by the estimated total amount of the allocation base for the period. (p. 89)

Raw materials Any materials that go into the final product. (p. 93)

Schedule of cost of goods manufactured A schedule that contains three elements of product costs—direct materials, direct labor, and manufacturing overhead—and that summarizes the portions of those costs that remain in ending Work in Process inventory and that are transferred out of Work in Process into Finished Goods. (p. 102)

Schedule of cost of goods sold A schedule that contains three elements of product costs—direct materials, direct labor, and manufacturing overhead—and that summarizes the portions of those costs that remain in ending Finished Goods inventory and that are transferred out of Finished Goods into Cost of Goods Sold. (p. 102)

Time ticket A document that is used to record the amount of time an employee spends on various activities. (p. 88)

Underapplied overhead A debit balance in the Manufacturing Overhead account that occurs when the amount of overhead cost actually incurred exceeds the amount of overhead cost applied to Work in Process during a period. (p. 104)

Work in process Units of product that are only partially complete and will require further work before they are ready for sale to the customer. (p. 93)

Questions

3–1 Why aren't actual manufacturing overhead costs traced to jobs just as direct materials and direct labor costs are traced to jobs?

3–2 Explain the four-step process used to compute a predetermined overhead rate.

3–3 What is the purpose of the job cost sheet in a job-order costing system?

3–4   Explain why some production costs must be assigned to products through an allocation process.

3–5   Why do companies use predetermined overhead rates rather than actual manufacturing overhead costs to apply overhead to jobs?

3–6   What factors should be considered in selecting a base to be used in computing the predetermined overhead rate?

3–7   If a company fully allocates all of its overhead costs to jobs, does this guarantee that a profit will be earned for the period?

3–8   What account is credited when overhead cost is applied to Work in Process? Would you expect the amount applied for a period to equal the actual overhead costs of the period? Why or why not?

3–9   What is underapplied overhead? Overapplied overhead? What disposition is made of these amounts at the end of the period?

3–10   Provide two reasons why overhead might be underapplied in a given year.

3–11   What adjustment is made for underapplied overhead on the schedule of cost of goods sold? What adjustment is made for overapplied overhead?

3–12   What is a plantwide overhead rate? Why are multiple overhead rates, rather than a plantwide overhead rate, used in some companies?

3–13   What happens to overhead rates based on direct labor when automated equipment replaces direct labor?

Multiple-choice questions are provided on the text website at www.mhhe.com/garrison15e.

 Applying Excel

Available with McGraw-Hill's *Connect*® Accounting.

The Excel worksheet form that appears below is to be used to recreate part of the example on pages 104–105. Download the workbook containing this form from the Online Learning Center at www.mhhe.com/garrison15e. *On the website you will also receive instructions about how to use this worksheet form.*

LO3–1, LO3–4, LO3–7

	A	B	C	D
1	Chapter 3: Applying Excel			
2				
3	Data			
4	Allocation base	Machine-hours		
5	Estimated manufacturing overhead cost	$300,000		
6	Estimated total amount of the allocation base	75,000	machine-hours	
7	Actual manufacturing overhead cost	$290,000		
8	Actual total amount of the allocation base	68,000	machine-hours	
9				
10	Enter a formula into each of the cells marked with a ? below			
11				
12	Computation of the predetermined overhead rate			
13	Estimated manufacturing overhead cost	?		
14	Estimated total amount of the allocation base	?	machine-hours	
15	Predetermined overhead rate	?	per machine-hour	
16				
17	Computation of underapplied or overapplied manufacturing overhead			
18	Actual manufacturing overhead cost	?		
19	Manufacturing overhead cost applied to Work in Process during the year.			
20	Predetermined overhead rate	?	per machine-hour	
21	Actual total amount of the allocation base	?	machine-hours	
22	Manufacturing overhead applied	?		
23	Underapplied (overapplied) manufacturing overhead	?		
24				

Chapter 3 Form / Filled in Chapter 3 Form / Chapter 3 Formulas

You should proceed to the requirements below only after completing your worksheet.

Required:

1. Check your worksheet by changing the estimated total amount of the allocation base in the Data area to 60,000 machine-hours, keeping all of the other data the same as in the original example. If your worksheet is operating properly, the predetermined overhead rate should now be $5.00 per machine-hour. If you do not get this answer, find the errors in your worksheet and correct them.

   How much is the underapplied (overapplied) manufacturing overhead? Did it change? Why or why not?

2. Determine the underapplied (overapplied) manufacturing overhead for a different company with the following data:

Allocation base	Machine-hours
Estimated manufacturing overhead cost	$100,000
Estimated total amount of the allocation base	50,000 machine-hours
Actual manufacturing overhead cost	$90,000
Actual total amount of the allocation base	40,000 machine-hours

3. What happens to the underapplied (overapplied) manufacturing overhead from part (2) if the estimated total amount of the allocation base is changed to 40,000 machine-hours and everything else remains the same? Why is the amount of underapplied (overapplied) manufacturing overhead different from part (2)?

4. Change the estimated total amount of the allocation base back to 50,000 machine-hours so that the data look exactly like they did in part (2). Now change the actual manufacturing overhead cost to $100,000. What is the underapplied (overapplied) manufacturing overhead now? Why is the amount of underapplied (overapplied) manufacturing overhead different from part (2)?

The Foundational 15   ACCOUNTING

Available with McGraw-Hill's *Connect® Accounting*.

LO3–1, LO3–2, LO3–3, LO3–4, LO3–5, LO3–6, LO3–7

Sweeten Company had no jobs in progress at the beginning of March and no beginning inventories. It started only two jobs during March—Job P and Job Q. Job P was completed and sold by the end of the March and Job Q was incomplete at the end of the March. The company uses a plantwide predetermined overhead rate based on direct labor-hours. The following additional information is available for the company as a whole and for Jobs P and Q (all data and questions relate to the month of March):

Estimated total fixed manufacturing overhead	$10,000
Estimated variable manufacturing overhead per direct labor-hour	$1.00
Estimated total direct labor-hours to be worked	2,000
Total actual manufacturing overhead costs incurred	$12,500

	Job P	Job Q
Direct materials	$13,000	$8,000
Direct labor cost	$21,000	$7,500
Actual direct labor-hours worked	1,400	500

1. What is the company's predetermined overhead rate?
2. How much manufacturing overhead was applied to Job P and Job Q?
3. What is the direct labor hourly wage rate?
4. If Job P includes 20 units, what is its unit product cost? What is the total amount of manufacturing cost assigned to Job Q as of the end of March (including applied overhead)?
5. Assume the ending raw materials inventory is $1,000 and the company does not use any indirect materials. Prepare the journal entries to record raw materials purchases and the issuance of direct materials for use in production.

6. Assume that the company does not use any indirect labor. Prepare the journal entry to record the direct labor costs added to production.
7. Prepare the journal entry to apply manufacturing overhead costs to production.
8. Assume the ending raw materials inventory is $1,000 and the company does not use any indirect materials. Prepare a schedule of cost of goods manufactured.
9. Prepare the journal entry to transfer costs from Work in Process to Finished Goods.
10. Prepare a completed Work in Process T-account including the beginning and ending balances and all debits and credits posted to the account.
11. Prepare a schedule of cost of goods sold. (Stop after computing the unadjusted cost of goods sold.)
12. Prepare the journal entry to transfer costs from Finished Goods to Cost of Goods Sold.
13. What is the amount of underapplied or overapplied overhead?
14. Prepare the journal entry to close the amount of underapplied or overapplied overhead to Cost of Goods Sold.
15. Assume that Job P includes 20 units that each sell for $3,000 and that the company's selling and administrative expenses in March were $14,000. Prepare an absorption costing income statement for March.

    Exercises

All applicable exercises are available with McGraw-Hill's *Connect® Accounting.*

EXERCISE 3–1 Compute the Predetermined Overhead Rate [LO3–1]

Harris Fabrics computes its predetermined overhead rate annually on the basis of direct labor-hours. At the beginning of the year, it estimated that 20,000 direct labor-hours would be required for the period's estimated level of production. The company also estimated $94,000 of fixed manufacturing overhead expenses for the coming period and variable manufacturing overhead of $2.00 per direct labor-hour. Harris's actual manufacturing overhead for the year was $123,900 and its actual total direct labor was 21,000 hours.

Required:
Compute the company's predetermined overhead rate for the year.

EXERCISE 3–2 Apply Overhead [LO3–2]

Luthan Company uses a predetermined overhead rate of $23.40 per direct labor-hour. This predetermined rate was based on a cost formula that estimated $257,400 of total manufacturing overhead for an estimated activity level of 11,000 direct labor-hours.

The company incurred actual total manufacturing overhead costs of $249,000 and 10,800 total direct labor-hours during the period.

Required:
Determine the amount of manufacturing overhead that would have been applied to all jobs during the period.

EXERCISE 3–3 Computing Job Costs [LO3–3]

Mickley Company's predetermined overhead rate is $14.00 per direct labor-hour and its direct labor wage rate is $12.00 per hour. The following information pertains to Job A-500:

Direct materials	$230
Direct labor	$108

Required:
1. What is the total manufacturing cost assigned to Job A-500?
2. If Job A-500 consists of 40 units, what is the average cost assigned to each unit included in the job?

EXERCISE 3–4 Prepare Journal Entries [LO3–4]

Larned Corporation recorded the following transactions for the just completed month.
a. $80,000 in raw materials were purchased on account.
b. $71,000 in raw materials were requisitioned for use in production. Of this amount, $62,000 was for direct materials and the remainder was for indirect materials.

116

Chapter 3

c.   Total labor wages of $112,000 were incurred. Of this amount, $101,000 was for direct labor and the remainder was for indirect labor.
d.   Additional manufacturing overhead costs of $175,000 were incurred.

Required:
Record the above transactions in journal entries.

EXERCISE 3–5 Prepare T-Accounts [LO3–5, LO3–7]
Jurvin Enterprises recorded the following transactions for the just completed month. The company had no beginning inventories.
a. $94,000 in raw materials were purchased for cash.
b. $89,000 in raw materials were requisitioned for use in production. Of this amount, $78,000 was for direct materials and the remainder was for indirect materials.
c.   Total labor wages of $132,000 were incurred and paid. Of this amount, $112,000 was for direct labor and the remainder was for indirect labor.
d.   Additional manufacturing overhead costs of $143,000 were incurred and paid.
e.   Manufacturing overhead costs of $152,000 were applied to jobs using the company's predetermined overhead rate.
f.   All of the jobs in progress at the end of the month were completed and shipped to customers.
g.   Any underapplied or overapplied overhead for the period was closed out to Cost of Goods Sold.

Required:
1.   Post the above transactions to T-accounts.
2.   Determine the cost of goods sold for the period.

EXERCISE 3–6 Schedules of Cost of Goods Manufactured and Cost of Goods Sold [LO3–6]
Primare Corporation has provided the following data concerning last month's manufacturing operations.

Purchases of raw materials	$30,000
Indirect materials included in manufacturing overhead	$5,000
Direct labor	$58,000
Manufacturing overhead applied to work in process	$87,000
Underapplied overhead	$4,000

Inventories	Beginning	Ending
Raw materials	$12,000	$18,000
Work in process	$56,000	$65,000
Finished goods	$35,000	$42,000

Required:
1.   Prepare a schedule of cost of goods manufactured for the month.
2.   Prepare a schedule of cost of goods sold for the month.

EXERCISE 3–7 Underapplied and Overapplied Overhead [LO3–7]
Osborn Manufacturing uses a predetermined overhead rate of $18.20 per direct labor-hour. This predetermined rate was based on a cost formula that estimates $218,400 of total manufacturing overhead for an estimated activity level of 12,000 direct labor-hours.

The company incurred actual total manufacturing overhead costs of $215,000 and 11,500 total direct labor-hours during the period.

Required:
1.   Determine the amount of underapplied or overapplied manufacturing overhead for the period.
2.   Assuming that the entire amount of the underapplied or overapplied overhead is closed out to Cost of Goods Sold, what would be the effect of the underapplied or overapplied overhead on the company's gross margin for the period?

EXERCISE 3–8 Applying Overhead; Computing Unit Product Cost [LO3–2, LO3–3]
A company assigns overhead cost to completed jobs on the basis of 125% of direct labor cost. The job cost sheet for Job 313 shows that $10,000 in direct materials has been used on the job and that $12,000 in direct labor cost has been incurred. A total of 1,000 units were produced in Job 313.

Required:
What is the total manufacturing cost assigned to Job 313? What is the unit product cost for Job 313?

EXERCISE 3–9 Journal Entries and T-accounts [LO3–2, LO3–4, LO3–5]

The Polaris Company uses a job-order costing system. The following data relate to October, the first month of the company's fiscal year.

a. Raw materials purchased on account, $210,000.
b. Raw materials issued to production, $190,000 ($178,000 direct materials and $12,000 indirect materials).
c. Direct labor cost incurred, $90,000; indirect labor cost incurred, $110,000.
d. Depreciation recorded on factory equipment, $40,000.
e. Other manufacturing overhead costs incurred during October, $70,000 (credit Accounts Payable).
f. The company applies manufacturing overhead cost to production on the basis of $8 per machine-hour. A total of 30,000 machine-hours were recorded for October.
g. Production orders costing $520,000 according to their job cost sheets were completed during October and transferred to Finished Goods.
h. Production orders that had cost $480,000 to complete according to their job cost sheets were shipped to customers during the month. These goods were sold on account at 25% above cost.

Required:
1. Prepare journal entries to record the information given above.
2. Prepare T-accounts for Manufacturing Overhead and Work in Process. Post the relevant information above to each account. Compute the ending balance in each account, assuming that Work in Process has a beginning balance of $42,000.

EXERCISE 3–10 Applying Overhead to a Job [LO3–2]

Sigma Corporation applies overhead cost to jobs on the basis of direct labor cost. Job V, which was started and completed during the current period, shows charges of $5,000 for direct materials, $8,000 for direct labor, and $6,000 for overhead on its job cost sheet. Job W, which is still in process at year-end, shows charges of $2,500 for direct materials and $4,000 for direct labor.

Required:
Should any overhead cost be added to Job W at year-end? If so, how much? Explain.

EXERCISE 3–11 Schedules of Cost of Goods Manufactured and Cost of Goods Sold; Income Statement [LO3–6]

The following data from the just completed year are taken from the accounting records of Mason Company:

Sales	$524,000
Direct labor cost	$70,000
Raw material purchases	$118,000
Selling expenses	$140,000
Administrative expenses	$63,000
Manufacturing overhead applied to work in process	$90,000
Actual manufacturing overhead costs	$80,000

Inventories	Beginning of Year	End of Year
Raw materials	$7,000	$15,000
Work in process	$10,000	$5,000
Finished goods	$20,000	$35,000

Required:
1. Prepare a schedule of cost of goods manufactured. Assume all raw materials used in production were direct materials.
2. Prepare a schedule of cost of goods sold.
3. Prepare an income statement.

EXERCISE 3–12 Applying Overhead; Cost of Goods Manufactured [LO3–2, LO3–6, LO3–7]
The following cost data relate to the manufacturing activities of Chang Company during the just completed year:

Manufacturing overhead costs incurred:	
Indirect materials	$ 15,000
Indirect labor	130,000
Property taxes, factory	8,000
Utilities, factory	70,000
Depreciation, factory	240,000
Insurance, factory	10,000
Total actual manufacturing overhead costs incurred	$473,000
Other costs incurred:	
Purchases of raw materials (both direct and indirect)	$400,000
Direct labor cost	$60,000
Inventories:	
Raw materials, beginning	$20,000
Raw materials, ending	$30,000
Work in process, beginning	$40,000
Work in process, ending	$70,000

The company uses a predetermined overhead rate to apply overhead cost to jobs. The rate for the year was $25 per machine-hour. A total of 19,400 machine-hours was recorded for the year.

Required:
1. Compute the amount of underapplied or overapplied overhead cost for the year.
2. Prepare a schedule of cost of goods manufactured for the year.

EXERCISE 3–13 Varying Predetermined Overhead Rates [LO3–1, LO3–2, LO3–3]
Kingsport Containers Company makes a single product that is subject to wide seasonal variations in demand. The company uses a job-order costing system and computes predetermined overhead rates on a quarterly basis using the number of units to be produced as the allocation base. Its estimated costs, by quarter, for the coming year are given below:

	Quarter			
	First	Second	Third	Fourth
Direct materials	$240,000	$120,000	$ 60,000	$180,000
Direct labor	128,000	64,000	32,000	96,000
Manufacturing overhead	300,000	220,000	180,000	?
Total manufacturing costs (a)	$668,000	$404,000	$272,000	$?
Number of units to be produced (b)	80,000	40,000	20,000	60,000
Estimated unit product cost (a) ÷ (b)	$8.35	$10.10	$13.60	?

Management finds the variation in quarterly unit product costs to be confusing and difficult to work with. It has been suggested that the problem lies with manufacturing overhead because it is the largest element of total manufacturing cost. Accordingly, you have been asked to find a more appropriate way of assigning manufacturing overhead cost to units of product.

Required:
1. Using the high-low method, estimate the fixed manufacturing overhead cost per quarter and the variable manufacturing overhead cost per unit. Create a cost formula to estimate the total manufacturing overhead cost for the fourth quarter. Compute the total manufacturing cost and unit product cost for the fourth quarter.
2. What is causing the estimated unit product cost to fluctuate from one quarter to the next?
3. How would you recommend stabilizing the company's unit product cost? Support your answer with computations that adapt the cost formula you created in requirement 1.

EXERCISE 3–14 Computing Predetermined Overhead Rates and Job Costs [LO3–1, LO3–2, LO3–3, LO3–7]

Moody Corporation uses a job-order costing system with a plantwide overhead rate based on machine-hours. At the beginning of the year, the company made the following estimates:

Machine-hours required to support estimated production	100,000
Fixed manufacturing overhead cost	$650,000
Variable manufacturing overhead cost per machine-hour	$3.00

Required:

1. Compute the predetermined overhead rate.
2. During the year, Job 400 was started and completed. The following information was available with respect to this job:

Direct materials requisitioned	$450
Direct labor cost	$210
Machine-hours used	40

Compute the total manufacturing cost assigned to Job 400.
3. During the year, the company worked a total of 146,000 machine-hours on all jobs and incurred actual manufacturing overhead costs of $1,350,000. What is the amount of underapplied or overapplied overhead for the year? If this amount were closed out entirely to Cost of Goods Sold would the journal entry increase or decrease net operating income?

EXERCISE 3–15 Departmental Overhead Rates [LO3–1, LO3–2, LO3–3]

White Company has two departments, Cutting and Finishing. The company uses a job-order costing system and computes a predetermined overhead rate in each department. The Cutting Department bases its rate on machine-hours, and the Finishing Department bases its rate on direct labor-hours. At the beginning of the year, the company made the following estimates:

	Department	
	Cutting	Finishing
Direct labor-hours	6,000	30,000
Machine-hours	48,000	5,000
Total fixed manufacturing overhead cost	$264,000	$366,000
Variable manufacturing overhead per machine-hour	$2.00	—
Variable manufacturing overhead per direct labor-hour	—	$4.00

Required:

1. Compute the predetermined overhead rate to be used in each department.
2. Assume that the overhead rates that you computed in (1) above are in effect. The job cost sheet for Job 203, which was started and completed during the year, showed the following:

	Department	
	Cutting	Finishing
Direct labor-hours	6	20
Machine-hours	80	4
Materials requisitioned	$500	$310
Direct labor cost	$70	$150

Compute the total manufacturing cost assigned to Job 203.
3. Would you expect substantially different amounts of overhead cost to be assigned to some jobs if the company used a plantwide overhead rate based on direct labor-hours, rather than using departmental rates? Explain. No computations are necessary.

120   Chapter 3

EXERCISE 3–16 Applying Overhead; Journal Entries; Disposition of Underapplied or Overapplied Overhead [LO3–4, LO3–5, LO3–7]

The following information is taken from the accounts of Latta Company. The entries in the T-accounts are summaries of the transactions that affected those accounts during the year.

Manufacturing Overhead					Work in Process			
(a)	460,000	(b)	390,000	Bal.	15,000	(c)	710,000
Bal.	70,000				260,000		
					85,000		
				(b)	390,000		
				Bal.	40,000		

Finished Goods					Cost of Goods Sold			
Bal.	50,000	(d)	640,000	(d)	640,000		
(c)	710,000						
Bal.	120,000						

The overhead that had been applied to production during the year is distributed among the ending balances in the accounts as follows:

Work in Process, ending	$ 19,500
Finished Goods, ending	58,500
Cost of Goods Sold	312,000
Overhead applied	$390,000

For example, of the $40,000 ending balance in Work in Process, $19,500 was overhead that had been applied during the year.

Required:
1. Identify reasons for entries (a) through (d).
2. Assume that the company closes any balance in the Manufacturing Overhead account directly to Cost of Goods Sold. Prepare the necessary journal entry.
3. Assume instead that the company allocates any balance in the Manufacturing Overhead account to the other accounts in proportion to the overhead applied in their ending balances. Prepare the necessary journal entry, with supporting computations.

EXERCISE 3–17 Plantwide and Departmental Overhead Rates; Job Costs [LO3–1, LO3–2, LO3–3]

Delph Company uses a job-order costing system and has two manufacturing departments—Molding and Fabrication. The company provided the following estimates at the beginning of the year:

	Molding	Fabrication	Total
Machine-hours	20,000	30,000	50,000
Fixed manufacturing overhead costs	$700,000	$210,000	$910,000
Variable manufacturing overhead per machine-hour	$3.00	$3.00	

During the year, the company had no beginning or ending inventories and it started, completed, and sold only two jobs—Job D-70 and Job C-200. It provided the following information related to those two jobs:

Job D-70	Molding	Fabrication	Total
Direct materials cost	$375,000	$325,000	$700,000
Direct labor cost	$200,000	$160,000	$360,000
Machine-hours	14,000	6,000	20,000

Job C-200	Molding	Fabrication	Total
Direct materials cost	$300,000	$250,000	$550,000
Direct labor cost	$175,000	$225,000	$400,000
Machine-hours	6,000	24,000	30,000

Delph had no overapplied or underapplied manufacturing overhead during the year.

Required:

1. Assume Delph uses a plantwide overhead rate based on machine-hours.
   a. Compute the predetermined plantwide overhead rate.
   b. Compute the total manufacturing costs assigned to Job D-70 and Job C-200.
   c. If Delph establishes bid prices that are 150% of total manufacturing costs, what bid price would it have established for Job D-70 and Job C-200?
   d. What is Delph's cost of goods sold for the year?
2. Assume Delph uses departmental overhead rates based on machine-hours.
   a. Compute the predetermined departmental overhead rates.
   b. Compute the total manufacturing costs assigned to Job D-70 and Job C-200.
   c. If Delph establishes bid prices that are 150% of total manufacturing costs, what bid price would it have established for Job D-70 and Job C-200?
   d. What is Delph's cost of goods sold for the year?
3. What managerial insights are revealed by the computations that you performed in this problem? (*Hint:* Do the cost of goods sold amounts that you computed in requirements 1 and 2 differ from one another? Do the bid prices that you computed in requirements 1 and 2 differ from one another? Why?)

EXERCISE 3–18 Applying Overhead; T-accounts; Journal Entries [LO3–1, LO3–2, LO3–4, LO3–5, LO3–7]
Harwood Company uses a job-order costing system. Overhead costs are applied to jobs on the basis of machine-hours. At the beginning of the year, management estimated that 80,000 machine-hours would be required for the period's estimated level of production. The company also estimated $128,000 of fixed manufacturing overhead expenses for the coming period and variable manufacturing overhead of $0.80 per machine-hour.

Required:

1. Compute the company's predetermined overhead rate.
2. Assume that during the year the company works only 75,000 machine-hours and incurs the following costs in the Manufacturing Overhead and Work in Process accounts:

Manufacturing Overhead		Work in Process	
(Maintenance) 21,000	?	(Direct materials) 710,000	
(Indirect materials) 8,000		(Direct labor) 90,000	
(Indirect labor) 60,000		(Overhead) ?	
(Utilities) 32,000			
(Insurance) 7,000			
(Depreciation) 56,000			

Copy the data in the T-accounts above onto your answer sheet. Compute the amount of overhead cost that would be applied to Work in Process for the year and make the entry in your T-accounts.
3. Compute the amount of underapplied or overapplied overhead for the year and show the balance in your Manufacturing Overhead T-account. Prepare a journal entry to close out the balance in this account to Cost of Goods Sold.
4. Explain why the manufacturing overhead was underapplied or overapplied for the year.

EXERCISE 3–19 Applying Overhead in a Service Company [LO3–1, LO3–2, LO3–3]
Leeds Architectural Consultants began operations on January 2. The following activity was recorded in the company's Work in Process account for the first month of operations:

Work in Process			
Costs of subcontracted work	230,000	To completed projects	390,000
Direct staff costs	75,000		
Studio overhead	120,000		

Leeds Architectural Consultants is a service firm, so the names of the accounts it uses are different from the names used in manufacturing companies. Costs of Subcontracted Work is comparable to Direct Materials; Direct Staff Costs is the same as Direct Labor; Studio Overhead is the same as Manufacturing Overhead; and Completed Projects is the same as Finished Goods. Apart from the difference in terms, the accounting methods used by the company are identical to the methods used by manufacturing companies.

Leeds Architectural Consultants uses a job-order costing system and applies studio overhead to Work in Process on the basis of direct staff costs. At the end of January, only one job was still in process. This job (Lexington Gardens Project) had been charged with $6,500 in direct staff costs.

Required:

1. Compute the predetermined overhead rate that was in use during January.
2. Complete the following job cost sheet for the partially completed Lexington Gardens Project.

> **Job Cost Sheet—Lexington Gardens Project**
> **As of January 31**
>
> Costs of subcontracted work . . . . $?
> Direct staff costs . . . .   ?
> Studio overhead . . . .   ?
> Total cost to January 31 . . . . $?

EXERCISE 3–20 Applying Overhead; Journal Entries; T-accounts [LO3–1, LO3–2, LO3–3, LO3–4, LO3–5]
Dillon Products manufactures various machined parts to customer specifications. The company uses a job-order costing system and applies overhead cost to jobs on the basis of machine-hours. At the beginning of the year, the company used a cost formula to estimate that it would incur $4,800,000 in manufacturing overhead costs at an activity level of 240,000 machine-hours.

The company spent the entire month of January working on a large order for 16,000 custom-made machined parts. The company had no work in process at the beginning of January. Cost data relating to January follow:

a. Raw materials purchased on account, $325,000.
b. Raw materials requisitioned for production, $290,000 (80% direct materials and 20% indirect materials).
c. Labor cost incurred in the factory, $180,000 (one-third direct labor and two-thirds indirect labor).
d. Depreciation recorded on factory equipment, $75,000.
e. Other manufacturing overhead costs incurred, $62,000 (credit Accounts Payable).
f. Manufacturing overhead cost was applied to production on the basis of 15,000 machine-hours actually worked during the month.
g. The completed job was moved into the finished goods warehouse on January 31 to await delivery to the customer. (In computing the dollar amount for this entry, remember that the cost of a completed job consists of direct materials, direct labor, and *applied* overhead.)

Required:

1. Prepare journal entries to record items (a) through (f) above [ignore item (g) for the moment].
2. Prepare T-accounts for Manufacturing Overhead and Work in Process. Post the relevant items from your journal entries to these T-accounts.
3. Prepare a journal entry for item (g) above.
4. Compute the unit product cost that will appear on the job cost sheet.

Problems

All applicable problems are available with McGraw-Hill's *Connect*® Accounting.

PROBLEM 3–21 T-Account Analysis of Cost Flows [LO3–1, LO3–5, LO3–6, LO3–7]
Selected T-accounts of Moore Company are given below for the just completed year:

Raw Materials			
Bal. 1/1	15,000	Credits	?
Debits	120,000		
Bal. 12/31	25,000		

Manufacturing Overhead			
Debits	230,000	Credits	?

Work in Process			
Bal. 1/1	20,000	Credits	470,000
Direct materials	90,000		
Direct labor	150,000		
Overhead	240,000		
Bal. 12/31	?		

Factory Wages Payable			
Debits	185,000	Bal. 1/1	9,000
		Credits	180,000
		Bal. 12/31	4,000

Finished Goods			
Bal. 1/1	40,000	Credits	?
Debits	?		
Bal. 12/31	60,000		

Cost of Goods Sold		
Debits	?	

Required:

1. What was the cost of raw materials put into production during the year?
2. How much of the materials in (1) above consisted of indirect materials?
3. How much of the factory labor cost for the year consisted of indirect labor?
4. What was the cost of goods manufactured for the year?
5. What was the cost of goods sold for the year (before considering underapplied or overapplied overhead)?
6. If overhead is applied to production on the basis of direct labor cost, what rate was in effect during the year?
7. Was manufacturing overhead underapplied or overapplied? By how much?
8. Compute the ending balance in the Work in Process inventory account. Assume that this balance consists entirely of goods started during the year. If $8,000 of this balance is direct labor cost, how much of it is direct materials cost? Manufacturing overhead cost?

PROBLEM 3–22 Predetermined Overhead Rate; Disposition of Underapplied or Overapplied Overhead [LO3–1, LO3–7]

Luzadis Company makes furniture using the latest automated technology. The company uses a job-order costing system and applies manufacturing overhead cost to products on the basis of machine-hours. The following estimates were used in preparing the predetermined overhead rate at the beginning of the year:

Machine-hours	75,000
Fixed manufacturing overhead cost	$795,000
Variable manufacturing overhead per computer-hour ...	$1.40

During the year, a glut of furniture on the market resulted in cutting back production and a buildup of furniture in the company's warehouse. The company's cost records revealed the following actual cost and operating data for the year:

Machine-hours	60,000
Manufacturing overhead cost	$850,000
Inventories at year-end:	
Raw materials	$30,000
Work in process (includes overhead applied of 36,000)	$100,000
Finished goods (includes overhead applied of 180,000)	$500,000
Cost of goods sold (includes overhead applied of 504,000)	$1,400,000

Chapter 3

Required:

1. Compute the company's predetermined overhead rate.
2. Compute the underapplied or overapplied overhead.
3. Assume that the company closes any underapplied or overapplied overhead directly to Cost of Goods Sold. Prepare the appropriate journal entry.
4. Assume that the company allocates any underapplied or overapplied overhead to Work in Process, Finished Goods, and Cost of Goods Sold on the basis of the amount of overhead applied that remains in each account at the end of the year. Prepare the journal entry to show the allocation for the year.
5. How much higher or lower will net operating income be if the underapplied or overapplied overhead is allocated rather than closed directly to Cost of Goods Sold?

PROBLEM 3–23 Schedules of Cost of Goods Manufactured and Cost of Goods Sold; Income Statement [LO3–6]

Superior Company provided the following account balances for the year ended December 31 (all raw materials are used in production as direct materials):

Selling expenses	$140,000
Purchases of raw materials	$290,000
Direct labor	?
Administrative expenses	$100,000
Manufacturing overhead applied to work in process	$285,000
Total actual manufacturing overhead costs	$270,000

Inventory balances at the beginning and end of the year were as follows:

	Beginning of Year	End of Year
Raw materials	$40,000	$10,000
Work in process	?	$35,000
Finished goods	$50,000	?

The total manufacturing costs for the year were $683,000; the cost of goods available for sale totaled $740,000; the unadjusted cost of goods sold totaled $660,000; and the net operating income was $30,000. The company's overapplied or underapplied overhead is closed entirely to Cost of Goods Sold.

Required:

Prepare schedules of cost of goods manufactured and cost of goods sold and an income statement. (*Hint:* Prepare the income statement and schedule of cost of goods sold first followed by the schedule of cost of goods manufactured.)

PROBLEM 3–24 Multiple Departments; Applying Overhead [LO3–1, LO3–2, LO3–3, LO3–7]

High Desert Potteryworks makes a variety of pottery products that it sells to retailers such as Home Depot. The company uses a job-order costing system in which predetermined overhead rates are used to apply manufacturing overhead cost to jobs. The predetermined overhead rate in the Molding Department is based on machine-hours, and the rate in the Painting Department is based on direct labor-hours. At the beginning of the year, the company's management made the following estimates:

	Department	
	Molding	Painting
Direct labor-hours	12,000	60,000
Machine-hours	70,000	8,000
Direct materials cost	$510,000	$650,000
Direct labor cost	$130,000	$420,000
Fixed manufacturing overhead cost	$497,000	$615,000
Variable manufacturing overhead per machine-hour	$1.50	–
Variable manufacturing overhead per direct labor-hour	–	$2.00

Job 205 was started on August 1 and completed on August 10. The company's cost records show the following information concerning the job:

	Department	
	Molding	Painting
Direct labor-hours	30	84
Machine-hours	110	20
Materials placed into production	$470	$332
Direct labor cost	$325	$588

Required:

1. Compute the predetermined overhead rate used during the year in the Molding Department. Compute the rate used in the Painting Department.
2. Compute the total overhead cost applied to Job 205.
3. What would be the total cost recorded for Job 205? If the job contained 50 units, what would be the unit product cost?
4. At the end of the year, the records of High Desert Potteryworks revealed the following *actual* cost and operating data for all jobs worked on during the year:

	Department	
	Molding	Painting
Direct labor-hours	10,000	62,000
Machine-hours	65,000	9,000
Direct materials cost	$430,000	$680,000
Direct labor cost	$108,000	$436,000
Manufacturing overhead cost	$570,000	$750,000

What was the amount of underapplied or overapplied overhead in each department at the end of the year?

PROBLEM 3–25 Schedule of Cost of Goods Manufactured; Overhead Analysis [LO3–1, LO3–2, LO3–3, LO3–6, LO3–7]

Gitano Products operates a job-order costing system and applies overhead cost to jobs on the basis of direct materials *used in production* (*not* on the basis of raw materials purchased). Its predetermined overhead rate was based on a cost formula that estimated $800,000 of manufacturing overhead for an estimated allocation base of $500,000 direct material dollars to be used in production. The company has provided the following data for the just completed year:

Purchase of raw materials	$510,000
Direct labor cost	$90,000
Manufacturing overhead costs:	
Indirect labor	$170,000
Property taxes	$48,000
Depreciation of equipment	$260,000
Maintenance	$95,000
Insurance	$7,000
Rent, building	$180,000

	Beginning	Ending
Raw Materials	$20,000	$80,000
Work in Process	$150,000	$70,000
Finished Goods	$260,000	$400,000

Required:
1. a. Compute the predetermined overhead rate for the year.
    b. Compute the amount of underapplied or overapplied overhead for the year.
2. Prepare a schedule of cost of goods manufactured for the year. Assume all raw materials are used in production as direct materials.
3. Compute the unadjusted cost of goods sold for the year. (Do not include any underapplied or overapplied overhead in your cost of goods sold figure.) What options are available for disposing of underapplied or overapplied overhead?
4. Job 215 was started and completed during the year. What price would have been charged to the customer if the job required $8,500 in direct materials and $2,700 in direct labor cost and the company priced its jobs at 25% above the job's cost according to the accounting system?
5. Direct materials made up $24,000 of the $70,000 ending Work in Process inventory balance. Supply the information missing below:

Direct materials	$24,000
Direct labor	?
Manufacturing overhead	?
Work in process inventory	$70,000

PROBLEM 3–26 Journal Entries; T-Accounts; Financial Statements [LO3–1, LO3–2, LO3–3, LO3–4, LO3–5, LO3–6, LO3–7]
Froya Fabrikker A/S of Bergen, Norway, is a small company that manufactures specialty heavy equipment for use in North Sea oil fields. The company uses a job-order costing system and applies manufacturing overhead cost to jobs on the basis of direct labor-hours. Its predetermined overhead rate was based on a cost formula that estimated $360,000 of manufacturing overhead for an estimated allocation base of 900 direct labor-hours. The following transactions took place during the year (all purchases and services were acquired on account):
a. Raw materials were purchased for use in production, $200,000.
b. Raw materials were requisitioned for use in production (all direct materials), $185,000.
c. Utility bills were incurred, $70,000 (90% related to factory operations, and the remainder related to selling and administrative activities).
d. Salary and wage costs were incurred:

Direct labor (975 hours)	$230,000
Indirect labor	$90,000
Selling and administrative salaries	$110,000

e. Maintenance costs were incurred in the factory, $54,000.
f. Advertising costs were incurred, $136,000.
g. Depreciation was recorded for the year, $95,000 (80% related to factory equipment, and the remainder related to selling and administrative equipment).
h. Rental cost incurred on buildings, $120,000 (85% related to factory operations, and the remainder related to selling and administrative facilities).
i. Manufacturing overhead cost was applied to jobs, $__?__.
j. Cost of goods manufactured for the year, $770,000.
k. Sales for the year (all on account) totaled $1,200,000. These goods cost $800,000 according to their job cost sheets.
The balances in the inventory accounts at the beginning of the year were:

Raw Materials	$30,000
Work in Process	$21,000
Finished Goods	$60,000

Required:
1. Prepare journal entries to record the preceding data.
2. Post your entries to T-accounts. (Don't forget to enter the beginning inventory balances above.) Determine the ending balances in the inventory accounts and in the Manufacturing Overhead account.

3. Prepare a schedule of cost of goods manufactured.
4. Prepare a journal entry to close any balance in the Manufacturing Overhead account to Cost of Goods Sold. Prepare a schedule of cost of goods sold.
5. Prepare an income statement for the year.
6. Job 412 was one of the many jobs started and completed during the year. The job required $8,000 in direct materials and 39 hours of direct labor time at a total direct labor cost of $9,200. The job contained only four units. If the company bills at a price 60% above the unit product cost on the job cost sheet, what price per unit would have been charged to the customer?

PROBLEM 3–27 Comprehensive Problem [LO3–1, LO3–2, LO3–4, LO3–5, LO3–7]

Gold Nest Company of Guandong, China, is a family-owned enterprise that makes birdcages for the South China market. The company sells its birdcages through an extensive network of street vendors who receive commissions on their sales. All of the company's transactions with customers, employees, and suppliers are conducted in cash; there is no credit.

The company uses a job-order costing system in which overhead is applied to jobs on the basis of direct labor cost. Its predetermined overhead rate is based on a cost formula that estimated $330,000 of manufacturing overhead for an estimated activity level of $200,000 direct labor dollars. At the beginning of the year, the inventory balances were as follows:

Raw materials	$25,000
Work in process	$10,000
Finished goods	$40,000

During the year, the following transactions were completed:
a. Raw materials purchased for cash, $275,000.
b. Raw materials requisitioned for use in production, $280,000 (materials costing $220,000 were charged directly to jobs; the remaining materials were indirect).
c. Costs for employee services were incurred as follows:

Direct labor	$180,000
Indirect labor	$72,000
Sales commissions	$63,000
Administrative salaries	$90,000

d. Rent for the year was $18,000 ($13,000 of this amount related to factory operations, and the remainder related to selling and administrative activities).
e. Utility costs incurred in the factory, $57,000.
f. Advertising costs incurred, $140,000.
g. Depreciation recorded on equipment, $100,000. ($88,000 of this amount was on equipment used in factory operations; the remaining $12,000 was on equipment used in selling and administrative activities.)
h. Manufacturing overhead cost was applied to jobs, $? .
i. Goods that had cost $675,000 to manufacture according to their job cost sheets were completed.
j. Sales for the year totaled $1,250,000. The total cost to manufacture these goods according to their job cost sheets was $700,000.

Required:
1. Prepare journal entries to record the transactions for the year.
2. Prepare T-accounts for inventories, Manufacturing Overhead, and Cost of Goods Sold. Post relevant data from your journal entries to these T-accounts (don't forget to enter the beginning balances in your inventory accounts). Compute an ending balance in each account.
3. Is Manufacturing Overhead underapplied or overapplied for the year? Prepare a journal entry to close any balance in the Manufacturing Overhead account to Cost of Goods Sold.
4. Prepare an income statement for the year. (Do not prepare a schedule of cost of goods manufactured; all of the information needed for the income statement is available in the journal entries and T-accounts you have prepared.)

Chapter 3

PROBLEM 3–28 Cost Flows; T-Accounts; Income Statement [LO3–1, LO3–2, LO3–5, LO3–6, LO3–7]
Supreme Videos, Inc., produces short musical videos for sale to retail outlets. The company's balance sheet accounts as of January 1, the beginning of its fiscal year, are given below.

Supreme Videos, Inc.
Balance Sheet
January 1

Assets

Current assets:		
Cash		$ 63,000
Accounts receivable		102,000
Inventories:		
Raw materials (film, costumes)	$ 30,000	
Videos in process	45,000	
Finished videos awaiting sale	81,000	156,000
Prepaid insurance		9,000
Total current assets		330,000
Studio and equipment	730,000	
Less accumulated depreciation	210,000	520,000
Total assets		$850,000

Liabilities and Stockholders' Equity

Accounts payable		$160,000
Capital stock	$420,000	
Retained earnings	270,000	690,000
Total liabilities and stockholders' equity		$850,000

Because the videos differ in length and in complexity of production, the company uses a job-order costing system to determine the cost of each video produced. Studio (manufacturing) overhead is charged to videos on the basis of camera-hours of activity. The company's predetermined overhead rate for the year is based on a cost formula that estimated $280,000 in manufacturing overhead for an estimated allocation base of 7,000 camera-hours. The following transactions were recorded for the year:

a. Film, costumes, and similar raw materials purchased on account, $185,000.
b. Film, costumes, and other raw materials issued to production, $200,000 (85% of this material was considered direct to the videos in production, and the other 15% was considered indirect).
c. Utility costs incurred in the production studio, $72,000.
d. Depreciation recorded on the studio, cameras, and other equipment, $84,000. Three-fourths of this depreciation related to actual production of the videos, and the remainder related to equipment used in marketing and administration.
e. Advertising expense incurred, $130,000.
f. Costs for salaries and wages were incurred as follows:

Direct labor (actors and directors)	$82,000
Indirect labor (carpenters to build sets,	
costume designers, and so forth)	$110,000
Administrative salaries	$95,000

g. Prepaid insurance expired during the year, $7,000 (80% related to production of videos, and 20% related to marketing and administrative activities).
h. Miscellaneous marketing and administrative expenses incurred, $8,600.
i. Studio (manufacturing) overhead was applied to videos in production. The company recorded 7,250 camera-hours of activity during the year.
j. Videos that cost $550,000 to produce according to their job cost sheets were transferred to the finished videos warehouse to await sale and shipment.
k. Sales for the year totaled $925,000 and were all on account. The total cost to produce these videos according to their job cost sheets was $600,000.

l. Collections from customers during the year totaled $850,000.

m. Payments to suppliers on account during the year, $500,000; payments to employees for salaries and wages, $285,000.

Required:

1. Prepare a T-account for each account on the company's balance sheet and enter the beginning balances.

2. Record the transactions directly into the T-accounts. Prepare new T-accounts as needed. Key your entries to the letters (a) through (m) above. Compute the ending balance in each account.

3. Is the Studio (manufacturing) Overhead account underapplied or overapplied for the year? Make an entry in the T-accounts to close any balance in the Studio Overhead account to Cost of Goods Sold.

4. Prepare an income statement for the year. (Do not prepare a schedule of cost of goods manufactured; all of the information needed for the income statement is available in the T-accounts.)

  Cases

All applicable cases are available with McGraw-Hill's Connect® Accounting.

CASE 3–29 Ethics and the Manager [LO3–1, LO3–2, LO3–7]

Terri Ronsin had recently been transferred to the Home Security Systems Division of National Home Products. Shortly after taking over her new position as divisional controller, she was asked to develop the division's predetermined overhead rate for the upcoming year. The accuracy of the rate is important because it is used throughout the year and any overapplied or underapplied overhead is closed out to Cost of Goods Sold at the end of the year. National Home Products uses direct labor-hours in all of its divisions as the allocation base for manufacturing overhead.

To compute the predetermined overhead rate, Terri divided her estimate of the total manufacturing overhead for the coming year by the production manager's estimate of the total direct labor-hours for the coming year. She took her computations to the division's general manager for approval but was quite surprised when he suggested a modification in the base. Her conversation with the general manager of the Home Security Systems Division, Harry Irving, went like this:

Ronsin: Here are my calculations for next year's predetermined overhead rate. If you approve, we can enter the rate into the computer on January 1 and be up and running in the job-order costing system right away this year.

Irving: Thanks for coming up with the calculations so quickly, and they look just fine. There is, however, one slight modification I would like to see. Your estimate of the total direct labor-hours for the year is 440,000 hours. How about cutting that to about 420,000 hours?

Ronsin: I don't know if I can do that. The production manager says she will need about 440,000 direct labor-hours to meet the sales projections for the year. Besides, there are going to be over 430,000 direct labor-hours during the current year and sales are projected to be higher next year.

Irving: Teri, I know all of that. I would still like to reduce the direct labor-hours in the base to something like 420,000 hours. You probably don't know that I had an agreement with your predecessor as divisional controller to shave 5% or so off the estimated direct labor-hours every year. That way, we kept a reserve that usually resulted in a big boost to net operating income at the end of the fiscal year in December. We called it our Christmas bonus. Corporate headquarters always seemed as pleased as punch that we could pull off such a miracle at the end of the year. This system has worked well for many years, and I don't want to change it now.

Required:

1. Explain how shaving 5% off the estimated direct labor-hours in the base for the predetermined overhead rate usually results in a big boost in net operating income at the end of the fiscal year.

2. Should Terri Ronsin go along with the general manager's request to reduce the direct labor-hours in the predetermined overhead rate computation to 420,000 direct labor-hours?

CASE 3–30 Plantwide versus Departmental Overhead Rates; Underapplied or Overapplied Overhead
[LO3–1, LO3–2, LO3–3, LO3–7]

"Blast it!" said David Wilson, president of Teledex Company. "We've just lost the bid on the Koopers job by $2,000. It seems we're either too high to get the job or too low to make any money on half the jobs we bid."

130

Chapter 3

Teledex Company manufactures products to customers' specifications and operates a job-order costing system. Manufacturing overhead cost is applied to jobs on the basis of direct labor cost. The following estimates were made at the beginning of the year:

| | Department | | | |
	Fabricating	Machining	Assembly	Total Plant
Direct labor	$200,000	$100,000	$300,000	$600,000
Manufacturing overhead	$350,000	$400,000	$90,000	$840,000

Jobs require varying amounts of work in the three departments. The Koopers job, for example, would have required manufacturing costs in the three departments as follows:

| | Department | | | |
	Fabricating	Machining	Assembly	Total Plant
Direct materials	$3,000	$200	$1,400	$4,600
Direct labor	$2,800	$500	$6,200	$9,500
Manufacturing overhead	?	?	?	?

The company uses a plantwide overhead rate to apply manufacturing overhead cost to jobs.

Required:

1. Assuming use of a plantwide overhead rate:
   a. Compute the rate for the current year.
   b. Determine the amount of manufacturing overhead cost that would have been applied to the Koopers job.
2. Suppose that instead of using a plantwide overhead rate, the company had used a separate predetermined overhead rate in each department. Under these conditions:
   a. Compute the rate for each department for the current year.
   b. Determine the amount of manufacturing overhead cost that would have been applied to the Koopers job.
3. Explain the difference between the manufacturing overhead that would have been applied to the Koopers job using the plantwide rate in question 1 (b) and using the departmental rates in question 2 (b).
4. Assume that it is customary in the industry to bid jobs at 150% of total manufacturing cost (direct materials, direct labor, and applied overhead). What was the company's bid price on the Koopers job? What would the bid price have been if departmental overhead rates had been used to apply overhead cost?
5. At the end of the year, the company assembled the following *actual* cost data relating to all jobs worked on during the year.

| | Department | | | |
	Fabricating	Machining	Assembly	Total Plant
Direct materials	$190,000	$16,000	$114,000	$320,000
Direct labor	$210,000	$108,000	$262,000	$580,000
Manufacturing overhead	$360,000	$420,000	$84,000	$864,000

Compute the underapplied or overapplied overhead for the year (a) assuming that a plantwide overhead rate is used, and (b) assuming that departmental overhead rates are used.

Appendix 3A: Activity-Based Absorption Costing

LO3–8

Use activity-based absorption costing to compute unit product costs.

Chapter 3 described how manufacturing companies use traditional absorption costing systems to calculate unit product costs for the purpose of valuing inventories and determining cost of goods sold for external financial reports. In this appendix, we contrast traditional absorption costing with an alternative approach called *activity-based absorption costing*. **Activity-based absorption costing** assigns all manufacturing overhead costs to products based on the *activities* performed to make those products. An **activity** is an event that causes the consumption of manufacturing overhead resources. Rather than relying on plant-wide or departmental cost pools, the activity-based approach accumulates each activity's overhead costs in *activity cost pools*. An **activity cost pool** is a "bucket" in which costs are accumulated that relate to a single activity. Each activity cost pool has one *activity measure*. An **activity measure** is an allocation base that is used as the denominator for an activity cost pool. The costs accumulated in the numerator of an activity cost pool divided by the quantity of the activity measure in its denominator equals what is called an *activity rate*. An activity rate is used to assign costs from an activity cost pool to products.

Activity-based absorption costing differs from traditional absorption costing in two ways. First, the activity-based approach uses more cost pools than a traditional approach. Second, the activity-based approach includes some activities and activity measures that *do not* relate to the volume of units produced, whereas the traditional approach relies exclusively on allocation bases that are driven by the volume of production. For example, the activity-based approach may include *batch-level activities*. A **batch-level activity** is performed each time a batch is handled or processed, regardless of how many units are in the batch. Batch-level activities include tasks such as placing purchase orders, setting up equipment, and transporting batches of component parts. Costs at the batch level depend on the number of batches processed rather than the number of units produced. The activity-based approach may also include *product-level activities*. A **product-level activity** relates to specific products and typically must be carried out regardless of how many batches are run or units of product are produced and sold. Product-level activities include tasks such as designing a product and making engineering design changes to a product. Costs at the product-level depend on the number of products supported rather than the number of batches run or the number of units of product produced and sold.

To illustrate the differences between traditional and activity-based absorption costing, we'll use an example focused on Maxtar Industries, a manufacturer of high-quality smoker/barbecue units. The company has two product lines—Premium and Standard. The company has traditionally applied manufacturing overhead costs to these products using a plantwide predetermined overhead rate based on direct labor-hours. Exhibit 3A–1 details how the unit product costs of the two product lines are computed using the company's

---

Basic Data

Total estimated manufacturing overhead cost	$1,520,000	
Total estimated direct labor-hours	400,000 DLHs	

	Premium	Standard
Direct materials per unit	$40.00	$30.00
Direct labor per unit	$24.00	$18.00
Direct labor-hours per unit	2.0 DLHs	1.5 DLHs
Units produced	50,000 units	200,000 units

Computation of the Predetermined Overhead Rate

$$\text{Predetermined overhead rate} = \frac{\text{Total estimated manufacturing overhead}}{\text{Total estimated amount of the allocation base}}$$

$$= \frac{\$1,520,000}{400,000 \text{ DLHs}} = \$3.80 \text{ per DLH}$$

Traditional Unit Product Costs

	Premium	Standard
Direct materials	$40.00	$30.00
Direct labor	24.00	18.00
Manufacturing overhead (2.0 DLHs × $3.80 per DLH; 1.5 DLHs × $3.80 per DLH)	7.60	5.70
Unit product cost	$71.60	$53.70

EXHIBIT 3A–1
Maxtar Industries' Traditional Costing System

Chapter 3

traditional costing system. The unit product cost of the Premium product line is $71.60 and the unit product cost of the Standard product line is $53.70 according to this traditional costing system.

Maxtar Industries has recently experimented with an activity-based absorption costing system that has three activity cost pools: (1) supporting direct labor; (2) setting up machines; and (3) parts administration. The top of Exhibit 3A–2 displays basic data concerning these activity cost pools. Note that the total estimated overhead cost in these three costs pools, $1,520,000, agrees with the total estimated overhead cost in the company's

EXHIBIT 3A–2
Maxtar Industries' Activity-Based Absorption Costing System

Basic Data

Activity Cost Pools and Activity Measures	Estimated Overhead Cost	Premium	Standard	Total
		Expected Activity		
Supporting direct labor (DLHs)	$ 800,000	100,000	300,000	400,000
Setting up machines (setups)	480,000	600	200	800
Parts administration (part types)	240,000	140	60	200
Total manufacturing overhead cost . . .	$1,520,000			

Computation of Activity Rates

Activity Cost Pools	(a) Estimated Overhead Cost	(b) Total Expected Activity	(a) ÷ (b) Activity Rate
Supporting direct labor . . .	$800,000	400,000 DLHs	$2 per DLH
Setting up machines	$480,000	800 setups	$600 per setup
Parts administration	$240,000	200 part types	$1,200 per part type

Assigning Overhead Costs to Products

Overhead Cost for the Premium Product

Activity Cost Pools	(a) Activity Rate	(b) Activity	(a) × (b) ABC Cost
Supporting direct labor . . .	$2 per DLH	100,000 DLHs	$200,000
Setting up machines	$600 per setup	600 setups	360,000
Parts administration	$1,200 per part type	140 part types	168,000
Total			$728,000

Overhead Cost for the Standard Product

Activity Cost Pools	(a) Activity Rate	(b) Activity	(a) × (b) ABC Cost
Supporting direct labor . .	$2 per DLH	300,000 DLHs	$600,000
Setting up machines	$600 per setup	200 setups	120,000
Parts administration	$1,200 per part type	60 part types	72,000
Total			$792,000

Activity-Based Absorption Costing Product Costs

	Premium	Standard
Direct materials	$40.00	$30.00
Direct labor	24.00	18.00
Manufacturing overhead ($728,000 ÷ 50,000 units; $792,000 ÷ 200,000 units)	14.56	3.96
Unit product cost	$78.56	$51.96

traditional costing system. The company's activity-based approach simply provides an alternative way to allocate the company's manufacturing overhead across the two products.

The activity rates for the three activity cost pools are computed in the second table in Exhibit 3A–2. For example, the total cost in the "setting up machines" activity cost pool, $480,000, is divided by the total activity associated with that cost pool, 800 setups, to determine the activity rate of $600 per setup.

The activity rates are used to allocate overhead costs to the two products in the third table in Exhibit 3A–2. For example, the activity rate for the "setting up machines" activity cost pool, $600 per setup, is multiplied by the Premium product line's 600 setups to determine the $360,000 machine setup cost allocated to the Premium product line.

The table at the bottom of Exhibit 3A–2 displays the overhead costs per unit and the activity-based unit product costs. The overhead cost per unit is determined by dividing the total overhead cost by the number of units produced. For example, the Premium product line's total overhead cost of $728,000 is divided by 50,000 units to determine the $14.56 overhead cost per unit. Note that the unit product costs differ from those computed using the company's traditional costing system in Exhibit 3A–1. Because the activity-based approach contains both a batch-level (setting up machines) and a product-level (parts administration) activity cost pool, the unit product costs under the activity-based approach follow the usual pattern in which overhead costs are shifted from the high-volume to the low-volume product. The unit product cost of the Standard product line, the high-volume product, has gone down from $53.70 under the traditional costing system to $51.96 under activity-based costing. In contrast, the unit product cost of the Premium product line, the low-volume product, has increased from $71.60 under the traditional costing system to $78.56 under activity-based costing. Instead of using direct labor-hours (which moves in tandem with the volume of the production) to assign all manufacturing overhead costs to products, the activity-based approach uses a batch-level activity measure and a product-level activity measure to assign the batch-level and product-level activity cost pools to the two products.

Glossary (Appendix 3A)

Activity An event that causes the consumption of manufacturing overhead resources. (p. 130)
Activity-based absorption costing A costing method that assigns all manufacturing overhead costs to products based on the *activities* performed to make those products. (p. 130)
Activity cost pool A "bucket" in which costs are accumulated that relate to a single activity. (p. 131)
Activity measure An allocation base that is used as the denominator for an activity cost pool. (p. 131)
Batch-level activity An activity that is performed each time a batch is handled or processed, regardless of how many units are in the batch. The amount of resources consumed depends on the number of batches run rather than on the number of units in the batch. (p. 131)
Product-level activity An activity that relates to specific products and typically must be carried out regardless of how many batches are run or units of product are produced and sold. (p. 131)

 Appendix 3A Exercises and Problems

All applicable exercises and problems are available with McGraw-Hill's Connect® Accounting.

EXERCISE 3A–1 Activity-Based Absorption Costing [LO3–8]

Fogerty Company makes two products, titanium Hubs and Sprockets. Data regarding the two products follow:

	Direct Labor-Hours per Unit	Annual Production
Hubs	0.80	10,000 units
Sprockets	0.40	40,000 units

134   Chapter 3

Additional information about the company follows:

a.   Hubs require $32 in direct materials per unit, and Sprockets require $18.
b.   The direct labor wage rate is $15 per hour.
c.   Hubs are more complex to manufacture than Sprockets and they require special processing.
d.   The company's activity-based absorption costing system has the following activity cost pools:

Activity Cost Pool (and Activity Measure)	Estimated Overhead Cost	Expected Activity		
		Hubs	Sprockets	Total
Machine setups (number of setups)	$72,000	100	300	400
Special processing (machine-hours)	$200,000	5,000	0	5,000
General factory (Direct labor-hours)	$816,000	8,000	16,000	24,000

Required:

1.   Compute the activity rate for each activity cost pool.
2.   Compute the unit product cost for Hubs and Sprockets using activity-based absorption costing.

EXERCISE 3A–2 Activity-Based Absorption Costing as an Alternative to Traditional Product Costing
[LO3–8]
Harrison Company makes two products and uses a traditional costing system in which a single plantwide predetermined overhead rate is computed based on direct labor-hours. Data for the two products for the upcoming year follow:

	Rascon	Parcel
Direct materials cost per unit	$13.00	$22.00
Direct labor cost per unit	$6.00	$3.00
Direct labor-hours per unit	0.40	0.20
Number of units produced	20,000	80,000

These products are customized to some degree for specific customers.

Required:

1.   The company's manufacturing overhead costs for the year are expected to be $576,000. Using the company's traditional costing system, compute the unit product costs for the two products.
2.   Management is considering an activity-based absorption costing system in which half of the overhead would continue to be allocated on the basis of direct labor-hours and half would be allocated on the basis of engineering design time. This time is expected to be distributed as follows during the upcoming year:

	Rascon	Parcel	Total
Engineering design time (in hours)	3,000	3,000	6,000

Compute the unit product costs for the two products using the proposed activity-based absorption costing system.
3.   Explain why the product costs differ between the two systems.

EXERCISE 3A–3 Activity-Based Absorption Costing as an Alternative to Traditional Product Costing
[LO3–8]
Stillicum Corporation makes ultra light-weight backpacking tents. Data concerning the company's two product lines appear below:

	Deluxe	Standard
Direct materials per unit	$72.00	$53.00
Direct labor per unit	$12.00	$9.60
Direct labor-hours per unit	1.0 DLHs	0.8 DLHs
Estimated annual production	10,000 units	50,000 units

The company has a traditional costing system in which manufacturing overhead is applied to units based on direct labor-hours. Data concerning manufacturing overhead and direct labor-hours for the upcoming year appear below:

Estimated total manufacturing overhead	$325,000
Estimated total direct labor-hours	50,000 DLHs

Required:
1. Determine the unit product costs of the Deluxe and Standard products under the company's traditional costing system.
2. The company is considering replacing its traditional costing system with an activity-based absorption costing system that would have the following three activity cost pools:

	Estimated	Expected Activity		
Activity Cost Pools and Activity Measures	Overhead Cost	Deluxe	Standard	Total
Supporting direct labor (direct labor-hours)	$200,000	10,000	40,000	50,000
Batch setups (setups)	75,000	200	100	300
Safety testing (tests)	50,000	30	70	100
Total manufacturing overhead cost	$325,000			

Determine the unit product costs of the Deluxe and Standard products under the activity-based absorption costing system.

PROBLEM 3A–4 Activity-Based Absorption Costing as an Alternative to Traditional Product Costing
[LO3–8]

Ellix Company manufactures two models of ultra-high fidelity speakers, the X200 model and the X99 model. Data regarding the two products follow:

Product	Direct Labor-Hours	Annual Production	Total Direct Labor-Hours
X200	1.8 DLHs per unit	5,000 units	9,000 DLHs
X99	0.9 DLHs per unit	30,000 units	27,000 DLHs
			36,000 DLHs

Additional information about the company follows:
a. Model X200 requires $72 in direct materials per unit, and model X99 requires $50.
b. The direct labor rate is $10 per hour.
c. The company has always used direct labor-hours as the base for applying manufacturing overhead cost to products.
d. Model X200 is more complex to manufacture than model X99 and requires the use of special equipment.
e. Because of the special work required in (d) above, the company is considering the use of activity-based absorption costing to apply manufacturing overhead cost to products. Three activity cost pools have been identified as follows:

Activity Cost Pool	Activity Measure	Estimated Total Cost	Estimated Total Activity		
			X200	X99	Total
Machine setups	Number of setups	$ 360,000	50	100	150
Special processing	Machine-hours	180,000	12,000	0	12,000
General factory	Direct labor-hours	1,260,000	9,000	27,000	36,000
		$1,800,000			

136

Chapter 3

Required:

1. Assume that the company continues to use direct labor-hours as the base for applying overhead cost to products.
   a. Compute the predetermined overhead rate.
   b. Compute the unit product cost of each model.
2. Assume that the company decides to use activity-based absorption costing to apply overhead cost to products.
   a. Compute the activity rate for each activity cost pool and determine the amount of overhead cost that would be applied to each model using the activity-based approach.
   b. Compute the unit product cost of each model.
3. Explain why overhead cost shifted from the high-volume model to the low-volume model under the activity-based approach.

PROBLEM 3A–5 Activity-Based Absorption Costing as an Alternative to Traditional Product Costing
[LO3–8]
Siegel Company manufactures a product that is available in both a deluxe model and a regular model. The company has manufactured the regular model for years. The deluxe model was introduced several years ago to tap a new segment of the market. Since introduction of the deluxe model, the company's profits have steadily declined and management has become increasingly concerned about the accuracy of its costing system. Sales of the deluxe model have been increasing rapidly.

Manufacturing overhead is assigned to products on the basis of direct labor-hours. For the current year, the company has estimated that it will incur $900,000 in manufacturing overhead cost and produce 5,000 units of the deluxe model and 40,000 units of the regular model. The deluxe model requires two hours of direct labor time per unit, and the regular model requires one hour. Material and labor costs per unit are as follows:

	Model	
	Deluxe	Regular
Direct materials	$40	$25
Direct labor	$14	$7

Required:

1. Using direct labor-hours as the base for assigning overhead cost to products, compute the predetermined overhead rate. Using this rate and other data from the problem, determine the unit product cost of each model.
2. Management is considering using activity-based absorption costing to apply manufacturing overhead cost to products. The activity-based system would have the following four activity cost pools:

Activity Cost Pool	Activity Measure	Estimated Overhead Cost
Purchasing	Purchase orders issued	$204,000
Processing	Machine-hours	182,000
Scrap/rework	Scrap/rework orders issued	379,000
Shipping	Number of shipments	135,000
		$900,000

	Expected Activity		
Activity Measure	Deluxe	Regular	Total
Purchase orders issued	200	400	600
Machine-hours	20,000	15,000	35,000
Scrap/rework orders issued	1,000	1,000	2,000
Number of shipments	250	650	900

Determine the predetermined overhead rate for each of the four activity cost pools.

3. Using the predetermined overhead rates you computed in part (2), do the following:
    a. Compute the total amount of manufacturing overhead cost that would be applied to each model using the activity-based absorption costing system. After these totals have been computed, determine the amount of manufacturing overhead cost per unit of each model.
    b. Compute the unit product cost of each model (direct materials, direct labor, and manufacturing overhead).
4. From the data you have developed in parts (1) through (3), identify factors that may account for the company's declining profits.

CASE 3A–6 Activity-Based Absorption Costing and Pricing [LO3–8]

Java Source, Inc. (JSI), is a processor and distributor of a variety of blends of coffee. The company buys coffee beans from around the world and roasts, blends, and packages them for resale. JSI offers a large variety of different coffees that it sells to gourmet shops in one-pound bags. The major cost of the coffee is raw materials. However, the company's predominantly automated roasting, blending, and packing processes require a substantial amount of manufacturing overhead. The company uses relatively little direct labor.

Some of JSI's coffees are very popular and sell in large volumes, while a few of the newer blends sell in very low volumes. JSI prices its coffees at manufacturing cost plus a markup of 25%, with some adjustments made to keep the company's prices competitive.

For the coming year, JSI's budget includes estimated manufacturing overhead cost of $2,200,000. JSI assigns manufacturing overhead to products on the basis of direct labor-hours. The expected direct labor cost totals $600,000, which represents 50,000 hours of direct labor time. Based on the sales budget and expected raw materials costs, the company will purchase and use $5,000,000 of raw materials (mostly coffee beans) during the year.

The expected costs for direct materials and direct labor for one-pound bags of two of the company's coffee products appear below.

	Kenya Dark	Viet Select
Direct materials	$4.50	$2.90
Direct labor (0.02 hours per bag)	$0.24	$0.24

JSI's controller believes that the company's traditional costing system may be providing misleading cost information. To determine whether or not this is correct, the controller has prepared an analysis of the year's expected manufacturing overhead costs, as shown in the following table:

Activity Cost Pool	Activity Measure	Expected Activity for the Year	Expected Cost for the Year
Purchasing	Purchase orders	2,000 orders	$ 560,000
Material handling	Number of setups	1,000 setups	193,000
Quality control	Number of batches	500 batches	90,000
Roasting	Roasting hours	95,000 roasting hours	1,045,000
Blending	Blending hours	32,000 blending hours	192,000
Packaging	Packaging hours	24,000 packaging hours	120,000
Total manufacturing overhead cost			$2,200,000

Data regarding the expected production of Kenya Dark and Viet Select coffee are presented below.

	Kenya Dark	Viet Select
Expected sales	80,000 pounds	4,000 pounds
Batch size	5,000 pounds	500 pounds
Setups	2 per batch	2 per batch
Purchase order size	20,000 pounds	500 pounds
Roasting time per 100 pounds	1.5 roasting hours	1.5 roasting hours
Blending time per 100 pounds	0.5 blending hours	0.5 blending hours
Packaging time per 100 pounds	0.3 packaging hours	0.3 packaging hours

Required:

1. Using direct labor-hours as the base for assigning manufacturing overhead cost to products, do the following:
    a. Determine the predetermined overhead rate that will be used during the year.
    b. Determine the unit product cost of one pound of the Kenya Dark coffee and one pound of the Viet Select coffee.
2. Using activity-based absorption costing as the basis for assigning manufacturing overhead cost to products, do the following:
    a. Determine the total amount of manufacturing overhead cost assigned to the Kenya Dark coffee and to the Viet Select coffee for the year.
    b. Using the data developed in (2a) above, compute the amount of manufacturing overhead cost per pound of the Kenya Dark coffee and the Viet Select coffee. Round all computations to the nearest whole cent.
    c. Determine the unit product cost of one pound of the Kenya Dark coffee and one pound of the Viet Select coffee.
3. Write a brief memo to the president of JSI explaining what you have found in (1) and (2) above and discussing the implications to the company of using direct labor as the base for assigning manufacturing overhead cost to products.

(CMA, adapted)

Appendix 3B: The Predetermined Overhead Rate and Capacity

LO3–9
Understand the implications of basing the predetermined overhead rate on activity at capacity rather than on estimated activity for the period.

Companies typically base their predetermined overhead rates on the estimated, or budgeted, amount of the allocation base for the upcoming period. This is the method that is used in the chapter, but it is a practice that is often criticized based on the accounting for fixed manufacturing overhead costs.[1] As we shall see, the critics argue that, in general, too much fixed manufacturing overhead cost is applied to products. To focus on this issue, we will make two simplifying assumptions in this appendix: (1) we will consider only fixed manufacturing overhead; and (2) we will assume that the actual fixed manufacturing overhead at the end of the period is the same as the estimated, or budgeted, fixed manufacturing overhead at the beginning of the period. Neither of these assumptions is entirely realistic. Ordinarily, some manufacturing overhead is variable and even fixed costs can differ from what was expected at the beginning of the period, but making those assumptions enables us to focus on the primary issues the critics raise.

An example will help us to understand the controversy. Prahad Corporation manufactures music CDs for local recording studios. The company's CD duplicating machine is capable of producing a new CD every 10 seconds from a master CD. The company leases the CD duplicating machine for $180,000 per year, and this is the company's only manufacturing overhead cost. With allowances for setups and maintenance, the machine is theoretically capable of producing up to 900,000 CDs per year. However, due to weak retail sales of CDs, the company's commercial customers are unlikely to order more than 600,000 CDs next year. The company uses machine time as the allocation base for applying manufacturing overhead to CDs. These data are summarized below:

Prahad Corporation Data	
Total manufacturing overhead cost	$180,000 per year
Allocation base—machine time per CD	10 seconds per CD
Capacity	900,000 CDs per year
Budgeted output for next year	600,000 CDs

[1] Statement of Financial Accounting Standards No. 151: *Inventory Costs* and International Accounting Standard 2: *Inventories* require allocating fixed manufacturing overhead costs to products based on normal capacity. Normal capacity reflects the level of output expected to be produced over numerous periods under normal circumstances. This definition mirrors the language used in this book that refers to basing the predetermined overhead rate on the estimated, or budgeted, amount of the allocation base for the upcoming period.

If Prahad follows common practice and computes its predetermined overhead rate using estimated or budgeted figures, then its predetermined overhead rate for next year would be $0.03 per second of machine time computed as follows:

$$\frac{\text{Predetermined}}{\text{overhead rate}} = \frac{\text{Estimated total manufacturing overhead cost}}{\text{Estimated total amount of the allocation base}}$$

$$= \frac{\$180,000}{600,000 \text{ CDs} \times 10 \text{ seconds per CD}}$$

$$= \$0.03 \text{ per second}$$

Because each CD requires 10 seconds of machine time, each CD will be charged for $0.30 of overhead cost.

Critics charge that there are two problems with this procedure. First, if predetermined overhead rates are based on budgeted activity and overhead includes significant fixed costs, then the unit product costs will fluctuate depending on the budgeted level of activity for the period. For example, if the budgeted output for the year was only 300,000 CDs, the predetermined overhead rate would be $0.06 per second of machine time or $0.60 per CD rather than $0.30 per CD. In general, if budgeted output falls, the overhead cost per unit will increase; it will appear that the CDs cost more to make. Managers may then be tempted to increase prices at the worst possible time—just as demand is falling.

Second, critics charge that under the traditional approach, products are charged for resources that they don't use. When the fixed costs of capacity are spread over estimated activity, the units that are produced must shoulder the costs of unused capacity. That is why the applied overhead cost per unit increases as the level of activity falls. The critics argue that products should be charged only for the capacity that they use; they should not be charged for the capacity they don't use. This can be accomplished by basing the predetermined overhead rate on capacity as follows:

$$\frac{\text{Predetermined overhead}}{\text{rate based on capacity}} = \frac{\text{Estimated total manufacturing overhead cost at capacity}}{\text{Estimated total amount of the allocation base at capacity}}$$

$$= \frac{\$180,000}{900,000 \text{ CDs} \times 10 \text{ seconds per CD}}$$

$$= \$0.02 \text{ per second}$$

It is important to realize that the numerator in this predetermined overhead rate is the estimated total manufacturing overhead cost *at capacity*. In general, the numerator in a predetermined overhead rate is the estimated total manufacturing overhead cost for the level of activity in the denominator. Ordinarily, the estimated total manufacturing overhead cost *at capacity* will be larger than the estimated total manufacturing overhead cost *at the estimated level of activity*. The estimated level of activity in this case was 600,000 CDs (or 6 million seconds of machine time), whereas capacity is 900,000 CDs (or 9 million seconds of machine time). The estimated total manufacturing overhead cost at 600,000 CDs was $180,000. This also happens to be the estimated total manufacturing overhead cost at 900,000 CDs, but that only happens because we have assumed that the manufacturing overhead is entirely fixed. If manufacturing overhead contained any variable element, the total manufacturing overhead would be larger at 900,000 CDs than at 600,000 CDs and, in that case, the predetermined overhead rate should reflect that fact.

At any rate, returning to the computation of the predetermined overhead rate based on capacity, the predetermined overhead rate is $0.02 per second and so the overhead cost applied to each CD would be $0.20. This charge is constant and would not be affected by the level of activity during a period. If output falls, the charge would still be $0.20 per CD.

This method will almost certainly result in underapplied overhead. If actual output at Prahad Corporation is 600,000 CDs, then only $120,000 of overhead cost would be applied to products ($0.20 per CD × 600,000 CDs). Because the actual overhead cost is $180,000, overhead would be underapplied by $60,000. Because we are assuming that

Chapter 3

manufacturing overhead is entirely fixed and that actual manufacturing overhead equals the manufacturing overhead as estimated at the beginning of the year, the underapplied overhead represents the cost of unused capacity. In other words, if there had been no unused capacity, there would have been no underapplied overhead. The critics suggest that the underapplied overhead that results from unused capacity should be separately disclosed on the income statement as the Cost of Unused Capacity—a period expense. Disclosing this cost as a lump sum of $60,000 on the income statement, rather than burying it in Cost of Goods Sold or ending inventories, makes it much more visible to managers. An example of such an income statement appears below:

Prahad Corporation Income Statement For the Year Ended December 31		
Sales[1]		$1,200,000
Cost of goods sold[2]		1,080,000
Gross margin		120,000
Other expenses:		
Cost of unused capacity[3]	$60,000	
Selling and administrative expenses[4]	90,000	150,000
Net operating loss		$ (30,000)

[1] Assume sales of 600,000 CDs at $2 per CD.
[2] Assume the unit product cost of the CDs is $1.80, including $0.20 for manufacturing overhead.
[3] See the calculations in the text on the prior page. Underapplied overhead is $60,000.
[4] Assume selling and administrative expenses total $90,000.

Appendix 3B: Exercises and Problems   connect
ACCOUNTING

All applicable exercises and problems are available with McGraw-Hill's
***Connect*® Accounting.**

EXERCISE 3B–1 Overhead Rate Based on Capacity [LO3–9]
Wixis Cabinets makes custom wooden cabinets for high-end stereo systems from specialty woods. The company uses a job-order costing system. The capacity of the plant is determined by the capacity of its constraint, which is time on the automated bandsaw that makes finely beveled cuts in wood according to the preprogrammed specifications of each cabinet. The bandsaw can operate up to 180 hours per month. The estimated total manufacturing overhead at capacity is $14,760 per month. The company bases its predetermined overhead rate on capacity, so its predetermined overhead rate is $82 per hour of bandsaw use.
The results of a recent month's operations appear below:

Sales	$43,740
Beginning inventories	$0
Ending inventories	$0
Direct materials	$5,350
Direct labor (all variable)	$8,860
Manufacturing overhead incurred	$14,220
Selling and administrative expense	$8,180
Actual hours of bandsaw use	150

Required:
1. Prepare an income statement following the example in Appendix 3B in which any underapplied overhead is directly recorded on the income statement as an expense.
2. Why is overhead ordinarily underapplied when the predetermined overhead rate is based on capacity?

EXERCISE 3B–2 Overhead Rates and Capacity Issues [LO3–1, LO3–2, LO3–7, LO3–9]

Security Pension Services helps clients to set up and administer pension plans that are in compliance with tax laws and regulatory requirements. The firm uses a job-order costing system in which overhead is applied to clients' accounts on the basis of professional staff hours charged to the accounts. Data concerning two recent years appear below:

	2012	2013
Estimated professional staff hours to be charged to clients' accounts	4,600	4,500
Estimated overhead cost	$310,500	$310,500
Professional staff hours available	6,000	6,000

"Professional staff hours available" is a measure of the capacity of the firm. Any hours available that are not charged to clients' accounts represent unused capacity. All of the firm's overhead is fixed.

Required:

1. Marta Brinksi is an established client whose pension plan was set up many years ago. In both 2012 and 2013, only 2.5 hours of professional staff time were charged to Ms. Brinksi's account. If the company bases its predetermined overhead rate on the estimated overhead cost and the estimated professional staff hours to be charged to clients, how much overhead cost would have been applied to Ms. Brinksi's account in 2012? In 2013?

2. Suppose that the company bases its predetermined overhead rate on the estimated overhead cost and the estimated professional staff hours to be charged to clients as in (1) above. Also suppose that the actual professional staff hours charged to clients' accounts and the actual overhead costs turn out to be exactly as estimated in both years. By how much would the overhead be underapplied or overapplied in 2012? In 2013?

3. Refer back to the data concerning Ms. Brinksi in (1) above. If the company bases its predetermined overhead rate on the *professional staff hours available*, how much overhead cost would have been applied to Ms. Brinksi's account in 2012? In 2013?

4. Suppose that the company bases its predetermined overhead rate on the professional staff hours available as in (3) above. Also suppose that the actual professional staff hours charged to clients' accounts and the actual overhead costs turn out to be exactly as estimated in both years. By how much would the overhead be underapplied or overapplied in 2012? In 2013?

PROBLEM 3B–3 Predetermined Overhead Rate and Capacity [LO3–1, LO3–2, LO3–7, LO3–9]

Platinum Tracks, Inc., is a small audio recording studio located in Los Angeles. The company handles work for advertising agencies—primarily for radio ads—and has a few singers and bands as clients. Platinum Tracks handles all aspects of recording from editing to making a digital master from which CDs can be copied. The competition in the audio recording industry in Los Angeles has always been tough, but it has been getting even tougher over the last several years. The studio has been losing customers to newer studios that are equipped with more up-to-date equipment and that are able to offer very attractive prices and excellent service. Summary data concerning the last two years of operations follow:

	2012	2013
Estimated hours of studio service	1,000	800
Estimated studio overhead cost	$160,000	$160,000
Actual hours of studio service provided	750	500
Actual studio overhead cost incurred	$160,000	$160,000
Hours of studio service at capacity	1,600	1,600

The company applies studio overhead to recording jobs on the basis of the hours of studio service provided. For example, 40 hours of studio time were required to record, edit, and master the *Verde Baja* music CD for a local Latino band. All of the studio overhead is fixed, and the actual overhead cost incurred was exactly as estimated at the beginning of the year in both 2012 and 2013.

Required:

1. Platinum Tracks computes its predetermined overhead rate at the beginning of each year based on the estimated studio overhead and the estimated hours of studio service for the year. How much overhead would have been applied to the Verde Baja job if it had been done in 2012? In 2013? By how much would overhead have been underapplied or overapplied in 2012? In 2013?

Chapter 3

2. The president of Platinum Tracks has heard that some companies in the industry have changed to a system of computing the predetermined overhead rate at the beginning of each year based on the hours of studio service that could be provided at capacity. He would like to know what effect this method would have on job costs. How much overhead would have been applied using this method to the Verde Baja job if it had been done in 2012? In 2013? By how much would overhead have been underapplied or overapplied in 2012 using this method? In 2013?

3. How would you interpret the underapplied or overapplied overhead that results from using studio hours at capacity to compute the predetermined overhead rate?

4. What fundamental business problem is Platinum Tracks facing? Which method of computing the predetermined overhead rate is likely to be more helpful in facing this problem? Explain.

CASE 3B–4 Ethics; Predetermined Overhead Rate and Capacity [LO3–2, LO3–7, LO3–9]

Pat Miranda, the new controller of Vault Hard Drives, Inc., has just returned from a seminar on the choice of the activity level in the predetermined overhead rate. Even though the subject did not sound exciting at first, she found that there were some important ideas presented that should get a hearing at her company. After returning from the seminar, she arranged a meeting with the production manager, J. Stevens, and the assistant production manager, Marvin Washington.

Pat: I ran across an idea that I wanted to check out with both of you. It's about the way we compute predetermined overhead rates.

J.: We're all ears.

Pat: We compute the predetermined overhead rate by dividing the estimated total factory overhead for the coming year, which is all a fixed cost, by the estimated total units produced for the coming year.

Marvin: We've been doing that as long as I've been with the company.

J.: And it has been done that way at every other company I've worked at, except at most places they divide by direct labor-hours.

Pat: We use units because it is simpler and we basically make one product with minor variations. But, there's another way to do it. Instead of basing the overhead rate on the estimated total units produced for the coming year, we could base it on the total units produced at capacity.

Marvin: Oh, the Marketing Department will love that. It will drop the costs on all of our products. They'll go wild over there cutting prices.

Pat: That is a worry, but I wanted to talk to both of you first before going over to Marketing.

J.: Aren't you always going to have a lot of underapplied overhead?

Pat: That's correct, but let me show you how we would handle it. Here's an example based on our budget for next year.

Budgeted (estimated) production	160,000 units
Budgeted sales	160,000 units
Capacity	200,000 units
Selling price	$60 per unit
Variable manufacturing cost	$15 per unit
Total manufacturing overhead cost (all fixed)	$4,000,000
Administrative and selling expenses (all fixed)	$2,700,000
Beginning inventories	$0

Traditional Approach to Computation of the Predetermined Overhead Rate

$$\frac{\text{Estimated total manufacturing overhead cost, \$4,000,000}}{\text{Estimated total units produced, 160,000}} = \$25 \text{ per unit}$$

Budgeted Income Statement		
Revenue (160,000 units × $60 per unit)		$9,600,000
Cost of goods sold:		
Variable manufacturing (160,000 units × $15 per unit)	$2,400,000	
Manufacturing overhead applied		
(160,000 units × $25 per unit)	4,000,000	6,400,000
Gross margin		3,200,000
Selling and administrative expenses		2,700,000
Net operating income		$ 500,000

New Approach to Computation of the Predetermined Overhead Rate
Using Capacity in the Denominator

$$\frac{\text{Estimated total manufacturing overhead cost at capacity, \$4,000,000}}{\text{Total units at capacity, 200,000}} = \$20 \text{ per unit}$$

Budgeted Income Statement		
Revenue (160,000 units × $60 per unit)		$9,600,000
Cost of goods sold:		
Variable manufacturing (160,000 units × $15 per unit) . . .	$2,400,000	
Manufacturing overhead applied		
(160,000 units × $20 per unit)	3,200,000	5,600,000
Gross margin		4,000,000
Cost of unused capacity [(200,000 units − 160,000 units)		
× $20 per unit]		800,000
Selling and administrative expenses		2,700,000
Net operating income		$ 500,000

J.: Whoa!! I don't think I like the looks of that "Cost of unused capacity." If that thing shows up on the income statement, someone from headquarters is likely to come down here looking for some people to lay off.

Marvin: I'm worried about something else too. What happens when sales are not up to expectations? Can we pull the "hat trick"?

Pat: I'm sorry, I don't understand.

J.: Marvin's talking about something that happens fairly regularly. When sales are down and profits look like they are going to be lower than the president told the owners they were going to be, the president comes down here and asks us to deliver some more profits.

Marvin: And we pull them out of our hat.

J.: Yeah, we just increase production until we get the profits we want.

Pat: I still don't understand. You mean you increase sales?

J.: Nope, we increase production. We're the production managers, not the sales managers.

Pat: I get it. Because you have produced more, the sales force has more units it can sell.

J.: Nope, the marketing people don't do a thing. We just build inventories and that does the trick.

Required:

In all of the questions below, assume that the predetermined overhead rate under the traditional method is $25 per unit, and under the new method it is $20 per unit. Also assume that under the traditional method any underapplied or overapplied overhead is taken directly to the income statement as an adjustment to Cost of Goods Sold.

1. Suppose actual production is 160,000 units. Compute the net operating incomes that would be realized under the traditional and new methods if actual sales are 150,000 units and everything else turns out as expected.

2. How many units would have to be produced under each of the methods in order to realize the budgeted net operating income of $500,000 if actual sales are 150,000 units and everything else turns out as expected?

3. What effect does the new method based on capacity have on the volatility of net operating income?

4. Will the "hat trick" be easier or harder to perform if the new method based on capacity is used?

5. Do you think the "hat trick" is ethical?

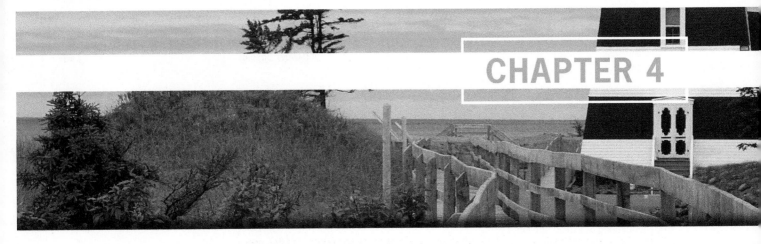

CHAPTER 4

Process Costing

Costing the "Quicker-Picker-Upper"

If you have ever spilled milk, there is a good chance that you used Bounty paper towels to clean up the mess. **Procter & Gamble (P&G)** manufactures Bounty in two main processing departments—Paper Making and Paper Converting. In the Paper Making Department, wood pulp is converted into paper and then spooled into 2,000 pound rolls. In the Paper Converting Department, two of the 2,000 pound rolls of paper are simultaneously unwound into a machine that creates a two-ply paper towel that is decorated, perforated, and embossed to create texture. The large sheets of paper towels that emerge from this process are wrapped around a cylindrical cardboard core measuring eight feet in length. Once enough sheets wrap around the core, the eight foot roll is cut into individual rolls of Bounty that are sent down a conveyor to be wrapped, packed, and shipped.

In this type of manufacturing environment, costs cannot be readily traced to individual rolls of Bounty; however, given the homogeneous nature of the product, the total costs incurred in the Paper Making Department can be spread uniformly across its output of 2,000 pound rolls of paper. Similarly, the total costs incurred in the Paper Converting Department (including the cost of the 2,000 pound rolls that are transferred in from the Paper Making Department) can be spread uniformly across the number of cases of Bounty produced.

P&G uses a similar costing approach for many of its products such as Tide, Crest toothpaste, and Dawn dishwashing liquid. ■

Source: Conversation with Brad Bays, formerly a Procter & Gamble financial executive.

LEARNING OBJECTIVES

After studying Chapter 4, you should be able to:

LO4–1 Record the flow of materials, labor, and overhead through a process costing system.

LO4–2 Compute the equivalent units of production using the weighted-average method.

LO4–3 Compute the cost per equivalent unit using the weighted-average method.

LO4–4 Assign costs to units using the weighted-average method.

LO4–5 Prepare a cost reconciliation report.

LO4–6 *(Appendix 4A) Compute the equivalent units of production using the FIFO method.*

LO4–7 *(Appendix 4A) Compute the cost per equivalent unit using the FIFO method.*

LO4–8 *(Appendix 4A) Assign costs to units using the FIFO method.*

LO4–9 *(Appendix 4A) Prepare a cost reconciliation report using the FIFO method.*

LO4–10 *(Appendix 4B) Allocate service department costs to operating departments using the direct method.*

LO4–11 *(Appendix 4B) Allocate service department costs to operating departments using the step-down method.*

Job-order costing and process costing are two common methods for determining unit product costs. As explained in the previous chapter, job-order costing is used when many different jobs or products are worked on each period. Examples of industries that use job-order costing include furniture manufacturing, special-order printing, shipbuilding, and many types of service organizations.

By contrast, **process costing** is used most commonly in industries that convert raw materials into homogeneous (i.e., uniform) products, such as bricks, soda, or paper, on a continuous basis. Examples of companies that would use process costing include Reynolds Consumer Products (aluminum ingots), Scott Paper (paper towels), General Mills (flour), ExxonMobil (gasoline and lubricating oils), Coppertone (sunscreens), and Kellogg's (breakfast cereals). In addition, process costing is sometimes used in companies with assembly operations. A form of process costing may also be used in utilities that produce gas, water, and electricity.

Our purpose in this chapter is to explain how product costing works in a process costing system.

Comparison of Job-Order and Process Costing

In some ways process costing is very similar to job-order costing, and in some ways it is very different. In this section, we focus on these similarities and differences to provide a foundation for the detailed discussion of process costing that follows.

Similarities between Job-Order and Process Costing

Much of what you learned in the previous chapter about costing and cost flows applies equally well to process costing in this chapter. We are not throwing out all that we have learned about costing and starting from "scratch" with a whole new system. The similarities between job-order and process costing can be summarized as follows:

1. Both systems have the same basic purposes—to assign material, labor, and manufacturing overhead costs to products and to provide a mechanism for computing unit product costs.
2. Both systems use the same basic manufacturing accounts, including Manufacturing Overhead, Raw Materials, Work in Process, and Finished Goods.
3. The flow of costs through the manufacturing accounts is basically the same in both systems.

As can be seen from this comparison, much of the knowledge that you have already acquired about costing is applicable to a process costing system. Our task now is to refine and extend your knowledge to process costing.

Differences between Job-Order and Process Costing

There are three differences between job-order and process costing. First, process costing is used when a company produces a continuous flow of units that are indistinguishable from one another. Job-order costing is used when a company produces many different jobs that have unique production requirements. Second, under process costing, it makes no sense to try to identify materials, labor, and overhead costs with a particular customer order (as we did with job-order costing) because each order is just one of many that are filled from a continuous flow of virtually identical units from the production line. Accordingly, process costing accumulates costs by department (rather than by order) and assigns these costs uniformly to all units that pass through the department during a period. Job cost sheets (which we used for job-order costing) are not used to accumulate costs. Third, process costing systems compute

EXHIBIT 4–1
Differences between Job-Order and Process Costing

Job-Order Costing	Process Costing
1. Many different jobs are worked on during each period, with each job having different production requirements.	1. A single product is produced either on a continuous basis or for long periods of time. All units of product are identical.
2. Costs are accumulated by individual job.	2. Costs are accumulated by department.
3. Unit costs are computed *by job* on the job cost sheet.	3. Unit costs are computed *by department.*

unit costs by department. This differs from job-order costing where unit costs are computed by job on the job cost sheet. Exhibit 4–1 summarizes the differences just described.

Cost Flows in Process Costing

Before going through a detailed example of process costing, it will be helpful to see how, in a general way, manufacturing costs flow through a process costing system.

Processing Departments

A **processing department** is an organizational unit where work is performed on a product and where materials, labor, or overhead costs are added to the product. For example, a **Nalley's** potato chip factory might have three processing departments—one for preparing potatoes, one for cooking, and one for inspecting and packaging. A brick factory might have two processing departments—one for mixing and molding clay into brick form and one for firing the molded brick. Some products and services may go through a number of processing departments, while others may go through only one or two. Regardless of the number of processing departments, they all have two essential features. First, the activity in the processing department is performed uniformly on all of the units passing through it. Second, the output of the processing department is homogeneous; in other words, all of the units produced are identical.

Products in a process costing environment, such as bricks or potato chips, typically flow in sequence from one department to another as in Exhibit 4–2.

EXHIBIT 4–2
Sequential Processing Departments

MONKS MAKE A LIVING SELLING BEER

The Trappist monks of St. Sixtus monastery in Belgium have been brewing beer since 1839. Customers must make an appointment with the monastery to buy a maximum of two 24-bottle cases per month. The scarce and highly prized beer sells for more than $15 per 11-ounce bottle.

The monk's brewing ingredients include water, malt, hops, sugar, and yeast. The sequential steps of the beer-making process include grinding and crushing the malt grain, brewing by adding water to the crushed malt, filtering to separate a liquid called wort from undissolved grain particles, boiling to sterilize the wort (including adding sugar to increase the density of the wort), fermentation by adding yeast to convert sugar into alcohol and carbon dioxide, storage where the beer is aged for at least three weeks, and bottling where more sugar and yeast are added to enable two weeks of additional fermentation in the bottle.

Unlike growth-oriented for-profit companies, the monastery has not expanded its production capacity since 1946, seeking instead to sell just enough beer to sustain the monks' modest lifestyle.

Source: John W. Miller, "Trappist Command: Thou Shalt Not Buy Too Much of Our Beer," *The Wall Street Journal*, November 29, 2007, pp. A1 and A14.

The Flow of Materials, Labor, and Overhead Costs

Cost accumulation is simpler in a process costing system than in a job-order costing system. In a process costing system, instead of having to trace costs to hundreds of different jobs, costs are traced to only a few processing departments.

A T-account model of materials, labor, and overhead cost flows in a process costing system is shown in Exhibit 4–3. Several key points should be noted from this exhibit. First, note that a separate Work in Process account is maintained for *each processing department*.

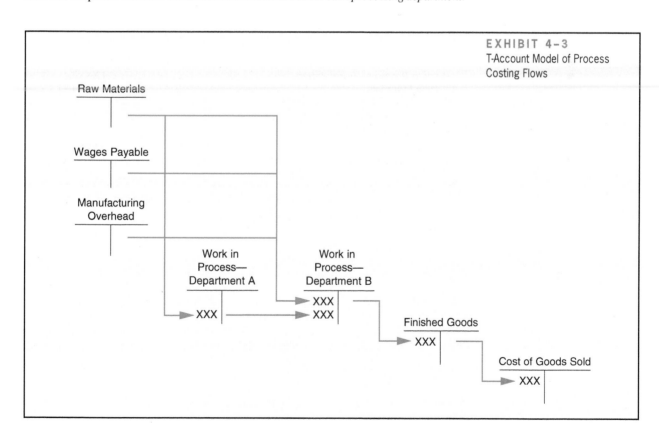

EXHIBIT 4–3
T-Account Model of Process Costing Flows

Chapter 4

In contrast, in a job-order costing system the entire company may have only one Work in Process account. Second, note that the completed production of the first processing department (Department A in the exhibit) is transferred to the Work in Process account of the second processing department (Department B). After further work in Department B, the completed units are then transferred to Finished Goods. (In Exhibit 4–3, we show only two processing departments, but a company can have many processing departments.)

Finally, note that materials, labor, and overhead costs can be added in *any* processing department—not just the first. Costs in Department B's Work in Process account consist of the materials, labor, and overhead costs incurred in Department B plus the costs attached to partially completed units transferred in from Department A (called transferred-in costs).

Materials, Labor, and Overhead Cost Entries

LO4–1
Record the flow of materials, labor, and overhead through a process costing system.

To complete our discussion of cost flows in a process costing system, in this section we show journal entries relating to materials, labor, and overhead costs at Megan's Classic Cream Soda, a company that has two processing departments—Formulating and Bottling. In the Formulating Department, ingredients are checked for quality and then mixed and injected with carbon dioxide to create bulk cream soda. In the Bottling Department, bottles are checked for defects, filled with cream soda, capped, visually inspected again for defects, and then packed for shipping.

Materials Costs   As in job-order costing, materials are drawn from the storeroom using a materials requisition form. Materials can be added in any processing department, although it is not unusual for materials to be added only in the first processing department, with subsequent departments adding only labor and overhead costs.

At Megan's Classic Cream Soda, some materials (i.e., water, flavors, sugar, and carbon dioxide) are added in the Formulating Department and some materials (i.e., bottles, caps, and packing materials) are added in the Bottling Department. The journal entry to record the materials used in the first processing department, the Formulating Department, is as follows:

Work in Process—Formulating	XXX	
Raw Materials		XXX

The journal entry to record the materials used in the second processing department, the Bottling Department, is as follows:

Work in Process—Bottling	XXX	
Raw Materials		XXX

Labor Costs   In process costing, labor costs are traced to departments—not to individual jobs. The following journal entry records the labor costs in the Formulating Department at Megan's Classic Cream Soda:

Work in Process—Formulating	XXX	
Salaries and Wages Payable		XXX

A similar entry would be made to record labor costs in the Bottling Department.

Overhead Costs   In process costing, as in job-order costing, predetermined overhead rates are usually used. Manufacturing overhead cost is applied according to the amount of the allocation base that is incurred in the department. The following journal entry records the overhead cost applied in the Formulating Department:

Work in Process—Formulating	XXX	
Manufacturing Overhead		XXX

A similar entry would be made to apply manufacturing overhead costs in the Bottling Department.

Completing the Cost Flows   Once processing has been completed in a department, the units are transferred to the next department for further processing, as illustrated in the T-accounts in Exhibit 4–3. The following journal entry transfers the cost of partially completed units from the Formulating Department to the Bottling Department:

| Work in Process—Bottling | XXX | |
| Work in Process—Formulating | | XXX |

After processing has been completed in the Bottling Department, the costs of the completed units are transferred to the Finished Goods inventory account:

| Finished Goods | XXX | |
| Work in Process—Bottling | | XXX |

Finally, when a customer's order is filled and units are sold, the cost of the units is transferred to Cost of Goods Sold:

| Cost of Goods Sold | XXX | |
| Finished Goods | | XXX |

To summarize, the cost flows between accounts are basically the same in a process costing system as they are in a job-order costing system. The only difference at this point is that in a process costing system each department has a separate Work in Process account.

THE DIFFERENCE BETWEEN LABOR RATES AND LABOR COST

The emergence of China as a global competitor has increased the need for managers to understand the difference between labor rates and labor cost. Labor rates reflect the amount paid to employees per hour or month. Labor costs measure the employee compensation paid per unit of output. For example, Tenneco has plants in Shanghai, China, and Litchfield, Michigan, that both manufacture exhaust systems for automobiles. The monthly labor rate per employee at the Shanghai plant ranges from $210–$250, whereas the same figure for the Litchfield plant ranges from $1,880–$4,064. A naïve interpretation of these labor rates would be to automatically assume that the Shanghai plant is the lower labor cost facility. A wiser comparison of the two plants' labor costs would account for the fact that the Litchfield plant produced 1.4 million exhaust systems in 2005 compared to 400,000 units at the Shanghai plant, while having only 20% more employees than the Shanghai plant.

Source: Alex Taylor III, "A Tale of Two Factories," *Fortune*, September 18, 2006, pp. 118–126.

We now turn our attention to Double Diamond Skis, a company that manufactures a high-performance deep-powder ski, and that uses process costing to determine its unit product costs. The company's production process is illustrated in Exhibit 4–4. Skis go through a sequence of five processing departments, starting with the Shaping and Milling Department and ending with the Finishing and Pairing Department. The basic idea in process costing is to add together all of the costs incurred in a department during a period and then to spread those costs uniformly across the units processed in that department during that period. As we shall see, applying this simple idea involves a few complications.

Equivalent Units of Production

After materials, labor, and overhead costs have been accumulated in a department, the department's output must be determined so that unit product costs can be computed. The difficulty is that a department usually has some partially completed units in its ending

EXHIBIT 4–4
The Production Process at Double Diamond Skis*

Shaping and Milling Department

Computer-assisted milling machines shape the wood core and aluminum sheets that serve as the backbone of the ski.

Graphics Application Department

Graphics are applied to the back of clear plastic top sheets using a heat-transfer process.

Molding Department

The wooden core and various layers are stacked in a mold, polyurethane foam is injected into the mold, and then the mold is placed in a press that fuses the parts together.

Grinding and Sanding Department

The semi-finished skis are tuned by stone grinding and belt sanding. The ski edges are beveled and polished.

Finishing and Pairing Department

A skilled technician selects skis to form a pair and adjusts the skis' camber.

Finished Goods

*Adapted from Bill Gout, Jesse James Doquilo, and Studio M D, "Capped Crusaders," *Skiing*, October 1993, pp. 138–144.

inventory. It does not seem reasonable to count these partially completed units as equivalent to fully completed units when counting the department's output. Therefore, these partially completed units are translated into an *equivalent* number of fully completed units. In process costing, this translation is done using the following formula:

$$\text{Equivalent units} = \text{Number of partially completed units} \times \text{Percentage completion}$$

As the formula states, **equivalent units** is the product of the number of partially completed units and the percentage completion of those units with respect to the processing in the department. Roughly speaking, the equivalent units is the number of complete units that could have been obtained from the materials and effort that went into the partially complete units.

For example, suppose the Molding Department at Double Diamond has 500 units in its ending work in process inventory that are 60% complete with respect to processing in the department. These 500 partially complete units are equivalent to 300 fully complete units (500 × 60% = 300). Therefore, the ending work in process inventory contains 300 equivalent units. These equivalent units are added to any units completed during the period to determine the department's output for the period—called the *equivalent units of production*.

Equivalent units of production for a period can be computed in different ways. In this chapter, we discuss the *weighted-average method*. In Appendix 4A, we discuss the *FIFO method*. The **FIFO method** of process costing is a method in which equivalent units and unit costs relate only to work done during the current period. In contrast, the **weighted-average method** blends together units and costs from the current period with units and costs from the prior period. In the weighted-average method, the **equivalent units of production** for a department are the number of units transferred to the next department (or to finished goods) plus the equivalent units in the department's ending work in process inventory.

Weighted-Average Method

Under the weighted-average method, a department's equivalent units are computed as follows:

LO4–2
Compute the equivalent units of production using the weighted-average method.

Weighted-Average Method
(a separate calculation is made for each cost category in each processing department)

$$\text{Equivalent units of production} = \text{Units transferred to the next department or to finished goods} + \text{Equivalent units in ending work in process inventory}$$

Note that the computation of the equivalent units of production involves adding the number of units transferred out of the department to the equivalent units in the department's ending inventory. There is no need to compute the equivalent units for the units transferred out of the department—they are 100% complete with respect to the work done in that department or they would not be transferred out. In other words, each unit transferred out of the department is counted as one equivalent unit.

Consider the Shaping and Milling Department at Double Diamond. This department uses computerized milling machines to precisely shape the wooden core and metal sheets that will be used to form the backbone of the ski. (See Exhibit 4–4 for an overview of the production process at Double Diamond.) The activity shown at the top of the next page took place in the department in May.

The first thing to note about the activity in the Shaping and Milling Department is the flow of units through the department. The department started with 200 units in beginning work in process inventory. During May, 5,000 units were started into production. This made a total of 5,200 units. Of this total, 4,800 units were completed and transferred to the next department during May and 400 units were still in the department at the end of the month as ending work in process inventory. In general, the units in

Shaping and Milling Department	Units	Percent Complete	
		Materials	Conversion
Beginning work in process inventory	200	55%	30%
Units started into production during May	5,000		
Units completed during May and transferred to the next department	4,800	100%*	100%*
Ending work in process inventory	400	40%	25%

*We always assume that units transferred out of a department are 100% complete with respect to the processing done in that department.

beginning work in process inventory plus the units started into production must equal the units in ending work in process inventory plus the units completed and transferred out. In equation form, this is:

$$\text{Units in beginning work in process inventory} + \text{Units started into production}$$
$$\text{or transferred in} = \text{Units in ending work in process inventory} + \text{Units completed}$$
$$\text{and transferred out}$$

Note the use of the term *conversion* in the table above. **Conversion cost**, as defined in an earlier chapter, is direct labor cost plus manufacturing overhead cost. In process costing, conversion cost is often treated as a single element of product cost.

Note that the beginning work in process inventory was 55% complete with respect to materials costs and 30% complete with respect to conversion costs. This means that 55% of the materials costs required to complete the units in the department had already been incurred. Likewise, 30% of the conversion costs required to complete the units had already been incurred.

Two equivalent unit figures must be computed—one for materials and one for conversion. These computations are shown in Exhibit 4–5.

Note that the computations in Exhibit 4–5 ignore the fact that the units in the beginning work in process inventory were partially complete. For example, the 200 units in beginning inventory were already 30% complete with respect to conversion costs. Nevertheless, the weighted-average method is concerned only with the 4,900 equivalent units that are in ending inventories and in units transferred to the next department; it is not concerned with the fact that the beginning inventory was already partially complete. In other words, the 4,900 equivalent units computed using the weighted-average method include work that was accomplished in prior periods. This is a key point concerning the weighted-average method and it is easy to overlook.

EXHIBIT 4–5 Equivalent Units of Production: Weighted-Average Method	Shaping and Milling Department	Materials	Conversion
	Units transferred to the next department	4,800	4,800
	Ending work in process inventory:		
	Materials: 400 units × 40% complete	160	
	Conversion: 400 units × 25% complete		100
	Equivalent units of production	4,960	4,900

GETTING LESS FOR THE SAME PRICE

When the prices of raw materials such as sugar and cotton increase during an economic downturn, companies realize that they cannot pass these cost increases on to customers in the form of higher prices. Instead, companies often respond to these circumstances by holding their prices constant while giving customers less for their money. For example, when the price of cotton increased Georgia-Pacific responded by decreasing the width of its Angel Soft Double Roll toilet paper from 4.27 inches to 4.00 inches. The company also reduced the number of sheets per roll from 352 to 300. Similarly, Procter & Gamble decreased the number of sheets in a roll of Charmin Ultra Soft Big Roll from 200 to 176.

These product size reductions not only lower raw material costs, but they also reduce shipping costs. Georgia-Pacific estimates that its smaller rolls of toilet paper enable it to transport 12–17% more units per truck, thereby saving 345,000 gallons of gasoline per year.

Source: Beth Kowitt, "When Less is . . . Less?" *Fortune*, November 15, 2010, p. 21.

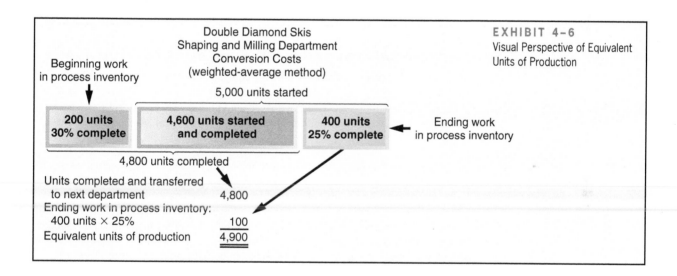

EXHIBIT 4–6
Visual Perspective of Equivalent Units of Production

Exhibit 4–6 provides another way of looking at the computation of equivalent units of production. This exhibit depicts the equivalent units computation for conversion costs. Study it carefully before going on.

Compute and Apply Costs

In the last section, we computed the equivalent units of production for materials and for conversion at Double Diamond Skis. In this section we will compute the cost per equivalent unit for materials and for conversion. We will then use these costs to value ending work in process and finished goods inventories. Exhibit 4–7 displays all of the data concerning May's operations in the Shaping and Milling Department that we will need to complete these tasks.

LO4–3
Compute the cost per equivalent unit using the weighted-average method.

EXHIBIT 4–7	Beginning work in process inventory:	
Shaping and Milling Department	Units in process	200
Data for May Operations	Completion with respect to materials	55%
	Completion with respect to conversion	30%
	Costs in beginning work in process inventory:	
	Materials cost	$ 9,600
	Conversion cost	5,575
	Total cost in beginning work in process inventory	$15,175
	Units started into production during the period	5,000
	Units completed and transferred out	4,800
	Costs added during the period:	
	Materials cost	$368,600
	Conversion cost	350,900
	Total cost added during the period	$719,500
	Ending work in process inventory:	
	Units in process	400
	Completion with respect to materials	40%
	Completion with respect to conversion	25%

Cost per Equivalent Unit—Weighted-Average Method

In the weighted-average method, the cost per equivalent unit is computed as follows:

Weighted-Average Method
(a separate calculation is made for each cost category in each processing department)

$$\text{Cost per equivalent unit} = \frac{\text{Cost of beginning work in process inventory} + \text{Cost added during the period}}{\text{Equivalent units of production}}$$

Note that the numerator is the sum of the cost of beginning work in process inventory and of the cost added during the period. Thus, the weighted-average method blends together costs from the prior and current periods. That is why it is called the weighted-average method; it averages together units and costs from both the prior and current periods.

The costs per equivalent unit for materials and for conversion are computed below for the Shaping and Milling Department for May:

Shaping and Milling Department Costs per Equivalent Unit		
	Materials	Conversion
Cost of beginning work in process inventory	$ 9,600	$ 5,575
Costs added during the period	368,600	350,900
Total cost (a)	$378,200	$356,475
Equivalent units of production (see Exhibit 4–5) (b)	4,960	4,900
Cost per equivalent unit (a) ÷ (b)	$76.25	$72.75

Applying Costs—Weighted-Average Method

LO4–4

Assign costs to units using the weighted-average method.

The costs per equivalent unit are used to value units in ending inventory and units that are transferred to the next department. For example, each unit transferred out of Double Diamond's Shaping and Milling Department to the Graphics Application Department, as depicted in Exhibit 4–4, will carry with it a cost of $149.00 ($76.25 for materials cost and $72.75 for conversion cost). Because 4,800 units were transferred out in May to the next department, the total cost assigned to those units would be $715,200 (= 4,800 units × $149.00 per unit).

A complete accounting of the costs of both ending work in process inventory and the units transferred out appears below:

Shaping and Milling Department
Costs of Ending Work in Process Inventory and the Units Transferred Out

	Materials	Conversion	Total
Ending work in process inventory:			
Equivalent units of production (materials:			
400 units × 40% complete; conversion:			
400 units × 25% complete) (a)	160	100	
Cost per equivalent unit (see page 154) (b)	$76.25	$72.75	
Cost of ending work in process inventory (a) × (b)	$12,200	$7,275	$19,475
Units completed and transferred out:			
Units transferred to the next department (a) ...	4,800	4,800	
Cost per equivalent unit (see above) (b)	$76.25	$72.75	
Cost of units transferred out (a) × (b)	$366,000	$349,200	$715,200

In each case, the equivalent units are multiplied by the cost per equivalent unit to determine the cost assigned to the units. This is done for each cost category—in this case, materials and conversion. The equivalent units for the units completed and transferred out are simply the number of units transferred to the next department because they would not have been transferred unless they were complete.

Cost Reconciliation Report

The costs assigned to ending work in process inventory and to the units transferred out reconcile with the costs we started with in Exhibit 4–7 as shown below:

LO4–5
Prepare a cost reconciliation report.

Shaping and Milling Department
Cost Reconciliation

Costs to be accounted for:	
Cost of beginning work in process inventory (Exhibit 4–7)	$ 15,175
Costs added to production during the period (Exhibit 4–7)	719,500
Total cost to be accounted for	$734,675
Costs accounted for as follows:	
Cost of ending work in process inventory (see above).............	$ 19,475
Cost of units transferred out (see above)	715,200
Total cost accounted for	$734,675

The $715,200 cost of the units transferred to the next department, Graphics Application, will be accounted for in that department as "costs transferred in." It will be treated in the process costing system as just another category of costs like materials or conversion costs. The only difference is that the costs transferred in will always be 100% complete with respect to the work done in the Shaping and Milling Department. Costs are passed on from one department to the next in this fashion, until they reach the last processing department, Finishing and Pairing. When the products are completed in this last department, their costs are transferred to finished goods.

Operation Costing

The costing systems discussed in Chapters 3 and 4 represent the two ends of a continuum. On one end is job-order costing, which is used by companies that produce many different products in one facility. On the other end is process costing, which is used by companies that produce homogeneous products in large quantities. Between these two extremes there are many hybrid systems that include characteristics of both job-order and process costing. One of these hybrids is called *operation costing*.

Operation costing is used in situations where products have some common characteristics and some individual characteristics. Shoes, for example, have common characteristics in that all styles involve cutting and sewing that can be done on a repetitive basis, using the same equipment and following the same basic procedures. Shoes also have individual characteristics—some are made of expensive leathers and others may be made using inexpensive synthetic materials. In a situation such as this, where products have some common characteristics but also must be processed individually, operation costing may be used to determine product costs.

As mentioned above, operation costing is a hybrid system that employs aspects of both job-order and process costing. Products are typically processed in batches when operation costing is used, with each batch charged for its own specific materials. In this sense, operation costing is similar to job-order costing. However, labor and overhead costs are accumulated by operation or by department, and these costs are assigned to units as in process costing. If shoes are being produced, each shoe is charged the same per unit conversion cost, regardless of the style involved, but it is charged with its specific materials cost. Thus, the company is able to distinguish between styles in terms of materials, but it is able to employ the simplicity of a process costing system for labor and overhead costs.

Examples of other products for which operation costing may be used include electronic equipment (such as semiconductors), textiles, clothing, and jewelry (such as rings, bracelets, and medallions). Products of this type are typically produced in batches, but they can vary considerably from model to model or from style to style in terms of the cost of materials.

Summary

Process costing is used in situations where homogeneous products or services are produced on a continuous basis. Costs flow through the manufacturing accounts in basically the same way in a process costing system as in a job-order costing system. However, costs are accumulated by department rather than by job in process costing.

In process costing, the equivalent units of production must be determined for each cost category in each department. Under the weighted-average method, the equivalent units of production equals the number of units transferred out to the next department or to finished goods plus the equivalent units in ending work in process inventory. The equivalent units in ending inventory equals the product of the number of partially completed units in ending work in process inventory and their percentage of completion with respect to the specific cost category.

Under the weighted-average method, the cost per equivalent unit for a specific cost category is computed by adding the cost of beginning work in process inventory and the cost added during the period and then dividing the result by the equivalent units of production. The cost per equivalent unit is then used to value the ending work in process inventory and the units transferred out to the next department or to finished goods.

The cost reconciliation report reconciles the cost of beginning inventory and the costs added to production during the period to the cost of ending inventory and the cost of units transferred out.

Costs are transferred from one department to the next until the last processing department. At that point, the cost of completed units is transferred to finished goods.

Review Problem: Process Cost Flows and Costing Units

Luxguard Home Paint Company produces exterior latex paint, which it sells in one-gallon containers. The company has two processing departments—Base Fab and Finishing. White paint, which is used as a base for all the company's paints, is mixed from raw ingredients in the

Base Fab Department. Pigments are then added to the basic white paint, the pigmented paint is squirted under pressure into one-gallon containers, and the containers are labeled and packed for shipping in the Finishing Department. Information relating to the company's operations for April follows:

a. Issued raw materials for use in production: Base Fab Department, $851,000; and Finishing Department, $629,000.

b. Incurred direct labor costs: Base Fab Department, $330,000; and Finishing Department, $270,000.

c. Applied manufacturing overhead cost: Base Fab Department, $665,000; and Finishing Department, $405,000.

d. Transferred basic white paint from the Base Fab Department to the Finishing Department, $1,850,000.

e. Transferred paint that had been prepared for shipping from the Finishing Department to Finished Goods, $3,200,000.

Required:

1. Prepare journal entries to record items (a) through (e) above.

2. Post the journal entries from (1) above to T-accounts. The balance in the Base Fab Department's Work in Process account on April 1 was $150,000; the balance in the Finishing Department's Work in Process account was $70,000. After posting entries to the T-accounts, find the ending balance in each department's Work in Process account.

3. Determine the cost of ending work in process inventories and of units transferred out of the Base Fab Department in April. The following additional information is available regarding production in the Base Fab Department during April:

Production data:	
Units (gallons) in process, April 1: materials 100% complete;	
labor and overhead 60% complete	30,000
Units (gallons) started into production during April	420,000
Units (gallons) completed and transferred to the	
Finishing Department	370,000
Units (gallons) in process, April 30: materials 50% complete;	
labor and overhead 25% complete	80,000
Cost data:	
Work in process inventory, April 1:	
Materials	$ 92,000
Labor	21,000
Overhead	37,000
Total cost of work in process inventory	$ 150,000
Cost added during April:	
Materials	$ 851,000
Labor	330,000
Overhead	665,000
Total cost added during April	$1,846,000

4. Prepare a cost reconciliation report for April.

Solution to Review Problem

1.	a.	Work in Process—Base Fab Department	851,000	
		Work in Process—Finishing Department	629,000	
		Raw Materials		1,480,000
	b.	Work in Process—Base Fab Department	330,000	
		Work in Process—Finishing Department	270,000	
		Salaries and Wages Payable		600,000
	c.	Work in Process—Base Fab Department	665,000	
		Work in Process—Finishing Department	405,000	
		Manufacturing Overhead		1,070,000
	d.	Work in Process—Finishing Department	1,850,000	
		Work in Process—Base Fab Department		1,850,000
	e.	Finished Goods	3,200,000	
		Work in Process—Finishing Department		3,200,000

Chapter 4

2.

Raw Materials			
Bal.	XXX	(a)	1,480,000

Salaries and Wages Payable		
	(b)	600,000

Work in Process— Base Fab Department

Bal.	150,000	(d)	1,850,000
(a)	851,000		
(b)	330,000		
(c)	665,000		
Bal.	146,000		

Manufacturing Overhead

(Various actual costs)		(c)	1,070,000

Work in Process—Finishing Department

Bal.	70,000	(e)	3,200,000
(a)	629,000		
(b)	270,000		
(c)	405,000		
(d)	1,850,000		
Bal.	24,000		

Finished Goods

Bal.	XXX	
(e)	3,200,000	

3. First, we must compute the equivalent units of production for each cost category:

Base Fab Department
Equivalent Units of Production

	Materials	Labor	Overhead
Units transferred to the next department	370,000	370,000	370,000
Ending work in process inventory (materials: 80,000 units × 50% complete; labor: 80,000 units × 25% complete; overhead: 80,000 units × 25% complete)	40,000	20,000	20,000
Equivalent units of production	410,000	390,000	390,000

Then we must compute the cost per equivalent unit for each cost category:

Base Fab Department
Costs per Equivalent Unit

	Materials	Labor	Overhead
Costs:			
Cost of beginning work in process inventory	$ 92,000	$ 21,000	$ 37,000
Costs added during the period	851,000	330,000	665,000
Total cost (a)	$943,000	$351,000	$702,000
Equivalent units of production (b)	410,000	390,000	390,000
Cost per equivalent unit (a) ÷ (b)..................	$2.30	$0.90	$1.80

The costs per equivalent unit can then be applied to the units in ending work in process inventory and the units transferred out as follows:

Base Fab Department
Costs of Ending Work in Process Inventory and the Units Transferred Out

	Materials	Labor	Overhead	Total
Ending work in process inventory:				
Equivalent units of production	40,000	20,000	20,000	
Cost per equivalent unit	$2.30	$0.90	$1.80	
Cost of ending work in process inventory	$92,000	$18,000	$36,000	$146,000
Units completed and transferred out:				
Units transferred to the next department	370,000	370,000	370,000	
Cost per equivalent unit	$2.30	$0.90	$1.80	
Cost of units completed and transferred out ...	$851,000	$333,000	$666,000	$1,850,000

4.

Base Fab Department Cost Reconciliation	
Costs to be accounted for:	
Cost of beginning work in process inventory	$ 150,000
Costs added to production during the period	1,846,000
Total cost to be accounted for	$1,996,000
Costs accounted for as follows:	
Cost of ending work in process inventory	$ 146,000
Cost of units transferred out	1,850,000
Total cost accounted for	$1,996,000

Glossary

Conversion cost Direct labor cost plus manufacturing overhead cost. (p. 152)

Equivalent units The product of the number of partially completed units and their percentage of completion with respect to a particular cost. Equivalent units are the number of complete whole units that could be obtained from the materials and effort contained in partially completed units. (p. 151)

Equivalent units of production (weighted-average method) The units transferred to the next department (or to finished goods) during the period plus the equivalent units in the department's ending work in process inventory. (p. 151)

FIFO method A process costing method in which equivalent units and unit costs relate only to work done during the current period. (p. 151)

Operation costing A hybrid costing system used when products have some common characteristics and some individual characteristics. (p. 156)

Process costing A costing method used when essentially homogeneous products are produced on a continuous basis. (p. 145)

Processing department An organizational unit where work is performed on a product and where materials, labor, or overhead costs are added to the product. (p. 146)

Weighted-average method A process costing method that blends together units and costs from both the current and prior periods. (p. 151)

Questions

4–1 Under what conditions would it be appropriate to use a process costing system?

4–2 In what ways are job-order and process costing similar?

4–3 Why is cost accumulation simpler in a process costing system than it is in a job-order costing system?

4–4 How many Work in Process accounts are maintained in a company that uses process costing?

4–5 Assume that a company has two processing departments—Mixing followed by Firing. Prepare a journal entry to show a transfer of work in process from the Mixing Department to the Firing Department.

4–6 Assume that a company has two processing departments—Mixing followed by Firing. Explain what costs might be added to the Firing Department's Work in Process account during a period.

4–7 What is meant by the term *equivalent units of production* when the weighted-average method is used?

4–8 Watkins Trophies, Inc., produces thousands of medallions made of bronze, silver, and gold. The medallions are identical except for the materials used in their manufacture. What costing system would you advise the company to use?

Multiple-choice questions are provided on the text website at www.mhhe.com/garrison15e.

Applying Excel |ACCOUNTING

Available with McGraw-Hill's *Connect® Accounting*.

LO4–2, LO4–3, LO4–4, LO4–5

The Excel worksheet form that appears below is to be used to recreate the extended example on pages 153–155. Download the workbook containing this form from the Online Learning Center at www.mhhe.com/garrison15e. *On the website you will also receive instructions about how to use this worksheet form.*

	A	B	C	D
1	Chapter 4: Applying Excel			
2				
3	Data			
4	Beginning work in process inventory:			
5	Units in process	200		
6	Completion with respect to materials	55%		
7	Completion with respect to conversion	30%		
8	Costs in the beginning work in process inventory:			
9	Materials cost	$9,600		
10	Conversion cost	$5,575		
11	Units started into production during the period	5,000		
12	Costs added to production during the period:			
13	Materials cost	$368,600		
14	Conversion cost	$350,900		
15	Ending work in process inventory:			
16	Units in process	400		
17	Completion with respect to materials	40%		
18	Completion with respect to conversion	25%		
19				
20	Enter a formula into each of the cells marked with a ? below			
21				
22	Weighted-Average method:			
23				
24	*Equivalent Units of Production*			
25		Materials	Conversion	
26	Units transferred to the next department	?	?	
27	Ending work in process inventory:			
28	Materials	?		
29	Conversion		?	
30	Equivalent units of production	?	?	
31				
32	*Costs per Equivalent Unit*			
33		Materials	Conversion	
34	Cost of beginning work in process inventory	?	?	
35	Costs added during the period	?	?	
36	Total cost	?	?	
37	Equivalent units of production	?	?	
38	Cost per equivalent unit	?	?	
39				
40	*Costs of Ending Work in Process Inventory and the Units Transferred Out*			
41		Materials	Conversion	Total
42	Ending work in process inventory:			
43	Equivalent units of production	?	?	
44	Cost per equivalent unit	?	?	
45	Cost of ending work in process inventory	?	?	?
46				
47	Units completed and transferred out:			
48	Units transferred to the next department	?	?	
49	Cost per equivalent unit	?	?	
50	Cost of units transferred out	?	?	?
51				
52	*Cost Reconciliation*			
53	Costs to be accounted for:			
54	Cost of beginning work in process inventory	?		
55	Costs added to production during the period	?		
56	Total cost to be accounted for	?		
57	Costs accounted for as follows:			
58	Cost of ending work in process inventory	?		
59	Cost of units transferred out	?		
60	Total cost accounted for	?		

◄ ◄ ► ►| Chapter 4 Form / Chapter 4 Formulas / Chapte

You should proceed to the requirements below only after completing your worksheet.

Required:
1. Check your worksheet by changing the beginning work in process inventory to 100 units, the units started into production during the period to 2,500 units, and the units in ending work in process inventory to 200 units, keeping all of the other data the same as in the original example. If your worksheet is operating properly, the cost per equivalent unit for materials should now be $152.50 and the cost per equivalent unit for conversion

should be $145.50. If you do not get these answers, find the errors in your worksheet and correct them.

How much is the total cost of the units transferred out? Did it change? Why or why not?

2.   Enter the following data from a different company into your worksheet:

Beginning work in process inventory:	
Units in process	200
Completion with respect to materials	100%
Completion with respect to conversion	20%
Costs in the beginning work in process inventory:	
Materials cost	$2,000
Conversion cost	$800
Units started into production during the period	1,800
Costs added during the period:	
Materials cost	$18,400
Conversion cost	$38,765
Ending work in process inventory:	
Units in process	100
Completion with respect to materials	100%
Completion with respect to conversion	30%

What is the cost of the units transferred out?

3.   What happens to the cost of the units transferred out in part (2) above if the percentage completion with respect to conversion for the beginning inventory is changed from 20% to 40% and everything else remains the same? What happens to the cost per equivalent unit for conversion? Explain.

       The Foundational 15

Available with McGraw-Hill's *Connect*® Accounting.

Clopack Company manufactures one product that goes through one processing department called Mixing. All raw materials are introduced at the start of work in the Mixing Department. The company uses the weighted-average method to account for units and costs. Its Work in Process T-account for the Mixing Department for June follows (all forthcoming questions pertain to June):   LO4–1, LO4–2, LO4–3, LO4–4, LO4–5

Work in Process—Mixing Department

June 1 balance	28,000	Completed and transferred to Finished Goods	?
Materials	120,000		
Direct labor	79,500		
Overhead	97,000		
June 30 balance	?		

The June 1 work in process inventory consisted of 5,000 pounds with $16,000 in materials cost and $12,000 in conversion cost. The June 1 work in process inventory was 100% complete with respect to materials and 50% complete with respect to conversion. During June, 37,500 pounds were started into production. The June 30 work in process inventory consisted of 8,000 pounds that were 100% complete with respect to materials and 40% complete with respect to conversion.

Required:

1.   Prepare the journal entries to record the raw materials used in production and the direct labor cost incurred.

2.   Prepare the journal entry to record the overhead cost applied to production.

3.   How many units were completed and transferred to finished goods during the period?

Chapter 4

4. Compute the equivalent units of production for materials.
5. Compute the equivalent units of production for conversion.
6. What is the amount of the cost of beginning work in process inventory plus the cost added during the period for materials?
7. What is the amount of the cost of beginning work in process inventory plus the cost added during the period for conversion?
8. What is the cost per equivalent unit for materials?
9. What is the cost per equivalent unit for conversion?
10. What is the cost of ending work in process inventory for materials?
11. What is the cost of ending work in process inventory for conversion?
12. What is the cost of materials transferred to finished goods?
13. What is the amount of conversion cost transferred to finished goods?
14. Prepare the journal entry to record the transfer of costs from Work in Process to Finished Goods.
15. What is the total cost to be accounted for? What is the total cost accounted for?

Exercises   connect
|ACCOUNTING

All applicable exercises are available with McGraw-Hill's _Connect_® _Accounting._

EXERCISE 4–1 Process Costing Journal Entries [LO4–1]
Quality Brick Company produces bricks in two processing departments—Molding and Firing. Information relating to the company's operations in March follows:
a.   Raw materials were issued for use in production: Molding Department, $23,000; and Firing Department, $8,000.
b.   Direct labor costs were incurred: Molding Department, $12,000; and Firing Department, $7,000.
c.   Manufacturing overhead was applied: Molding Department, $25,000; and Firing Department, $37,000.
d.   Unfired, molded bricks were transferred from the Molding Department to the Firing Department. According to the company's process costing system, the cost of the unfired, molded bricks was $57,000.
e.   Finished bricks were transferred from the Firing Department to the finished goods warehouse. According to the company's process costing system, the cost of the finished bricks was $103,000.
f.   Finished bricks were sold to customers. According to the company's process costing system, the cost of the finished bricks sold was $101,000.

Required:
Prepare journal entries to record items (a) through (f) above.

EXERCISE 4–2 Computation of Equivalent Units—Weighted-Average Method [LO4–2]
Clonex Labs, Inc., uses a process costing system. The following data are available for one department for October:

		Percent Completed	
	Units	Materials	Conversion
Work in process, October 1	30,000	65%	30%
Work in process, October 31	15,000	80%	40%

The department started 175,000 units into production during the month and transferred 190,000 completed units to the next department.

Required:
Compute the equivalent units of production for October assuming that the company uses the weighted-average method of accounting for units and costs.

EXERCISE 4–3 Cost per Equivalent Unit—Weighted-Average Method [LO4–3]

Superior Micro Products uses the weighted-average method in its process costing system. Data for the Assembly Department for May appear below:

	Materials	Labor	Overhead
Work in process, May 1	$18,000	$5,500	$27,500
Cost added during May	$238,900	$80,300	$401,500
Equivalent units of production	35,000	33,000	33,000

Required:
1. Compute the cost per equivalent unit for materials, for labor, and for overhead.
2. Compute the total cost per equivalent whole unit.

EXERCISE 4–4 Applying Costs to Units—Weighted-Average Method [LO4–4]

Data concerning a recent period's activity in the Prep Department, the first processing department in a company that uses process costing, appear below:

	Materials	Conversion
Equivalent units of production in ending work in process	2,000	800
Cost per equivalent unit	$13.86	$4.43

A total of 20,100 units were completed and transferred to the next processing department during the period.

Required:
Compute the cost of the units transferred to the next department during the period and the cost of ending work in process inventory.

EXERCISE 4–5 Cost Reconciliation Report—Weighted-Average Method [LO4–5]

Maria Am Corporation uses a process costing system. The Baking Department is one of the processing departments in its strudel manufacturing facility. In June in the Baking Department, the cost of beginning work in process inventory was $3,570, the cost of ending work in process inventory was $2,860, and the cost added to production was $43,120.

Required:
Prepare a cost reconciliation report for the Baking Department for June.

EXERCISE 4–6 Equivalent Units—Weighted-Average Method [LO4–2]

Hielta Oy, a Finnish company, processes wood pulp for various manufacturers of paper products. Data relating to tons of pulp processed during June are provided below:

		Percent Completed	
	Tons of Pulp	Materials	Labor and Overhead
Work in process, June 1	20,000	90%	80%
Work in process, June 30	30,000	60%	40%
Started into production during June ...	190,000		

Required:
1. Compute the number of tons of pulp completed and transferred out during June.
2. Compute the equivalent units of production for materials and for labor and overhead for June.

EXERCISE 4–7 Process Costing Journal Entries [LO4–1]

Chocolaterie de Geneve, SA, is located in a French-speaking canton in Switzerland. The company makes chocolate truffles that are sold in popular embossed tins. The company has two processing departments—Cooking and Molding. In the Cooking Department, the raw ingredients for the truffles are mixed and then cooked in special candy-making vats. In the Molding Department, the melted chocolate and other ingredients from the Cooking Department are carefully poured into

Chapter 4

molds and decorative flourishes are applied by hand. After cooling, the truffles are packed for sale. The company uses a process costing system. The T-accounts below show the flow of costs through the two departments in April:

Work in Process—Cooking

Balance 4/1	8,000	Transferred out	160,000
Direct materials	42,000		
Direct labor	50,000		
Overhead	75,000		

Work in Process—Molding

Balance 4/1	4,000	Transferred out	240,000
Transferred in	160,000		
Direct labor	36,000		
Overhead	45,000		

Required:

Prepare journal entries showing the flow of costs through the two processing departments during April.

EXERCISE 4–8 Equivalent Units and Cost per Equivalent Unit—Weighted-Average Method [LO4–2, LO4–3, LO4–4]

Helix Corporation produces prefabricated flooring in a series of steps carried out in production departments. All of the material that is used in the first production department is added at the beginning of processing in that department. Data for May for the first production department follow:

	Units	Percent Complete	
		Materials	Conversion
Work in process inventory, May 1	5,000	100%	40%
Work in process inventory, May 31	10,000	100%	30%

Materials cost in work in process inventory, May 1	$1,500
Conversion cost in work in process inventory, May 1	$4,000
Units started into production	180,000
Units transferred to the next production department	175,000
Materials cost added during May	$54,000
Conversion cost added during May	$352,000

Required:

1. Assume that the company uses the weighted-average method of accounting for units and costs. Determine the equivalent units for May for the first process.
2. Compute the costs per equivalent unit for May for the first process.
3. Determine the total cost of ending work in process inventory and the total cost of units transferred to the next process in May.

EXERCISE 4–9 Equivalent Units and Cost per Equivalent Unit—Weighted-Average Method [LO4–2, LO4–3]

Pureform, Inc., manufactures a product that passes through two departments. Data for a recent month for the first department follow:

	Units	Materials	Labor	Overhead
Work in process inventory, beginning	5,000	$4,320	$1,040	$1,790
Units started in process	45,000			
Units transferred out	42,000			
Work in process inventory, ending	8,000			
Cost added during the month		$52,800	$21,500	$32,250

The beginning work in process inventory was 80% complete with respect to materials and 60% complete with respect to labor and overhead. The ending work in process inventory was 75% complete with respect to materials and 50% complete with respect to labor and overhead.

Required:

Assume that the company uses the weighted-average method of accounting for units and costs.
1. Compute the equivalent units for the month for the first department.
2. Determine the costs per equivalent unit for the month.

EXERCISE 4–10 Equivalent Units—Weighted-Average Method [LO4–2]

Alaskan Fisheries, Inc., processes salmon for various distributors. Two departments are involved—Cleaning and Packing. Data relating to pounds of salmon processed in the Cleaning Department during July are presented below:

		Percent Completed	
	Pounds of Salmon	Materials	Labor and Overhead
Work in process inventory, July 1	20,000	100%	30%
Work in process inventory, July 31	25,000	100%	60%

A total of 380,000 pounds of salmon were started into processing during July. All materials are added at the beginning of processing in the Cleaning Department.

Required:

Compute the equivalent units for July for both materials and labor and overhead assuming that the company uses the weighted-average method of accounting for units.

EXERCISE 4–11 Comprehensive Exercise; Second Production Department—Weighted-Average Method [LO4–2, LO4–3, LO4–4, LO4–5]

Scribners Corporation produces fine papers in three production departments—Pulping, Drying, and Finishing. In the Pulping Department, raw materials such as wood fiber and rag cotton are mechanically and chemically treated to separate their fibers. The result is a thick slurry of fibers. In the Drying Department, the wet fibers transferred from the Pulping Department are laid down on porous webs, pressed to remove excess liquid, and dried in ovens. In the Finishing Department, the dried paper is coated, cut, and spooled onto reels. The company uses the weighted-average method in its process costing system. Data for March for the Drying Department follow:

		Percent Completed	
	Units	Pulping	Conversion
Work in process inventory, March 1	5,000	100%	20%
Work in process inventory, March 31	8,000	100%	25%
Pulping cost in work in process inventory, March 1		$4,800	
Conversion cost in work in process inventory, March 1		$500	
Units transferred to the next production department		157,000	
Pulping cost added during March		$102,450	
Conversion cost added during March		$31,300	

No materials are added in the Drying Department. Pulping cost represents the costs of the wet fibers transferred in from the Pulping Department. Wet fiber is processed in the Drying Department in batches; each unit in the above table is a batch and one batch of wet fibers produces a set amount of dried paper that is passed on to the Finishing Department.

Required:

1. Determine the equivalent units for March for pulping and conversion.
2. Compute the costs per equivalent unit for March for pulping and conversion.
3. Determine the total cost of ending work in process inventory and the total cost of units transferred to the Finishing Department in March.
4. Prepare a cost reconciliation report for the Drying Department for March.

166

Chapter 4

EXERCISE 4–12 Cost Assignment; Cost Reconciliation—Weighted-Average Method [LO4–2, LO4–4, LO4–5]

Superior Micro Products uses the weighted-average method in its process costing system. During January, the Delta Assembly Department completed its processing of 25,000 units and transferred them to the next department. The cost of beginning inventory and the costs added during January amounted to $599,780 in total. The ending inventory in January consisted of 3,000 units, which were 80% complete with respect to materials and 60% complete with respect to labor and over-head. The costs per equivalent unit for the month were as follows:

	Materials	Labor	Overhead
Cost per equivalent unit	$12.50	$3.20	$6.40

Required:
1. Compute the equivalent units of materials, labor, and overhead in the ending inventory for the month.
2. Compute the cost of ending inventory and of the units transferred to the next department for January.
3. Prepare a cost reconciliation for January. (Note: You will not be able to break the cost to be accounted for into the cost of beginning inventory and costs added during the month.)

Problems   ACCOUNTING

All applicable problems are available with McGraw-Hill's *Connect® Accounting*.

PROBLEM 4–13 Comprehensive Problem; Second Production Department—Weighted-Average Method [LO4–2, LO4–3, LO4–4, LO4–5]

Old Country Links Inc. produces sausages in three production departments—Mixing, Casing and Curing, and Packaging. In the Mixing Department, meats are prepared and ground and then mixed with spices. The spiced meat mixture is then transferred to the Casing and Curing Department, where the mixture is force-fed into casings and then hung and cured in climate-controlled smoking chambers. In the Packaging Department, the cured sausages are sorted, packed, and labeled. The company uses the weighted-average method in its process costing system. Data for September for the Casing and Curing Department follow:

	Units	Percent Completed		
		Mixing	Materials	Conversion
Work in process inventory, September 1	1	100%	90%	80%
Work in process inventory, September 30	1	100%	80%	70%

	Mixing	Materials	Conversion
Work in process inventory, September 1	$1,670	$90	$605
Cost added during September	$81,460	$6,006	$42,490

Mixing cost represents the costs of the spiced meat mixture transferred in from the Mixing Depart-ment. The spiced meat mixture is processed in the Casing and Curing Department in batches; each unit in the above table is a batch and one batch of spiced meat mixture produces a set amount of sausages that are passed on to the Packaging Department. During September, 50 batches (i.e., units) were completed and transferred to the Packaging Department.

Required:
1. Determine the equivalent units for September for mixing, materials, and conversion. Do not round off your computations.
2. Compute the costs per equivalent unit for September for mixing, materials, and conversion.

3. Determine the total cost of ending work in process inventory and the total cost of units transferred to the Packaging Department in September.
4. Prepare a cost reconciliation report for the Casing and Curing Department for September.

PROBLEM 4–14 Analysis of Work in Process T-account—Weighted-Average Method [LO4–1, LO4–2, LO4–3, LO4–4]
Weston Products manufactures an industrial cleaning compound that goes through three processing departments—Grinding, Mixing, and Cooking. All raw materials are introduced at the start of work in the Grinding Department. The Work in Process T-account for the Grinding Department for May is given below:

Work in Process—Grinding Department			
Inventory, May 1	21,800	Completed and transferred to the Mixing Department	?
Materials	133,400		
Conversion	225,500		
Inventory, May 31	?		

The May 1 work in process inventory consisted of 18,000 pounds with $14,600 in materials cost and $7,200 in conversion cost. The May 1 work in process inventory was 100% complete with respect to materials and 30% complete with respect to conversion. During May, 167,000 pounds were started into production. The May 31 inventory consisted of 15,000 pounds that were 100% complete with respect to materials and 60% complete with respect to conversion. The company uses the weighted-average method to account for units and costs.

Required:
1. Determine the equivalent units of production for May.
2. Determine the costs per equivalent unit for May.
3. Determine the cost of the units completed and transferred to the Mixing Department during May.

PROBLEM 4–15 Comprehensive Problem—Weighted-Average Method [LO4–2, LO4–3, LO4–4, LO4–5]
Sunspot Beverages, Ltd., of Fiji makes blended tropical fruit drinks in two stages. Fruit juices are extracted from fresh fruits and then blended in the Blending Department. The blended juices are then bottled and packed for shipping in the Bottling Department. The following information pertains to the operations of the Blending Department for June.

		Percent Completed	
	Units	Materials	Conversion
Work in process, beginning	20,000	100%	75%
Started into production	180,000		
Completed and transferred out	160,000		
Work in process, ending	40,000	100%	25%
		Materials	Conversion
Work in process, beginning		$25,200	$24,800
Cost added during June		$334,800	$238,700

Required:
Assume that the company uses the weighted-average method.
1. Determine the equivalent units for June for the Blending Department.
2. Compute the costs per equivalent unit for the Blending Department.
3. Determine the total cost of ending work in process inventory and the total cost of units transferred to the Bottling Department.
4. Prepare a cost reconciliation report for the Blending Department for June.

PROBLEM 4–16 Comprehensive Problem—Weighted-Average Method [LO4–2, LO4–3, LO4–4, LO4–5]
Builder Products, Inc., manufactures a caulking compound that goes through three processing stages prior to completion. Information on work in the first department, Cooking, is given below for May:

Production data:	
Pounds in process, May 1; materials 100% complete;	
conversion 80% complete	10,000
Pounds started into production during May	100,000
Pounds completed and transferred out	?
Pounds in process, May 31; materials 60% complete;	
conversion 20% complete	15,000
Cost data:	
Work in process inventory, May 1:	
Materials cost	$1,500
Conversion cost	$7,200
Cost added during May:	
Materials cost	$154,500
Conversion cost	$90,800

The company uses the weighted-average method.

Required:
1. Compute the equivalent units of production.
2. Compute the costs per equivalent unit for the month.
3. Determine the cost of ending work in process inventory and of the units transferred out to the next department.
4. Prepare a cost reconciliation report for the month.

PROBLEM 4–17 Cost Flows [LO4–1]
Lubricants, Inc., produces a special kind of grease that is widely used by race car drivers. The grease is produced in two processing departments: Refining and Blending. Raw materials are introduced at various points in the Refining Department.

The following incomplete Work in Process account is available for the Refining Department for March:

Work in Process—Refining Department

March 1 balance	38,000	Completed and transferred to Blending	?
Materials	495,000		
Direct labor	72,000		
Overhead	181,000		
March 31 balance	?		

The March 1 work in process inventory in the Refining Department consists of the following elements: materials, $25,000; direct labor, $4,000; and overhead, $9,000.

Costs incurred during March in the Blending Department were: materials used, $115,000; direct labor, $18,000; and overhead cost applied to production, $42,000.

Required:
1. Prepare journal entries to record the costs incurred in both the Refining Department and Blending Department during March. Key your entries to the items (a) through (g) below.
   a. Raw materials were issued for use in production.
   b. Direct labor costs were incurred.
   c. Manufacturing overhead costs for the entire factory were incurred, $225,000. (Credit Accounts Payable.)
   d. Manufacturing overhead cost was applied to production using a predetermined overhead rate.
   e. Units that were complete with respect to processing in the Refining Department were transferred to the Blending Department, $740,000.

f.   Units that were complete with respect to processing in the Blending Department were transferred to Finished Goods, $950,000.

g.   Completed units were sold on account, $1,500,000. The Cost of Goods Sold was $900,000.

2. Post the journal entries from (1) above to T-accounts. The following account balances existed at the beginning of March. (The beginning balance in the Refining Department's Work in Process account is given on the prior page.)

Raw Materials	$618,000
Work in Process—Blending Department	$65,000
Finished Goods	$20,000

After posting the entries to the T-accounts, find the ending balance in the inventory accounts and the manufacturing overhead account.

PROBLEM 4–18 Interpreting a Report—Weighted-Average Method [LO4–2, LO4–3, LO4–4]

Cooperative San José of southern Sonora state in Mexico makes a unique syrup using cane sugar and local herbs. The syrup is sold in small bottles and is prized as a flavoring for drinks and for use in desserts. The bottles are sold for $12 each. The first stage in the production process is carried out in the Mixing Department, which removes foreign matter from the raw materials and mixes them in the proper proportions in large vats. The company uses the weighted-average method in its process costing system.

A hastily prepared report for the Mixing Department for April appears below:

Units to be accounted for:	
Work in process, April 1 (materials 90% complete;	
conversion 80% complete)	30,000
Started into production	200,000
Total units to be accounted for	230,000
Units accounted for as follows:	
Transferred to next department	190,000
Work in process, April 30 (materials 75% complete;	
conversion 60% complete)	40,000
Total units accounted for	230,000
Cost Reconciliation	
Cost to be accounted for:	
Work in process, April 1	$ 98,000
Cost added during the month	827,000
Total cost to be accounted for	$925,000
Cost accounted for as follows:	
Work in process, April 30	$119,400
Transferred to next department	805,600
Total cost accounted for	$925,000

Management would like some additional information about Cooperative San José's operations.

Required:

1. What were the equivalent units for the month?

2. What were the costs per equivalent unit for the month? The beginning inventory consisted of the following costs: materials, $67,800; and conversion cost, $30,200. The costs added during the month consisted of: materials, $579,000; and conversion cost, $248,000.

3. How many of the units transferred to the next department were started and completed during the month?

4. The manager of the Mixing Department stated, "Materials prices jumped from about $2.50 per unit in March to $3 per unit in April, but due to good cost control I was able to hold our materials cost to less than $3 per unit for the month." Should this manager be rewarded for good cost control? Explain.

Chapter 4

Cases

All applicable cases are available with McGraw-Hill's *Connect*® *Accounting*.

CASE 4–19 Second Department—Weighted-Average Method [LO4–2, LO4–3, LO4–4]
"I think we goofed when we hired that new assistant controller," said Ruth Scarpino, president of Provost Industries. "Just look at this report that he prepared for last month for the Finishing Department. I can't understand it."

Finishing Department costs:	
Work in process inventory, April 1, 450 units; materials	
100% complete; conversion 60% complete	$ 8,208*
Costs transferred in during the month from the	
preceding department, 1,950 units	17,940
Materials cost added during the month	6,210
Conversion costs incurred during the month	13,920
Total departmental costs	$46,278
Finishing Department costs assigned to:	
Units completed and transferred to finished goods,	
1,800 units at $25.71 per unit	$46,278
Work in process inventory, April 30, 600 units;	
materials 0% complete; conversion 35% complete	0
Total departmental costs assigned	$46,278

*Consists of cost transferred in, $4,068; materials cost, $1,980; and conversion cost, $2,160.

"He's struggling to learn our system," replied Frank Harrop, the operations manager. "The problem is that he's been away from process costing for a long time, and it's coming back slowly."

"It's not just the format of his report that I'm concerned about. Look at that $25.71 unit cost that he's come up with for April. Doesn't that seem high to you?" said Ms. Scarpino.

"Yes, it does seem high; but on the other hand, I know we had an increase in materials prices during April, and that may be the explanation," replied Mr. Harrop. "I'll get someone else to redo this report and then we may be able to see what's going on."

Provost Industries manufactures a ceramic product that goes through two processing departments—Molding and Finishing. The company uses the weighted-average method in its process costing.

Required:
1. Prepare a report for the Finishing Department showing how much cost should have been assigned to the units completed and transferred to finished goods, and how much cost should have been assigned to ending work in process inventory in the Finishing Department.
2. Explain to the president why the unit cost on the new assistant controller's report is so high.

CASE 4–20 Ethics and the Manager, Understanding the Impact of Percentage Completion on Profit—Weighted-Average Method [LO4–2, LO4–3, LO4–4]
Gary Stevens and Mary James are production managers in the Consumer Electronics Division of General Electronics Company, which has several dozen plants scattered in locations throughout the world. Mary manages the plant located in Des Moines, Iowa, while Gary manages the plant in El Segundo, California. Production managers are paid a salary and get an additional bonus equal to 5% of their base salary if the entire division meets or exceeds its target profits for the year. The bonus is determined in March after the company's annual report has been prepared and issued to stockholders.

Shortly after the beginning of the new year, Mary received a phone call from Gary that went like this:
Gary: How's it going, Mary?
Mary: Fine, Gary. How's it going with you?

Gary: Great! I just got the preliminary profit figures for the division for last year and we are within $200,000 of making the year's target profits. All we have to do is pull a few strings, and we'll be over the top!

Mary: What do you mean?

Gary: Well, one thing that would be easy to change is your estimate of the percentage completion of your ending work in process inventories.

Mary: I don't know if I can do that, Gary. Those percentage completion figures are supplied by Tom Winthrop, my lead supervisor, who I have always trusted to provide us with good estimates. Besides, I have already sent the percentage completion figures to corporate headquarters.

Gary: You can always tell them there was a mistake. Think about it, Mary. All of us managers are doing as much as we can to pull this bonus out of the hat. You may not want the bonus check, but the rest of us sure could use it.

The final processing department in Mary's production facility began the year with no work in process inventories. During the year, 210,000 units were transferred in from the prior processing department and 200,000 units were completed and sold. Costs transferred in from the prior department totaled $39,375,000. No materials are added in the final processing department. A total of $20,807,500 of conversion cost was incurred in the final processing department during the year.

Required:

1. Tom Winthrop estimated that the units in ending inventory in the final processing department were 30% complete with respect to the conversion costs of the final processing department. If this estimate of the percentage completion is used, what would be the Cost of Goods Sold for the year?

2. Does Gary Stevens want the estimated percentage completion to be increased or decreased? Explain why.

3. What percentage completion would result in increasing reported net operating income by $200,000 over the net operating income that would be reported if the 30% figure were used?

4. Do you think Mary James should go along with the request to alter estimates of the percentage completion? Why or why not?

Appendix 4A: FIFO Method

The FIFO method of process costing differs from the weighted-average method in two ways: (1) the computation of equivalent units, and (2) the way in which costs of beginning inventory are treated. The FIFO method is generally considered more accurate than the weighted-average method, but it is more complex. The complexity is not a problem for computers, but the FIFO method is a little more difficult to understand and to learn than the weighted-average method.

Equivalent Units—FIFO Method

LO4–6
Compute the equivalent units of production using the FIFO method.

The computation of equivalent units under the FIFO method differs from the computation under the weighted-average method in two ways.

First, the "units transferred out" is divided into two parts. One part consists of the units from the beginning inventory that were completed and transferred out, and the other part consists of the units that were both *started* and *completed* during the current period.

Second, full consideration is given to the amount of work expended during the current period on units in the *beginning* work in process inventory as well as on units in the ending inventory. Thus, under the FIFO method, both beginning and ending inventories are converted to an equivalent units basis. For the beginning inventory, the equivalent units represent the work done to *complete* the units; for the ending inventory, the equivalent units represent the work done to bring the units to a stage of partial completion at the end of the period (the same as with the weighted-average method).

Chapter 4

The formula for computing the equivalent units of production under the FIFO method is more complex than under the weighted-average method:

FIFO Method
(a separate calculation is made for each cost category
in each processing department)

Equivalent units of production = Equivalent units to complete beginning work in process inventory*

+ Units started and completed during the period

+ Equivalent units in ending work in process inventory

$$\begin{matrix} \text{*Equivalent units to} \\ \text{complete beginning work} \\ \text{in process inventory} \end{matrix} = \begin{matrix} \text{Units in beginning} \\ \text{work in process} \\ \text{inventory} \end{matrix} \times \left(100\% - \begin{matrix} \text{Percentage completion} \\ \text{of beginning work in} \\ \text{process inventory} \end{matrix} \right)$$

Or, the equivalent units of production can also be determined as follows:

Equivalent units of production = Units transferred out

+ Equivalent units in ending work in process inventory

− Equivalent units in beginning work in process inventory

To illustrate the FIFO method, refer again to the data for the Shaping and Milling Department at Double Diamond Skis. The department completed and transferred 4,800 units to the Graphics Application Department during May. Because 200 of these units came from the beginning inventory, the Shaping and Milling Department must have started and completed 4,600 units during May. The 200 units in the beginning inventory were 55% complete with respect to materials and only 30% complete with respect to conversion costs when the month started. Thus, to complete these units the department must have added another 45% of materials costs (100% − 55% = 45%) and another 70% of conversion costs (100% − 30% = 70%). Following this line of reasoning, the equivalent units for the department for May would be computed as shown in Exhibit 4A–1.

EXHIBIT 4A–1 Equivalent Units of Production: FIFO Method		Materials	Conversion
To complete beginning work in process inventory:			
Materials: 200 units × (100% − 55%)*		90	
Conversion: 200 units × (100% − 30%)*			140
Units started and completed during the period		4,600[†]	4,600[†]
Ending work in process inventory:			
Materials: 400 units × 40% complete		160	
Conversion: 400 units × 25% complete			100
Equivalent units of production		4,850	4,840

*This is the work needed to complete the units in beginning inventory.
[†] 5,000 units started − 400 units in ending work in process = 4,600 units started and completed. This can also be computed as 4,800 units completed and transferred to the next department − 200 units in beginning work in process inventory. The FIFO method assumes that the units in beginning inventory are finished first.

Comparison of Equivalent Units of Production under the Weighted-Average and FIFO Methods

Stop at this point and compare the data in Exhibit 4A–1 with the data in Exhibit 4–5 in the chapter, which shows the computation of equivalent units under the weighted-average method. Also refer to Exhibit 4A–2, which compares the two methods.

The essential difference between the two methods is that the weighted-average method blends work and costs from the prior period with work and costs in the current period, whereas the FIFO method separates the two periods. To see this more clearly, consider the following reconciliation of the two calculations of equivalent units:

Shaping and Milling Department	Materials	Conversion
Equivalent units—weighted-average method	4,960	4,900
Less equivalent units in beginning work in process inventory:		
200 units × 55%	110	
200 units × 30%		60
Equivalent units of production—FIFO method	4,850	4,840

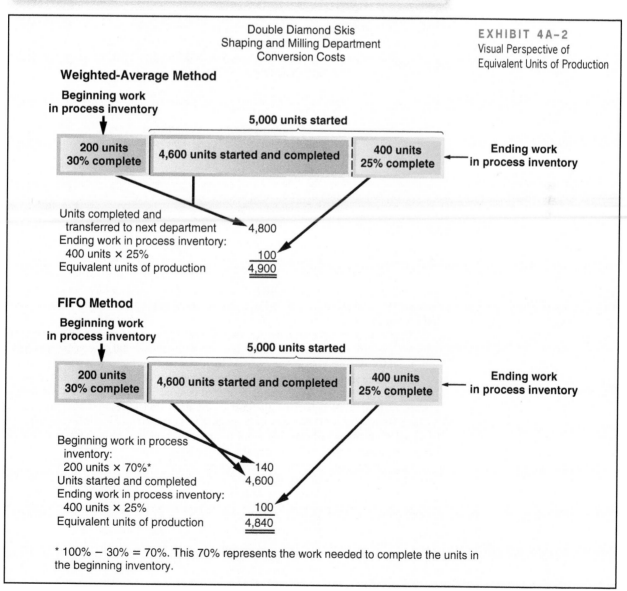

Double Diamond Skis
Shaping and Milling Department
Conversion Costs

EXHIBIT 4A–2
Visual Perspective of
Equivalent Units of Production

Weighted-Average Method

Beginning work in process inventory

5,000 units started

| 200 units 30% complete | 4,600 units started and completed | 400 units 25% complete |

Ending work in process inventory

Units completed and transferred to next department 4,800
Ending work in process inventory:
  400 units × 25% 100
Equivalent units of production 4,900

FIFO Method

Beginning work in process inventory

5,000 units started

| 200 units 30% complete | 4,600 units started and completed | 400 units 25% complete |

Ending work in process inventory

Beginning work in process inventory:
  200 units × 70%* 140
Units started and completed 4,600
Ending work in process inventory:
  400 units × 25% 100
Equivalent units of production 4,840

* 100% − 30% = 70%. This 70% represents the work needed to complete the units in the beginning inventory.

Chapter 4

As shown in the reconciliation of the two costing methods, it is evident that the FIFO method removes the equivalent units that were already in beginning inventory from the equivalent units as defined using the weighted-average method. Thus, the FIFO method isolates the equivalent units that are due to work performed during the current period. The weighted-average method blends together the equivalent units already in beginning inventory with the equivalent units that are due to work performed in the current period.

Cost per Equivalent Unit—FIFO Method

LO4–7
Compute the cost per equivalent unit using the FIFO method.

In the FIFO method, the cost per equivalent unit is computed as follows:

FIFO Method
(a separate calculation is made for each cost category in each processing department)

$$\text{Cost per equivalent unit} = \frac{\text{Cost added during the period}}{\text{Equivalent units of production}}$$

Unlike the weighted-average method, in the FIFO method the cost per equivalent unit is based only on the costs incurred in the department in the current period.

The costs per equivalent unit for materials and for conversion are computed below for the Shaping and Milling Department for May:

Shaping and Milling Department Costs per Equivalent Unit—FIFO method		
	Materials	Conversion
Cost added during the period (a)	$368,600	$350,900
Equivalent units of production (b)	4,850	4,840
Cost per equivalent unit (a) ÷ (b)	$76.00	$72.50

Applying Costs—FIFO Method

LO4–8
Assign costs to units using the FIFO method.

The costs per equivalent unit are used to value units in ending inventory and units that are transferred to the next department. For example, each unit transferred out of the Shaping and Milling Department to the Graphics Application Department will carry with it a cost of $148.50—$76.00 for materials cost and $72.50 for conversion cost. Because 4,800 units were transferred out in May to the next department, the total cost assigned to those units would be $712,800 (4,800 units × $148.50 per unit).

A complete accounting of the costs of both ending work in process inventory and the units transferred out appears on the next page. It is more complicated than the weighted-average method. This is because the cost of the units transferred out consists of three separate components: (1) the cost of beginning work in process inventory; (2) the cost to complete the units in beginning work in process inventory; and (3) the cost of units started and completed during the period.

Again, note that the cost of the units transferred out consists of three distinct components—the cost of beginning work in process inventory, the cost to complete the units in beginning inventory, and the cost of units started and completed during the period. This is a major difference between the weighted-average and FIFO methods.

Shaping and Milling Department
Costs of Ending Work in Process Inventory and Units Transferred Out—FIFO Method

	Materials	Conversion	Total
Ending work in process inventory:			
Equivalent units of production (see Exhibit 4A–1) (a)	160	100	
Cost per equivalent unit (see page 174) (b)	$76.00	$72.50	
Cost of ending work in process inventory (a) × (b)	$12,160	$7,250	$19,410
Units transferred out:			
Cost in beginning work in process inventory	$9,600	$5,575	$15,175
Cost to complete the units in beginning work in process inventory:			
Equivalent units of production required to complete the units in beginning inventory (see Exhibit 4A–1) (a)	90	140	
Cost per equivalent unit (see page 174) (b)	$76.00	$72.50	
Cost to complete the units in beginning inventory (a) × (b)	$6,840	$10,150	$16,990
Cost of units started and completed this period:			
Units started and completed this period (see Exhibit 4A–1) (a)	4,600	4,600	
Cost per equivalent unit (see page 174) (b)	$76.00	$72.50	
Cost of units started and completed this period (a) × (b)	$349,600	$333,500	$683,100
Total cost of units transferred out			$715,265

Cost Reconciliation Report—FIFO Method

The costs assigned to ending work in process inventory and to the units transferred out reconcile with the costs we started with in Exhibit 4–7 as shown below:

LO4–9
Prepare a cost reconciliation report using the FIFO method.

Shaping and Milling Department
Cost Reconciliation

Costs to be accounted for:	
Cost of beginning work in process inventory (Exhibit 4–7)	$ 15,175
Costs added to production during the period (Exhibit 4–7)	719,500
Total cost to be accounted for	$734,675
Costs accounted for as follows:	
Cost of ending work in process inventory (see above)	$ 19,410
Cost of units transferred out (see above)	715,265
Total cost accounted for	$734,675

The $715,265 cost of the units transferred to the next department, Graphics Application, will be accounted for in that department as "costs transferred in." As in the weighted-average method, this cost will be treated in the process costing system as just another category of costs, like materials or conversion costs. The only difference is that the costs transferred in will always be 100% complete with respect to the work done in the Graphics Applications Department. Costs are passed on from one department to the next in this fashion, until they reach the last processing department, Finishing and Pairing. When the products are completed in this last department, their costs are transferred to finished goods.

176   Chapter 4

A Comparison of Costing Methods

In most situations, the weighted-average and FIFO methods will produce very similar unit costs. If there never are any ending inventories, the two methods will produce identical results. The reason for this is that without any ending inventories, no costs can be carried forward into the next period and the weighted-average method will base unit costs on just the current period's costs—just as in the FIFO method. If there *are* ending inventories, either erratic input prices or erratic production levels would also be required to generate much of a difference in unit costs under the two methods. This is because the weighted-average method will blend the unit costs from the prior period with the unit costs of the current period. Unless these unit costs differ greatly, the blending will not make much difference.

Nevertheless, from the standpoint of cost control, the FIFO method is superior to the weighted-average method. Current performance should be evaluated based on costs of the current period only but the weighted-average method mixes costs of the current period with costs of the prior period. Thus, under the weighted-average method, the manager's apparent performance in the current period is influenced by what happened in the prior period. This problem does not arise under the FIFO method because the FIFO method makes a clear distinction between costs of prior periods and costs incurred during the current period. For the same reason, the FIFO method also provides more up-to-date cost data for decision-making purposes.

On the other hand, the weighted-average method is simpler to apply than the FIFO method, but computers can handle the additional calculations with ease once they have been appropriately programmed.

Appendix 4A Exercises and Problems

All applicable exercises and problems are available with McGraw-Hill's *Connect*® Accounting.

EXERCISE 4A–1 Computation of Equivalent Units—FIFO Method [LO4–6]
Refer to the data for Clonex Labs, Inc., in Exercise 4–2.

Required:
Compute the equivalent units of production for October assuming that the company uses the FIFO method of accounting for units and costs.

EXERCISE 4A–2 Cost per Equivalent Unit—FIFO Method [LO4–7]
Superior Micro Products uses the FIFO method in its process costing system. Data for the Assembly Department for May appear below:

	Materials	Labor	Overhead
Cost added during May	$193,320	$62,000	$310,000
Equivalent units of production	27,000	25,000	25,000

Required:
Compute the cost per equivalent unit for materials, labor, overhead, and in total.

EXERCISE 4A–3 Applying Costs to Units—FIFO Method [LO4–8]
Data concerning a recent period's activity in the Assembly Department, the first processing department in a company that uses process costing, appear below:

	Materials	Conversion
Cost of work in process inventory at the beginning of the period	$3,200	$650
Equivalent units of production in the ending work in process inventory . . .	400	200
Equivalent units of production required to complete the beginning work in process inventory	600	1,200
Cost per equivalent unit for the period	$2.32	$0.75

A total of 26,000 units were completed and transferred to the next processing department during the period. Beginning work in process inventory consisted of 2,000 units and ending work in process inventory consisted of 1,000 units.

Required:

Using the FIFO method, compute the cost of the units transferred to the next department during the period and the cost of ending work in process inventory.

EXERCISE 4A–4 Cost Reconciliation Report—FIFO Method [LO4–9]

Schroeder Baking Corporation uses a process costing system in its large-scale baking operations. The Mixing Department is one of the company's processing departments. In the Mixing Department in July, the cost of beginning work in process inventory was $1,460, the cost of ending work in process inventory was $3,120, and the cost added to production was $36,540.

Required:

Prepare a cost reconciliation report for the Mixing Department for July.

EXERCISE 4A–5 Computation of Equivalent Units—FIFO Method [LO4–6]

MediSecure, Inc., produces clear plastic containers for pharmacies in a process that starts in the Molding Department. Data concerning that department's operations in the most recent period appear below:

Beginning work in process:	
Units in process	500
Completion with respect to materials	80%
Completion with respect to conversion	40%
Units started into production during the month	153,600
Units completed and transferred out	153,700
Ending work in process:	
Units in process	400
Completion with respect to materials	75%
Completion with respect to conversion	20%

Required:

MediSecure uses the FIFO method in its process costing system. Compute the equivalent units of production for the period for the Molding Department.

EXERCISE 4A–6 Equivalent Units—FIFO Method [LO4–6]

Refer to the data for Alaskan Fisheries, Inc., in Exercise 4–10.

Required:

Compute the equivalent units for July for the Cleaning Department assuming that the company uses the FIFO method of accounting for units.

EXERCISE 4A–7 Equivalent Units and Cost per Equivalent Unit—FIFO Method [LO4–6, LO4–7]

Refer to the data for Pureform, Inc., in Exercise 4–9.

Required:

Assume that the company uses the FIFO method of accounting for units and costs.
1. Compute the equivalent units for the month for the first processing department.
2. Determine the costs per equivalent unit for the month.

EXERCISE 4A–8 Equivalent Units—FIFO Method [LO4–6]

Refer to the data for Hielta Oy in Exercise 4–6. Assume that the company uses the FIFO method in its process costing system.

Required:

1. Compute the number of tons of pulp completed and transferred out during June.
2. Compute the equivalent units of production for materials and for labor and overhead for June.

Chapter 4

EXERCISE 4A–9 Equivalent Units; Applying Costs—FIFO Method [LO4–6, LO4–7, LO4–8]
Jarvene Corporation uses the FIFO method in its process costing system. The following data are for the most recent month of operations in one of the company's processing departments:

Units in beginning inventory	400
Units started into production	3,000
Units in ending inventory	300
Units transferred to the next department	3,100

	Materials	Conversion
Percentage completion of beginning inventory	80%	40%
Percentage completion of ending inventory	70%	60%

The cost of beginning inventory according to the company's costing system was $11,040 of which $8,120 was for materials and the remainder was for conversion cost. The costs added during the month amounted to $132,730. The costs per equivalent unit for the month were:

	Materials	Conversion
Cost per equivalent unit	$25.40	$18.20

Required:
1. Compute the total cost per equivalent unit for the month.
2. Compute the equivalent units of material and of conversion in the ending inventory.
3. Compute the equivalent units of material and of conversion that were required to complete the beginning inventory.
4. Determine the number of units started and completed during the month.
5. Determine the costs of ending inventory and units transferred out.

PROBLEM 4A–10 Equivalent Units; Applying Costs; Cost Reconciliation Report—FIFO Method [LO4–6, LO4–7, LO4–8, LO4–9]
Selzik Company makes super-premium cake mixes that go through two processing departments, Blending and Packaging. The following activity was recorded in the Blending Department during July:

Production data:	
Units in process, July 1 (materials 100% complete; conversion 30% complete) ...	10,000
Units started into production	170,000
Units in process, July 31 (materials 100% complete; conversion 40% complete) ...	20,000
Cost data:	
Work in process inventory, July 1:	
Materials cost	$8,500
Conversion cost	$4,900
Cost added during the month:	
Materials cost	$139,400
Conversion cost	$244,200

All materials are added at the beginning of work in the Blending Department. The company uses the FIFO method in its process costing system.

Required:
1. Determine the equivalent units for July for the Blending Department.
2. Compute the costs per equivalent unit for July for the Blending Department.
3. Determine the total cost of ending work in process inventory and the total cost of units transferred to the next process for the Blending Department in July.
4. Prepare a cost reconciliation report for the Blending Department for July.

PROBLEM 4A–11 Equivalent Units; Cost per Equivalent Unit; Applying Costs—FIFO Method [LO4–6, LO4–7, LO4–8, LO4–9]
Refer to the data for the Blending Department of Sunspots Beverages, Ltd., in Problem 4–15. Assume that the company uses the FIFO method rather than the weighted-average method in its process costing system.

Required:
1. Determine the equivalent units for June for the Blending Department.
2. Compute the costs per equivalent unit for June for the Blending Department.
3. Determine the total cost of ending work in process inventory and the total cost of units transferred to the next process for the Blending Department in June.
4. Prepare a cost reconciliation report for the Blending Department for June.

CASE 4A–12 Second Department—FIFO Method [LO4–6, LO4–7, LO4–8]
Refer to the data for Provost Industries in Case 4–19. Assume that the company uses the FIFO method in its process costing system.

Required:
1. Prepare a report for the Finishing Department for April showing how much cost should have been assigned to the units completed and transferred to finished goods and how much cost should have been assigned to the ending work in process inventory.
2. As stated in the case, the company experienced an increase in materials prices during April. Would the effects of this price increase tend to show up more under the weighted-average method or under the FIFO method? Why?

Appendix 4B: Service Department Allocations

Most large organizations have both *operating departments* and *service departments*. The central purposes of the organization are carried out in the operating departments. In contrast, service departments do not directly engage in operating activities. Instead, they provide services or assistance to the operating departments. Examples of operating departments include the Surgery Department at Mt. Sinai Hospital, the Geography Department at the University of Washington, the Marketing Department at Allstate Insurance Company, and production departments at manufacturers such as Mitsubishi, Hewlett-Packard, and Michelin. In process costing, the processing departments are all operating departments. Examples of service departments include Cafeteria, Internal Auditing, Human Resources, Cost Accounting, and Purchasing.

The overhead costs of operating departments commonly include allocations of costs from the service departments. To the extent that service department costs are classified as production costs, they should be included in unit product costs and thus, must be allocated to operating departments in a process costing system.

Three approaches are used to allocate the costs of service departments to other departments: the direct method, the step-down method, and the reciprocal method. These three methods are discussed in the following sections. However, before getting into the details of these methods, we will discuss *interdepartmental services*.

Interdepartmental Services

Many service departments provide services to each other, as well as to operating departments. For example, the Cafeteria Department provides meals for all employees, including those assigned to other service departments, as well as to employees of the operating departments. In turn, the Cafeteria Department may receive services from other service departments, such as from Custodial Services or from Personnel. Services provided between service departments are known as *interdepartmental* or *reciprocal services*.

180

Chapter 4

Direct Method

LO4–10

Allocate service department
costs to operating departments
using the direct method.

The *direct method* is the simplest of the three cost allocation methods. It ignores the services provided by a service department to other service departments (e.g., interdepartmental services) and allocates all service department costs directly to operating departments. Even if a service department (such as Personnel) provides a large amount of service to another service department (such as the cafeteria), no allocations are made between the two departments. Rather, all costs are allocated *directly* to the operating departments, bypassing the other service departments; hence, the term *direct method.*

For an example of the direct method, consider Mountain View Hospital, which has two service departments and two operating departments as shown below. The hospital allocates its Hospital Administration costs on the basis of employee-hours and its Custodial Services costs on the basis of square feet occupied.

	Service Departments		Operating Departments		
	Hospital Administration	Custodial Services	Laboratory	Patient Care	Total
Departmental costs before allocation	$360,000	$90,000	$261,000	$689,000	$1,400,000
Employee hours ...	12,000	6,000	18,000	30,000	66,000
Space occupied— square feet	10,000	200	5,000	45,000	60,200

The direct method of allocating the hospital's service department costs to the operating departments is shown in Exhibit 4B–1. Several things should be noted in this exhibit. First, the employee-hours of the Hospital Administration Department and the Custodial Services Department are ignored when allocating the costs of Hospital Administration using the direct method. *Under the direct method, any of the allocation base attributable to the service departments themselves is ignored; only the amount of the allocation base attributable to the operating departments is used in the allocation.* Note that the same rule is used when allocating the costs of the Custodial Services Department. Even though the Hospital Administration and Custodial Services departments occupy some space, this is ignored when the Custodial Services costs are allocated. Finally, note that after all allocations have been completed, all of the service department costs are contained in the two operating departments.

EXHIBIT 4B–1
Direct Method of Allocation

	Service Departments		Operating Departments		
	Hospital Administration	Custodial Services	Laboratory	Patient Care	Total
Departmental costs before allocation	$360,000	$90,000	$261,000	$689,000	$1,400,000
Allocation:					
Hospital Administration costs ($^{18}/_{48}$, $^{30}/_{48}$)*	(360,000)		135,000	225,000	
Custodial Services costs ($^{5}/_{50}$, $^{45}/_{50}$)†		(90,000)	9,000	81,000	
Total cost after allocation	$ 0	$ 0	$405,000	$995,000	$1,400,000

———
*Based on the employee-hours in the two operating departments, which are 18,000 hours + 30,000 hours = 48,000 hours.
†Based on the square feet occupied by the two operating departments, which is 5,000 square feet + 45,000 square feet = 50,000 square feet.

Although the direct method is simple, it is less accurate than the other methods because it ignores interdepartmental services.

Step-Down Method

LO4–11
Allocate service department costs to operating departments using the step-down method.

Unlike the direct method, the *step-down method* provides for allocation of a service department's costs to other service departments, as well as to operating departments. The step-down method is sequential. The sequence typically begins with the department that provides the greatest amount of service to other service departments. After its costs have been allocated, the process continues, step by step, ending with the department that provides the least amount of services to other service departments. This step procedure is illustrated in Exhibit 4B–2.

Exhibit 4B–3 shows the details of the step-down method. Note the following three key points about these allocations. First, under Allocation in Exhibit 4B–3, you see two allocations, or steps. In the first step, the costs of Hospital Administration are allocated

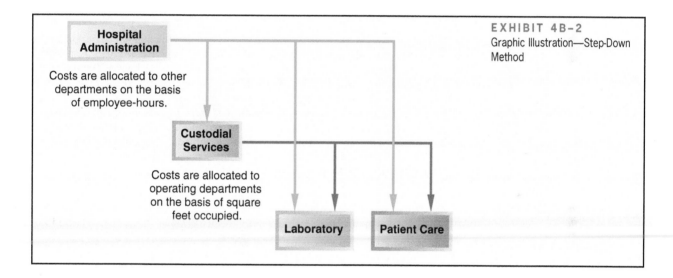

EXHIBIT 4B–2
Graphic Illustration—Step-Down Method

Hospital Administration

Costs are allocated to other departments on the basis of employee-hours.

Custodial Services

Costs are allocated to operating departments on the basis of square feet occupied.

Laboratory   **Patient Care**

EXHIBIT 4B–3
Step-Down Method of Allocation

	Service Departments		Operating Departments		
	Hospital Administration	Custodial Services	Laboratory	Patient Care	Total
Departmental costs before allocation	$360,000	$ 90,000	$261,000	$ 689,000	$1,400,000
Allocation:					
Hospital Administration costs ($6/54$, $18/54$, $30/54$)* ..	(360,000)	40,000	120,000	200,000	
Custodial Services costs ($5/50$, $45/50$)†		(130,000)	13,000	117,000	
Total cost after allocation	$ 0	$ 0	$394,000	$1,006,000	$1,400,000

*Based on the employee-hours in Custodial Services and the two operating departments, which are 6,000 hours + 18,000 hours + 30,000 hours = 54,000 hours.
  As in Exhibit 4B–1, this allocation is based on the square feet occupied by the two operating departments.

182

Chapter 4

to another service department (Custodial Services) as well as to the operating departments. In contrast to the direct method, the allocation base for Hospital Administration costs now includes the employee-hours for Custodial Services as well as for the operating departments. However, the allocation base still excludes the employee-hours for Hospital Administration itself. *In both the direct and step-down methods, any amount of the allocation base attributable to the service department whose cost is being allocated is always ignored.* Second, looking again at Exhibit 4B–3, note that in the second step under the Allocation heading, the cost of Custodial Services is allocated to the two operating departments, and none of the cost is allocated to Hospital Administration even though Hospital Administration occupies space in the building. *In the step-down method, any amount of the allocation base that is attributable to a service department whose cost has already been allocated is ignored.* After a service department's costs have been allocated, costs of other service departments are not reallocated back to it. Third, note that the cost of Custodial Services allocated to other departments in the second step ($130,000) in Exhibit 4B–3 includes the costs of Hospital Administration that were allocated to Custodial Services in the first step in Exhibit 4B–3.

Reciprocal Method

The *reciprocal method* gives full recognition to interdepartmental services. Under the step-down method only partial recognition of interdepartmental services is possible. The step-down method always allocates costs forward—never backward. The reciprocal method, by contrast, allocates service department costs in *both* directions. Thus, because Custodial Services in the prior example provides services for Hospital Administration, part of Custodial Services' costs will be allocated *back* to Hospital Administration if the reciprocal method is used. At the same time, part of Hospital Administration's costs will be allocated *forward* to Custodial Services. Reciprocal allocation requires the use of simultaneous linear equations and is beyond the scope of this book. Examples of the reciprocal method can be found in more advanced cost accounting texts.

Appendix 4B Exercises and Problems

All applicable exercises and problems are available with McGraw-Hill's *Connect*® *Accounting*.

EXERCISE 4B–1 Direct Method [LO4–10]
Seattle Western University has provided the following data to be used in its service department cost allocations:

	Service Departments		Operating Departments	
	Administration	Facility Services	Undergraduate Programs	Graduate Programs
Departmental costs before allocations	$2,400,000	$1,600,000	$26,800,000	$5,700,000
Student credit-hours			20,000	5,000
Space occupied—square feet	25,000	10,000	70,000	30,000

Required:
Using the direct method, allocate the costs of the service departments to the two operating departments. Allocate the costs of Administration on the basis of student credit-hours and Facility Services costs on the basis of space occupied.

Process Costing **183**

EXERCISE 4B–2 Step-Down Method [LO4–11]

Madison Park Co-op, a whole foods grocery and gift shop, has provided the following data to be used in its service department cost allocations:

	Service Departments		Operating Departments	
	Administration	Janitorial	Groceries	Gifts
Departmental costs before allocations ...	$150,000	$40,000	$2,320,000	$950,000
Employee-hours	320	160	3,100	740
Space occupied—square feet	250	100	4,000	1,000

Required:

Using the step-down method, allocate the costs of the service departments to the two operating departments. Allocate Administration first on the basis of employee-hours and then Janitorial on the basis of space occupied.

EXERCISE 4B–3 Step-Down Method [LO4–11]

The Ferre Publishing Company has three service departments and two operating departments. Selected data from a recent period on the five departments follow:

	Service Departments			Operating Departments		
	Administration	Janitorial	Maintenance	Binding	Printing	Total
Costs	$140,000	$105,000	$48,000	$275,000	$430,000	$998,000
Number of employees	60	35	140	315	210	760
Square feet of space occupied	15,000	10,000	20,000	40,000	100,000	185,000
Hours of press time				30,000	60,000	90,000

The company allocates service department costs by the step-down method in the following order: Administration (number of employees), Janitorial (space occupied), and Maintenance (hours of press time).

Required:

Using the step-down method, allocate the service department costs to the operating departments.

EXERCISE 4B–4 Direct Method [LO4–10]

Refer to the data for the Ferre Publishing Company in Exercise 4B–3.

Required:

Assuming that the company uses the direct method rather than the step-down method to allocate service department costs, how much cost would be assigned to each operating department?

PROBLEM 4B–5 Step-Down Method [LO4–11]

Woodbury Hospital has three service departments and three operating departments. Estimated cost and operating data for all departments in the hospital for the forthcoming quarter are presented in the table below:

	Service Departments			Operating Departments			
	Housekeeping Services	Food Services	Admin. Services	Laboratory	Radiology	General Hospital	Total
Variable costs	$ 0	$193,860	$158,840	$243,600	$304,800	$ 74,500	$ 975,600
Fixed costs	87,000	107,200	90,180	162,300	215,700	401,300	1,063,680
Total cost	$87,000	$301,060	$249,020	$405,900	$520,500	$475,800	$2,039,280
Meals served			800	2,000	1,000	68,000	71,800
Percentage of peak-period needs—Food Services			0.8%	2.4%	1.6%	95.2%	100%
Square feet of space	5,000	13,000	6,500	10,000	7,500	108,000	150,000
Files processed				14,000	7,000	25,000	46,000
Percentage of peak-period needs—Admin. Services				30%	20%	50%	100%

Chapter 4

The costs of the service departments are allocated by the step-down method using the allocation bases and in the order shown in the following table:

Service Department	Costs Incurred	Allocation Bases
Housekeeping Services	Fixed	Square feet of space
Food Services	Variable	Meals served
	Fixed	Peak-period needs—Food Services
Administrative Services	Variable	Files processed
	Fixed	Peak-period needs—Admin. Services

All billing in the hospital is done through Laboratory, Radiology, or General Hospital. The hospital's administrator wants the costs of the three service departments allocated to these three billing centers.

Required:
Using the step-down method, prepare the cost allocation desired by the hospital administrator. Include under each billing center the direct costs of the center, as well as the costs allocated from the service departments.

PROBLEM 4B–6 Step-Down Method versus Direct Method; Predetermined Overhead Rates [LO4–10, LO4–11]
The Sendai Co., Ltd., of Japan has budgeted costs in its various departments as follows for the coming year:

Factory Administration	$270,000
Custodial Services	68,760
Personnel	28,840
Maintenance	45,200
Machining—overhead	376,300
Assembly—overhead	175,900
Total cost	$965,000

The company allocates service department costs to other departments in the order listed below.

Department	Number of Employees	Total Labor-Hours	Square Feet of Space Occupied	Direct Labor-Hours	Machine-Hours
Factory Administration	12	—	5,000	—	—
Custodial Services	4	3,000	2,000	—	—
Personnel	5	5,000	3,000	—	—
Maintenance	25	22,000	10,000	—	—
Machining	40	30,000	70,000	20,000	70,000
Assembly	60	90,000	20,000	80,000	10,000
	146	150,000	110,000	100,000	80,000

Machining and Assembly are operating departments; the other departments are service departments. Factory Administration is allocated on the basis of labor-hours; Custodial Services on the basis of square feet occupied; Personnel on the basis of number of employees; and Maintenance on the basis of machine-hours.

Required:
1. Allocate service department costs to consuming departments by the step-down method. Then compute predetermined overhead rates in the operating departments using a machine-hours basis in Machining and a direct labor-hours basis in Assembly.

2. Repeat (1) above, this time using the direct method. Again compute predetermined overhead rates in Machining and Assembly.
3. Assume that the company doesn't bother with allocating service department costs but simply computes a single plantwide overhead rate based on total overhead costs (both service department and operating department costs) divided by total direct labor-hours. Compute the plantwide overhead rate.
4. Suppose a job requires machine and labor time as follows:

	Machine-Hours	Direct Labor-Hours
Machining Department	190	25
Assembly Department	10	75
Total hours	200	100

Using the overhead rates computed in (1), (2), and (3) above, compute the amount of overhead cost that would be assigned to the job if the overhead rates were developed using the step-down method, the direct method, and the plantwide method.

CASE 4B–7 Step-Down Method versus Direct Method [LO4–10, LO4–11]

"This is really an odd situation," said Jim Carter, general manager of Highland Publishing Company. "We get most of the jobs we bid on that require a lot of press time in the Printing Department, yet profits on those jobs are never as high as they ought to be. On the other hand, we lose most of the jobs we bid on that require a lot of time in the Binding Department. I would be inclined to think that the problem is with our overhead rates, but we're already computing separate overhead rates for each department. So what else could be wrong?"

Highland Publishing Company is a large organization that offers a variety of printing and binding work. The Printing and Binding departments are supported by three service departments. The costs of these service departments are allocated to other departments in the order listed below. (For each service department, use the allocation base that provides the best measure of service provided, as discussed in the chapter.)

Department	Total Labor-Hours	Square Feet of Space Occupied	Number of Employees	Machine-Hours	Direct Labor-Hours
Personnel	20,000	4,000	10		
Custodial Services ...	30,000	6,000	15		
Maintenance	50,000	20,000	25		
Printing	90,000	80,000	40	150,000	60,000
Binding	260,000	40,000	120	30,000	175,000
	450,000	150,000	210	180,000	235,000

Budgeted overhead costs in each department for the current year are shown below:

Personnel	$ 360,000
Custodial Services	141,000
Maintenance	201,000
Printing	525,000
Binding	373,500
Total budgeted cost	$1,600,500

Because of its simplicity, the company has always used the direct method to allocate service department costs to the two operating departments.

Chapter 4

Required:

1. Using the step-down method, allocate the service department costs to the consuming departments. Then compute predetermined overhead rates for the current year using machine-hours as the allocation base in the Printing Department and direct labor-hours as the allocation base in the Binding Department.
2. Repeat (1) above, this time using the direct method. Again compute predetermined overhead rates in the Printing and Binding departments.
3. Assume that during the current year the company bids on a job that requires machine and labor time as follows:

	Machine-Hours	Direct Labor-Hours
Printing Department	15,400	900
Binding Department	800	2,000
Total hours	16,200	2,900

a. Determine the amount of overhead cost that would be assigned to the job if the company used the overhead rates developed in (1) above. Then determine the amount of overhead cost that would be assigned to the job if the company used the overhead rates developed in (2) above.
b. Explain to Mr. Carter, the general manager, why the step-down method provides a better basis for computing predetermined overhead rates than the direct method.

CHAPTER 5

Cost-Volume-Profit Relationships

Moreno Turns Around the Los Angeles Angels

When Arturo Moreno bought Major League Baseball's Los Angeles Angels in 2003, the team was drawing 2.3 million fans and losing $5.5 million per year. Moreno immediately cut prices to attract more fans and increase profits. In his first spring training game, he reduced the price of selected tickets from $12 to $6. By increasing attendance, Moreno understood that he would sell more food and souvenirs. He dropped the price of draft beer by $2 and cut the price of baseball caps from $20 to $7.

The Angels now consistently draw about 3.4 million fans per year. This growth in attendance helped double stadium sponsorship revenue to $26 million, and it motivated the Fox Sports Network to pay the Angels $500 million to broadcast all of its games for the next ten years. Since Moreno bought the Angels, annual revenues have jumped from $127 million to $212 million, and the team's operating loss of $5.5 million has been transformed to a profit of $10.3 million. ■

Source: Matthew Craft, "Moreno's Math," Forbes, May 11, 2009, pp. 84–87.

LEARNING OBJECTIVES

After studying Chapter 5, you should be able to:

LO5–1 Explain how changes in activity affect contribution margin and net operating income.

LO5–2 Prepare and interpret a cost-volume-profit (CVP) graph and a profit graph.

LO5–3 Use the contribution margin ratio (CM ratio) to compute changes in contribution margin and net operating income resulting from changes in sales volume.

LO5–4 Show the effects on net operating income of changes in variable costs, fixed costs, selling price, and volume.

LO5–5 Determine the break-even point.

LO5–6 Determine the level of sales needed to achieve a desired target profit.

LO5–7 Compute the margin of safety and explain its significance.

LO5–8 Compute the degree of operating leverage at a particular level of sales and explain how it can be used to predict changes in net operating income.

LO5–9 Compute the break-even point for a multiproduct company and explain the effects of shifts in the sales mix on contribution margin and the break-even point.

Chapter 5

Cost-volume-profit (CVP) analysis helps managers make many important decisions such as what products and services to offer, what prices to charge, what marketing strategy to use, and what cost structure to maintain. Its primary purpose is to estimate how profits are affected by the following five factors:

1. Selling prices.
2. Sales volume.
3. Unit variable costs.
4. Total fixed costs.
5. Mix of products sold.

To simplify CVP calculations, managers typically adopt the following assumptions with respect to these factors[1]:

1. Selling price is constant. The price of a product or service will not change as volume changes.
2. Costs are linear and can be accurately divided into variable and fixed elements. The variable element is constant per unit. The fixed element is constant in total over the entire relevant range.
3. In multiproduct companies, the mix of products sold remains constant.

While these assumptions may be violated in practice, the results of CVP analysis are often "good enough" to be quite useful. Perhaps the greatest danger lies in relying on simple CVP analysis when a manager is contemplating a large change in sales volume that lies outside the relevant range. However, even in these situations the CVP model can be adjusted to take into account anticipated changes in selling prices, variable costs per unit, total fixed costs, and the sales mix that arise when the estimated sales volume falls outside the relevant range.

To help explain the role of CVP analysis in business decisions, we'll now turn our attention to the case of Acoustic Concepts, Inc., a company founded by Prem Narayan.

MANAGERIAL ACCOUNTING IN ACTION
THE ISSUE

ACOUSTIC
concepts
inc

Prem, who was a graduate student in engineering at the time, started Acoustic Concepts to market a radical new speaker he had designed for automobile sound systems. The speaker, called the Sonic Blaster, uses an advanced microprocessor and proprietary software to boost amplification to awesome levels. Prem contracted with a Taiwanese electronics manufacturer to produce the speaker. With seed money provided by his family, Prem placed an order with the manufacturer and ran advertisements in auto magazines.

The Sonic Blaster was an immediate success, and sales grew to the point that Prem moved the company's headquarters out of his apartment and into rented quarters in a nearby industrial park. He also hired a receptionist, an accountant, a sales manager, and a small sales staff to sell the speakers to retail stores. The accountant, Bob Luchinni, had worked for several small companies where he had acted as a business advisor as well as accountant and bookkeeper. The following discussion occurred soon after Bob was hired:

Prem: Bob, I've got a lot of questions about the company's finances that I hope you can help answer.

Bob: We're in great shape. The loan from your family will be paid off within a few months.

Prem: I know, but I am worried about the risks I've taken on by expanding operations. What would happen if a competitor entered the market and our sales slipped? How far could sales drop without putting us into the red? Another question I've been trying to resolve is how much our sales would have to increase to justify the big marketing campaign the sales staff is pushing for.

Bob: Marketing always wants more money for advertising.

---

[1] One additional assumption often used in manufacturing companies is that inventories do not change. The number of units produced equals the number of units sold.

Prem: And they are always pushing me to drop the selling price on the speaker. I agree with them that a lower price will boost our sales volume, but I'm not sure the increased volume will offset the loss in revenue from the lower price.

Bob: It sounds like these questions are all related in some way to the relationships among our selling prices, our costs, and our volume. I shouldn't have a problem coming up with some answers.

Prem: Can we meet again in a couple of days to see what you have come up with?

Bob: Sounds good. By then I'll have some preliminary answers for you as well as a model you can use for answering similar questions in the future.

The Basics of Cost-Volume-Profit (CVP) Analysis

Bob Luchinni's preparation for his forthcoming meeting with Prem begins with the contribution income statement. The contribution income statement emphasizes the behavior of costs and therefore is extremely helpful to managers in judging the impact on profits of changes in selling price, cost, or volume. Bob will base his analysis on the following contribution income statement he prepared last month:

	Total	Per Unit
Acoustic Concepts, Inc. Contribution Income Statement For the Month of June		
Sales (400 speakers)	$100,000	$250
Variable expenses	60,000	150
Contribution margin	40,000	$100
Fixed expenses	35,000	
Net operating income	$ 5,000	

Notice that sales, variable expenses, and contribution margin are expressed on a per unit basis as well as in total on this contribution income statement. The per unit figures will be very helpful to Bob in some of his calculations. Note that this contribution income statement has been prepared for management's use inside the company and would not ordinarily be made available to those outside the company.

Contribution Margin

Contribution margin is the amount remaining from sales revenue after variable expenses have been deducted. Thus, it is the amount available to cover fixed expenses and then to provide profits for the period. Notice the sequence here—contribution margin is used *first* to cover the fixed expenses, and then whatever remains goes toward profits. If the contribution margin is not sufficient to cover the fixed expenses, then a loss occurs for the period. To illustrate with an extreme example, assume that Acoustic Concepts sells only one speaker during a particular month. The company's income statement would appear as follows:

LO5–1
Explain how changes in activity affect contribution margin and net operating income.

	Total	Per Unit
Contribution Income Statement Sales of 1 Speaker		
Sales (1 speaker)	$ 250	$250
Variable expenses	150	150
Contribution margin	100	$100
Fixed expenses	35,000	
Net operating loss	$(34,900)	

For each additional speaker the company sells during the month, $100 more in contribution margin becomes available to help cover the fixed expenses. If a second speaker is sold, for example, then the total contribution margin will increase by $100 (to a total of $200) and the company's loss will decrease by $100, to $34,800:

Contribution Income Statement
Sales of 2 Speakers

	Total	Per Unit
Sales (2 speakers)	$ 500	$250
Variable expenses	300	150
Contribution margin	200	$100
Fixed expenses	35,000	
Net operating loss	$(34,800)	

If enough speakers can be sold to generate $35,000 in contribution margin, then all of the fixed expenses will be covered and the company will *break even* for the month—that is, it will show neither profit nor loss but just cover all of its costs. To reach the break-even point, the company will have to sell 350 speakers in a month because each speaker sold yields $100 in contribution margin:

Contribution Income Statement
Sales of 350 Speakers

	Total	Per Unit
Sales (350 speakers)	$87,500	$250
Variable expenses	52,500	150
Contribution margin	35,000	$100
Fixed expenses	35,000	
Net operating income	$ 0	

Computation of the break-even point is discussed in detail later in the chapter; for the moment, note that the **break-even point** is the level of sales at which profit is zero.

Once the break-even point has been reached, net operating income will increase by the amount of the unit contribution margin for each additional unit sold. For example, if 351 speakers are sold in a month, then the net operating income for the month will be $100 because the company will have sold 1 speaker more than the number needed to break even:

Contribution Income Statement
Sales of 351 Speakers

	Total	Per Unit
Sales (351 speakers)	$87,750	$250
Variable expenses	52,650	150
Contribution margin	35,100	$100
Fixed expenses	35,000	
Net operating income	$ 100	

If 352 speakers are sold (2 speakers above the break-even point), the net operating income for the month will be $200. If 353 speakers are sold (3 speakers above the break-even point), the net operating income for the month will be $300, and so forth. To estimate the profit at any sales volume above the break-even point, multiply the number of units sold in excess of the break-even point by the unit contribution margin. The result represents the anticipated profits for the period. Or, to estimate the effect of a planned increase in sales on profits, simply multiply the increase in units sold by the unit contribution margin. The result will be the expected increase in profits. To illustrate, if Acoustic Concepts is currently selling 400 speakers per month and plans to increase sales to 425 speakers per month, the anticipated impact on profits can be computed as follows:

Increased number of speakers to be sold	25
Contribution margin per speaker	× $100
Increase in net operating income	$ 2,500

These calculations can be verified as follows:

	Sales Volume 400 Speakers	425 Speakers	Difference (25 Speakers)	Per Unit
Sales (@ $250 per speaker)	$100,000	$106,250	$6,250	$250
Variable expenses (@ $150 per speaker)	60,000	63,750	3,750	150
Contribution margin	40,000	42,500	2,500	$100
Fixed expenses	35,000	35,000	0	
Net operating income	$ 5,000	$ 7,500	$2,500	

To summarize, if sales are zero, the company's loss would equal its fixed expenses. Each unit that is sold reduces the loss by the amount of the unit contribution margin. Once the break-even point has been reached, each additional unit sold increases the company's profit by the amount of the unit contribution margin.

CVP Relationships in Equation Form

The contribution format income statement can be expressed in equation form as follows:

$$\text{Profit} = (\text{Sales} - \text{Variable expenses}) - \text{Fixed expenses}$$

For brevity, we use the term *profit* to stand for net operating income in equations.

When a company has only a *single* product, as at Acoustic Concepts, we can further refine the equation as follows:

$$\text{Sales} = \text{Selling price per unit} \times \text{Quantity sold} = P \times Q$$

$$\text{Variable expenses} = \text{Variable expenses per unit} \times \text{Quantity sold} = V \times Q$$

$$\text{Profit} = (P \times Q - V \times Q) - \text{Fixed expenses}$$

We can do all of the calculations of the previous section using this simple equation. For example, on the previous page we computed that the net operating income (profit) at sales of 351 speakers would be $100. We can arrive at the same conclusion using the above equation as follows:

$$\text{Profit} = (P \times Q - V \times Q) - \text{Fixed expenses}$$

$$\text{Profit} = (\$250 \times 351 - \$150 \times 351) - \$35,000$$

$$= (\$250 - \$150) \times 351 - \$35,000$$

$$= (\$100) \times 351 - \$35,000$$

$$= \$35,100 - \$35,000 = \$100$$

192

Chapter 5

It is often useful to express the simple profit equation in terms of the unit contribution margin (Unit CM) as follows:

Unit CM = Selling price per unit − Variable expenses per unit = $P - V$

Profit = $(P \times Q - V \times Q)$ − Fixed expenses

Profit = $(P - V) \times Q$ − Fixed expenses

Profit = Unit CM $\times Q$ − Fixed expenses

We could also have used this equation to determine the profit at sales of 351 speakers as follows:

$$\text{Profit} = \text{Unit CM} \times Q - \text{Fixed expenses}$$

$$= \$100 \times 351 - \$35,000$$

$$= \$35,100 - \$35,000 = \$100$$

For those who are comfortable with algebra, the quickest and easiest approach to solving the problems in this chapter may be to use the simple profit equation in one of its forms.

CVP Relationships in Graphic Form

LO5–2

Prepare and interpret a cost-volume-profit (CVP) graph and a profit graph.

The relationships among revenue, cost, profit, and volume are illustrated on a **cost-volume-profit (CVP) graph**. A CVP graph highlights CVP relationships over wide ranges of activity. To help explain his analysis to Prem Narayan, Bob Luchinni prepared a CVP graph for Acoustic Concepts.

Preparing the CVP Graph In a CVP graph (sometimes called a *break-even chart*), unit volume is represented on the horizontal (X) axis and dollars on the vertical (Y) axis. Preparing a CVP graph involves the three steps depicted in Exhibit 5–1:

1. Draw a line parallel to the volume axis to represent total fixed expense. For Acoustic Concepts, total fixed expenses are $35,000.
2. Choose some volume of unit sales and plot the point representing total expense (fixed and variable) at the sales volume you have selected. In Exhibit 5–1, Bob Luchinni chose a volume of 600 speakers. Total expense at that sales volume is:

Fixed expense	$ 35,000
Variable expense (600 speakers × $150 per speaker)	90,000
Total expense	$125,000

After the point has been plotted, draw a line through it back to the point where the fixed expense line intersects the dollars axis.
3. Again choose some sales volume and plot the point representing total sales dollars at the activity level you have selected. In Exhibit 5–1, Bob Luchinni again chose a volume of 600 speakers. Sales at that volume total $150,000 (600 speakers × $250 per speaker). Draw a line through this point back to the origin.

The interpretation of the completed CVP graph is given in Exhibit 5–2. The anticipated profit or loss at any given level of sales is measured by the vertical distance between the total revenue line (sales) and the total expense line (variable expense plus fixed expense).

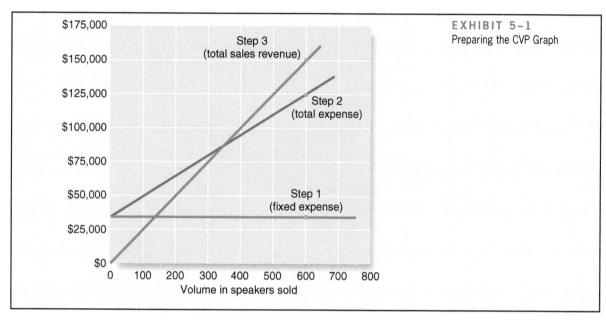

EXHIBIT 5–1
Preparing the CVP Graph

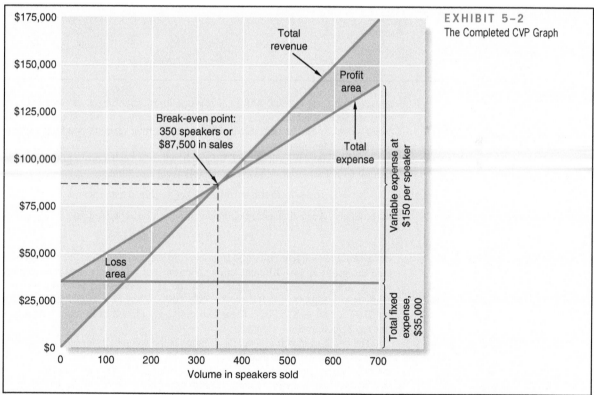

EXHIBIT 5–2
The Completed CVP Graph

The break-even point is where the total revenue and total expense lines cross. The break-even point of 350 speakers in Exhibit 5–2 agrees with the break-even point computed earlier.

As discussed earlier, when sales are below the break-even point—in this case, 350 units—the company suffers a loss. Note that the loss (represented by the vertical distance

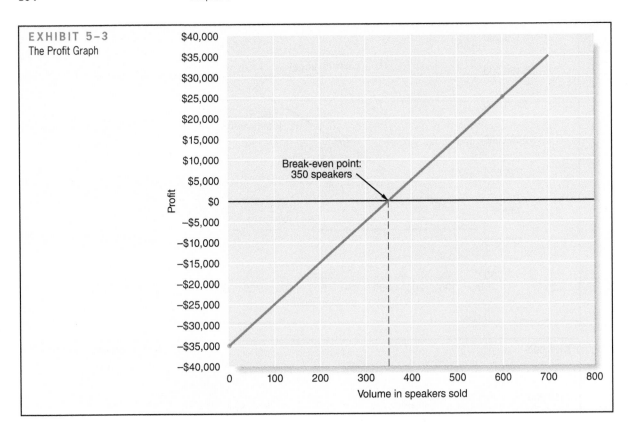

EXHIBIT 5–3
The Profit Graph

between the total expense and total revenue lines) gets bigger as sales decline. When sales are above the break-even point, the company earns a profit and the size of the profit (represented by the vertical distance between the total revenue and total expense lines) increases as sales increase.

An even simpler form of the CVP graph, which we call a profit graph, is presented in Exhibit 5–3. That graph is based on the following equation:

$$\text{Profit} = \text{Unit CM} \times Q - \text{Fixed expenses}$$

In the case of Acoustic Concepts, the equation can be expressed as:

$$\text{Profit} = \$100 \times Q - \$35,000$$

Because this is a linear equation, it plots as a single straight line. To plot the line, compute the profit at two different sales volumes, plot the points, and then connect them with a straight line. For example, when the sales volume is zero (i.e., $Q = 0$), the profit is $- \$35,000$ (= $\$100 \times 0 - \$35,000$). When Q is 600, the profit is $\$25,000$ (= $\$100 \times 600 - \$35,000$). These two points are plotted in Exhibit 5–3 and a straight line has been drawn through them.

The break-even point on the profit graph is the volume of sales at which profit is zero and is indicated by the dashed line on the graph. Note that the profit steadily increases to the right of the break-even point as the sales volume increases and that the loss becomes steadily worse to the left of the break-even point as the sales volume decreases.

LO5–3

Use the contribution margin ratio (CM ratio) to compute changes in contribution margin and net operating income resulting from changes in sales volume.

Contribution Margin Ratio (CM Ratio)

In the previous section, we explored how cost-volume-profit relationships can be visualized. In this section, we show how the *contribution margin ratio* can be used in cost-volume-profit calculations. As the first step, we have added a column to Acoustic Concepts' contribution format income statement in which sales revenues, variable expenses, and contribution margin are expressed as a percentage of sales:

	Total	Per Unit	Percent of Sales
Sales (400 speakers)	$100,000	$250	100%
Variable expenses	60,000	150	60%
Contribution margin	40,000	$100	40%
Fixed expenses	35,000		
Net operating income	$ 5,000		

The contribution margin as a percentage of sales is referred to as the **contribution margin ratio (CM ratio)**. This ratio is computed as follows:

$$\text{CM ratio} = \frac{\text{Contribution margin}}{\text{Sales}}$$

For Acoustic Concepts, the computations are:

$$\text{CM ratio} = \frac{\text{Total contribution margin}}{\text{Total sales}} = \frac{\$40,000}{\$100,000} = 40\%$$

In a company such as Acoustic Concepts that has only one product, the CM ratio can also be computed on a per unit basis as follows:

$$\text{CM ratio} = \frac{\text{Unit contribution margin}}{\text{Unit selling price}} = \frac{\$100}{\$250} = 40\%$$

The CM ratio shows how the contribution margin will be affected by a change in total sales. Acoustic Concepts' CM ratio of 40% means that for each dollar increase in sales, total contribution margin will increase by 40 cents ($1 sales × CM ratio of 40%). Net operating income will also increase by 40 cents, assuming that fixed costs are not affected by the increase in sales. Generally, the effect of a change in sales on the contribution margin is expressed in equation form as:

$$\text{Change in contribution margin} = \text{CM ratio} \times \text{Change in sales}$$

As this illustration suggests, *the impact on net operating income of any given dollar change in total sales can be computed by applying the CM ratio to the dollar change.* For example, if Acoustic Concepts plans a $30,000 increase in sales during the coming month, the contribution margin should increase by $12,000 ($30,000 increase in sales × CM ratio of 40%). As we noted above, net operating income will also increase by $12,000 if fixed costs do not change. This is verified by the following table:

	Sales Volume			Percent of Sales
	Present	Expected	Increase	
Sales	$100,000	$130,000	$30,000	100%
Variable expenses	60,000	78,000*	18,000	60%
Contribution margin	40,000	52,000	12,000	40%
Fixed expenses	35,000	35,000	0	
Net operating income	$ 5,000	$ 17,000	$12,000	

*$130,000 expected sales ÷ $250 per unit = 520 units. 520 units × $150 per unit = $78,000.

Chapter 5

The relation between profit and the CM ratio can also be expressed using the following equations:

$$\text{Profit} = \text{CM ratio} \times \text{Sales} - \text{Fixed expenses}^2$$

or, in terms of changes,

$$\text{Change in profit} = \text{CM ratio} \times \text{Change in sales} - \text{Change in fixed expenses}$$

For example, at sales of $130,000, the profit is expected to be $17,000 as shown below:

$$\text{Profit} = \text{CM ratio} \times \text{Sales} - \text{Fixed expenses}$$
$$= 0.40 \times \$130,000 - \$35,000$$
$$= \$52,000 - \$35,000 = \$17,000$$

Again, if you are comfortable with algebra, this approach will often be quicker and easier than constructing contribution format income statements.

The CM ratio is particularly valuable in situations where the dollar sales of one product must be traded off against the dollar sales of another product. In this situation, products that yield the greatest amount of contribution margin per dollar of sales should be emphasized.

Some Applications of CVP Concepts

LO5–4
Show the effects on net operating income of changes in variable costs, fixed costs, selling price, and volume.

Bob Luchinni, the accountant at Acoustic Concepts, wanted to demonstrate to the company's president Prem Narayan how the concepts developed on the preceding pages can be used in planning and decision making. Bob gathered the following basic data:

	Per Unit	Percent of Sales
Selling price	$250	100%
Variable expenses	150	60%
Contribution margin	$100	40%

Recall that fixed expenses are $35,000 per month. Bob Luchinni will use these data to show the effects of changes in variable costs, fixed costs, sales price, and sales volume on the company's profitability in a variety of situations.

Before proceeding further, however, we need to introduce another concept—the *variable expense ratio*. The **variable expense ratio** is the ratio of variable expenses to sales. It can be computed by dividing the total variable expenses by the total sales, or in a single product analysis, it can be computed by dividing the variable expenses per unit by the unit selling price. In the case of Acoustic Concepts, the variable expense ratio is 0.60; that is, variable expense is 60% of sales. Expressed as an equation, the definition of the variable expense ratio is:

$$\text{Variable expense ratio} = \frac{\text{Variable expenses}}{\text{Sales}}$$

---

[2] This equation can be derived using the basic profit equation and the definition of the CM ratio as follows:

Profit = (Sales − Variable expenses) − Fixed expenses

Profit = Contribution margin − Fixed expenses

Profit = $\dfrac{\text{Contribution margin}}{\text{Sales}} \times \text{Sales} - \text{Fixed expenses}$

Profit = CM ratio × Sales − Fixed expenses

This leads to a useful equation that relates the CM ratio to the variable expense ratio as follows:

$$\text{CM ratio} = \frac{\text{Contribution margin}}{\text{Sales}}$$

$$\text{CM ratio} = \frac{\text{Sales} - \text{Variable expenses}}{\text{Sales}}$$

$$\text{CM ratio} = 1 - \text{Variable expense ratio}$$

Change in Fixed Cost and Sales Volume   Acoustic Concepts is currently selling 400 speakers per month at $250 per speaker for total monthly sales of $100,000. The sales manager feels that a $10,000 increase in the monthly advertising budget would increase monthly sales by $30,000 to a total of 520 units. Should the advertising budget be increased? The table below shows the financial impact of the proposed change in the monthly advertising budget.

	Current Sales	Sales with Additional Advertising Budget	Difference	Percent of Sales
Sales	$100,000	$130,000	$30,000	100%
Variable expenses	60,000	78,000*	18,000	60%
Contribution margin	40,000	52,000	12,000	40%
Fixed expenses	35,000	45,000†	10,000	
Net operating income	$ 5,000	$ 7,000	$ 2,000	

*520 units × $150 per unit = $78,000.
†$35,000 + additional $10,000 monthly advertising budget = $45,000.

Assuming no other factors need to be considered, the increase in the advertising budget should be approved because it would increase net operating income by $2,000. There are two shorter ways to arrive at this solution. The first alternative solution follows:

Alternative Solution 1

Expected total contribution margin:	
$130,000 × 40% CM ratio	$52,000
Present total contribution margin:	
$100,000 × 40% CM ratio	40,000
Increase in total contribution margin	12,000
Change in fixed expenses:	
Less incremental advertising expense	10,000
Increased net operating income	$ 2,000

Because in this case only the fixed costs and the sales volume change, the solution can also be quickly derived as follows:

Alternative Solution 2

Incremental contribution margin:	
$30,000 × 40% CM ratio	$12,000
Less incremental advertising expense	10,000
Increased net operating income	$ 2,000

Notice that this approach does not depend on knowledge of previous sales. Also note that it is unnecessary under either shorter approach to prepare an income statement. Both of the alternative solutions involve **incremental analysis**—they consider only the costs and revenues that will change if the new program is implemented. Although in each case a new income statement could have been prepared, the incremental approach is simpler and more direct and focuses attention on the specific changes that would occur as a result of the decision.

Change in Variable Costs and Sales Volume   Refer to the original data. Recall that Acoustic Concepts is currently selling 400 speakers per month. Prem is considering the use of higher-quality components, which would increase variable costs (and thereby reduce the contribution margin) by $10 per speaker. However, the sales manager predicts that using higher-quality components would increase sales to 480 speakers per month. Should the higher-quality components be used?

The $10 increase in variable costs would decrease the unit contribution margin by $10—from $100 down to $90.

Solution

Expected total contribution margin with higher-quality components:	
480 speakers × $90 per speaker	$43,200
Present total contribution margin:	
400 speakers × $100 per speaker	40,000
Increase in total contribution margin	$ 3,200

According to this analysis, the higher-quality components should be used. Because fixed costs would not change, the $3,200 increase in contribution margin shown above should result in a $3,200 increase in net operating income.

Change in Fixed Cost, Selling Price, and Sales Volume   Refer to the original data and recall again that Acoustic Concepts is currently selling 400 speakers per month. To increase sales, the sales manager would like to cut the selling price by $20 per speaker and increase the advertising budget by $15,000 per month. The sales manager believes that if these two steps are taken, unit sales will increase by 50% to 600 speakers per month. Should the changes be made?

A decrease in the selling price of $20 per speaker would decrease the unit contribution margin by $20 down to $80.

Solution

Expected total contribution margin with lower selling price:	
600 speakers × $80 per speaker	$48,000
Present total contribution margin:	
400 speakers × $100 per speaker	40,000
Incremental contribution margin	8,000
Change in fixed expenses:	
Less incremental advertising expense	15,000
Reduction in net operating income	$ (7,000)

According to this analysis, the changes should not be made. The $7,000 reduction in net operating income that is shown above can be verified by preparing comparative income statements as shown on the next page.

	Present 400 Speakers per Month		Expected 600 Speakers per Month		
	Total	Per Unit	Total	Per Unit	Difference
Sales	$100,000	$250	$138,000	$230	$38,000
Variable expenses	60,000	150	90,000	150	30,000
Contribution margin	40,000	$100	48,000	$ 80	8,000
Fixed expenses	35,000		50,000*		15,000
Net operating income (loss)	$ 5,000		$ (2,000)		$ (7,000)

*35,000 + Additional monthly advertising budget of $15,000 = $50,000.

Change in Variable Cost, Fixed Cost, and Sales Volume

Refer to Acoustic Concepts' original data. As before, the company is currently selling 400 speakers per month. The sales manager would like to pay salespersons a sales commission of $15 per speaker sold, rather than the flat salaries that now total $6,000 per month. The sales manager is confident that the change would increase monthly sales by 15% to 460 speakers per month. Should the change be made?

Solution Changing the sales staff's compensation from salaries to commissions would affect both fixed and variable expenses. Fixed expenses would decrease by $6,000, from $35,000 to $29,000. Variable expenses per unit would increase by $15, from $150 to $165, and the unit contribution margin would decrease from $100 to $85.

Expected total contribution margin with sales staff on commissions:	
460 speakers × $85 per speaker	$39,100
Present total contribution margin:	
400 speakers × $100 per speaker	40,000
Decrease in total contribution margin	(900)
Change in fixed expenses:	
Add salaries avoided if a commission is paid	6,000
Increase in net operating income	$ 5,100

According to this analysis, the changes should be made. Again, the same answer can be obtained by preparing comparative income statements:

	Present 400 Speakers per Month		Expected 460 Speakers per Month		
	Total	Per Unit	Total	Per Unit	Difference
Sales	$100,000	$250	$115,000	$250	$15,000
Variable expenses	60,000	150	75,900	165	15,900
Contribution margin	40,000	$100	39,100	$ 85	900
Fixed expenses	35,000		29,000		(6,000)*
Net operating income	$ 5,000		$ 10,100		$ 5,100

*Note: A *reduction* in fixed expenses has the effect of *increasing* net operating income.

200   Chapter 5

Change in Selling Price

Change in Selling Price   Refer to the original data where Acoustic Concepts is currently selling 400 speakers per month. The company has an opportunity to make a bulk sale of 150 speakers to a wholesaler if an acceptable price can be negotiated. This sale would not disturb the company's regular sales and would not affect the company's total fixed expenses. What price per speaker should be quoted to the wholesaler if Acoustic Concepts is seeking a profit of $3,000 on the bulk sale?

Solution

Variable cost per speaker	$150
Desired profit per speaker:	
$3,000 ÷ 150 speakers	20
Quoted price per speaker	$170

Notice that fixed expenses are not included in the computation. This is because fixed expenses are not affected by the bulk sale, so all of the additional contribution margin increases the company's profits.

IN BUSINESS

MANAGING RISK IN THE BOOK PUBLISHING INDUSTRY

Greenleaf Book Group is a book publishing company in Austin, Texas, that attracts authors who are willing to pay publishing costs and forgo up-front advances in exchange for a larger royalty rate on each book sold. For example, assume a typical publisher prints 10,000 copies of a new book that it sells for $12.50 per unit. The publisher pays the author an advance of $20,000 to write the book and then incurs $60,000 of expenses to market, print, and edit the book. The publisher also pays the author a 20% royalty (or $2.50 per unit) on each book sold above 8,000 units. In this scenario, the publisher must sell 6,400 books to break even (= $80,000 in fixed costs ÷ $12.50 per unit). If all 10,000 copies are sold, the author earns $25,000 (= $20,000 advance + 2,000 copies × $2.50) and the publisher earns $40,000 (= $125,000 − $60,000 − $20,000 − $5,000).

Greenleaf alters the financial arrangement described above by requiring the author to assume the risk of poor sales. It pays the author a 70% royalty on all units sold (or $8.75 per unit), but the author forgoes the $20,000 advance and pays Greenleaf $60,000 to market, print, and edit the book. If the book flops, the author fails to recover her production costs. If all 10,000 units are sold, the author earns $27,500 (= $10,000 units × $8.75 − $60,000) and Greenleaf earns $37,500 (= 10,000 units × ($12.50 − $8.75)).

Source: Christopher Steiner, "Book It," *Forbes*, September 7, 2009, p. 58.

Break-Even and Target Profit Analysis

Managers use break-even and target profit analysis to answer questions such as how much would we have to sell to avoid incurring a loss or how much would we have to sell to make a profit of $10,000 per month? We'll discuss break-even analysis first followed by target profit analysis.

Break-Even Analysis

LO5–5
Determine the break-even point.

Earlier in the chapter we defined the break-even point as *the level of sales at which the company's profit is zero*. To calculate the break-even point (in unit sales and dollar sales), managers can use either of two approaches, the equation method or the formula method. We'll demonstrate both approaches using the data from Acoustic Concepts.

The Equation Method   The equation method relies on the basic profit equation introduced earlier in the chapter. Since Acoustic Concepts has only one product, we'll use the contribution margin form of this equation to perform the break-even calculations. Remembering that Acoustic Concepts' unit contribution margin is $100, and its fixed expenses are $35,000, the company's break-even point is computed as follows:

$$\text{Profit} = \text{Unit CM} \times Q - \text{Fixed expense}$$
$$\$0 = \$100 \times Q - \$35,000$$
$$\$100 \times Q = \$0 + \$35,000$$
$$Q = \$35,000 \div \$100$$
$$Q = 350$$

Thus, as we determined earlier in the chapter, Acoustic Concepts will break even (or earn zero profit) at a sales volume of 350 speakers per month.

The Formula Method   The formula method is a shortcut version of the equation method. It centers on the idea discussed earlier in the chapter that each unit sold provides a certain amount of contribution margin that goes toward covering fixed expenses. In a single product situation, the formula for computing the unit sales to break even is:

$$\text{Units sales to break even} = \frac{\text{Fixed expenses}^3}{\text{Unit CM}}$$

In the case of Acoustic Concepts, the unit sales needed to break even is computed as follows:

$$\text{Units sales to break even} = \frac{\text{Fixed expenses}}{\text{Unit CM}}$$
$$= \frac{\$35,000}{\$100}$$
$$= 350$$

Notice that 350 units is the same answer that we got when using the equation method. This will always be the case because the formula method and equation method are mathematically equivalent. The formula method simply skips a few steps in the equation method.

Break-Even in Dollar Sales   In addition to finding the break-even point in unit sales, we can also find the break-even point in dollar sales using three methods. First, we could solve for the break-even point in *unit* sales using the equation method or formula method and then simply multiply the result by the selling price. In the case of Acoustic Concepts, the break-even point in dollar sales using this approach would be computed as 350 speakers × $250 per speaker, or $87,500 in total sales.

Second, we can use the equation method to compute the break-even point in dollar sales. Remembering that Acoustic Concepts' contribution margin ratio is 40% and its fixed expenses are $35,000, the equation method calculates the break-even point in dollar sales as follows:

$$\text{Profit} = \text{CM ratio} \times \text{Sales} - \text{Fixed expenses}$$
$$\$0 = 0.40 \times \text{Sales} - \$35,000$$
$$0.40 \times \text{Sales} = \$0 + \$35,000$$
$$\text{Sales} = \$35,000 \div 0.40$$
$$\text{Sales} = \$87,500$$

---

[3] This formula can be derived as follows:
$$\text{Profit} = \text{Unit CM} \times Q - \text{Fixed expenses}$$
$$\$0 = \text{Unit CM} \times Q - \text{Fixed expenses}$$
$$\text{Unit CM} \times Q = \$0 + \text{Fixed expenses}$$
$$Q = \text{Fixed expenses} \div \text{Unit CM}$$

Chapter 5

Third, we can use the formula method to compute the dollar sales needed to break even as shown below:

$$\text{Dollar sales to break even} = \frac{\text{Fixed expenses}^4}{\text{CM ratio}}$$

In the case of Acoustic Concepts, the computations are performed as follows:

$$\text{Dollar sales to break even} = \frac{\text{Fixed expenses}}{\text{CM ratio}}$$

$$= \frac{\$35,000}{0.40}$$

$$= \$87,500$$

Again, you'll notice that the break-even point in dollar sales ($87,500) is the same under all three methods. This will always be the case because these methods are mathematically equivalent.

LO5–6

Determine the level of sales needed to achieve a desired target profit.

Target Profit Analysis

Target profit analysis is one of the key uses of CVP analysis. In **target profit analysis**, we estimate what sales volume is needed to achieve a specific target profit. For example, suppose Prem Narayan of Acoustic Concepts would like to estimate the sales needed to attain a target profit of $40,000 per month. To determine the unit sales and dollar sales needed to achieve a target profit, we can rely on the same two approaches that we have been discussing thus far, the equation method or the formula method.

The Equation Method   To compute the unit sales required to achieve a target profit of $40,000 per month, Acoustic Concepts can use the same profit equation that was used for its break-even analysis. Remembering that the company's contribution margin per unit is $100 and its total fixed expenses are $35,000, the equation method could be applied as follows:

$$\text{Profit} = \text{Unit CM} \times Q - \text{Fixed expense}$$

$$\$40,000 = \$100 \times Q - \$35,000$$

$$\$100 \times Q = \$40,000 + \$35,000$$

$$Q = \$75,000 \div \$100$$

$$Q = 750$$

Thus, the target profit can be achieved by selling 750 speakers per month. Notice that the only difference between this equation and the equation used for Acoustic Concepts' break-even calculation is the profit figure. In the break-even scenario, the profit is $0, whereas in the target profit scenario the profit is $40,000.

---

4 This formula can be derived as follows:

$$\text{Profit} = \text{CM ratio} \times \text{Sales} - \text{Fixed expenses}$$

$$\$0 = \text{CM ratio} \times \text{Sales} - \text{Fixed expenses}$$

$$\text{CM ratio} \times \text{Sales} = \$0 + \text{Fixed expenses}$$

$$\text{Sales} = \text{Fixed expenses} \div \text{CM ratio}$$

The Formula Method In general, in a single product situation, we can compute the sales volume required to attain a specific target profit using the following formula:

$$\text{Units sales to attain the target profit} = \frac{\text{Target profit} + \text{Fixed expenses}}{\text{Unit CM}}$$

In the case of Acoustic Concepts, the unit sales needed to attain a target profit of 40,000 is computed as follows:

$$\text{Units sales to attain the target profit} = \frac{\text{Target profit} + \text{Fixed expenses}}{\text{Unit CM}}$$

$$= \frac{\$40,000 + \$35,000}{\$100}$$

$$= 750$$

Target Profit Analysis in Terms of Dollar Sales When quantifying the dollar sales needed to attain a target profit we can apply the same three methods that we used for calculating the dollar sales needed to break even. First, we can solve for the *unit* sales needed to attain the target profit using the equation method or formula method and then simply multiply the result by the selling price. In the case of Acoustic Concepts, the dollar sales to attain its target profit would be computed as 750 speakers × $250 per speaker, or $187,500 in total sales.

Second, we can use the equation method to compute the dollar sales needed to attain the target profit. Remembering that Acoustic Concepts' target profit is $40,000, its contribution margin ratio is 40%, and its fixed expenses are $35,000, the equation method calculates the answer as follows:

$$\text{Profit} = \text{CM ratio} \times \text{Sales} - \text{Fixed expenses}$$

$$\$40,000 = 0.40 \times \text{Sales} - \$35,000$$

$$0.40 \times \text{Sales} = \$40,000 + \$35,000$$

$$\text{Sales} = \$75,000 \div 0.40$$

$$\text{Sales} = \$187,500$$

Third, we can use the formula method to compute the dollar sales needed to attain the target profit as shown below:

$$\text{Dollar sales to attain a target profit} = \frac{\text{Target profit} + \text{Fixed expenses}}{\text{CM ratio}}$$

In the case of Acoustic Concepts, the computations would be:

$$\text{Dollar sales to attain a target profit} = \frac{\text{Target profit} + \text{Fixed expenses}}{\text{CM ratio}}$$

$$= \frac{\$40,000 + \$35,000}{\$0.40}$$

$$= \$187,500$$

Again, you'll notice that the answers are the same regardless of which method we use. This is because all of the methods discussed are simply different roads to the same destination.

204   Chapter 5

SNAP FITNESS GROWS IN A WEAK ECONOMY

When Bally's Total Fitness was filing for bankruptcy, Snap Fitness was expanding to more than 900 clubs in the United States with 400,000 members. The secret to Snap Fitness' success is its "no frills" approach to exercise. Each club typically has five treadmills, two stationary bikes, five elliptical machines, and weight equipment while bypassing amenities such as on-site child care, juice bars, and showers. Each club is usually staffed only 25–40 hours per week and it charges a membership fee of $35 per month.

To open a new Snap Fitness location, each franchise owner has an initial capital outlay of $120,000 for various types of equipment and a one-time licensing fee of $15,000. The franchisee also pays Snap (the parent company) a royalty fee of $400 per month plus $0.50 for each membership. Snap also collects one-time fees of $5 for each new member's "billing setup" and $5 for each security card issued. If a new club attracts 275 members, it can break even in as little as three months. Can you estimate the underlying calculations related to this break-even point?

Source: Nicole Perlroth, "Survival of the Fittest," *Forbes*, January 12, 2009, pp. 54–55.

The Margin of Safety

LO5–7

Compute the margin of safety and explain its significance.

The **margin of safety** is the excess of budgeted or actual sales dollars over the break-even volume of sales dollars. It is the amount by which sales can drop before losses are incurred. The higher the margin of safety, the lower the risk of not breaking even and incurring a loss. The formula for the margin of safety is:

$$\text{Margin of safety in dollars} = \text{Total budgeted (or actual) sales} - \text{Break-even sales}$$

The margin of safety can also be expressed in percentage form by dividing the margin of safety in dollars by total dollar sales:

$$\text{Margin of safety percentage} = \frac{\text{Margin of safety in dollars}}{\text{Total budgeted (or actual) sales in dollars}}$$

The calculation of the margin of safety for Acoustic Concepts is:

Sales (at the current volume of 400 speakers) (a)	$100,000
Break-even sales (at 350 speakers)	87,500
Margin of safety in dollars (b)	$ 12,500
Margin of safety percentage, (b) ÷ (a)	12.5%

This margin of safety means that at the current level of sales and with the company's current prices and cost structure, a reduction in sales of $12,500, or 12.5%, would result in just breaking even.

In a single-product company like Acoustic Concepts, the margin of safety can also be expressed in terms of the number of units sold by dividing the margin of safety in dollars by the selling price per unit. In this case, the margin of safety is 50 speakers ($12,500 ÷ $250 per speaker = 50 speakers).

COMPUTING MARGIN OF SAFETY FOR A SMALL BUSINESS

Sam Calagione owns Dogfish Head Craft Brewery, a microbrewery in Rehobeth Beach, Delaware. He charges distributors as much as $100 per case for his premium beers such as World Wide Stout. The high-priced microbrews bring in $800,000 in operating income on revenue of $7 million. Calagione reports that his raw ingredients and labor costs for one case of World Wide Stout are $30 and $16, respectively. Bottling and packaging costs are $6 per case. Gas and electric costs are about $10 per case.

If we assume that World Wide Stout is representative of all Dogfish microbrews, then we can compute the company's margin of safety in five steps. First, variable cost as a percentage of sales is 62% [($30 + $16 + $6 + $10)/$100]. Second, the contribution margin ratio is 38% (1 − 0.62). Third, Dogfish's total fixed cost is $1,860,000 [($7,000,000 × 0.38) − $800,000]. Fourth, the break-even point in dollar sales is $4,894,737 ($1,860,000/0.38). Fifth, the margin of safety is $2,105,263 ($7,000,000 − $4,894,737).

Source: Patricia Huang, "Château Dogfish," *Forbes*, February 28, 2005, pp. 57–59.

Prem Narayan and Bob Luchinni met to discuss the results of Bob's analysis.

MANAGERIAL ACCOUNTING IN ACTION
THE WRAP-UP

ACOUSTIC
concepts

Prem: Bob, everything you have shown me is pretty clear. I can see what impact the sales manager's suggestions would have on our profits. Some of those suggestions are quite good and others are not so good. I am concerned that our margin of safety is only 50 speakers. What can we do to increase this number?

Bob: Well, we have to increase total sales or decrease the break-even point or both.

Prem: And to decrease the break-even point, we have to either decrease our fixed expenses or increase our unit contribution margin?

Bob: Exactly.

Prem: And to increase our unit contribution margin, we must either increase our selling price or decrease the variable cost per unit?

Bob: Correct.

Prem: So what do you suggest?

Bob: Well, the analysis doesn't tell us which of these to do, but it does indicate we have a potential problem here.

Prem: If you don't have any immediate suggestions, I would like to call a general meeting next week to discuss ways we can work on increasing the margin of safety. I think everyone will be concerned about how vulnerable we are to even small downturns in sales.

CVP Considerations in Choosing a Cost Structure

Cost structure refers to the relative proportion of fixed and variable costs in an organization. Managers often have some latitude in trading off between these two types of costs. For example, fixed investments in automated equipment can reduce variable labor costs. In this section, we discuss the choice of a cost structure. We also introduce the concept of *operating leverage*.

Cost Structure and Profit Stability

Which cost structure is better—high variable costs and low fixed costs, or the opposite? No single answer to this question is possible; each approach has its advantages. To show what we mean, refer to the following contribution format income statements for two blueberry farms. Bogside Farm depends on migrant workers to pick its berries by hand, whereas Sterling Farm has invested in expensive berry-picking machines. Consequently, Bogside Farm has higher variable costs, but Sterling Farm has higher fixed costs:

	Bogside Farm		Sterling Farm	
	Amount	Percent	Amount	Percent
Sales	$100,000	100%	$100,000	100%
Variable expenses	60,000	60%	30,000	30%
Contribution margin	40,000	40%	70,000	70%
Fixed expenses	30,000		60,000	
Net operating income	$ 10,000		$ 10,000	

Which farm has the better cost structure? The answer depends on many factors, including the long-run trend in sales, year-to-year fluctuations in the level of sales, and the attitude of the owners toward risk. If sales are expected to exceed $100,000 in the future, then Sterling Farm probably has the better cost structure. The reason is that its CM ratio is higher, and its profits will therefore increase more rapidly as sales increase. To illustrate, assume that each farm experiences a 10% increase in sales without any increase in fixed costs. The new income statements would be as follows:

	Bogside Farm		Sterling Farm	
	Amount	Percent	Amount	Percent
Sales	$110,000	100%	$110,000	100%
Variable expenses	66,000	60%	33,000	30%
Contribution margin	44,000	40%	77,000	70%
Fixed expenses	30,000		60,000	
Net operating income	$ 14,000		$ 17,000	

Sterling Farm has experienced a greater increase in net operating income due to its higher CM ratio even though the increase in sales was the same for both farms.

What if sales drop below $100,000? What are the farms' break-even points? What are their margins of safety? The computations needed to answer these questions are shown below using the formula method:

	Bogside Farm	Sterling Farm
Fixed expenses	$ 30,000	$ 60,000
Contribution margin ratio	÷ 0.40	÷ 0.70
Dollar sales to break even	$ 75,000	$ 85,714
Total current sales (a)	$100,000	$100,000
Break-even sales	75,000	85,714
Margin of safety in sales dollars (b)	$ 25,000	$ 14,286
Margin of safety percentage (b) ÷ (a)	25.0%	14.3%

Bogside Farm's margin of safety is greater and its contribution margin ratio is lower than Sterling Farm. Therefore, Bogside Farm is less vulnerable to downturns than Sterling Farm. Due to its lower contribution margin ratio, Bogside Farm will not lose contribution margin as rapidly as Sterling Farm when sales decline. Thus, Bogside Farm's profit will be less volatile. We saw earlier that this is a drawback when sales increase, but it provides more protection when sales drop. And because its break-even point is lower, Bogside Farm can suffer a larger sales decline before losses emerge.

To summarize, without knowing the future, it is not obvious which cost structure is better. Both have advantages and disadvantages. Sterling Farm, with its higher fixed costs and lower variable costs, will experience wider swings in net operating income as sales fluctuate, with greater profits in good years and greater losses in bad years. Bogside Farm, with its lower fixed costs and higher variable costs, will enjoy greater profit stability and will be more protected from losses during bad years, but at the cost of lower net operating income in good years.

Operating Leverage

A lever is a tool for multiplying force. Using a lever, a massive object can be moved with only a modest amount of force. In business, *operating leverage* serves a similar purpose. **Operating leverage** is a measure of how sensitive net operating income is to a given percentage change in dollar sales. Operating leverage acts as a multiplier. If operating leverage is high, a small percentage increase in sales can produce a much larger percentage increase in net operating income.

Operating leverage can be illustrated by returning to the data for the two blueberry farms. We previously showed that a 10% increase in sales (from $100,000 to $110,000 in each farm) results in a 70% increase in the net operating income of Sterling Farm (from $10,000 to $17,000) and only a 40% increase in the net operating income of Bogside Farm (from $10,000 to $14,000). Thus, for a 10% increase in sales, Sterling Farm experiences a much greater percentage increase in profits than does Bogside Farm. Therefore, Sterling Farm has greater operating leverage than Bogside Farm.

The **degree of operating leverage** at a given level of sales is computed by the following formula:

$$\text{Degree of operating leverage} = \frac{\text{Contribution margin}}{\text{Net operating income}}$$

The degree of operating leverage is a measure, at a given level of sales, of how a percentage change in sales volume will affect profits. To illustrate, the degree of operating leverage for the two farms at $100,000 sales would be computed as follows:

$$\text{Bogside Farm:} \frac{\$40,000}{\$10,000} = 4$$

$$\text{Sterling Farm:} \frac{\$70,000}{\$10,000} = 7$$

Because the degree of operating leverage for Bogside Farm is 4, the farm's net operating income grows four times as fast as its sales. In contrast, Sterling Farm's net operating income grows seven times as fast as its sales. Thus, if sales increase by 10%, then we can expect the net operating income of Bogside Farm to increase by four times this amount, or by 40%, and the net operating income of Sterling Farm to increase by seven times this amount, or by 70%. In general, this relation between the percentage change in sales and the percentage change in net operating income is given by the following formula:

$$\frac{\text{Percentage change in}}{\text{net operating income}} = \frac{\text{Degree of}}{\text{operating leverage}} \times \frac{\text{Percentage}}{\text{change in sales}}$$

Bogside Farm: Percentage change in net operating income = 4 × 10% = 40%

Sterling Farm: Percentage change in net operating income = 7 × 10% = 70%

What is responsible for the higher operating leverage at Sterling Farm? The only difference between the two farms is their cost structure. If two companies have the same total revenue and same total expense but different cost structures, then the company with

LO5–8
Compute the degree of operating leverage at a particular level of sales and explain how it can be used to predict changes in net operating income.

208

Chapter 5

the higher proportion of fixed costs in its cost structure will have higher operating lever-age. Referring back to the original example on page 206, when both farms have sales of $100,000 and total expenses of $90,000, one-third of Bogside Farm's costs are fixed but two-thirds of Sterling Farm's costs are fixed. As a consequence, Sterling's degree of oper-ating leverage is higher than Bogside's.

The degree of operating leverage is not a constant; it is greatest at sales levels near the break-even point and decreases as sales and profits rise. The following table shows the degree of operating leverage for Bogside Farm at various sales levels. (Data used ear-lier for Bogside Farm are shown in color.)

Sales	$75,000	$80,000	$100,000	$150,000	$225,000
Variable expenses	45,000	48,000	60,000	90,000	135,000
Contribution margin (a)	30,000	32,000	40,000	60,000	90,000
Fixed expenses	30,000	30,000	30,000	30,000	30,000
Net operating income (b)	$ 0	$ 2,000	$ 10,000	$ 30,000	$ 60,000
Degree of operating leverage, (a) ÷ (b)	∞	16	4	2	1.5

Thus, a 10% increase in sales would increase profits by only 15% (10% × 1.5) if sales were previously $225,000, as compared to the 40% increase we computed earlier at the $100,000 sales level. The degree of operating leverage will continue to decrease the far-ther the company moves from its break-even point. At the break-even point, the degree of operating leverage is infinitely large ($30,000 contribution margin ÷ $0 net operating income = ∞).

The degree of operating leverage can be used to quickly estimate what impact various percentage changes in sales will have on profits, without the necessity of preparing detailed income statements. As shown by our examples, the effects of operating leverage can be dramatic. If a company is near its break-even point, then even small percentage increases in sales can yield large percentage increases in profits. *This explains why management will often work very hard for only a small increase in sales volume.* If the degree of operating leverage is 5, then a 6% increase in sales would translate into a 30% increase in profits.

IN BUSINESS

THE DANGERS OF A HIGH DEGREE OF OPERATING LEVERAGE

In recent years, computer chip manufacturers have poured more than $75 billion into construct-ing new manufacturing facilities to meet the growing demand for digital devices such as iPhones and Blackberrys. Because 70% of the costs of running these facilities are fixed, a sharp drop in customer demand forces these companies to choose between two undesirable options. They can slash production levels and absorb large amounts of unused capacity costs, or they can continue producing large volumes of output in spite of shrinking demand, thereby flooding the market with excess supply and lowering prices. Either choice distresses investors who tend to shy away from computer chip makers in economic downturns.

Source: Bruce Einhorn, "Chipmakers on the Edge," *BusinessWeek*, January 5, 2009, pp. 30–31.

Structuring Sales Commissions

Companies usually compensate salespeople by paying them a commission based on sales, a salary, or a combination of the two. Commissions based on sales dollars can lead to lower profits. To illustrate, consider Pipeline Unlimited, a producer of surfing equipment. Salespersons sell the company's products to retail sporting goods stores throughout North America and the Pacific Basin. Data for two of the company's surfboards, the XR7 and Turbo models, appear below:

	Model	
	XR7	Turbo
Selling price	$695	$749
Variable expenses	344	410
Contribution margin	$351	$339

Which model will salespeople push hardest if they are paid a commission of 10% of sales revenue? The answer is the Turbo because it has the higher selling price and hence the larger commission. On the other hand, from the standpoint of the company, profits will be greater if salespeople steer customers toward the XR7 model because it has the higher contribution margin.

To eliminate such conflicts, commissions can be based on contribution margin rather than on selling price. If this is done, the salespersons will want to sell the mix of products that maximizes contribution margin. Providing that fixed costs are not affected by the sales mix, maximizing the contribution margin will also maximize the company's profit.[5] In effect, by maximizing their own compensation, salespersons will also maximize the company's profit.

Sales Mix

Before concluding our discussion of CVP concepts, we need to consider the impact of changes in *sales mix* on a company's profit.

The Definition of Sales Mix

The term **sales mix** refers to the relative proportions in which a company's products are sold. The idea is to achieve the combination, or mix, that will yield the greatest profits. Most companies have many products, and often these products are not equally profitable. Hence, profits will depend to some extent on the company's sales mix. Profits will be greater if high-margin rather than low-margin items make up a relatively large proportion of total sales.

Changes in the sales mix can cause perplexing variations in a company's profits. A shift in the sales mix from high-margin items to low-margin items can cause total profits to decrease even though total sales may increase. Conversely, a shift in the sales mix from low-margin items to high-margin items can cause the reverse effect—total profits may increase even though total sales decrease. It is one thing to achieve a particular sales volume; it is quite another to sell the most profitable mix of products.

LO5–9
Compute the break-even point for a multiproduct company and explain the effects of shifts in the sales mix on contribution margin and the break-even point.

---

[5] This also assumes the company has no production constraint. If it does, the sales commissions should be modified. See the Profitability Appendix at the end of the book.

IN BUSINESS

NETBOOK SALES CANNIBALIZE PC SALES

When computer manufacturers introduced the "netbook," they expected it to serve as a consumer's third computer—complementing home and office personal computers (PCs) rather than replacing them. However, when the economy soured many customers decided to buy lower-priced netbooks instead of PCs, which in turn adversely affected the financial performance of many companies. For example, when Microsoft failed to achieve its sales goals, the company partially blamed growing netbook sales and declining PC sales for its troubles. Microsoft's Windows operating system for netbooks sells for $15–$25 per device, which is less than half the cost of the company's least expensive Windows operating system for PCs.

Source: Olga Kharif, "Small, Cheap—and Frighteningly Popular," *BusinessWeek*, December 8, 2008, p. 64.

Sales Mix and Break-Even Analysis

If a company sells more than one product, break-even analysis is more complex than discussed to this point. The reason is that different products will have different selling prices, different costs, and different contribution margins. Consequently, the break-even point depends on the mix in which the various products are sold. To illustrate, consider Virtual Journeys Unlimited, a small company that sells two DVDs: the Monuments DVD, a tour of the United States' most popular National Monuments; and the Parks DVD, which tours the United States' National Parks. The company's September sales, expenses, and break-even point are shown in Exhibit 5–4.

As shown in the exhibit, the break-even point is $60,000 in sales, which was computed by dividing the company's fixed expenses of $27,000 by its overall CM ratio of 45%. However, this is the break-even only if the company's sales mix does not change. Currently, the Monuments DVD is responsible for 20% and the Parks DVD for 80% of the company's dollar sales. Assuming this sales mix does not change, if total sales are $60,000, the sales of the Monuments DVD would be $12,000 (20% of $60,000) and the sales of the Parks DVD would be $48,000 (80% of $60,000). As shown in Exhibit 5–4, at these levels of sales, the company would indeed break even. But $60,000 in sales represents the break-even point for the company only if the sales mix does not change. *If the sales mix changes, then the break-even point will also usually change.* This is illustrated by the results for October in which the sales mix shifted away from the more profitable Parks DVD (which has a 50% CM ratio) toward the less profitable Monuments CD (which has a 25% CM ratio). These results appear in Exhibit 5–5.

Although sales have remained unchanged at $100,000, the sales mix is exactly the reverse of what it was in Exhibit 5–4, with the bulk of the sales now coming from the less profitable Monuments DVD. Notice that this shift in the sales mix has caused both the overall CM ratio and total profits to drop sharply from the prior month even though total sales are the same. The overall CM ratio has dropped from 45% in September to only 30% in October, and net operating income has dropped from $18,000 to only $3,000. In addition, with the drop in the overall CM ratio, the company's break-even point is no longer $60,000 in sales. Because the company is now realizing less average contribution margin per dollar of sales, it takes more sales to cover the same amount of fixed costs. Thus, the break-even point has increased from $60,000 to $90,000 in sales per year.

In preparing a break-even analysis, an assumption must be made concerning the sales mix. Usually the assumption is that it will not change. However, if the sales mix is expected to change, then this must be explicitly considered in any CVP computations.

EXHIBIT 5–4
Multiproduct Break-Even Analysis

Virtual Journeys Unlimited
Contribution Income Statement
For the Month of September

	Monuments DVD		Parks DVD		Total	
	Amount	Percent	Amount	Percent	Amount	Percent
Sales	$20,000	100%	$80,000	100%	$100,000	100%
Variable expenses	15,000	75%	40,000	50%	55,000	55%
Contribution margin	$ 5,000	25%	$40,000	50%	45,000	45%
Fixed expenses					27,000	
Net operating income					$ 18,000	

Computation of the break-even point:

$$\frac{\text{Fixed expenses}}{\text{Overall CM ratio}} = \frac{\$27,000}{0.45} = \$60,000$$

Verification of the break-even point:

	Monuments DVD	Parks DVD	Total
Current dollar sales	$20,000	$80,000	$100,000
Percentage of total dollar sales	20%	80%	100%
Sales at the break-even point	$12,000	$48,000	$60,000

	Monuments DVD		Parks DVD		Total	
	Amount	Percent	Amount	Percent	Amount	Percent
Sales	$12,000	100%	$48,000	100%	$ 60,000	100%
Variable expenses	9,000	75%	24,000	50%	33,000	55%
Contribution margin	$ 3,000	25%	$24,000	50%	27,000	45%
Fixed expenses					27,000	
Net operating income					$ 0	

EXHIBIT 5–5
Multiproduct Break-Even Analysis: A Shift in Sales Mix (see Exhibit 5–4)

Virtual Journeys Unlimited
Contribution Income Statement
For the Month of October

	Monuments DVD		Parks DVD		Total	
	Amount	Percent	Amount	Percent	Amount	Percent
Sales	$80,000	100%	$20,000	100%	$100,000	100%
Variable expenses	60,000	75%	10,000	50%	70,000	70%
Contribution margin	$20,000	25%	$10,000	50%	30,000	30%
Fixed expenses					27,000	
Net operating income					$ 3,000	

Computation of the break-even point:

$$\frac{\text{Fixed expenses}}{\text{Overall CM ratio}} = \frac{\$27,000}{0.30} = \$90,000$$

212   Chapter 5

Summary

CVP analysis is based on a simple model of how profits respond to prices, costs, and volume. This model can be used to answer a variety of critical questions such as what is the company's break-even volume, what is its margin of safety, and what is likely to happen if specific changes are made in prices, costs, and volume.

A CVP graph depicts the relationships between unit sales on the one hand and fixed expenses, variable expenses, total expenses, total sales, and profits on the other hand. The profit graph is simpler than the CVP graph and shows how profits depend on sales. The CVP and profit graphs are useful for developing intuition about how costs and profits respond to changes in sales.

The contribution margin ratio is the ratio of the total contribution margin to total sales. This ratio can be used to quickly estimate what impact a change in total sales would have on net operating income. The ratio is also useful in break-even analysis.

Break-even analysis is used to estimate how much sales would have to be to just break even. The unit sales required to break even can be estimated by dividing the fixed expense by the unit contribution margin. Target profit analysis is used to estimate how much sales would have to be to attain a specified target profit. The unit sales required to attain the target profit can be estimated by dividing the sum of the target profit and fixed expense by the unit contribution margin.

The margin of safety is the amount by which the company's current sales exceeds break-even sales.

The degree of operating leverage allows quick estimation of what impact a given percentage change in sales would have on the company's net operating income. The higher the degree of operating leverage, the greater is the impact on the company's profits. The degree of operating leverage is not constant—it depends on the company's current level of sales.

The profits of a multiproduct company are affected by its sales mix. Changes in the sales mix can affect the break-even point, margin of safety, and other critical factors.

Review Problem: CVP Relationships

Voltar Company manufactures and sells a specialized cordless telephone for high electromagnetic radiation environments. The company's contribution format income statement for the most recent year is given below:

	Total	Per Unit	Percent of Sales
Sales (20,000 units)	$1,200,000	$60	100%
Variable expenses	900,000	45	? %
Contribution margin	300,000	$15	? %
Fixed expenses	240,000		
Net operating income	$ 60,000		

Management is anxious to increase the company's profit and has asked for an analysis of a number of items.

Required:
1. Compute the company's CM ratio and variable expense ratio.
2. Compute the company's break-even point in both unit sales and dollar sales. Use the equation method.
3. Assume that sales increase by $400,000 next year. If cost behavior patterns remain unchanged, by how much will the company's net operating income increase? Use the CM ratio to compute your answer.
4. Refer to the original data. Assume that next year management wants the company to earn a profit of at least $90,000. How many units will have to be sold to meet this target profit?
5. Refer to the original data. Compute the company's margin of safety in both dollar and percentage form.

6. a. Compute the company's degree of operating leverage at the present level of sales.
   b. Assume that through a more intense effort by the sales staff, the company's sales increase by 8% next year. By what percentage would you expect net operating income to increase? Use the degree of operating leverage to obtain your answer.
   c. Verify your answer to (b) by preparing a new contribution format income statement showing an 8% increase in sales.

7. In an effort to increase sales and profits, management is considering the use of a higher-quality speaker. The higher-quality speaker would increase variable costs by $3 per unit, but management could eliminate one quality inspector who is paid a salary of $30,000 per year. The sales manager estimates that the higher-quality speaker would increase annual sales by at least 20%.
   a. Assuming that changes are made as described above, prepare a projected contribution format income statement for next year. Show data on a total, per unit, and percentage basis.
   b. Compute the company's new break-even point in both unit sales and dollar sales. Use the formula method.
   c. Would you recommend that the changes be made?

Solution to Review Problem

1.

$$\text{CM ratio} = \frac{\text{Unit contribution margin}}{\text{Unit selling price}} = \frac{\$15}{\$60} = 25\%$$

$$\text{Variable expense ratio} = \frac{\text{Variable expense}}{\text{Selling price}} = \frac{\$45}{\$60} = 75\%$$

2.

$$\text{Profit} = \text{Unit CM} \times Q - \text{Fixed expenses}$$

$$\$0 = (\$60 - \$45) \times Q - \$240,000$$

$$\$15Q = \$240,000$$

$$Q = \$240,000 \div \$15$$

$$Q = 16,000 \text{ units; or at } \$60 \text{ per unit, } \$960,000$$

3.

Increase in sales	$400,000
Multiply by the CM ratio	× 25%
Expected increase in contribution margin	$100,000

Because the fixed expenses are not expected to change, net operating income will increase by the entire $100,000 increase in contribution margin computed above.

4. Equation method:

$$\text{Profit} = \text{Unit CM} \times Q - \text{Fixed expenses}$$

$$\$90,000 = (\$60 - \$45) \times Q - \$240,000$$

$$\$15Q = \$90,000 + \$240,000$$

$$Q = \$330,000 \div \$15$$

$$Q = 22,000 \text{ units}$$

Formula method:

$$\frac{\text{Unit sales to attain}}{\text{the target profit}} = \frac{\text{Target profit} + \text{Fixed expenses}}{\text{Contribution margin per unit}} = \frac{\$90,000 + \$240,000}{\$15 \text{ per unit}} = 22,000 \text{ units}$$

5.

$$\text{Margin of safety in dollars} = \text{Total sales} - \text{Break-even sales}$$

$$= \$1,200,000 - \$960,000 = \$240,000$$

$$\text{Margin of safety percentage} = \frac{\text{Margin of safety in dollars}}{\text{Total sales}} = \frac{\$240,000}{\$1,200,000} = 20\%$$

214   Chapter 5

6. a. Degree of operating leverage $= \dfrac{\text{Contribution margin}}{\text{Net operating income}} = \dfrac{\$300,000}{\$60,000} = 5$

  b.

Expected increase in sales	8%
Degree of operating leverage	× 5
Expected increase in net operating income	40%

  c. If sales increase by 8%, then 21,600 units (20,000 × 1.08 = 21,600) will be sold next year. The new contribution format income statement would be as follows:

	Total	Per Unit	Percent of Sales
Sales (21,600 units)	$1,296,000	$60	100%
Variable expenses	972,000	45	75%
Contribution margin	324,000	$15	25%
Fixed expenses	240,000		
Net operating income	$ 84,000		

Thus, the $84,000 expected net operating income for next year represents a 40% increase over the $60,000 net operating income earned during the current year:

$$\frac{\$84,000 - \$60,000}{\$60,000} = \frac{\$24,000}{\$60,000} = 40\% \text{ increase}$$

Note that the increase in sales from 20,000 to 21,600 units has increased *both* total sales and total variable expenses.

7. a. A 20% increase in sales would result in 24,000 units being sold next year: 20,000 units × 1.20 = 24,000 units.

	Total	Per Unit	Percent of Sales
Sales (24,000 units)	$1,440,000	$60	100%
Variable expenses	1,152,000	48*	80%
Contribution margin	288,000	$12	20%
Fixed expenses	210,000†		
Net operating income	$ 78,000		

*$45 + $3 = $48; $48 ÷ $60 = 80%.
†$240,000 − $30,000 = $210,000.

Note that the change in per unit variable expenses results in a change in both the per unit contribution margin and the CM ratio.

  b. Unit sales to break even $= \dfrac{\text{Fixed expenses}}{\text{Unit contribution margin}}$

$$= \frac{\$210,000}{\$12 \text{ per unit}} = 17,500 \text{ units}$$

  Dollar sales to break even $= \dfrac{\text{Fixed expenses}}{\text{CM ratio}}$

$$= \frac{\$210,000}{0.20} = \$1,050,000$$

  c. Yes, based on these data, the changes should be made. The changes increase the company's net operating income from the present $60,000 to $78,000 per year. Although the changes also result in a higher break-even point (17,500 units as compared to the present 16,000 units), the company's margin of safety actually becomes greater than before:

  Margin of safety in dollars = Total sales − Break-even sales

$$= \$1,440,000 - \$1,050,000 = \$390,000$$

As shown in (5) on the prior page, the company's present margin of safety is only $240,000. Thus, several benefits will result from the proposed changes.

Glossary

Break-even point The level of sales at which profit is zero. (p. 190)

Contribution margin ratio (CM ratio) A ratio computed by dividing contribution margin by dollar sales. (p. 195)

Cost-volume-profit (CVP) graph A graphical representation of the relationships between an organization's revenues, costs, and profits on the one hand and its sales volume on the other hand. (p. 192)

Degree of operating leverage A measure, at a given level of sales, of how a percentage change in sales will affect profits. The degree of operating leverage is computed by dividing contribution margin by net operating income. (p. 207)

Incremental analysis An analytical approach that focuses only on those costs and revenues that change as a result of a decision. (p. 198)

Margin of safety The excess of budgeted or actual dollar sales over the break-even dollar sales. (p. 204)

Operating leverage A measure of how sensitive net operating income is to a given percentage change in dollar sales. (p. 207)

Sales mix The relative proportions in which a company's products are sold. Sales mix is computed by expressing the sales of each product as a percentage of total sales. (p. 209)

Target profit analysis Estimating what sales volume is needed to achieve a specific target profit. (p. 202)

Variable expense ratio A ratio computed by dividing variable expenses by dollar sales. (p. 196)

Questions

5–1 What is meant by a product's contribution margin ratio? How is this ratio useful in planning business operations?

5–2 Often the most direct route to a business decision is an incremental analysis. What is meant by an *incremental analysis?*

5–3 In all respects, Company A and Company B are identical except that Company A's costs are mostly variable, whereas Company B's costs are mostly fixed. When sales increase, which company will tend to realize the greatest increase in profits? Explain.

5–4 What is meant by the term *operating leverage?*

5–5 What is meant by the term *break-even point?*

5–6 In response to a request from your immediate supervisor, you have prepared a CVP graph portraying the cost and revenue characteristics of your company's product and operations. Explain how the lines on the graph and the break-even point would change if (*a*) the selling price per unit decreased, (*b*) fixed cost increased throughout the entire range of activity portrayed on the graph, and (*c*) variable cost per unit increased.

5–7 What is meant by the margin of safety?

5–8 What is meant by the term *sales mix?* What assumption is usually made concerning sales mix in CVP analysis?

5–9 Explain how a shift in the sales mix could result in both a higher break-even point and a lower net income.

Multiple-choice questions are provided on the text website at www.mhhe.com/garrison15e.

 Applying Excel

Available with McGraw-Hill's *Connect® Accounting.*

The Excel worksheet form that appears on the next page is to be used to recreate portions of the Review Problem on pages 212–214. Download the workbook containing this form from the Online Learning Center at www.mhhe.com/garrison15e. *On the website you will also receive instructions about how to use this worksheet form.*

L05–6, L05–7, L05–8

Chapter 5

	A	B	C	D
1	Chapter 5: Applying Excel			
2				
3	**Data**			
4	Unit sales	20,000	units	
5	Selling price per unit	$60	per unit	
6	Variable expenses per unit	$45	per unit	
7	Fixed expenses	$240,000		
8				
9	*Enter a formula into each of the cells marked with a ? below*			
10	**Review Problem: CVP Relationships**			
11				
12	*Compute the CM ratio and variable expense ratio*			
13	Selling price per unit	?	per unit	
14	Variable expenses per unit	?	per unit	
15	Contribution margin per unit	?	per unit	
16				
17	CM ratio	?		
18	Variable expense ratio	?		
19				
20	*Compute the break-even*			
21	Break-even in unit sales	?	units	
22	Break-even in dollar sales	?		
23				
24	*Compute the margin of safety*			
25	Margin of safety in dollars	?		
26	Margin of safety percentage	?		
27				
28	*Compute the degree of operating leverage*			
29	Sales	?		
30	Variable expenses	?		
31	Contribution margin	?		
32	Fixed expenses	?		
33	Net operating income	?		
34				
35	Degree of operating leverage	?		
36				

H ◄ ► H   Chapter 5 Form   Filled in Chapter 5 Form

You should proceed to the requirements below only after completing your worksheet.

Required:

1. Check your worksheet by changing the fixed expenses to $270,000. If your worksheet is operating properly, the degree of operating leverage should be 10. If you do not get this answer, find the errors in your worksheet and correct them. How much is the margin of safety percentage? Did it change? Why or why not?

2. Enter the following data from a different company into your worksheet:

Unit sales	10,000 units
Selling price per unit	$120 per unit
Variable expenses per unit	$72 per unit
Fixed expenses	$420,000

What is the margin of safety percentage? What is the degree of operating leverage?

3. Using the degree of operating leverage and without changing anything in your worksheet, calculate the percentage change in net operating income if unit sales increase by 15%.

4. Confirm the calculations you made in part (3) above by increasing the unit sales in your worksheet by 15%. What is the new net operating income and by what percentage did it increase?

5. Thad Morgan, a motorcycle enthusiast, has been exploring the possibility of relaunching the Western Hombre brand of cycle that was popular in the 1930s. The retro-look cycle would be sold for $10,000 and at that price, Thad estimates 600 units would be sold each year. The variable cost to produce and sell the cycles would be $7,500 per unit. The annual fixed cost would be $1,200,000.

    a. Using your worksheet, what would be the break-even unit sales, the margin of safety in dollars, and the degree of operating leverage?

    b. Thad is worried about the selling price. Rumors are circulating that other retro brands of cycles may be revived. If so, the selling price for the Western Hombre would have to be reduced to $9,000 to compete effectively. In that event, Thad would also reduce fixed expenses by $300,000 by reducing advertising expenses, but he still hopes to sell 600 units per year. Do you think this is a good plan? Explain. Also, explain the degree of operating leverage that appears on your worksheet.

 The Foundational 15

Available with McGraw-Hill's *Connect*® Accounting.

Oslo Company prepared the following contribution format income statement based on a sales volume of 1,000 units (the relevant range of production is 500 units to 1,500 units):

LO5–1, LO5–3, LO5–4, LO5–5, LO5–6, LO5–7, LO5–8

Sales	$20,000
Variable expenses	12,000
Contribution margin	8,000
Fixed expenses	6,000
Net operating income	$ 2,000

Required:
(Answer each question independently and always refer to the original data unless instructed otherwise.)

1. What is the contribution margin per unit?
2. What is the contribution margin ratio?
3. What is the variable expense ratio?
4. If sales increase to 1,001 units, what would be the increase in net operating income?
5. If sales decline to 900 units, what would be the net operating income?
6. If the selling price increases by $2 per unit and the sales volume decreases by 100 units, what would be the net operating income?
7. If the variable cost per unit increases by $1, spending on advertising increases by $1,500, and unit sales increase by 250 units, what would be the net operating income?
8. What is the break-even point in unit sales?
9. What is the break-even point in dollar sales?
10. How many units must be sold to achieve a target profit of $5,000?
11. What is the margin of safety in dollars? What is the margin of safety percentage?
12. What is the degree of operating leverage?
13. Using the degree of operating leverage, what is the estimated percent increase in net operating income of a 5% increase in sales?
14. Assume that the amounts of the company's total variable expenses and total fixed expenses were reversed. In other words, assume that the total variable expenses are $6,000 and the total fixed expenses are $12,000. Under this scenario and assuming that total sales remain the same, what is the degree of operating leverage?
15. Using the degree of operating leverage that you computed in the previous question, what is the estimated percent increase in net operating income of a 5% increase in sales?

Exercises   connect
|ACCOUNTING

All applicable exercises are available with McGraw-Hill's *Connect® Accounting*.

EXERCISE 5–1 Preparing a Contribution Format Income Statement [LO5–1]
Whirly Corporation's most recent income statement is shown below:

	Total	Per Unit
Sales (10,000 units)	$350,000	$35.00
Variable expenses	200,000	20.00
Contribution margin	150,000	$15.00
Fixed expenses	135,000	
Net operating income	$ 15,000	

Required:
Prepare a new contribution format income statement under each of the following conditions (consider each case independently):
1. The sales volume increases by 100 units.
2. The sales volume decreases by 100 units.
3. The sales volume is 9,000 units.

EXERCISE 5–2 Prepare a Cost-Volume-Profit (CVP) Graph [LO5–2]
Karlik Enterprises distributes a single product whose selling price is $24 and whose variable expense is $18 per unit. The company's monthly fixed expense is $24,000.

Required:
1. Prepare a cost-volume-profit graph for the company up to a sales level of 8,000 units.
2. Estimate the company's break-even point in unit sales using your cost-volume-profit graph.

EXERCISE 5–3 Prepare a Profit Graph [LO5–2]
Jaffre Enterprises distributes a single product whose selling price is $16 and whose variable expense is $11 per unit. The company's fixed expense is $16,000 per month.

Required:
1. Prepare a profit graph for the company up to a sales level of 4,000 units.
2. Estimate the company's break-even point in unit sales using your profit graph.

EXERCISE 5–4 Computing and Using the CM Ratio [LO5–3]
Last month when Holiday Creations, Inc., sold 50,000 units, total sales were $200,000, total variable expenses were $120,000, and fixed expenses were $65,000.

Required:
1. What is the company's contribution margin (CM) ratio?
2. Estimate the change in the company's net operating income if it were to increase its total sales by $1,000.

EXERCISE 5–5 Changes in Variable Costs, Fixed Costs, Selling Price, and Volume [LO5–4]
Data for Hermann Corporation are shown below:

	Per Unit	Percent of Sales
Selling price	$90	100%
Variable expenses	63	70
Contribution margin	$27	30%

Fixed expenses are $30,000 per month and the company is selling 2,000 units per month.

Required:
1. The marketing manager argues that a $5,000 increase in the monthly advertising budget would increase monthly sales by $9,000. Should the advertising budget be increased?
2. Refer to the original data. Management is considering using higher-quality components that would increase the variable expense by $2 per unit. The marketing manager believes that the higher-quality product would increase sales by 10% per month. Should the higher-quality components be used?

EXERCISE 5–6 Compute the Break-Even Point [LO5–5]

Mauro Products distributes a single product, a woven basket whose selling price is $15 and whose variable expense is $12 per unit. The company's monthly fixed expense is $4,200.

Required:
1. Solve for the company's break-even point in unit sales using the equation method.
2. Solve for the company's break-even point in dollar sales using the equation method and the CM ratio.
3. Solve for the company's break-even point in unit sales using the formula method.
4. Solve for the company's break-even point in dollar sales using the formula method and the CM ratio.

EXERCISE 5–7 Compute the Level of Sales Required to Attain a Target Profit [LO5–6]

Lin Corporation has a single product whose selling price is $120 and whose variable expense is $80 per unit. The company's monthly fixed expense is $50,000.

Required:
1. Using the equation method, solve for the unit sales that are required to earn a target profit of $10,000.
2. Using the formula method, solve for the unit sales that are required to earn a target profit of $15,000.

EXERCISE 5–8 Compute the Margin of Safety [LO5–7]

Molander Corporation is a distributor of a sun umbrella used at resort hotels. Data concerning the next month's budget appear below:

Selling price	$30 per unit
Variable expenses	$20 per unit
Fixed expenses	$7,500 per month
Unit sales	1,000 units per month

Required:
1. Compute the company's margin of safety.
2. Compute the company's margin of safety as a percentage of its sales.

EXERCISE 5–9 Compute and Use the Degree of Operating Leverage [LO5–8]

Engberg Company installs lawn sod in home yards. The company's most recent monthly contribution format income statement follows:

	Amount	Percent of Sales
Sales	$80,000	100%
Variable expenses	32,000	40%
Contribution margin	48,000	60%
Fixed expenses	38,000	
Net operating income	$10,000	

Required:
1. Compute the company's degree of operating leverage.
2. Using the degree of operating leverage, estimate the impact on net operating income of a 5% increase in sales.
3. Verify your estimate from part (2) above by constructing a new contribution format income statement for the company assuming a 5% increase in sales.

Chapter 5

EXERCISE 5–10 Compute the Break-Even Point for a Multiproduct Company [LO5–9]
Lucido Products markets two computer games: Claimjumper and Makeover. A contribution format income statement for a recent month for the two games appears below:

	Claimjumper	Makeover	Total
Sales	$30,000	$70,000	$100,000
Variable expenses	20,000	50,000	70,000
Contribution margin	$10,000	$20,000	30,000
Fixed expenses			24,000
Net operating income			$ 6,000

Required:
1. Compute the overall contribution margin (CM) ratio for the company.
2. Compute the overall break-even point for the company in dollar sales.
3. Verify the overall break-even point for the company by constructing a contribution format income statement showing the appropriate levels of sales for the two products.

EXERCISE 5–11 Missing Data; Basic CVP Concepts [LO5–1, LO5–9]
Fill in the missing amounts in each of the eight case situations below. Each case is independent of the others. (*Hint:* One way to find the missing amounts would be to prepare a contribution format income statement for each case, enter the known data, and then compute the missing items.)
a.   Assume that only one product is being sold in each of the four following case situations:

Case	Units Sold	Sales	Variable Expenses	Contribution Margin per Unit	Fixed Expenses	Net Operating Income (Loss)
1........	15,000	$180,000	$120,000	?	$50,000	?
2........	?	$100,000	?	$10	$32,000	$8,000
3........	10,000	?	$70,000	$13	?	$12,000
4........	6,000	$300,000	?	?	$100,000	$(10,000)

b.   Assume that more than one product is being sold in each of the four following case situations:

Case	Sales	Variable Expenses	Average Contribution Margin Ratio	Fixed Expenses	Net Operating Income (Loss)
1................	$500,000	?	20%	?	$7,000
2................	$400,000	$260,000	?	$100,000	?
3................	?	?	60%	$130,000	$20,000
4................	$600,000	$420,000	?	?	$(5,000)

EXERCISE 5–12 Multiproduct Break-Even Analysis [LO5–9]
Olongapo Sports Corporation distributes two premium golf balls—the Flight Dynamic and the Sure Shot. Monthly sales and the contribution margin ratios for the two products follow:

	Product		
	Flight Dynamic	Sure Shot	Total
Sales	$150,000	$250,000	$400,000
CM ratio	80%	36%	?

Fixed expenses total $183,750 per month.

Required:
1. Prepare a contribution format income statement for the company as a whole. Carry computations to one decimal place.
2. Compute the break-even point for the company based on the current sales mix.
3. If sales increase by $100,000 a month, by how much would you expect net operating income to increase? What are your assumptions?

EXERCISE 5–13 Using a Contribution Format Income Statement [LO5–1, LO5–4]
Miller Company's most recent contribution format income statement is shown below:

	Total	Per Unit
Sales (20,000 units)	$300,000	$15.00
Variable expenses	180,000	9.00
Contribution margin	120,000	$ 6.00
Fixed expenses	70,000	
Net operating income	$ 50,000	

Required:
Prepare a new contribution format income statement under each of the following conditions (consider each case independently):
1. The number of units sold increases by 15%.
2. The selling price decreases by $1.50 per unit, and the number of units sold increases by 25%.
3. The selling price increases by $1.50 per unit, fixed expenses increase by $20,000, and the number of units sold decreases by 5%.
4. The selling price increases by 12%, variable expenses increase by 60 cents per unit, and the number of units sold decreases by 10%.

EXERCISE 5–14 Break-Even and Target Profit Analysis [LO5–3, LO5–4, LO5–5, LO5–6]
Lindon Company is the exclusive distributor for an automotive product that sells for $40 per unit and has a CM ratio of 30%. The company's fixed expenses are $180,000 per year. The company plans to sell 16,000 units this year.

Required:
1. What are the variable expenses per unit?
2. Using the equation method:
   a. What is the break-even point in unit sales and in dollar sales?
   b. What amount of unit sales and dollar sales is required to earn an annual profit of $60,000?
   c. Assume that by using a more efficient shipper, the company is able to reduce its variable expenses by $4 per unit. What is the company's new break-even point in unit sales and in dollar sales?
3. Repeat (2) above using the formula method.

EXERCISE 5–15 Operating Leverage [LO5–4, LO5–8]
Magic Realm, Inc., has developed a new fantasy board game. The company sold 15,000 games last year at a selling price of $20 per game. Fixed expenses associated with the game total $182,000 per year, and variable expenses are $6 per game. Production of the game is entrusted to a printing contractor. Variable expenses consist mostly of payments to this contractor.

Required:
1. Prepare a contribution format income statement for the game last year and compute the degree of operating leverage.
2. Management is confident that the company can sell 18,000 games next year (an increase of 3,000 games, or 20%, over last year). Compute:
   a. The expected percentage increase in net operating income for next year.
   b. The expected total dollar net operating income for next year. (Do not prepare an income statement; use the degree of operating leverage to compute your answer.)

222   Chapter 5

EXERCISE 5–16 Break-Even Analysis and CVP Graphing [LO5–2, LO5–4, LO5–5]
The Hartford Symphony Guild is planning its annual dinner-dance. The dinner-dance committee has assembled the following expected costs for the event:

Dinner (per person)	$18
Favors and program (per person)	$2
Band	$2,800
Rental of ballroom	$900
Professional entertainment during intermission	$1,000
Tickets and advertising	$1,300

The committee members would like to charge $35 per person for the evening's activities.

Required:
1. Compute the break-even point for the dinner-dance (in terms of the number of persons who must attend).
2. Assume that last year only 300 persons attended the dinner-dance. If the same number attend this year, what price per ticket must be charged in order to break even?
3. Refer to the original data ($35 ticket price per person). Prepare a CVP graph for the dinner-dance from zero tickets up to 600 tickets sold.

EXERCISE 5–17 Break-Even and Target Profit Analysis [LO5–4, LO5–5, LO5–6]
Outback Outfitters sells recreational equipment. One of the company's products, a small camp stove, sells for $50 per unit. Variable expenses are $32 per stove, and fixed expenses associated with the stove total $108,000 per month.

Required:
1. Compute the break-even point in unit sales and in dollar sales.
2. If the variable expenses per stove increase as a percentage of the selling price, will it result in a higher or a lower break-even point? Why? (Assume that the fixed expenses remain unchanged.)
3. At present, the company is selling 8,000 stoves per month. The sales manager is convinced that a 10% reduction in the selling price would result in a 25% increase in monthly sales of stoves. Prepare two contribution format income statements, one under present operating conditions, and one as operations would appear after the proposed changes. Show both total and per unit data on your statements.
4. Refer to the data in (3) above. How many stoves would have to be sold at the new selling price to yield a minimum net operating income of $35,000 per month?

EXERCISE 5–18 Break-Even and Target Profit Analysis; Margin of Safety; CM Ratio [LO5–1, LO5–3, LO5–5, LO5–6, LO5–7]
Menlo Company distributes a single product. The company's sales and expenses for last month follow:

	Total	Per Unit
Sales	$450,000	$30
Variable expenses	180,000	12
Contribution margin	270,000	$18
Fixed expenses	216,000	
Net operating income	$ 54,000	

Required:
1. What is the monthly break-even point in unit sales and in dollar sales?
2. Without resorting to computations, what is the total contribution margin at the break-even point?
3. How many units would have to be sold each month to earn a target profit of $90,000? Use the formula method. Verify your answer by preparing a contribution format income statement at the target sales level.
4. Refer to the original data. Compute the company's margin of safety in both dollar and percentage terms.
5. What is the company's CM ratio? If sales increase by $50,000 per month and there is no change in fixed expenses, by how much would you expect monthly net operating income to increase?

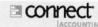 **Problems**

All applicable problems are available with McGraw-Hill's *Connect® Accounting*.

PROBLEM 5–19 Break-Even Analysis; Pricing [LO5–1, LO5–4, LO5–5]

Minden Company introduced a new product last year for which it is trying to find an optimal selling price. Marketing studies suggest that the company can increase sales by 5,000 units for each $2 reduction in the selling price. The company's present selling price is $70 per unit, and variable expenses are $40 per unit. Fixed expenses are $540,000 per year. The present annual sales volume (at the $70 selling price) is 15,000 units.

Required:
1. What is the present yearly net operating income or loss?
2. What is the present break-even point in unit sales and in dollar sales?
3. Assuming that the marketing studies are correct, what is the maximum annual profit that the company can earn? At how many units and at what selling price per unit would the company generate this profit?
4. What would be the break-even point in unit sales and in dollar sales using the selling price you determined in (3) above (e.g., the selling price at the level of maximum profits)? Why is this break-even point different from the break-even point you computed in (2) above?

PROBLEM 5–20 Various CVP Questions: Break-Even Point; Cost Structure; Target Sales [LO5–1, LO5–3, LO5–4, LO5–5, LO5–6, LO5–8]

Northwood Company manufactures basketballs. The company has a ball that sells for $25. At present, the ball is manufactured in a small plant that relies heavily on direct labor workers. Thus, variable expenses are high, totaling $15 per ball, of which 60% is direct labor cost.

Last year, the company sold 30,000 of these balls, with the following results:

Sales (30,000 balls)	$750,000
Variable expenses	450,000
Contribution margin	300,000
Fixed expenses	210,000
Net operating income	$ 90,000

Required:
1. Compute (a) the CM ratio and the break-even point in balls, and (b) the degree of operating leverage at last year's sales level.
2. Due to an increase in labor rates, the company estimates that variable expenses will increase by $3 per ball next year. If this change takes place and the selling price per ball remains constant at $25, what will be the new CM ratio and break-even point in balls?
3. Refer to the data in (2) above. If the expected change in variable expenses takes place, how many balls will have to be sold next year to earn the same net operating income, $90,000, as last year?
4. Refer again to the data in (2) above. The president feels that the company must raise the selling price of its basketballs. If Northwood Company wants to maintain the same CM ratio as last year, what selling price per ball must it charge next year to cover the increased labor costs?
5. Refer to the original data. The company is discussing the construction of a new, automated manufacturing plant. The new plant would slash variable expenses per ball by 40%, but it would cause fixed expenses per year to double. If the new plant is built, what would be the company's new CM ratio and new break-even point in balls?
6. Refer to the data in (5) above.
   a. If the new plant is built, how many balls will have to be sold next year to earn the same net operating income, $90,000, as last year?
   b. Assume the new plant is built and that next year the company manufactures and sells 30,000 balls (the same number as sold last year). Prepare a contribution format income statement and compute the degree of operating leverage.
   c. If you were a member of top management, would you have been in favor of constructing the new plant? Explain.

224

Chapter 5

PROBLEM 5–21 Sales Mix; Multiproduct Break-Even Analysis [LO5–9]
Gold Star Rice, Ltd., of Thailand exports Thai rice throughout Asia. The company grows three varieties of rice—Fragrant, White, and Loonzain. Budgeted sales by product and in total for the coming month are shown below:

	Product							
	White		Fragrant		Loonzain		Total	
Percentage of total sales	20%		52%		28%		100%	
Sales	$150,000	100%	$390,000	100%	$210,000	100%	$750,000	100%
Variable expenses	108,000	72%	78,000	20%	84,000	40%	270,000	36%
Contribution margin	$ 42,000	28%	$312,000	80%	$126,000	60%	480,000	64%
Fixed expenses							449,280	
Net operating income							$30,720	

$$\frac{\text{Dollar sales to}}{\text{break even}} = \frac{\text{Fixed expenses}}{\text{CM ratio}} = \frac{\$449,280}{0.64} = \$702,000$$

As shown by these data, net operating income is budgeted at $30,720 for the month and break-even sales at $702,000.

Assume that actual sales for the month total $750,000 as planned. Actual sales by product are: White, $300,000; Fragrant, $180,000; and Loonzain, $270,000.

Required:
1. Prepare a contribution format income statement for the month based on actual sales data. Present the income statement in the format shown above.
2. Compute the break-even point in dollar sales for the month based on your actual data.
3. Considering the fact that the company met its $750,000 sales budget for the month, the president is shocked at the results shown on your income statement in (1) above. Prepare a brief memo for the president explaining why both the operating results and the break-even point in dollar sales are different from what was budgeted.

PROBLEM 5–22 Basics of CVP Analysis; Cost Structure [LO5–1, LO5–3, LO5–4, LO5–5, LO5–6]
Due to erratic sales of its sole product—a high-capacity battery for laptop computers—PEM, Inc., has been experiencing difficulty for some time. The company's contribution format income statement for the most recent month is given below:

Sales (19,500 units × $30 per unit)	$585,000
Variable expenses	409,500
Contribution margin	175,500
Fixed expenses	180,000
Net operating loss	$ (4,500)

Required:
1. Compute the company's CM ratio and its break-even point in both unit sales and dollar sales.
2. The president believes that a $16,000 increase in the monthly advertising budget, combined with an intensified effort by the sales staff, will result in an $80,000 increase in monthly sales. If the president is right, what will be the effect on the company's monthly net operating income or loss? (Use the incremental approach in preparing your answer.)
3. Refer to the original data. The sales manager is convinced that a 10% reduction in the selling price, combined with an increase of $60,000 in the monthly advertising budget, will double unit sales. What will the new contribution format income statement look like if these changes are adopted?
4. Refer to the original data. The Marketing Department thinks that a fancy new package for the laptop computer battery would help sales. The new package would increase packaging costs by 75 cents per unit. Assuming no other changes, how many units would have to be sold each month to earn a profit of $9,750?

5. Refer to the original data. By automating, the company could reduce variable expenses by $3 per unit. However, fixed expenses would increase by $72,000 each month.
    a. Compute the new CM ratio and the new break-even point in both unit sales and dollar sales.
    b. Assume that the company expects to sell 26,000 units next month. Prepare two contribution format income statements, one assuming that operations are not automated and one assuming that they are. (Show data on a per unit and percentage basis, as well as in total, for each alternative.)
    c. Would you recommend that the company automate its operations? Explain.

PROBLEM 5–23 Basics of CVP Analysis [LO5–1, LO5–3, LO5–4, LO5–5, LO5–8]

Feather Friends, Inc., distributes a high-quality wooden birdhouse that sells for $20 per unit. Variable expenses are $8 per unit, and fixed expenses total $180,000 per year.

Required:

Answer the following independent questions:
1. What is the product's CM ratio?
2. Use the CM ratio to determine the break-even point in dollar sales.
3. Due to an increase in demand, the company estimates that sales will increase by $75,000 during the next year. By how much should net operating income increase (or net loss decrease) assuming that fixed expenses do not change?
4. Assume that the operating results for last year were:

Sales	$400,000
Variable expenses	160,000
Contribution margin	240,000
Fixed expenses	180,000
Net operating income	$ 60,000

    a. Compute the degree of operating leverage at the current level of sales.
    b. The president expects sales to increase by 20% next year. By what percentage should net operating income increase?
5. Refer to the original data. Assume that the company sold 18,000 units last year. The sales manager is convinced that a 10% reduction in the selling price, combined with a $30,000 increase in advertising, would increase annual unit sales by one-third. Prepare two contribution format income statements, one showing the results of last year's operations and one showing the results of operations if these changes are made. Would you recommend that the company do as the sales manager suggests?
6. Refer to the original data. Assume again that the company sold 18,000 units last year. The president does not want to change the selling price. Instead, he wants to increase the sales commission by $1 per unit. He thinks that this move, combined with some increase in advertising, would increase annual sales by 25%. By how much could advertising be increased with profits remaining unchanged? Do not prepare an income statement; use the incremental analysis approach.

PROBLEM 5–24 Break-Even and Target Profit Analysis [LO5–5, LO5–6]

The Shirt Works sells a large variety of tee shirts and sweatshirts. Steve Hooper, the owner, is thinking of expanding his sales by hiring high school students, on a commission basis, to sell sweatshirts bearing the name and mascot of the local high school.

These sweatshirts would have to be ordered from the manufacturer six weeks in advance, and they could not be returned because of the unique printing required. The sweatshirts would cost Hooper $8 each with a minimum order of 75 sweatshirts. Any additional sweatshirts would have to be ordered in increments of 75.

Since Hooper's plan would not require any additional facilities, the only costs associated with the project would be the costs of the sweatshirts and the costs of the sales commissions. The selling price of the sweatshirts would be $13.50 each. Hooper would pay the students a commission of $1.50 for each shirt sold.

Required:

1. To make the project worthwhile, Hooper would require a $1,200 profit for the first three months of the venture. What level of unit sales and dollar sales would be required to reach this target net operating income? Show all computations.
2. Assume that the venture is undertaken and an order is placed for 75 sweatshirts. What would be Hooper's break-even point in unit sales and in dollar sales? Show computations and explain the reasoning behind your answer.

226

Chapter 5

PROBLEM 5–25 Changes in Fixed and Variable Expenses; Break-Even and Target Profit Analysis
[LO5–4, LO5–5, LO5–6]

Neptune Company produces toys and other items for use in beach and resort areas. A small, inflatable toy has come onto the market that the company is anxious to produce and sell. The new toy will sell for $3 per unit. Enough capacity exists in the company's plant to produce 16,000 units of the toy each month. Variable expenses to manufacture and sell one unit would be $1.25, and fixed expenses associated with the toy would total $35,000 per month.

The company's Marketing Department predicts that demand for the new toy will exceed the 16,000 units that the company is able to produce. Additional manufacturing space can be rented from another company at a fixed expense of $1,000 per month. Variable expenses in the rented facility would total $1.40 per unit, due to somewhat less efficient operations than in the main plant.

Required:
1. Compute the monthly break-even point for the new toy in unit sales and in dollar sales.
2. How many units must be sold each month to make a monthly profit of $12,000?
3. If the sales manager receives a bonus of 10 cents for each unit sold in excess of the break-even point, how many units must be sold each month to earn a return of 25% on the monthly investment in fixed expenses?

PROBLEM 5–26 Basic CVP Analysis; Graphing [LO5–1, LO5–2, LO5–4, LO5–5]

The Fashion Shoe Company operates a chain of women's shoe shops that carry many styles of shoes that are all sold at the same price. Sales personnel in the shops are paid a substantial commission on each pair of shoes sold (in addition to a small base salary) in order to encourage them to be aggressive in their sales efforts.

The following worksheet contains cost and revenue data for Shop 48 and is typical of the company's many outlets:

	Per Pair of Shoes
Selling price	$30.00
Variable expenses:	
Invoice cost	$13.50
Sales commission	4.50
Total variable expenses	$18.00
	Annual
Fixed expenses:	
Advertising	$ 30,000
Rent	20,000
Salaries	100,000
Total fixed expenses	$150,000

Required:
1. Calculate the annual break-even point in unit sales and in dollar sales for Shop 48.
2. Prepare a CVP graph showing cost and revenue data for Shop 48 from zero shoes up to 17,000 pairs of shoes sold each year. Clearly indicate the break-even point on the graph.
3. If 12,000 pairs of shoes are sold in a year, what would be Shop 48's net operating income or loss?
4. The company is considering paying the store manager of Shop 48 an incentive commission of 75 cents per pair of shoes (in addition to the salesperson's commission). If this change is made, what will be the new break-even point in unit sales and in dollar sales?
5. Refer to the original data. As an alternative to (4) above, the company is considering paying the store manager 50 cents commission on each pair of shoes sold in excess of the break-even point. If this change is made, what will be the shop's net operating income or loss if 15,000 pairs of shoes are sold?
6. Refer to the original data. The company is considering eliminating sales commissions entirely in its shops and increasing fixed salaries by $31,500 annually. If this change is made, what will be the new break-even point in unit sales and in dollar sales for Shop 48? Would you recommend that the change be made? Explain.

PROBLEM 5–27 Sales Mix; Break-Even Analysis; Margin of Safety [LO5–7, LO5–9]

Island Novelties, Inc., of Palau makes two products, Hawaiian Fantasy and Tahitian Joy. Present revenue, cost, and sales data for the two products follow:

	Hawaiian Fantasy	Tahitian Joy
Selling price per unit	$15	$100
Variable expenses per unit	$9	$20
Number of units sold annually	20,000	5,000

Fixed expenses total $475,800 per year.

Required:

1. Assuming the sales mix given above, do the following:
   a. Prepare a contribution format income statement showing both dollar and percent columns for each product and for the company as a whole.
   b. Compute the break-even point in dollar sales for the company as a whole and the margin of safety in both dollars and percent.
2. The company has developed a new product to be called Samoan Delight. Assume that the company could sell 10,000 units at $45 each. The variable expenses would be $36 each. The company's fixed expenses would not change.
   a. Prepare another contribution format income statement, including sales of the Samoan Delight (sales of the other two products would not change).
   b. Compute the company's new break-even point in dollar sales and the new margin of safety in both dollars and percent.
3. The president of the company examines your figures and says, "There's something strange here. Our fixed expenses haven't changed and you show greater total contribution margin if we add the new product, but you also show our break-even point going up. With greater contribution margin, the break-even point should go down, not up. You've made a mistake somewhere." Explain to the president what has happened.

PROBLEM 5–28 Sales Mix; Commission Structure; Multiproduct Break-Even Analysis [LO5–9]

Carbex, Inc., produces cutlery sets out of high-quality wood and steel. The company makes a standard cutlery set and a deluxe set and sells them to retail department stores throughout the country. The standard set sells for $60, and the deluxe set sells for $75. The variable expenses associated with each set are given below.

	Standard	Deluxe
Production costs	$15.00	$30.00
Sales commissions (15% of sales price)	$9.00	$11.25

The company's fixed expenses each month are:

Advertising	$105,000
Depreciation	$21,700
Administrative	$63,000

Salespersons are paid on a commission basis to encourage them to be aggressive in their sales efforts. Mary Parsons, the financial vice president, watches sales commissions carefully and has noted that they have risen steadily over the last year. For this reason, she was shocked to find that even though sales have increased, profits for the current month—May—are down substantially from April. Sales, in sets, for the last two months are given below:

	Standard	Deluxe	Total
April	4,000	2,000	6,000
May	1,000	5,000	6,000

228

Chapter 5

Required:
1. Prepare contribution format income statements for April and May. Use the following headings:

	Standard		Deluxe		Total	
	Amount	Percent	Amount	Percent	Amount	Percent
Sales ...						
Etc						

Place the fixed expenses only in the Total column. Do not show percentages for the fixed expenses.

2. Explain the difference in net operating incomes between the two months, even though the same total number of sets was sold in each month.
3. What can be done to the sales commissions to improve the sales mix?
   a. Using April's sales mix, what is the break-even point in dollar sales?
   b. Without doing any calculations, explain whether the break-even points would be higher or lower with May's sales mix than April's sales mix.

PROBLEM 5–29 Changes in Cost Structure; Break-Even Analysis; Operating Leverage; Margin of Safety [LO5–4, LO5–5, LO5–7, LO5–8]
Morton Company's contribution format income statement for last month is given below:

Sales (15,000 units × $30 per unit)	$450,000
Variable expenses	315,000
Contribution margin	135,000
Fixed expenses	90,000
Net operating income	$ 45,000

The industry in which Morton Company operates is quite sensitive to cyclical movements in the economy. Thus, profits vary considerably from year to year according to general economic conditions. The company has a large amount of unused capacity and is studying ways of improving profits.

Required:
1. New equipment has come onto the market that would allow Morton Company to automate a portion of its operations. Variable expenses would be reduced by $9 per unit. However, fixed expenses would increase to a total of $225,000 each month. Prepare two contribution format income statements, one showing present operations and one showing how operations would appear if the new equipment is purchased. Show an Amount column, a Per Unit column, and a Percent column on each statement. Do not show percentages for the fixed expenses.
2. Refer to the income statements in (1) above. For both present operations and the proposed new operations, compute (a) the degree of operating leverage, (b) the break-even point in dollar sales, and (c) the margin of safety in both dollar and percentage terms.
3. Refer again to the data in (1) above. As a manager, what factor would be paramount in your mind in deciding whether to purchase the new equipment? (Assume that enough funds are available to make the purchase.)
4. Refer to the original data. Rather than purchase new equipment, the marketing manager argues that the company's marketing strategy should be changed. Rather than pay sales commissions, which are currently included in variable expenses, the company would pay salespersons fixed salaries and would invest heavily in advertising. The marketing manager claims this new approach would increase unit sales by 30% without any change in selling price; the company's new monthly fixed expenses would be $180,000; and its net operating income would increase by 20%. Compute the break-even point in dollar sales for the company under the new marketing strategy. Do you agree with the marketing manager's proposal?

PROBLEM 5–30 Graphing; Incremental Analysis; Operating Leverage [LO5–2, LO5–4, LO5–5, LO5–6, LO5–8]
Angie Silva has recently opened The Sandal Shop in Brisbane, Australia, a store that specializes in fashionable sandals. Angie has just received a degree in business and she is anxious to apply the principles she has learned to her business. In time, she hopes to open a chain of sandal shops. As a first step, she has prepared the following analysis for her new store:

Sales price per pair of sandals	$40
Variable expenses per pair of sandals	16
Contribution margin per pair of sandals	$24
Fixed expenses per year:	
Building rental	$15,000
Equipment depreciation	7,000
Selling	20,000
Administrative	18,000
Total fixed expenses	$60,000

Required:
1. How many pairs of sandals must be sold each year to break even? What does this represent in total sales dollars?
2. Prepare a CVP graph or a profit graph for the store from zero pairs up to 4,000 pairs of sandals sold each year. Indicate the break-even point on your graph.
3. Angie has decided that she must earn at least $18,000 the first year to justify her time and effort. How many pairs of sandals must be sold to reach this target profit?
4. Angie now has two salespersons working in the store—one full time and one part time. It will cost her an additional $8,000 per year to convert the part-time position to a full-time position. Angie believes that the change would bring in an additional $25,000 in sales each year. Should she convert the position? Use the incremental approach. (Do not prepare an income statement.)
5. Refer to the original data. During the first year, the store sold only 3,000 pairs of sandals and reported the following operating results:

Sales (3,000 pairs)	$120,000
Variable expenses	48,000
Contribution margin	72,000
Fixed expenses	60,000
Net operating income	$ 12,000

  a. What is the store's degree of operating leverage?
  b. Angie is confident that with a more intense sales effort and with a more creative advertising program she can increase sales by 50% next year. What would be the expected percentage increase in net operating income? Use the degree of operating leverage to compute your answer.

PROBLEM 5–31 Interpretive Questions on the CVP Graph [LO5–2, LO5–5]
A CVP graph such as the one shown below is a useful technique for showing relationships among an organization's costs, volume, and profits.

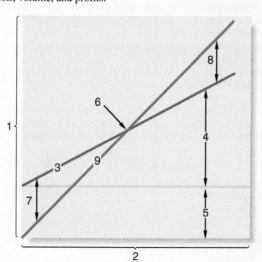

230   Chapter 5

Required:
1. Identify the numbered components in the CVP graph.
2. State the effect of each of the following actions on line 3, line 9, and the break-even point. For line 3 and line 9, state whether the action will cause the line to:

> Remain unchanged.
> Shift upward.
> Shift downward.
> Have a steeper slope (i.e., rotate upward).
> Have a flatter slope (i.e., rotate downward).
> Shift upward *and* have a steeper slope.
> Shift upward *and* have a flatter slope.
> Shift downward *and* have a steeper slope.
> Shift downward *and* have a flatter slope.

In the case of the break-even point, state whether the action will cause the break-even point to:

> Remain unchanged.
> Increase.
> Decrease.
> Probably change, but the direction is uncertain.

Treat each case independently.

x. *Example.*   Fixed expenses are reduced by $5,000 per period.
    Answer (see choices above):   Line 3:   Shift downward.
                                     Line 9:   Remain unchanged.
                                     Break-even point: Decrease.

a. The unit selling price is increased from $18 to $20.
b. Unit variable expenses are decreased from $12 to $10.
c. Fixed expenses are increased by $3,000 per period.
d. Two thousand more units are sold during the period than were budgeted.
e. Due to paying salespersons a commission rather than a flat salary, fixed expenses are reduced by $8,000 per period and unit variable expenses are increased by $3.
f. Due to an increase in the cost of materials, both unit variable expenses and the selling price are increased by $2.
g. Advertising costs are increased by $10,000 per period, resulting in a 10% increase in the number of units sold.
h. Due to automating an operation previously done by workers, fixed expenses are increased by $12,000 per period and unit variable expenses are reduced by $4.

Cases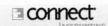

All applicable cases are available with McGraw-Hill's *Connect® Accounting.*

CASE 5–32 Break-Evens for Individual Products in a Multiproduct Company [LO5–5, LO5–9]

Cheryl Montoya picked up the phone and called her boss, Wes Chan, the vice president of marketing at Piedmont Fasteners Corporation: "Wes, I'm not sure how to go about answering the questions that came up at the meeting with the president yesterday."

"What's the problem?"

"The president wanted to know the break-even point for each of the company's products, but I am having trouble figuring them out."

"I'm sure you can handle it, Cheryl. And, by the way, I need your analysis on my desk tomorrow morning at 8:00 sharp in time for the follow-up meeting at 9:00."

Piedmont Fasteners Corporation makes three different clothing fasteners in its manufacturing facility in North Carolina. Data concerning these products appear below:

	Velcro	Metal	Nylon
Normal annual sales volume	100,000	200,000	400,000
Unit selling price	$1.65	$1.50	$0.85
Variable expense per unit	$1.25	$0.70	$0.25

Total fixed expenses are $400,000 per year.

All three products are sold in highly competitive markets, so the company is unable to raise its prices without losing unacceptable numbers of customers.

The company has an extremely effective lean production system, so there are no beginning or ending work in process or finished goods inventories.

Required:

1. What is the company's over-all break-even point in dollar sales?
2. Of the total fixed expenses of $400,000, $20,000 could be avoided if the Velcro product is dropped, $80,000 if the Metal product is dropped, and $60,000 if the Nylon product is dropped. The remaining fixed expenses of $240,000 consist of common fixed expenses such as administrative salaries and rent on the factory building that could be avoided only by going out of business entirely.
   a. What is the break-even point in unit sales for each product?
   b. If the company sells exactly the break-even quantity of each product, what will be the overall profit of the company? Explain this result.

CASE 5–33 Cost Structure; Break-Even and Target Profit Analysis [LO5–4, LO5–5, LO5–6]

Pittman Company is a small but growing manufacturer of telecommunications equipment. The company has no sales force of its own; rather, it relies completely on independent sales agents to market its products. These agents are paid a sales commission of 15% for all items sold.

Barbara Cheney, Pittman's controller, has just prepared the company's budgeted income statement for next year. The statement follows:

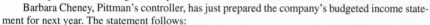

Pittman Company		
Budgeted Income Statement		
For the Year Ended December 31		
Sales		$16,000,000
Manufacturing expenses:		
Variable	$7,200,000	
Fixed overhead	2,340,000	9,540,000
Gross margin		6,460,000
Selling and administrative expenses:		
Commissions to agents	2,400,000	
Fixed marketing expenses	120,000*	
Fixed administrative expenses	1,800,000	4,320,000
Net operating income		2,140,000
Fixed interest expenses		540,000
Income before income taxes		1,600,000
Income taxes (30%)		480,000
Net income		$ 1,120,000

*Primarily depreciation on storage facilities.

As Barbara handed the statement to Karl Vecci, Pittman's president, she commented, "I went ahead and used the agents' 15% commission rate in completing these statements, but we've just learned that they refuse to handle our products next year unless we increase the commission rate to 20%."

"That's the last straw," Karl replied angrily. "Those agents have been demanding more and more, and this time they've gone too far. How can they possibly defend a 20% commission rate?"

"They claim that after paying for advertising, travel, and the other costs of promotion, there's nothing left over for profit," replied Barbara.

"I say it's just plain robbery," retorted Karl. "And I also say it's time we dumped those guys and got our own sales force. Can you get your people to work up some cost figures for us to look at?"

"We've already worked them up," said Barbara. "Several companies we know about pay a 7.5% commission to their own salespeople, along with a small salary. Of course, we would have to handle all promotion costs, too. We figure our fixed expenses would increase by $2,400,000 per year, but that would be more than offset by the $3,200,000 (20% × $16,000,000) that we would avoid on agents' commissions."

The breakdown of the $2,400,000 cost follows:

Salaries:	
Sales manager	$ 100,000
Salespersons	600,000
Travel and entertainment	400,000
Advertising	1,300,000
Total	$2,400,000

"Super," replied Karl. "And I noticed that the $2,400,000 is just what we're paying the agents under the old 15% commission rate."

"It's even better than that," explained Barbara. "We can actually save $75,000 a year because that's what we're having to pay the auditing firm now to check out the agents' reports. So our overall administrative expenses would be less."

"Pull all of these numbers together and we'll show them to the executive committee tomorrow," said Karl. "With the approval of the committee, we can move on the matter immediately."

Required:

1. Compute Pittman Company's break-even point in dollar sales for next year assuming:
   a. The agents' commission rate remains unchanged at 15%.
   b. The agents' commission rate is increased to 20%.
   c. The company employs its own sales force.
2. Assume that Pittman Company decides to continue selling through agents and pays the 20% commission rate. Determine the volume of sales that would be required to generate the same net income as contained in the budgeted income statement for next year.
3. Determine the volume of sales at which net income would be equal regardless of whether Pittman Company sells through agents (at a 20% commission rate) or employs its own sales force.
4. Compute the degree of operating leverage that the company would expect to have on December 31 at the end of next year assuming:
   a. The agents' commission rate remains unchanged at 15%.
   b. The agents' commission rate is increased to 20%.
   c. The company employs its own sales force.
   Use income *before* income taxes in your operating leverage computation.
5. Based on the data in (1) through (4) above, make a recommendation as to whether the company should continue to use sales agents (at a 20% commission rate) or employ its own sales force. Give reasons for your answer.

(CMA, adapted)

CHAPTER 6

Variable Costing and Segment Reporting: Tools for Management

Misguided Incentives in the Auto Industry

When the economy tanks, automakers, such as General Motors and Chrysler, often "flood the market" with a supply of vehicles that far exceeds customer demand. They pursue this course of action even though it tarnishes their brand image and increases their auto storage costs, tire replacement costs, customer rebate costs, and advertising costs. This begs the question why would managers knowingly produce more vehicles than are demanded by customers?

In the auto industry, a manager's bonus is often influenced by her company's reported profits; thus, there is a strong incentive to boost profits by producing more units. How can this be done you ask? It would seem logical that producing more units would have no impact on profits unless the units were sold, right? Wrong! As we will discover in this chapter, absorption costing—the most widely used method of determining product costs—can artificially increase profits when managers choose to increase the quantity of units produced. ■

Source: Marielle Segarra, "Lots of Trouble," CFO, March 2012, pp. 29–30.

LEARNING OBJECTIVES

After studying Chapter 6, you should be able to:

LO6–1 Explain how variable costing differs from absorption costing and compute unit product costs under each method.

LO6–2 Prepare income statements using both variable and absorption costing.

LO6–3 Reconcile variable costing and absorption costing net operating incomes and explain why the two amounts differ.

LO6–4 Prepare a segmented income statement that differentiates traceable fixed costs from common fixed costs and use it to make decisions.

LO6–5 Compute companywide and segment break-even points for a company with traceable fixed costs.

LO6–6 *(Appendix 6A)* Prepare an income statement using super-variable costing and reconcile this approach with variable costing.

234   Chapter 6

This chapter describes two applications of the contribution format income statements that were introduced in earlier chapters. First, it explains how manufacturing companies can prepare *variable costing* income statements, which rely on the contribution format, for internal decision making purposes. The variable costing approach will be contrasted with *absorption costing* income statements, which were discussed in Chapter 3 and are generally used for external reports. Ordinarily, variable costing and absorption costing produce different net operating income figures, and the difference can be quite large. In addition to showing how these two methods differ, we will describe the advantages of variable costing for internal reporting purposes and we will show how management decisions can be affected by the costing method chosen.

Second, the chapter explains how the contribution format can be used to prepare segmented income statements. In addition to companywide income statements, managers need to measure the profitability of individual *segments* of their organizations. A **segment** is a part or activity of an organization about which managers would like cost, revenue, or profit data. This chapter explains how to create contribution format income statements that report profit data for business segments, such as divisions, individual stores, geographic regions, customers, and product lines.

Overview of Variable and Absorption Costing

LO6–1

Explain how variable costing differs from absorption costing and compute unit product costs under each method.

As you begin to read about variable and absorption costing income statements in the coming pages, focus your attention on three key concepts. First, both income statement formats include product costs and period costs, although they define these cost classifications differently. Second, variable costing income statements are grounded in the contribution format. They categorize expenses based on cost behavior—variable expenses are reported separately from fixed expenses. Absorption costing income statements ignore variable and fixed cost distinctions. Third, as mentioned in the paragraph above, variable and absorption costing net operating income figures often differ from one another. The reason for these differences always relates to the fact the variable costing and absorption costing income statements account for fixed manufacturing overhead differently. *Pay very close attention to the two different ways that variable costing and absorption costing account for fixed manufacturing overhead.*

Variable Costing

Under **variable costing**, only those manufacturing costs that vary with output are treated as product costs. This would usually include direct materials, direct labor, and the variable portion of manufacturing overhead. Fixed manufacturing overhead is not treated as a product cost under this method. Rather, fixed manufacturing overhead is treated as a period cost and, like selling and administrative expenses, it is expensed in its entirety each period. Consequently, the cost of a unit of product in inventory or in cost of goods sold under the variable costing method does not contain any fixed manufacturing overhead cost. Variable costing is sometimes referred to as *direct costing* or *marginal costing*.

Absorption Costing

As discussed in Chapter 3, **absorption costing** treats *all* manufacturing costs as product costs, regardless of whether they are variable or fixed. The cost of a unit of product under the absorption costing method consists of direct materials, direct labor, and *both* variable and fixed manufacturing overhead. Thus, absorption costing allocates a portion of fixed manufacturing overhead cost to each unit of product, along with the variable manufacturing costs. Because absorption costing includes all manufacturing costs in product costs, it is frequently referred to as the *full cost* method.

Selling and Administrative Expenses

Selling and administrative expenses are never treated as product costs, regardless of the costing method. Thus, under absorption and variable costing, variable and fixed selling and administrative expenses are always treated as period costs and are expensed as incurred.

Summary of Differences   The essential difference between variable costing and absorption costing, as illustrated in Exhibit 6–1, is how each method accounts for fixed manufacturing overhead costs—all other costs are treated the same under the two methods. In absorption costing, fixed manufacturing overhead costs are included as part of the costs of work in process inventories. When units are completed, these costs are transferred to finished goods and only when the units are sold do these costs flow through to the income statement as part of cost of goods sold. In variable costing, fixed manufacturing overhead costs are considered to be period costs—just like selling and administrative costs—and are taken immediately to the income statement as period expenses.

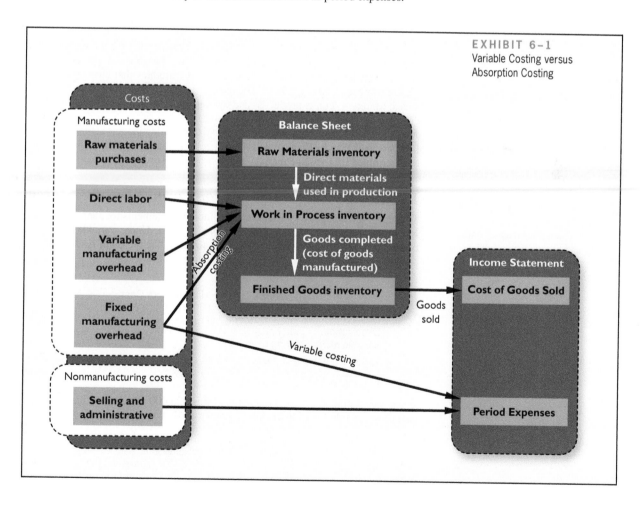

EXHIBIT 6–1
Variable Costing versus
Absorption Costing

Variable and Absorption Costing—An Example

To illustrate the difference between variable costing and absorption costing, consider Weber Light Aircraft, a company that produces light recreational aircraft. Data concerning the company's operations appear below:

	Per Aircraft	Per Month
Selling price	$100,000	
Direct materials	$19,000	
Direct labor	$5,000	
Variable manufacturing overhead	$1,000	
Fixed manufacturing overhead		$70,000
Variable selling and administrative expenses	$10,000	
Fixed selling and administrative expenses		$20,000

	January	February	March
Beginning inventory	0	0	1
Units produced	1	2	4
Units sold	1	1	5
Ending inventory	0	1	0

As you review the data above, it is important to realize that for the months of January, February, and March, the selling price per aircraft, variable cost per aircraft, and total monthly fixed expenses never change. The only variables that change in this example are the number of units produced (January = 1 unit produced; February = 2 units produced; March = 4 units produced) and the number of units sold (January = 1 unit sold; February = 1 unit sold; March = 5 units sold).

We will first construct the company's variable costing income statements for January, February, and March. Then we will show how the company's net operating income would be determined for the same months using absorption costing.

Variable Costing Contribution Format Income Statement

LO6–2

Prepare income statements using both variable and absorption costing.

To prepare the company's variable costing income statements for January, February, and March we begin by computing the unit product cost. Under variable costing, product costs consist solely of variable production costs. At Weber Light Aircraft, the variable production cost per unit is $25,000, determined as follows:

Variable Costing Unit Product Cost	
Direct materials	$19,000
Direct labor	5,000
Variable manufacturing overhead	1,000
Variable costing unit product cost	$25,000

Since each month's variable production cost is $25,000 per aircraft, the variable costing cost of goods sold for all three months can be easily computed as follows:

Variable Costing Cost of Goods Sold			
	January	February	March
Variable production cost (a)	$25,000	$25,000	$25,000
Units sold (b)	1	1	5
Variable cost of goods sold (a) × (b)	$25,000	$25,000	$125,000

And the company's total selling and administrative expense would be derived as follows:

Selling and Administrative Expenses	January	February	March
Variable selling and administrative expense (@ $10,000 per unit sold)	$10,000	$10,000	$50,000
Fixed selling and administrative expense	20,000	20,000	20,000
Total selling and administrative expense	$30,000	$30,000	$70,000

Putting it all together, the variable costing income statements would appear as shown in Exhibit 6–2. Notice, the contribution format has been used in these income statements. Also, the monthly fixed manufacturing overhead costs ($70,000) have been recorded as a period expense in the month incurred.

Variable Costing Contribution Format Income Statements	January	February	March
Sales	$100,000	$100,000	$500,000
Variable expenses:			
Variable cost of goods sold	25,000	25,000	125,000
Variable selling and administrative expense	10,000	10,000	50,000
Total variable expenses	35,000	35,000	175,000
Contribution margin	65,000	65,000	325,000
Fixed expenses:			
Fixed manufacturing overhead	70,000	70,000	70,000
Fixed selling and administrative expense	20,000	20,000	20,000
Total fixed expenses	90,000	90,000	90,000
Net operating income (loss)	$ (25,000)	$ (25,000)	$235,000

EXHIBIT 6–2
Variable Costing Income Statements

A simple method for understanding how Weber Light Aircraft computed its variable costing net operating income figures is to focus on the contribution margin per aircraft sold, which is computed as follows:

Contribution Margin per Aircraft Sold		
Selling price per aircraft		$100,000
Variable production cost per aircraft	$25,000	
Variable selling and administrative expense per aircraft	10,000	35,000
Contribution margin per aircraft		$ 65,000

The variable costing net operating income for each period can always be computed by multiplying the number of units sold by the contribution margin per unit and then subtracting total fixed costs. For Weber Light Aircraft these computations would appear as follows:

	January	February	March
Number of aircraft sold	1	1	5
Contribution margin per aircraft	× $65,000	× $65,000	× $65,000
Total contribution margin	$65,000	$65,000	$325,000
Total fixed expenses	90,000	90,000	90,000
Net operating income (loss)	$(25,000)	$(25,000)	$235,000

Notice, January and February have the same net operating loss. This occurs because one aircraft was sold in each month and, as previously mentioned, the selling price per aircraft, variable cost per aircraft, and total monthly fixed expenses remain constant.

238

Absorption Costing Income Statement

As we begin the absorption costing portion of the example, remember that the only reason absorption costing income differs from variable costing is that the methods account for fixed manufacturing overhead differently. Under absorption costing, fixed manufacturing overhead is included in product costs. In variable costing, fixed manufacturing overhead is not included in product costs and instead is treated as a period expense just like selling and administrative expenses.

The first step in preparing Weber's absorption costing income statements for January, February, and March is to determine the company's unit product costs for each month as follows[1]:

Absorption Costing Unit Product Cost			
	January	February	March
Direct materials	$19,000	$19,000	$19,000
Direct labor	5,000	5,000	5,000
Variable manufacturing overhead	1,000	1,000	1,000
Fixed manufacturing overhead ($70,000 ÷ 1 unit produced in January; $70,000 ÷ 2 units produced in February; $70,000 ÷ 4 units produced in March) ...	70,000	35,000	17,500
Absorption costing unit product cost	$95,000	$60,000	$42,500

Notice that in each month, Weber's fixed manufacturing overhead cost of $70,000 is divided by the number of units produced to determine the fixed manufacturing overhead cost per unit.

Given these unit product costs, the company's absorption costing net operating income in each month would be determined as shown in Exhibit 6–3.

The sales for all three months in Exhibit 6–3 are the same as the sales shown in the variable costing income statements. The January cost of goods sold consists of one unit produced during January at a cost of $95,000 according to the absorption costing system. The February cost of goods sold consists of one unit produced during February at a cost of $60,000 according to the absorption costing system. The March cost of goods sold ($230,000) consists of one unit produced during February at an absorption cost of $60,000 plus four units produced in March with a total absorption cost of $170,000 (= 4 units produced × $42,500 per unit). The selling and administrative expenses equal the amounts reported in the variable costing income statements; however they are reported as one amount rather than being separated into variable and fixed components.

EXHIBIT 6–3
Absorption Costing Income
Statements

Absorption Costing Income Statements			
	January	February	March
Sales	$100,000	$100,000	$500,000
Cost of goods sold ($95,000 × 1 unit; $60,000 × 1 unit; $60,000 × 1 unit + $42,500 × 4 units) ...	95,000	60,000	230,000
Gross margin	5,000	40,000	270,000
Selling and administrative expenses	30,000	30,000	70,000
Net operating income (loss)	$ (25,000)	$ 10,000	$200,000

---

[1] For simplicity, we assume in this section that an actual costing system is used in which actual costs are spread over the units produced during the period. If a predetermined overhead rate were used, the analysis would be similar, but more complex.

Note that even though sales were exactly the same in January and February and the cost structure did not change, net operating income was $35,000 higher in February than in January under absorption costing. This occurs because one aircraft produced in February is not sold until March. This aircraft has $35,000 of fixed manufacturing overhead attached to it that was incurred in February, but will not be recorded as part of cost of goods sold until March.

Contrasting the variable costing and absorption costing income statements in Exhibits 6–2 and 6–3, note that net operating income is the same in January under variable costing and absorption costing, but differs in the other two months. We will discuss this in some depth shortly. Also note that the format of the variable costing income statement differs from the absorption costing income statement. An absorption costing income statement categorizes costs by function—manufacturing versus selling and administrative. All of the manufacturing costs flow through the absorption costing cost of goods sold and all of the selling and administrative expenses are listed separately as period expenses. In contrast, in the contribution approach, costs are categorized according to how they behave. All of the variable expenses are listed together and all of the fixed expenses are listed together. The variable expenses category includes manufacturing costs (i.e., variable cost of goods sold) as well as selling and administrative expenses. The fixed expenses category also includes both manufacturing costs and selling and administrative expenses.

IN BUSINESS

THE BEHAVIORAL SIDE OF CALCULATING UNIT PRODUCT COSTS

Andreas STIHL, a manufacturer of chain saws and other landscaping products, asked its U.S. subsidiary, STIHL Inc., to replace its absorption costing income statements with the variable costing approach. From a computer systems standpoint, the change was not disruptive because STIHL used an enterprise system called SAP that accommodates both absorption and variable costing. However, from a behavioral standpoint, STIHL felt the change could be very disruptive. For example, STIHL's senior managers were keenly aware that the variable costing approach reported lower unit product costs than the absorption costing approach. Given this reality, the sales force might be inclined to erroneously conclude that each product had magically become more profitable, thereby justifying ill-advised price reductions. Because of behavioral concerns such as this, STIHL worked hard to teach its employees how to interpret a variable costing income statement.

Source: Carl S. Smith, "Going for GPK: STIHL Moves Toward This Costing System in the United States," *Strategic Finance*, April 2005, pp. 36–39.

Reconciliation of Variable Costing with Absorption Costing Income

As noted earlier, variable costing and absorption costing net operating incomes may not be the same. In the case of Weber Light Aircraft, the net operating incomes are the same in January, but differ in the other two months. These differences occur because under absorption costing some fixed manufacturing overhead is capitalized in inventories (i.e., included in product costs) rather than being immediately expensed on the income statement. If inventories increase during a period, under absorption costing some of the fixed manufacturing overhead of the current period will be *deferred* in ending inventories. For example, in February two aircraft were produced and each carried with it $35,000 (= $70,000 ÷ 2 aircraft produced) in fixed manufacturing overhead. Since only one aircraft was sold, $35,000 of this fixed manufacturing overhead was on February's absorption costing income statement as part of cost of goods sold, but $35,000 would have been on the balance sheet as part of finished goods inventories. In contrast, under variable costing *all* of the $70,000 of fixed manufacturing overhead appeared on the February income

LO6–3
Reconcile variable costing and absorption costing net operating incomes and explain why the two amounts differ.

Chapter 6

statement as a period expense. Consequently, net operating income was higher under absorption costing than under variable costing by $35,000 in February. This was reversed in March when four units were produced, but five were sold. In March, under absorption costing $105,000 of fixed manufacturing overhead was included in cost of goods sold ($35,000 for the unit produced in February and sold in March plus $17,500 for each of the four units produced and sold in March), but only $70,000 was recognized as a period expense under variable costing. Hence, the net operating income in March was $35,000 lower under absorption costing than under variable costing.

In general, when the units produced exceed unit sales and hence inventories increase, net operating income is higher under absorption costing than under variable costing. This occurs because some of the fixed manufacturing overhead of the period is *deferred* in inventories under absorption costing. In contrast, when unit sales exceed the units produced and hence inventories decrease, net operating income is lower under absorption costing than under variable costing. This occurs because some of the fixed manufacturing overhead of previous periods is *released* from inventories under absorption costing. When the units produced and unit sales are equal, no change in inventories occurs and absorption costing and variable costing net operating incomes are the same.[2]

Variable costing and absorption costing net operating incomes can be reconciled by determining how much fixed manufacturing overhead was deferred in, or released from, inventories during the period:

Fixed Manufacturing Overhead Deferred in, or Released from, Inventories under Absorption Costing			
	January	February	March
Fixed manufacturing overhead in ending inventories	$0	$35,000	$ 0
Fixed manufacturing overhead in beginning inventories	0	0	35,000
Fixed manufacturing overhead deferred in (released from) inventories	$0	$35,000	$(35,000)

In equation form, the fixed manufacturing overhead that is deferred in or released from inventories can be determined as follows:

$$\begin{array}{ccc} \text{Manufacturing overhead} & \text{Fixed manufacturing} & \text{Fixed manufacturing} \\ \text{deferred in} & = \quad \text{overhead in} \quad - & \text{overhead in} \\ \text{(released from) inventory} & \text{ending inventories} & \text{beginning inventories} \end{array}$$

The reconciliation would then be reported as shown in Exhibit 6–4:

EXHIBIT 6–4
Reconciliation of Variable Costing and Absorption Costing Net Operating Incomes

Reconciliation of Variable Costing and Absorption Costing Net Operating Incomes			
	January	February	March
Variable costing net operating income (loss)	$(25,000)	$(25,000)	$235,000
Add (deduct) fixed manufacturing overhead deferred in (released from) inventory under absorption costing	0	35,000	(35,000)
Absorption costing net operating income (loss) . . .	$(25,000)	$ 10,000	$200,000

---

[2] These general statements about the relation between variable costing and absorption costing net operating income assume LIFO is used to value inventories. Even when LIFO is not used, the general statements tend to be correct. Although U.S. GAAP allows LIFO and FIFO inventory flow assumptions, International Financial Reporting Standards do not allow a LIFO inventory flow assumption.

Relation between Production and Sales for the Period	Effect on Inventories	Relation between Absorption and Variable Costing Net Operating Incomes
Units produced = Units sold	No change in inventories	Absorption costing net operating income = Variable costing net operating income
Units produced > Units sold	Inventories increase	Absorption costing net operating income > Variable costing net operating income*
Units produced < Units sold	Inventories decrease	Absorption costing net operating income < Variable costing net operating income†

*Net operating income is higher under absorption costing because fixed manufacturing overhead cost is *deferred* in inventory under absorption costing as inventories increase.
†Net operating income is lower under absorption costing because fixed manufacturing overhead cost is *released* from inventory under absorption costing as inventories decrease.

EXHIBIT 6–5
Comparative Income Effects—Absorption and Variable Costing

Again note that the difference between variable costing net operating income and absorption costing net operating income is entirely due to the amount of fixed manufacturing overhead that is deferred in, or released from, inventories during the period under absorption costing. Changes in inventories affect absorption costing net operating income—they do not affect variable costing net operating income, providing that variable manufacturing costs per unit are stable.

The reasons for differences between variable and absorption costing net operating incomes are summarized in Exhibit 6–5. When the units produced equal the units sold, as in January for Weber Light Aircraft, absorption costing net operating income will equal variable costing net operating income. This occurs because when production equals sales, all of the fixed manufacturing overhead incurred in the current period flows through to the income statement under both methods. For companies that use Lean Production, the number of units produced tends to equal the number of units sold. This occurs because goods are produced in response to customer orders, thereby eliminating finished goods inventories and reducing work in process inventory to almost nothing. So, when a company uses Lean Production differences in variable costing and absorption costing net operating income will largely disappear.

When the units produced exceed the units sold, absorption costing net operating income will exceed variable costing net operating income. This occurs because inventories have increased; therefore, under absorption costing some of the fixed manufacturing overhead incurred in the current period is deferred in ending inventories on the balance sheet, whereas under variable costing all of the fixed manufacturing overhead incurred in the current period flows through to the income statement. In contrast, when the units produced are less than the units sold, absorption costing net operating income will be less than variable costing net operating income. This occurs because inventories have decreased; therefore, under absorption costing fixed manufacturing overhead that had been deferred in inventories during a prior period flows through to the current period's income statement together with all of the fixed manufacturing overhead incurred during the current period. Under variable costing, just the fixed manufacturing overhead of the current period flows through to the income statement.

LEAN MANUFACTURING SHRINKS INVENTORIES

Conmed, a surgical device maker in Utica, New York, switched to lean manufacturing by replacing its assembly lines with U-shaped production cells. It also started producing only enough units to satisfy customer demand rather than producing as many units as possible and storing them in warehouses. The company calculated that its customers use one of its disposable surgical devices every 90 seconds, so that is precisely how often it produces a new unit. Its assembly area for fluid-injection devices used to occupy 3,300 square feet of space and contained $93,000 worth of parts. Now the company produces its fluid-injection devices in 660 square feet of space while maintaining only $6,000 of parts inventory.

When Conmed adopted lean manufacturing, it substantially reduced its finished goods inventories. What impact do you think this initial reduction in inventories may have had on net operating income? Why?

Source: Pete Engardio, "Lean and Mean Gets Extreme," *BusinessWeek*, March 23 and 30, 2009, pp. 60–62.

Advantages of Variable Costing and the Contribution Approach

Variable costing, together with the contribution approach, offers appealing advantages for internal reports. This section discusses three of those advantages.

Enabling CVP Analysis

CVP analysis requires that we break costs down into their fixed and variable components. Because variable costing income statements categorize costs as fixed and variable, it is much easier to use this income statement format to perform CVP analysis than attempting to use the absorption costing format, which mixes together fixed and variable costs.

Moreover, absorption costing net operating income may or may not agree with the results of CVP analysis. For example, let's suppose that you are interested in computing the sales that would be necessary to generate a target profit of $235,000 at Weber Light Aircraft. A CVP analysis based on the January variable costing income statement from Exhibit 6–2 would proceed as follows:

Sales (a)	$100,000
Contribution margin (b)	$65,000
Contribution margin ratio (b) ÷ (a)	65%
Total fixed expenses	$90,000

$$\text{Dollar sales to attain target profit} = \frac{\text{Target profit} + \text{Fixed expenses}}{\text{CM ratio}}$$

$$= \frac{\$235,000 + \$90,000}{0.65} = \$500,000$$

Thus, a CVP analysis based on the January variable costing income statement predicts that the net operating income would be $235,000 when sales are $500,000. And indeed, the net operating income under variable costing *is* $235,000 when the sales are $500,000 in March. However, the net operating income under absorption costing is *not* $235,000 in March, even though the sales are $500,000. Why is this? The reason is that under absorption costing, net operating income can be distorted by changes in inventories. In March, inventories decreased, so some of the fixed manufacturing overhead that had been deferred in February's ending inventories was released to the March income statement, resulting in a net operating income that is $35,000 lower than the $235,000 predicted by CVP analysis. If inventories had increased in March, the opposite would have occurred— the absorption costing net operating income would have been higher than the $235,000 predicted by CVP analysis.

Explaining Changes in Net Operating Income

The variable costing income statements in Exhibit 6–2 are clear and easy to understand. All other things the same, when sales go up, net operating income goes up. When sales go down, net operating income goes down. When sales are constant, net operating income is constant. The number of units produced does not affect net operating income.

Absorption costing income statements can be confusing and are easily misinterpreted. Look again at the absorption costing income statements in Exhibit 6–3; a manager might wonder why net operating income went up from January to February even though sales were exactly the same. Was it a result of lower selling costs, more efficient operations, or was it some other factor? In fact, it was simply because the number of units produced exceeded the number of units sold in February and so some of the fixed manufacturing overhead costs were deferred in inventories in that month. These costs have not gone away—they will eventually flow through to the income statement in a later period when inventories go down. There is no way to tell this from the absorption costing income statements.

To avoid mistakes when absorption costing is used, readers of financial statements should be alert to changes in inventory levels. Under absorption costing, if inventories increase, fixed manufacturing overhead costs are deferred in inventories, which in turn increases net operating income. If inventories decrease, fixed manufacturing overhead costs are released from inventories, which in turn decreases net operating income. Thus, when absorption costing is used, fluctuations in net operating income can be caused by changes in inventories as well as changes in sales.

Supporting Decision Making

The variable costing method correctly identifies the additional variable costs that will be incurred to make one more unit. It also emphasizes the impact of fixed costs on profits. The total amount of fixed manufacturing costs appears explicitly on the income statement, highlighting that the whole amount of fixed manufacturing costs must be covered for the company to be truly profitable. In the Weber Light Aircraft example, the variable costing income statements correctly report that the cost of producing another unit is $25,000 and they explicitly recognize that $70,000 of fixed manufactured overhead must be covered to earn a profit.

Under absorption costing, fixed manufacturing overhead costs appear to be variable with respect to the number of units sold, but they are not. For example, in January, the absorption unit product cost at Weber Light Aircraft is $95,000, but the variable portion of this cost is only $25,000. The fixed overhead costs of $70,000 are commingled with variable production costs, thereby obscuring the impact of fixed overhead costs on profits. Because absorption unit product costs are stated on a per unit basis, managers may mistakenly believe that if another unit is produced, it will cost the company $95,000. But of course it would not. The cost of producing another unit would be only $25,000. Misinterpreting absorption unit product costs as variable can lead to many problems, including inappropriate pricing decisions and decisions to drop products that are in fact profitable.

Segmented Income Statements and the Contribution Approach

LO6-4

Prepare a segmented income statement that differentiates traceable fixed costs from common fixed costs and use it to make decisions.

In the remainder of the chapter, we'll learn how to use the contribution approach to construct income statements for business segments. These segmented income statements are useful for analyzing the profitability of segments, making decisions, and measuring the performance of segment managers.

Traceable and Common Fixed Costs and the Segment Margin

You need to understand three new terms to prepare segmented income statements using the contribution approach—*traceable fixed cost, common fixed cost,* and *segment margin.*

A **traceable fixed cost** of a segment is a fixed cost that is incurred because of the existence of the segment—if the segment had never existed, the fixed cost would not have been incurred; and if the segment were eliminated, the fixed cost would disappear. Examples of traceable fixed costs include the following:

- The salary of the Fritos product manager at PepsiCo is a *traceable* fixed cost of the Fritos business segment of PepsiCo.
- The maintenance cost for the building in which Boeing 747s are assembled is a *traceable* fixed cost of the 747 business segment of Boeing.
- The liability insurance at Disney World is a *traceable* fixed cost of the Disney World business segment of The Walt Disney Corporation.

A **common fixed cost** is a fixed cost that supports the operations of more than one segment, but is not traceable in whole or in part to any one segment. Even if a segment were entirely eliminated, there would be no change in a true common fixed cost. For example:

- The salary of the CEO of General Motors is a *common* fixed cost of the various divisions of General Motors.
- The cost of heating a Safeway or Kroger grocery store is a *common* fixed cost of the store's various departments—groceries, produce, bakery, meat, and so forth.
- The cost of the receptionist's salary at an office shared by a number of doctors is a *common* fixed cost of the doctors. The cost is traceable to the office, but not to individual doctors.

To prepare a segmented income statement, variable expenses are deducted from sales to yield the contribution margin for the segment. The contribution margin tells us what happens to profits as volume changes—holding a segment's capacity and fixed costs constant. The contribution margin is especially useful in decisions involving temporary uses of capacity such as special orders. These types of decisions often involve only variable costs and revenues—the two components of contribution margin.

The **segment margin** is obtained by deducting the traceable fixed costs of a segment from the segment's contribution margin. It represents the margin available after a segment has covered all of its own costs. *The segment margin is the best gauge of the long-run profitability of a segment* because it includes only those costs that are caused by the segment. If a segment can't cover its own costs, then that segment probably should be dropped (unless it has important side effects on other segments). Notice, common fixed costs are not allocated to segments.

From a decision-making point of view, the segment margin is most useful in major decisions that affect capacity such as dropping a segment. By contrast, as we noted earlier, the contribution margin is most useful in decisions involving short-run changes in volume, such as pricing special orders that involve temporary use of existing capacity.

HAS THE INTERNET KILLED CATALOGS?

Smith & Hawken, an outdoor-accessories retailer, has experienced growing Internet sales and declining catalog sales. These trends seem consistent with conventional wisdom, which suggests that the Internet will make catalogs obsolete. Yet, Smith & Hawken, like many retailers with growing Internet sales, has no plans to discontinue its catalogs. In fact, the total number of catalogs mailed in the United States by all companies has jumped from 16.6 billion in 2002 to 19.2 billion in 2005. Why?

Catalog shoppers and Internet shoppers are not independent customer segments. Catalog shoppers frequently choose to complete their sales transactions online rather than placing telephone orders. This explains why catalogs remain a compelling marketing medium even though catalog sales are declining for many companies. If retailers separately analyze catalog sales and Internet sales, they may discontinue the catalogs segment while overlooking the adverse impact of this decision on Internet segment margins.

Source: Louise Lee, "Catalogs, Catalogs, Everywhere," *BusinessWeek*, December 4, 2006, pp. 32–34.

Identifying Traceable Fixed Costs

The distinction between traceable and common fixed costs is crucial in segment reporting because traceable fixed costs are charged to segments and common fixed costs are not. In an actual situation, it is sometimes hard to determine whether a cost should be classified as traceable or common.

The general guideline is to treat as traceable costs *only those costs that would disappear over time if the segment itself disappeared.* For example, if one division within a company were sold or discontinued, it would no longer be necessary to pay that division manager's salary. Therefore the division manager's salary would be classified as a traceable fixed cost of the division. On the other hand, the president of the company undoubtedly would continue to be paid even if one of many divisions was dropped. In fact, he or she might even be paid more if dropping the division was a good idea. Therefore, the president's salary is common to the company's divisions and should not be charged to them.

When assigning costs to segments, the key point is to resist the temptation to allocate costs (such as depreciation of corporate facilities) that are clearly common and that will continue regardless of whether the segment exists or not. *Any allocation of common costs to segments reduces the value of the segment margin as a measure of long-run segment profitability and segment performance.*

Traceable Costs Can Become Common Costs

Fixed costs that are traceable to one segment may be a common cost of another segment. For example, United Airlines might want a segmented income statement that shows the segment margin for a particular flight from Chicago to Paris further broken down into first-class, business-class, and economy-class segment margins. The airline must pay a substantial landing fee at Charles DeGaulle airport in Paris. This fixed landing fee is a traceable cost of the flight, but it is a common cost of the first-class, business-class, and economy-class segments. Even if the first-class cabin is empty, the entire landing fee must be paid. So the landing fee is not a traceable cost of the first-class cabin. But on the other hand, paying the fee is necessary in order to have any first-class, business-class, or economy-class passengers. So the landing fee is a common cost of these three classes.

IN BUSINESS

SEGMENT REPORTING AT THE VILAR PERFORMING ARTS CENTER

The Vilar Performing Arts Center is a 535-seat theater located in Beaver Creek, Colorado, that presents an unusually wide variety of performances categorized into six business segments—Family Series, Broadway Series, Theatre/Comedy Series, Dance Series, Classical Series, and Concert Series. The executive director of the Vilar, Kris Sabel, must decide which shows to book, what financial terms to offer to the artists, what contributions are likely from underwriters (i.e., donors), and what prices to charge for tickets. He evaluates the profitability of the segments using segmented income statements that include traceable costs (such as the costs of transporting, lodging, and feeding the artists) and exclude common costs (such as the salaries of Kris and his staff, depreciation on the theater, and general marketing expenses).

Data concerning the Classical Series segment for one season appears below:

Number of shows	4
Number of seats budgeted	863
Number of seats sold	655
Average seats sold per show	164
Ticket sales	$ 46,800
Underwriting (donors)	65,000
Total income	$111,800
Artists fees	78,870
Other traceable expenses	11,231
Classical Series segment margin	$ 21,699

Although the Classical Series sold an average of only 164 seats per show, its overall segment margin ($21,699) is positive thanks to $65,000 of underwriting revenues from donors. Had common costs been allocated to the Classical Series, it may have appeared unprofitable and been discontinued—resulting in fewer shows during the season; less diverse programming; disappointment among a small, but dedicated, number of fans; and lower overall income for the Vilar due to the loss of its Classical Series segment margin.

Segmented Income Statements—An Example

ProphetMax, Inc., is a rapidly growing computer software company. Exhibit 6–6 shows its variable costing income statement for the most recent month. As the company has grown, its senior managers have asked for segmented income statements that could be used to make decisions and evaluate managerial performance. ProphetMax's controller responded by creating examples of contribution format income statements segmented by the company's divisions, product lines, and sales channels. She created Exhibit 6–7 to explain that ProphetMax's profits can be segmented into its two divisions—the Business Products Division and the Consumer Products Division. The Consumer Products Division's profits can be further segmented into the Clip Art and Computer Games product lines. Finally, the Computer Games product line's profits (within the Consumer Products Division) can be segmented into the Online and Retail Stores sales channels.

Levels of Segmented Income Statements

Exhibit 6–8, on page 248, contains the controller's segmented income statements for the segments depicted in Exhibit 6–7. The contribution format income statement for the entire company appears at the very top of the exhibit under the column labeled Total Company. Notice, the net operating income shown in this column ($13,500) is the same as the net operating income shown in Exhibit 6–6. Immediately to the right of the Total Company column are two columns—one for each of the two divisions. We can see that the Business Products Division's traceable fixed expenses are $90,000 and the Consumer

Variable Costing and Segment Reporting: Tools for Management   **247**

ProphetMax, Inc. Variable Costing Income Statement	
Sales	$500,000
Variable expenses:	
Variable cost of goods sold	180,000
Other variable expenses	50,000
Total variable expenses	230,000
Contribution margin	270,000
Fixed expenses	256,500
Net operating income	$ 13,500

EXHIBIT 6–6
ProphetMax, Inc. Variable Costing Income Statement

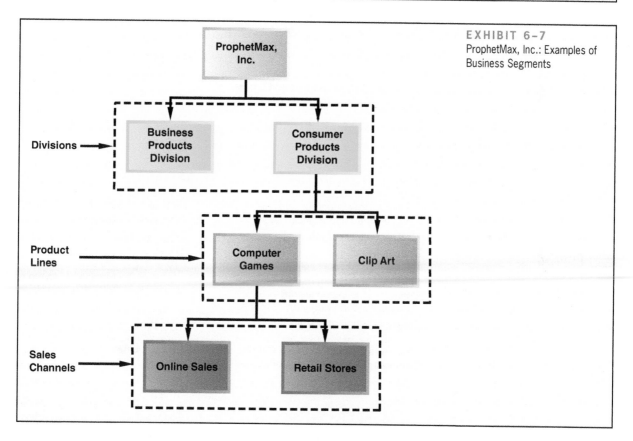

EXHIBIT 6–7
ProphetMax, Inc.: Examples of Business Segments

Products Division's are $81,000. These $171,000 of traceable fixed expenses (as shown in the Total Company column) plus the $85,500 of common fixed expenses not traceable to individual divisions equals ProphetMax's total fixed expenses ($256,500) as shown in Exhibit 6–6. We can also see that the Business Products Division's segment margin is $60,000 and the Consumer Products Division's is $39,000. These segment margins show the company's divisional managers how much each of their divisions is contributing to the company's profits.

The middle portion of Exhibit 6–8 further segments the Consumer Products Division into its two product lines, Clip Art and Computer Games. The dual nature of some fixed costs can be seen in this portion of the exhibit. Notice, in the top portion of Exhibit 6–8 when segments are defined as divisions, the Consumer Products Division has $81,000 in traceable fixed expenses. However, when we drill down to the product lines (in the

EXHIBIT 6–8
ProphetMax, Inc.—Segmented Income Statements in the Contribution Format

Segments Defined as Divisions

	Total Company	Divisions	
		Business Products Division	Consumer Products Division
Sales	$500,000	$300,000	$200,000
Variable expenses:			
Variable cost of goods sold	180,000	120,000	60,000
Other variable expenses	50,000	30,000	20,000
Total variable expenses	230,000	150,000	80,000
Contribution margin	270,000	150,000	120,000
Traceable fixed expenses	171,000	90,000	81,000
Divisional segment margin	99,000	$ 60,000	$ 39,000
Common fixed expenses not traceable to individual divisions	85,500		
Net operating income	$ 13,500		

Segments Defined as Product Lines of the Consumer Products Division

	Consumer Products Division	Product Line	
		Clip Art	Computer Games
Sales	$200,000	$75,000	$125,000
Variable expenses:			
Variable cost of goods sold	60,000	20,000	40,000
Other variable expenses	20,000	5,000	15,000
Total variable expenses	80,000	25,000	55,000
Contribution margin	120,000	50,000	70,000
Traceable fixed expenses	70,000	30,000	40,000
Product-line segment margin	50,000	$20,000	$ 30,000
Common fixed expenses not traceable to individual product lines	11,000		
Divisional segment margin	$ 39,000		

Segments Defined as Sales Channels for One Product Line, Computer Games, of the Consumer Products Division

	Computer Games	Sales Channels	
		Online Sales	Retail Stores
Sales	$125,000	$100,000	$25,000
Variable expenses:			
Variable cost of goods sold	40,000	32,000	8,000
Other variable expenses	15,000	5,000	10,000
Total variable expenses	55,000	37,000	18,000
Contribution margin	70,000	63,000	7,000
Traceable fixed expenses	25,000	15,000	10,000
Sales-channel segment margin	45,000	$ 48,000	$ (3,000)
Common fixed expenses not traceable to individual sales channels	15,000		
Product-line segment margin	$ 30,000		

middle portion of the exhibit), only $70,000 of the $81,000 cost that was traceable to the Consumer Products Division is traceable to the product lines. The other $11,000 becomes a common fixed cost of the two product lines of the Consumer Products Division.

Why would $11,000 of traceable fixed costs become a common fixed cost when the division is divided into product lines? The $11,000 is the monthly depreciation expense on a machine that is used to encase products in tamper-proof packages for the consumer market. The depreciation expense is a traceable cost of the Consumer Products Division as a whole, but it is a common cost of the division's two product lines. Even if one of the product lines were discontinued entirely, the machine would still be used to wrap the remaining products. Therefore, none of the depreciation expense can really be traced to individual products. Conversely, the $70,000 traceable fixed cost can be traced to the individual product lines because it consists of the costs of product-specific advertising. A total of $30,000 was spent on advertising clip art and $40,000 was spent on advertising computer programs.

The bottom portion of Exhibit 6–8 further segments the Computer Games product line into two sales channels, Online Sales and Retail Stores. The dual nature of some fixed costs can also be seen in this portion of the exhibit. In the middle portion of Exhibit 6–8 when segments are defined as product lines, the Computer Games product line has $40,000 in traceable fixed expenses. However, when we look at the sales channels in the bottom portion of the exhibit, only $25,000 of the $40,000 that was traceable to Computer Games is traceable to the sales channels. The other $15,000 becomes a common fixed cost of the two sales channels for the Computer Games product line.

Segmented Income Statements—Decision Making and Break-Even Analysis

Once a company prepares contribution format segmented income statements, it can use those statements to make decisions and perform break-even analysis.

Decision Making

Let's refer again to the bottom portion of Exhibit 6–8 to illustrate how segmented income statements support decision making. Notice that the Online Sales segment has a segment margin of $48,000 and the Retail Stores segment has a segment margin of $(3,000). Let's assume that ProphetMax wants to know the profit impact of discontinuing the sale of computer games through its Retail Stores sales channel. The company believes that online sales of its computer games will increase 10% if it discontinues the Retail Stores sales channel. It also believes that the Business Products Division and Clip Art product line will be unaffected by this decision. How would you compute the profit impact of this decision?

The first step is to calculate the profit impact of the Retail Stores sales channel disappearing. If this sales channel disappears, we assume its sales, variable expenses, and traceable fixed expenses would all disappear. The quickest way to summarize these financial impacts is to focus on the Retail Stores' segment margin. In other words, if the Retail Stores sales channel disappears, then its negative segment margin of $3,000 would also disappear. This would increase ProphetMax's net operating income by $3,000. The second step is to calculate the profit impact of increasing online sales of computer games by 10%. To perform this calculation, we assume that the Online Sales total traceable fixed expenses ($15,000) remain constant and its contribution margin ratio remains constant at 63% (= $63,000 ÷ $100,000). If online sales increase $10,000 (= $100,000 × 10%), then the Online Sales segment's contribution margin will increase by $6,300 (= $10,000 × 63%). The overall profit impact of discontinuing the Retail Stores sales channel can be summarized as follows:

Avoidance of the retail segment's loss	$3,000
Online Sales additional contribution margin	6,300
Increase in ProphetMax's net operating income	$9,300

LO6–5
Compute companywide and segment break-even points for a company with traceable fixed costs.

Break-Even Analysis

In Chapter 5, we learned how to compute a companywide break-even point for a multi-product company with no traceable fixed expenses. Now we are going to use the Prophet-Max, Inc., data in Exhibit 6–8 to explain how to compute companywide and segment break-even points for a company with traceable fixed expenses. The formula for computing a companywide break-even point is as follows:

$$\frac{\text{Dollar sales for company}}{\text{to break even}} = \frac{\text{Traceable fixed expenses} + \text{Common fixed expenses}}{\text{Overall CM ratio}}$$

In the case of ProphetMax, we should begin by reviewing the information in the Total Company column in the top portion of Exhibit 6–8. This column of data indicates that ProphetMax's total traceable fixed expenses are $171,000 and its total common fixed expenses are $85,500. Furthermore, the company's overall contribution margin of $270,000 divided by its total sales of $500,000 equals its overall CM ratio of 0.54. Given this information, ProphetMax's companywide break-even point is computed as follows:

$$\frac{\text{Dollar sales for company}}{\text{to break even}} = \frac{\text{Traceable fixed expenses} + \text{Common fixed expenses}}{\text{Overall CM ratio}}$$

$$= \frac{\$171,000 + \$85,500}{0.54}$$

$$= \frac{\$256,500}{0.54}$$

$$= \$475,000$$

It is important to emphasize that this computation assumes a constant sales mix. In other words, in the ProphetMax example, it assumes that 60% of the total sales ($300,000 ÷ $500,000) will always come from the Business Products Division and 40% of the total sales ($200,000 ÷ $500,000) will always come from the Consumer Products Division.

To compute the break-even point for a business segment, the formula is as follows:

$$\frac{\text{Dollar sales for a segment}}{\text{to break even}} = \frac{\text{Segment traceable fixed expenses}}{\text{Segment CM ratio}}$$

In the case of ProphetMax's Business Products Division, we should begin by reviewing the information in the Business Products Division column in the top portion of Exhibit 6–8. This column of data indicates that the Business Products Division's traceable fixed expenses are $90,000 and its CM ratio is 0.50 ($150,000 ÷ $300,000). Given this information, the Business Products Division's break-even point is computed as follows:

$$\frac{\text{Dollar sales for a segment}}{\text{to break even}} = \frac{\text{Segment traceable fixed expenses}}{\text{Segment CM ratio}}$$

$$= \frac{\$90,000}{0.50}$$

$$= \$180,000$$

The same calculation can be performed for the Consumer Products Division using data from the Consumer Products Division column in the top portion of Exhibit 6–8. Given that the Consumer Products Division's traceable fixed expenses are $81,000 and its CM ratio is 0.60 ($120,000 ÷ $200,000), its break-even point is computed as follows:

$$\frac{\text{Dollar sales for a segment}}{\text{to break even}} = \frac{\text{Segment traceable fixed expenses}}{\text{Segment CM ratio}}$$

$$= \frac{\$81,000}{0.60}$$

$$= \$135,000$$

Notice that the sum of the segment break-even sales figures of $315,000 ($180,000 + $135,000) is less than the companywide break-even point of $475,000. This occurs because the segment break-even calculations *do not include the company's common fixed expenses.* The exclusion of the company's common fixed expenses can be verified by preparing income statements based on each segment's break-even dollar sales as follows:

	Total Company	Business Products Division	Consumer Products Division
Sales	$315,000	$180,000	$135,000
Variable expenses	144,000	90,000	54,000
Contribution margin	171,000	90,000	81,000
Traceable fixed expenses	171,000	90,000	81,000
Segment margin	0	$ 0	$ 0
Common fixed expenses	85,500		
Net operating loss	$ (85,500)		

When each segment achieves its break-even point, the company's overall net operating loss of $85,500 equals its common fixed expenses of $85,500. This reality can often lead managers astray when making decisions. In an attempt to "cover the company's common fixed expenses," managers will often allocate common fixed expenses to business segments when performing break-even calculations and making decisions. *This is a mistake!* Allocating common fixed expenses to business segments artificially inflates each segment's break-even point. This may cause managers to erroneously discontinue business segments where the inflated break-even point appears unobtainable. The decision to retain or discontinue a business segment should be based on the sales and expenses that would disappear if the segment were dropped. Because common fixed expenses *will persist even if a business segment is dropped,* they should not be allocated to business segments when making decisions.

Segmented Income Statements—Common Mistakes

All of the costs attributable to a segment—and only those costs—should be assigned to the segment. Unfortunately, companies often make mistakes when assigning costs to segments. They omit some costs, inappropriately assign traceable fixed costs, and arbitrarily allocate common fixed costs.

Omission of Costs

The costs assigned to a segment should include all costs attributable to that segment from the company's entire value chain. All of these functions, from research and development, through product design, manufacturing, marketing, distribution, and customer service, are required to bring a product or service to the customer and generate revenues.

However, only manufacturing costs are included in product costs under absorption costing, which is widely regarded as required for external financial reporting. To avoid having to maintain two costing systems and to provide consistency between internal and external reports, many companies also use absorption costing for their internal reports such as segmented income statements. As a result, such companies omit from their profitability analysis part or all of the "upstream" costs in the value chain, which consist of research and development and product design, and the "downstream" costs, which consist of marketing, distribution, and customer service. Yet these nonmanufacturing costs are just as essential in determining product profitability as are the manufacturing costs. These upstream and downstream costs, which are usually included in selling and administrative expenses on absorption costing income statements, can represent half or more of the total costs of an organization. If either the upstream or downstream costs are omitted in profitability analysis, then the product is undercosted and management may unwittingly develop and maintain products that in the long run result in losses.

Inappropriate Methods for Assigning Traceable Costs among Segments

In addition to omitting costs, many companies do not correctly handle traceable fixed expenses on segmented income statements. First, they do not trace fixed expenses to segments even when it is feasible to do so. Second, they use inappropriate allocation bases to allocate traceable fixed expenses to segments.

Failure to Trace Costs Directly   Costs that can be traced directly to a specific segment should be charged directly to that segment and should not be allocated to other segments. For example, the rent for a branch office of an insurance company should be charged directly to the branch office rather than included in a companywide overhead pool and then spread throughout the company.

Inappropriate Allocation Base   Some companies use arbitrary allocation bases to allocate costs to segments. For example, some companies allocate selling and administrative expenses on the basis of sales revenues. Thus, if a segment generates 20% of total company sales, it would be allocated 20% of the company's selling and administrative expenses as its "fair share." This same basic procedure is followed if cost of goods sold or some other measure is used as the allocation base.

Costs should be allocated to segments for internal decision-making purposes only when the allocation base actually drives the cost being allocated (or is very highly correlated with the real cost driver). For example, sales should be used to allocate selling and administrative expenses only if a 10% increase in sales will result in a 10% increase in selling and administrative expenses. To the extent that selling and administrative expenses are not driven by sales volume, these expenses will be improperly allocated—with a disproportionately high percentage of the selling and administrative expenses assigned to the segments with the largest sales.

Arbitrarily Dividing Common Costs among Segments

The third business practice that leads to distorted segment costs is the practice of assigning nontraceable costs to segments. For example, some companies allocate the common costs of the corporate headquarters building to products on segment reports. However, in a multiproduct company, no single product is likely to be responsible for any significant amount of this cost. Even if a product were eliminated entirely, there would usually be no significant effect on any of the costs of the corporate headquarters building. In short, there is no cause-and-effect relation between the cost of the corporate headquarters building and the existence of any one product. As a consequence, any allocation of the cost of the corporate headquarters building to the products must be arbitrary.

Common costs like the costs of the corporate headquarters building are necessary, of course, to have a functioning organization. The practice of arbitrarily allocating common costs to segments is often justified on the grounds that "someone" has to "cover the common costs." While it is undeniably true that a company must cover its common costs to earn a profit, arbitrarily allocating common costs to segments does not ensure that this will happen. In fact, adding a share of common costs to the real costs of a segment may make an otherwise profitable segment appear to be unprofitable. If a manager eliminates the apparently unprofitable segment, the real traceable costs of the segment will be saved, but its revenues will be lost. And what happens to the common fixed costs that were allocated to the segment? They don't disappear; they are reallocated to the remaining segments of the company. That makes all of the remaining segments appear to be less profitable—possibly resulting in dropping other segments. The net effect will be to reduce the overall profits of the company and make it even more difficult to "cover the common costs."

Additionally, common fixed costs are not manageable by the manager to whom they are arbitrarily allocated; they are the responsibility of higher-level managers. When common fixed costs are allocated to managers, they are held responsible for those costs even though they cannot control them.

Income Statements—An External Reporting Perspective

Companywide Income Statements

Practically speaking, absorption costing is required for external reports according to U.S. generally accepted accounting principles (GAAP).[3] Furthermore, International Financial Reporting Standards (IFRS) explicitly require companies to use absorption costing. Probably because of the cost and possible confusion of maintaining two separate costing systems—one for external reporting and one for internal reporting—most companies use absorption costing for their external and internal reports.

With all of the advantages of the contribution approach, you may wonder why the absorption approach is used at all. While the answer is partly due to adhering to tradition, absorption costing is also attractive to many accountants and managers because they believe it better matches costs with revenues. Advocates of absorption costing argue that *all* manufacturing costs must be assigned to products in order to properly match the costs of producing units of product with their revenues when they are sold. The fixed costs of depreciation, taxes, insurance, supervisory salaries, and so on, are just as essential to manufacturing products as are the variable costs.

Advocates of variable costing argue that fixed manufacturing costs are not really the costs of any particular unit of product. These costs are incurred to have the *capacity* to make products during a particular period and will be incurred even if nothing is made during the period. Moreover, whether a unit is made or not, the fixed manufacturing costs will be exactly the same. Therefore, variable costing advocates argue that fixed manufacturing costs are not part of the costs of producing a particular unit of product, and thus, the matching principle dictates that fixed manufacturing costs should be charged to the current period.

Segmented Financial Information

U.S. GAAP and IFRS require that publicly traded companies include segmented financial and other data in their annual reports and that the segmented reports prepared for external users *must use the same methods and definitions that the companies use in internal segmented reports that are prepared to aid in making operating decisions.* This is a very unusual stipulation because companies are not ordinarily required to report the same data to external users that are used for internal decision-making purposes. This requirement creates incentives for publicly traded companies to avoid using the contribution format for internal segmented reports. Segmented contribution format income statements contain vital information that companies are often very reluctant to release to the public (and hence competitors). In addition, this requirement creates problems in reconciling internal and external reports.

---

[3] The Financial Accounting Standards Board (FASB) has created a single source of authoritative nongovernmental U.S. generally accepted accounting principles (GAAP) called the FASB Accounting Standards Codification (FASB codification). Although the FASB codification does not explicitly disallow variable costing, it does explicitly prohibit companies from excluding all manufacturing overhead costs from product costs. It also provides an in-depth discussion of fixed overhead allocation to products, thereby implying that absorption costing is required for external reports. Although some companies expense significant elements of fixed manufacturing costs on their external reports, practically speaking, U.S. GAAP requires absorption costing for external reports.

3M REPORTS SEGMENTED PROFITABILITY TO SHAREHOLDERS

In 2009, 3M Company reported segmented profitability to its shareholders by product lines and geographic areas. A portion of the company's segmented information is summarized below (all numbers are in millions):

	Net Sales	Net Operating Income
Product Lines:		
Industrial and transportation	$7,116	$1,238
Health care	$4,294	$1,350
Consumer and office	$3,471	$748
Safety, security, and protection services	$3,180	$745
Display and graphics	$3,132	$590
Electro and communications	$2,276	$322
Geographic Areas:		
United States	$8,509	$1,640
Asia Pacific	$6,120	$1,528
Europe, Middle East and Africa	$5,972	$1,003
Latin America and Canada	$2,516	$631

3M's annual report does not report the gross margins or contribution margins for its business segments. Why do you think this is the case?

Source: 3M Company, 2009 Annual Report.

Summary

Variable and absorption costing are alternative methods of determining unit product costs. Under variable costing, only those manufacturing costs that vary with output are treated as product costs. This includes direct materials, variable overhead, and ordinarily direct labor. Fixed manufacturing overhead is treated as a period cost and it is expensed on the income statement as incurred. By contrast, absorption costing treats fixed manufacturing overhead as a product cost, along with direct materials, direct labor, and variable overhead. Under both costing methods, selling and administrative expenses are treated as period costs and they are expensed on the income statement as incurred.

Because absorption costing treats fixed manufacturing overhead as a product cost, a portion of fixed manufacturing overhead is assigned to each unit as it is produced. If units of product are unsold at the end of a period, then the fixed manufacturing overhead cost attached to those units is carried with them into the inventory account and deferred to a future period. When these units are later sold, the fixed manufacturing overhead cost attached to them is released from the inventory account and charged against income as part of cost of goods sold. Thus, under absorption costing, it is possible to defer a portion of the fixed manufacturing overhead cost from one period to a future period through the inventory account.

Unfortunately, this shifting of fixed manufacturing overhead cost between periods can cause erratic fluctuations in net operating income and can result in confusion and unwise decisions. To guard against mistakes when they interpret income statement data, managers should be alert to changes in inventory levels or unit product costs during the period.

Segmented income statements provide information for evaluating the profitability and performance of divisions, product lines, sales territories, and other segments of a company. Under the contribution approach, variable costs and fixed costs are clearly distinguished from each other and only those costs that are traceable to a segment are assigned to the segment. A cost is considered traceable to a segment only if the cost is caused by the segment and could be avoided by eliminating the segment. Fixed common costs are not allocated to segments. The segment margin consists of revenues, less variable expenses, less traceable fixed expenses of the segment.

The dollar sales required for a segment to break even is computed by dividing the segment's traceable fixed expenses by its contribution margin ratio. A company's common fixed expenses should not be allocated to segments when performing break-even calculations because they will not change in response to segment-level decisions.

Review Problem 1: Contrasting Variable and Absorption Costing

Dexter Corporation produces and sells a single product, a wooden hand loom for weaving small items such as scarves. Selected cost and operating data relating to the product for two years are given below:

Selling price per unit	$50
Manufacturing costs:	
Variable per unit produced:	
Direct materials	$11
Direct labor	$6
Variable manufacturing overhead	$3
Fixed manufacturing overhead per year	$120,000
Selling and administrative expenses:	
Variable per unit sold	$4
Fixed per year	$70,000

	Year 1	Year 2
Units in beginning inventory	0	2,000
Units produced during the year	10,000	6,000
Units sold during the year	8,000	8,000
Units in ending inventory	2,000	0

Required:
1. Assume the company uses absorption costing.
   a. Compute the unit product cost in each year.
   b. Prepare an income statement for each year.
2. Assume the company uses variable costing.
   a. Compute the unit product cost in each year.
   b. Prepare an income statement for each year.
3. Reconcile the variable costing and absorption costing net operating incomes.

Solution to Review Problem 1

1. a. Under absorption costing, all manufacturing costs, variable and fixed, are included in unit product costs:

	Year 1	Year 2
Direct materials	$11	$11
Direct labor	6	6
Variable manufacturing overhead	3	3
Fixed manufacturing overhead		
($120,000 ÷ 10,000 units)	12	
($120,000 ÷ 6,000 units)		20
Absorption costing unit product cost	$32	$40

b. The absorption costing income statements follow:

	Year 1	Year 2
Sales (8,000 units × $50 per unit)	$400,000	$400,000
Cost of goods sold (8,000 units × $32 per unit);		
(2,000 units × $32 per unit) +		
(6,000 units × $40 per unit)	256,000	304,000
Gross margin	144,000	96,000
Selling and administrative expenses		
(8,000 units × $4 per unit + $70,000)	102,000	102,000
Net operating income (loss)	$ 42,000	$ (6,000)

2. a. Under variable costing, only the variable manufacturing costs are included in unit product costs:

	Year 1	Year 2
Direct materials	$11	$11
Direct labor	6	6
Variable manufacturing overhead	3	3
Variable costing unit product cost	$20	$20

b. The variable costing income statements follow:

	Year 1		Year 2	
Sales (8,000 units × $50 per unit)		$400,000		$400,000
Variable expenses:				
Variable cost of goods sold				
(8,000 units × $20 per unit)	$160,000		$160,000	
Variable selling and administrative				
expenses (8,000 units × $4 per unit) . . .	32,000	192,000	32,000	192,000
Contribution margin		208,000		208,000
Fixed expenses:				
Fixed manufacturing overhead	120,000		120,000	
Fixed selling and administrative				
expenses	70,000	190,000	70,000	190,000
Net operating income		$ 18,000		$ 18,000

3. The reconciliation of the variable and absorption costing net operating incomes follows:

	Year 1	Year 2
Fixed manufacturing overhead in ending inventories	$24,000	$ 0
Fixed manufacturing overhead in beginning inventories . . .	0	24,000
Fixed manufacturing overhead deferred in		
(released from) inventories	$24,000	$(24,000)

	Year 1	Year 2
Variable costing net operating income	$18,000	$18,000
Add fixed manufacturing overhead costs deferred		
in inventory under absorption costing		
(2,000 units × $12 per unit)	24,000	
Deduct fixed manufacturing overhead costs released		
from inventory under absorption costing		
(2,000 units × $12 per unit)		(24,000)
Absorption costing net operating income (loss)	$42,000	$ (6,000)

Review Problem 2: Segmented Income Statements

The business staff of the law firm Frampton, Davis & Smythe has constructed the following report that breaks down the firm's overall results for last month into two business segments—family law and commercial law:

	Company Total	Family Law	Commercial Law
Revenues from clients	$1,000,000	$400,000	$600,000
Variable expenses	220,000	100,000	120,000
Contribution margin	780,000	300,000	480,000
Traceable fixed expenses	670,000	280,000	390,000
Segment margin	110,000	20,000	90,000
Common fixed expenses	60,000	24,000	36,000
Net operating income (loss)	$ 50,000	$ (4,000)	$ 54,000

However, this report is not quite correct. The common fixed expenses such as the managing partner's salary, general administrative expenses, and general firm advertising have been allocated to the two segments based on revenues from clients.

Required:

1. Redo the segment report, eliminating the allocation of common fixed expenses. Would the firm be better off financially if the family law segment were dropped? (Note: Many of the firm's commercial law clients also use the firm for their family law requirements such as drawing up wills.)
2. The firm's advertising agency has proposed an ad campaign targeted at boosting the revenues of the family law segment. The ad campaign would cost $20,000, and the advertising agency claims that it would increase family law revenues by $100,000. The managing partner of Frampton, Davis & Smythe believes this increase in business could be accommodated without any increase in fixed expenses. Estimate the effect this ad campaign would have on the family law segment margin and on the firm's overall net operating income.
3. Compute the companywide break-even point in dollar sales and the dollar sales required for each business segment to break even.

Solution to Review Problem 2

1. The corrected segmented income statement appears below:

	Company Total	Family Law	Commercial Law
Revenues from clients	$1,000,000	$400,000	$600,000
Variable expenses	220,000	100,000	120,000
Contribution margin	780,000	300,000	480,000
Traceable fixed expenses	670,000	280,000	390,000
Segment margin	110,000	$ 20,000	$ 90,000
Common fixed expenses	60,000		
Net operating income	$ 50,000		

No, the firm would not be financially better off if the family law practice were dropped. The family law segment is covering all of its own costs and is contributing $20,000 per month to covering the common fixed expenses of the firm. While the segment margin for family law

Chapter 6

is much lower than for commercial law, it is still profitable. Moreover, family law may be a service that the firm must provide to its commercial clients in order to remain competitive.

2. The ad campaign would increase the family law segment margin by $55,000 as follows:

Increased revenues from clients	$100,000
Family law contribution margin ratio ($300,000 ÷ $400,000)	× 75%
Increased contribution margin	$ 75,000
Less cost of the ad campaign	20,000
Increased segment margin	$ 55,000

Because there would be no increase in fixed expenses (including common fixed expenses), the increase in overall net operating income is also $55,000.

3. The companywide break-even point is computed as follows:

$$\frac{\text{Dollar sales for company}}{\text{to break even}} = \frac{\text{Traceable fixed expenses} + \text{Common fixed expenses}}{\text{Overall CM ratio}}$$

$$= \frac{\$670,000 + \$60,000}{0.78}$$

$$= \frac{\$730,000}{0.78}$$

$$= \$935,897 \text{ (rounded)}$$

The break-even point for the family law segment is computed as follows:

$$\frac{\text{Dollar sales for a segment}}{\text{to break even}} = \frac{\text{Segment traceable fixed expenses}}{\text{Segment CM ratio}}$$

$$= \frac{\$280,000}{0.75}$$

$$= \$373,333 \text{ (rounded)}$$

The break-even point for the commercial law segment is computed as follows:

$$\frac{\text{Dollar sales for a segment}}{\text{to break even}} = \frac{\text{Segment traceable fixed expenses}}{\text{Segment CM ratio}}$$

$$= \frac{\$390,000}{0.80}$$

$$= \$487,500$$

Glossary

Absorption costing A costing method that includes all manufacturing costs—direct materials, direct labor, and both variable and fixed manufacturing overhead—in unit product costs. (p. 234)

Common fixed cost A fixed cost that supports more than one business segment, but is not traceable in whole or in part to any one of the business segments. (p. 244)

Variable Costing and Segment Reporting: Tools for Management   **259**

Segment Any part or activity of an organization about which managers seek cost, revenue, or profit data. (p. 234)

Segment margin A segment's contribution margin less its traceable fixed costs. It represents the margin available after a segment has covered all of its own traceable costs. (p. 244)

Traceable fixed cost A fixed cost that is incurred because of the existence of a particular business segment and that would be eliminated if the segment were eliminated. (p. 244)

Variable costing A costing method that includes only variable manufacturing costs—direct materials, direct labor, and variable manufacturing overhead—in unit product costs. (p. 234)

Questions

6–1 What is the basic difference between absorption costing and variable costing?

6–2 Are selling and administrative expenses treated as product costs or as period costs under variable costing?

6–3 Explain how fixed manufacturing overhead costs are shifted from one period to another under absorption costing.

6–4 What are the arguments in favor of treating fixed manufacturing overhead costs as product costs?

6–5 What are the arguments in favor of treating fixed manufacturing overhead costs as period costs?

6–6 If the units produced and unit sales are equal, which method would you expect to show the higher net operating income, variable costing or absorption costing? Why?

6–7 If the units produced exceed unit sales, which method would you expect to show the higher net operating income, variable costing or absorption costing? Why?

6–8 If fixed manufacturing overhead costs are released from inventory under absorption costing, what does this tell you about the level of production in relation to the level of sales?

6–9 Under absorption costing, how is it possible to increase net operating income without increasing sales?

6–10 How does Lean Production reduce or eliminate the difference in reported net operating income between absorption and variable costing?

6–11 What is a segment of an organization? Give several examples of segments.

6–12 What costs are assigned to a segment under the contribution approach?

6–13 Distinguish between a traceable cost and a common cost. Give several examples of each.

6–14 Explain how the segment margin differs from the contribution margin.

6–15 Why aren't common costs allocated to segments under the contribution approach?

6–16 How is it possible for a cost that is traceable to a segment to become a common cost if the segment is divided into further segments?

6–17 Should a company allocate its common fixed expenses to business segments when computing the break-even point for those segments? Why?

Multiple-choice questions are provided on the text website at www.mhhe.com/garrison15e.

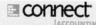 **Applying Excel**

Available with McGraw-Hill's *Connect*® Accounting.

The Excel worksheet form that appears on the next page is to be used to recreate portions of Review Problem 1 on pages 255–256. Download the workbook containing this form from the Online Learning Center at www.mhhe.com/garrison15e. *On the website you will also receive instructions about how to use this worksheet form.*   LO6–2

	A	B	C	D	E	F
1	Chapter 6: Applying Excel					
2						
3	**Data**					
4	Selling price per unit	$50				
5	Manufacturing costs:					
6	Variable per unit produced:					
7	Direct materials	$11				
8	Direct labor	$6				
9	Variable manufacturing overhead	$3				
10	Fixed manufacturing overhead per year	$120,000				
11	Selling and administrative expenses:					
12	Variable per unit sold	$4				
13	Fixed per year	$70,000				
14						
15		Year 1	Year 2			
16	Units in beginning inventory	0				
17	Units produced during the year	10,000	6,000			
18	Units sold during the year	8,000	8,000			
19						
20	Enter a formula into each of the cells marked with a ? below					
21	**Review Problem 1: Contrasting Variable and Absorption Costing**					
22						
23	*Compute the Ending Inventory*					
24		Year 1	Year 2			
25	Units in beginning inventory	0	?			
26	Units produced during the year	?	?			
27	Units sold during the year	?	?			
28	Units in ending inventory	?	?			
29						
30	*Compute the Absorption Costing Unit Product Cost*					
31		Year 1	Year 2			
32	Direct materials	?	?			
33	Direct labor	?	?			
34	Variable manufacturing overhead	?	?			
35	Fixed manufacturing overhead	?	?			
36	Absorption costing unit product cost	?	?			
37						
38	*Construct the Absorption Costing Income Statement*					
39		Year 1	Year 2			
40	Sales	?	?			
41	Cost of goods sold	?	?			
42	Gross margin	?	?			
43	Selling and administrative expenses	?	?			
44	Net operating income	?	?			
45						
46	*Compute the Variable Costing Unit Product Cost*					
47		Year 1	Year 2			
48	Direct materials	?	?			
49	Direct labor	?	?			
50	Variable manufacturing overhead	?	?			
51	Variable costing unit product cost	?	?			
52						
53	*Construct the Variable Costing Income Statement*					
54		Year 1		Year 2		
55	Sales		?		?	
56	Variable expenses:					
57	Variable cost of goods sold	?		?		
58	Variable selling and administrative expenses	?	?	?	?	
59	Contribution margin		?		?	
60	Fixed expenses:					
61	Fixed manufacturing overhead	?		?		
62	Fixed selling and administrative expenses	?	?	?	?	
63	Net operating income		?		?	
64						

Chapter 6 Form   Filled in Chapter 6 Form   Chapter 6

You should proceed to the requirements below only after completing your worksheet. The LIFO inventory flow assumption is used throughout this problem.

Required:

1. Check your worksheet by changing the units sold in the Data to 6,000 for Year 2. The cost of goods sold under absorption costing for Year 2 should now be $240,000. If it isn't, check cell C41. The formula in this cell should be =IF(C26<C27,C26*C36+(C27-C26)*B36,C27*C36). If your worksheet is operating properly, the net operating income under both absorption costing and variable costing should be $(34,000) for Year 2. That is, the loss in Year 2 is $34,000 under both systems. If you do not get these answers, find the errors in your worksheet and correct them.

    Why is the absorption costing net operating income now equal to the variable costing net operating income in Year 2?

2. Enter the following data from a different company into your worksheet:

Data		
Selling price per unit	$75	
Manufacturing costs:		
Variable per unit produced:		
Direct materials	$12	
Direct labor	$5	
Variable manufacturing overhead	$7	
Fixed manufacturing overhead per year	$150,000	
Selling and administrative expenses:		
Variable per unit sold	$1	
Fixed per year	$60,000	
	Year 1	Year 2
Units in beginning inventory	0	
Units produced during the year	15,000	10,000
Units sold during the year	12,000	12,000

Is the net operating income under variable costing different in Year 1 and Year 2? Why or why not? Explain the relation between the net operating income under absorption costing and variable costing in Year 1. Explain the relation between the net operating income under absorption costing and variable costing in Year 2.

3. At the end of Year 1, the company's board of directors set a target for Year 2 of net operating income of $500,000 under absorption costing. If this target is met, a hefty bonus would be paid to the CEO of the company. Keeping everything else the same from part (2) above, change the units produced in Year 2 to 50,000 units. Would this change result in a bonus being paid to the CEO? Do you think this change would be in the best interests of the company? What is likely to happen in Year 3 to the absorption costing net operating income if sales remain constant at 12,000 units per year?

 ACCOUNTING   **The Foundational 15**

Available with McGraw-Hill's Connect® Accounting.

Diego Company manufactures one product that is sold for $80 per unit in two geographic regions—the East and West regions. The following information pertains to the company's first year of operations in which it produced 40,000 units and sold 35,000 units.

LO6–1, LO6–2, LO6–3, LO6–4

Variable costs per unit:	
Manufacturing:	
Direct materials	$24
Direct labor	$14
Variable manufacturing overhead	$2
Variable selling and administrative	$4
Fixed costs per year:	
Fixed manufacturing overhead	$800,000
Fixed selling and administrative expenses	$496,000

The company sold 25,000 units in the East region and 10,000 units in the West region. It determined that $250,000 of its fixed selling and administrative expenses is traceable to the West region, $150,000 is traceable to the East region, and the remaining $96,000 is a common fixed cost. The company will continue to incur the total amount of its fixed manufacturing overhead costs as long as it continues to produce any amount of its only product.

Required:
Answer each question independently based on the original data unless instructed otherwise. You do not need to prepare a segmented income statement until question 13.

1. What is the unit product cost under variable costing?
2. What is the unit product cost under absorption costing?
3. What is the company's total contribution margin under variable costing?
4. What is the company's net operating income under variable costing?
5. What is the company's total gross margin under absorption costing?
6. What is the company's net operating income under absorption costing?
7. What is the amount of the difference between the variable costing and absorption costing net operating incomes? What is the cause of this difference?
8. What is the company's break-even point in unit sales? Is it above or below the actual sales volume? Compare the break-even sales volume to your answer for question 6 and comment.
9. If the sales volumes in the East and West regions had been reversed, what would be the company's overall break-even point in unit sales?
10. What would have been the company's variable costing net operating income if it had produced and sold 35,000 units? You do not need to perform any calculations to answer this question.
11. What would have been the company's absorption costing net operating income if it had produced and sold 35,000 units? You do not need to perform any calculations to answer this question.
12. If the company produces 5,000 fewer units than it sells in its second year of operations, will absorption costing net operating income be higher or lower than variable costing net operating income in Year 2? Why? No calculations are necessary.
13. Prepare a contribution format segmented income statement that includes a Total column and columns for the East and West regions.
14. Diego is considering eliminating the West region because an internally generated report suggests the region's total *gross margin* in the first year of operations was $50,000 less than its traceable fixed selling and administrative expenses. Diego believes that if it drops the West region, the East region's sales will grow by 5% in Year 2. Using the contribution approach for analyzing segment profitability and assuming all else remains constant in Year 2, what would be the profit impact of dropping the West region in Year 2?
15. Assume the West region invests $30,000 in a new advertising campaign in Year 2 that increases its unit sales by 20%. If all else remains constant, what would be the profit impact of pursuing the advertising campaign?

Exercises   connect
|ACCOUNTING

All applicable exercises are available with McGraw-Hill's *Connect*® Accounting.

EXERCISE 6–1 Variable and Absorption Costing Unit Product Costs [LO6–1]
Ida Sidha Karya Company is a family-owned company located in the village of Gianyar on the island of Bali in Indonesia. The company produces a handcrafted Balinese musical instrument called a gamelan that is similar to a xylophone. The gamelans are sold for $850. Selected data for the company's operations last year follow:

Units in beginning inventory	0
Units produced	250
Units sold	225
Units in ending inventory	25
Variable costs per unit:	
Direct materials	$100
Direct labor	$320
Variable manufacturing overhead	$40
Variable selling and administrative	$20
Fixed costs:	
Fixed manufacturing overhead	$60,000
Fixed selling and administrative	$20,000

Required:
1. Assume that the company uses absorption costing. Compute the unit product cost for one gamelan.
2. Assume that the company uses variable costing. Compute the unit product cost for one gamelan.

EXERCISE 6–2 Variable Costing Income Statement; Explanation of Difference in Net Operating Income [LO6–2]

Refer to the data in Exercise 6–1 for Ida Sidha Karya Company. The absorption costing income statement prepared by the company's accountant for last year appears below:

Sales	$191,250
Cost of goods sold	157,500
Gross margin	33,750
Selling and administrative expense	24,500
Net operating income	$ 9,250

Required:
1. Determine how much of the ending inventory consists of fixed manufacturing overhead cost deferred in inventory to the next period.
2. Prepare an income statement for the year using variable costing. Explain the difference in net operating income between the two costing methods.

EXERCISE 6–3 Reconciliation of Absorption and Variable Costing Net Operating Incomes [LO6–3]

Jorgansen Lighting, Inc., manufactures heavy-duty street lighting systems for municipalities. The company uses variable costing for internal management reports and absorption costing for external reports to shareholders, creditors, and the government. The company has provided the following data:

	Year 1	Year 2	Year 3
Inventories:			
Beginning (units)	200	170	180
Ending (units)	170	180	220
Variable costing net operating income	$1,080,400	$1,032,400	$996,400

The company's fixed manufacturing overhead per unit was constant at $560 for all three years.

Required:
1. Determine each year's absorption costing net operating income. Present your answer in the form of a reconciliation report.
2. In Year 4, the company's variable costing net operating income was $984,400 and its absorption costing net operating income was $1,012,400. Did inventories increase or decrease during Year 4? How much fixed manufacturing overhead cost was deferred or released from inventory during Year 4?

EXERCISE 6–4 Basic Segmented Income Statement [LO6–4]

Royal Lawncare Company produces and sells two packaged products, Weedban and Greengrow. Revenue and cost information relating to the products follow:

	Product	
	Weedban	Greengrow
Selling price per unit	$6.00	$7.50
Variable expenses per unit	$2.40	$5.25
Traceable fixed expenses per year	$45,000	$21,000

Common fixed expenses in the company total $33,000 annually. Last year the company produced and sold 15,000 units of Weedban and 28,000 units of Greengrow.

Required:
Prepare a contribution format income statement segmented by product lines.

Chapter 6

EXERCISE 6–5 Companywide and Segment Break-Even Analysis [LO6–5]

Piedmont Company segments its business into two regions—North and South. The company prepared the contribution format segmented income statement shown below:

	Total Company	North	South
Sales	$600,000	$400,000	$200,000
Variable expenses	360,000	280,000	80,000
Contribution margin	240,000	120,000	120,000
Traceable fixed expenses	120,000	60,000	60,000
Segment margin	120,000	$ 60,000	$ 60,000
Common fixed expenses	50,000		
Net operating income	$ 70,000		

Required:
1. Compute the companywide break-even point in dollar sales.
2. Compute the break-even point in dollar sales for the North region.
3. Compute the break-even point in dollar sales for the South region.

EXERCISE 6–6 Variable and Absorption Costing Unit Product Costs and Income Statements [LO6–1, LO6–2]

Lynch Company manufactures and sells a single product. The following costs were incurred during the company's first year of operations:

Variable costs per unit:	
Manufacturing:	
Direct materials	$6
Direct labor	$9
Variable manufacturing overhead	$3
Variable selling and administrative	$4
Fixed costs per year:	
Fixed manufacturing overhead	$300,000
Fixed selling and administrative	$190,000

During the year, the company produced 25,000 units and sold 20,000 units. The selling price of the company's product is $50 per unit.

Required:
1. Assume that the company uses absorption costing:
   a. Compute the unit product cost.
   b. Prepare an income statement for the year.
2. Assume that the company uses variable costing:
   a. Compute the unit product cost.
   b. Prepare an income statement for the year.

EXERCISE 6–7 Segmented Income Statement [LO6–4]

Shannon Company segments its income statement into its North and South Divisions. The company's overall sales, contribution margin ratio, and net operating income are $500,000, 46%, and $10,000, respectively. The North Division's contribution margin and contribution margin ratio are $150,000 and 50%, respectively. The South Division's segment margin is $30,000. The company has $90,000 of common fixed expenses that cannot be traced to either division.

Required:
Prepare an income statement for Shannon Company that uses the contribution format and is segmented by divisions. In addition, for the company as a whole and for each segment, show each item on the segmented income statements as a percent of sales.

EXERCISE 6–8 Deducing Changes in Inventories [LO6–3]

Parker Products Inc, a manufacturer, reported $123 million in sales and a loss of $18 million in its annual report to shareholders. According to a CVP analysis prepared for management, the company's break-even point is $115 million in sales.

Required:

Assuming that the CVP analysis is correct, is it likely that the company's inventory level increased, decreased, or remained unchanged during the year? Explain.

EXERCISE 6–9 Variable and Absorption Costing Unit Product Costs and Income Statements
[LO6–1, LO6–2, LO6–3]

Walsh Company manufactures and sells one product. The following information pertains to each of the company's first two years of operations:

Variable costs per unit:	
Manufacturing:	
Direct materials	$25
Direct labor	$15
Variable manufacturing overhead	$5
Variable selling and administrative	$2
Fixed costs per year:	
Fixed manufacturing overhead	$250,000
Fixed selling and administrative expenses	$80,000

During its first year of operations, Walsh produced 50,000 units and sold 40,000 units. During its second year of operations, it produced 40,000 units and sold 50,000 units. The selling price of the company's product is $60 per unit.

Required:

1. Assume the company uses variable costing:
   a. Compute the unit product cost for Year 1 and Year 2.
   b. Prepare an income statement for Year 1 and Year 2.
2. Assume the company uses absorption costing:
   a. Compute the unit product cost for Year 1 and Year 2.
   b. Prepare an income statement for Year 1 and Year 2.
3. Explain the difference between variable costing and absorption costing net operating income in Year 1. Also, explain why the two net operating income figures differ in Year 2.

EXERCISE 6–10 Companywide and Segment Break-Even Analysis [LO6–5]

Crossfire Company segments its business into two regions—East and West. The company prepared the contribution format segmented income statement shown below:

	Total Company	East	West
Sales	$900,000	$600,000	$300,000
Variable expenses	675,000	480,000	195,000
Contribution margin	225,000	120,000	105,000
Traceable fixed expenses	141,000	50,000	91,000
Segment margin	84,000	$ 70,000	$ 14,000
Common fixed expenses	59,000		
Net operating income	$ 25,000		

Required:

1. Compute the companywide break-even point dollar in sales.
2. Compute the break-even point in dollar sales for the East region.
3. Compute the break-even point in dollar sales for the West region.
4. Prepare a new segmented income statement based on the break-even dollar sales that you computed in requirements 2 and 3. Use the same format as shown above. What is Crossfire's net operating income in your new segmented income statement?
5. Do you think that Crossfire should allocate its common fixed expenses to the East and West regions when computing the break-even points for each region? Why?

266

Chapter 6

EXERCISE 6–11 Segmented Income Statement [LO6–4]

Wingate Company, a wholesale distributor of electronic equipment, has been experiencing losses for some time, as shown by its most recent monthly contribution format income statement, which follows:

Sales	$1,000,000
Variable expenses	390,000
Contribution margin	610,000
Fixed expenses	625,000
Net operating income (loss)	$ (15,000)

In an effort to isolate the problem, the president has asked for an income statement segmented by division. Accordingly, the Accounting Department has developed the following information:

	Division		
	East	Central	West
Sales	$250,000	$400,000	$350,000
Variable expenses as a percentage of sales	52%	30%	40%
Traceable fixed expenses	$160,000	$200,000	$175,000

Required:
1. Prepare a contribution format income statement segmented by divisions, as desired by the president.
2. As a result of a marketing study, the president believes that sales in the West Division could be increased by 20% if monthly advertising in that division were increased by $15,000. Would you recommend the increased advertising? Show computations to support your answer.

EXERCISE 6–12 Variable Costing Income Statement; Reconciliation [LO6–2, LO6–3]

Whitman Company has just completed its first year of operations. The company's absorption costing income statement for the year appears below:

Whitman Company
Income Statement

Sales (35,000 units × $25 per unit)	$875,000
Cost of goods sold (35,000 units × $16 per unit)	560,000
Gross margin	315,000
Selling and administrative expenses	280,000
Net operating income	$ 35,000

The company's selling and administrative expenses consist of $210,000 per year in fixed expenses and $2 per unit sold in variable expenses. The $16 per unit product cost given above is computed as follows:

Direct materials	$ 5
Direct labor	6
Variable manufacturing overhead	1
Fixed manufacturing overhead ($160,000 ÷ 40,000 units)	4
Absorption costing unit product cost	$16

Required:
1. Redo the company's income statement in the contribution format using variable costing.
2. Reconcile any difference between the net operating income on your variable costing income statement and the net operating income on the absorption costing income statement above.

EXERCISE 6–13 Inferring Costing Method; Unit Product Cost [LO6–1]

Sierra Company incurs the following costs to produce and sell a single product.

Variable costs per unit:	
Direct materials	$9
Direct labor	$10
Variable manufacturing overhead	$5
Variable selling and administrative expenses	$3
Fixed costs per year:	
Fixed manufacturing overhead	$150,000
Fixed selling and administrative expenses	$400,000

During the last year, 25,000 units were produced and 22,000 units were sold. The Finished Goods inventory account at the end of the year shows a balance of $72,000 for the 3,000 unsold units.

Required:

1. Is the company using absorption costing or variable costing to cost units in the Finished Goods inventory account? Show computations to support your answer.
2. Assume that the company wishes to prepare financial statements for the year to issue to its stockholders.
    a. Is the $72,000 figure for Finished Goods inventory the correct amount to use on these statements for external reporting purposes? Explain.
    b. At what dollar amount *should* the 3,000 units be carried in the inventory for external reporting purposes?

EXERCISE 6–14 Variable Costing Unit Product Cost and Income Statement; Break-Even [LO6–1, LO6–2]

Chuck Wagon Grills, Inc., makes a single product—a handmade specialty barbecue grill that it sells for $210. Data for last year's operations follow:

Units in beginning inventory	0
Units produced	20,000
Units sold	19,000
Units in ending inventory	1,000
Variable costs per unit:	
Direct materials	$ 50
Direct labor	80
Variable manufacturing overhead	20
Variable selling and administrative	10
Total variable cost per unit	$160
Fixed costs:	
Fixed manufacturing overhead	$700,000
Fixed selling and administrative	285,000
Total fixed costs	$985,000

Required:

1. Assume that the company uses variable costing. Compute the unit product cost for one barbecue grill.
2. Assume that the company uses variable costing. Prepare a contribution format income statement for the year.
3. What is the company's break-even point in terms of the number of barbecue grills sold?

EXERCISE 6–15 Absorption Costing Unit Product Cost and Income Statement [LO6–1, LO6–2]

Refer to the data in Exercise 6–14 for Chuck Wagon Grills. Assume in this exercise that the company uses absorption costing.

Required:

1. Compute the unit product cost for one barbecue grill.
2. Prepare an income statement.

268

Chapter 6

EXERCISE 6–16 Working with a Segmented Income Statement; Break-Even Analysis [LO6–4, LO6–5]
Raner, Harris, & Chan is a consulting firm that specializes in information systems for medical and dental clinics. The firm has two offices—one in Chicago and one in Minneapolis. The firm classifies the direct costs of consulting jobs as variable costs. A contribution format segmented income statement for the company's most recent year is given below:

	Total Company		Office Chicago		Office Minneapolis	
Sales	$450,000	100%	$150,000	100%	$300,000	100%
Variable expenses	225,000	50%	45,000	30%	180,000	60%
Contribution margin	225,000	50%	105,000	70%	120,000	40%
Traceable fixed expenses	126,000	28%	78,000	52%	48,000	16%
Office segment margin	99,000	22%	$ 27,000	18%	$ 72,000	24%
Common fixed expenses not traceable to offices	63,000	14%				
Net operating income	$ 36,000	8%				

Required:
1. Compute the companywide break-even point in dollar sales. Also, compute the break-even point for the Chicago office and for the Minneapolis office. Is the companywide break-even point greater than, less than, or equal to the sum of the Chicago and Minneapolis break-even points? Why?
2. By how much would the company's net operating income increase if Minneapolis increased its sales by $75,000 per year? Assume no change in cost behavior patterns.
3. Refer to the original data. Assume that sales in Chicago increase by $50,000 next year and that sales in Minneapolis remain unchanged. Assume no change in fixed costs.
   a. Prepare a new segmented income statement for the company using the above format. Show both amounts and percentages.
   b. Observe from the income statement you have prepared that the contribution margin ratio for Chicago has remained unchanged at 70% (the same as in the above data) but that the segment margin ratio has changed. How do you explain the change in the segment margin ratio?

EXERCISE 6–17 Working with a Segmented Income Statement [LO6–4]
Refer to the data in Exercise 6–16. Assume that Minneapolis' sales by major market are:

	Minneapolis		Market Medical		Market Dental	
Sales	$300,000	100%	$200,000	100%	$100,000	100%
Variable expenses	180,000	60%	128,000	64%	52,000	52%
Contribution margin	120,000	40%	72,000	36%	48,000	48%
Traceable fixed expenses	33,000	11%	12,000	6%	21,000	21%
Market segment margin	87,000	29%	$ 60,000	30%	$ 27,000	27%
Common fixed expenses not traceable to markets	15,000	5%				
Office segment margin	$ 72,000	24%				

The company would like to initiate an intensive advertising campaign in one of the two market segments during the next month. The campaign would cost $5,000. Marketing studies indicate that such a campaign would increase sales in the Medical market by $40,000 or increase sales in the Dental market by $35,000.

Required:
1. In which of the markets would you recommend that the company focus its advertising campaign? Show computations to support your answer.
2. In Exercise 6–16, Minneapolis shows $48,000 in traceable fixed expenses. What happened to the $48,000 in this exercise?

Variable Costing and Segment Reporting: Tools for Management   **269**

Problems

All applicable problems are available with McGraw-Hill's *Connect*® *Accounting*.

PROBLEM 6–18 Variable and Absorption Costing Unit Product Costs and Income Statements
[LO6–1, LO6–2]

Haas Company manufactures and sells one product. The following information pertains to each of the company's first three years of operations:

Variable costs per unit:	
Manufacturing:	
Direct materials	$20
Direct labor	$12
Variable manufacturing overhead	$4
Variable selling and administrative	$2
Fixed costs per year:	
Fixed manufacturing overhead	$960,000
Fixed selling and administrative expenses	$240,000

During its first year of operations, Haas produced 60,000 units and sold 60,000 units. During its second year of operations, it produced 75,000 units and sold 50,000 units. In its third year, Haas produced 40,000 units and sold 65,000 units. The selling price of the company's product is $58 per unit.

Required:
1. Compute the company's break-even point in units sold.
2. Assume the company uses variable costing:
   a. Compute the unit product cost for Year 1, Year 2, and Year 3.
   b. Prepare an income statement for Year 1, Year 2, and Year 3.
3. Assume the company uses absorption costing:
   a. Compute the unit product cost for Year 1, Year 2, and Year 3.
   b. Prepare an income statement for Year 1, Year 2, and Year 3.
4. Compare the net operating income figures that you computed in requirements 2 and 3 to the break-even point that you computed in requirement 1. Which net operating income figures seem counterintuitive? Why?

PROBLEM 6–19 Variable Costing Income Statement; Reconciliation [LO6–2, LO6–3]
During Heaton Company's first two years of operations, the company reported absorption costing net operating income as follows:

	Year 1	Year 2
Sales (@ $25 per unit)	$1,000,000	$1,250,000
Cost of goods sold (@ $18 per unit)	720,000	900,000
Gross margin	280,000	350,000
Selling and administrative expenses*	210,000	230,000
Net operating income	$ 70,000	$ 120,000

*$2 per unit variable; $130,000 fixed each year.

The company's $18 unit product cost is computed as follows:

Direct materials	$ 4
Direct labor	7
Variable manufacturing overhead	1
Fixed manufacturing overhead ($270,000 ÷ 45,000 units)	6
Absorption costing unit product cost	$18

Forty percent of fixed manufacturing overhead consists of wages and salaries; the remainder consists of depreciation charges on production equipment and buildings.

270   Chapter 6

Production and cost data for the two years are:

	Year 1	Year 2
Units produced	45,000	45,000
Units sold	40,000	50,000

Required:
1. Prepare a variable costing contribution format income statement for each year.
2. Reconcile the absorption costing and the variable costing net operating income figures for each year.

PROBLEM 6–20 Variable and Absorption Costing Unit Product Costs and Income Statements; Explanation of Difference in Net Operating Income [LO6–1, LO6–2, LO6–3]
High Country, Inc., produces and sells many recreational products. The company has just opened a new plant to produce a folding camp cot that will be marketed throughout the United States. The following cost and revenue data relate to May, the first month of the plant's operation:

Beginning inventory	0
Units produced	10,000
Units sold	8,000
Selling price per unit	$75
Selling and administrative expenses:	
Variable per unit	$6
Fixed (per month)	$200,000
Manufacturing costs:	
Direct materials cost per unit	$20
Direct labor cost per unit	$8
Variable manufacturing overhead cost per unit	$2
Fixed manufacturing overhead cost (per month)	$100,000

Management is anxious to see how profitable the new camp cot will be and has asked that an income statement be prepared for May.

Required:
1. Assume that the company uses absorption costing.
   a. Determine the unit product cost.
   b. Prepare an income statement for May.
2. Assume that the company uses variable costing.
   a. Determine the unit product cost.
   b. Prepare a contribution format income statement for May.
3. Explain the reason for any difference in the ending inventory balances under the two costing methods and the impact of this difference on reported net operating income.

PROBLEM 6–21 Segment Reporting and Decision-Making [LO6–4]
Vulcan Company's contribution format income statement for June is given below:

Vulcan Company Income Statement For the Month Ended June 30	
Sales	$750,000
Variable expenses	336,000
Contribution margin	414,000
Fixed expenses	378,000
Net operating income	$ 36,000

Management is disappointed with the company's performance and is wondering what can be done to improve profits. By examining sales and cost records, you have determined the following:
a. The company is divided into two sales territories—Northern and Southern. The Northern territory recorded $300,000 in sales and $156,000 in variable expenses during June; the remaining sales and variable expenses were recorded in the Southern territory. Fixed expenses of $120,000 and $108,000 are traceable to the Northern and Southern territories, respectively. The rest of the fixed expenses are common to the two territories.

Variable Costing and Segment Reporting: Tools for Management

b.   The company is the exclusive distributor for two products—Paks and Tibs. Sales of Paks and Tibs totaled $50,000 and $250,000, respectively, in the Northern territory during June. Variable expenses are 22% of the selling price for Paks and 58% for Tibs. Cost records show that $30,000 of the Northern territory's fixed expenses are traceable to Paks and $40,000 to Tibs, with the remainder common to the two products.

Required:

1.   Prepare contribution format segmented income statements first showing the total company broken down between sales territories and then showing the Northern territory broken down by product line. In addition, for the company as a whole and for each segment, show each item on the segmented income statements as a percent of sales.
2.   Look at the statement you have prepared showing the total company segmented by sales territory. What insights revealed by this statement should be brought to the attention of management?
3.   Look at the statement you have prepared showing the Northern territory segmented by product lines. What insights revealed by this statement should be brought to the attention of management?

PROBLEM 6–22 Prepare and Reconcile Variable Costing Statements [LO6–1, LO6–2, LO6–3]

Denton Company manufactures and sells a single product. Cost data for the product are given below:

Variable costs per unit:	
Direct materials	$ 7
Direct labor	10
Variable manufacturing overhead	5
Variable selling and administrative	3
Total variable cost per unit	$25
Fixed costs per month:	
Fixed manufacturing overhead	$315,000
Fixed selling and administrative	245,000
Total fixed cost per month	$560,000

The product sells for $60 per unit. Production and sales data for July and August, the first two months of operations, follow:

	Units Produced	Units Sold
July	17,500	15,000
August	17,500	20,000

The company's Accounting Department has prepared absorption costing income statements for July and August as presented below:

	July	August
Sales	$900,000	$1,200,000
Cost of goods sold	600,000	800,000
Gross margin	300,000	400,000
Selling and administrative expenses	290,000	305,000
Net operating income	$ 10,000	$ 95,000

Required:

1.   Determine the unit product cost under:
     a.   Absorption costing.
     b.   Variable costing.
2.   Prepare contribution format variable costing income statements for July and August.
3.   Reconcile the variable costing and absorption costing net operating income figures.
4.   The company's Accounting Department has determined the company's break-even point to be 16,000 units per month, computed as follows:

$$\frac{\text{Fixed cost per month}}{\text{Unit contribution margin}} = \frac{\$560,000}{\$35 \text{ per unit}} = 16,000 \text{ units}$$

272

Chapter 6

"I'm confused," said the president. "The accounting people say that our break-even point is 16,000 units per month, but we sold only 15,000 units in July, and the income statement they prepared shows a $10,000 profit for that month. Either the income statement is wrong or the break-even point is wrong." Prepare a brief memo for the president, explaining what happened on the July absorption costing income statement.

PROBLEM 6–23 Absorption and Variable Costing; Production Constant, Sales Fluctuate [LO6–1, LO6–2, LO6–3]

Tami Tyler opened Tami's Creations, Inc., a small manufacturing company, at the beginning of the year. Getting the company through its first quarter of operations placed a considerable strain on Ms. Tyler's personal finances. The following income statement for the first quarter was prepared by a friend who has just completed a course in managerial accounting at State University.

Tami's Creations, Inc. Income Statement For the Quarter Ended March 31		
Sales (28,000 units)		$1,120,000
Variable expenses:		
Variable cost of goods sold	$462,000	
Variable selling and administrative	168,000	630,000
Contribution margin		490,000
Fixed expenses:		
Fixed manufacturing overhead	300,000	
Fixed selling and administrative	200,000	500,000
Net operating loss		$ (10,000)

Ms. Tyler is discouraged over the loss shown for the quarter, particularly because she had planned to use the statement as support for a bank loan. Another friend, a CPA, insists that the company should be using absorption costing rather than variable costing and argues that if absorption costing had been used the company probably would have reported at least some profit for the quarter.

At this point, Ms. Tyler is manufacturing only one product, a swimsuit. Production and cost data relating to the swimsuit for the first quarter follow:

Units produced	30,000
Units sold	28,000
Variable costs per unit:	
Direct materials	$3.50
Direct labor	$12.00
Variable manufacturing overhead	$1.00
Variable selling and administrative	$6.00

Required:

1. Complete the following:
   a. Compute the unit product cost under absorption costing.
   b. Redo the company's income statement for the quarter using absorption costing.
   c. Reconcile the variable and absorption costing net operating income (loss) figures.
2. Was the CPA correct in suggesting that the company really earned a "profit" for the quarter? Explain.
3. During the second quarter of operations, the company again produced 30,000 units but sold 32,000 units. (Assume no change in total fixed costs.)
   a. Prepare a contribution format income statement for the quarter using variable costing.
   b. Prepare an income statement for the quarter using absorption costing.
   c. Reconcile the variable costing and absorption costing net operating incomes.

PROBLEM 6–24 Companywide and Segment Break-Even Analysis; Decision Making [LO6–4, LO6–5]

Toxaway Company is a merchandiser that segments its business into two divisions—Commercial and Residential. The company's accounting intern was asked to prepare segmented income statements that the company's divisional managers could use to calculate their break-even points and make decisions. She took the prior month's companywide income statement and prepared the absorption format segmented income statement shown below:

	Total Company	Commercial	Residential
Sales	$750,000	$250,000	$500,000
Cost of goods sold	500,000	140,000	360,000
Gross margin	250,000	110,000	140,000
Selling and administrative expenses	240,000	104,000	136,000
Net operating income	$ 10,000	$ 6,000	$ 4,000

In preparing these statements, the intern determined that Toxaway's only variable selling and administrative expense is a 10% sales commission on all sales. The company's total fixed expenses include $72,000 of common fixed expenses that would continue to be incurred even if the Commercial or Residential segments are discontinued, $38,000 of fixed expenses that would be avoided if the Residential segment is dropped, and $55,000 of fixed expenses that would be avoided if the Commericial segment is dropped.

Required:

1. Do you agree with the intern's decision to use an absorption format for her segmented income statement? Why?
2. Based on the intern's segmented income statement, can you determine how she allocated the company's common fixed expenses to the Commercial and Residential segments? Do you agree with her decision to allocate the common fixed expenses to the Commercial and Residential segments?
3. Redo the intern's segmented income statement using the contribution format.
4. Compute the companywide break-even point in dollar sales.
5. Compute the break-even point in dollar sales for the Commercial Division and for the Residential Division.
6. Assume the company decided to pay its sales representatives in the Commercial and Residential Divisions a total monthly salary of $15,000 and $30,000, respectively, and to lower its companywide sales commission percentage from 10% to 5%. Calculate the new break-even point in dollar sales for the Commercial Division and the Residential Division.

PROBLEM 6–25 Prepare and Interpret Income Statements; Changes in Both Sales and Production; Lean Production [LO6–1, LO6–2, LO6–3]

Starfax, Inc., manufactures a small part that is widely used in various electronic products such as home computers. Operating results for the first three years of activity were as follows (absorption costing basis):

	Year 1	Year 2	Year 3
Sales	$800,000	$640,000	$800,000
Cost of goods sold	580,000	400,000	620,000
Gross margin	220,000	240,000	180,000
Selling and administrative expenses	190,000	180,000	190,000
Net operating income (loss)	$ 30,000	$ 60,000	$ (10,000)

In the latter part of Year 2, a competitor went out of business and in the process dumped a large number of units on the market. As a result, Starfax's sales dropped by 20% during Year 2 even though production increased during the year. Management had expected sales to remain constant at 50,000 units; the increased production was designed to provide the company with a buffer of protection against unexpected spurts in demand. By the start of Year 3, management could see that inventory was excessive and that spurts in demand were unlikely. To reduce the excessive inventories, Starfax cut back production during Year 3, as shown below:

	Year 1	Year 2	Year 3
Production in units	50,000	60,000	40,000
Sales in units	50,000	40,000	50,000

274   Chapter 6

Additional information about the company follows:

a.   The company's plant is highly automated. Variable manufacturing expenses (direct materials, direct labor, and variable manufacturing overhead) total only $2 per unit, and fixed manufacturing overhead expenses total $480,000 per year.

b.   Fixed manufacturing overhead costs are applied to units of product on the basis of each year's production. That is, a new fixed manufacturing overhead rate is computed each year.

c.   Variable selling and administrative expenses were $1 per unit sold in each year. Fixed selling and administrative expenses totaled $140,000 per year.

d.   The company uses a FIFO inventory flow assumption.

Starfax's management can't understand why profits doubled during Year 2 when sales dropped by 20% and why a loss was incurred during Year 3 when sales recovered to previous levels.

Required:

1.   Prepare a contribution format variable costing income statement for each year.

2.   Refer to the absorption costing income statements above.

   a.   Compute the unit product cost in each year under absorption costing. (Show how much of this cost is variable and how much is fixed.)

   b.   Reconcile the variable costing and absorption costing net operating income figures for each year.

3.   Refer again to the absorption costing income statements. Explain why net operating income was higher in Year 2 than it was in Year 1 under the absorption approach, in light of the fact that fewer units were sold in Year 2 than in Year 1.

4.   Refer again to the absorption costing income statements. Explain why the company suffered a loss in Year 3 but reported a profit in Year 1 although the same number of units was sold in each year.

5.   a.   Explain how operations would have differed in Year 2 and Year 3 if the company had been using Lean Production, with the result that ending inventory was zero.

   b.   If Lean Production had been used during Year 2 and Year 3 and the predetermined overhead rate is based on 50,000 units per year, what would the company's net operating income (or loss) have been in each year under absorption costing? Explain the reason for any differences between these income figures and the figures reported by the company in the statements above.

PROBLEM 6–26 Restructuring a Segmented Income Statement [LO6–4]
Losses have been incurred at Millard Corporation for some time. In an effort to isolate the problem and improve the company's performance, management has requested that the monthly income statement be segmented by sales region. The company's first effort at preparing a segmented statement is given below. This statement is for May, the most recent month of activity.

	Sales Region		
	West	Central	East
Sales	$450,000	$800,000	$ 750,000
Regional expenses (traceable):			
Cost of goods sold	162,900	280,000	376,500
Advertising	108,000	200,000	210,000
Salaries	90,000	88,000	135,000
Utilities	13,500	12,000	15,000
Depreciation	27,000	28,000	30,000
Shipping expense	17,100	32,000	28,500
Total regional expenses	418,500	640,000	795,000
Regional income (loss) before corporate expenses	31,500	160,000	(45,000)
Corporate expenses:			
Advertising (general)	18,000	32,000	30,000
General administrative expense	50,000	50,000	50,000
Total corporate expenses	68,000	82,000	80,000
Net operating income (loss)	$ (36,500)	$ 78,000	$(125,000)

Cost of goods sold and shipping expense are both variable; other costs are all fixed.

Millard Corporation is a wholesale distributor of office products. It purchases office products from manufacturers and distributes them in the three regions given above. The three regions are about the same size, and each has its own manager and sales staff. The products that the company distributes vary widely in profitability.

Required:

1. List any disadvantages or weaknesses that you see to the statement format illustrated on the previous page.
2. Explain the basis that is apparently being used to allocate the corporate expenses to the regions. Do you agree with these allocations? Explain.
3. Prepare a new contribution format segmented income statement for May. Show a Total column as well as data for each region. In addition, for the company as a whole and for each sales region, show each item on the segmented income statement as a percent of sales.
4. Analyze the statement that you prepared in part (3) above. What points that might help to improve the company's performance would you bring to management's attention?

PROBLEM 6–27 Incentives Created by Absorption Costing; Ethics and the Manager [LO6–2]
Carlos Cavalas, the manager of Echo Products' Brazilian Division, is trying to set the production schedule for the last quarter of the year. The Brazilian Division had planned to sell 3,600 units during the year, but by September 30 only the following activity had been reported:

	Units
Inventory, January 1	0
Production	2,400
Sales	2,000
Inventory, September 30	400

The division can rent warehouse space to store up to 1,000 units. The minimum inventory level that the division should carry is 50 units. Mr. Cavalas is aware that production must be at least 200 units per quarter in order to retain a nucleus of key employees. Maximum production capacity is 1,500 units per quarter.

Demand has been soft, and the sales forecast for the last quarter is only 600 units. Due to the nature of the division's operations, fixed manufacturing overhead is a major element of product cost.

Required:

1. Assume that the division is using variable costing. How many units should be scheduled for production during the last quarter of the year? (The basic formula for computing the required production for a period in a company is: Expected sales + Desired ending inventory − Beginning inventory = Required production.) Show computations and explain your answer. Will the number of units scheduled for production affect the division's reported income or loss for the year? Explain.
2. Assume that the division is using absorption costing and that the divisional manager is given an annual bonus based on divisional operating income. If Mr. Cavalas wants to maximize his division's operating income for the year, how many units should be scheduled for production during the last quarter? [See the formula in (1) above.] Explain.
3. Identify the ethical issues involved in the decision Mr. Cavalas must make about the level of production for the last quarter of the year.

PROBLEM 6–28 Basic Segment Reporting; Activity-Based Cost Assignment [LO6–4]
Diversified Products, Inc., has recently acquired a small publishing company that offers three books for sale—a cookbook, a travel guide, and a handy speller. Each book sells for $10. The publishing company's most recent monthly income statement is given on the next page:

		Product Line		
	Total Company	Cookbook	Travel Guide	Handy Speller
Sales	$300,000	$90,000	$150,000	$60,000
Expenses:				
Printing costs	102,000	27,000	63,000	12,000
Advertising	36,000	13,500	19,500	3,000
General sales	18,000	5,400	9,000	3,600
Salaries	33,000	18,000	9,000	6,000
Equipment depreciation	9,000	3,000	3,000	3,000
Sales commissions	30,000	9,000	15,000	6,000
General administration	42,000	14,000	14,000	14,000
Warehouse rent	12,000	3,600	6,000	2,400
Depreciation—office facilities	3,000	1,000	1,000	1,000
Total expenses	285,000	94,500	139,500	51,000
Net operating income (loss)	$ 15,000	$ (4,500)	$ 10,500	$ 9,000

The following additional information is available about the company:

a. Only printing costs and sales commissions are variable; all other costs are fixed. The printing costs (which include materials, labor, and variable overhead) are traceable to the three product lines as shown in the statement above. Sales commissions are 10% of sales for any product.

b. The same equipment is used to produce all three books, so the equipment depreciation cost has been allocated equally among the three product lines. An analysis of the company's activities indicates that the equipment is used 30% of the time to produce cookbooks, 50% of the time to produce travel guides, and 20% of the time to produce handy spellers.

c. The warehouse is used to store finished units of product, so the rental cost has been allocated to the product lines on the basis of sales dollars. The warehouse rental cost is $3 per square foot per year. The warehouse contains 48,000 square feet of space, of which 7,200 square feet is used by the cookbook line, 24,000 square feet by the travel guide line, and 16,800 square feet by the handy speller line.

d. The general sales cost above includes the salary of the sales manager and other sales costs not traceable to any specific product line. This cost has been allocated to the product lines on the basis of sales dollars.

e. The general administration cost and depreciation of office facilities both relate to administration of the company as a whole. These costs have been allocated equally to the three product lines.

f. All other costs are traceable to the three product lines in the amounts shown on the statement above.

The management of Diversified Products, Inc., is anxious to improve the publishing company's 5% return on sales.

Required:

1. Prepare a new contribution format segmented income statement for the month. Adjust allocations of equipment depreciation and of warehouse rent as indicated by the additional information provided.

2. After seeing the income statement in the main body of the problem, management has decided to eliminate the cookbook because it is not returning a profit, and to focus all available resources on promoting the travel guide.

   a. Based on the statement you have prepared, do you agree with the decision to eliminate the cookbook? Explain.

   b. Based on the statement you have prepared, do you agree with the decision to focus all available resources on promoting the travel guide? Assume that an ample market is available for all three product lines. (*Hint:* Compute the contribution margin ratio for each product.)

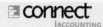 **Cases**

All applicable cases are available with McGraw-Hill's *Connect® Accounting*.

CASE 6–29 Variable and Absorption Costing Unit Product Costs and Income Statements [LO6–1, LO6–2]
O'Brien Company manufactures and sells one product. The following information pertains to each of the company's first three years of operations:

Variable costs per unit:	
Manufacturing:	
Direct materials	$32
Direct labor	$20
Variable manufacturing overhead	$4
Variable selling and administrative	$3
Fixed costs per year:	
Fixed manufacturing overhead	$660,000
Fixed selling and administrative expenses	$120,000

During its first year of operations, O'Brien produced 100,000 units and sold 80,000 units. During its second year of operations, it produced 75,000 units and sold 90,000 units. In its third year, O'Brien produced 80,000 units and sold 75,000 units. The selling price of the company's product is $75 per unit.

Required:
1. Assume the company uses variable costing and a FIFO inventory flow assumption (FIFO means first-in first-out. In other words, it assumes that the oldest units in inventory are sold first):
    a. Compute the unit product cost for Year 1, Year 2, and Year 3.
    b. Prepare an income statement for Year 1, Year 2, and Year 3.
2. Assume the company uses variable costing and a LIFO inventory flow assumption (LIFO means last-in first-out. In other words, it assumes that the newest units in inventory are sold first):
    a. Compute the unit product cost for Year 1, Year 2, and Year 3.
    b. Prepare an income statement for Year 1, Year 2, and Year 3.
3. Assume the company uses absorption costing and a FIFO inventory flow assumption (FIFO means first-in first-out. In other words, it assumes that the oldest units in inventory are sold first):
    a. Compute the unit product cost for Year 1, Year 2, and Year 3.
    b. Prepare an income statement for Year 1, Year 2, and Year 3.
4. Assume the company uses absorption costing and a LIFO inventory flow assumption (LIFO means last-in first-out. In other words, it assumes that the newest units in inventory are sold first):
    a. Compute the unit product cost for Year 1, Year 2, and Year 3.
    b. Prepare an income statement for Year 1, Year 2, and Year 3.

CASE 6–30 Service Organization; Segment Reporting [LO6–4]
Music Teachers, Inc., is an educational association for music teachers that has 20,000 members. The association operates from a central headquarters but has local membership chapters throughout the United States. Monthly meetings are held by the local chapters to discuss recent developments on topics of interest to music teachers. The association's journal, Teachers' Forum, is issued monthly with features about recent developments in the field. The association publishes books and reports and also sponsors professional courses that qualify for continuing

Chapter 6

professional education credit. The association's statement of revenues and expenses for the current year is presented below.

Music Teachers, Inc. Statement of Revenues and Expenses For the Year Ended November 30	
Revenues	$3,275,000
Expenses:	
Salaries	920,000
Personnel costs	230,000
Occupancy costs	280,000
Reimbursement of member costs to local chapters	600,000
Other membership services	500,000
Printing and paper	320,000
Postage and shipping	176,000
Instructors' fees	80,000
General and administrative	38,000
Total expenses	3,144,000
Excess of revenues over expenses	$ 131,000

The board of directors of Music Teachers, Inc., has requested that a segmented income statement be prepared showing the contribution of each segment to the association. The association has four segments: Membership Division, Magazine Subscriptions Division, Books and Reports Division, and Continuing Education Division. Mike Doyle has been assigned responsibility for preparing the segmented income statement, and he has gathered the following data prior to its preparation.

a. Membership dues are $100 per year, of which $20 is considered to cover a one-year subscription to the association's journal. Other benefits include membership in the association and chapter affiliation. The portion of the dues covering the magazine subscription ($20) should be assigned to the Magazine Subscription Division.

b. One-year subscriptions to Teachers' Forum were sold to nonmembers and libraries at $30 per subscription. A total of 2,500 of these subscriptions were sold last year. In addition to subscriptions, the magazine generated $100,000 in advertising revenues. The costs per magazine subscription were $7 for printing and paper and $4 for postage and shipping.

c. A total of 28,000 technical reports and professional texts were sold by the Books and Reports Division at an average unit selling price of $25. Average costs per publication were $4 for printing and paper and $2 for postage and shipping.

d. The association offers a variety of continuing education courses to both members and nonmembers. The one-day courses had a tuition cost of $75 each and were attended by 2,400 students. A total of 1,760 students took two-day courses at a tuition cost of $125 for each student. Outside instructors were paid to teach some courses.

e. Salary costs and space occupied by division follow:

	Salaries	Space Occupied (square feet)
Membership	$210,000	2,000
Magazine Subscriptions	150,000	2,000
Books and Reports	300,000	3,000
Continuing Education	180,000	2,000
Corporate staff	80,000	1,000
Total	$920,000	10,000

Personnel costs are 25% of salaries in the separate divisions as well as for the corporate staff. The $280,000 in occupancy costs includes $50,000 in rental cost for a warehouse used by the Books and Reports Division for storage purposes.

f.   Printing and paper costs other than for magazine subscriptions and for books and reports relate to the Continuing Education Division.

g.   General and administrative expenses include costs relating to overall administration of the association as a whole. The company's corporate staff does some mailing of materials for general administrative purposes.

The expenses that can be traced or assigned to the corporate staff, as well as any other expenses that are not traceable to the segments, will be treated as common costs. It is not necessary to distinguish between variable and fixed costs.

Required:

1.   Prepare a contribution format segmented income statement for Music Teachers, Inc. This statement should show the segment margin for each division as well as results for the association as a whole.

2.   Give arguments for and against allocating all costs of the association to the four divisions.

(CMA, adapted)

Appendix 6A: Super-Variable Costing

In the discussion of variable costing in this chapter we have assumed that direct labor and a portion of manufacturing overhead are variable costs that should be attached to products. However, these assumptions about cost behavior may not be true. For example, it may be easier and more accurate to assume that *all* manufacturing overhead costs are fixed costs because the variable portion of these costs is insignificant or too difficult to estimate. Furthermore, many companies' labor costs (including direct and indirect labor) are more fixed than variable due to labor regulations, labor contracts, or management policy. In countries such as France, Germany, Spain, and Japan, management often has little flexibility in adjusting the labor force to changes in business activity. Even in countries such as the United States and the United Kingdom, where management usually has greater latitude to adjust the size of its labor force, many managers choose to view labor as a fixed cost. They make this choice because the cost savings from terminating or laying off employees during a short-term business downturn may be swamped by the negative effects on employee morale and by the costs of later finding and training suitable replacements. Moreover, treating employees as variable costs subtly fosters the attitude that employees are expendable and replaceable like materials rather than unique, difficult-to-replace assets.

Super-variable costing is a variation on variable costing in which direct labor and manufacturing overhead costs are considered to be fixed. **Super-variable costing** classifies all direct labor and manufacturing overhead costs as fixed period costs and *only direct materials as a variable product cost*. To simplify, in this appendix we also assume that selling and administrative expenses are entirely fixed.

LO6–6
Prepare an income statement using super-variable costing and reconcile this approach with variable costing.

Super-Variable Costing and Variable Costing—An Example

To illustrate the difference between treating direct labor as a fixed cost (as in super-variable costing) and treating direct labor as a variable cost (as in variable costing), we will use a modified version of the Weber Light Aircraft example from the main body of the chapter. Data concerning the company's operations appear below:

	Per Aircraft	Per Month
Selling price	$100,000	
Direct materials	$19,000	
Direct labor		$20,000
Fixed manufacturing overhead		$74,000
Fixed selling and administrative expense		$40,000

	January	February	March
Beginning inventory	0	0	1
Units produced	2	2	2
Units sold	2	1	3
Ending inventory	0	1	0

The key thing to notice here is that direct labor is a fixed cost—$20,000 per month. Also, notice that Weber Light Aircraft has no variable manufacturing overhead costs and no variable selling and administrative expenses. For the months of January, February, and March, the company's selling price per aircraft, variable cost per aircraft, monthly production in units, and total monthly fixed expenses never change. The only thing that changes in this example is the number of units sold (January = 2 units sold; February = 1 unit sold; March = 3 units sold).

We will first construct the company's super-variable costing income statements for January, February, and March. Then we will show how the company's net operating income would be determined for the same months using variable costing if it were incorrectly assumed that direct labor is a variable cost. As you'll see, both income statements rely on the contribution format.

Super-Variable Costing Income Statements

To prepare the company's super-variable costing income statements for each month we follow four steps. First, we compute sales by multiplying the number of units sold by the selling price per unit, which in this example is $100,000 per unit. Second, we compute the variable cost of goods sold by multiplying the number of units sold by the unit product cost, which in this example is the direct materials cost of $19,000 per unit. Third, we compute the contribution margin by subtracting the variable cost of goods sold from sales. Fourth, we compute net operating income by subtracting all fixed expenses from the contribution margin.

Using these four steps, Weber's super-variable costing income statements for each month would appear as shown in Exhibit 6A–1. Notice that the only variable expense is variable cost of goods sold, which is the $19,000 of direct materials per unit sold. For example, in March, the unit product cost of $19,000 is multiplied by three units sold to obtain the variable cost of goods sold of $57,000. The total monthly fixed manufacturing expenses of $94,000 include $20,000 of direct labor and $74,000 of fixed manufacturing overhead.

EXHIBIT 6A–1 Super-Variable Costing Income Statements		January	February	March
Sales (@ $100,000 per unit)		$200,000	$100,000	$300,000
Variable cost of goods sold (@ $19,000 per unit)		38,000	19,000	57,000
Contribution margin		162,000	81,000	243,000
Fixed expenses:				
Fixed manufacturing expenses		94,000	94,000	94,000
Fixed selling and administrative expenses . . .		40,000	40,000	40,000
Total fixed expenses		134,000	134,000	134,000
Net operating income (loss)		$ 28,000	$ (53,000)	$109,000

Variable Costing Income Statements

The variable costing income statements in this example differ from the super-variable costing income statements in one important respect—we will assume that direct labor is incorrectly classified as a variable cost and is included in unit product costs. Because the monthly direct labor cost is $20,000 and two aircraft are produced each month, if direct labor costs are included in unit product costs, then Weber Light Aircraft will assign

	January	February	March	
Sales (@ $100,000 per unit)	$200,000	$100,000	$300,000	**EXHIBIT 6A–2**
Variable cost of goods sold				Variable Costing Income
(@ $29,000 per unit)	58,000	29,000	87,000	Statements
Contribution margin	142,000	71,000	213,000	
Fixed expenses:				
Fixed manufacturing overhead	74,000	74,000	74,000	
Fixed selling and administrative expenses . . .	40,000	40,000	40,000	
Total fixed expenses	114,000	114,000	114,000	
Net operating income (loss)	$ 28,000	$ (43,000)	$ 99,000	

$10,000 of direct labor cost to each aircraft that it produces. Thus, the company's unit product costs under variable costing would be computed as follows:

	January	February	March
Direct materials	$19,000	$19,000	$19,000
Direct labor	10,000	10,000	10,000
Unit product cost	$29,000	$29,000	$29,000

Given these unit product cost figures, the company's variable costing income statements would be computed as shown in Exhibit 6A–2. For example, in March, the unit product cost of $29,000 is multiplied by three units sold to obtain the variable cost of goods sold of $87,000. The total fixed manufacturing overhead of $74,000 and total fixed selling and administrative expenses of $40,000 are both recorded as period expenses.

Reconciliation of Super-Variable Costing and Variable Costing Income

The super-variable costing and variable costing net operating incomes are both $28,000 in January. However, in February, the super-variable costing income is $10,000 lower than the variable costing income and the opposite holds true in March. In other words, the super-variable costing income in March is $10,000 higher than the variable costing income.

Why do these two costing methods produce different net operating incomes? The answer can be found in the accounting for direct labor costs. Super-variable costing treats direct labor as a fixed period expense whereas variable costing treats direct labor as a variable product cost. In other words, super-variable costing records the entire direct labor cost of $20,000 as an expense on each month's income statement. Conversely, variable costing assigns $10,000 of direct labor cost to each unit produced. The $10,000 assigned to each unit produced remains in inventory on the balance sheet until the unit is sold—at which point the $10,000 assigned to it is transferred to variable cost of goods sold on the income statement. Given this background, the super-variable costing and variable costing incomes for each month can be reconciled as follows:

	January	February	March
Direct labor cost in ending inventory			
(@ $10,000 per unit)	$ 0	$10,000	$ 0
− Direct labor cost in beginning inventory			
(@ $10,000 per unit)	0	0	10,000
= Direct labor cost deferred in			
(released from) inventory	$ 0	$10,000	$(10,000)

282 Chapter 6

	January	February	March
Super-variable costing net operating income (loss)	$28,000	$(53,000)	$109,000
Direct labor deferred in (released from) inventory	0	10,000	(10,000)
Variable costing net operating income (loss) ...	$28,000	$(43,000)	$ 99,000

In January, both costing methods report the same net operating income ($28,000). This occurs because each method expenses $20,000 of direct labor in the income statement. In February, super-variable costing income is $10,000 less than variable costing income. This difference arises because super-variable costing expenses $20,000 of direct labor in the income statement, whereas variable costing expenses only $10,000 of direct labor in the income statement ($10,000 per unit × 1 unit sold) and defers $10,000 of direct labor on the balance sheet ($10,000 per unit × 1 unit produced but not sold). In March, super-variable costing income is $10,000 greater than variable costing income. This difference arises because super-variable costing expenses $20,000 of direct labor on the income statement, whereas variable costing expenses $30,000 of direct labor on the income statement ($10,000 per unit × 3 unit sold). Notice that one of the units sold in March was actually produced in February. Under variable costing, the $10,000 of direct labor attached to the unit produced in February is released from inventory and included in variable cost of goods sold for March.

In summary, the key issue considered in this appendix is how a company treats direct labor costs. If a company treats direct labor as a variable cost, the cost system may encourage managers to treat labor costs as an expense to be minimized when sales decline and this may result in reduced morale and eventual problems when business picks up. Second, in practice management may have little ability to adjust the direct labor force even if they wanted to, resulting in a situation in which direct labor costs are in fact fixed. In either case, treating direct labor costs as variable can lead to bad decisions. The super-variable costing approach overcomes this problem by treating labor costs as fixed costs.

Glossary (Appendix 6A)

Super-variable costing A costing method that classifies all direct labor and manufacturing overhead costs as fixed period costs and *only direct materials as a variable product cost.* (p. 279)

Appendix 6A Exercises and Problems |ACCOUNTING

All applicable exercises and problems are available with McGraw-Hill's Connect® Accounting.

EXERCISE 6A–1 Super-Variable Costing Income Statement [LO6–6]
Zola Company manufactures and sells one product. The following information pertains to the company's first year of operations:

Variable cost per unit:	
Direct materials	$18
Fixed costs per year:	
Direct labor	$200,000
Fixed manufacturing overhead	$250,000
Fixed selling and administrative expenses	$80,000

The company does not incur any variable manufacturing overhead costs or variable selling and administrative expenses. During its first year of operations, Zola produced 25,000 units and sold 20,000 units. The selling price of the company's product is $50 per unit.

Required:
1. Assume the company uses super-variable costing:
   a. Compute the unit product cost for the year.
   b. Prepare an income statement for the year.

EXERCISE 6A–2 Super-Variable Costing and Variable Costing Unit Product Costs and Income Statements [LO6–2, LO6–6]
Lyons Company manufactures and sells one product. The following information pertains to the company's first year of operations:

Variable cost per unit:	
Direct materials	$13
Fixed costs per year:	
Direct labor	$750,000
Fixed manufacturing overhead	$420,000
Fixed selling and administrative expenses	$110,000

The company does not incur any variable manufacturing overhead costs or variable selling and administrative expenses. During its first year of operations, Lyons produced 60,000 units and sold 52,000 units. The selling price of the company's product is $40 per unit.

Required:
1. Assume the company uses super-variable costing:
   a. Compute the unit product cost for the year.
   b. Prepare an income statement for the year.
2. Assume the company uses a variable costing system that assigns $12.50 of direct labor cost to each unit produced:
   a. Compute the unit product cost for the year.
   b. Prepare an income statement for the year.
3. Prepare a reconciliation that explains the difference between the super-variable costing and variable costing net operating incomes.

EXERCISE 6A–3 Super-Variable Costing and Variable Costing Unit Product Costs and Income Statements [LO6–2, LO6–6]
Kelly Company manufactures and sells one product. The following information pertains to each of the company's first two years of operations:

Variable cost per unit:	
Direct materials	$12
Fixed costs per year:	
Direct labor	$500,000
Fixed manufacturing overhead	$450,000
Fixed selling and administrative expenses	$180,000

The company does not incur any variable manufacturing overhead costs or variable selling and administrative expenses. During its first year of operations, Kelly produced 50,000 units and sold 40,000 units. During its second year of operations, it produced 50,000 units and sold 60,000 units. The selling price of the company's product is $50 per unit.

Required:
1. Assume the company uses super-variable costing:
   a. Compute the unit product cost for Year 1 and Year 2.
   b. Prepare an income statement for Year 1 and Year 2.

284

Chapter 6

2. Assume the company uses a variable costing system that assigns $10 of direct labor cost to each unit produced:
   a. Compute the unit product cost for Year 1 and Year 2.
   b. Prepare an income statement for Year 1 and Year 2.
3. Prepare a reconciliation that explains the difference between the super-variable costing and variable costing net operating incomes in Years 1 and 2.

PROBLEM 6A–4 Super-Variable Costing and Variable Costing Unit Product Costs and Income Statements [LO6–2, LO6–6]

Ogilvy Company manufactures and sells one product. The following information pertains to each of the company's first three years of operations:

Variable cost per unit:	
Direct materials	$16
Fixed costs per year:	
Direct labor	$540,000
Fixed manufacturing overhead	$822,000
Fixed selling and administrative expenses	$370,000

The company does not incur any variable manufacturing overhead costs or variable selling and administrative expenses. During its first year of operations, Ogilvy produced 60,000 units and sold 60,000 units. During its second year of operations, it produced 60,000 units and sold 55,000 units. In its third year, Ogilvy produced 60,000 units and sold 65,000 units. The selling price of the company's product is $45 per unit.

Required:
1. Assume the company uses super-variable costing:
   a. Compute the unit product cost for Year 1, Year 2, and Year 3.
   b. Prepare an income statement for Year 1, Year 2, and Year 3.
2. Assume the company uses a variable costing system that assigns $9 of direct labor cost to each unit produced:
   a. Compute the unit product cost for Year 1, Year 2, and Year 3.
   b. Prepare an income statement for Year 1, Year 2, and Year 3.
3. Prepare a reconciliation that explains the difference between the super-variable costing and variable costing net operating incomes in Years 1, 2, and 3.

PROBLEM 6A–5 Super-Variable Costing, Variable Costing, and Absorption Costing Income Statements [LO6–2, LO6–6]

Bracey Company manufactures and sells one product. The following information pertains to the company's first year of operations:

Variable cost per unit:	
Direct materials	$19
Fixed costs per year:	
Direct labor	$250,000
Fixed manufacturing overhead	$300,000
Fixed selling and administrative expenses	$90,000

The company does not incur any variable manufacturing overhead costs or variable selling and administrative expenses. During its first year of operations, Bracey produced 20,000 units and sold 18,000 units. The selling price of the company's product is $55 per unit.

Required:

1. Assume the company uses super-variable costing:
   a. Compute the unit product cost for the year.
   b. Prepare an income statement for the year.
2. Assume the company uses a variable costing system that assigns $12.50 of direct labor cost to each unit produced:
   a. Compute the unit product cost for the year.
   b. Prepare an income statement for the year.
3. Assume the company uses an absorption costing system that assigns $12.50 of direct labor cost and $15.00 of fixed manufacturing overhead cost to each unit produced:
   a. Compute the unit product cost for the year.
   b. Prepare an income statement for the year.
4. Prepare a reconciliation that explains the difference between the super-variable costing and variable costing net operating incomes. Prepare another reconciliation that explains the difference between the super-variable costing and absorption costing net operating incomes.

CHAPTER 7

Activity-Based Costing: A Tool to Aid Decision Making

Managing Product Complexity

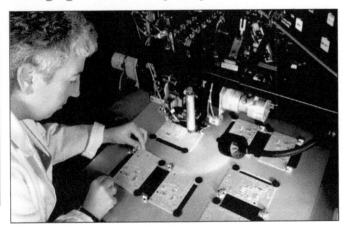

Managers often understand that increasing the variety of raw material inputs used in their products increases costs. For example, **General Mills** studied its 50 varieties of Hamburger Helper and concluded that it could lower costs by discontinuing half of them without alienating customers. **Seagate** studied seven varieties of its computer hard drives and found that only 2% of their parts could be shared by more than one hard drive. The engineers fixed the problem by redesigning the hard drives so that they used more common component parts. Instead of using 61 types of screws to make the hard drives, the engineers reduced the number of screws needed to 19. Eventually all Seagate products were designed so that 75% of their component parts were shared with other product lines.

Activity-based costing systems quantify the increase in costs, such as procurement costs, material handling costs, and assembly costs that are caused by inefficient product designs and other factors. ■

Sources: Mina Kimes, "Cereal Cost Cutters," Fortune, November 10, 2008, p. 24; Erika Brown, "Drive Fast, Drive Hard," Forbes, January 9, 2006, pp. 92–96.

LEARNING OBJECTIVES

After studying Chapter 7, you should be able to:

LO7–1 Understand activity-based costing and how it differs from a traditional costing system.

LO7–2 Assign costs to cost pools using a first-stage allocation.

LO7–3 Compute activity rates for cost pools.

LO7–4 Assign costs to a cost object using a second-stage allocation.

LO7–5 Use activity-based costing to compute product and customer margins.

LO7–6 (Appendix 7A) Prepare an action analysis report using activity-based costing data and interpret the report.

This chapter introduces the concept of *activity-based costing* which has been embraced by a wide variety of organizations including Charles Schwab, Citigroup, Lowe's, Coca-Cola, J&B Wholesale, Fairchild Semiconductor, Assan Aluminum, Sysco Foods, Fisher Scientific International, and Peregrine Outfitters. **Activity-based costing (ABC)** is a costing method that is designed to provide managers with cost information for strategic and other decisions that potentially affect capacity and therefore "fixed" as well as variable costs. Activity-based costing is ordinarily used as a supplement to, rather than as a replacement for, a company's usual costing system. Most organizations that use activity-based costing have two costing systems—the official costing system that is used for preparing external financial reports and the activity-based costing system that is used for internal decision making and for managing activities.

This chapter focuses primarily on ABC applications in manufacturing to provide a contrast with the material presented in earlier chapters. More specifically, Chapters 3 and 4 focused on traditional absorption costing systems used by manufacturing companies to calculate unit product costs for the purpose of valuing inventories and determining cost of goods sold for external financial reports. In contrast, this chapter explains how manufacturing companies can use activity-based costing rather than traditional methods to calculate unit product costs for the purposes of managing overhead and making decisions. Chapter 6 had a similar purpose. That chapter focused on how to use variable costing to aid decisions that do not affect fixed costs. This chapter extends that idea to show how activity-based costing can be used to aid decisions that potentially affect fixed costs as well as variable costs.

Activity-Based Costing: An Overview

As stated above, traditional absorption costing is designed to provide data for external financial reports. In contrast, activity-based costing is designed to be used for internal decision making. As a consequence, activity-based costing differs from traditional absorption costing in three ways. In activity-based costing:

LO7–1
Understand activity-based costing and how it differs from a traditional costing system.

1. Nonmanufacturing as well as manufacturing costs may be assigned to products, but only on a cause-and-effect basis.
2. Some manufacturing costs may be excluded from product costs.
3. Numerous overhead cost pools are used, each of which is allocated to products and other cost objects using its own unique measure of activity.

Each of these departures from traditional absorption costing will be discussed in turn.

Nonmanufacturing Costs and Activity-Based Costing

In traditional absorption costing, manufacturing costs are assigned to products and non-manufacturing costs are not assigned to products. Conversely, in activity-based costing, we recognize that many nonmanufacturing costs relate to selling, distributing, and servicing specific products. Thus, ABC includes manufacturing *and* nonmanufacturing costs when calculating the entire cost of a product rather than just its manufacturing cost.

There are two types of nonmanufacturing costs that ABC systems assign to products. First, ABC systems trace all direct nonmanufacturing costs to products. Commissions paid to salespersons, shipping costs, and warranty repair costs are examples of nonmanufacturing costs that can be directly traced to individual products. Second, ABC systems allocate indirect nonmanufacturing costs to products whenever the products have presumably caused the costs to be incurred. In fact, in this chapter, we emphasize this point by expanding the definition of *overhead* to include all indirect costs—manufacturing and nonmanufacturing.

In summary, ABC product cost calculations include all direct costs that can be traced to products and all indirect costs that are caused by products. The need to distinguish between manufacturing and nonmanufacturing costs disappears—which is very different from earlier chapters that focused solely on determining the manufacturing cost of a product.

Manufacturing Costs and Activity-Based Costing

In traditional absorption costing systems, *all* manufacturing costs are assigned to products—even manufacturing costs that are not caused by the products. For example, in Chapter 3 we learned that a predetermined plantwide overhead rate is computed by dividing *all* budgeted manufacturing overhead costs by a measure of budgeted activity such as direct labor-hours. This approach spreads *all* manufacturing overhead costs across products based on each product's direct labor-hour usage. In contrast, activity-based costing systems purposely do not assign two types of manufacturing overhead costs to products.

Manufacturing overhead includes costs such as the factory security guard's wages, the plant controller's salary, and the cost of supplies used by the plant manager's secretary. These types of costs are assigned to products in a traditional absorption costing system even though they are totally unaffected by which products are made during a period. In contrast, activity-based costing systems do not arbitrarily assign these types of costs, which are called *organization-sustaining* costs, to products. Activity-based costing treats these types of costs as period expenses rather than product costs.

Additionally, in a traditional absorption costing system, the costs of unused, or idle, capacity are assigned to products. If the budgeted level of activity declines, the overhead rate and unit product costs increase as the increasing costs of idle capacity are spread over a smaller base. In contrast, in activity-based costing, products are only charged for the costs of the capacity they use—not for the costs of capacity they don't use. This provides more stable unit product costs and is consistent with the goal of assigning to products only the costs of the resources that they use.[1]

Exhibit 7–1 summarizies the two departures from traditional absorption costing that we have discussed thus far. The top portion of the exhibit shows that traditional absorption costing treats all manufacturing costs as product costs and all nonmanufacturing costs as period costs. The bottom portion of the exhibit shows that activity-based costing expands the definition of *overhead* to include all indirect costs—manufacturing and nonmanufacturing. The overhead costs that are caused by products are allocated to them, whereas any overhead costs that are not caused by products are treated as period costs. It also shows that ABC treats direct nonmanufacturing costs as product costs rather than period costs.

Now we turn our attention to the third and final difference between traditional absorption costing and activity-based costing.

Cost Pools, Allocation Bases, and Activity-Based Costing

Throughout the 19th century and most of the 20th century, cost system designs were simple and satisfactory. Typically, either one plantwide overhead cost pool or a number of departmental overhead cost pools were used to assign overhead costs to products. The plantwide and departmental approaches always had one thing in common—they relied on allocation bases such as direct labor-hours and machine-hours for allocating overhead costs to products. In the labor-intensive production processes of many years ago, direct labor was the most common choice for an overhead allocation base because it represented a large component of product costs, direct labor-hours were closely tracked, and

---

[1] Appendix 3B discusses how the costs of idle capacity can be accounted for as a period cost in an income statement. This treatment highlights the cost of idle capacity rather than burying it in inventory and cost of goods sold. The procedures laid out in this chapter for activity-based costing have the same end effect.

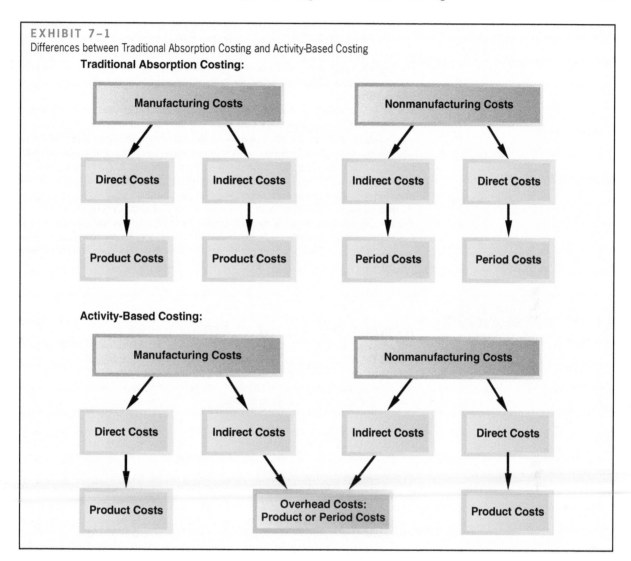

EXHIBIT 7–1
Differences between Traditional Absorption Costing and Activity-Based Costing

many managers believed that direct labor-hours, the total volume of units produced, and overhead costs were highly correlated. (Three variables, such as direct labor-hours, the total volume of units produced, and overhead costs, are highly correlated if they tend to move together.) Given that most companies at the time were producing a very limited variety of products that required similar resources to produce, allocation bases such as direct labor-hours, or even machine-hours, worked fine because, in fact, there was probably little difference in the overhead costs attributable to different products.

Then conditions began to change. As a percentage of total cost, direct labor began declining and overhead began increasing. Many tasks previously done by direct laborers were being performed by automated equipment—a component of overhead. Companies began creating new products and services at an ever-accelerating rate that differed in volume, batch size, and complexity. Managing and sustaining this product diversity required investing in many more overhead resources, such as production schedulers and product design engineers, that had no obvious connection to direct labor-hours or machine-hours. In this new environment, continuing to rely exclusively on a limited number of overhead cost pools and traditional allocation bases posed the risk that reported unit product costs would be distorted and, therefore, misleading when used for decision-making purposes.

Activity-based costing, thanks to advances in technology that make more complex cost systems feasible, provides an alternative to the traditional plantwide and departmental approaches to defining cost pools and selecting allocation bases. The activity-based approach has appeal in today's business environment because it uses more cost pools and unique measures of activity to better understand the costs of managing and sustaining product diversity.

In activity-based costing, an **activity** is any event that causes the consumption of overhead resources. An **activity cost pool** is a "bucket" in which costs are accumulated that relate to a single activity measure in the ABC system. An **activity measure** is an allocation base in an activity-based costing system. The term *cost driver* is also used to refer to an activity measure because the activity measure should "drive" the cost being allocated. The two most common types of activity measures are *transaction drivers* and *duration drivers.* **Transaction drivers** are simple counts of the number of times an activity occurs, such as the number of bills sent out to customers. **Duration drivers** measure the amount of time required to perform an activity, such as the time spent preparing individual bills for customers. In general, duration drivers are more accurate measures of resource consumption than transaction drivers, but they take more effort to record. For that reason, transaction drivers are often used in practice.

IN BUSINESS

A CRITICAL PERSPECTIVE OF ABC

Marconi is a Portuguese telecommunications company that encountered problems with its ABC system. The company's production managers felt that 23% of the costs included in the system were common costs that should not be allocated to products and that allocating these costs to products was not only inaccurate, but also irrelevant to their operational cost reduction efforts. Furthermore, Marconi's front-line workers resisted the ABC system because they felt it might be used to weaken their autonomy and to justify downsizing, outsourcing, and work intensification. They believed that ABC created a "turkeys queuing for Christmas syndrome" because they were expected to volunteer information to help create a cost system that could eventually lead to their demise. These two complications created a third problem—the data necessary to build the ABC cost model was provided by disgruntled and distrustful employees. Consequently, the accuracy of the data was questionable at best. In short, Marconi's experiences illustrate some of the challenges that complicate real-world ABC implementations.

Source: Maria Major and Trevor Hopper, "Managers Divided: Implementing ABC in a Portuguese Telecommunications Company," *Management Accounting Research*, June 2005, pp. 205–229.

Traditional cost systems rely exclusively on allocation bases that are driven by the volume of production. On the other hand, activity-based costing defines five levels of activity—unit-level, batch-level, product-level, customer-level, and organization-sustaining—that largely do *not* relate to the volume of units produced. The costs and corresponding activity measures for unit-level activities do relate to the volume of units produced; however, the remaining categories do not. These levels are described as follows:[2]

1. **Unit-level activities** are performed each time a unit is produced. The costs of unit-level activities should be proportional to the number of units produced. For example, providing power to run processing equipment would be a unit-level activity because power tends to be consumed in proportion to the number of units produced.

2. **Batch-level activities** are performed each time a batch is handled or processed, regardless of how many units are in the batch. For example, tasks such as placing

---

[2]   Robin Cooper, "Cost Classification in Unit-Based and Activity-Based Manufacturing Cost Systems," *Journal of Cost Management,* Fall 1990, pp. 4–14.

purchase orders, setting up equipment, and arranging for shipments to customers are batch-level activities. They are incurred once for each batch (or customer order). Costs at the batch level depend on the number of batches processed rather than on the number of units produced, the number of units sold, or other measures of volume. For example, the cost of setting up a machine for batch processing is the same regardless of whether the batch contains one or thousands of items.

3. **Product-level activities** relate to specific products and typically must be carried out regardless of how many batches are run or units of product are produced or sold. For example, activities such as designing a product, advertising a product, and maintaining a product manager and staff are all product-level activities.

4. **Customer-level activities** relate to specific customers and include activities such as sales calls, catalog mailings, and general technical support that are not tied to any specific product.

5. **Organization-sustaining activities** are carried out regardless of which customers are served, which products are produced, how many batches are run, or how many units are made. This category includes activities such as heating the factory, cleaning executive offices, providing a computer network, arranging for loans, preparing annual reports to shareholders, and so on.

Many companies throughout the world continue to base overhead allocations on direct labor-hours or machine-hours. In situations where overhead costs and direct labor-hours are highly correlated or in situations where the goal of the overhead allocation process is to prepare external financial reports, this practice makes sense. However, if plantwide overhead costs do not move in tandem with plantwide direct labor-hours or machine-hours, product costs will be distorted—with the potential of distorting decisions made within the company.

DINING IN THE CANYON

Western River Expeditions (www.westernriver.com) runs river rafting trips on the Colorado, Green, and Salmon rivers. One of its most popular trips is a six-day trip down the Grand Canyon, which features famous rapids such as Crystal and Lava Falls as well as the awesome scenery accessible only from the bottom of the Grand Canyon. The company runs trips of one or two rafts, each of which carries two guides and up to 18 guests. The company provides all meals on the trip, which are prepared by the guides.

In terms of the hierarchy of activities, a guest can be considered as a unit and a raft as a batch. In that context, the wages paid to the guides are a batch-level cost because each raft requires two guides regardless of the number of guests in the raft. Each guest is given a mug to use during the trip and to take home at the end of the trip as a souvenir. The cost of the mug is a unit-level cost because the number of mugs given away is strictly proportional to the number of guests on a trip.

What about the costs of food served to guests and guides—is this a unit-level cost, a batch-level cost, a product-level cost, or an organization-sustaining cost? At first glance, it might be thought that food costs are a unit-level cost—the greater the number of guests, the higher the food costs. However, that is not quite correct. Standard menus have been created for each day of the trip. For example, the first night's menu might consist of shrimp cocktail, steak, cornbread, salad, and cheesecake. The day before a trip begins, all of the food needed for the trip is taken from the central warehouse and packed in modular containers. It isn't practical to finely adjust the amount of food for the actual number of guests planned to be on a trip—most of the food comes prepackaged in large lots. For example, the shrimp cocktail menu may call for two large bags of frozen shrimp per raft and that many bags will be packed regardless of how many guests are expected on the raft. Consequently, the costs of food are not a unit-level cost that varies with the number of guests actually on a trip. Instead, the costs of food are a batch-level cost.

Source: Conversations with Western River Expeditions personnel.

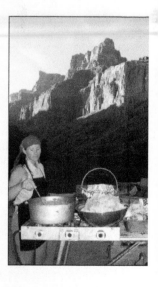

292   Chapter 7

Designing an Activity-Based Costing (ABC) System

There are three essential characteristics of a successful activity-based costing implementation. First, top managers must strongly support the ABC implementation because their leadership is instrumental in properly motivating all employees to embrace the need to change. Second, top managers should ensure that ABC data is linked to how people are evaluated and rewarded. If employees continue to be evaluated and rewarded using traditional (non-ABC) cost data, they will quickly get the message that ABC is not important and they will abandon it. Third, a cross-functional team should be created to design and implement the ABC system. The team should include representatives from each area that will use ABC data, such as the marketing, production, engineering, and accounting departments. These cross-functional employees possess intimate knowledge of many parts of an organization's operations that is necessary for designing an effective ABC system. Furthermore, tapping the knowledge of cross-functional managers lessens their resistance to ABC because they feel included in the implementation process. Time after time, when accountants have attempted to implement an ABC system on their own without top-management support and cross-functional involvement, the results have been ignored.

IN BUSINESS

IMPLEMENTING ACTIVITY-BASED COSTING IN CHINA

Xu Ji Electric Company is publicly traded on China's Shen Zhen Stock Exchange. From 2001–2003, it successfully implemented an activity-based costing (ABC) system because top-level managers continuously supported the new system—particularly during a challenging phase when the ABC software encountered problems. The ABC adoption was also aided by Xu Ji's decision to drive the implementation using a top-down approach, which is aligned with the company's cultural norm of deferring to and supporting the hierarchical chain of command.

Xu Ji's experience is similar to Western ABC implementations that have consistently recognized the necessity of top-level management support. However, contrary to Xu Ji's experience, many Western managers do not readily support the top-down implementation of new management innovations in their organizations. They prefer to be involved in the decision-making processes that introduce change into their organizations.

Source: Lana Y.J. Liu and Fei Pan, "The Implementation of Activity-Based Costing in China: An Innovation Action Research Approach," *The British Accounting Review* 39, 2007, pp. 249–264.

MANAGERIAL ACCOUNTING IN ACTION
THE ISSUE

Classic Brass, Inc., makes two main product lines for luxury yachts—standard stanchions and custom compass housings. The president of the company, John Towers, recently attended a management conference at which activity-based costing was discussed. Following the conference, he called a meeting of the company's top managers to discuss what he had learned. Attending the meeting were production manager Susan Richter, the marketing manager Tom Olafson, and the accounting manager Mary Goodman. He began the conference by distributing the company's income statement that Mary Goodman had prepared a few hours earlier (see Exhibit 7–2):

John: Well, it's official. Our company has sunk into the red for the first time in its history—a loss of $1,250.
Tom: I don't know what else we can do! Given our successful efforts to grow sales of the custom compass housings, I was expecting to see a boost to our bottom line, not a net loss. Granted, we have been losing even more bids than usual for standard stanchions because of our recent price increase, but . . .
John: Do you think our prices for standard stanchions are too high?

EXHIBIT 7-2
Classic Brass Income Statement

Classic Brass
Income Statement
Year Ended December 31, 2014

Sales		$3,200,000
Cost of goods sold:		
Direct materials	$ 975,000	
Direct labor	351,250	
Manufacturing overhead*	1,000,000	2,326,250
Gross margin		873,750
Selling and administrative expenses:		
Shipping expenses	65,000	
General administrative expenses	510,000	
Marketing expenses	300,000	875,000
Net operating loss		$ (1,250)

*The company's traditional cost system allocates manufacturing overhead to products using a plantwide overhead rate and machine-hours as the allocation base. Inventory levels did not change during the year.

Tom: No, I don't think our prices are too high. I think our competitors' prices are too low. In fact, I'll bet they are pricing below their cost.

Susan: Why would our competitors price below their cost?

Tom: They are out to grab market share.

Susan: What good is more market share if they are losing money on every unit sold?

John: I think Susan has a point. Mary, what is your take on this?

Mary: If our competitors are pricing standard stanchions below cost, shouldn't they be losing money rather than us? If our company is the one using accurate information to make informed decisions while our competitors are supposedly clueless, then why is our "bottom line" taking a beating? Unfortunately, I think we may be the ones relying on distorted cost data, not our competitors.

John: Based on what I heard at the conference that I just attended, I am inclined to agree. One of the presentations at the conference dealt with activity-based costing. As the speaker began describing the usual insights revealed by activity-based costing systems, I was sitting in the audience getting an ill feeling in my stomach.

Mary: Honestly John, I have been claiming for years that our existing cost system is okay for external reporting, but it is dangerous to use it for internal decision making. It sounds like you are on board now, right?

John: Yes.

Mary: Well then, how about if all of you commit the time and energy to help me build a fairly simple activity-based costing system that may shed some light on the problems we are facing?

John: Let's do it. I want each of you to appoint one of your top people to a special "ABC team" to investigate how we cost products.

Like most other ABC implementations, the ABC team decided that its new ABC system would supplement, rather than replace, the existing cost accounting system, which would continue to be used for external financial reports. The new ABC system would be used to prepare special reports for management decisions such as bidding on new business.

The accounting manager drew the chart appearing in Exhibit 7-3 to explain the general structure of the ABC model to her team members. Cost objects such as products generate activities. For example, a customer order for a custom compass housing requires the activity of preparing a production order. Such an activity consumes resources. A production order uses a sheet of paper and takes time to fill out. And consumption of resources causes costs. The greater the number of sheets used to fill out production orders and

EXHIBIT 7–3
The Activity-Based Costing Model

the greater the amount of time devoted to filling out such orders, the greater the cost. Activity-based costing attempts to trace through these relationships to identify how products and customers affect costs.

As in most other companies, the ABC team at Classic Brass felt that the company's traditional cost accounting system adequately measured the direct materials and direct labor costs of products because these costs are directly traced to products. Therefore, the ABC study would be concerned solely with the other costs of the company—manufacturing overhead and selling and administrative costs.

The team felt it was important to carefully plan how it would go about implementing the new ABC system at Classic Brass. Accordingly, it broke down the implementation process into five steps:

Steps for Implementing Activity-Based Costing:

1. Define activities, activity cost pools, and activity measures.
2. Assign overhead costs to activity cost pools.
3. Calculate activity rates.
4. Assign overhead costs to cost objects using the activity rates and activity measures.
5. Prepare management reports.

Step 1: Define Activities, Activity Cost Pools, and Activity Measures

The first major step in implementing an ABC system is to identify the activities that will form the foundation for the system. This can be difficult and time-consuming and involves a great deal of judgment. A common procedure is for the individuals on the ABC implementation team to interview people who work in overhead departments and ask them to describe their major activities. Ordinarily, this results in a very long list of activities.

The length of such lists of activities poses a problem. On the one hand, the greater the number of activities tracked in the ABC system, the more accurate the costs are likely to be. On the other hand, a complex system involving large numbers of activities is costly to design, implement, maintain, and use. Consequently, the original lengthy list of activities is usually reduced to a handful by combining similar activities. For example, several actions may be involved in handling and moving raw materials—from receiving raw materials on the loading dock to sorting them into the appropriate bins in the storeroom. All of these activities might be combined into a single activity called material handling.

When combining activities in an ABC system, activities should be grouped together at the appropriate level. Batch-level activities should not be combined with unit-level activities or product-level activities with batch-level activities and so on. In general, it is best to combine only those activities that are highly correlated with each other within a level. For example, the number of customer orders received is likely to be highly correlated with the number of completed customer orders shipped, so these two batch-level activities (receiving and shipping orders) can usually be combined with little loss of accuracy.

At Classic Brass, the ABC team, in consultation with top managers, selected the following *activity cost pools* and *activity measures:*

Activity Cost Pools at Classic Brass	
Activity Cost Pool	Activity Measure
Customer orders	Number of customer orders
Product design	Number of product designs
Order size	Machine-hours
Customer relations	Number of active customers
Other	Not applicable

The *Customer Orders* cost pool will be assigned all costs of resources that are consumed by taking and processing customer orders, including costs of processing paperwork and any costs involved in setting up machines for specific orders. The activity measure for this cost pool is the number of customer orders received. This is a batch-level activity because each order generates work that occurs regardless of whether the order is for one unit or 1,000 units.

The *Product Design* cost pool will be assigned all costs of resources consumed by designing products. The activity measure for this cost pool is the number of products designed. This is a product-level activity because the amount of design work on a new product does not depend on the number of units ultimately ordered or batches ultimately run.

The *Order Size* cost pool will be assigned all costs of resources consumed as a consequence of the number of units produced, including the costs of miscellaneous factory supplies, power to run machines, and some equipment depreciation. This is a unit-level activity because each unit requires some of these resources. The activity measure for this cost pool is machine-hours.

The *Customer Relations* cost pool will be assigned all costs associated with maintaining relations with customers, including the costs of sales calls and the costs of entertaining customers. The activity measure for this cost pool is the number of customers the company has on its active customer list. The Customer Relations cost pool represents a customer-level activity.

The *Other* cost pool will be assigned all overhead costs that are not associated with customer orders, product design, the size of the orders, or customer relations. These costs mainly consist of organization-sustaining costs and the costs of unused, idle capacity. These costs *will not* be assigned to products because they represent resources that are *not* consumed by products.

It is unlikely that any other company would use exactly the same activity cost pools and activity measures that were selected by Classic Brass. Because of the amount of judgment involved, the number and definitions of the activity cost pools and activity measures used by companies vary considerably.

The Mechanics of Activity-Based Costing

Step 2: Assign Overhead Costs to Activity Cost Pools

Exhibit 7–4 shows the annual overhead costs (both manufacturing and nonmanufacturing) that Classic Brass intends to assign to its activity cost pools. Notice the data in the exhibit are organized by department (e.g., Production, General Administrative, and Marketing). This is because the data have been extracted from the company's general ledger. General ledgers

LO7–2

Assign costs to cost pools using a first-stage allocation.

EXHIBIT 7–4			
Annual Overhead Costs (Both Manufacturing and Nonmanufacturing) at Classic Brass	**Production Department:**		
	Indirect factory wages	$500,000	
	Factory equipment depreciation	300,000	
	Factory utilities	120,000	
	Factory building lease	80,000	$1,000,000
	General Administrative Department:		
	Administrative wages and salaries	400,000	
	Office equipment depreciation	50,000	
	Administrative building lease	60,000	510,000
	Marketing Department:		
	Marketing wages and salaries	250,000	
	Selling expenses	50,000	300,000
	Total overhead cost		$1,810,000

usually classify costs within the departments where the costs are incurred. For example, salaries, supplies, rent, and so forth incurred in the marketing department are charged to that department. The functional orientation of the general ledger mirrors the presentation of costs in the absorption income statement in Exhibit 7–2. In fact, you'll notice the total costs for the Production Department in Exhibit 7–4 ($1,000,000) equal the total manufacturing overhead costs from the income statement in Exhibit 7–2. Similarly, the total costs for the General Administrative and Marketing Departments in Exhibit 7–4 ($510,000 and $300,000) equal the marketing and general and administrative expenses shown in Exhibit 7–2.

Three costs included in the income statement in Exhibit 7–2—direct materials, direct labor, and shipping—are excluded from the costs shown in Exhibit 7–4. The ABC team purposely excluded these costs from Exhibit 7–4 because the existing cost system can accurately trace direct materials, direct labor, and shipping costs to products. There is no need to incorporate these direct costs in the activity-based allocations of indirect costs.

Classic Brass's activity-based costing system will divide the nine types of overhead costs in Exhibit 7–4 among its activity cost pools via an allocation process called *first-stage allocation*. The **first-stage allocation** in an ABC system is the process of assigning functionally organized overhead costs derived from a company's general ledger to the activity cost pools.

First-stage allocations are usually based on the results of interviews with employees who have first-hand knowledge of the activities. For example, Classic Brass needs to allocate $500,000 of indirect factory wages to its five activity cost pools. These allocations will be more accurate if the employees who are classified as indirect factory workers (e.g., supervisors, engineers, and quality inspectors) are asked to estimate what percentage of their time is spent dealing with customer orders, with product design, with processing units of product (i.e., order size), and with customer relations. These interviews are conducted with considerable care. Those who are interviewed must thoroughly understand what the activities encompass and what is expected of them in the interview. In addition, departmental managers are typically interviewed to determine how the non-personnel costs should be distributed across the activity cost pools. For example, the Classic Brass production manager would be interviewed to determine how the $300,000 of factory equipment depreciation (shown in Exhibit 7–4) should be allocated to the activity cost pools. The key question that the production manager would need to answer is "What percentage of the available machine capacity is consumed by each activity such as the number of customer orders or the number of units processed (i.e., size of orders)?"

The results of the interviews at Classic Brass are displayed in Exhibit 7–5. For example, factory equipment depreciation is distributed 20% to Customer Orders, 60% to Order Size, and 20% to the Other cost pool. The resource in this instance is machine time. According to the estimates made by the production manager, 60% of the total available

EXHIBIT 7–5
Results of Interviews: Distribution
of Resource Consumption
across Activity Cost Pools

	A	B	C	D	E	F	G	H
1				*Activity Cost Pools*				
2		*Customer Orders*	*Product Design*	*Order Size*	*Customer Relations*	*Other*	*Totals*	
3								
4	Production Department:							
5	Indirect factory wages	25%	40%	20%	10%	5%	100%	
6	Factory equipment depreciation	20%	0%	60%	0%	20%	100%	
7	Factory utilities	0%	10%	50%	0%	40%	100%	
8	Factory building lease	0%	0%	0%	0%	100%	100%	
9								
10	General Administrative Department:							
11	Administrative wages and salaries	15%	5%	10%	30%	40%	100%	
12	Office equipment depreciation	30%	0%	0%	25%	45%	100%	
13	Administrative building lease	0%	0%	0%	0%	100%	100%	
14								
15	Marketing Department:							
16	Marketing wages and salaries	22%	8%	0%	60%	10%	100%	
17	Selling expenses	10%	0%	0%	70%	20%	100%	
18								

Exhibit 7-5 / Exhibit 7-6 / Exhibit 7-7 / Exhibit 7-9 / Exhibit 7-10 / Exhibit 7-11 / Exhibit 7-11 (2)

EXHIBIT 7–6
First-Stage Allocations to Activity
Cost Pools

	A	B	C	D	E	F	G	H
1				*Activity Cost Pools*				
2		*Customer Orders*	*Product Design*	*Order Size*	*Customer Relations*	*Other*	*Totals*	
3								
4	Production Department:							
5	Indirect factory wages	$ 125,000	$ 200,000	$ 100,000	$ 50,000	$ 25,000	$ 500,000	
6	Factory equipment depreciation	60,000	0	180,000	0	60,000	300,000	
7	Factory utilities	0	12,000	60,000	0	48,000	120,000	
8	Factory building lease	0	0	0	0	80,000	80,000	
9								
10	General Administrative Department:							
11	Administrative wages and salaries	60,000	20,000	40,000	120,000	160,000	400,000	
12	Office equipment depreciation	15,000	0	0	12,500	22,500	50,000	
13	Administrative building lease	0	0	0	0	60,000	60,000	
14								
15	Marketing Department:							
16	Marketing wages and salaries	55,000	20,000	0	150,000	25,000	250,000	
17	Selling expenses	5,000	0	0	35,000	10,000	50,000	
18								
19	Total	$ 320,000	$ 252,000	$ 380,000	$ 367,500	$ 490,500	$ 1,810,000	
20								
21								

Exhibit 7-5 / **Exhibit 7-6** / Exhibit 7-7 / Exhibit 7-9 / Exhibit 7-10 / Exhibit 7-11 / Exhibit 7-11 (2)

Exhibit 7–5 shows that Customer Orders consume 25% of the
resources represented by the $500,000 of indirected factory wages.

25% × $500,000 = $125,000

Other entries in the table are computed in a similar fashion.

IN BUSINESS

AN ABC APPLICATION IN THE CONSTRUCTION INDUSTRY

Researchers from the United States and the Republic of Korea studied how a Korean manufacturer assigned the indirect costs of supplying reinforced steel bars (also called *rebar*) to various construction projects. The company's traditional cost system assigned all indirect costs to projects using rebar tonnage as the allocation base. Its ABC system had 10 activities that assigned indirect costs to projects using activity measures such as number of orders, number of sheets, number of distributing runs, number of production runs, and number of inspections.

The traditional and ABC systems assigned the following overhead costs to three construction projects called Commercial, High-Rise Condo, and Heavy Civil:

	Commercial	High-Rise Condo	Heavy Civil
Traditional cost system allocations	$ 64,587	$ 50,310	$91,102
ABC allocations	90,466	61,986	53,548
Difference	$(25,879)	$(11,676)	$37,554

Notice that the traditional cost system was undercosting the Commercial and High-Rise Condo projects relative to the ABC system. It was also overcosting the Heavy Civil project by $37,554 when compared to the ABC system.

Source: Yong-Woo Kim, Seungheon Han, "Sungwon Shin, and Kunhee Choi, "A Case Study of Activity-Based Costing in Allocation Rebar Fabrication Costs to Projects," *Construction Management and Economics*, May 2010, pp. 449–461.

machine time was used to actually process units to fill orders. This percentage is entered in the Order Size column. Each customer order requires setting up, which also requires machine time. This activity consumes 20% of the total available machine time and is entered under the Customer Orders column. The remaining 20% of available machine time represents idle time and is entered under the Other column.

Exhibit 7–5 and many of the other exhibits in this chapter are presented in the form of Excel spreadsheets. All of the calculations required in activity-based costing can be done by hand. Nevertheless, setting up an activity-based costing system on a spreadsheet or using special ABC software can save a lot of work—particularly in situations involving many activity cost pools and in organizations that periodically update their ABC systems.

We will not go into the details of how all of the percentages in Exhibit 7–5 were determined. However, note that 100% of the factory building lease has been assigned to the Other cost pool. Classic Brass has a single production facility. It has no plans to expand or to sublease any excess space. The cost of this production facility is treated as an organization-sustaining cost because there is no way to avoid even a portion of this cost if a particular product or customer were to be dropped. (Remember that organization-sustaining costs are assigned to the Other cost pool and are not allocated to products.) In contrast, some companies have separate facilities for manufacturing specific products. The costs of these separate facilities could be directly traced to the specific products.

Once the percentage distributions in Exhibit 7–5 have been established, it is easy to allocate costs to the activity cost pools. The results of this first-stage allocation are displayed in Exhibit 7–6. Each cost is allocated across the activity cost pools by multiplying it by the percentages in Exhibit 7–5. For example, the indirect factory wages of $500,000 are multiplied by the 25% entry under Customer Orders in Exhibit 7–5 to arrive at the $125,000 entry under Customer Orders in Exhibit 7–6. Similarly, the indirect factory wages of $500,000 are multiplied by the 40% entry under Product Design in Exhibit 7–5 to arrive at the $200,000 entry under Product Design in Exhibit 7–6. All of the entries in Exhibit 7–6 are computed in this way.

Now that the first-stage allocations to the activity cost pools have been completed, the next step is to compute the activity rates.

Step 3: Calculate Activity Rates

The activity rates that will be used for assigning overhead costs to products and customers are computed in Exhibit 7–7. The ABC team determined the total activity for each cost pool that would be required to produce the company's present product mix and to serve its present customers. These numbers are listed in Exhibit 7–7. For example, the ABC team found that 400 new product designs are required each year to serve the company's present customers. The activity rates are computed by dividing the *total* cost for each activity by its *total* activity. For example, the $320,000 total annual cost for the Customer Orders cost pool (which was computed in Exhibit 7–6) is divided by the total of 1,000 customer orders per year to arrive at the activity rate of $320 per customer order. Similarly, the $252,000 *total* cost for the Product Design cost pool is divided by the *total* number of designs (i.e., 400 product designs) to determine the activity rate of $630 per design. Note that an activity rate is not computed for the Other category of costs. This is because the *Other* cost pool consists of organization-sustaining costs and costs of idle capacity that are not allocated to products and customers.

The rates in Exhibit 7–7 indicate that *on average* a customer order consumes resources that cost $320; a product design consumes resources that cost $630; a unit of product consumes resources that cost $19 per machine-hour; and maintaining relations with a customer consumes resources that cost $1,470. Note that these are *average* figures. Some members of the ABC design team at Classic Brass argued that it would be unfair to charge all new products the same $630 product design cost regardless of how much design time they actually require. After discussing the pros and cons, the team concluded that it would not be worth the effort at the present time to keep track of actual design time spent on each new product. They felt that the benefits of increased accuracy would not be great enough to justify the higher cost of implementing and maintaining the more detailed costing system. Similarly, some team members were uncomfortable assigning the same $1,470 cost to each customer. Some customers are undemanding—ordering standard products well in advance of their needs. Others are very demanding and consume large amounts of marketing and administrative staff time. These are generally customers who order customized products, who tend to order at the last minute, and who change their minds. While everyone agreed with this observation, the data that would be required to measure individual customers' demands on resources were not currently available. Rather than delay implementation of the ABC system, the team decided to defer such refinements to a later date.

Before proceeding further, it would be helpful to get a better idea of the overall process of assigning costs to products and other cost objects in an ABC system. Exhibit 7–8 provides

LO7–3
Compute activity rates for cost pools.

EXHIBIT 7–7
Computation of Activity Rates

	A	B	C	D	E	F	G
1	*Activity Cost Pools*	*(a)* *Total Cost**	*(b)* *Total Activity*		*(a) ÷ (b)* *Activity Rate*		
2	Customer orders	$320,000	1,000	orders	$320	per order	
3	Product design	$252,000	400	designs	$630	per design	
4	Order size	$380,000	20,000	MHs	$19	per MH	
5	Customer relations	$367,500	250	customers	$1,470	per customer	
6	Other	$490,500	Not applicable		Not applicable		
7							
8	*From Exhibit 7-6.						
9							

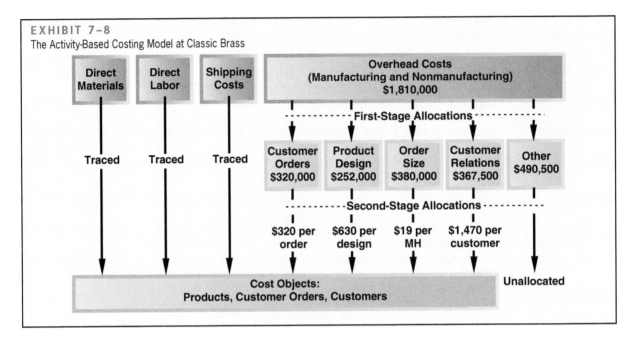

EXHIBIT 7–8
The Activity-Based Costing Model at Classic Brass

a visual perspective of the ABC system at Classic Brass. We recommend that you carefully go over this exhibit. In particular, note that the Other category, which contains organization-sustaining costs and costs of idle capacity, is not allocated to products or customers.

Step 4: Assign Overhead Costs to Cost Objects

LO7–4

Assign costs to a cost object using a second-stage allocation.

The fourth step in the implementation of activity-based costing is called *second-stage allocation*. In the **second-stage allocation**, activity rates are used to apply overhead costs to products and customers. First, we will illustrate how to assign costs to products followed by an example of how to assign costs to customers.

The data needed by the ABC team to assign overhead costs to Classic Brass's two products—standard stanchions and custom compass housings—are as follows:

Standard Stanchions

1. This product line does not require any new design resources.
2. 30,000 units were ordered during the year, comprising 600 separate orders.
3. Each stanchion requires 35 minutes of machine time for a total of 17,500 machine-hours.

Custom Compass Housings

1. This is a custom product that requires new design resources.
2. There were 400 orders for custom compass housings. Orders for this product are placed separately from orders for standard stanchions.
3. There were 400 custom designs prepared. One custom design was prepared for each order.
4. Because some orders were for more than one unit, a total of 1,250 custom compass housings were produced during the year. A custom compass housing requires an average of 2 machine-hours for a total of 2,500 machine-hours.

Notice, 600 customer orders were placed for standard stanchions and 400 customer orders were placed for custom compass housings, for a total of 1,000 customer orders. All 400 product designs related to custom compass housings; none related to standard stanchions. Producing 30,000 standard stanchions required 17,500 machine-hours and

HOW MUCH DOES IT COST TO HANDLE A PIECE OF LUGGAGE?

It costs an airline about $15 to carry a piece of checked luggage from one destination another. The activity "transporting luggage" consists of numerous sub-activities such as tagging bags, sorting them, placing them on carts, transporting bags planeside, loading them into the airplane, and delivering them to carousels and connecting flights.

A variety of employees invest a portion of their labor hours "transporting luggage" including ground personnel, check-in agents, service clerks, baggage service managers, and maintenance workers. In total, labor costs comprise $9 per bag. Airlines also spend millions of dollars on baggage equipment, sorting systems, carts, tractors, and conveyors, as well as rental costs related to bag rooms, carousels, and offices. They also pay to deliver misplaced bags to customers' homes and to compensate customers for lost bags that are never found. These expenses add up to about $4 per bag. The final expense related to transporting luggage is fuel costs, which average about $2 per bag.

Many major airlines now charge fees for checked bags. United Airlines expects to collect $275 million annually for its first and second bag fees.

Source: Scott McCartney, "What It Costs an Airline to Fly Your Luggage," *The Wall Street Journal*, November 25, 2008, p. D1 and D8.

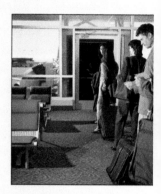

producing 1,250 custom compass housings required 2,500 machine-hours, for a total of 20,000 machine-hours.

Exhibit 7–9 illustrates how overhead costs are assigned to the standard stanchions and custom compass housings. For example, the exhibit shows that $192,000 of overhead costs are assigned from the Customer Orders activity cost pool to the standard stanchions ($320 per order × 600 orders). Similarly, $128,000 of overhead costs are assigned from the Customer Orders activity cost pool to the custom compass housings

EXHIBIT 7–9
Assigning Overhead Costs to Products

	A	B	C	D	E	F	G
1	**Overhead Cost for the Standard Stanchions**						
2	*Activity Cost Pools*	*(a)* *Activity Rate**		*(b)* *Activity*		*(a) × (b)* *ABC Cost*	
3	Customer orders	$320	per order	600	orders	$ 192,000	
4	Product design	$630	per design	0	designs	0	
5	Order size	$19	per MH	17,500	MHs	332,500	
6	Total					$ 524,500	
7							
8	**Overhead Cost for the Custom Compass Housing**						
9	*Activity Cost Pools*	*(a)* *Activity Rate**		*(b)* *Activity*		*(a) × (b)* *ABC Cost*	
10	Customer orders	$320	per order	400	orders	$ 128,000	
11	Product design	$630	per design	400	designs	252,000	
12	Order size	$19	per MH	2,500	MHs	47,500	
13	Total					$ 427,500	
14							
15	*From Exhibit 7-7.						
16							

Exhibit 7-5 / Exhibit 7-6 / Exhibit 7-7 / **Exhibit 7-9** / Exhibit 7-10 / Exhibit 7-11 / Exh

Chapter 7

($320 per order × 400 orders). The Customer Orders cost pool contained a total of $320,000 (see Exhibit 7–6 or 7–7) and this total amount has been assigned to the two products ($192,000 + $128,000 = $320,000).

Exhibit 7–9 shows that a total of $952,000 of overhead costs is assigned to Classic Brass's two product lines—$524,500 to standard stanchions and $427,500 to custom compass housings. This amount is less than the $1,810,000 of overhead costs included in the ABC system. Why? The total amount of overhead assigned to products does not match the total amount of overhead cost in the ABC system because the ABC team purposely did not assign the $367,500 of Customer Relations and $490,500 of Other costs to products. The Customer Relations activity is a customer-level activity and the Other activity is an organization-sustaining activity—neither activity is caused by products. As shown below, when the Customer Relations and Other activity costs are added to the $952,000 of overhead costs assigned to products, the total is $1,810,000.

	Standard Stanchions	Custom Compass Housings	Total
Overhead Costs Assigned to Products			
Customer orders	$192,000	$128,000	$ 320,000
Product design	0	252,000	252,000
Order size.........................	332,500	47,500	380,000
Subtotal	$524,500	$427,500	952,000
Overhead Costs not Assigned to Products			
Customer relations			367,500
Other			490,500
Subtotal			858,000
Total overhead cost			$1,810,000

Next, we describe another example of second-stage allocation—assigning activity costs to customers. The data needed by Classic Brass to assign overhead costs to one of its customers—Windward Yachts—are as follows:

Windward Yachts

1. The company placed a total of three orders.
   a. Two orders were for 150 standard stanchions per order.
   b. One order was for a single custom compass housing unit.
2. A total of 177 machine-hours were used to fulfill the three customer orders.
   a. The 300 standard stanchions required 175 machine-hours.
   b. The custom compass housing required 2 machine-hours.
3. Windward Yachts is one of 250 customers served by Classic Brass.

Exhibit 7–10 illustrates how the ABC system assigns overhead costs to this customer. As shown in Exhibit 7–10, the ABC team calculated that $6,423 of overhead costs should be assigned to Windward Yachts. The exhibit shows that Windward Yachts is assigned $960 ($320 per order × 3 orders) of overhead costs from the Customer Orders activity cost pool; $630 ($630 per design × 1 design) from the Product Design cost pool; $3,363 ($19 per machine-hour × 177 machine-hours) from the Order Size cost pool; and $1,470 ($1,470 per customer × 1 customer) from the Customer Relations cost pool.

EXHIBIT 7–10
Assigning Overhead Costs to Customers

	A	B	C	D	E	F
1	**Overhead Cost for Windward Yachts**					
2						
3	*Activity Cost Pools*	*(a)* *Activity Rate**		*(b)* *Activity*		*(a) × (b)* *ABC Cost*
4	Customer orders	$320	per order	3	orders	$ 960
5	Product design	$630	per design	1	designs	630
6	Order size	$19	per MH	177	MHs	3,363
7	Customer relations	$1,470	per customer	1	customer	1,470
8	Total overhead cost assigned to customer					$ 6,423
9						
10	*From Exhibit 7-7.					
11						

Exhibit 7-5 / Exhibit 7-6 / Exhibit 7-7 / Exhibit 7-9 / **Exhibit 7-10** / Exhibit 7-11 / Exhibit 7-

With second-stage allocations complete, the ABC design team was ready to turn its attention to creating reports that would help explain the company's first ever net operating loss.

Step 5: Prepare Management Reports

LO7–5
Use activity-based costing to compute product and customer margins.

The most common management reports prepared with ABC data are product and customer profitability reports. These reports help companies channel their resources to their most profitable growth opportunities while at the same time highlighting products and customers that drain profits. We begin by illustrating a product profitability report followed by a customer profitability report.

The Classic Brass ABC team realized that the profit from a product, also called the *product margin,* is a function of the product's sales and the direct and indirect costs that the product causes. The ABC cost allocations shown in Exhibit 7–9 only summarize each product's indirect (i.e., overhead) costs. Therefore, to compute a product's profit (i.e., product margin), the design team needed to gather each product's sales and direct costs in addition to the overhead costs previously computed. The pertinent sales and direct cost data for each product are shown below. Notice the numbers in the total column agree with the income statement in Exhibit 7–2.

	Standard Stanchions	Custom Compass Housings	Total
Sales	$2,660,000	$540,000	$3,200,000
Direct costs:			
Direct materials	$905,500	$69,500	$975,000
Direct labor	$263,750	$87,500	$351,250
Shipping	$60,000	$5,000	$65,000

Having gathered the above data, the design team created the product profitability report shown in Exhibit 7–11. The report revealed that standard stanchions are profitable, with a positive product margin of $906,250, whereas the custom compass housings are unprofitable, with a negative product margin of $49,500. Keep in mind that the product profitability report purposely does not include the costs in the Customer Relations and Other activity cost pools. These costs, which total $858,000, were excluded from the

---

EXHIBIT 7-11
Product Margins—Activity-Based
Costing

	A	B	C	D	E	F	
1	Product Margins—Activity-Based Costing						
2		Standard Stanchions			Custom Compass Housings		
3	Sales		$ 2,660,000			$ 540,000	
4	Costs:						
5	Direct materials	$ 905,500			$ 69,500		
6	Direct labor	263,750			87,500		
7	Shipping	60,000			5,000		
8	Customer orders (from Exhibit 7-9)	192,000			128,000		
9	Product design (from Exhibit 7-9)	-			252,000		
10	Order size (from Exhibit 7-9)	332,500			47,500		
11	Total cost		1,753,750			589,500	
12	Product margin		$ 906,250			$ (49,500)	
13							

◄ ◄ ► ►| Exhibit 7-5 ╱ Exhibit 7-6 ╱ Exhibit 7-7 ╱ Exhibit 7-9 ╱ Exhibit 7-10 ╱ **Exhibit 7-11** ╱ Exhib ◄ ► |

---

report because they are not caused by the products. Customer Relations costs are caused by customers, not products. The Other costs are organization-sustaining costs and unused capacity costs that are not caused by any particular product.

The product margins can be reconciled with the company's net operating loss as follows:

	Standard Stanchions	Custom Compass Housings	Total
Sales (See Exhibit 7–11)	$2,660,000	$540,000	$3,200,000
Total costs (See Exhibit 7–11)	1,753,750	589,500	2,343,250
Product margins (See Exhibit 7–11)	$ 906,250	$ (49,500)	856,750
Overhead costs not assigned to products:			
Customer relations			367,500
Other			490,500
Total			858,000
Net operating loss			$ (1,250)

Next, the design team created a customer profitability report for Windward Yachts. Similar to the product profitability report, the design team needed to gather data concerning sales to Windward Yachts and the direct material, direct labor, and shipping costs associated with those sales. Those data are presented below:

	Windward Yachts
Sales	$11,350
Direct costs:	
Direct material costs	$2,123
Direct labor costs	$1,900
Shipping costs	$205

IS ACTIVITY-BASED COSTING STILL BEING USED?

Researchers surveyed 348 managers to determine which costing methods their companies use. The table below shows the percentage of respondents whose companies use the various costing methods to assign departmental costs to cost objects such as products.

			Departments				
Costing Method	Research and Development	Product and Process Design	Production	Sales and Marketing	Distribution	Customer Service	Shared Services
Activity-based	13.0%	14.7%	18.3%	17.3%	17.2%	21.8%	23.0%
Standard[1]	17.6%	20.7%	42.0%	18.1%	28.4%	18.5%	23.0%
Normal[2]	4.6%	8.6%	9.9%	7.9%	6.0%	8.1%	5.6%
Actual[3]	23.1%	25.0%	23.7%	23.6%	26.7%	16.9%	15.9%
Other	1.9%	0.9%	0.0%	0.8%	0.9%	1.6%	2.4%
Not allocated	39.8%	30.2%	6.1%	32.3%	20.7%	33.1%	30.2%

[1]Standard costing is used for the variance computations in Chapter 10.
[2]Normal costing is used for the job-order costing computations in Chapter 3.
[3]Actual costing is used to create the absorption and variable costing income statements in Chapter 6.

The results show that 18.3% of respondents use ABC to allocate production costs to cost objects and 42% use standard costing for the same purpose. ABC is used by at least 13% of respondents within all functional departments across the value chain. Many companies do not allocate nonproduction costs to cost objects.

Source: William O. Stratton, Denis Desroches, Raef Lawson, and Toby Hatch, "Activity-Based Costing: Is It Still Relevant?" *Management Accounting Quarterly*, Spring 2009, pp. 31–40.

Using these data and the data from Exhibit 7–10, the design team created the customer profitability report shown in Exhibit 7–12. The report revealed that the customer margin for Windward Yachts is $699. A similar report could be prepared for each of

	A	B	C
1	**Customer Margin—Activity-Based Costing**		
2			*Windward Yachts*
3	Sales		$11,350
4	Costs:		
5	Direct materials	$ 2,123	
6	Direct labor	1,900	
7	Shipping	205	
8	Customer orders (from Exhibit 7-10)	960	
9	Product design (from Exhibit 7-10)	630	
10	Order size (from Exhibit 7-10)	3,363	
11	Customer relations (from Exhibit 7-10)	1,470	10,651
12	Customer margin		$ 699
13			

Exhibit 7-12   Exhibit 7-13   Exhibit 7-14   Exhibit 7A-1   Ex

EXHIBIT 7–12
Customer Margin—Activity-Based Costing

Classic Brass's 250 customers, thereby enabling the company to cultivate relationships with its most profitable customers, while taking steps to reduce the negative impact of unprofitable customers.

Comparison of Traditional and ABC Product Costs

The ABC team used a two-step process to compare its traditional and ABC product costs. First, the team reviewed the product margins reported by the traditional cost system. Then, it contrasted the differences between the traditional and ABC product margins.

Product Margins Computed Using the Traditional Cost System

Classic Brass's traditional cost system assigns only manufacturing costs to products—this includes direct materials, direct labor, and manufacturing overhead. Selling and administrative costs are not assigned to products. Exhibit 7–13 shows the product margins reported by Classic Brass's traditional cost system. We will explain how these margins were calculated in three steps. First, the sales and direct materials and direct labor cost data are the same numbers used by the ABC team to prepare Exhibit 7–11. In other words, the traditional cost system and the ABC system treat these three pieces of revenue and cost data identically.

Second, the traditional cost system uses a plantwide overhead rate to assign manufacturing overhead costs to products. The numerator for the plantwide overhead rate is $1,000,000, which is the total amount of manufacturing overhead shown on the income statement in Exhibit 7–2. The footnote in Exhibit 7–2 mentions that the traditional cost system uses machine-hours to assign manufacturing overhead costs to products. The Order Size activity in Exhibit 7–7 used 20,000 machine-hours as its level of activity. These same 20,000 machine-hours would be used in the denominator of the plantwide overhead rate, which is computed as follows:

$$\text{Plantwide overhead rate} = \frac{\text{Total estimated manufacturing overhead}}{\text{Total estimated machine-hours}}$$

$$= \frac{\$1,000,000}{20,000 \text{ machine-hours}}$$

$$= \$50 \text{ per machine-hour}$$

Because 17,500 machine-hours were worked on standard stanchions, this product line is assigned $875,000 (17,500 machine-hours × $50 per machine-hour) of manufacturing overhead cost. Similarly, the custom compass housings required 2,500 machine-hours, so this product line is assigned $125,000 (2,500 machine-hours × $50 per machine-hour) of manufacturing overhead cost. The sales of each product minus its cost of goods sold equals the product margin of $615,750 for standard stanchions and $258,000 for custom compass housings.

Notice, the net operating loss of $1,250 shown in Exhibit 7–13 agrees with the loss reported in the income statement in Exhibit 7–2 and with the loss shown in the table beneath Exhibit 7–11. The company's *total* sales, *total* costs, and its resulting net operating loss are the same regardless of whether you are looking at the absorption income statement in Exhibit 7–2, the ABC product profitability analysis depicted on page 304, or the traditional product profitability analysis in Exhibit 7–13. Although the "total pie" remains constant across the traditional and ABC systems, what differs is how the pie is divided between the two product lines. The traditional product margin calculations suggest that standard stanchions are generating a product margin of $615,750 and the custom compass housings a product margin of $258,000. However, these product margins differ

EXHIBIT 7–13
Product Margins—Traditional Costing System

	A	B	C	D	E	F	G	H	I
1	**Product Margins—Traditional Cost System**								
2		*Standard Stanchions*			*Custom Compass Housings*			*Total*	
3	Sales		$2,660,000			$ 540,000			$3,200,000
4	Cost of goods sold:								
5	Direct materials	$ 905,500			$ 69,500			$ 975,000	
6	Direct labor	263,750			87,500			351,250	
7	Manufacturing overhead	875,000	2,044,250		125,000	282,000		1,000,000	2,326,250
8	Product margin		$ 615,750			$ 258,000			873,750
9	Selling and administrative								875,000
10	Net operating income								$ (1,250)
11									

Exhibit 7-12 | **Exhibit 7-13** | Exhibit 7-14 | Exhibit 7A-1 | Exhibit 7A-2

from the ABC product margins reported in Exhibit 7–11. Indeed, the traditional cost system is sending misleading signals to Classic Brass's managers about each product's profitability. Let's explain why.

The Differences between ABC and Traditional Product Costs

The changes in product margins caused by switching from the traditional cost system to the activity-based costing system are shown below:

	Standard Stanchions	Custom Compass Housings
Product margins—traditional	$615,750	$ 258,000
Product margins—ABC	906,250	(49,500)
Change in reported product margins	$290,500	$(307,500)

The traditional cost system overcosts the standard stanchions and consequently reports an artificially low product margin for this product. The switch to an activity-based view of product profitability increases the product margin on standard stanchions by $290,500. In contrast, the traditional cost system undercosts the custom compass housings and reports an artificially high product margin for this product. The switch to activity-based costing decreases the product margin on custom compass housings by $307,500.

The reasons for the change in reported product margins between the two costing methods are revealed in Exhibit 7–14. The top portion of the exhibit shows each product's direct and indirect cost assignments as reported by the traditional cost system in Exhibit 7–13. For example, Exhibit 7–14 includes the following costs for standard stanchions: direct materials, $905,500; direct labor, $263,750; and manufacturing overhead, $875,000. Each of these costs corresponds with those reported in Exhibit 7–13. Notice, the selling and administrative costs of $875,000 are purposely not allocated to products because these costs are considered to be period costs when using traditional costing. Similarly, the bottom portion of Exhibit 7–14 summarizes the direct and indirect cost assignments as reported by the activity-based costing system in Exhibit 7–11. The only new information in Exhibit 7–14 is shown in the two columns of percentages. The first column of percentages shows the percentage of each cost assigned to standard stanchions. For example, the $905,500 of direct materials cost traced to standard stanchions is 92.9% of the company's total direct materials cost of $975,000. The second column of percentages does the same thing for custom compass housings.

EXHIBIT 7–14
A Comparison of Traditional and
Activity-Based Cost Assignments

	Standard Stanchions		Custom Compass Housings		
	(a)	(a) ÷ (c)	(b)	(b) ÷ (c)	(c)
Traditional Cost System	Amount	%	Amount	%	Total
Direct materials	$ 905,500	92.9%	$ 69,500	7.1%	$ 975,000
Direct labor	263,750	75.1%	87,500	24.9%	351,250
Manufacturing overhead	875,000	87.5%	125,000	12.5%	1,000,000
Total cost assigned to products	$2,044,250		$282,000		2,326,250
Selling and administrative					875,000
Total cost					$3,201,250
Activity-Based Costing System					
Direct costs:					
Direct materials	$ 905,500	92.9%	$ 69,500	7.1%	$ 975,000
Direct labor	263,750	75.1%	87,500	24.9%	351,250
Shipping	60,000	92.3%	5,000	7.7%	65,000
Indirect costs:					
Customer orders	192,000	60.0%	128,000	40.0%	320,000
Product design	0	0.0%	252,000	100.0%	252,000
Order size	332,500	87.5%	47,500	12.5%	380,000
Total cost assigned to products	$1,753,750		$589,500		2,343,250
Costs not assigned to products:					
Customer relations					367,500
Other					490,500
Total cost					$3,201,250

There are three reasons why the traditional and activity-based costing systems report different product margins. First, Classic Brass's traditional cost system allocates all manufacturing overhead costs to products. This forces both products to absorb all manufacturing overhead costs regardless of whether they actually consumed the costs that were allocated to them. The ABC system does not assign the manufacturing overhead costs consumed by the Customer Relations activity to products because these costs are caused by customers, not specific products. It also does not assign the manufacturing overhead costs included in the Other activity to products because these organization-sustaining and unused capacity costs are not caused by any particular product. From an ABC point of view, assigning these costs to products is inherently arbitrary and counterproductive.

Second, Classic Brass's traditional cost system allocates all of the manufacturing overhead costs using a volume-related allocation base—machine-hours—that may or may not reflect what actually causes the costs. In other words, in the traditional system, 87.5% of each manufacturing overhead cost is implicitly assigned to standard stanchions and 12.5% is assigned to custom compass housings. For example, the traditional cost system inappropriately assigns 87.5% of the costs of the Customer Orders activity (a batch-level activity) to standard stanchions even though the ABC system revealed that standard stanchions caused only 60% of these costs. Conversely, the traditional cost system assigns only 12.5% of these costs to custom compass housings even though this product caused 40% of these costs. Similarly, the traditional cost system assigns 87.5% of the costs of the Product Design activity (a product-level activity) to standard stanchions even though the standard stanchions caused none (0%) of these costs. All (100%) of the costs of the Product Design activity, rather than just 12.5%, should be assigned to custom compass housings. The result is that traditional cost systems overcost high-volume products (such as the standard stanchions) and undercost low-volume products (such as the custom compass housings) because they assign batch-level and product-level costs using volume-related allocation bases.

The third reason the product margins differ between the two cost systems is that the ABC system assigns the nonmanufacturing overhead costs caused by products to those products on a cause-and-effect basis. The traditional cost system disregards these costs because they are classified as period costs. The ABC system directly traces shipping costs to products and includes the nonmanufacturing overhead costs caused by products in the activity cost pools that are assigned to products.

MANAGERIAL ACCOUNTING IN ACTION
THE WRAP-UP

The ABC design team presented the results of its work in a meeting attended by all of the top managers of Classic Brass, including the president John Towers, the production manager Susan Richter, the marketing manager Tom Olafson, and the accounting manager Mary Goodman. The ABC team brought with them copies of the chart showing the ABC design (Exhibit 7–8), and the table comparing the traditional and ABC cost assignments (Exhibit 7–14). After the formal presentation by the ABC team, the following discussion took place:

John: I would like to personally thank the ABC team for all of the work they have done and for an extremely interesting presentation. I am now beginning to wonder about a lot of the decisions we have made in the past using our old cost accounting system. According to the ABC analysis, we had it all backwards. We are losing money on the custom products and making a fistful on the standard products.

Mary: I have to admit that I had no idea that the Product Design work for custom compass housings was so expensive! I knew burying these costs in our plantwide overhead rate was penalizing standard stanchions, but I didn't understand the magnitude of the problem.

Susan: I never did believe we were making a lot of money on the custom jobs. You ought to see all of the problems they create for us in production.

Tom: I hate to admit it, but the custom jobs always seem to give us headaches in marketing, too.

John: If we are losing money on custom compass housings, why not suggest to our customers that they go elsewhere for that kind of work?

Tom: Wait a minute, we would lose a lot of sales.

Susan: So what, we would save a lot more costs.

Mary: Maybe yes, maybe no. Some of the costs would not disappear if we were to drop the custom business.

Tom: Like what?

Mary: Well Tom, I believe you said that about 10% of your time is spent dealing with new products. As a consequence, 10% of your salary was allocated to the Product Design cost pool. If we were to drop all of the products requiring design work, would you be willing to take a 10% pay cut?

Tom: I trust you're joking.

Mary: Do you see the problem? Just because 10% of your time is spent on custom products doesn't mean that the company would save 10% of your salary if the custom products were dropped. Before we take a drastic action like dropping the custom products, we should identify which costs are really relevant.

John: I think I see what you are driving at. We wouldn't want to drop a lot of products only to find that our costs really haven't changed much. It is true that dropping the products would free up resources like Tom's time, but we had better be sure we have some good use for those resources *before* we take such an action.

As this discussion among the managers of Classic Brass illustrates, caution should be exercised before taking action based on an ABC analysis such as the one shown in Exhibits 7–11 and 7–12. The product and customer margins computed in these exhibits are a useful starting point for further analysis, but managers need to know what costs are really affected before taking any action such as dropping a product or customer or changing the prices of products or services. Appendix 7A shows how an *action analysis report* can be constructed to help managers make such decisions. An **action analysis report** provides more detail about costs and how they might adjust to changes in activity than the ABC analysis presented in Exhibits 7–11 and 7–12.

IN BUSINESS

AN ABC IMPLEMENTATION IN THAILAND

APS, a parawood furniture factory located in the Songkhla Province of Southern Thailand, employs over 250 workers to make more than 100 types of furniture. The company's traditional cost system assigns indirect manufacturing costs to products based on each product's total sales. Its ABC system relies on various volume-related and non-volume-related activity measures, such as direct labor-hours, number of setups, and number of trips, to assign overhead costs to products.

The company's traditional and ABC systems assigned per-unit overhead costs to its five best-selling products as follows:

	Tile Top Table	Side Chair	Telephone Table	Plant Tree with Grooves	Computer Desk
Traditional cost system allocations	$7.08	$2.21	$3.53	$3.65	$4.53
ABC allocations	2.18	1.13	1.32	1.80	6.07
Difference	$4.90	$1.08	$2.21	$1.85	$(1.54)

Given that all five of these products have high sales volumes, it is not surprising to see that the traditional cost system has overcosted four of them.

Source: Sakesun Suthummanon, Wanida Ratanamanee, Nirachara Boonyanuwat, and Pieanpon Saritprit, "Applying Activity-Based Costing (ABC) to a Parawood Furniture Factory," *The Engineering Economist*, Volume 56 (2011), pp. 80–93.

Targeting Process Improvements

Activity-based costing can also be used to identify activities that would benefit from process improvements. When used in this way, activity-based costing is often called *activity-based management*. Basically, **activity-based management** involves focusing on activities to eliminate waste, decrease processing time, and reduce defects. Activity-based management is used in organizations as diverse as manufacturing companies, hospitals, and the U.S. Marine Corps.

The first step in any improvement program is to decide what to improve. The activity rates computed in activity-based costing can provide valuable clues concerning where there is waste and opportunity for improvement. For example, looking at the activity rates in Exhibit 7–7, managers at Classic Brass may conclude that $320 to process a customer order is far too expensive for an activity that adds no value to the product. As a consequence, they may target their process improvement efforts toward the Customer Orders activity.[3]

---

[3] In chapter 12, we introduce the Theory of Constraints, which is a powerful tool that helps companies target their process improvement efforts on the most profitable opportunities.

Benchmarking is another way to leverage the information in activity rates. **Benchmarking** is a systematic approach to identifying the activities with the greatest room for improvement. It is based on comparing the performance in an organization with the performance of other, similar organizations known for their outstanding performance. If a particular part of the organization performs far below the world-class standard, managers will be likely to target that area for improvement.

Activity-Based Costing and External Reports

Although activity-based costing generally provides more accurate product costs than traditional costing methods, it is infrequently used for external reports for a number of reasons. First, external reports are less detailed than internal reports prepared for decision making. On the external reports, individual product costs are not reported. Cost of goods sold and inventory valuations are disclosed, but they are not broken down by product. If some products are undercosted and some are overcosted, the errors tend to offset each other when the product costs are added together.

Second, it is often very difficult to make changes in a company's accounting system. The official cost accounting systems in most large companies are usually embedded in complex computer programs that have been modified in-house over the course of many years. It is extremely difficult to make changes in such computer programs without causing numerous bugs.

Third, an ABC system such as the one described in this chapter does not conform to generally accepted accounting principles (GAAP). As discussed in prior chapters, product costs computed for external reports must include all of the manufacturing costs and only manufacturing costs; but in an ABC system as described in this chapter, product costs exclude some manufacturing costs and include some nonmanufacturing costs. It is possible to adjust the ABC data at the end of the period to conform to GAAP, but that requires more work.

Fourth, auditors are likely to be uncomfortable with allocations that are based on interviews with the company's personnel. Such subjective data can be easily manipulated by management to make earnings and other key variables look more favorable.

For all of these reasons, most companies confine their ABC efforts to special studies for management, and they do not attempt to integrate activity-based costing into their formal cost accounting systems.

The Limitations of Activity-Based Costing

Implementing an activity-based costing system is a major project that requires substantial resources. And once implemented, an activity-based costing system is more costly to maintain than a traditional costing system—data concerning numerous activity measures must be periodically collected, checked, and entered into the system. The benefits of increased accuracy may not outweigh these costs.

Activity-based costing produces numbers, such as product margins, that are at odds with the numbers produced by traditional costing systems. But managers are accustomed to using traditional costing systems to run their operations and traditional costing systems are often used in performance evaluations. Essentially, activity-based costing changes the rules of the game. It is a fact of human nature that changes in organizations, particularly those that alter the rules of the game, inevitably face resistance. This underscores the importance of top management support and the full participation of line managers, as well as the accounting staff, in any activity-based costing initiative. If activity-based costing is viewed as an accounting initiative that does not have the full support of top management, it is doomed to failure.

Chapter 7

In practice, most managers insist on fully allocating all costs to products, customers, and other costing objects in an activity-based costing system—including the costs of idle capacity and organization-sustaining costs. This results in overstated costs and understated margins and mistakes in pricing and other critical decisions.

Activity-based costing data can easily be misinterpreted and must be used with care when used in making decisions. Costs assigned to products, customers, and other cost objects are only *potentially* relevant. Before making any significant decisions using activity-based costing data, managers must identify which costs are really relevant for the decision at hand. See Appendix 7A for more details.

As discussed in the previous section, reports generated by the best activity-based costing systems do not conform to external reporting requirements. Consequently, an organization involved in activity-based costing should have two cost systems—one for internal use and one for preparing external reports. This is costlier than maintaining just one system and may cause confusion about which system is to be believed and relied on.

Summary

Traditional cost accounting methods suffer from several defects that can result in distorted costs for decision-making purposes. All manufacturing costs—even those that are not caused by any specific product—are allocated to products. Nonmanufacturing costs that are caused by products are not assigned to products. And finally, traditional methods tend to place too much reliance on unit-level allocation bases such as direct labor and machine-hours. This results in overcosting high-volume products and undercosting low-volume products and can lead to mistakes when making decisions.

Activity-based costing estimates the costs of the resources consumed by cost objects such as products and customers. The activity-based costing approach assumes that cost objects generate activities that in turn consume costly resources. Activities form the link between costs and cost objects. Activity-based costing is concerned with overhead—both manufacturing overhead and selling and administrative overhead. The accounting for direct labor and direct materials is usually the same under traditional and ABC costing methods.

To build an ABC system, companies typically choose a small set of activities that summarize much of the work performed in overhead departments. Associated with each activity is an activity cost pool. To the extent possible, overhead costs are directly traced to these activity cost pools. The remaining overhead costs are allocated to the activity cost pools in the first-stage allocation. Interviews with managers often form the basis for these allocations.

An activity rate is computed for each cost pool by dividing the costs assigned to the cost pool by the measure of activity for the cost pool. Activity rates provide useful information to managers concerning the costs of performing overhead activities. A particularly high cost for an activity may trigger efforts to improve the way the activity is carried out in the organization.

In the second-stage allocation, activity rates are used to apply costs to cost objects such as products and customers. The costs computed under activity-based costing are often quite different from the costs generated by a company's traditional cost accounting system. While the ABC system is almost certainly more accurate, managers should nevertheless exercise caution before making decisions based on the ABC data. Some of the costs may not be avoidable and hence would not be relevant.

Review Problem: Activity-Based Costing

Ferris Corporation makes a single product—a fire-resistant commercial filing cabinet—that it sells to office furniture distributors. The company has a simple ABC system that it uses for internal decision making. The company has two overhead departments whose costs are listed on the following page:

Activity-Based Costing: A Tool to Aid Decision Making   **313**

Manufacturing overhead	$500,000
Selling and administrative overhead	300,000
Total overhead costs	$800,000

The company's ABC system has the following activity cost pools and activity measures:

Activity Cost Pool	Activity Measure
Assembling units	Number of units
Processing orders	Number of orders
Supporting customers	Number of customers
Other	Not applicable

Costs assigned to the "Other" activity cost pool have no activity measure; they consist of the costs of unused capacity and organization-sustaining costs—neither of which are assigned to orders, customers, or the product.

Ferris Corporation distributes the costs of manufacturing overhead and selling and administrative overhead to the activity cost pools based on employee interviews, the results of which are reported below:

Distribution of Resource Consumption Across Activity Cost Pools					
	Assembling Units	Processing Orders	Supporting Customers	Other	Total
Manufacturing overhead	50%	35%	5%	10%	100%
Selling and administrative overhead	10%	45%	25%	20%	100%
Total activity	1,000 units	250 orders	100 customers		

Required:

1. Perform the first-stage allocation of overhead costs to the activity cost pools as in Exhibit 7–6.
2. Compute activity rates for the activity cost pools as in Exhibit 7–7.
3. OfficeMart is one of Ferris Corporation's customers. Last year, OfficeMart ordered filing cabinets four different times. OfficeMart ordered a total of 80 filing cabinets during the year. Construct a table as in Exhibit 7–10 showing the overhead costs attributable to OfficeMart.
4. The selling price of a filing cabinet is $595. The cost of direct materials is $180 per filing cabinet, and direct labor is $50 per filing cabinet. What is the customer margin of OfficeMart? See Exhibit 7–12 for an example of how to complete this report.

Solution to Review Problem

1. The first-stage allocation of costs to the activity cost pools appears below:

	Activity Cost Pools				
	Assembling Units	Processing Orders	Supporting Customers	Other	Total
Manufacturing overhead . . .	$250,000	$175,000	$ 25,000	$ 50,000	$500,000
Selling and administrative overhead	30,000	135,000	75,000	60,000	300,000
Total cost	$280,000	$310,000	$100,000	$110,000	$800,000

314

Chapter 7

2. The activity rates for the activity cost pools are:

Activity Cost Pools	(a) Total Cost	(b) Total Activity	(a) ÷ (b) Activity Rate
Assembling units	$280,000	1,000 units	$280 per unit
Processing orders	$310,000	250 orders	$1,240 per order
Supporting customers	$100,000	100 customers	$1,000 per customer

3. The overhead cost attributable to OfficeMart would be computed as follows:

Activity Cost Pools	(a) Activity Rate	(b) Activity	(a) × (b) ABC Cost
Assembling units	$280 per unit	80 units	$22,400
Processing orders	$1,240 per order	4 orders	$4,960
Supporting customers	$1,000 per customer	1 customer	$1,000

4. The customer margin can be computed as follows:

Sales ($595 per unit × 80 units)		$47,600
Costs:		
Direct materials ($180 per unit × 80 units)	$14,400	
Direct labor ($50 per unit × 80 units)	4,000	
Assembling units (above)	22,400	
Processing orders (above)	4,960	
Supporting customers (above)	1,000	46,760
Customer margin		$ 840

Glossary

Action analysis report A report showing what costs have been assigned to a cost object, such as a product or customer, and how difficult it would be to adjust the cost if there is a change in activity. (p. 310)

Activity An event that causes the consumption of overhead resources in an organization. (p. 290)

Activity-based costing (ABC) A costing method based on activities that is designed to provide managers with cost information for strategic and other decisions that potentially affect capacity and therefore fixed as well as variable costs. (p. 287)

Activity-based management (ABM) A management approach that focuses on managing activities as a way of eliminating waste and reducing delays and defects. (p. 310)

Activity cost pool A "bucket" in which costs are accumulated that relate to a single activity measure in an activity-based costing system. (p. 290)

Activity measure An allocation base in an activity-based costing system; ideally, a measure of the amount of activity that drives the costs in an activity cost pool. (p. 290)

Batch-level activities Activities that are performed each time a batch of goods is handled or processed, regardless of how many units are in the batch. The amount of resource consumed depends on the number of batches run rather than on the number of units in the batch. (p. 290)

Benchmarking A systematic approach to identifying the activities with the greatest potential for improvement. (p. 311)

Customer-level activities Activities that are carried out to support customers, but that are not related to any specific product. (p. 291)

Duration driver A measure of the amount of time required to perform an activity. (p. 290)

First-stage allocation The process by which overhead costs are assigned to activity cost pools in an activity-based costing system. (p. 296)

Organization-sustaining activities Activities that are carried out regardless of which customers are served, which products are produced, how many batches are run, or how many units are made. (p. 291)

Product-level activities Activities that relate to specific products that must be carried out regardless of how many units are produced and sold or batches run. (p. 291)

Second-stage allocation The process by which activity rates are used to apply costs to products and customers in activity-based costing. (p. 300)

Transaction driver A simple count of the number of times an activity occurs. (p. 290)

Unit-level activities Activities that are performed each time a unit is produced. (p. 290)

Questions

7–1 In what fundamental ways does activity-based costing differ from traditional costing methods such as job-order costing as described in Chapter 3?

7–2 Why is direct labor a poor base for allocating overhead in many companies?

7–3 Why are top management support and cross-functional involvement crucial when attempting to implement an activity-based costing system?

7–4 What are unit-level, batch-level, product-level, customer-level, and organization-sustaining activities?

7–5 What types of costs should not be assigned to products in an activity-based costing system?

7–6 Why are there two stages of allocation in activity-based costing?

7–7 Why is the first stage of the allocation process in activity-based costing often based on interviews?

7–8 When activity-based costing is used, why do manufacturing overhead costs often shift from high-volume products to low-volume products?

7–9 How can the activity rates (i.e., cost per activity) for the various activities be used to target process improvements?

7–10 Why is the activity-based costing described in this chapter unacceptable for external financial reports?

Multiple-choice questions are provided on the text website at www.mhhe.com/garrison15e.

 Applying Excel

Available with McGraw-Hill's *Connect® Accounting*.

The Excel worksheet form that appears on the next page is to be used to recreate the Review Problem on pages 312–314. Download the workbook containing this form from the Online Learning Center at www.mhhe.com/garrison15e. *On the website you will also receive instructions about how to use this worksheet form.*

You should proceed to the requirements below only after completing your worksheet.

L07–1, L07–2, L07–3, L07–4

Required:

1. Check your worksheet by doubling the units ordered in cell B16 to 160. The customer margin under activity-based costing should now be $7,640 and the traditional costing product margin should be $(21,600). If you do not get these results, find the errors in your worksheet and correct them.
    a. Why has the customer margin under activity-based costing more than doubled when the number of units ordered is doubled?
    b. Why has the traditional costing product margin exactly doubled from a loss of $10,800 to a loss of $21,600?
    c. Which costing system, activity-based costing or traditional costing, provides a more accurate picture of what happens to profits as the number of units ordered increases? Explain.

316

Chapter 7

	A	B	C	D	E	F	G
1	Chapter 7: Applying Excel						
2							
3	**Data**						
4	Manufacturing overhead	$500,000					
5	Selling and administrative overhead	$300,000					
6							
7		*Assembling Units*	*Processing Orders*	*Supporting Customers*	*Other*		
8	Manufacturing overhead	50%	35%	5%	10%		
9	Selling and administrative overhead	10%	45%	25%	20%		
10	Total activity	1,000	250	100			
11		units	orders	customers			
12							
13	OfficeMart orders:						
14	Customers	1	customer				
15	Orders	4	orders				
16	Number of filing cabinets ordered in total	80	units				
17	Selling price	$595					
18	Direct materials	$180					
19	Direct labor	$50					
20							
21	*Enter a formula into each of the cells marked with a ? below*						
22	**Review Problem: Activity-Based Costing**						
23							
24	*Perform the first stage allocations*						
25		*Assembling Units*	*Processing Orders*	*Supporting Customers*	*Other*	*Total*	
26	Manufacturing overhead	?	?	?	?	?	
27	Selling and administrative overhead	?	?	?	?	?	
28	Total cost	?	?	?	?	?	
29							
30	*Compute the activity rates*						
31	*Activity Cost Pools*	*Total Cost*	*Total Activity*		*Activity Rate*		
32	Assembling units	?	? units		? per unit		
33	Processing orders	?	? orders		? per order		
34	Supporting customers	?	? customers		? per customer		
35							
36	*Compute the overhead cost attributable to the OfficeMart orders*						
37	*Activity Cost Pools*	*Activity Rate*			*Activity*	*ABC Cost*	
38	Assembling units	? per unit			? units	?	
39	Processing orders	? per order			? orders	?	
40	Supporting customers	? per customer			? customer	?	
41							
42	*Determine the customer margin for the OfficeMart orders under Activity-Based Costing*						
43	Sales		?				
44	Costs:						
45	Direct materials	?					
46	Direct labor	?					
47	Unit-related overhead	?					
48	Order-related overhead	?					
49	Customer-related overhead	?	?				
50	Customer margin		?				
51							
52	*Determine the product margin for the OfficeMart orders under a traditional cost system*						
53	Manufacturing overhead	?					
54	Total activity	? units					
55	Manufacturing overhead per unit	? per unit					
56							
57	Sales		?				
58	Costs:						
59	Direct materials	?					
60	Direct labor	?					
61	Manufacturing overhead	?	?				
62	Traditional costing product margin		?				
63							

◄ ◄ ► ►| **Chapter 7 Form** / Filled in Chapter 7 Form / Chapter 7 Formulas

2. Let's assume that OfficeMart places different orders next year, purchasing higher-end filing cabinets more frequently, but in smaller quantities per order. Enter the following data into your worksheet:

Data

Manufacturing overhead	$500,000			
Selling and administrative overhead ...	$300,000			

	Assembling Units	Processing Orders	Supporting Customers	Other
Manufacturing overhead	50%	35%	5%	10%
Selling and administrative overhead	10%	45%	25%	20%
Total activity	1,000 units	250 orders	100 customers	

OfficeMart orders:

Customers	1 customer
Orders.........................	20 orders
Total number of filing cabinets ordered ...	80 units
Selling price	$795
Direct materials	$185
Direct labor......................	$90

    a. What is the customer margin under activity-based costing?
    b. What is the product margin under the traditional cost system?
    c. Explain why the profitability picture looks much different now than it did when OfficeMart was ordering less expensive filing cabinets less frequently, but in larger quantities per order.

3. Using the data you entered in part (2), change the percentage of selling and administrative overhead attributable to processing orders from 45% to 30% and the percentage attributable to supporting customers from 25% to 40%. That portion of the worksheet should look like this:

	Assembling Units	Processing Orders	Supporting Customers	Other
Manufacturing overhead	50%	35%	5%	10%
Selling and administrative overhead ...	10%	30%	40%	20%
Total activity	1,000 units	250 orders	100 customers	

    a. Relative to the results from part (2), what has happened to the customer margin under activity-based costing? Why?
    b. Relative to the results from part (2), what has happened to the product margin under the traditional cost system? Why?

 The Foundational 15

Available with McGraw-Hill's *Connect*® Accounting.

Hickory Company manufactures two products—14,000 units of Product Y and 6,000 units of Product Z. The company uses a plantwide overhead rate based on direct labor-hours. It is considering implementing an activity-based costing (ABC) system that allocates all of its manufacturing overhead to four cost pools. The following additional information is available for the company as a whole and for Products Y and Z:

LO7–1, LO7–3, LO7–4

Activity Cost Pool	Activity Measure	Estimated Overhead Cost	Expected Activity
Machining	Machine-hours	$200,000	10,000 MHs
Machine setups	Number of setups	$100,000	200 setups
Product design	Number of products	$84,000	2 products
General factory	Direct labor-hours	$300,000	12,000 DLHs

318   Chapter 7

Activity Measure	Product Y	Product Z
Machine-hours	7,000	3,000
Number of setups	50	150
Number of products	1	1
Direct labor-hours	8,000	4,000

Required:

1. What is the company's plantwide overhead rate?
2. Using the plantwide overhead rate, how much manufacturing overhead cost is allocated to Product Y? How much is allocated to Product Z?
3. What is the activity rate for the Machining activity cost pool?
4. What is the activity rate for the Machine Setups activity cost pool?
5. What is the activity rate for the Product Design activity cost pool?
6. What is the activity rate for the General Factory activity cost pool?
7. Which of the four activities is a batch-level activity? Why?
8. Which of the four activities is a product-level activity? Why?
9. Using the ABC system, how much total manufacturing overhead cost would be assigned to Product Y?
10. Using the ABC system, how much total manufacturing overhead cost would be assigned to Product Z?
11. Using the plantwide overhead rate, what percentage of the total overhead cost is allocated to Product Y? What percentage is allocated to Product Z?
12. Using the ABC system, what percentage of the Machining costs is assigned to Product Y? What percentage is assigned to Product Z? Are these percentages similar to those obtained in requirement 11? Why?
13. Using the ABC system, what percentage of Machine Setups cost is assigned to Product Y? What percentage is assigned to Product Z? Are these percentages similar to those obtained in requirement 11? Why?
14. Using the ABC system, what percentage of the Product Design cost is assigned to Product Y? What percentage is assigned to Product Z? Are these percentages similar to those obtained in requirement 11? Why?
15. Using the ABC system, what percentage of the General Factory cost is assigned to Product Y? What percentage is assigned to Product Z? Are these percentages similar to those obtained in requirement 11? Why?

Exercises   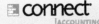 connect
|ACCOUNTING

All applicable exercises are available with McGraw-Hill's *Connect® Accounting*.

EXERCISE 7–1 ABC Cost Hierarchy [LO7–1]
The following activities occur at Greenwich Corporation, a company that manufactures a variety of products.
a. Receive raw materials from suppliers.
b. Manage parts inventories.
c. Do rough milling work on products.
d. Interview and process new employees in the personnel department.
e. Design new products.
f. Perform periodic preventive maintenance on general-use equipment.
g. Use the general factory building.
h. Issue purchase orders for a job.

Required:
Classify each of the activities above as either a unit-level, batch-level, product-level, or organization-sustaining activity.

EXERCISE 7–2 First Stage Allocation [LO7–2]
SecuriCorp operates a fleet of armored cars that make scheduled pickups and deliveries in the Los Angeles area. The company is implementing an activity-based costing system that has four activity cost pools: Travel, Pickup and Delivery, Customer Service, and Other. The activity measures are miles for the Travel cost pool, number of pickups and deliveries for the Pickup and Delivery

Activity-Based Costing: A Tool to Aid Decision Making   **319**

cost pool, and number of customers for the Customer Service cost pool. The Other cost pool has no activity measure because it is an organization-sustaining activity. The following costs will be assigned using the activity-based costing system:

Driver and guard wages	$ 720,000
Vehicle operating expense	280,000
Vehicle depreciation	120,000
Customer representative salaries and expenses	160,000
Office expenses	30,000
Administrative expenses	320,000
Total cost	$1,630,000

The distribution of resource consumption across the activity cost pools is as follows:

	Travel	Pickup and Delivery	Customer Service	Other	Totals
Driver and guard wages	50%	35%	10%	5%	100%
Vehicle operating expense	70%	5%	0%	25%	100%
Vehicle depreciation	60%	15%	0%	25%	100%
Customer representative salaries and expenses	0%	0%	90%	10%	100%
Office expenses	0%	20%	30%	50%	100%
Administrative expenses	0%	5%	60%	35%	100%

Required:
Complete the first stage allocations of costs to activity cost pools as illustrated in Exhibit 7–6.

EXERCISE 7–3 Compute Activity Rates [LO7–3]

Green Thumb Gardening is a small gardening service that uses activity-based costing to estimate costs for pricing and other purposes. The proprietor of the company believes that costs are driven primarily by the size of customer lawns, the size of customer garden beds, the distance to travel to customers, and the number of customers. In addition, the costs of maintaining garden beds depends on whether the beds are low maintenance beds (mainly ordinary trees and shrubs) or high maintenance beds (mainly flowers and exotic plants). Accordingly, the company uses the five activity cost pools listed below:

Activity Cost Pool	Activity Measure
Caring for lawn	Square feet of lawn
Caring for garden beds–low maintenance	Square feet of low maintenance beds
Caring for garden beds–high maintenance	Square feet of high maintenance beds
Travel to jobs	Miles
Customer billing and service	Number of customers

The company has already completed its first stage allocations of costs and has summarized its annual costs and activity as follows:

Activity Cost Pool	Estimated Overhead Cost	Expected Activity
Caring for lawn	$72,000	150,000 square feet of lawn
Caring for garden beds–low maintenance	$26,400	20,000 square feet of low maintenance beds
Caring for garden beds–high maintenance	$41,400	15,000 square feet of high maintenance beds
Travel to jobs	$3,250	12,500 miles
Customer billing and service	$8,750	25 customers

Chapter 7

Required:
Compute the activity rate for each of the activity cost pools.

EXERCISE 7–4 Second-Stage Allocation [LO7–4]
Klumper Corporation is a diversified manufacturer of industrial goods. The company's activity-based costing system contains the following six activity cost pools and activity rates:

Activity Cost Pool	Activity Rates
Supporting direct labor	$6.00 per direct labor-hour
Machine processing	$4.00 per machine-hour
Machine setups	$50.00 per setup
Production orders	$90.00 per order
Shipments	$14.00 per shipment
Product sustaining	$840.00 per product

Activity data have been supplied for the following two products:

	Total Expected Activity	
	K425	M67
Number of units produced per year ...	200	2,000
Direct labor-hours	80	500
Machine-hours	100	1,500
Machine setups	1	4
Production orders	1	4
Shipments	1	10
Product sustaining	1	1

Required:
Determine the total overhead cost that would be assigned to each of the products listed above in the activity-based costing system.

EXERCISE 7–5 Product and Customer Profitability Analysis [LO7–4, LO7–5]
Thermal Rising, Inc., makes paragliders for sale through specialty sporting goods stores. The company has a standard paraglider model, but also makes custom-designed paragliders. Management has designed an activity-based costing system with the following activity cost pools and activity rates:

Activity Cost Pool	Activity Rate
Supporting direct labor	$26 per direct labor-hour
Order processing	$284 per order
Custom design processing	$186 per custom design
Customer service	$379 per customer

Management would like an analysis of the profitability of a particular customer, Big Sky Outfitters, which has ordered the following products over the last 12 months:

	Standard Model	Custom Design
Number of gliders	20	3
Number of orders	1	3
Number of custom designs	0	3
Direct labor-hours per glider	26.35	28.00
Selling price per glider	$1,850	$2,400
Direct materials cost per glider	$564	$634

The company's direct labor rate is $19.50 per hour.

Required:

Using the company's activity-based costing system, compute the customer margin of Big Sky Outfitters.

EXERCISE 7–6 Cost Hierarchy [LO7–1]

CD Express, Inc., provides CD duplicating services to software companies. The customer provides a master CD from which CD Express makes copies. An order from a customer can be for a single copy or for thousands of copies. Most jobs are broken down into batches to allow smaller jobs, with higher priorities, to have access to the machines.

A number of activities carried out at CD Express are listed below.

a. Sales representatives' periodic visits to customers to keep them informed about the services provided by CD Express.
b. Ordering labels from the printer for a particular CD.
c. Setting up the CD duplicating machine to make copies from a particular master CD.
d. Loading the automatic labeling machine with labels for a particular CD.
e. Visually inspecting CDs and placing them by hand into protective plastic cases prior to shipping.
f. Preparation of the shipping documents for the order.
g. Periodic maintenance of equipment.
h. Lighting and heating the company's production facility.
i. Preparation of quarterly financial reports.

Required:

Classify each of the activities above as either a unit-level, batch-level, product-level, customer-level, or organization-sustaining activity. An order to duplicate a particular CD is a product-level activity. Assume the order is large enough that it must be broken down into batches.

EXERCISE 7–7 First-Stage Allocations [LO7–2]

The operations vice president of Security Home Bank has been interested in investigating the efficiency of the bank's operations. She has been particularly concerned about the costs of handling routine transactions at the bank and would like to compare these costs at the bank's various branches. If the branches with the most efficient operations can be identified, their methods can be studied and then replicated elsewhere. While the bank maintains meticulous records of wages and other costs, there has been no attempt thus far to show how those costs are related to the various services provided by the bank. The operations vice president has asked your help in conducting an activity-based costing study of bank operations. In particular, she would like to know the cost of opening an account, the cost of processing deposits and withdrawals, and the cost of processing other customer transactions.

The Westfield branch of Security Home Bank has submitted the following cost data for last year:

Teller wages	$160,000
Assistant branch manager salary	75,000
Branch manager salary	80,000
Total	$315,000

Virtually all other costs of the branch—rent, depreciation, utilities, and so on—are organization-sustaining costs that cannot be meaningfully assigned to individual customer transactions such as depositing checks.

In addition to the cost data above, the employees of the Westfield branch have been interviewed concerning how their time was distributed last year across the activities included in the activity-based costing study. The results of those interviews appear below:

Distribution of Resource Consumption Across Activities

	Opening Accounts	Processing Deposits and Withdrawals	Processing Other Customer Transactions	Other Activities	Total
Teller wages	5%	65%	20%	10%	100%
Assistant branch manager salary . . .	15%	5%	30%	50%	100%
Branch manager salary	5%	0%	10%	85%	100%

Required:

Prepare the first-stage allocation for the activity-based costing study. (See Exhibit 7–6 for an example of a first-stage allocation.)

EXERCISE 7–8 Computing and Interpreting Activity Rates [LO7–3]

(This exercise is a continuation of Exercise 7–7; it should be assigned *only* if Exercise 7–7 is also assigned.) The manager of the Westfield branch of Security Home Bank has provided the following data concerning the transactions of the branch during the past year:

Activity	Total Activity at the Westfield Branch
Opening accounts	500 new accounts opened
Processing deposits and withdrawals	100,000 deposits and withdrawals processed
Processing other customer transactions . . .	5,000 other customer transactions processed

The lowest costs reported by other branches for these activities are displayed below:

Activity	Lowest Cost among All Security Home Bank Branches
Opening accounts	$26.75 per new account
Processing deposits and withdrawals	$1.24 per deposit or withdrawal
Processing other customer transactions	$11.86 per other customer transaction

Required:

1. Using the first-stage allocation from Exercise 7–7 and the above data, compute the activity rates for the activity-based costing system. (Use Exhibit 7–7 as a guide.) Round all computations to the nearest whole cent.
2. What do these results suggest to you concerning operations at the Westfield branch?

EXERCISE 7–9 Second-Stage Allocation to an Order [LO7–4]

Durban Metal Products, Ltd., of the Republic of South Africa makes specialty metal parts used in applications ranging from the cutting edges of bulldozer blades to replacement parts for Land Rovers. The company uses an activity-based costing system for internal decision-making purposes. The company has four activity cost pools as listed below:

Activity Cost Pool	Activity Measure	Activity Rate
Order size	Number of direct labor-hours	$16.85 per direct labor-hour
Customer orders	Number of customer orders	$320.00 per customer order
Product testing	Number of testing hours	$89.00 per testing hour
Selling	Number of sales calls	$1,090.00 per sales call

The managing director of the company would like information concerning the cost of a recently completed order for heavy-duty trailer axles. The order required 200 direct labor-hours, 4 hours of product testing, and 2 sales calls.

Required:

Prepare a report summarizing the overhead costs assigned to the order for heavy-duty trailer axles. What is the total overhead cost assigned to the order?

EXERCISE 7–10 Customer Profitability Analysis [LO7–3, LO7–4, LO7–5]

Worley Company buys surgical supplies from a variety of manufacturers and then resells and delivers these supplies to hundreds of hospitals. Worley sets its prices for all hospitals by marking up its cost of goods sold to those hospitals by 5%. For example, if a hospital buys supplies from Worley that had cost Worley $100 to buy from manufacturers, Worley would charge the hospital $105 to purchase these supplies.

For years, Worley believed that the 5% markup covered its selling and administrative expenses and provided a reasonable profit. However, in the face of declining profits Worley decided to implement an activity-based costing system to help improve its understanding of customer profitability. The company broke its selling and administrative expenses into five activities as shown below:

Activity Cost Pool (Activity Measure)	Total Cost	Total Activity
Customer deliveries (Number of deliveries)	$ 500,000	5,000 deliveries
Manual order processing (Number of manual orders) . . .	248,000	4,000 orders
Electronic order processing (Number of electronic orders)	200,000	12,500 orders
Line item picking (Number of line items picked)	450,000	450,000 line items
Other organization-sustaining costs (None)	602,000	
Total selling and administrative expenses	$2,000,000	

Worley gathered the data below for two of the many hospitals that it serves—University and Memorial (both hospitals purchased a total quantity of medical supplies that had cost Worley $30,000 to buy from its manufacturers):

	Activity	
Activity Measure	University	Memorial
Number of deliveries	10	25
Number of manual orders	0	30
Number of electronic orders	15	0
Number of line items picked	120	250

Required:
1. Compute the total revenue that Worley would receive from University and Memorial.
2. Compute the activity rate for each activity cost pool.
3. Compute the total activity costs that would be assigned to University and Memorial.
4. Compute Worley's customer margin for University and Memorial. (*Hint:* Do not overlook the $30,000 cost of goods sold that Worley incurred serving each hospital.)
5. Describe the purchasing behaviors that are likely to characterize Worley's least profitable customers.

EXERCISE 7–11 Second-Stage Allocation and Margin Calculations [LO7–4, LO7–5]
Foam Products, Inc., makes foam seat cushions for the automotive and aerospace industries. The company's activity-based costing system has four activity cost pools, which are listed below along with their activity measures and activity rates:

Activity Cost Pool	Activity Measure	Activity Rate
Supporting direct labor	Number of direct labor-hours	$5.55 per direct labor-hour
Batch processing	Number of batches	$107.00 per batch
Order processing	Number of orders	$275.00 per order
Customer service	Number of customers	$2,463.00 per customer

The company just completed a single order from Interstate Trucking for 1,000 custom seat cushions. The order was produced in two batches. Each seat cushion required 0.25 direct labor-hours. The selling price was $20 per unit, the direct materials cost was $8.50 per unit, and the direct labor cost was $6.00 per unit. This was Interstate Trucking's only order during the year.

Required:
Using Exhibit 7–12 as a guide, prepare a report showing the customer margin on sales to Interstate Trucking for the year.

324

Chapter 7

EXERCISE 7–12 Activity Measures [LO7–1]

Various activities at Ming Corporation, a manufacturing company, are listed below. Each activity has been classified as a unit-level, batch-level, product-level, or customer-level activity.

Activity	Level of Activity	Examples of Activity Measures
a. Direct labor workers assemble a product	Unit	
b. Products are designed by engineers	Product	
c. Equipment is set up	Batch	
d. Machines are used to shape and cut materials	Unit	
e. Monthly bills are sent out to regular customers	Customer	
f. Materials are moved from the receiving dock to production lines	Batch	
g. All completed units are inspected for defects	Unit	

Required:
Complete the table by providing an example of an activity measure for each activity.

EXERCISE 7–13 Computing ABC Product Costs [LO7–3, LO7–4]

Fogerty Company makes two products, titanium Hubs and Sprockets. Data regarding the two products follow:

	Direct Labor-Hours per Unit	Annual Production
Hubs	0.80	10,000 units
Sprockets	0.40	40,000 units

Additional information about the company follows:
a. Hubs require $32 in direct materials per unit, and Sprockets require $18.
b. The direct labor wage rate is $15 per hour.
c. Hubs are more complex to manufacture than Sprockets and they require special equipment.
d. The ABC system has the following activity cost pools:

Activity Cost Pool (Activity Measure)	Estimated Overhead Cost	Hubs	Sprockets	Total
Machine setups (number of setups)	$72,000	100	300	400
Special processing (machine-hours)	$200,000	5,000	0	5,000
General factory (organization-sustaining)	$816,000	NA	NA	NA

Required:
1. Compute the activity rate for each activity cost pool. Did you compute an activity rate for all of the activity cost pools? Why?
2. Determine the unit product cost of each product according to the ABC system.

EXERCISE 7–14 Calculating and Interpreting Activity-Based Costing Data [LO7–3, LO7–4]

Hiram's Lakeside is a popular restaurant located on Lake Washington in Seattle. The owner of the restaurant has been trying to better understand costs at the restaurant and has hired a student intern to conduct an activity-based costing study. The intern, in consultation with the owner, identified three major activities and then completed the first-stage allocations of costs to the activity cost pools. The results appear below.

Activity Cost Pool	Activity Measure	Total Cost	Total Activity
Serving a party of diners	Number of parties served	$33,000	6,000 parties
Serving a diner	Number of diners served	$138,000	15,000 diners
Serving drinks	Number of drinks ordered	$24,000	10,000 drinks

The above costs include all of the costs of the restaurant except for organization-sustaining costs such as rent, property taxes, and top-management salaries.

A group of diners who ask to sit at the same table are counted as a party. Some costs, such as the costs of cleaning linen, are the same whether one person is at a table or the table is full. Other costs, such as washing dishes, depend on the number of diners served.

Prior to the activity-based costing study, the owner knew very little about the costs of the restaurant. She knew that the total cost for the month (including organization-sustaining costs) was $240,000 and that 15,000 diners had been served. Therefore, the average cost per diner was $16.

Required:

1. According to the activity-based costing system, what is the total cost of serving each of the following parties of diners?
   a. A party of four diners who order three drinks in total.
   b. A party of two diners who do not order any drinks.
   c. A lone diner who orders two drinks.
2. Convert the total costs you computed in (1) above to costs per diner. In other words, what is the average cost per diner for serving each of the following parties?
   a. A party of four diners who order three drinks in total.
   b. A party of two diners who do not order any drinks.
   c. A lone diner who orders two drinks.
3. Why do the costs per diner for the three different parties differ from each other and from the overall average cost of $16 per diner?

EXERCISE 7–15 Comprehensive Activity-Based Costing Exercise [LO7–2, LO7–3, LO7–4, LO7–5]
Advanced Products Corporation has supplied the following data from its activity-based costing system:

Overhead Costs	
Wages and salaries	$300,000
Other overhead costs	100,000
Total overhead costs	$400,000

Activity Cost Pool	Activity Measure	Total Activity for the Year
Supporting direct labor	Number of direct labor-hours	20,000 DLHs
Order processing	Number of customer orders	400 orders
Customer support	Number of customers	200 customers
Other	This is an organization-sustaining activity	Not applicable

Distribution of Resource Consumption Across Activities

	Supporting Direct Labor	Order Processing	Customer Support	Other	Total
Wages and salaries	40%	30%	20%	10%	100%
Other overhead costs . . .	30%	10%	20%	40%	100%

During the year, Advanced Products completed one order for a new customer, Shenzhen Enterprises. This customer did not order any other products during the year. Data concerning that order follow:

Data concerning the Shenzhen Enterprises Order	
Units ordered	10 units
Direct labor-hours	2 DLHs per unit
Selling price	$300 per unit
Direct materials	$180 per unit
Direct labor	$50 per unit

326   Chapter 7

Required:
1. Using Exhibit 7–6 as a guide, prepare a report showing the first-stage allocations of overhead costs to the activity cost pools.
2. Using Exhibit 7–7 as a guide, compute the activity rates for the activity cost pools.
3. Prepare a report showing the overhead costs for the order from Shenzhen Enterprises including customer support costs.
4. Using Exhibit 7–12 as a guide, prepare a report showing the customer margin for Shenzhen Enterprises.

Problems connect
ACCOUNTING

All applicable problems are available with McGraw-Hill's *Connect*® Accounting.

PROBLEM 7–16 Comparing Traditional and Activity-Based Product Margins [LO7–1, LO7–3, LO7–4, LO7–5]

Hi-Tek Manufacturing Inc. makes two types of industrial component parts—the B300 and the T500. An absorption costing income statement for the most recent period is shown below:

Hi-Tek Manufacturing Inc.	
Income Statement	
Sales	$2,100,000
Cost of goods sold	1,600,000
Gross margin	500,000
Selling and administrative expenses	550,000
Net operating loss	$ (50,000)

Hi-Tek produced and sold 70,000 units of B300 at a price of $20 per unit and 17,500 units of T500 at a price of $40 per unit. The company's traditional cost system allocates manufacturing overhead to products using a plantwide overhead rate and direct labor dollars as the allocation base. Additional information relating to the company's two product lines is shown below:

	B300	T500	Total
Direct materials	$436,300	$251,700	$ 688,000
Direct labor	$200,000	$104,000	304,000
Manufacturing overhead			608,000
Cost of goods sold			$1,600,000

The company has created an activity-based costing system to evaluate the profitability of its products. Hi-Tek's ABC implementation team concluded that $50,000 and $100,000 of the company's advertising expenses could be directly traced to B300 and T500, respectively. The remainder of the selling and administrative expenses was organization-sustaining in nature. The ABC team also distributed the company's manufacturing overhead to four activities as shown below:

Activity Cost Pool (and Activity Measure)	Manufacturing Overhead	Activity B300	Activity T500	Activity Total
Machining (machine-hours)	$213,500	90,000	62,500	152,500
Setups (setup hours)	157,500	75	300	375
Product-sustaining (number of products)	120,000	1	1	2
Other (organization-sustaining costs)	117,000	NA	NA	NA
Total manufacturing overhead cost	$608,000			

Required:
1. Using Exhibit 7–13 as a guide, compute the product margins for the B300 and T500 under the company's traditional costing system.
2. Using Exhibit 7–11 as a guide, compute the product margins for B300 and T500 under the activity-based costing system.
3. Using Exhibit 7–14 as a guide, prepare a quantitative comparison of the traditional and activity-based cost assignments. Explain why the traditional and activity-based cost assignments differ.

PROBLEM 7–17 Comparing Traditional and Activity-Based Product Margins [LO7–1, LO7–3, LO7–4, LO7–5]

Smoky Mountain Corporation makes two types of hiking boots—Xtreme and the Pathfinder. Data concerning these two product lines appear below:

	Xtreme	Pathfinder
Selling price per unit	$140.00	$99.00
Direct materials per unit	$72.00	$53.00
Direct labor per unit	$24.00	$12.00
Direct labor-hours per unit	2.0 DLHs	1.0 DLHs
Estimated annual production and sales	20,000 units	80,000 units

The company has a traditional costing system in which manufacturing overhead is applied to units based on direct labor-hours. Data concerning manufacturing overhead and direct labor-hours for the upcoming year appear below:

Estimated total manufacturing overhead	$1,980,000
Estimated total direct labor-hours	120,000 DLHs

Required:
1. Using Exhibit 7–13 as a guide, compute the product margins for the Xtreme and the Pathfinder products under the company's traditional costing system.
2. The company is considering replacing its traditional costing system with an activity-based costing system that would assign its manufacturing overhead to the following four activity cost pools (the Other cost pool includes organization-sustaining costs and idle capacity costs):

	Estimated	Expected Activity		
Activities and Activity Measures	Overhead Cost	Xtreme	Pathfinder	Total
Supporting direct labor (direct labor-hours) ...	$ 783,600	40,000	80,000	120,000
Batch setups (setups)	495,000	200	100	300
Product sustaining (number of products) ...	602,400	1	1	2
Other	99,000	NA	NA	NA
Total manufacturing overhead cost	$1,980,000			

Using Exhibit 7–11 as a guide, compute the product margins for the Xtreme and the Pathfinder products under the activity-based costing system.
3. Using Exhibit 7–14 as a guide, prepare a quantitative comparison of the traditional and activity-based cost assignments. Explain why the traditional and activity-based cost assignments differ.

PROBLEM 7–18 Activity-Based Costing and Bidding on Jobs [LO7–2, LO7–3, LO7–4]

Mercer Asbestos Removal Company removes potentially toxic asbestos insulation and related products from buildings. There has been a long-simmering dispute between the company's estimator and the work supervisors. The on-site supervisors claim that the estimators do not adequately distinguish between routine work such as removal of asbestos insulation around heating pipes in older homes and nonroutine work such as removing asbestos-contaminated ceiling plaster in industrial buildings. The on-site supervisors believe that nonroutine work is far more expensive than routine work and should bear higher customer charges. The estimator sums up his position in this way: "My job is to measure the area to be cleared of asbestos. As directed by top management, I simply multiply the square footage by $2.50 to determine the bid price. Since our average cost is only $2.175 per square foot, that leaves enough cushion to take care of the additional costs of nonroutine work that shows up. Besides, it is difficult to know what is routine or not routine until you actually start tearing things apart."

To shed light on this controversy, the company initiated an activity-based costing study of all of its costs. Data from the activity-based costing system follow:

Activity Cost Pool	Activity Measure	Total Activity
Removing asbestos	Thousands of square feet	800 thousand square feet
Estimating and job setup	Number of jobs	500 jobs
Working on nonroutine jobs	Number of nonroutine jobs	100 nonroutine jobs
Other (costs of idle capacity and organization-sustaining costs) . . .	None	

Note: The 100 nonroutine jobs are included in the total of 500 jobs. Both nonroutine jobs and routine jobs require estimating and setup.

Costs for the Year

Wages and salaries	$ 300,000
Disposal fees	700,000
Equipment depreciation	90,000
On-site supplies	50,000
Office expenses	200,000
Licensing and insurance	400,000
Total cost	$1,740,000

Distribution of Resource Consumption Across Activities

	Removing Asbestos	Estimating and Job Setup	Working on Nonroutine Jobs	Other	Total
Wages and salaries	50%	10%	30%	10%	100%
Disposal fees	60%	0%	40%	0%	100%
Equipment depreciation . . .	40%	5%	20%	35%	100%
On-site supplies	60%	30%	10%	0%	100%
Office expenses	10%	35%	25%	30%	100%
Licensing and insurance . . .	30%	0%	50%	20%	100%

Required:
1. Using Exhibit 7–6 as a guide, perform the first-stage allocation of costs to the activity cost pools.
2. Using Exhibit 7–7 as a guide, compute the activity rates for the activity cost pools.
3. Using the activity rates you have computed, determine the total cost and the average cost per thousand square feet of each of the following jobs according to the activity-based costing system.
   a.   A routine 1,000-square-foot asbestos removal job.
   b.   A routine 2,000-square-foot asbestos removal job.
   c.   A nonroutine 2,000-square-foot asbestos removal job.
4. Given the results you obtained in (3) above, do you agree with the estimator that the company's present policy for bidding on jobs is adequate?

PROBLEM 7–19 Second Stage Allocations and Product Margins [LO7–4, LO7–5]

Pixel Studio, Inc., is a small company that creates computer-generated animations for films and television. Much of the company's work consists of short commercials for television, but the company also does realistic computer animations for special effects in movies.

The young founders of the company have become increasingly concerned with the economics of the business—particularly since many competitors have sprung up recently in the local area. To help understand the company's cost structure, an activity-based costing system has been designed. Three major activities are carried out in the company: animation concept, animation production, and contract administration. The animation concept activity is carried out at the contract proposal stage when the company bids on projects. This is an intensive activity that involves individuals from all parts of the company in creating story boards and prototype stills to be shown to the prospective client. Once a project is accepted by the client, the animation goes into production and contract administration begins. Almost all of the work involved in animation production is done by the technical staff, whereas the administrative staff is largely responsible for contract administration. The activity cost pools and their activity measures are listed below:

Activity Cost Pool	Activity Measure	Activity Rate
Animation concept	Number of proposals	$6,040 per proposal
Animation production	Minutes of completed animation	$7,725 per minute
Contract administration	Number of contracts	$6,800 per contract

These activity rates include all of the company's costs, except for the costs of idle capacity and organization-sustaining costs. There are no direct labor or direct materials costs.

Preliminary analysis using these activity rates has indicated that the local commercial segment of the market may be unprofitable. This segment is highly competitive. Producers of local commercials may ask three or four companies like Pixel Studio to bid, which results in an unusually low ratio of accepted contracts to bids. Furthermore, the animation sequences tend to be much shorter for local commercials than for other work. Since animation work is billed at fairly standard rates according to the running time of the completed animation, this means that the revenues from these short projects tend to be below average. Data concerning activity in the local commercial market appear below:

Activity Measure	Local Commercials
Number of proposals	25
Minutes of completed animation	5
Number of contracts	10

The total sales from the 10 contracts for local commercials was $180,000.

Required:

1. Determine the cost of serving the local commercial market.
2. Prepare a report showing the margin earned serving the local commercial market. (Remember, this company has no direct materials or direct labor costs.)
3. What would you recommend to management concerning the local commercial market?

PROBLEM 7–20 Evaluating the Profitability of Services [LO7–2, LO7–3, LO7–4, LO7–5]

Gallatin Carpet Cleaning is a small, family-owned business operating out of Bozeman, Montana. For its services, the company has always charged a flat fee per hundred square feet of carpet cleaned. The current fee is $28 per hundred square feet. However, there is some question about whether the company is actually making any money on jobs for some customers—particularly those located on remote ranches that require considerable travel time. The owner's daughter, home for the summer from college, has suggested investigating this question using activity-based

Chapter 7

costing. After some discussion, a simple system consisting of four activity cost pools seemed to be adequate. The activity cost pools and their activity measures appear below:

Activity Cost Pool	Activity Measure	Activity for the Year
Cleaning carpets	Square feet cleaned (00s)	20,000 hundred square feet
Travel to jobs	Miles driven	60,000 miles
Job support	Number of jobs	2,000 jobs
Other (costs of idle capacity and organization-sustaining costs) . . .	None	Not applicable

The total cost of operating the company for the year is $430,000, which includes the following costs:

Wages	$150,000
Cleaning supplies	40,000
Cleaning equipment depreciation	20,000
Vehicle expenses	80,000
Office expenses	60,000
President's compensation	80,000
Total cost	$430,000

Resource consumption is distributed across the activities as follows:

Distribution of Resource Consumption Across Activities

	Cleaning Carpets	Travel to Jobs	Job Support	Other	Total
Wages	70%	20%	0%	10%	100%
Cleaning supplies	100%	0%	0%	0%	100%
Cleaning equipment depreciation . .	80%	0%	0%	20%	100%
Vehicle expenses	0%	60%	0%	40%	100%
Office expenses	0%	0%	45%	55%	100%
President's compensation	0%	0%	40%	60%	100%

Job support consists of receiving calls from potential customers at the home office, scheduling jobs, billing, resolving issues, and so on.

Required:

1. Using Exhibit 7–6 as a guide, prepare the first-stage allocation of costs to the activity cost pools.
2. Using Exhibit 7–7 as a guide, compute the activity rates for the activity cost pools.
3. The company recently completed a 5 hundred square foot carpet-cleaning job at the Flying N ranch—a 75-mile round-trip journey from the company's offices in Bozeman. Compute the cost of this job using the activity-based costing system.
4. The revenue from the Flying N ranch was $140 (5 hundred square feet @ $28 per hundred square feet). Using Exhibit 7–12 as a guide, prepare a report showing the margin from this job.
5. What do you conclude concerning the profitability of the Flying N ranch job? Explain.
6. What advice would you give the president concerning pricing jobs in the future?

Appendix 7A: ABC Action Analysis

A conventional ABC analysis, such as the one presented in Exhibits 7–11 and 7–12 in the chapter, has several important limitations. Referring back to Exhibit 7–11, recall that the custom compass housings show a negative product margin of $49,500. Because of this apparent loss, managers were considering dropping this product. However, as the discussion among the managers revealed, it is unlikely that all of the $589,500 cost of the product would be avoided if it were dropped. Some of these costs would continue even if the product were totally eliminated. *Before* taking action, it is vital to identify which costs would be avoided and which costs would continue. Only those costs that can be avoided are relevant in the decision. Moreover, many of the costs are managed costs that would require explicit management action to eliminate. If the custom compass housings product line were eliminated, the direct materials cost would be avoided without any explicit management action—the materials simply wouldn't be ordered. On the other hand, if the custom compass housings were dropped, explicit management action would be required to eliminate the salaries of overhead workers that are assigned to this product.

Simply shifting these managed costs to other products would not solve anything. These costs would have to be eliminated or redeployed to increase sales to have any benefit to the company. While eliminating the cost is obviously beneficial, redeploying the resources is only beneficial if the resources are used to expand the output of a work center that has been operating at full capacity. If the resources are redeployed to a work center with idle capacity, the additional resources would only increase the excess capacity in that work center—which has no direct benefit to the company.

In addition, if some overhead costs need to be eliminated as a result of dropping a product, specific managers must be held responsible for eliminating those costs or the reductions are unlikely to occur. If no one is specifically held responsible for eliminating the costs, they will almost certainly continue to be incurred. Without external pressure, managers usually avoid cutting costs in their areas of responsibility. The action analysis report developed in this appendix is intended to help top managers identify what costs are relevant in a decision and to place responsibility for the elimination of those costs on the appropriate managers.

LO7–6
Prepare an action analysis report using activity-based costing data and interpret the report.

Activity Rates—Action Analysis Report

Constructing an action analysis report begins with the results of the first-stage allocation, which is reproduced as Exhibit 7A–1 (page 332). In contrast to the conventional ABC analysis covered in the chapter, the calculation of the activity rates for an action analysis report is a bit more involved. In addition to computing an overall activity rate for each activity cost pool, an activity rate is computed for each cell in Exhibit 7A–1. The computations of activity rates for the action analysis are carried out in Exhibit 7A–2 (page 332). For example, the $125,000 cost of indirect factory wages for the Customer Orders cost pool is divided by the total activity for that cost pool—1,000 orders—to arrive at the activity rate of $125 per customer order for indirect factory wages. Similarly, the $200,000 cost of indirect factory wages for the Product Design cost pool is divided by the total activity for that cost pool—400 designs—to arrive at the activity rate of $500 per design for indirect factory wages. Note that the totals at the bottom of Exhibit 7A–2 agree with the overall activity rates in Exhibit 7–7 in the chapter. Exhibit 7A–2, which shows the activity rates for the action analysis report, contains more detail than Exhibit 7–7, which contains the activity rates for the conventional ABC analysis.

Assignment of Overhead Costs to Products—Action Analysis Report

Computing the overhead costs to be assigned to products for an action analysis report also involves more detail than for a conventional ABC analysis. The computations for Classic Brass are carried out in Exhibit 7A–3. For example, the activity rate of $125 per customer

EXHIBIT 7A–1
First-Stage Allocations to Activity Cost Pools

	A	B	C	D	E	F	G
1		Activity Cost Pools					
2		Customer Orders	Product Design	Order Size	Customer Relations	Other	Total
4	Production Department:						
5	Indirect factory wages	$ 125,000	$ 200,000	$ 100,000	$ 50,000	$ 25,000	$ 500,000
6	Factory equipment depreciation	60,000	0	180,000	0	60,000	300,000
7	Factory utilities	0	12,000	60,000	0	48,000	120,000
8	Factory building lease	0	0	0	0	80,000	80,000
10	General Administrative Department:						
11	Administrative wages and salaries	60,000	20,000	40,000	120,000	160,000	400,000
12	Office equipment depreciation	15,000	0	0	12,500	22,500	50,000
13	Administrative building lease	0	0	0	0	60,000	60,000
15	Marketing Department:						
16	Marketing wages and salaries	55,000	20,000	0	150,000	25,000	250,000
17	Selling expenses	5,000	0	0	35,000	10,000	50,000
19	Total cost	$ 320,000	$ 252,000	$ 380,000	$ 367,500	$ 490,500	$ 1,810,000
20							

H ◀ ▶ H   Exhibit 7A-1   Exhibit 7A-2   Exhibit 7A-3A   Exhibit 7A-3B   Exhibit ◀

EXHIBIT 7A–2
Computation of the Activity Rates
for the Action Analysis Report

	A	B	C	D	E	F
1		Activity Cost Pools				
2		Customer Orders	Product Design	Order Size	Customer Relations	Other
4	Total activity	1,000 orders	400 product designs	20,000 machine-hours	250 active customers	Not applicable*
7	Production Department:					
8	Indirect factory wages	$ 125	500	$ 5	$ 200	
9	Factory equipment depreciation	60	0	9	0	
10	Factory utilities	0	30	3	0	
11	Factory building lease	0	0	0	0	
13	General Administrative Department:					
14	Administrative wages and salaries	60	50	2	480	
15	Office equipment depreciation	15	0	0	50	
16	Administrative building lease	0	0	0	0	
18	Marketing Department:					
19	Marketing wages and salaries	55	50	0	600	
20	Selling expenses	5	0	0	140	
22	Total (conventional ABC analysis)	$ 320	$ 630	$ 19	$ 1,470	
24	*Activity rates are not computed for the Other cost pool since these costs will not be allocated further.					

H ◀ ▶ H   Exhibit 7A-1   Exhibit 7A-2   Exhibit 7A-3A   Exhibit 7A-3B   Exhibit 7A-5   Activity rates ◀ ▶

$125,000 ÷ 1,000 **orders** = $125 **per order.**

Other entries in the table are computed similarly.

order for indirect factory wages is multiplied by 600 orders for the standard stanchions to arrive at the cost of $75,000 for indirect factory wages in Exhibit 7A–3. Instead of just a single cost number for each cost pool as in the conventional ABC analysis, we now have an entire cost matrix showing much more detail. Note that the column totals for the cost matrix in Exhibit 7A–3 agree with the ABC costs for standard stanchions in Exhibit 7–9.

Activity-Based Costing: A Tool to Aid Decision Making   **333**

	A	B	C	D	E	F
1	**Action Analysis Cost Matrix for Standard Stanchions**					
3			*Activity Cost Pools*			
4		*Customer Orders*	*Product Design*	*Order Size*	*Customer Relations*	*Total*
6	Total activity for stanchions	600 orders	product designs	17,500 machine-hours	Not applicable	
9	Production Department:					
10	Indirect factory wages	$ 75,000	$ 0	$ 87,500		$ 162,500
11	Factory equipment depreciation	36,000	0	157,500		193,500
12	Factory utilities	0	0	52,500		52,500
13	Factory building lease	0	0	0		0
15	General Administrative Department:					
16	Administrative wages and salaries	36,000	0	35,000		71,000
17	Office equipment depreciation	9,000	0	0		9,000
18	Administrative building lease	0	0	0		0
20	Marketing Department:					
21	Marketing wages and salaries	33,000	0	0		33,000
22	Selling expenses	3,000	0	0		3,000
24	Total (conventional ABC analysis)	$ 192,000	$ 0	$ 332,500		$ 524,500

◄ ◄ ► ►◄ / Exhibit 7A-1 / Exhibit 7A-2 / **Exhibit 7A-3A** / Exhibit 7A ◄

From Exhibit 7A–2, the activity rate for indirect factory wages for the Customer Orders cost pool is $125 per order.

$125 per order × 600 orders = $75,000

Other entries in the table are computed in a similar way.

	A	B	C	D	E	F
1	**Action Analysis Cost Matrix for the Custom Compass Housings**					
3			*Activity Cost Pools*			
4		*Customer Orders*	*Product Design*	*Order Size*	*Customer Relations*	*Total*
6	Total activity for custom compass housings	400 order	400 product design	2,500 machine-hours	Not applicable	
9	Production Department:					
10	Indirect factory wages	$ 50,000	$ 200,000	$ 12,500		$ 262,500
11	Factory equipment depreciation	24,000	0	22,500		46,500
12	Factory utilities	0	12,000	7,500		19,500
13	Factory building lease	0	0	0		0
15	General Administrative Department:					
16	Administrative wages and salaries	24,000	20,000	5,000		49,000
17	Office equipment depreciation	6,000	0	0		6,000
18	Administrative building lease	0	0	0		0
20	Marketing Department:					
21	Marketing wages and salaries	22,000	20,000	0		42,000
22	Selling expenses	2,000	0	0		2,000
24	Total (conventional ABC analysis)	$ 128,000	$ 252,000	$ 47,500		$ 427,500

◄ ◄ ► ►◄ / Exhibit 7A-2 / Exhibit 7A-3A / **Exhibit 7A-3B** / Exhibit 7A- ◄

From Exhibit 7A–2, the activity rate for indirect factory wages for the Customer Orders cost pool is $125 per order.

$125 per order × 400 orders = $50,000

Other entries in the table are computed in a similar way.

334   Chapter 7

Indeed, the conventional ABC analysis of Exhibit 7–11 can be easily constructed using the column totals at the bottom of the cost matrices in Exhibit 7A–3. In contrast, the action analysis report will be based on the row totals at the right of the cost matrices in Exhibit 7A–3. In addition, the action analysis report will include a simple color-coding scheme that will help managers identify how easily the various costs can be adjusted.

Ease of Adjustment Codes

The ABC team constructed Exhibit 7A–4 to aid managers in the use of the ABC data. In this exhibit, each cost has been assigned an *ease of adjustment code*—Green, Yellow, or Red. The **ease of adjustment code** reflects how easily the cost could be adjusted to changes in activity.[4] "Green" costs are those costs that would adjust more or less automatically to changes in activity without any action by managers. For example, direct materials costs would adjust to changes in orders without any action being taken by managers. If a customer does not order stanchions, the direct materials for the stanchions would not be required and would not be ordered. "Yellow" costs are those costs that could be adjusted in response to changes in activity, but such adjustments require management action; the adjustment is not automatic. The ABC team believes, for example, that direct labor costs should be included in the Yellow category. Managers must make difficult decisions and take explicit action to increase or decrease, in aggregate, direct labor costs—particularly because the company has a no lay-off policy. "Red" costs are costs that could be adjusted to changes in activity only with a great deal of difficulty, and the adjustment would require management action. The building leases fall into this category because it would be very difficult and expensive to break the leases.

The Action Analysis View of the ABC Data

Looking at Exhibit 7A–3, the totals on the right-hand side of the table indicate that the $427,500 of overhead cost for the custom compass housings consists of $262,500 of indirect factory wages, $46,500 of factory equipment depreciation, and so on. These data

---

EXHIBIT 7A–4
Ease of Adjustment Codes

Green: *Costs that adjust automatically to changes in activity without management action.*

   Direct materials
   Shipping costs

Yellow: *Costs that could, in principle, be adjusted to changes in activity, but management action would be required.*

   Direct labor
   Indirect factory wages
   Factory utilities
   Administrative wages and salaries
   Office equipment depreciation
   Marketing wages and salaries
   Selling expenses

Red: *Costs that would be very difficult to adjust to changes in activity and management action would be required.*

   Factory equipment depreciation
   Factory building lease
   Administrative building lease

---

[4] The idea of using colors to code how easily costs can be adjusted was suggested to us at a seminar put on by Boeing and by an article by Alfred King, "Green Dollars and Blue Dollars: The Paradox of Cost Reduction," *Journal of Cost Management*, Fall 1993, pp. 44–52.

	A	B	C	
1	Custom Compass Housings			
2	Sales (from Exhibit 7-11)		$ 540,000	
3				
4	Green costs:			
5	Direct materials (from Exhibit 7-11)	$ 69,500		
6	Shipping (from Exhibit 7-11)	5,000	74,500	
7	Green margin		465,500	
8				
9	Yellow costs:			
10	Direct labor (from Exhibit 7-11)	87,500		
11	Indirect factory wages (from Exhibit 7A-3)	262,500		
12	Factory utilities (from Exhibit 7A-3)	19,500		
13	Administrative wages and salaries (from Exhibit 7A-3)	49,000		
14	Office equipment depreciation (from Exhibit 7A-3)	6,000		
15	Marketing wages and salaries (from Exhibit 7A-3)	42,000		
16	Selling expenses (from Exhibit 7A-3)	2,000	468,500	
17	Yellow margin		(3,000)	
18				
19	Red costs:			
20	Factory equipment depreciation (from Exhibit 7A-3)	46,500		
21	Factory building lease (from Exhibit 7A-3)	0		
22	Administrative building lease (from Exhibit 7A-3)	0	46,500	
23	Red margin		$ (49,500)	
24				

◄ ◄ ► ►| Exhibit 7A-5 / Activity rates / Stanchio ◄

EXHIBIT 7A–5
Action Analysis of Custom Compass Housings: Activity-Based Costing System

are displayed in Exhibit 7A–5, which shows an action analysis of the custom compass housings product. An action analysis report shows what costs have been assigned to the cost object, such as a product or customer, and how difficult it would be to adjust the cost if there is a change in activity. Note that the Red margin at the bottom of Exhibit 7A–5, $(49,500), is exactly the same as the product margin for the custom compass housings in Exhibit 7–11 in the chapter.

The cost data in the action analysis in Exhibit 7A–5 are arranged by the color coded ease of adjustment. All of the Green costs—those that adjust more or less automatically to changes in activity—appear together at the top of the list of costs. These costs total $74,500 and are subtracted from the sales of $540,000 to yield a Green margin of $465,500. The same procedure is followed for the Yellow and Red costs. This action analysis indicates what costs would have to be cut and how difficult it would be to cut them if the custom compass housings product were dropped. Prior to making any decision about dropping products, the managers responsible for the costs must agree to either eliminate the resources represented by those costs or to transfer the resources to an area in the organization that really needs the resources. If managers do not make such a commitment, it is likely that the costs would continue to be incurred. As a result, the company would lose the sales from the products without really eliminating the costs.

After the action analysis was prepared by the ABC team, top management at Classic Brass met once again to review the results of the ABC analysis.

John: When we last met, we had discussed the advisability of discontinuing the custom compass housings product line. I understand that the ABC team has done some additional analysis to help us in making this decision.

Mary: That's right. The action analysis report we put together indicates how easy it would be to adjust each cost and where specific cost savings would have to come from if we were to drop the custom compass housings.

John: What's this red margin at the bottom of the action analysis? Isn't that a product margin?

**MANAGERIAL
ACCOUNTING IN ACTION**
THE WRAP-UP

Mary: Yes, it is. However, we call it a red margin because we should stop and think very, very carefully before taking any actions based on that margin.

John: Why is that?

Mary: As an example, we subtracted the costs of factory equipment depreciation to arrive at that red margin. We doubt that we could avoid any of that cost if we were to drop custom orders. We use the same machines on custom orders that we use on standard products. The factory equipment has no resale value, and it does not wear out through use.

John: What about this yellow margin?

Mary: Yellow means proceed with a great deal of caution. To get to the yellow margin we deducted from sales numerous costs that could be adjusted only if the managers involved are willing to eliminate resources or shift them to another department in an effort to grow sales.

John: If I understand the yellow margin correctly, the apparent loss of $3,000 on the custom compass housings is the result of the indirect factory wages of $262,500.

Susan: Right, that's basically the wages of our design engineers.

John: I am uncomfortable with the idea of laying off any of our designers for numerous reasons. So where does that leave us?

Mary: What about raising prices on our custom products?

Tom: We should be able to do that. We have been undercutting the competition to make sure that we won bids on custom work because we thought it was a very profitable thing to do.

John: Why don't we just charge directly for design work?

Tom: Some of our competitors already do that. However, I don't think we would be able to charge enough to cover our design costs.

John: Can we do anything to make our design work more efficient so it costs us less? I'm not going to lay anyone off, but if we make the design process more efficient, we could lower the charge for design work and spread those costs across more customers.

Susan: That may be possible. I'll form a process improvement team to look at it.

John: Let's get some benchmark data on design costs. If we set our minds to it, I'm sure we can be world class in no time.

Susan: Okay. Mary, will you help with the benchmark data?

Mary: Sure.

John: Let's meet again in about a week to discuss our progress. Is there anything else on the agenda for today?

The points raised in the preceding discussion are extremely important. By measuring the resources consumed by products (and other cost objects), an ABC system provides a much better basis for decision making than a traditional cost accounting system that spreads overhead costs around without much regard for what might be causing the overhead. A well-designed ABC system provides managers with estimates of potentially relevant costs that can be a very useful starting point for management analysis.

Summary (Appendix 7A)

The action analysis report illustrated in this appendix is a valuable addition to the ABC toolkit. An action analysis report provides more information for decision making than a conventional ABC analysis. The action analysis report makes it clear where costs would have to be adjusted in the organization as a result of an action. In a conventional ABC analysis, a cost such as $320 for processing an order represents costs from many parts of the organization. If an order is dropped, there will be little pressure to actually eliminate the $320 cost unless it is clear where the costs are incurred and which managers would be responsible for reducing the cost. In contrast, an action analysis report traces the costs to where they are incurred in the organization and makes it much easier to assign responsibility to managers for reducing costs. In addition, an action analysis report provides information concerning how easily a cost can be adjusted. Costs that cannot be adjusted are not relevant in a decision.

Exhibit 7A–6 summarizes all of the steps required to create both an action analysis report as illustrated in this appendix and an activity analysis as shown in the chapter.

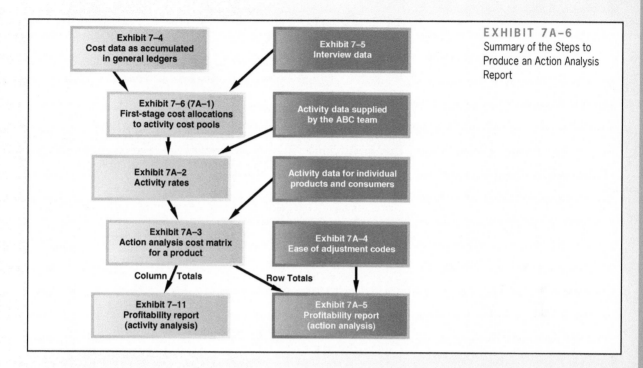

Summary of the Steps to
Produce an Action Analysis
Report

Review Problem: Activity Analysis Report

Refer to the data for Ferris Corporation in the Review Problem at the end of the chapter on pages 312–314.

Required:

1. Compute activity rates for Ferris Corporation as in Exhibit 7A–2.
2. Using Exhibit 7A–3 as a guide, construct a table showing the overhead costs for the OfficeMart orders described in requirement (3) of the Review Problem at the end of the chapter.
3. The management of Ferris Corporation has assigned ease of adjustment codes to costs as follows:

Cost	Ease of Adjustment Code
Direct materials	Green
Direct labor	Yellow
Manufacturing overhead	Yellow
Selling and administrative overhead	Red

Using Exhibit 7A–5 as a guide, prepare an action analysis of the OfficeMart orders.

Solution to Review Problem

1. The activity rates for the activity cost pools are:

	Assembling Units	Processing Orders	Supporting Customers
Total activity	1,000 units	250 orders	100 customers
Manufacturing overhead	$250	$ 700	$ 250
Selling and administrative overhead ...	30	540	750
Total	$280	$1,240	$1,000

338 Chapter 7

2. The overhead cost for the four orders of a total of 80 filing cabinets would be computed as follows:

	Assembling Units	Processing Orders	Supporting Customers	Total
Activity	80 units	4 orders	1 customer	
Manufacturing overhead	$20,000	$2,800	$ 250	$23,050
Selling and administrative overhead . . .	2,400	2,160	750	5,310
Total	$22,400	$4,960	$1,000	$28,360

3. The action analysis report is:

Sales		$47,600
Green costs:		
Direct materials	$14,400	14,400
Green margin		33,200
Yellow costs:		
Direct labor	4,000	
Manufacturing overhead	23,050	27,050
Yellow margin		6,150
Red costs:		
Selling and administrative overhead . . .	5,310	5,310
Red margin		$ 840

Glossary (Appendix 7A)

Ease of adjustment codes Costs are coded as Green, Yellow, or Red—depending on how easily the cost could be adjusted to changes in activity. "Green" costs adjust automatically to changes in activity. "Yellow" costs could be adjusted in response to changes in activity, but such adjustments require management action; the adjustment is not automatic. "Red" costs could be adjusted to changes in activity only with a great deal of difficulty and would require management action. (p. 334)

Appendix 7A Exercises and Problems

All applicable exercises and problems are available with McGraw-Hill's *Connect*® *Accounting*.

EXERCISE 7A–1 Preparing an Action Analysis Report [LO7–6]
Fairway Golf Corporation produces private label golf clubs for pro shops throughout North America. The company uses activity-based costing to evaluate the profitability of serving its customers. This analysis is based on categorizing the company's costs as follows, using the ease of adjustment color coding scheme described in Appendix 7A:

	Ease of Adjustment Code
Direct materials	Green
Direct labor	Yellow
Indirect labor	Yellow
Factory equipment depreciation	Red
Factory administration	Red
Selling and administrative wages and salaries	Red
Selling and administrative depreciation	Red
Marketing expenses	Yellow

Management would like to evaluate the profitability of a particular customer—Shaker Run Golf Club of Lebanon, Ohio. Over the last twelve months this customer submitted one order for 100 golf clubs that had to be produced in four batches due to differences in product labeling requested by the customer. Summary data concerning the order appear below:

Number of clubs	100
Number of orders	1
Number of batches	4
Direct labor-hours per club	0.3
Selling price per club	$50.00
Direct materials cost per club	$29.50
Direct labor rate per hour	$20.50

A cost analyst working in the controller's office at the company has already produced the action analysis cost matrix for the Shaker Run Golf Club that appears below:

Action Analysis Cost Matrix for Shaker Run Golf Club

	Activity Cost Pools				
	Supporting Direct labor	Batch Processing	Order Processing	Customer Service	Total
Activity	30 direct labor-hours	4 batches	1 order	1 customer	
Manufacturing overhead:					
Indirect labor	$ 35.40	$53.70	$ 6.80	$ 0.00	$ 95.90
Factory equipment depreciation ...	102.80	0.90	0.00	0.00	103.70
Factory administration	18.50	0.50	12.00	228.00	259.00
Selling and administrative overhead:					
Wages and salaries	11.00	0.00	36.00	382.00	429.00
Depreciation	0.00	0.00	6.00	24.00	30.00
Marketing expenses	117.70	0.00	54.00	369.00	540.70
Total	$285.40	$55.10	$114.80	$1,003.00	$1,458.30

Required:

Prepare an action analysis report showing the profitability of the Shaker Run Golf Club. Include direct materials and direct labor costs in the report. Use Exhibit 7A–5 as a guide for organizing the report.

EXERCISE 7A–2 Second-Stage Allocation Using the Action Analysis Approach [LO7–4, LO7–6]
This exercise should be assigned in conjunction with Exercise 7–9.

The results of the first-stage allocation of the activity-based costing system at Durban Metal Products, Ltd., in which the activity rates were computed, appear below:

	Order Size	Customer Orders	Product Testing	Selling
Manufacturing overhead:				
Indirect labor	$ 8.25	$180.00	$30.00	$ 0.00
Factory depreciation	8.00	0.00	40.00	0.00
Factory utilities	0.10	0.00	1.00	0.00
Factory administration	0.00	48.00	18.00	30.00
Selling and administrative:				
Wages and salaries	0.50	80.00	0.00	800.00
Depreciation	0.00	12.00	0.00	40.00
Taxes and insurance	0.00	0.00	0.00	20.00
Selling expenses	0.00	0.00	0.00	200.00
Total overhead cost	$16.85	$320.00	$89.00	$1,090.00

340

Chapter 7

Required:

1. Using Exhibit 7A–3 as a guide, prepare a report showing the overhead cost of the order for heavy-duty trailer axles discussed in Exercise 7–9. What is the total overhead cost of the order according to the activity-based costing system?

2. Explain the two different perspectives this report gives to managers concerning the nature of the overhead costs involved in the order. (*Hint:* Look at the row and column totals of the report you have prepared.)

EXERCISE 7A–3 Second-Stage Allocations and Margin Calculations Using the Action Analysis Approach [LO7–4, LO7–6]

Refer to the data for Foam Products, Inc., in Exercise 7–11 and the following additional details concerning the activity rates in the activity-based costing system:

	Activity Rates			
	Supporting Direct Labor	Batch Processing	Order Processing	Customer Service
Manufacturing overhead:				
Indirect labor	$0.60	$ 60.00	$ 20.00	$ 0.00
Factory equipment depreciation	4.00	17.00	0.00	0.00
Factory administration	0.10	7.00	25.00	150.00
Selling and administrative overhead:				
Wages and salaries	0.40	20.00	160.00	1,600.00
Depreciation	0.00	3.00	10.00	38.00
Marketing expenses	0.45	0.00	60.00	675.00
Total	$5.55	$107.00	$275.00	$2,463.00

Management has provided its ease of adjustment codes for the purpose of preparing action analyses.

	Ease of Adjustment Codes
Direct materials	Green
Direct labor	Yellow
Manufacturing overhead:	
Indirect labor	Yellow
Factory equipment depreciation	Red
Factory administration	Red
Selling and administrative overhead:	
Wages and salaries	Red
Depreciation	Red
Marketing expenses	Yellow

Required:

Using Exhibit 7A–5 as a guide, prepare an action analysis report for Interstate Trucking similar to those prepared for products.

EXERCISE 7A–4 Comprehensive Activity-Based Costing Exercise [LO7–2, LO7–3, LO7–4, LO7–6]

Refer to the data for Advanced Products Corporation in Exercise 7–15.

Required:

1. Using Exhibit 7A–1 as a guide, prepare a report showing the first-stage allocations of overhead costs to the activity cost pools.

2. Using Exhibit 7A–2 as a guide, compute the activity rates for the activity cost pools.

3. Using Exhibit 7A–3 as a guide, prepare a report showing the overhead costs for the order from Shenzhen Enterprises including customer support costs.

4. Using Exhibit 7–12 as a guide, prepare a report showing the customer margin for Shenzhen Enterprises.

Activity-Based Costing: A Tool to Aid Decision Making

5. Using Exhibit 7A–5 as a guide, prepare an action analysis report showing the customer margin for Shenzhen Enterprises. Direct materials should be coded as a Green cost, direct labor and wages and salaries as Yellow costs, and other overhead costs as a Red cost.
6. What action, if any, do you recommend as a result of the above analyses?

EXERCISE 7A–5 Second Stage Allocations and Product Margins [LO7–4, LO7–6]

Refer to the data for Pixel Studio, Inc., in Problem 7–19. In addition, the company has provided the following details concerning its activity rates:

	Activity Rates		
	Animation Concept	Animation Production	Contract Administration
Technical staff salaries	$4,000	$6,000	$1,600
Animation equipment depreciation	360	1,125	0
Administrative wages and salaries	1,440	150	4,800
Supplies costs	120	300	160
Facility costs	120	150	240
Total	$6,040	$7,725	$6,800

Management has provided the following ease of adjustment codes for the various costs:

	Ease of Adjustment Code
Technical staff salaries	Red
Animation equipment depreciation	Red
Administrative wages and salaries	Yellow
Supplies costs	Green
Facility costs	Red

These codes created some controversy. In particular, some administrators objected to coding their own salaries Yellow, while the technical staff salaries were coded Red. However, the founders of the firm overruled these objections by pointing out that "our technical staff is our most valuable asset. Good animators are extremely difficult to find, and they would be the last to go if we had to cut back."

Required:

1. Using Exhibit 7A–3 as a guide, determine the cost of the local commercials market. (Think of the local commercial market as a product.)
2. Using Exhibit 7A–5 as a guide, prepare an action analysis report concerning the local commercial market. (This company has no direct materials or direct labor costs.)
3. What would you recommend to management concerning the local commercial market?

CHAPTER 8

Master Budgeting

Planning for a Crisis—Civil War Trust

The Civil War Trust (CWT) is a private, nonprofit organization with 70,000 members that works to preserve the nation's remaining Civil War battlefields—many of which are threatened by commercial development such as shopping centers, houses, industrial parks, and casinos. To forestall development, the CWT typically purchases the land or development rights to the land. The CWT has saved over 25,000 acres from development, including, for example, 698 acres of battlefield at Gettysburg.

CWT's management team was particularly concerned about the budget proposal for 2009, which was to be presented to the board of directors in the fall of 2008. The CWT is wholly supported by contributions from its members and many of those members had been adversely affected by the ongoing financial crisis that followed the collapse of the subprime mortgage market. Consequently, the funds that would be available for operations in 2009 were particularly difficult to predict. Accordingly, the budget for 2009 contained three variations based on progressively pessimistic economic assumptions. The more pessimistic budgets were called contingent budgets. As 2008 progressed and member contributions declined somewhat from previous levels, CWT switched to the first contingent budget. This contingent budget required a number of actions to reduce costs including a hiring freeze and a salary freeze, but maintained an aggressive program of protecting battlefield acreage through purchases of land and development rights. Fortunately, the CWT did not have to switch to the most pessimistic budget— which would have involved layoffs and other extraordinary cost-saving measures.

Instead of reacting in a panic mode to unfavorable developments, CWT used the budgeting process to carefully plan in advance for a number of possible contingencies. ■

Sources: Communications with James Lighthizer, president, and David Duncan, director of membership and development, Civil War Trust; and the CWT website, www.civilwar.org.

LEARNING OBJECTIVES

After studying Chapter 8, you should be able to:

LO8–1 Understand why organizations budget and the processes they use to create budgets.

LO8–2 Prepare a sales budget, including a schedule of expected cash collections.

LO8–3 Prepare a production budget.

LO8–4 Prepare a direct materials budget, including a schedule of expected cash disbursements for purchases of materials.

LO8–5 Prepare a direct labor budget.

LO8–6 Prepare a manufacturing overhead budget.

LO8–7 Prepare a selling and administrative expense budget.

LO8–8 Prepare a cash budget.

LO8–9 Prepare a budgeted income statement.

LO8–10 Prepare a budgeted balance sheet.

I n this chapter, we describe how organizations strive to achieve their financial goals by preparing a number of budgets that together form an integrated business plan known as the *master budget*. The master budget is an essential management tool that communicates management's plans throughout the organization, allocates resources, and coordinates activities.

What Is a Budget?

A **budget** is a detailed plan for the future that is usually expressed in formal quantitative terms. Individuals sometimes create household budgets that balance their income and expenditures for food, clothing, housing, and so on while providing for some savings. Once the budget is established, actual spending is compared to the budget to make sure the plan is being followed. Companies use budgets in a similar way, although the amount of work and underlying details far exceed a personal budget.

LO8–1
Understand why organizations budget and the processes they use to create budgets.

Budgets are used for two distinct purposes—*planning* and *control*. **Planning** involves developing goals and preparing various budgets to achieve those goals. **Control** involves gathering feedback to ensure that the plan is being properly executed or modified as circumstances change. To be effective, a good budgeting system must provide for both planning and control. Good planning without effective control is a waste of time and effort.

Advantages of Budgeting

Organizations realize many benefits from budgeting, including:

1. Budgets *communicate* management's plans throughout the organization.
2. Budgets force managers to *think about* and *plan* for the future. In the absence of the necessity to prepare a budget, many managers would spend all of their time dealing with day-to-day emergencies.
3. The budgeting process provides a means of *allocating resources* to those parts of the organization where they can be used most effectively.
4. The budgeting process can uncover potential *bottlenecks* before they occur.
5. Budgets *coordinate* the activities of the entire organization by *integrating* the plans of its various parts. Budgeting helps to ensure that everyone in the organization is pulling in the same direction.
6. Budgets define goals and objectives that can serve as *benchmarks* for evaluating subsequent performance.

IN BUSINESS

EXECUTING STRATEGY WITH BUDGETS

Robert DeMartini, the CEO of New Balance, set a goal of tripling his company's revenues to $3 billion in four years. He tripled the company's annual advertising budget and doubled its consumer research budget in an effort to attract more young customers. These decisions represented a strategic shift for New Balance, which usually spends less than $20 million per year in advertising compared to competitors such as Nike and Adidas, which annually invest $184 million and $80 million, respectively.

One reason companies prepare budgets is to allocate resources across departments in a manner that supports strategic priorities. DeMartini used the budget to send a clear signal that his marketing department was expected to play a huge role in achieving the company's revenue growth targets. As time progresses, he will compare the company's actual revenue growth from young consumers to the marketing department's expenditures to see if his strategy is working or requires adjustment.

Source: Stephanie Kang, "New Balance Steps up Marketing Drive," *The Wall Street Journal*, March 21, 2008, p. B3.

Responsibility Accounting

Most of what we say in this chapter and in the next three chapters is concerned with *responsibility accounting*. The basic idea underlying **responsibility accounting** is that a manager should be held responsible for those items—and *only* those items—that the manager can actually control to a significant extent. Each line item (i.e., revenue or cost) in the budget is the responsibility of a manager who is held responsible for subsequent deviations between budgeted goals and actual results. In effect, responsibility accounting *personalizes* accounting information by holding individuals responsible for revenues and costs. This concept is central to any effective planning and control system. Someone must be held responsible for each cost or else no one will be responsible and the cost will inevitably grow out of control.

What happens if actual results do not measure up to the budgeted goals? The manager is not necessarily penalized. However, the manager should take the initiative to understand the sources of significant favorable or unfavorable discrepancies, should take steps to correct unfavorable discrepancies and to exploit and replicate favorable discrepancies, and should be prepared to explain discrepancies and the steps taken to correct or exploit them to higher management. The point of an effective responsibility accounting system is to make sure that nothing "falls through the cracks," that the organization reacts quickly and appropriately to deviations from its plans, and that the organization learns from the feedback it gets by comparing budgeted goals to actual results. The point is *not* to penalize individuals for missing targets.

IN BUSINESS

SMALL BUSINESSES ARE CUTTING THE NUMBER OF EMPLOYEES

Costume Specialists had to decrease its workforce by 20% when the economy tanked. However, when sales began to surge the company did not budget for a workforce expansion because it had learned to function more efficiently with fewer employees. Many other small businesses have also "tightened their budgeting belts" by choosing to operate with fewer employees. In some cases, these companies have used methods such as cross-training their employees to improve efficiency. However, in other cases they are using contract workers instead of hiring full-time employees to avoid the cost of providing full-time employees with fringe benefits such as health insurance.

Source: Sarah E. Needleman, "Entrepreneurs Prefer to Keep Staffs Lean," *The Wall Street Journal*, March 2, 2010, p. B5.

Choosing a Budget Period

Operating budgets ordinarily cover a one-year period corresponding to the company's fiscal year. Many companies divide their budget year into four quarters. The first quarter is then subdivided into months, and monthly budgets are developed. The last three quarters may be carried in the budget as quarterly totals only. As the year progresses, the figures for the second quarter are broken down into monthly amounts, then the third-quarter figures are broken down, and so forth. This approach has the advantage of requiring periodic review and reappraisal of budget data throughout the year.

Continuous or *perpetual budgets* are sometimes used. A **continuous** or **perpetual budget** is a 12-month budget that rolls forward one month (or quarter) as the current month (or quarter) is completed. In other words, one month (or quarter) is added to the end of the budget as each month (or quarter) comes to a close. This approach keeps managers focused at least one year ahead so that they do not become too narrowly focused on short-term results.

In this chapter, we will look at one-year operating budgets. However, using basically the same techniques, operating budgets can be prepared for periods that extend over many years. It may be difficult to accurately forecast sales and other data much beyond a year, but even rough estimates can be invaluable in uncovering potential problems and opportunities that would otherwise be overlooked.

The Self-Imposed Budget

The success of a budget program is largely determined by the way a budget is developed. Oftentimes, the budget is imposed from above, with little participation by lower-level managers. However, in the most successful budget programs, managers actively participate in preparing their own budgets. Imposing expectations from above and then penalizing employees who do not meet those expectations will generate resentment rather than cooperation and commitment. In fact, many managers believe that being empowered to create their own *self-imposed budgets* is the most effective method of budget preparation. A **self-imposed budget** or **participative budget** is a budget that is prepared with the full cooperation and participation of managers at all levels.

Self-imposed budgets have a number of advantages:

1. Individuals at all levels of the organization are recognized as members of the team whose views and judgments are valued by top management.
2. Budget estimates prepared by front-line managers are often more accurate and reliable than estimates prepared by top managers who have less intimate knowledge of markets and day-to-day operations.
3. Motivation is generally higher when individuals participate in setting their own goals than when the goals are imposed from above. Self-imposed budgets create commitment.
4. A manager who is not able to meet a budget that has been imposed from above can always say that the budget was unrealistic and impossible to meet. With a self-imposed budget, this claim cannot be made.

Self-imposed budgeting has two important limitations. First, lower-level managers may make suboptimal budgeting recommendations if they lack the broad strategic perspective possessed by top managers. Second, self-imposed budgeting may allow lower-level managers to create too much *budgetary slack*. Because the manager who creates the budget will be held accountable for actual results that deviate from the budget, the manager will have a natural tendency to submit a budget that is easy to attain (i.e., the manager will build slack into the budget). For this reason, budgets prepared by lower-level managers should be scrutinized by higher levels of management. Questionable items should be discussed and modified as appropriate. Without such a review, self-imposed budgets may fail to support the organization's strategy or may be too slack, resulting in suboptimal performance.

Unfortunately, many companies do not use self-imposed budgeting. Instead, top managers often initiate the budgeting process by issuing profit targets. Lower-level managers are directed to prepare budgets that meet those targets. The difficulty is that the targets set by top managers may be unrealistically high or may allow too much slack. If the targets are too high and employees know they are unrealistic, motivation will suffer. If the targets allow too much slack, waste will occur. Unfortunately, top managers are often not in a position to know whether the targets are appropriate. Admittedly, a self-imposed budgeting system may lack sufficient strategic direction and lower-level managers may be tempted to build slack into their budgets. Nevertheless, because of the motivational advantages of self-imposed budgets, top managers should be cautious about imposing inflexible targets from above.

Human Factors in Budgeting

The success of a budget program also depends on whether top management uses the budget to pressure or blame employees. Using budgets to blame employees breeds hostility, tension, and mistrust rather than cooperation and productivity. Unfortunately, the budget is too often used as a pressure device and excessive emphasis is placed on "meeting the budget" under all circumstances. Rather than being used as a weapon, the budget should be used as a positive instrument to assist in establishing goals, measuring operating results, and isolating areas that need attention.

346   Chapter 8

The budgeting process is also influenced by the fact that bonuses are often based on meeting and exceeding budgets. Typically, no bonus is paid unless the budget is met. The bonus often increases when the budget target is exceeded, but the bonus is usually capped out at some level. For obvious reasons, managers who have such a bonus plan or whose performance is evaluated based on meeting budget targets usually prefer to be evaluated based on highly achievable budgets. Moreover, highly achievable budgets may help build a manager's confidence and generate greater commitment to the budget while also reducing the likelihood that a manager will engage in undesirable behavior at the end of budgetary periods to secure bonus compensation. So, while some experts argue that budget targets should be very challenging and should require managers to stretch to meet their goals, in practice, most companies set their budget targets at "highly achievable" levels.

The Master Budget: An Overview

The **master budget** consists of a number of separate but interdependent budgets that formally lay out the company's sales, production, and financial goals. The master budget culminates in a cash budget, a budgeted income statement, and a budgeted balance sheet. Exhibit 8–1 provides an overview of the various parts of the master budget and how they are related.

EXHIBIT 8–1
The Master Budget
Interrelationships

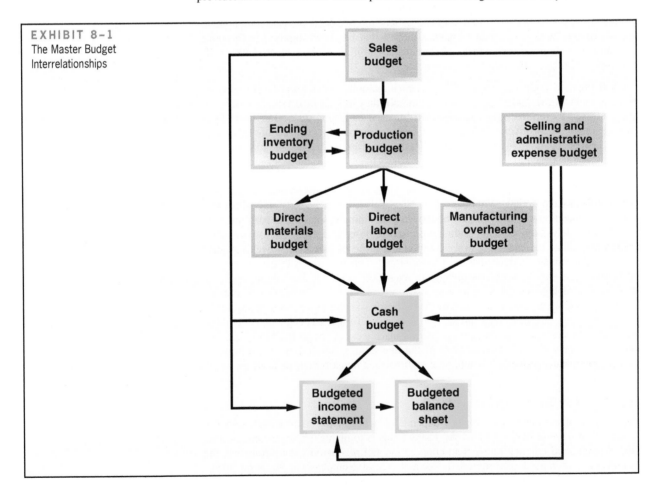

The first step in the budgeting process is the preparation of the **sales budget**, which is a detailed schedule showing the expected sales for the budget period. An accurate sales budget is the key to the entire budgeting process. As illustrated in Exhibit 8–1, all other parts of the master budget depend on the sales budget. If the sales budget is inaccurate, the rest of the budget will be inaccurate. The sales budget is based on the company's sales forecast, which may require the use of sophisticated mathematical models and statistical tools that are beyond the scope of this course.

The sales budget influences the variable portion of the selling and administrative expense budget and it feeds into the production budget, which defines how many units need to be produced during the budget period. The production budget in turn is used to determine the direct materials, direct labor, and manufacturing overhead budgets. Once a company has prepared these three manufacturing cost budgets, it can prepare the ending finished goods inventory budget.

The master budget concludes with the preparation of a cash budget, income statement, and balance sheet. Information from the sales budget, selling and administrative expense budget, and the manufacturing cost budgets all influence the preparation of the *cash budget*. A **cash budget** is a detailed plan showing how cash resources will be acquired and used. The budgeted income statement provides an estimate of net income for the budget period and it relies on information from the sales budget, ending finished goods inventory budget, selling and administrative expense budget, and the cash budget. The final schedule of the master budget is the balance sheet, which estimates a company's assets, liabilities, and stockholders' equity at the end of a budget period.

Seeing the Big Picture

The 10 schedules contained in a master budget can be overwhelming; therefore, it is important to see the big picture in two respects. First, a master budget for a manufacturing company is designed to answer 10 key questions as follows:

1. How much sales revenue will we earn?
2. How much cash will we collect from customers?
3. How much raw material will we need to purchase?
4. How much manufacturing cost (including direct materials, direct labor, and manufacturing overhead) will we incur?
5. How much cash will we pay to our suppliers and our direct laborers, and how much will we pay for manufacturing overhead resources?
6. What is the total cost that will be transferred from finished goods inventory to cost of goods sold?
7. How much selling and administrative expense will we incur and how much cash will we pay related to those expenses?
8. How much money will we borrow from or repay to lenders—including interest?
9. How much net operating income will we earn?
10. What will our balance sheet look like at the end of the budget period?

Second, it is important to understand that many of the schedules in a master budget hinge on a variety of estimates and assumptions that managers must make when preparing those schedules. Exhibit 8–2 summarizes the questions that underlie these estimates and assumptions for seven of the schedules included in a master budget. As you study the forthcoming budget schedules, keep these two "big picture" insights in mind—that the budget is designed to answer 10 key questions and that it is based on various estimates and assumptions—because they will help you understand *why* and *how* a master budget is created.

EXHIBIT 8–2
Estimates and Assumptions for a Master Budget

Sales budget:
1. What are the budgeted unit sales?
2. What is the budgeted selling price per unit?
3. What percentage of accounts receivable will be collected in the current and subsequent periods?

Production budget:
1. What percentage of next period's unit sales needs to be maintained in ending finished goods inventory?

Direct materials budget:
1. How many units of raw material are needed to make one unit of finished goods?
2. What is the budgeted cost for one unit of raw material?
3. What percentage of next period's production needs should be maintained in ending raw materials inventory?
4. What percentage of raw material purchases will be paid in the current and subsequent periods?

Direct labor budget:
1. How many direct labor-hours are required per unit of finished goods?
2. What is the budgeted direct labor wage rate per hour?

Manufacturing overhead budget:
1. What is the budgeted variable overhead cost per unit of the allocation base?
2. What is the total budgeted fixed overhead cost per period?
3. What is the budgeted depreciation expense on factory assets per period?

Selling and administrative expense budget:
1. What is the budgeted variable selling and administrative expense per unit sold?
2. What is the total budgeted fixed selling and administrative expense per period?
3. What is the budgeted depreciation expense on non-factory assets per period?

Cash budget:
1. What is the budgeted minimum cash balance?
2. What are our estimated expenditures for noncurrent asset purchases and dividends?
3. What is the estimated interest rate on borrowed funds?

Preparing the Master Budget

**MANAGERIAL
ACCOUNTING IN ACTION**
THE ISSUE

Tom Wills is the majority stockholder and chief executive officer of Hampton Freeze, Inc., a company he started in 2012. The company makes premium popsicles using only natural ingredients and featuring exotic flavors such as tangy tangerine and minty mango. The company's business is highly seasonal, with most of the sales occurring in spring and summer.

In 2013, the company's second year of operations, a major cash crunch in the first and second quarters almost forced the company into bankruptcy. In spite of this cash crunch, 2013 turned out to be a very successful year in terms of both cash flow and net income. Partly as a result of that harrowing experience, Tom decided toward the end of 2013 to hire a professional financial manager. Tom interviewed several promising candidates for the job and settled on Larry Giano, who had considerable experience in the packaged foods industry. In the job interview, Tom questioned Larry about the steps he would take to prevent a recurrence of the 2013 cash crunch:

Tom: As I mentioned earlier, we are going to end 2013 with a very nice profit. What you may not know is that we had some very big financial problems this year.
Larry: Let me guess. You ran out of cash sometime in the first or second quarter.
Tom: How did you know?
Larry: Most of your sales are in the second and third quarter, right?

Tom: Sure, everyone wants to buy popsicles in the spring and summer, but nobody wants them when the weather turns cold.

Larry: So you don't have many sales in the first quarter?

Tom: Right.

Larry: And in the second quarter, which is the spring, you are producing like crazy to fill orders?

Tom: Sure.

Larry: Do your customers, the grocery stores, pay you the day you make your deliveries?

Tom: Are you kidding? Of course not.

Larry: So in the first quarter, you don't have many sales. In the second quarter, you are producing like crazy, which eats up cash, but you aren't paid by your customers until long after you have paid your employees and suppliers. No wonder you had a cash problem. I see this pattern all the time in food processing because of the seasonality of the business.

Tom: So what can we do about it?

Larry: The first step is to predict the magnitude of the problem before it occurs. If we can predict early in the year what the cash shortfall is going to be, we can go to the bank and arrange for credit before we really need it. Bankers tend to be leery of panicky people who show up begging for emergency loans. They are much more likely to make the loan if you look like you are in control of the situation.

Tom: How can we predict the cash shortfall?

Larry: You can put together a cash budget. In fact, while you're at it, you might as well do a master budget. You'll find it well worth the effort because we can use a master budget to estimate the financial statement implications of numerous "what-if" questions. For example, with the click of a mouse we can answer questions such as: What-if unit sales are 10% less than our original forecast, what will be the impact on profits? Or, what if we increase our selling price by 15% and unit sales drop by 5%, what will be the impact on profits?

Tom: That sounds great Larry! Not only do we need a cash budget, but I would love to have a master budget that could quickly answer the types of "what-if" questions that you just described. As far as I'm concerned, the sooner you get started, the better.

With the full backing of Tom Wills, Larry Giano set out to create a master budget for the company for the year 2014. In his planning for the budgeting process, Larry drew up the following list of documents that would be a part of the master budget:

1. A sales budget, including a schedule of expected cash collections.
2. A production budget (a merchandise purchases budget would be used in a merchandising company).
3. A direct materials budget, including a schedule of expected cash disbursements for purchases of materials.
4. A direct labor budget.
5. A manufacturing overhead budget.
6. An ending finished goods inventory budget.
7. A selling and administrative expense budget.
8. A cash budget.
9. A budgeted income statement.
10. A budgeted balance sheet.

Larry felt it was important to have everyone's cooperation in the budgeting process, so he asked Tom to call a companywide meeting to explain the budgeting process. At the meeting there was initially some grumbling, but Tom was able to convince nearly everyone of the necessity for planning and getting better control over spending. It helped that the cash crisis earlier in the year was still fresh in everyone's minds. As much as some people disliked the idea of budgets, they liked their jobs more.

EXHIBIT 8–3
Hampton Freeze: The Beginning Balance Sheet

	A	B	C
1	**Hampton Freeze, Inc.**		
2	**Balance Sheet**		
3	**December 31, 2013**		
4			
5	**Assets**		
6	Current assets:		
7	Cash	$ 42,500	
8	Accounts receivable	90,000	
9	Raw materials inventory (21,000 pounds)	4,200	
10	Finished goods inventory (2,000 cases)	26,000	
11	Total current assets		$162,700
12	Plant and equipment:		
13	Land	80,000	
14	Buildings and equipment	700,000	
15	Accumulated depreciation	(292,000)	
16	Plant and equipment, net		488,000
17	Total assets		$650,700
18			
19	**Liabilities and Stockholders' Equity**		
20	Current liabilities:		
21	Accounts payable		$ 25,800
22	Stockholders' equity:		
23	Common stock	$ 175,000	
24	Retained earnings	449,900	
25	Total stockholders' equity		624,900
26	Total liabilities and stockholders' equity		$650,700
27			

Beginning Balance Sheet / Budgeting Assump

In the months that followed, Larry worked closely with all of the managers involved in the master budget, gathering data from them and making sure that they understood and fully supported the parts of the master budget that would affect them.

The interdependent documents that Larry Giano prepared for Hampton Freeze are Schedules 1 through 10 of the company's master budget. In this section, we will study these schedules as well as the beginning balance sheet and the budgeting assumptions that Larry included in his master budget to help answer the types of "what-if" questions that he discussed with Tom Wills.

The Beginning Balance Sheet

Exhibit 8–3 shows the first tab included in Larry's Microsoft Excel master budget file. It contains Hampton Freeze's beginning balance sheet as of December 31, 2013. Larry included this balance sheet in his master budget file so that he could link some of this data to subsequent schedules. For example, as you'll eventually see, he used cell references within Excel to link the beginning accounts receivable balance of $90,000 to the schedule of expected cash collections. He also used cell references to link the beginning cash balance of $42,500 to the cash budget.

The Budgeting Assumptions

Exhibit 8–4 shows the second tab included in Larry's master budget file. It is labeled Budgeting Assumptions and it contains all of Hampton Freeze's answers to the questions summarized in Exhibit 8–2. The data included in Exhibit 8–4 summarize the estimates and assumptions that provide the foundation for Hampton Freeze's entire master

EXHIBIT 8-4
Hampton Freeze: Budgeting Assumptions

	A	B	C	D	E	F
1	Hampton Freeze, Inc.					
2	Budgeting Assumptions					
3	For the Year Ended December 31, 2014					
4						
5		*All 4 Quarters*		*Quarter*		
			1	*2*	*3*	*4*
6	*Sales Budget*					
7	Budgeted sales in cases		10,000	30,000	40,000	20,000
8	Selling price per case	$ 20.00				
9	Percentage of sales collected in the quarter of sale	70%				
10	Percentage of sales collected in the quarter after sale	30%				
11						
12	*Production Budget*					
13	Percentage of next quarter's sales in ending finished goods inventory	20%				
14						
15	*Direct Materials Budget*					
16	Pounds of sugar per case	15				
17	Cost per pound of sugar	$ 0.20				
18	Percentage of next quarter's production needs in ending inventory	10%				
19	Percentage of purchases paid in the quarter purchased	50%				
20	Percentage of purchases paid in the quarter after purchase	50%				
21						
22	*Direct Labor Budget*					
23	Direct labor-hours required per case	0.40				
24	Direct labor cost per hour	$ 15.00				
25						
26	*Manufacturing Overhead Budget*					
27	Variable manufacturing overhead per direct labor-hour	$ 4.00				
28	Fixed manufacturing overhead per quarter	$ 60,600				
29	Depreciation per quarter	$ 15,000				
30						
31						
32	*Selling and Administrative Expense Budget*					
33	Variable selling and administrative expense per case	$ 1.80				
34	Fixed selling and administrative expense per quarter:					
35	Advertising	$ 20,000				
36	Executive salaries	$ 55,000				
37	Insurance	$ 10,000				
38	Property tax	$ 4,000				
39	Depreciation	$ 10,000				
40						
41	*Cash Budget*					
42	Minimum cash balance	$ 30,000				
43	Equipment purchases		$ 50,000	$ 40,000	$ 20,000	$ 20,000
44	Dividends	$ 8,000				
45	Simple interest rate per quarter	3%				
46						

Beginning Balance Sheet **Budgeting Assumptions** Schedule 1 Schedule 2 Sche

*For simplicity, we assume that all quarterly estimates, except quarterly unit sales and equipment purchases, will be the same for all four quarters.

budget, so it is important to familiarize yourself with this information now. Beginning with the estimates underlying the sales budget, Exhibit 8–4 shows that Hampton Freeze's budgeted quarterly unit sales are 10,000, 30,000, 40,000, and 20,000 cases. Its budgeted selling price is $20 per case. The company expects to collect 70% of its credit sales in the quarter of sale, and the remaining 30% of credit sales will be collected in the quarter after sale.

Exhibit 8–4 also shows that the production budget is based on the assumption that Hampton Freeze will maintain ending finished goods inventory equal to 20% of the next quarter's unit sales. In terms of the company's only direct material, high fructose sugar, it budgets 15 pounds of sugar per case of popsicles at a cost of $0.20 per pound.[1]

---

[1] While popsicle manufacturing is likely to involve other raw materials, such as popsicle sticks and packaging materials, for simplicity, we have limited our scope to high fructose sugar.

352

Chapter 8

It expects to maintain ending raw materials inventory equal to 10% of the raw materials needed to satisfy the following quarter's production. In addition, the company plans to pay for 50% of its material purchases within the month of purchase and the remaining 50% in the following month.

Continuing with a summary of Exhibit 8–4, the two key assumptions underlying the direct labor budget are that 0.40 direct labor-hours are required per case of popsicles and the direct labor cost per hour is $15. The manufacturing overhead budget is based on three underlying assumptions—the variable overhead cost per direct labor-hour is $4.00, the total fixed overhead per quarter is $60,600, and the quarterly depreciation on factory assets is $15,000. Exhibit 8–4 also shows that the budgeted variable selling and administrative expense per case of popsicles is $1.80 and the fixed selling and administrative expenses per quarter include advertising ($20,000), executive salaries ($55,000), insurance ($10,000), property tax ($4,000), and depreciation expense ($10,000). The remaining budget assumptions depicted in Exhibit 8–4 pertain to the cash budget. The company expects to maintain a minimum cash balance each quarter of $30,000; it plans to make quarterly equipment purchases of $50,000, $40,000, $20,000, and $20,000;[2] it plans to pay quarterly dividends of $8,000; and it expects to pay simple interest on borrowed money of 3% per quarter.

Before reading further, it is important to understand why Larry created the Budgeting Assumptions tab shown in Exhibit 8–4. He did it because it simplifies the process of using a master budget to answer "what-if" questions. For example, assume that Larry wanted to answer the question: What-if we increase the selling price per unit by $2 and expect sales to drop by 1,000 units per quarter, what would be the impact on profits? With a properly constructed Budgeting Assumptions tab, Larry would only need to make a few adjustments to the data within this tab and the formulas embedded in each of the budget schedules would automatically update the projected financial results. This is much simpler than attempting to adjust data inputs within each of the master budget schedules.

The Sales Budget

LO8–2
Prepare a sales budget, including a schedule of expected cash collections.

Schedule 1 contains Hampton Freeze's sales budget for 2014. As you study this schedule, keep in mind that all of its numbers are derived from cell references to the Budgeting Assumptions tab and formulas—none of the numbers appearing in the schedule were actually keyed into their respective cells. Furthermore, it bears emphasizing that all remaining schedules in the master budget are prepared in the same fashion—they rely almost exclusively on cell references and formulas.

For the year, Hampton Freeze expects to sell 100,000 cases of popsicles at a price of $20 per case for total budgeted sales of $2,000,000. The budgeted unit sales for each quarter (10,000, 30,000, 40,000, and 20,000) come from cells C7 through F7 in the Budgeting Assumptions tab shown in Exhibit 8–4, and the selling price per case ($20.00) comes from cell B8 in the Budgeting Assumptions tab. Schedule 1 also shows that the company's expected cash collections for 2014 are $1,970,000. The accounts receivable balance of $90,000 that is collected in the first quarter comes from cell B8 of the beginning balance sheet shown in Exhibit 8–3. All other cash collections rely on the estimated cash collection percentages from cells B9 and B10 of the Budgeting Assumptions tab. For example, Schedule 1 shows that the budgeted sales for the first quarter equal $200,000. In the first quarter, Hampton Freeze expects to collect 70% of this amount, or $140,000. In the second quarter, the company expects to collect the remaining 30% of this amount, or $60,000.

---

[2] For simplicity, we assume that depreciation on these newly acquired assets is included in the quarterly depreciation estimates included in the Budgeting Assumptions tab.

SCHEDULE 1

	A	B	C	D	E	F
1			Hampton Freeze, Inc.			
2			Sales Budget			
3			For the Year Ended December 31, 2014			
4						
5				Quarter		
6		1	2	3	4	Year
7	Budgeted unit sales (in cases)	10,000	30,000	40,000	20,000	100,000
8	Selling price per unit	$ 20.00	$ 20.00	$ 20.00	$ 20.00	$ 20.00
9	Total sales	$200,000	$600,000	$800,000	$400,000	$2,000,000
10						
11		70%	30%			
12		Schedule of Expected Cash Collections				
13	Beginning accounts receivable[1]	$ 90,000				$ 90,000
14	First-quarter sales[2]	140,000	$ 60,000			200,000
15	Second-quarter sales[3]		420,000	$ 180,000		600,000
16	Third-quarter sales[4]			560,000	$ 240,000	800,000
17	Fourth-quarter sales[5]	-	-	-	280,000	280,000
18	Total cash collections[6]	$230,000	$480,000	$740,000	$520,000	$1,970,000

Budgeting Assumptions   Schedule 1   Schedule 2   Schedule 3   Sc

[1]Cash collections from last year's fourth-quarter sales. See the beginning balance sheet in Exhibit 8–3.
[2]$200,000 × 70%; $200,000 × 30%.
[3]$600,000 × 70%; $600,000 × 30%.
[4]$800,000 × 70%; $800,000 × 30%.
[5]$400,000 × 70%.
[6]Uncollected fourth-quarter sales ($120,000) appear as accounts receivable on the company's end-of-year budgeted balance sheet (see Schedule 10 on page 366).

The Production Budget

The production budget is prepared after the sales budget. The **production budget** lists the number of units that must be produced to satisfy sales needs and to provide for the desired ending finished goods inventory. Production needs can be determined as follows:

LO8–3
Prepare a production budget.

Budgeted unit sales	XXXX
Add desired units of ending finished goods inventory . . .	XXXX
Total needs	XXXX
Less units of beginning finished goods inventory	XXXX
Required production in units	XXXX

Note the production requirements are influenced by the desired level of the ending finished goods inventory. Inventories should be carefully planned. Excessive inventories tie up funds and create storage problems. Insufficient inventories can lead to lost sales or last-minute, high-cost production efforts.

Schedule 2 contains the production budget for Hampton Freeze. The budgeted sales data come from cells B7 through E7 of the sales budget. The desired ending finished goods inventory for the first quarter of 6,000 cases is computed by multiplying budgeted sales from the second quarter (30,000 cases) by the desired ending finished goods inventory percentage (20%) shown in cell B13 of the Budgeting Assumptions tab. The total needs for the first quarter (16,000 cases) are determined by adding together the budgeted sales of 10,000 cases for the quarter and the desired ending inventory of 6,000 cases. As discussed above, the ending inventory is intended to provide some cushion in the event

SCHEDULE 2

	A	B	C	D	E	F
		Hampton Freeze, Inc.				
3						
4		Production Budget				
5		For the Year Ended December 31, 2014				
6		(in cases)				
7						Assumed
8				Quarter		
9		1	2	3	4	Year
10	Budgeted unit sales (Schedule 1)	10,000	30,000	40,000	20,000	100,000
11	Add desired units of ending finished goods inventory*	6,000	8,000	4,000	3,000	3,000
12	Total needs	16,000	38,000	44,000	23,000	103,000
13	Less units of beginning finished goods inventory†	2,000	6,000	8,000	4,000	2,000
14	Required production in units	14,000	32,000	36,000	19,000	101,000

Budgeting Assumptions | Schedule 1 | **Schedule 2** | Schedule 3 | Sch

*Twenty percent of next quarter's sales. For example, the second-quarter sales are 30,000 cases. Therefore, the desired ending inventory of finished goods for the first quarter would be 20% × 30,000 cases = 6,000 cases.
†The beginning inventory in each quarter is the same as the prior quarter's ending inventory.

that problems develop in production or sales increase unexpectedly. Because the company already has 2,000 cases in beginning finished goods inventory (as shown in the beginning balance sheet in Exhibit 8–3), only 14,000 cases need to be produced in the first quarter.

Pay particular attention to the Year column to the right of the production budget in Schedule 2. In some cases (e.g., budgeted sales, total needs, and required production), the amount listed for the year is the sum of the quarterly amounts for the item. In other cases, (e.g., desired units of ending finished goods inventory and units of beginning finished goods inventory), the amount listed for the year is not simply the sum of the quarterly amounts. From the standpoint of the entire year, the beginning finished goods inventory is the same as the beginning finished goods inventory for the first quarter—it is *not* the sum of the beginning finished goods inventories for all four quarters. Similarly, from the standpoint of the entire year, the ending finished goods inventory, which Larry Giano assumed to be 3,000 units, is the same as the ending finished goods inventory for the fourth quarter—it is *not* the sum of the ending finished goods inventories for all four quarters. It is important to pay attention to such distinctions in all schedules that follow.

Inventory Purchases—Merchandising Company

Hampton Freeze prepares a production budget because it is a *manufacturing* company. If it were a *merchandising* company, instead it would prepare a **merchandise purchases budget** showing the amount of goods to be purchased from suppliers during the period. The format of the merchandise purchases budget is shown below:

Budgeted cost of goods sold	XXXX
Add desired ending merchandise inventory	XXXX
Total needs	XXXX
Less beginning merchandise inventory	XXXX
Required purchases	XXXX

A merchandising company would prepare a merchandise purchases budget, such as the one above, for each item carried in stock. The merchandise purchases budget can be expressed in dollars (as shown above) or in units. The top line of a merchandise purchases budget based on units would say Budgeted unit sales instead of Budgeted cost of goods sold.

A merchandise purchases budget is usually accompanied by a schedule of expected cash disbursements for merchandise purchases. The format of this schedule mirrors the approach used for the schedule of expected cash disbursements for purchases of materials that is illustrated at the bottom of Schedule 3 on page 356.

The Direct Materials Budget

A *direct materials budget* is prepared after the production requirements have been computed. The **direct materials budget** details the raw materials that must be purchased to fulfill the production budget and to provide for adequate inventories. The required purchases of raw materials are computed as follows:

LO8–4

Prepare a direct materials budget, including a schedule of expected cash disbursements for purchases of materials.

Required production in units of finished goods	XXXX
Units of raw materials needed per unit of finished goods . .	XXXX
Units of raw materials needed to meet production	XXXX
Add desired units of ending raw materials inventory	XXXX
Total units of raw materials needed	XXXX
Less units of beginning raw materials inventory	XXXX
Units of raw materials to be purchased	XXXX
Unit cost of raw materials	XXXX
Cost of raw materials to be purchased	XXXX

Schedule 3 contains the direct materials budget for Hampton Freeze. The first line of this budget contains the required production for each quarter, which is taken directly from cells B14 through E14 of the production budget (Schedule 2). The second line of the direct materials budget recognizes that 15 pounds of sugar (see cell B16 from the Budgeting Assumptions tab) are required to make one case of popsicles. The third line of the budget presents the raw materials needed to meet production. For example, in the first quarter, the required production of 14,000 cases is multiplied by 15 pounds to equal 210,000 pounds of sugar needed to meet production. The fourth line shows the desired units of ending raw materials inventory. For the first quarter this amount is computed by multiplying the raw materials needed to meet production in the second quarter of 480,000 pounds by the desired ending inventory percentage of 10% as shown in cell B18 of the Budgeting Assumptions tab. The desired units of ending raw materials inventory of 48,000 pounds is added to 210,000 pounds to provide the total units of raw materials needed of 258,000 pounds. However, because the company already has 21,000 pounds of sugar in beginning inventory (as shown in cell A9 in the beginning balance sheet in Exhibit 8–3), only 237,000 pounds of sugar need to be purchased in the first quarter. Because the budgeted cost of raw materials per pound is $0.20 (see cell B17 from the Budgeting Assumptions tab), the cost of raw material to be purchased in the first quarter is $47,400. For the entire year, the company plans to purchase $303,300 of raw materials.

Schedule 3 also shows that the company's expected cash disbursements for material purchases for 2014 are $301,200. The accounts payable balance of $25,800 that is paid in the first quarter comes from cell C21 of the beginning balance sheet shown in Exhibit 8–3. All other cash disbursement computations rely on the estimated cash payment percentages (both of which are 50%) from cells B19 and B20 of the Budgeting Assumptions tab. For example, Schedule 3 shows that the budgeted raw material purchases for the first quarter equal $47,400. In the first quarter, Hampton Freeze expects to pay 50% of this amount, or $23,700. In the second quarter, the company expects to pay the remaining 50% of this amount, or $23,700.

SCHEDULE 3

	A	B	C	D	E	F	G
3		Hampton Freeze, Inc.					
4		Direct Materials Budget					
5		For the Year Ended December 31, 2014					
6						Assumed	
7				Quarter			
8			1	2	3	4	Year
9	Required production in cases (Schedule 2)	14,000	32,000	36,000	19,000	101,000
10	Units of raw materials needed per case	15	15	15	15	15
11	Units of raw materials needed to meet production	210,000	480,000	540,000	285,000	1,515,000
12	Add desired units of ending raw materials inventory[1]	48,000 10%	54,000 10%	28,500 10%	22,500	22,500
13	Total units of raw materials needed	258,000	534,000	568,500	307,500	1,537,500
14	Less units of beginning raw materials inventory	21,000	48,000	54,000	28,500	21,000
15	Units of raw materials to be purchased	237,000	486,000	514,500	279,000	1,516,500
16	Cost of raw materials per pound	$ 0.20	$ 0.20	$ 0.20	$ 0.20	$ 0.20
17	Cost of raw materials to be purchased	$47,400	$97,200	$102,900	$55,800	$ 303,300
18							
19			50%	50%			
20	**Schedule of Expected Cash Disbursements for Purchases of Materials**						
21							
22	Beginning accounts payable[2]	$25,800				$ 25,800
23	First-quarter purchases[3]	23,700	$23,700			47,400
24	Second-quarter purchases[4]		48,600	$ 48,600		97,200
25	Third-quarter purchases[5]			51,450	$51,450	102,900
26	Fourth-quarter purchases[6]				27,900	27,900
27	Total cash disbursements for materials	$49,500	$72,300	$100,050	$79,350	$ 301,200

Schedule 3 / Schedule 4 / Schedule 5 / Schedule 6 / Schedule 7 / S

[1]Ten percent of the next quarter's production needs. For example, the second-quarter production needs are 480,000 pounds. Therefore, the desired ending inventory for the first quarter would be 10% × 480,000 pounds = 48,000 pounds.
[2]Cash payments for last year's fourth-quarter purchases. See the beginning-of-year balance sheet in Exhibit 8–3 on page 350.
[3]$47,400 × 50%; $47,400 × 50%.
[4]$97,200 × 50%; $97,200 × 50%.
[5]$102,900 × 50%; $102,900 × 50%.
[6]$55,800 × 50%. Unpaid fourth-quarter purchases ($27,900) appear as accounts payable on the company's end-of-year budgeted balance sheet (see Schedule 10 on page 366).

The Direct Labor Budget

LO8–5
Prepare a direct labor budget.

The **direct labor budget** shows the direct labor-hours required to satisfy the production budget. By knowing in advance how much labor time will be needed throughout the budget year, the company can develop plans to adjust the labor force as the situation requires. Companies that neglect the budgeting process run the risk of facing labor shortages or having to hire and lay off workers at awkward times. Erratic labor policies lead to insecurity, low morale, and inefficiency.

The direct labor budget for Hampton Freeze is shown in Schedule 4. The first line in the direct labor budget consists of the required production for each quarter, which is taken directly from cells B14 through E14 of the production budget (Schedule 2). The direct labor requirement for each quarter is computed by multiplying the number of units to be produced in each quarter by the 0.40 direct labor-hours required to make one unit (see cell B23 from the Budgeting Assumptions tab). For example, 14,000 cases are to be produced in the first quarter and each case requires 0.40 direct labor-hours, so a total of 5,600 direct labor-hours (14,000 cases × 0.40 direct labor-hours per case) will be required in the first quarter. The direct labor requirements are then translated into budgeted direct labor costs. How this is done will depend on the company's labor policy. In Schedule 4, Hampton Freeze has assumed that the direct labor force will be adjusted as the work requirements change from quarter to quarter. In that case, the direct labor cost is computed by simply multiplying the direct labor-hour requirements by the direct labor rate of $15 per hour (see cell B24 from the Budgeting Assumptions tab). For example, the direct labor cost in the first quarter is $84,000 (5,600 direct labor-hours × $15 per direct labor-hour).

SCHEDULE 4

	Hampton Freeze, Inc. Direct Labor Budget For the Year Ended December 31, 2014					
			Quarter			
		1	2	3	4	Year
7 Required production in cases (Schedule 2)		14,000	32,000	36,000	19,000	101,000
8 Direct labor-hours per case		0.40	0.40	0.40	0.40	0.40
9 Total direct labor-hours needed		5,600	12,800	14,400	7,600	40,400
10 Direct labor cost per hour		$ 15.00	$ 15.00	$ 15.00	$ 15.00	$ 15.00
11 Total direct labor cost		$ 84,000	$ 192,000	$ 216,000	$ 114,000	$ 606,000

Schedule 1 | Schedule 2 | Schedule 3 | **Schedule 4** | Schedule 5 | Schedule

*This schedule assumes that the direct labor workforce will be fully adjusted to the total direct labor-hours needed each quarter.

However, many companies have employment policies or contracts that prevent them from laying off and rehiring workers as needed. Suppose, for example, that Hampton Freeze has 25 workers who are classified as direct labor, but each of them is guaranteed at least 480 hours of pay each quarter at a rate of $15 per hour. In that case, the minimum direct labor cost for a quarter would be computed as follows:

$$25 \text{ workers} \times 480 \text{ hours per worker} \times \$15 \text{ per hour} = \$180,000$$

Note that in this case the direct costs shown in the first and fourth quarters of Schedule 4 would have to be increased to $180,000.

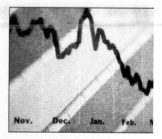

IN BUSINESS

MANAGING LABOR COSTS IN A DIFFICULT ECONOMY

When the economy sours, many companies choose to lay off employees. While this tactic lowers costs in the short run, it also lowers the morale and productivity of retained employees, sacrifices the institutional knowledge possessed by terminated employees, and increases future recruiting and training costs. Hypertherm Inc. has not fired a permanent employee since its founding in 1968, instead responding to economic hardship by eliminating overtime, cutting temporary staff, delaying capital investments, shifting cross-trained employees to new job responsibilities, and implementing a four-day work week. Hypertherm's employees regularly share their process improvement ideas with the company because they know if they eliminate non–value-added portions of their job responsibilities the company will redeploy them rather than eliminate non–value-added labor costs by firing them.

Source: Cari Tuna, "Some Firms Cut Costs Without Resorting to Layoffs," *The Wall Street Journal*, December 15, 2008, p. B4.

The Manufacturing Overhead Budget

The **manufacturing overhead budget** lists all costs of production other than direct materials and direct labor. Schedule 5 shows the manufacturing overhead budget for Hampton Freeze. At Hampton Freeze, manufacturing overhead is separated into variable and fixed components. As shown in the Budgeting Assumptions tab (Exhibit 8–4), the variable component is $4 per direct labor-hour and the fixed component is $60,600 per quarter. Because the variable component of manufacturing overhead depends on direct labor, the first line in the manufacturing overhead budget consists of the budgeted direct labor-hours from cells B9 through E9 of the direct labor budget (Schedule 4). The budgeted direct labor-hours in each quarter are multiplied by the variable rate to determine the variable component of manufacturing overhead. For example, the variable manufacturing overhead for the first quarter is $22,400 (5,600 direct labor-hours × $4.00 per direct labor-hour). This is added to the fixed manufacturing overhead for the quarter to determine the total manufacturing overhead for the quarter of $83,000 ($22,400 + $60,600).

LO8–6

Prepare a manufacturing overhead budget.

SCHEDULE 5

A	B	C	D	E	F
1	Hampton Freeze, Inc.				
2	Manufacturing Overhead Budget				
3	For the Year Ended December 31, 2014				
4					
5			Quarter		
6		1	2	3	4	Year
7 Budgeted direct labor-hours (Schedule 4)	5,600	12,800	14,400	7,600	40,400
8 Variable manufacturing overhead rate	$ 4.00	$ 4.00	$ 4.00	$ 4.00	$ 4.00
9 Variable manufacturing overhead	$ 22,400	$ 51,200	$ 57,600	$ 30,400	$ 161,600
10 Fixed manufacturing overhead	60,600	60,600	60,600	60,600	242,400
11 Total manufacturing overhead	83,000	111,800	118,200	91,000	404,000
12 Less depreciation	15,000	15,000	15,000	15,000	60,000
13 Cash disbursements for manufacturing overhead	$ 68,000	$ 96,800	$ 103,200	$ 76,000	$ 344,000
14					
15 Total manufacturing overhead (a)					$ 404,000
16 Budgeted direct labor-hours (b)					40,400
17 Predetermined overhead rate for the year (a)÷(b)					$10.00
18					
19					

Schedule 3 / Schedule 4 / **Schedule 5** / Schedule 6 / Schedule 7 / Schedule 8

A few words about fixed costs and the budgeting process are in order. In most cases, fixed costs are the costs of supplying capacity to make products, process purchase orders, handle customer calls, and so on. The amount of capacity that will be required depends on the expected level of activity for the period. If the expected level of activity is greater than the company's current capacity, then fixed costs may have to be increased. Or, if the expected level is appreciably below the company's current capacity, then it may be desirable to decrease fixed costs if possible. However, once the level of the fixed costs has been determined in the budget, the costs really are fixed. The time to adjust fixed costs is during the budgeting process. An activity-based costing system can help to determine the appropriate level of fixed costs at budget time by answering questions like, "How many clerks will we need to process the anticipated number of purchase orders next year?" For simplicity, all of the budgeting examples in this book assume that the appropriate levels of fixed costs have already been determined.

The last line of Schedule 5 for Hampton Freeze shows the budgeted cash disbursements for manufacturing overhead. Because some of the overhead costs are not cash outflows, the total budgeted manufacturing overhead costs must be adjusted to determine the cash disbursements for manufacturing overhead. At Hampton Freeze, the only significant noncash manufacturing overhead cost is depreciation, which is $15,000 per quarter (see cell B29 in the Budgeting Assumptions tab). These noncash depreciation charges are deducted from the total budgeted manufacturing overhead to determine the expected cash disbursements. Hampton Freeze pays all overhead costs involving cash disbursements in the quarter incurred. Note that the company's predetermined overhead rate for the year is $10 per direct labor-hour, which is determined by dividing the total budgeted manufacturing overhead for the year by the total budgeted direct labor-hours for the year.

The Ending Finished Goods Inventory Budget

After completing Schedules 1–5, Larry Giano had all of the data he needed to compute the unit product cost for the units produced during the budget year. This computation was needed for two reasons: first, to help determine cost of goods sold on the budgeted income statement; and second, to value ending inventories on the budgeted balance sheet. The cost of unsold units is computed on the **ending finished goods inventory budget**.[3]

---

[3] For simplicity, the beginning balance sheet and the ending finished goods inventory budget both report a unit product cost of $13. For purposes of answering "what-if" questions, this schedule would assume a FIFO inventory flow. In other words, the ending inventory would consist solely of units that are produced during the budget year.

SCHEDULE 6

	A	B	C	D	E	F	G	H	I
1				Hampton Freeze, Inc.					
2				Ending Finished Goods Inventory Budget					
3				(absorption costing basis)					
4				For the Year Ended December 31, 2014					
5									
6		Item	Quantity			Cost		Total	
7	Production cost per case:								
8	Direct materials		15.00	pounds	$ 0.20	per pound	$	3.00	
9	Direct labor		0.40	hours	$15.00	per hour		6.00	
10	Manufacturing overhead		0.40	hours	$10.00	per hour		4.00	
11	Unit product cost						$	13.00	
12									
13	Budgeted finished goods inventory:								
14	Ending finished goods inventory in cases (Schedule 2)							3,000	
15	Unit product cost (see above)						$	13.00	
16	Ending finished goods inventory in dollars						$	39,000	
17									

Schedule 3 / Schedule 4 / Schedule 5 / **Schedule 6** / Sch

Larry Giano considered using variable costing to prepare Hampton Freeze's budget statements, but he decided to use absorption costing instead because the bank would very likely require absorption costing. He also knew that it would be easy to convert the absorption costing financial statements to a variable costing basis later. At this point, the primary concern was to determine what financing, if any, would be required in 2014 and then to arrange for that financing from the bank.

The unit product cost computations are shown in Schedule 6. For Hampton Freeze, the absorption costing unit product cost is $13 per case of popsicles—consisting of $3 of direct materials, $6 of direct labor, and $4 of manufacturing overhead. The manufacturing overhead is applied to units of product at the rate of $10 per direct labor-hour. The budgeted carrying cost of the ending inventory is $39,000.

The Selling and Administrative Expense Budget

The **selling and administrative expense budget** lists the budgeted expenses for areas other than manufacturing. In large organizations, this budget would be a compilation of many smaller, individual budgets submitted by department heads and other persons responsible for selling and administrative expenses. For example, the marketing manager would submit a budget detailing the advertising expenses for each budget period.

Schedule 7 contains the selling and administrative expense budget for Hampton Freeze. Like the manufacturing overhead budget, the selling and administrative expense budget is divided into variable and fixed cost components. Consequently, budgeted sales in cases for each quarter are entered at the top of the schedule. These data are taken from cells B7 through E7 of the sales budget (Schedule 1). The budgeted variable selling and administrative expenses are determined by multiplying the budgeted cases sold by the variable selling and administrative expense of $1.80 per case (see cell B33 from the Budgeting Assumptions tab). For example, the budgeted variable selling and administrative

LO8–7
Prepare a selling and administrative expense budget.

SCHEDULE 7

	A	B	C	D	E	F
1	Hampton Freeze, Inc.					
2	Selling and Administrative Expense Budget					
3	For the Year Ended December 31, 2014					
4						
5				Quarter		
6		1	2	3	4	Year
7	Budgeted units sales (Schedule 1)	10,000	30,000	40,000	20,000	100,000
8	Variable selling and administrative expense per case	$ 1.80	$ 1.80	$ 1.80	$ 1.80	$ 1.80
9	Variable selling and administrative expense	$ 18,000	$ 54,000	$ 72,000	$ 36,000	$180,000
10	Fixed selling and administrative expenses:					
11	Advertising	20,000	20,000	20,000	20,000	80,000
12	Executive salaries	55,000	55,000	55,000	55,000	220,000
13	Insurance	10,000	10,000	10,000	10,000	40,000
14	Property taxes	4,000	4,000	4,000	4,000	16,000
15	Depreciation	10,000	10,000	10,000	10,000	40,000
16	Total fixed selling and administrative expenses	99,000	99,000	99,000	99,000	396,000
17	Total selling and administrative expenses	117,000	153,000	171,000	135,000	576,000
18	Less depreciation	10,000	10,000	10,000	10,000	40,000
19	Cash disbursements for selling and administrative expenses	$107,000	$143,000	$161,000	$125,000	$536,000
20						

Schedule 5 / Schedule 6 / **Schedule 7** / Schedule 8 / Schedule 9 / Schedule 10

expense for the first quarter is $18,000 (10,000 cases × $1.80 per case). The fixed selling and administrative expenses of $99,000 per quarter (see cells B35 through B39 from the Budgeting Assumptions tab) are then added to the variable selling and administrative expenses to arrive at the total budgeted selling and administrative expenses. Finally, to determine the cash disbursements for selling and administrative items, the total budgeted selling and administrative expense is adjusted by subtracting any noncash selling and administrative expenses (in this case, just depreciation).[4]

The Cash Budget

LO8–8
Prepare a cash budget.

The cash budget is composed of four major sections:

1. The receipts section.
2. The disbursements section.
3. The cash excess or deficiency section.
4. The financing section.

The receipts section lists all of the cash inflows, except from financing, expected during the budget period. Generally, the major source of receipts is from sales. The disbursements section summarizes all cash payments that are planned for the budget period. These payments include raw materials purchases, direct labor payments, manufacturing overhead costs, and so on, as contained in their respective budgets. In addition, other cash disbursements such as equipment purchases and dividends are listed.

---

[4] Other adjustments might need to be made for differences between cash flows on the one hand and revenues and expenses on the other hand. For example, if property taxes are paid twice a year in installments of $8,000 each, the expense for property tax would have to be "backed out" of the total budgeted selling and administrative expenses and the cash installment payments added to the appropriate quarters to determine the cash disbursements. Similar adjustments might also need to be made in the manufacturing overhead budget. We generally ignore these complications in this chapter.

The cash excess or deficiency section is computed as follows:

Beginning cash balance	XXXX
Add cash receipts	XXXX
Total cash available	XXXX
Less cash disbursements	XXXX
Excess (deficiency) of cash available over disbursements	XXXX

If a cash deficiency exists during any budget period or if there is a cash excess during any budget period that is less than the minimum required cash balance, the company will need to borrow money. Conversely, if there is a cash excess during any budget period that is greater than the minimum required cash balance, the company can invest the excess funds or repay principal and interest to lenders.

IN BUSINESS

MISMATCHED CASH FLOWS—CLIMBING THE HILLS AND VALLEYS

The Washington Trails Association (WTA) is a private, nonprofit organization primarily concerned with protecting and maintaining hiking trails in the state of Washington. Some 2,000 WTA volunteer workers donate more than 80,000 hours per year maintaining trails in rugged landscapes on federal, state, and private lands. The organization is supported by membership dues, voluntary contributions, grants, and some contract work for government.

The organization's income and expenses are erratic—although somewhat predictable—over the course of the year as shown in the chart below. Expenses tend to be highest in the spring and summer when most of the trail maintenance work is done. However, income spikes in December well after the expenses have been incurred. With cash outflows running ahead of cash inflows for much of the year, it is very important for the WTA to carefully plan its cash budget and to maintain adequate cash reserves to be able to pay its bills.

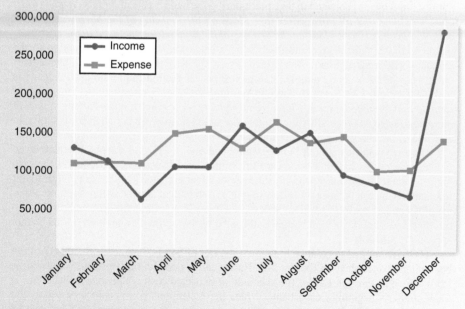

Note: Total income and total expense are approximately equal over the course of the year.

Sources: Conversation with Elizabeth Lunney, President of the Washington Trails Association; WTA documents; and the WTA website www.wta.org.

SCHEDULE 8

Hampton Freeze, Inc.
Cash Budget
For the Year Ended December 31, 2014

	Schedule	Quarter				Year
		1	2	3	4	
Beginning cash balance		$ 42,500	$ 36,000	$ 33,900	$ 165,650	$ 42,500
Add cash receipts:						
Collections from customers	1	230,000	480,000	740,000	520,000	1,970,000
Total cash available		272,500	516,000	773,900	685,650	2,012,500
Less cash disbursements:						
Direct materials	3	49,500	72,300	100,050	79,350	301,200
Direct labor	4	84,000	192,000	216,000	114,000	606,000
Manufacturing overhead	5	68,000	96,800	103,200	76,000	344,000
Selling and administrative	7	107,000	143,000	161,000	125,000	536,000
Equipment purchases		50,000	40,000	20,000	20,000	130,000
Dividends		8,000	8,000	8,000	8,000	32,000
Total cash disbursements		366,500	552,100	608,250	422,350	1,949,200
Excess (deficiency) of cash available over disbursements		(94,000)	(36,100)	165,650	263,300	63,300
Financing:						
Borrowings (at the beginnings of quarters)		130,000	70,000	-	-	200,000
Repayments (at end of the year)		-	-	-	(200,000)	(200,000)
Interest		-	-	-	(21,900)	(21,900)
Total financing		130,000	70,000	-	(221,900)	(21,900)
Ending cash balance		$ 36,000	$ 33,900	$ 165,650	$ 41,400	$ 41,400

Schedule 5 / Schedule 6 / Schedule 7 / **Schedule 8** / Schedule 9 / Schedule 10

The financing section of the cash budget details the borrowings and principal and interest repayments projected to take place during the budget period. *In this chapter, we'll always assume that all borrowings take place on the first day of the borrowing period and all repayments take place on the last day of the final period included in the cash budget.* To calculate borrowings and interest payments, you'll need to pay attention to the company's desired minimum cash balance and to the terms of the company's loan agreement with the bank. For example, Hampton Freeze's desired minimum cash balance is $30,000 (see cell B42 in the Budgeting Assumptions tab). Furthermore, *we are going to assume that Hampton Freeze's loan agreement stipulates that it must borrow money in increments of $10,000* and that it must pay simple interest of 3% per quarter (as shown in cell B43 of the Budgeting Assumptions tab).[5]

The cash balances at both the beginning and end of the year may be adequate even though a serious cash deficit occurs at some point during the year. Consequently, the cash budget should be broken down into time periods that are short enough to capture major fluctuations in cash balances. While a monthly cash budget is most common, some organizations budget cash on a weekly or even daily basis. At Hampton Freeze, Larry Giano has prepared a quarterly cash budget that can be further refined as necessary. This budget appears in Schedule 8.[6]

The beginning cash balance in the first quarter of $42,500 agrees with cell B7 of the beginning balance sheet in Exhibit 8–3. Each quarter's collections from customers come from cells B18 through E18 of the schedule of expected cash collections in Schedule 1. Each quarter's beginning cash balance plus the collections from customers equals the total cash available. For example, in the first quarter, the beginning cash balance of

---

[5] We use simple interest rather than compound interest throughout the chapter for simplicity.

[6] The format for the statement of cash flows, which is discussed in a later chapter, may also be used for the cash budget.

$42,500 plus the collections from customers of $230,000 equals the total cash available of $272,500.

The disbursements section of the cash budget includes six types of cash disbursements. Each quarter's cash disbursements for direct materials come from cells B27 through E27 of the schedule of expected cash disbursements for materials (see Schedule 3). The quarterly cash payments for direct labor were calculated in cells B11 through E11 of the direct labor budget (see Schedule 4), whereas the quarterly cash payments related to manufacturing overhead were calculated in cells B13 through E13 of the manufacturing overhead budget (see Schedule 5). The quarterly cash payments for selling and administrative expenses come from cells B19 through E19 of the selling and administrative expense budget (see Schedule 7). So putting it all together, in the first quarter, the cash disbursements for direct materials ($49,500), direct labor ($84,000), manufacturing overhead ($68,000), and selling and administrative expenses ($107,000), plus equipment purchases of $50,000 and a dividend of $8,000 (see cells C43 and B44 from the Budgeting Assumptions tab) equals the total cash disbursements of $366,500.

Each quarter's total cash available minus its total disbursements equals the excess (deficiency) of cash available over disbursements. For example, in the first quarter the total cash available of $272,500 minus the total disbursements of $366,500 results in a cash deficiency of $94,000. The excess or deficiency of cash directly influences whether Hampton Freeze will need to borrow money as shown in the Financing section of the cash budget.

The first row in the financing section of the cash budget relates to projected borrowings. In any period where a company's excess of cash available over disbursements is greater than its desired minimum cash balance, the company will not need to borrow money during that period. In the case of Hampton Freeze, the company wants to maintain a minimum cash balance of $30,000; therefore, it will not need to borrow money in any quarter where its excess of cash available over disbursements is greater than $30,000. However, in the first quarter of 2014 Hampton Freeze estimates that it will have a cash deficiency of $94,000; consequently, the company's minimum required borrowings at the beginning of the first quarter would be computed as follows:

Required Borrowings at the Beginning of the First Quarter

Desired ending cash balance	$ 30,000
Plus deficiency of cash available over disbursements	94,000
Minimum required borrowings	$124,000

Recall that the bank requires that loans be made in increments of $10,000. Because Hampton Freeze needs to borrow at least $124,000, it will have to borrow $130,000.

In the second quarter of 2014 Hampton Freeze estimates that it will have another cash deficiency of $36,100; therefore, the company's minimum required borrowings at the beginning of the second quarter would be computed as follows:

Required Borrowings at the Beginning of the Second Quarter

Desired ending cash balance	$30,000
Plus deficiency of cash available over disbursements	36,100
Minimum required borrowings	$66,100

Again, recall that the bank requires that loans be made in increments of $10,000. Because Hampton Freeze needs to borrow at least $66,100 at the beginning of the second quarter, the company will have to borrow $70,000 from the bank.

In the third and fourth quarters, Hampton Freeze has an excess of cash available over disbursements that is greater than $30,000, so it will not need to borrow money in these two quarters. Notice that in the third quarter Hampton Freeze has excess cash of $165,650, yet the cash budget does not include any principal or interest repayments during this quarter. This occurs because in this chapter, we always assume that the company will, as far as it is able, repay the loan plus accumulated interest on the *last day of the final period* included in the cash budget. Because Hampton Freeze has excess cash of $263,300 in the fourth quarter, on the last day of the fourth quarter, it would be able to repay the $200,000 that it borrowed from the lender plus $21,900 of interest computed as follows:

Interest on the $130,000 borrowed at the beginning of the first quarter:	
$130,000 × 0.01 per month × 12 months*	$15,600
Interest on the $70,000 borrowed at the beginning of the second quarter:	
$70,000 × 0.01 per month × 9 months*	6,300
Total interest accrued to the end of the fourth quarter	$21,900

* Simple, rather than compounded, interest is assume for simplicity

The ending cash balance for each period is computed by taking the excess (deficiency) of cash available over disbursements plus the total financing. For example, in the first quarter, Hampton Freeze's cash deficiency of $(94,000) plus its total financing of $130,000 equals its ending cash balance of $36,000. The ending cash balance for each quarter then becomes the beginning cash balance for the next quarter. Also notice that the amounts under the Year column in the cash budget are not always the sum of the amounts for the four quarters. In particular, the beginning cash balance for the year is the same as the beginning cash balance for the first quarter and the ending cash balance for the year is the same as the ending cash balance for the fourth quarter.

IN BUSINESS

NEW INSPECTIONS PINCH CASH FLOWS

Herald Metal and Plastic Works is a Chinese toy manufacturer that produces Star Wars action figures and G.I. Joes for Hasbro Inc. in the United States. The company used to ship its toys to America immediately after they rolled off the production line. However, this changed when American consumers discovered that some Chinese companies were using poisonous lead-based paint in their manufacturing processes. The Chinese government now requires toy manufacturers to store finished goods in warehouses for anywhere from three weeks to two months until its inspectors certify them for export.

Herald Metal and Plastic Works borrows money from lenders to buy raw materials and pay laborers to make its toys. The company is struggling to repay its loans because the government's inspection process delays cash receipts from customers.

Source: Chi-Chu Tschang, "Bottlenecks in Toyland," *BusinessWeek*, October 15, 2007, p. 52.

The Budgeted Income Statement

LO8–9
Prepare a budgeted income statement.

Schedule 9 contains the budgeted income statement for Hampton Freeze. All of the revenues and expenses shown on the budgeted income statement come from the data in the beginning balance sheet and the data developed in Schedules 1–8. The sales of

SCHEDULE 9

	A	B	C
1	Hampton Freeze, Inc.		
2	Budgeted Income Statement		
3	For the Year Ended December 31, 2014		
4			
5		*Schedules*	
6	Sales	1	$ 2,000,000
7	Cost of goods sold	1, 6	1,300,000
8	Gross margin		700,000
9	Selling and administrative expenses	7	576,000
10	Net operating Income		124,000
11	Interest expense	8	21,900
12	Net Income		$ 102,100
13			

Schedule 8 | **Schedule 9** | Schedule 10

$2,000,000 come from cell F9 of the sales budget (Schedule 1). The cost of goods sold of $1,300,000 is computed in two steps. First, cost of goods sold includes the 2,000 units of finished goods inventory from the beginning balance sheet, which have a total cost of $26,000 (see Exhibit 8–3). Second, it includes 98,000 units produced and sold in 2014 multiplied by $13 per unit (see Schedule 6), for a total of $1,274,000. Combining these two steps, the total cost of the 100,000 units sold (see Schedule 1) is $1,300,000 ($26,000 + $1,274,000).[7] The selling and administrative expenses of $576,000 come from cell F17 of the selling and administrative expenses budget (Schedule 7). Finally, the interest expense of $21,900 comes from cell G23 of the cash budget (Schedule 8).

The budgeted income statement is one of the key schedules in the budget process. It shows the company's planned profit and serves as a benchmark against which subsequent company performance can be measured. Because Larry Giano created a Budgeting Assumptions tab in his Excel file and linked all of his budget schedules together using properly constructed Excel formulas, he can make changes to his underlying budgeting assumptions and instantly see the impact of the change on all of the schedules and on net income. For example, if Larry wanted to estimate the profit impact if fourth quarter sales are 18,000 cases instead of 20,000 cases, he would simply change the 20,000 cases shown in cell F7 of his Budgeting Assumptions worksheet to 18,000 cases. The revised net income of $87,045 would instantly appear in cell C12 of the budgeted income statement.

The Budgeted Balance Sheet

The budgeted balance sheet is developed using data from the balance sheet from the beginning of the budget period (see Exhibit 8–3) and data contained in the various schedules. Hampton Freeze's budgeted balance sheet accompanied by explanations of how the numbers were derived is presented in Schedule 10.

After completing the master budget, Larry Giano took the documents to Tom Wills, chief executive officer of Hampton Freeze, for his review.

LO8–10
Prepare a budgeted balance sheet.

MANAGERIAL ACCOUNTING IN ACTION
THE WRAP-UP

---

[7] This explanation assumes a FIFO inventory flow assumption.

SCHEDULE 10

	A	B	C	D	E
1	Hampton Freeze, Inc.				
2	Budgeted Balance Sheet				
3	December 31, 2014				
4					
5	*Assets*				
6	Current assets:				
7	Cash	$ 41,400	(a)		
8	Accounts receivable	120,000	(b)		
9	Raw materials inventory	4,500	(c)		
10	Finished goods inventory	39,000	(d)		
11	Total current assets			$ 204,900	
12	Plant and equipment:				
13	Land	80,000	(e)		
14	Buildings and equipment	830,000	(f)		
15	Accumulated depreciation	(392,000)	(g)		
16	Plant and equipment, net			518,000	
17	Total assets			$ 722,900	
18					
19	*Liabilities and Stockholders' Equity*				
20	Current liabilities:				
21	Accounts payable (raw materials)			$ 27,900	(h)
22	Stockholders' equity:				
23	Common stock, no par	$ 175,000	(i)		
24	Retained earnings	520,000	(j)		
25	Total stockholders' equity			695,000	
26	Total liabilities and stockholders' equity			$ 722,900	
27					

Schedule 8 / Schedule 9 / **Schedule 10**

Explanations of December 31, 2014, balance sheet figures:
(a) From cell G25 of the cash budget (Schedule 8).
(b) Thirty percent of fourth-quarter sales, from Schedule 1 ($400,000 × 30% = $120,000).
(c) From the direct materials budget (Schedule 3). Cell E12 multiplied by cell E16. In other words, 22,500 pounds × $0.20 per pound = $4,500.
(d) From cell H16 of the ending finished goods inventory budget (Schedule 6).
(e) From cell B13 of the beginning balance sheet (Exhibit 8–3).
(f) Cell B14 of the beginning balance sheet (Exhibit 8–3) plus cell G16 from the cash budget (Schedule 8). In other words, $700,000 + $130,000 = $830,000.
(g) The beginning balance of $292,000 (from cell B15 of the beginning balance sheet in Exhibit 8–3) plus the depreciation of $60,000 included in cell F12 of the manufacturing overhead budget (Schedule 5) plus depreciation expense of $40,000 included in cell F18 in the selling and administrative expense budget (Schedule 8). In other words, $292,000 + $60,000 + $40,000 = $392,000.
(h) One-half of fourth-quarter raw materials purchases, from Schedule 3.
(i) From cell B23 of the beginning balance sheet (Exhibit 8–3).
(j)

December 31, 2013, balance	$449,900
Add net income, from cell C12 of Schedule 9	102,100
	552,000
Deduct dividends paid, from cell G17 of Schedule 8	32,000
December 31, 2014, balance	$520,000

Master Budgeting **367**

Larry: Here's the budget. Overall, the income is excellent, and the net cash flow for the entire year is positive.

Tom: Yes, but I see on this cash budget that we have the same problem with negative cash flows in the first and second quarters that we had last year.

Larry: That's true. I don't see any way around that problem. However, there is no doubt in my mind that if you take this budget to the bank today, they'll approve an open line of credit that will allow you to borrow enough money to make it through the first two quarters without any problem.

Tom: Are you sure? They didn't seem very happy to see me last year when I came in for an emergency loan.

Larry: Did you repay the loan on time?

Tom: Sure.

Larry: I don't see any problem. You won't be asking for an emergency loan this time. The bank will have plenty of warning. And with this budget, you have a solid plan that shows when and how you are going to pay off the loan. Trust me, they'll go for it. Also, keep in mind that the master budget contains all the embedded formulas you'll need to answer the types of "what-if" questions that we discussed earlier. If you want to calculate the financial impact of changing any of your master budget's underlying estimates or assumptions, you can do it with the click of a mouse!

Tom: This sounds fabulous Larry. Thanks for all of your work on this project.

LOCAL MUNICIPALITIES CLOSE BUDGET DEFICITS

Municipalities across the Unites States face a combined budget deficit of $56 to $86 billion. Many cities are responding to their budget shortfalls by outsourcing services to avoid the crushing cost of providing employee benefits. For example, San Jose, California, decided to put a dent in its $118 million budget deficit by outsourcing its janitorial services. The town of Lakewood, California, contracts 40% of its municipal services to outside vendors. Maywood, California, took the drastic step of outsourcing all of its public services to outside contractors. This small town of 40,000 residents terminated all municipal employees and hired the Los Angeles County Sheriff to oversee public safety.

Sources: Tamara Audi, "Cities Rent Police, Janitors to Save Cash," *The Wall Street Journal*, July 19, 2010, p. A3.

Summary

This chapter describes the budgeting process and shows how the various operating budgets relate to each other. The sales budget is the foundation for a master budget. Once the sales budget has been set, the production budget and the selling and administrative expense budget can be prepared because they depend on how many units are to be sold. The production budget determines how many units are to be produced, so after it is prepared, the various manufacturing cost budgets can be prepared. All of these budgets feed into the cash budget and the budgeted income statement and balance sheet. The parts of the master budget are connected in many ways. For example, the schedule of expected cash collections, which is completed in connection with the sales budget, provides data for both the cash budget and the budgeted balance sheet.

The material in this chapter is just an introduction to master budgeting. In later chapters, we will see how budgets are used to control day-to-day operations and how they are used in performance evaluation.

Review Problem: Budget Schedules

Mynor Corporation manufactures and sells a seasonal product that has peak sales in the third quarter. The following information concerns operations for Year 2—the coming year—and for the first two quarters of Year 3:

a. The company's single product sells for $8 per unit. Budgeted unit sales for the next six quarters are as follows (all sales are on credit):

	Year 2 Quarter				Year 3 Quarter	
	1	2	3	4	1	2
Budgeted unit sales	40,000	60,000	100,000	50,000	70,000	80,000

b. Sales are collected in the following pattern: 75% in the quarter the sales are made, and the remaining 25% in the following quarter. On January 1, Year 2, the company's balance sheet showed $65,000 in accounts receivable, all of which will be collected in the first quarter of the year. Bad debts are negligible and can be ignored.

c. The company desires an ending finished goods inventory at the end of each quarter equal to 30% of the budgeted unit sales for the next quarter. On December 31, Year 1, the company had 12,000 units on hand.

d. Five pounds of raw materials are required to complete one unit of product. The company requires ending raw materials inventory at the end of each quarter equal to 10% of the following quarter's production needs. On December 31, Year 1, the company had 23,000 pounds of raw materials on hand.

e. The raw material costs $0.80 per pound. Raw material purchases are paid for in the following pattern: 60% paid in the quarter the purchases are made, and the remaining 40% paid in the following quarter. On January 1, Year 2, the company's balance sheet showed $81,500 in accounts payable for raw material purchases, all of which will be paid for in the first quarter of the year.

Required:
Prepare the following budgets and schedules for the year, showing both quarterly and total figures:
1. A sales budget and a schedule of expected cash collections.
2. A production budget.
3. A direct materials budget and a schedule of expected cash payments for purchases of materials.

Solution to Review Problem

1. The sales budget is prepared as follows:

	Year 2 Quarter				Year
	1	2	3	4	
Budgeted unit sales	40,000	60,000	100,000	50,000	250,000
Selling price per unit	× $8	× $8	× $8	× $8	× $8
Total sales	$320,000	$480,000	$800,000	$400,000	$2,000,000

Based on the budgeted sales above, the schedule of expected cash collections is prepared as follows:

	Year 2 Quarter				Year
	1	2	3	4	
Beginning accounts receivable	$ 65,000				$ 65,000
First-quarter sales ($320,000 × 75%, 25%)	240,000	$ 80,000			320,000
Second-quarter sales ($480,000 × 75%, 25%)		360,000	$120,000		480,000
Third-quarter sales ($800,000 × 75%, 25%)			600,000	$200,000	800,000
Fourth-quarter sales ($400,000 × 75%)				300,000	300,000
Total cash collections	$305,000	$440,000	$720,000	$500,000	$1,965,000

2. Based on the sales budget in units, the production budget is prepared as follows:

	Year 2 Quarter					Year 3 Quarter	
	1	2	3	4	Year	1	2
Budgeted unit sales	40,000	60,000	100,000	50,000	250,000	70,000	80,000
Add desired ending finished goods inventory*	18,000	30,000	15,000	21,000†	21,000	24,000	
Total needs	58,000	90,000	115,000	71,000	271,000	94,000	
Less beginning finished goods inventory	12,000	18,000	30,000	15,000	12,000	21,000	
Required production	46,000	72,000	85,000	56,000	259,000	73,000	

*30% of the following quarter's budgeted unit sales.
†30% of the budgeted Year 3 first-quarter sales.

3. Based on the production budget, raw materials will need to be purchased during the year as follows:

	Year 2 Quarter					Year 3 Quarter
	1	2	3	4	Year 2	1
Required production in units of finished goods	46,000	72,000	85,000	56,000	259,000	73,000
Units of raw materials needed per unit of finished goods	× 5	× 5	× 5	× 5	× 5	× 5
Units of raw materials needed to meet production	230,000	360,000	425,000	280,000	1,295,000	365,000
Add desired units of ending raw materials inventory*	36,000	42,500	28,000	36,500†	36,500	
Total units of raw materials needed	266,000	402,500	453,000	316,500	1,331,500	
Less units of beginning raw materials inventory	23,000	36,000	42,500	28,000	23,000	
Units of raw materials to be purchased	243,000	366,500	410,500	288,500	1,308,500	
Unit cost of raw materials	× $0.80	× $0.80	× $0.80	× $0.80	× $0.80	
Cost of raw materials to be purchased	$194,400	$293,200	$328,400	$230,800	$1,046,800	

*10% of the following quarter's production needs in pounds.
†10% of the Year 3 first-quarter production needs in pounds.

Based on the raw material purchases above, expected cash payments are computed as follows:

	Year 2 Quarter				
	1	2	3	4	Year 2
Beginning accounts payable	$ 81,500				$ 81,500
First-quarter purchases ($194,400 × 60%, 40%)	116,640	$ 77,760			194,400
Second-quarter purchases ($293,200 × 60%, 40%)		175,920	$117,280		293,200
Third-quarter purchases ($328,400 × 60%, 40%)			197,040	$131,360	328,400
Fourth-quarter purchases ($230,800 × 60%)				138,480	138,480
Total cash disbursements	$198,140	$253,680	$314,320	$269,840	$1,035,980

Glossary

Budget A detailed plan for the future that is usually expressed in formal quantitative terms. (p. 343)

Cash budget A detailed plan showing how cash resources will be acquired and used over a specific time period. (p. 346)

Continuous budget A 12-month budget that rolls forward one month as the current month is completed. (p. 344)

Control The process of gathering feedback to ensure that a plan is being properly executed or modified as circumstances change. (p. 343)

Direct labor budget A detailed plan that shows the direct labor-hours required to fulfill the production budget. (p. 355)

370   Chapter 8

Direct materials budget A detailed plan showing the amount of raw materials that must be purchased to fulfill the production budget and to provide for adequate inventories. (p. 355)

Ending finished goods inventory budget A budget showing the dollar amount of unsold finished goods inventory that will appear on the ending balance sheet. (p. 358)

Manufacturing overhead budget A detailed plan showing the production costs, other than direct materials and direct labor, that will be incurred over a specified time period. (p. 357)

Master budget A number of separate but interdependent budgets that formally lay out the company's sales, production, and financial goals and that culminates in a cash budget, budgeted income statement, and budgeted balance sheet. (p. 346)

Merchandise purchases budget A detailed plan used by a merchandising company that shows the amount of goods that must be purchased from suppliers during the period. (p. 354)

Participative budget See *Self-imposed budget.* (p. 345)

Perpetual budget See *Continuous budget.* (p. 344)

Planning Developing goals and preparing budgets to achieve those goals. (p. 343)

Production budget A detailed plan showing the number of units that must be produced during a period in order to satisfy both sales and inventory needs. (p. 352)

Responsibility accounting A system of accountability in which managers are held responsible for those items of revenue and cost—and only those items—over which they can exert significant control. The managers are held responsible for differences between budgeted and actual results. (p. 344)

Sales budget A detailed schedule showing expected sales expressed in both dollars and units. (p. 346)

Self-imposed budget A method of preparing budgets in which managers prepare their own budgets. These budgets are then reviewed by higher-level managers, and any issues are resolved by mutual agreement. (p. 345)

Selling and administrative expense budget A detailed schedule of planned expenses that will be incurred in areas other than manufacturing during a budget period. (p. 359)

Questions

8–1 What is a budget? What is budgetary control?

8–2 Discuss some of the major benefits to be gained from budgeting.

8–3 What is meant by the term *responsibility accounting?*

8–4 What is a master budget? Briefly describe its contents.

8–5 Why is the sales forecast the starting point in budgeting?

8–6 "As a practical matter, planning and control mean exactly the same thing." Do you agree? Explain.

8–7 Why is it a good idea to create a "Budgeting Assumptions" tab when creating a master budget in Microsoft Excel?

8–8 What is a self-imposed budget? What are the major advantages of self-imposed budgets? What caution must be exercised in their use?

8–9 How can budgeting assist a company in planning its workforce staffing levels?

8–10 "The principal purpose of the cash budget is to see how much cash the company will have in the bank at the end of the year." Do you agree? Explain.

Multiple-choice questions are provided on the text website at www.mhhe.com/garrison15e.

Applying Excel

Available with McGraw-Hill's *Connect* Accounting.

LO8-2, LO8-3, LO8-4

The Excel worksheet form that appears on the next page is to be used to recreate the Review Problem on pages 368–369. Download the workbook containing this form from the Online Learning Center at www.mhhe.com/garrison15e. *On the website you will also receive instructions about how to use this worksheet form.*

	A	B	C	D	E	F	G	H	I
1	Chapter 8: Applying Excel								
2									
3	Data		Year 2 Quarter				Year 3 Quarter		
4			1	2	3	4	1	2	
5	Budgeted unit sales		40,000	60,000	100,000	50,000	70,000	80,000	
6									
7	• Selling price per unit	$8							
8	• Accounts receivable, beginning balance	$65,000							
9	• Sales collected in the quarter sales are made	75%							
10	• Sales collected in the quarter after sales are made	25%							
11	• Desired ending finished goods inventory is	30%	of the budgeted unit sales of the next quarter						
12	• Finished goods inventory, beginning	12,000	units						
13	• Raw materials required to produce one unit	5	pounds						
14	• Desired ending inventory of raw materials is	10%	of the next quarter's production needs						
15	• Raw materials inventory, beginning	23,000	pounds						
16	• Raw material costs	$0.80	per pound						
17	• Raw materials purchases are paid	60%	in the quarter the purchases are made						
18	and	40%	in the quarter following purchase						
19	• Accounts payable for raw materials, beginning balance	$81,500							
20									
21	*Enter a formula into each of the cells marked with a ? below*								
22	**Review Problem: Budget Schedules**								
23									
24	Construct the sales budget		Year 2 Quarter				Year 3 Quarter		
25			1	2	3	4	1	2	
26	Budgeted unit sales		?	?	?	?	?	?	
27	Selling price per unit		?	?	?	?	?	?	
28	Total sales		?	?	?	?	?	?	
29									
30	Construct the schedule of expected cash collections		Year 2 Quarter						
31			1	2	3	4	Year		
32	Beginning balance accounts receivable		?				?		
33	First-quarter sales		?	?			?		
34	Second-quarter sales			?	?		?		
35	Third-quarter sales				?	?	?		
36	Fourth-quarter sales					?	?		
37	Total cash collections		?	?	?	?	?		
38									
39	Construct the production budget		Year 2 Quarter					Year 3 Quarter	
40			1	2	3	4	Year	1	2
41	Budgeted unit sales		?	?	?	?	?	?	?
42	Add desired ending finished goods inventory		?	?	?	?	?	?	
43	Total needs		?	?	?	?	?	?	
44	Less beginning finished goods inventory		?	?	?	?	?	?	
45	Required production in units		?	?	?	?	?	?	
46									
47	Construct the raw materials purchases budget		Year 2 Quarter					Year 3 Quarter	
48			1	2	3	4	Year	1	
49	Required production (units)		?	?	?	?	?	?	
50	Raw materials required to produce one unit (pounds)		?	?	?	?	?	?	
51	Production needs (pounds)		?	?	?	?	?	?	
52	Add desired ending inventory of raw materials (pounds)		?	?	?	?	?		
53	Total needs (pounds)		?	?	?	?	?		
54	Less beginning inventory of raw materials (pounds)		?	?	?	?	?		
55	Raw materials to be purchased (pounds)		?	?	?	?	?		
56	Cost of raw materials per pound		?	?	?	?	?		
57	Cost of raw materials to be purchased		?	?	?	?	?		
58									
59	Construct the schedule of expected cash payments		Year 2 Quarter						
60			1	2	3	4	Year		
61	Beginning balance accounts payable		?				?		
62	First-quarter purchases		?	?			?		
63	Second-quarter purchases			?	?		?		
64	Third-quarter purchases				?	?	?		
65	Fourth-quarter purchases					?	?		
66	Total cash disbursements		?	?	?	?	?		
67									

H ◀ ▶ H Chapter 8 Form / Filled in Chapter 8 Form / Chapter 8 Formulas / Chapter 8 Requiremen

You should proceed to the requirements below only after completing your worksheet.

Required:

1. Check your worksheet by changing the budgeted unit sales in Quarter 2 of Year 2 in cell C5 to 75,000 units. The total expected cash collections for the year should now be $2,085,000. If you do not get this answer, find the errors in your worksheet and correct them. Have the total cash disbursements for the year changed? Why or why not?

2. The company has just hired a new marketing manager who insists that unit sales can be dramatically increased by dropping the selling price from $8 to $7. The marketing manager would like to use the following projections in the budget:

Data	Year 2 Quarter				Year 3 Quarter	
	1	2	3	4	1	2
Budgeted unit sales	50,000	70,000	120,000	80,000	90,000	100,000
Selling price per unit	$7					

Chapter 8

a. What are the total expected cash collections for the year under this revised budget?
b. What is the total required production for the year under this revised budget?
c. What is the total cost of raw materials to be purchased for the year under this revised budget?
d. What are the total expected cash disbursements for raw materials for the year under this revised budget?
e. After seeing this revised budget, the production manager cautioned that due to the limited availability of a complex milling machine, the plant can produce no more than 90,000 units in any one quarter. Is this a potential problem? If so, what can be done about it?

The Foundational 15

Available with McGraw-Hill's *Connect*® Accounting.

LO8–2, LO8–3, LO8–4, LO8–5, LO8–7, LO8–9, LO8–10

Morganton Company makes one product and it provided the following information to help prepare the master budget for its first four months of operations:

a. The budgeted selling price per unit is $70. Budgeted unit sales for June, July, August, and September are 8,400, 10,000, 12,000, and 13,000 units, respectively. All sales are on credit.
b. Forty percent of credit sales are collected in the month of the sale and 60% in the following month.
c. The ending finished goods inventory equals 20% of the following month's unit sales.
d. The ending raw materials inventory equals 10% of the following month's raw materials production needs. Each unit of finished goods requires 5 pounds of raw materials. The raw materials cost $2.00 per pound.
e. Thirty percent of raw materials purchases are paid for in the month of purchase and 70% in the following month.
f. The direct labor wage rate is $15 per hour. Each unit of finished goods requires two direct labor-hours.
g. The variable selling and administrative expense per unit sold is $1.80. The fixed selling and administrative expense per month is $60,000.

Required:
1. What are the budgeted sales for July?
2. What are the expected cash collections for July?
3. What is the accounts receivable balance at the end of July?
4. According to the production budget, how many units should be produced in July?
5. If 61,000 pounds of raw materials are needed to meet production in August, how many pounds of raw materials should be purchased in July?
6. What is the estimated cost of raw materials purchases for July?
7. If the cost of raw material purchases in June is $88,880, what are the estimated cash disbursements for raw materials purchases in July?
8. What is the estimated accounts payable balance at the end of July?
9. What is the estimated raw materials inventory balance at the end of July?
10. What is the total estimated direct labor cost for July assuming the direct labor workforce is adjusted to match the hours required to produce the forecasted number of units produced?
11. If the company always uses an estimated predetermined plantwide overhead rate of $10 per direct labor-hour, what is the estimated unit product cost?
12. What is the estimated finished goods inventory balance at the end of July?
13 What is the estimated cost of goods sold and gross margin for July?
14. What is the estimated total selling and administrative expense for July?
15. What is the estimated net operating income for July?

Exercises

All applicable exercises are available with McGraw-Hill's *Connect*® Accounting.

EXERCISE 8–1 Schedule of Expected Cash Collections [LO8–2]
Silver Company makes a product that is very popular as a Mother's Day gift. Thus, peak sales occur in May of each year, as shown in the company's sales budget for the second quarter given below:

	April	May	June	Total
Budgeted sales (all on account)	$300,000	$500,000	$200,000	$1,000,000

From past experience, the company has learned that 20% of a month's sales are collected in the month of sale, another 70% are collected in the month following sale, and the remaining 10% are collected in the second month following sale. Bad debts are negligible and can be ignored. February sales totaled $230,000, and March sales totaled $260,000.

Required:

1. Prepare a schedule of expected cash collections from sales, by month and in total, for the second quarter.
2. Assume that the company will prepare a budgeted balance sheet as of June 30. Compute the accounts receivable as of that date.

EXERCISE 8–2 Production Budget [LO8–3]

Down Under Products, Ltd., of Australia has budgeted sales of its popular boomerang for the next four months as follows:

	Sales in Units
April	50,000
May	75,000
June	90,000
July	80,000

The company is now in the process of preparing a production budget for the second quarter. Past experience has shown that end-of-month inventory levels must equal 10% of the following month's sales. The inventory at the end of March was 5,000 units.

Required:

Prepare a production budget for the second quarter; in your budget, show the number of units to be produced each month and for the quarter in total.

EXERCISE 8–3 Direct Materials Budget [LO8–4]

Three grams of musk oil are required for each bottle of Mink Caress, a very popular perfume made by a small company in western Siberia. The cost of the musk oil is $1.50 per gram. Budgeted production of Mink Caress is given below by quarters for Year 2 and for the first quarter of Year 3:

	Year 2				Year 3
	First	Second	Third	Fourth	First
Budgeted production, in bottles	60,000	90,000	150,000	100,000	70,000

Musk oil has become so popular as a perfume ingredient that it has become necessary to carry large inventories as a precaution against stock-outs. For this reason, the inventory of musk oil at the end of a quarter must be equal to 20% of the following quarter's production needs. Some 36,000 grams of musk oil will be on hand to start the first quarter of Year 2.

Required:

Prepare a direct materials budget for musk oil, by quarter and in total, for Year 2. At the bottom of your budget, show the amount of purchases for each quarter and for the year in total.

EXERCISE 8–4 Direct Labor Budget [LO8–5]

The production manager of Rordan Corporation has submitted the following forecast of units to be produced by quarter for the upcoming fiscal year:

	1st Quarter	2nd Quarter	3rd Quarter	4th Quarter
Units to be produced	8,000	6,500	7,000	7,500

Each unit requires 0.35 direct labor-hours, and direct laborers are paid $12.00 per hour.

Required:

1. Construct the company's direct labor budget for the upcoming fiscal year, assuming that the direct labor workforce is adjusted each quarter to match the number of hours required to produce the forecasted number of units produced.

Chapter 8

2. Construct the company's direct labor budget for the upcoming fiscal year, assuming that the direct labor workforce is not adjusted each quarter. Instead, assume that the company's direct labor workforce consists of permanent employees who are guaranteed to be paid for at least 2,600 hours of work each quarter. If the number of required direct labor-hours is less than this number, the workers are paid for 2,600 hours anyway. Any hours worked in excess of 2,600 hours in a quarter are paid at the rate of 1.5 times the normal hourly rate for direct labor.

EXERCISE 8–5 Manufacturing Overhead Budget [LO8–6]
The direct labor budget of Yuvwell Corporation for the upcoming fiscal year contains the following details concerning budgeted direct labor-hours:

	1st Quarter	2nd Quarter	3rd Quarter	4th Quarter
Budgeted direct labor-hours	8,000	8,200	8,500	7,800

The company's variable manufacturing overhead rate is $3.25 per direct labor-hour and the company's fixed manufacturing overhead is $48,000 per quarter. The only noncash item included in fixed manufacturing overhead is depreciation, which is $16,000 per quarter.

Required:
1. Construct the company's manufacturing overhead budget for the upcoming fiscal year.
2. Compute the company's manufacturing overhead rate (including both variable and fixed manufacturing overhead) for the upcoming fiscal year. Round off to the nearest whole cent.

EXERCISE 8–6 Selling and Administrative Expense Budget [LO8–7]
The budgeted unit sales of Weller Company for the upcoming fiscal year are provided below:

	1st Quarter	2nd Quarter	3rd Quarter	4th Quarter
Budgeted unit sales	15,000	16,000	14,000	13,000

The company's variable selling and administrative expense per unit is $2.50. Fixed selling and administrative expenses include advertising expenses of $8,000 per quarter, executive salaries of $35,000 per quarter, and depreciation of $20,000 per quarter. In addition, the company will make insurance payments of $5,000 in the first quarter and $5,000 in the third quarter. Finally, property taxes of $8,000 will be paid in the second quarter.

Required:
Prepare the company's selling and administrative expense budget for the upcoming fiscal year.

EXERCISE 8–7 Cash Budget [LO8–8]
Garden Depot is a retailer that is preparing its budget for the upcoming fiscal year. Management has prepared the following summary of its budgeted cash flows:

	1st Quarter	2nd Quarter	3rd Quarter	4th Quarter
Total cash receipts	$180,000	$330,000	$210,000	$230,000
Total cash disbursements	$260,000	$230,000	$220,000	$240,000

The company's beginning cash balance for the upcoming fiscal year will be $20,000. The company requires a minimum cash balance of $10,000 and may borrow any amount needed from a local bank at a quarterly interest rate of 3%. The company may borrow any amount at the beginning of any quarter and may repay its loans, or any part of its loans, at the end of any quarter. Interest payments are due on any principal at the time it is repaid. For simplicity, assume that interest is not compounded.

Required:
Prepare the company's cash budget for the upcoming fiscal year.

EXERCISE 8–8 Budgeted Income Statement [LO8–9]

Gig Harbor Boating is the wholesale distributor of a small recreational catamaran sailboat. Management has prepared the following summary data to use in its annual budgeting process:

Budgeted unit sales	460
Selling price per unit	$1,950
Cost per unit	$1,575
Variable selling and administrative expenses (per unit)	$75
Fixed selling and administrative expenses (per year)	$105,000
Interest expense for the year	$14,000

Required:

Prepare the company's budgeted income statement. Use the absorption costing income statement format shown in Schedule 9.

EXERCISE 8–9 Budgeted Balance Sheet [LO8–10]

The management of Mecca Copy, a photocopying center located on University Avenue, has compiled the following data to use in preparing its budgeted balance sheet for next year:

	Ending Balances
Cash	?
Accounts receivable	$8,100
Supplies inventory	$3,200
Equipment	$34,000
Accumulated depreciation	$16,000
Accounts payable	$1,800
Common stock	$5,000
Retained earnings	?

The beginning balance of retained earnings was $28,000, net income is budgeted to be $11,500, and dividends are budgeted to be $4,800.

Required:

Prepare the company's budgeted balance sheet.

EXERCISE 8–10 Production and Direct Materials Budgets [LO8–3, LO8–4]

Pearl Products Limited of Shenzhen, China, manufactures and distributes toys throughout South East Asia. Three cubic centimeters (cc) of solvent H300 are required to manufacture each unit of Supermix, one of the company's products. The company is now planning raw materials needs for the third quarter, the quarter in which peak sales of Supermix occur. To keep production and sales moving smoothly, the company has the following inventory requirements:

a. The finished goods inventory on hand at the end of each month must be equal to 3,000 units of Supermix plus 20% of the next month's sales. The finished goods inventory on June 30 is budgeted to be 10,000 units.

b. The raw materials inventory on hand at the end of each month must be equal to one-half of the following month's production needs for raw materials. The raw materials inventory on June 30 is budgeted to be 54,000 cc of solvent H300.

c. The company maintains no work in process inventories.

A sales budget for Supermix for the last six months of the year follows.

	Budgeted Sales in Units
July	35,000
August	40,000
September	50,000
October	30,000
November	20,000
December	10,000

Required:

1. Prepare a production budget for Supermix for the months July, August, September, and October.
2. Examine the production budget that you prepared in (1) above. Why will the company produce more units than it sells in July and August, and fewer units than it sells in September and October?
3. Prepare a direct materials budget showing the quantity of solvent H300 to be purchased for July, August, and September, and for the quarter in total.

EXERCISE 8–11 Cash Budget Analysis [LO8–8]

A cash budget, by quarters, is given below for a retail company (000 omitted). The company requires a minimum cash balance of at least $5,000 to start each quarter.

	Quarter				
	1	2	3	4	Year
Cash balance, beginning	$ 6	$?	$?	$?	$?
Add collections from customers	?	?	96	?	323
Total cash available	71	?	?	?	?
Less disbursements:					
Purchase of inventory	35	45	?	35	?
Selling and administrative expenses	?	30	30	?	113
Equipment purchases	8	8	10	?	36
Dividends	2	2	2	2	?
Total disbursements	?	85	?	?	?
Excess (deficiency) of cash available over disbursements	(2)	?	11	?	?
Financing:					
Borrowings	?	15	—	—	?
Repayments (including interest)*	—	—	(?)	(17)	(?)
Total financing	?	?	?	?	?
Cash balance, ending	$?	$?	$?	$?	$?

*Interest will total $1,000 for the year.

Required:
Fill in the missing amounts in the above table.

EXERCISE 8–12 Schedules of Expected Cash Collections and Disbursements; Income Statement; Balance Sheet [LO8–2, LO8–4, LO8–9, LO8–10]

Beech Corporation is a merchandising company that is preparing a master budget for the third quarter of the calendar year. The company's balance sheet as of June 30th is shown below:

Beech Corporation Balance Sheet June 30	
Assets	
Cash	$ 90,000
Accounts receivable	136,000
Inventory	62,000
Plant and equipment, net of depreciation	210,000
Total assets	$498,000
Liabilities and Stockholders' Equity	
Accounts payable	$ 71,100
Common stock	327,000
Retained earnings	99,900
Total liabilities and stockholders' equity	$498,000

Beech's managers have made the following additional assumptions and estimates:

1. Estimated sales for July, August, September, and October will be $210,000, $230,000, $220,000, and $240,000, respectively.

2. All sales are on credit and all credit sales are collected. Each month's credit sales are collected 35% in the month of sale and 65% in the month following the sale. All of the accounts receivable at June 30 will be collected in July.

3. Each month's ending inventory must equal 30% of the cost of next month's sales. The cost of goods sold is 60% of sales. The company pays for 40% of its merchandise purchases in the month of the purchase and the remaining 60% in the month following the purchase. All of the accounts payable at June 30 will be paid in July.

4. Monthly selling and administrative expenses are always $60,000. Each month $5,000 of this total amount is depreciation expense and the remaining $55,000 relates to expenses that are paid in the month they are incurred.

5. The company does not plan to borrow money or pay or declare dividends during the quarter ended September 30. The company does not plan to issue any common stock or repurchase its own stock during the quarter ended September 30.

Required:

1. Prepare a schedule of expected cash collections for July, August, and September. Also compute total cash collections for the quarter ended September 30.
2. a. Prepare a merchandise purchases budget for July, August, and September. Also compute total merchandise purchases for the quarter ended September 30.
   b. Prepare a schedule of expected cash disbursements for merchandise purchases for July, August, and September. Also compute total cash disbursements for merchandise purchases for the quarter ended September 30.
3. Prepare an income statement for the quarter ended September 30. Use the absorption format shown in Schedule 9.
4. Prepare a balance sheet as of September 30.

EXERCISE 8–13 Schedules of Expected Cash Collections and Disbursements; Income Statement; Balance Sheet [LO8–2, LO8–4, LO8–9, LO8–10]

Refer to the data for Beech Corporation in Exercise 8–12. The company is considering making the following changes to the assumptions underlying its master budget:

1. Each month's credit sales are collected 45% in the month of sale and 55% in the month following the sale.
2. Each month's ending inventory must equal 20% of the cost of next month's sales.
3. The company pays for 30% of its merchandise purchases in the month of the purchase and the remaining 70% in the month following the purchase.

All other information from Exercise 8–12 that is not mentioned above remains the same.

Required:

Using the new assumptions described above, complete the following requirements:

1. Prepare a schedule of expected cash collections for July, August, and September. Also compute total cash collections for the quarter ended September 30.
2. a. Prepare a merchandise purchases budget for July, August, and September. Also compute total merchandise purchases for the quarter ended September 30.
   b. Prepare a schedule of expected cash disbursements for merchandise purchases for July, August, and September. Also compute total cash disbursements for merchandise purchases for the quarter ended September 30.
3. Prepare an income statement for the quarter ended September 30. Use the absorption format shown in Schedule 9.
4. Prepare a balance sheet as of September 30.

EXERCISE 8–14 Sales and Production Budgets [LO8–2, LO8–3]

The marketing department of Jessi Corporation has submitted the following sales forecast for the upcoming fiscal year (all sales are on account):

	1st Quarter	2nd Quarter	3rd Quarter	4th Quarter
Budgeted unit sales	11,000	12,000	14,000	13,000

378

Chapter 8

The selling price of the company's product is $18.00 per unit. Management expects to collect 65% of sales in the quarter in which the sales are made, 30% in the following quarter, and 5% of sales are expected to be uncollectible. The beginning balance of accounts receivable, all of which is expected to be collected in the first quarter, is $70,200.

The company expects to start the first quarter with 1,650 units in finished goods inventory. Management desires an ending finished goods inventory in each quarter equal to 15% of the next quarter's budgeted sales. The desired ending finished goods inventory for the fourth quarter is 1,850 units.

Required:
1. Prepare the company's sales budget and schedule of expected cash collections.
2. Prepare the company's production budget for the upcoming fiscal year.

EXERCISE 8–15 Direct Labor and Manufacturing Overhead Budgets [LO8–5, LO8–6]

The Production Department of Hruska Corporation has submitted the following forecast of units to be produced by quarter for the upcoming fiscal year:

	1st Quarter	2nd Quarter	3rd Quarter	4th Quarter
Units to be produced	12,000	10,000	13,000	14,000

Each unit requires 0.2 direct labor-hours and direct laborers are paid $12.00 per hour.

In addition, the variable manufacturing overhead rate is $1.75 per direct labor-hour. The fixed manufacturing overhead is $86,000 per quarter. The only noncash element of manufacturing overhead is depreciation, which is $23,000 per quarter.

Required:
1. Prepare the company's direct labor budget for the upcoming fiscal year, assuming that the direct labor workforce is adjusted each quarter to match the number of hours required to produce the forecasted number of units produced.
2. Prepare the company's manufacturing overhead budget.

EXERCISE 8–16 Direct Materials and Direct Labor Budgets [LO8–4, LO8–5]

The production department of Zan Corporation has submitted the following forecast of units to be produced by quarter for the upcoming fiscal year:

	1st Quarter	2nd Quarter	3rd Quarter	4th Quarter
Units to be produced	5,000	8,000	7,000	6,000

In addition, 6,000 grams of raw materials inventory is on hand at the start of the 1st Quarter and the beginning accounts payable for the 1st Quarter is $2,880.

Each unit requires 8 grams of raw material that costs $1.20 per gram. Management desires to end each quarter with an inventory of raw materials equal to 25% of the following quarter's production needs. The desired ending inventory for the 4th Quarter is 8,000 grams. Management plans to pay for 60% of raw material purchases in the quarter acquired and 40% in the following quarter. Each unit requires 0.20 direct labor-hours and direct laborers are paid $11.50 per hour.

Required:
1. Prepare the company's direct materials budget and schedule of expected cash disbursements for purchases of materials for the upcoming fiscal year.
2. Prepare the company's direct labor budget for the upcoming fiscal year, assuming that the direct labor workforce is adjusted each quarter to match the number of hours required to produce the forecasted number of units produced.

Problems

All applicable problems are available with McGraw-Hill's *Connect® Accounting*.

PROBLEM 8–17 Cash Budget; Income Statement; Balance Sheet [LO8–2, LO8–4, LO8–8, LO8–9, LO8–10]

Minden Company is a wholesale distributor of premium European chocolates. The company's balance sheet as of April 30 is given below:

Minden Company
Balance Sheet
April 30

Assets

Cash	$ 9,000
Accounts receivable	54,000
Inventory	30,000
Buildings and equipment, net of depreciation	207,000
Total assets	$300,000

Liabilities and Stockholders' Equity

Accounts payable	$ 63,000
Note payable	14,500
Common stock	180,000
Retained earnings	42,500
Total liabilities and stockholders' equity	$300,000

The company is in the process of preparing a budget for May and has assembled the following data:
a. Sales are budgeted at $200,000 for May. Of these sales, $60,000 will be for cash; the remainder will be credit sales. One-half of a month's credit sales are collected in the month the sales are made, and the remainder is collected in the following month. All of the April 30 accounts receivable will be collected in May.
b. Purchases of inventory are expected to total $120,000 during May. These purchases will all be on account. Forty percent of all purchases are paid for in the month of purchase; the remainder are paid in the following month. All of the April 30 accounts payable to suppliers will be paid during May.
c. The May 31 inventory balance is budgeted at $40,000.
d. Selling and administrative expenses for May are budgeted at $72,000, exclusive of depreciation. These expenses will be paid in cash. Depreciation is budgeted at $2,000 for the month.
e. The note payable on the April 30 balance sheet will be paid during May, with $100 in interest. (All of the interest relates to May.)
f. New refrigerating equipment costing $6,500 will be purchased for cash during May.
g. During May, the company will borrow $20,000 from its bank by giving a new note payable to the bank for that amount. The new note will be due in one year.

Required:
1. Prepare a cash budget for May. Support your budget with a schedule of expected cash collections from sales and a schedule of expected cash disbursements for merchandise purchases.
2. Prepare a budgeted income statement for May. Use the absorption costing income statement format as shown in Schedule 9.
3. Prepare a budgeted balance sheet as of May 31.

380

Chapter 8

PROBLEM 8–18 Cash Budget; Income Statement; Balance Sheet; Changing Assumptions [LO8–2, LO8–4, LO8–8, LO8–9, LO8–10]

Refer to the data for Minden Company in Problem 8–17. The company is considering making the following changes to the assumptions underlying its master budget:
1. Sales are budgeted for $220,000 for May.
2. Each month's credit sales are collected 60% in the month of sale and 40% in the month following the sale.
3. The company pays for 50% of its merchandise purchases in the month of the purchase and the remaining 50% in the month following the purchase.

All other information from Problem 8–17 that is not mentioned above remains the same.

Required:
Using the new assumptions described above, complete the following requirements:
1. Prepare a cash budget for May. Support your budget with a schedule of expected cash collections from sales and a schedule of expected cash disbursements for merchandise purchases.
2. Prepare a budgeted income statement for May. Use the absorption costing income statement format as shown in Schedule 9.
4. Prepare a budgeted balance sheet as of May 31.

PROBLEM 8–19 Schedules of Expected Cash Collections and Disbursements [LO8–2, LO8–4, LO8–8]

You have been asked to prepare a December cash budget for Ashton Company, a distributor of exercise equipment. The following information is available about the company's operations:
a. The cash balance on December 1 is $40,000.
b. Actual sales for October and November and expected sales for December are as follows:

	October	November	December
Cash sales	$65,000	$70,000	$83,000
Sales on account	$400,000	$525,000	$600,000

Sales on account are collected over a three-month period as follows: 20% collected in the month of sale, 60% collected in the month following sale, and 18% collected in the second month following sale. The remaining 2% is uncollectible.
c. Purchases of inventory will total $280,000 for December. Thirty percent of a month's inventory purchases are paid during the month of purchase. The accounts payable remaining from November's inventory purchases total $161,000, all of which will be paid in December.
d. Selling and administrative expenses are budgeted at $430,000 for December. Of this amount, $50,000 is for depreciation.
e. A new web server for the Marketing Department costing $76,000 will be purchased for cash during December, and dividends totaling $9,000 will be paid during the month.
f. The company maintains a minimum cash balance of $20,000. An open line of credit is available from the company's bank to bolster the cash position as needed.

Required:
1. Prepare a schedule of expected cash collections for December.
2. Prepare a schedule of expected cash disbursements for merchandise purchases for December.
3. Prepare a cash budget for December. Indicate in the financing section any borrowing that will be needed during the month. Assume that any interest will not be paid until the following month.

PROBLEM 8–20 Evaluating a Company's Budget Procedures [LO8–1]

Springfield Corporation operates on a calendar-year basis. It begins the annual budgeting process in late August, when the president establishes targets for total sales dollars and net operating income before taxes for the next year.

The sales target is given to the Marketing Department, where the marketing manager formulates a sales budget by product line in both units and dollars. From this budget, sales quotas by product line in units and dollars are established for each of the corporation's sales districts.

The marketing manager also estimates the cost of the marketing activities required to support the target sales volume and prepares a tentative marketing expense budget.

The executive vice president uses the sales and profit targets, the sales budget by product line, and the tentative marketing expense budget to determine the dollar amounts that can be devoted to manufacturing and corporate office expense. The executive vice president prepares the budget for corporate expenses, and then forwards to the Production Department the product-line sales budget in units and the total dollar amount that can be devoted to manufacturing.

The production manager meets with the factory managers to develop a manufacturing plan that will produce the required units when needed within the cost constraints set by the executive vice president. The budgeting process usually comes to a halt at this point because the Production Department does not consider the financial resources allocated to it to be adequate.

When this standstill occurs, the vice president of finance, the executive vice president, the marketing manager, and the production manager meet to determine the final budgets for each of the areas. This normally results in a modest increase in the total amount available for manufacturing costs, while the marketing expense and corporate office expense budgets are cut. The total sales and net operating income figures proposed by the president are seldom changed. Although the participants are seldom pleased with the compromise, these budgets are final. Each executive then develops a new detailed budget for the operations in his or her area.

None of the areas has achieved its budget in recent years. Sales often run below the target. When budgeted sales are not achieved, each area is expected to cut costs so that the president's profit target can still be met. However, the profit target is seldom met because costs are not cut enough. In fact, costs often run above the original budget in all functional areas. The president is disturbed that Springfield has not been able to meet the sales and profit targets. He hired a consultant with considerable relevant industry experience. The consultant reviewed the budgets for the past four years. He concluded that the product-line sales budgets were reasonable and that the cost and expense budgets were adequate for the budgeted sales and production levels.

Required:
1. Discuss how the budgeting process as employed by Springfield Corporation contributes to the failure to achieve the president's sales and profit targets.
2. Suggest how Springfield Corporation's budgeting process could be revised to correct the problem.
3. Should the functional areas be expected to cut their costs when sales volume falls below budget? Explain your answer.

(CMA, adapted)

PROBLEM 8–21 Schedule of Expected Cash Collections; Cash Budget [LO8–2, LO8–8]

The president of the retailer Prime Products has just approached the company's bank with a request for a $30,000, 90-day loan. The purpose of the loan is to assist the company in acquiring inventories. Because the company has had some difficulty in paying off its loans in the past, the loan officer has asked for a cash budget to help determine whether the loan should be made. The following data are available for the months April through June, during which the loan will be used:
a. On April 1, the start of the loan period, the cash balance will be $24,000. Accounts receivable on April 1 will total $140,000, of which $120,000 will be collected during April and $16,000 will be collected during May. The remainder will be uncollectible.
b. Past experience shows that 30% of a month's sales are collected in the month of sale, 60% in the month following sale, and 8% in the second month following sale. The other 2% represents bad debts that are never collected. Budgeted sales and expenses for the three-month period follow:

	April	May	June
Sales (all on account)	$300,000	$400,000	$250,000
Merchandise purchases	$210,000	$160,000	$130,000
Payroll	$20,000	$20,000	$18,000
Lease payments	$22,000	$22,000	$22,000
Advertising	$60,000	$60,000	$50,000
Equipment purchases	—	—	$65,000
Depreciation	$15,000	$15,000	$15,000

c. Merchandise purchases are paid in full during the month following purchase. Accounts payable for merchandise purchases during March, which will be paid during April, total $140,000.
d. In preparing the cash budget, assume that the $30,000 loan will be made in April and repaid in June. Interest on the loan will total $1,200.

Required:

1. Prepare a schedule of expected cash collections for April, May, and June, and for the three months in total.
2. Prepare a cash budget, by month and in total, for the three-month period.
3. If the company needs a minimum cash balance of $20,000 to start each month, can the loan be repaid as planned? Explain.

PROBLEM 8–22 Cash Budget with Supporting Schedules [LO8–2, LO8–4, LO8–8]

Garden Sales, Inc., sells garden supplies. Management is planning its cash needs for the second quarter. The company usually has to borrow money during this quarter to support peak sales of lawn care equipment, which occur during May. The following information has been assembled to assist in preparing a cash budget for the quarter:

a. Budgeted monthly absorption costing income statements for April–July are:

	April	May	June	July
Sales	$600,000	$900,000	$500,000	$400,000
Cost of goods sold	420,000	630,000	350,000	280,000
Gross margin	180,000	270,000	150,000	120,000
Selling and administrative expenses:				
Selling expense	79,000	120,000	62,000	51,000
Administrative expense*	45,000	52,000	41,000	38,000
Total selling and administrative expenses	124,000	172,000	103,000	89,000
Net operating income	$ 56,000	$ 98,000	$ 47,000	$ 31,000

*Includes $20,000 of depreciation each month.

b. Sales are 20% for cash and 80% on account.
c. Sales on account are collected over a three-month period with 10% collected in the month of sale; 70% collected in the first month following the month of sale; and the remaining 20% collected in the second month following the month of sale. February's sales totaled $200,000, and March's sales totaled $300,000.
d. Inventory purchases are paid for within 15 days. Therefore, 50% of a month's inventory purchases are paid for in the month of purchase. The remaining 50% is paid in the following month. Accounts payable at March 31 for inventory purchases during March total $126,000.
e. Each month's ending inventory must equal 20% of the cost of the merchandise to be sold in the following month. The merchandise inventory at March 31 is $84,000.
f. Dividends of $49,000 will be declared and paid in April.
g. Land costing $16,000 will be purchased for cash in May.
h. The cash balance at March 31 is $52,000; the company must maintain a cash balance of at least $40,000 at the end of each month.
i. The company has an agreement with a local bank that allows the company to borrow in increments of $1,000 at the beginning of each month, up to a total loan balance of $200,000. The interest rate on these loans is 1% per month and for simplicity we will assume that interest is not compounded. The company would, as far as it is able, repay the loan plus accumulated interest at the end of the quarter.

Required:

1. Prepare a schedule of expected cash collections for April, May, and June, and for the quarter in total.
2. Prepare the following for merchandise inventory:
    a. A merchandise purchases budget for April, May, and June.
    b. A schedule of expected cash disbursements for merchandise purchases for April, May, and June, and for the quarter in total.
3. Prepare a cash budget for April, May, and June as well as in total for the quarter.

PROBLEM 8–23 Cash Budget with Supporting Schedules; Changing Assumptions [LO8–2, LO8–4, LO8–8]

Refer to the data for Garden Sales, Inc., in Problem 8–22. The company's president is interested in knowing how reducing inventory levels and collecting accounts receivable sooner will impact the cash budget. He revises the cash collection and ending inventory assumptions as follows:

1. Sales continue to be 20% for cash and 80% on credit. However, credit sales from April, May, and June are collected over a three-month period with 25% collected in the month of sale, 65% collected in the month following sale, and 10% in the second month following sale. Credit sales from February and March are collected during the second quarter using the collection percentages specified in Problem 8–22.

2. The company maintains its ending inventory levels for April, May, and June at 15% of the cost of merchandise to be sold in the following month. The merchandise inventory at March 31 remains $84,000 and accounts payable for inventory purchases at March 31 remains $126,000.

All other information from Problem 8–22 that is not referred to above remains the same.

Required:

1. Using the president's new assumptions in (1) above, prepare a schedule of expected cash collections for April, May, and June and for the quarter in total.

2. Using the president's new assumptions in (2) above, prepare the following for merchandise inventory:
   a. A merchandise purchases budget for April, May, and June.
   b. A schedule of expected cash disbursements for merchandise purchases for April, May, and June and for the quarter in total.

3. Using the president's new assumptions, prepare a cash budget for April, May, and June, and for the quarter in total.

4. Prepare a brief memorandum for the president explaining how his revised assumptions affect the cash budget.

PROBLEM 8–24 Behavioral Aspects of Budgeting; Ethics and the Manager [LO8–1]

Norton Company, a manufacturer of infant furniture and carriages, is in the initial stages of preparing the annual budget for next year. Scott Ford has recently joined Norton's accounting staff and is interested to learn as much as possible about the company's budgeting process. During a recent lunch with Marge Atkins, sales manager, and Pete Granger, production manager, Ford initiated the following conversation.

Ford: Since I'm new around here and am going to be involved with the preparation of the annual budget, I'd be interested to learn how the two of you estimate sales and production numbers.

Atkins: We start out very methodically by looking at recent history, discussing what we know about current accounts, potential customers, and the general state of consumer spending. Then, we add that usual dose of intuition to come up with the best forecast we can.

Granger: I usually take the sales projections as the basis for my projections. Of course, we have to make an estimate of what this year's ending inventories will be, which is sometimes difficult.

Ford: Why does that present a problem? There must have been an estimate of ending inventories in the budget for the current year.

Granger: Those numbers aren't always reliable because Marge makes some adjustments to the sales numbers before passing them on to me.

Ford: What kind of adjustments?

Atkins: Well, we don't want to fall short of the sales projections so we generally give ourselves a little breathing room by lowering the initial sales projection anywhere from 5% to 10%.

Granger: So, you can see why this year's budget is not a very reliable starting point. We always have to adjust the projected production rates as the year progresses and, of course, this changes the ending inventory estimates. By the way, we make similar adjustments to expenses by adding at least 10% to the estimates; I think everyone around here does the same thing.

Required:

1. Marge Atkins and Pete Granger have described the use of what is sometimes called *budgetary slack.*
   a. Explain why Atkins and Granger behave in this manner and describe the benefits they expect to realize from the use of budgetary slack.
   b. Explain how the use of budgetary slack can adversely affect Atkins and Granger.

2. As a management accountant, Scott Ford believes that the behavior described by Marge Atkins and Pete Granger may be unethical. By referring to the IMA's Statement of Ethical Professional Practice in Chapter 1, explain why the use of budgetary slack may be unethical.

(CMA, adapted)

384

Chapter 8

PROBLEM 8–25 Schedule of Expected Cash Collections; Cash Budget [LO8–2, LO8–8]

Herbal Care Corp., a distributor of herb-based sunscreens, is ready to begin its third quarter, in which peak sales occur. The company has requested a $40,000, 90-day loan from its bank to help meet cash requirements during the quarter. Since Herbal Care has experienced difficulty in paying off its loans in the past, the loan officer at the bank has asked the company to prepare a cash budget for the quarter. In response to this request, the following data have been assembled:

a. On July 1, the beginning of the third quarter, the company will have a cash balance of $44,500.
b. Actual sales for the last two months and budgeted sales for the third quarter follow (all sales are on account):

May (actual)	$250,000
June (actual)	$300,000
July (budgeted)	$400,000
August (budgeted)	$600,000
September (budgeted)	$320,000

Past experience shows that 25% of a month's sales are collected in the month of sale, 70% in the month following sale, and 3% in the second month following sale. The remainder is uncollectible.

c. Budgeted merchandise purchases and budgeted expenses for the third quarter are given below:

	July	August	September
Merchandise purchases	$240,000	$350,000	$175,000
Salaries and wages	$45,000	$50,000	$40,000
Advertising	$130,000	$145,000	$80,000
Rent payments	$9,000	$9,000	$9,000
Depreciation	$10,000	$10,000	$10,000

Merchandise purchases are paid in full during the month following purchase. Accounts payable for merchandise purchases on June 30, which will be paid during July, total $180,000.

d. Equipment costing $10,000 will be purchased for cash during July.
e. In preparing the cash budget, assume that the $40,000 loan will be made in July and repaid in September. Interest on the loan will total $1,200.

Required:

1. Prepare a schedule of expected cash collections for July, August, and September and for the quarter in total.
2. Prepare a cash budget, by month and in total, for the third quarter.
3. If the company needs a minimum cash balance of $20,000 to start each month, can the loan be repaid as planned? Explain.

PROBLEM 8–26 Cash Budget with Supporting Schedules [LO8–2, LO8–4, LO8–7, LO8–8]

Westex Products is a wholesale distributor of industrial cleaning products. When the treasurer of Westex Products approached the company's bank late in the current year seeking short-term financing, he was told that money was very tight and that any borrowing over the next year would have to be supported by a detailed statement of cash collections and disbursements. The treasurer also was told that it would be very helpful to the bank if borrowers would indicate the quarters in which they would be needing funds, as well as the amounts that would be needed, and the quarters in which repayments could be made.

Because the treasurer is unsure as to the particular quarters in which bank financing will be needed, he has assembled the following information to assist in preparing a detailed cash budget:

a. Budgeted sales and merchandise purchases for next year, as well as actual sales and purchases for the last quarter of the current year, are:

	Sales	Merchandise Purchases
Current Year:		
Fourth quarter actual	$200,000	$126,000
Next year:		
First quarter estimated	$300,000	$186,000
Second quarter estimated	$400,000	$246,000
Third quarter estimated	$500,000	$305,000
Fourth quarter estimated	$200,000	$126,000

b. All sales are on account. The company normally collects 65% of a quarter's sales before the quarter ends and another 33% in the following quarter. The remainder is uncollectible. This pattern of collections is now being experienced in the current year's fourth-quarter actual data.

c. Eighty percent of a quarter's merchandise purchases are paid for within the quarter. The remainder is paid for in the following quarter.

d. Selling and administrative expenses for next year are budgeted at $50,000 per quarter plus 15% of sales. Of the fixed amount, $20,000 each quarter is depreciation.

e. The company will pay $10,000 in dividends each quarter.

f. Land purchases of $75,000 will be made in the second quarter, and purchases of $48,000 will be made in the third quarter. These purchases will be for cash.

g. The Cash account contained $10,000 at the end of the current year. The treasurer feels that this represents a minimum balance that must be maintained.

h. The company has an agreement with a local bank that allows the company to borrow in increments of $1,000 at the beginning of each quarter, up to a total loan balance of $100,000. The interest rate on these loans is 2.5% per quarter and for simplicity we will assume that interest is not compounded. The company would, as far as it is able, repay the loan plus accumulated interest at the end of the year.

i. At present, the company has no loans outstanding.

Required:
1. Prepare the following by quarter and in total for next year:
   a. A schedule of expected cash collections.
   b. A schedule of expected cash disbursements for merchandise purchases.
2. Compute the expected cash disbursements for selling and administrative expenses, by quarter and in total, for next year.
3. Prepare a cash budget, by quarter and in total, for next year.

PROBLEM 8–27 Completing a Master Budget [LO8–2, LO8–4, LO8–7, LO8–8, LO8–9, LO8–10]
The following data relate to the operations of Shilow Company, a wholesale distributor of consumer goods:

Current assets as of March 31:	
Cash	$8,000
Accounts receivable	$20,000
Inventory	$36,000
Building and equipment, net	$120,000
Accounts payable	$21,750
Common stock	$150,000
Retained earnings	$12,250

a. The gross margin is 25% of sales.
b. Actual and budgeted sales data:

March (actual)	$50,000
April	$60,000
May	$72,000
June	$90,000
July	$48,000

c. Sales are 60% for cash and 40% on credit. Credit sales are collected in the month following sale. The accounts receivable at March 31 are a result of March credit sales.

d. Each month's ending inventory should equal 80% of the following month's budgeted cost of goods sold.

e. One-half of a month's inventory purchases is paid for in the month of purchase; the other half is paid for in the following month. The accounts payable at March 31 are the result of March purchases of inventory.

f. Monthly expenses are as follows: commissions, 12% of sales; rent, $2,500 per month; other expenses (excluding depreciation), 6% of sales. Assume that these expenses are paid monthly. Depreciation is $900 per month (includes depreciation on new assets).

g. Equipment costing $1,500 will be purchased for cash in April.

386

Chapter 8

h.   Management would like to maintain a minimum cash balance of at least $4,000 at the end
     of each month. The company has an agreement with a local bank that allows the company to
     borrow in increments of $1,000 at the beginning of each month, up to a total loan balance of
     $20,000. The interest rate on these loans is 1% per month and for simplicity we will assume
     that interest is not compounded. The company would, as far as it is able, repay the loan plus
     accumulated interest at the end of the quarter.

Required:
Using the preceding data:
1.   Complete the following schedule:

Schedule of Expected Cash Collections				
	April	May	June	Quarter
Cash sales	$36,000			
Credit sales	20,000			
Total collections	$56,000			

2.   Complete the following:

Merchandise Purchases Budget				
	April	May	June	Quarter
Budgeted cost of goods sold	$45,000*	$54,000		
Add desired ending inventory	43,200†			
Total needs	88,200			
Less beginning inventory	36,000			
Required purchases	$52,200			

*For April sales: $60,000 sales × 75% cost ratio = $45,000.
†$54,000 × 80% = $43,200

Schedule of Expected Cash Disbursements—Merchandise Purchases				
	April	May	June	Quarter
March purchases	$21,750			$21,750
April purchases	26,100	$26,100		52,200
May purchases				
June purchases				
Total disbursements	$47,850			

3.   Complete the following cash budget:

Cash Budget				
	April	May	June	Quarter
Beginning cash balance	$ 8,000			
Add cash collections	56,000			
Total cash available	64,000			
Less cash disbursements:				
For inventory	47,850			
For expenses	13,300			
For equipment	1,500			
Total cash disbursements	62,650			
Excess (deficiency) of cash	1,350			
Financing:				
Etc.				

4. Prepare an absorption costing income statement, similar to the one shown in Schedule 9 in the chapter, for the quarter ended June 30.
5. Prepare a balance sheet as of June 30.

PROBLEM 8–28 Integration of the Sales, Production, and Direct Materials Budgets [LO8–2, LO8–3, LO8–4]
Milo Company manufactures beach umbrellas. The company is preparing detailed budgets for the third quarter and has assembled the following information to assist in the budget preparation:
a. The Marketing Department has estimated sales as follows for the remainder of the year (in units):

July	30,000	October	20,000
August	70,000	November	10,000
September	50,000	December	10,000

The selling price of the beach umbrellas is $12 per unit.
b. All sales are on account. Based on past experience, sales are collected in the following pattern:

30% in the month of sale
65% in the month following sale
5% uncollectible

Sales for June totaled $300,000.
c. The company maintains finished goods inventories equal to 15% of the following month's sales. This requirement will be met at the end of June.
d. Each beach umbrella requires 4 feet of Gilden, a material that is sometimes hard to acquire. Therefore, the company requires that the ending inventory of Gilden be equal to 50% of the following month's production needs. The inventory of Gilden on hand at the beginning and end of the quarter will be:

June 30	72,000 feet
September 30	? feet

e. Gilden costs $0.80 per foot. One-half of a month's purchases of Gilden is paid for in the month of purchase; the remainder is paid for in the following month. The accounts payable on July 1 for purchases of Gilden during June will be $76,000.

Required:
1. Prepare a sales budget, by month and in total, for the third quarter. (Show your budget in both units and dollars.) Also prepare a schedule of expected cash collections, by month and in total, for the third quarter.
2. Prepare a production budget for each of the months July–October.
3. Prepare a direct materials budget for Gilden, by month and in total, for the third quarter. Also prepare a schedule of expected cash disbursements for Gilden, by month and in total, for the third quarter.

PROBLEM 8–29 Completing a Master Budget [LO8–2, LO8–4, LO8–7, LO8–8, LO8–9, LO8–10]
Hillyard Company, an office supplies specialty store, prepares its master budget on a quarterly basis. The following data have been assembled to assist in preparing the master budget for the first quarter:
a. As of December 31 (the end of the prior quarter), the company's general ledger showed the following account balances:

	Debits	Credits
Cash	$ 48,000	
Accounts receivable	224,000	
Inventory	60,000	
Buildings and equipment (net)	370,000	
Accounts payable		$ 93,000
Common stock		500,000
Retained earnings		109,000
	$702,000	$702,000

b. Actual sales for December and budgeted sales for the next four months are as follows:

December (actual)	$280,000
January	$400,000
February	$600,000
March	$300,000
April	$200,000

c. Sales are 20% for cash and 80% on credit. All payments on credit sales are collected in the month following sale. The accounts receivable at December 31 are a result of December credit sales.

d. The company's gross margin is 40% of sales. (In other words, cost of goods sold is 60% of sales.)

e. Monthly expenses are budgeted as follows: salaries and wages, $27,000 per month: advertising, $70,000 per month; shipping, 5% of sales; other expenses, 3% of sales. Depreciation, including depreciation on new assets acquired during the quarter, will be $42,000 for the quarter.

f. Each month's ending inventory should equal 25% of the following month's cost of goods sold.

g. One-half of a month's inventory purchases is paid for in the month of purchase; the other half is paid in the following month.

h. During February, the company will purchase a new copy machine for $1,700 cash. During March, other equipment will be purchased for cash at a cost of $84,500.

i. During January, the company will declare and pay $45,000 in cash dividends.

j. Management wants to maintain a minimum cash balance of $30,000. The company has an agreement with a local bank that allows the company to borrow in increments of $1,000 at the beginning of each month. The interest rate on these loans is 1% per month and for simplicity we will assume that interest is not compounded. The company would, as far as it is able, repay the loan plus accumulated interest at the end of the quarter.

Required:

Using the data above, complete the following statements and schedules for the first quarter:

1. Schedule of expected cash collections:

	January	February	March	Quarter
Cash sales	$ 80,000			
Credit sales	224,000			
Total cash collections	$304,000			

2. a. Merchandise purchases budget:

	January	February	March	Quarter
Budgeted cost of goods sold	$240,000*	$360,000		
Add desired ending inventory	90,000†			
Total needs	330,000			
Less beginning inventory	60,000			
Required purchases	$270,000			

*$400,000 sales × 60% cost ratio = $240,000.
†$360,000 × 25% = $90,000.

b. Schedule of expected cash disbursements for merchandise purchases:

	January	February	March	Quarter
December purchases	$ 93,000			$ 93,000
January purchases	135,000	135,000		270,000
February purchases		—		
March purchases		—		
Total cash disbursements for purchases	$228,000			

3.   Cash budget:

	January	February	March	Quarter
Beginning cash balance	$ 48,000			
Add cash collections	304,000			
Total cash available	352,000			
Less cash disbursements:				
Purchases of inventory	228,000			
Selling and administrative expenses	129,000			
Purchases of equipment	—			
Cash dividends	45,000			
Total cash disbursements	402,000			
Excess (deficiency) of cash	(50,000)			
Financing:				
Etc.				

4.   Prepare an absorption costing income statement for the quarter ending March 31 as shown in Schedule 9 in the chapter.

5.   Prepare a balance sheet as of March 31.

 Cases

All applicable cases are available with McGraw-Hill's _Connect® Accounting_.

CASE 8–30 Evaluating a Company's Budget Procedures [LO8–1]

Tom Emory and Jim Morris strolled back to their plant from the administrative offices of Ferguson & Son Manufacturing Company. Tom is manager of the machine shop in the company's factory; Jim is manager of the equipment maintenance department.

The men had just attended the monthly performance evaluation meeting for plant department heads. These meetings had been held on the third Tuesday of each month since Robert Ferguson, Jr., the president's son, had become plant manager a year earlier.

As they were walking, Tom Emory spoke: "Boy, I hate those meetings! I never know whether my department's accounting reports will show good or bad performance. I'm beginning to expect the worst. If the accountants say I saved the company a dollar, I'm called 'Sir,' but if I spend even a little too much—boy, do I get in trouble. I don't know if I can hold on until I retire."

Tom had just been given the worst evaluation he had ever received in his long career with Ferguson & Son. He was the most respected of the experienced machinists in the company. He had been with Ferguson & Son for many years and was promoted to supervisor of the machine shop when the company expanded and moved to its present location. The president (Robert Ferguson, Sr.) had often stated that the company's success was due to the high-quality work of machinists like Tom. As supervisor, Tom stressed the importance of craftsmanship and told his workers that he wanted no sloppy work coming from his department.

When Robert Ferguson, Jr., became the plant manager, he directed that monthly performance comparisons be made between actual and budgeted costs for each department. The departmental budgets were intended to encourage the supervisors to reduce inefficiencies and to seek cost reduction opportunities. The company controller was instructed to have his staff "tighten" the budget slightly whenever a department attained its budget in a given month; this was done to reinforce the plant manager's desire to reduce costs. The young plant manager often stressed the importance of continued progress toward attaining the budget; he also made it known that he kept a file of these performance reports for future reference when he succeeded his father.

Tom Emory's conversation with Jim Morris continued as follows:

Emory: I really don't understand. We've worked so hard to meet the budget, and the minute we do so they tighten it on us. We can't work any faster and still maintain quality. I think my men are ready to quit trying. Besides, those reports don't tell the whole story. We always seem to be interrupting the big jobs for all those small rush orders. All that setup and machine adjustment time is killing us. And quite frankly, Jim, you were no help. When our hydraulic press broke down last month, your people were nowhere to be found. We had to take it apart ourselves and got stuck with all that idle time.

Morris: I'm sorry about that, Tom, but you know my department has had trouble making budget, too. We were running well behind at the time of that problem, and if we'd spent a day on that old machine, we would never have made it up. Instead we made the scheduled inspections of the fork-lift trucks because we knew we could do those in less than the budgeted time.

Emory: Well, Jim, at least you have some options. I'm locked into what the scheduling department assigns to me and you know they're being harassed by sales for those special orders. Incidentally, why didn't your report show all the supplies you guys wasted last month when you were working in Bill's department?

Morris: We're not out of the woods on that deal yet. We charged the maximum we could to other work and haven't even reported some of it yet.

Emory: Well, I'm glad you have a way of getting out of the pressure. The accountants seem to know everything that's happening in my department, sometimes even before I do. I thought all that budget and accounting stuff was supposed to help, but it just gets me into trouble. It's all a big pain. I'm trying to put out quality work; they're trying to save pennies.

Required:

1. Identify the problems that appear to exist in Ferguson & Son Manufacturing Company's budgetary control system and explain how the problems are likely to reduce the effectiveness of the system.
2. Explain how Ferguson & Son Manufacturing Company's budgetary control system could be revised to improve its effectiveness.

(CMA, adapted)

CASE 8–31 Master Budget with Supporting Schedules [LO8–2, LO8–4, LO8–8, LO8–9, LO8–10]
You have just been hired as a new management trainee by Earrings Unlimited, a distributor of earrings to various retail outlets located in shopping malls across the country. In the past, the company has done very little in the way of budgeting and at certain times of the year has experienced a shortage of cash.

Since you are well trained in budgeting, you have decided to prepare comprehensive budgets for the upcoming second quarter in order to show management the benefits that can be gained from an integrated budgeting program. To this end, you have worked with accounting and other areas to gather the information assembled below.

The company sells many styles of earrings, but all are sold for the same price—$10 per pair. Actual sales of earrings for the last three months and budgeted sales for the next six months follow (in pairs of earrings):

January (actual)	20,000	June (budget)	50,000
February (actual)	26,000	July (budget)	30,000
March (actual)	40,000	August (budget)	28,000
April (budget)	65,000	September (budget)	25,000
May (budget)	100,000		

The concentration of sales before and during May is due to Mother's Day. Sufficient inventory should be on hand at the end of each month to supply 40% of the earrings sold in the following month.

Suppliers are paid $4 for a pair of earrings. One-half of a month's purchases is paid for in the month of purchase; the other half is paid for in the following month. All sales are on credit, with no discount, and payable within 15 days. The company has found, however, that only 20% of a month's sales are collected in the month of sale. An additional 70% is collected in the following month, and the remaining 10% is collected in the second month following sale. Bad debts have been negligible.

Monthly operating expenses for the company are given below:

Variable:	
Sales commissions	4% of sales
Fixed:	
Advertising	$200,000
Rent	$18,000
Salaries	$106,000
Utilities	$7,000
Insurance	$3,000
Depreciation	$14,000

Insurance is paid on an annual basis, in November of each year.

The company plans to purchase $16,000 in new equipment during May and $40,000 in new equipment during June; both purchases will be for cash. The company declares dividends of $15,000 each quarter, payable in the first month of the following quarter.

A listing of the company's ledger accounts as of March 31 is given below:

Assets

Cash	$ 74,000
Accounts receivable ($26,000 February sales;	346,000
$320,000 March sales)	
Inventory	104,000
Prepaid insurance	21,000
Property and equipment (net)	950,000
Total assets	$1,495,000

Liabilities and Stockholders' Equity

Accounts payable	$ 100,000
Dividends payable	15,000
Common stock	800,000
Retained earnings	580,000
Total liabilities and stockholders' equity	$1,495,000

The company maintains a minimum cash balance of $50,000. All borrowing is done at the beginning of a month; any repayments are made at the end of a month.

The company has an agreement with a bank that allows the company to borrow in increments of $1,000 at the beginning of each month. The interest rate on these loans is 1% per month and for simplicity we will assume that interest is not compounded. At the end of the quarter, the company would pay the bank all of the accumulated interest on the loan and as much of the loan as possible (in increments of $1,000), while still retaining at least $50,000 in cash.

Required:

Prepare a master budget for the three-month period ending June 30. Include the following detailed budgets:

1. a. A sales budget, by month and in total.
   b. A schedule of expected cash collections from sales, by month and in total.
   c. A merchandise purchases budget in units and in dollars. Show the budget by month and in total.
   d. A schedule of expected cash disbursements for merchandise purchases, by month and in total.
2. A cash budget. Show the budget by month and in total. Determine any borrowing that would be needed to maintain the minimum cash balance of $50,000.
3. A budgeted income statement for the three-month period ending June 30. Use the contribution approach.
4. A budgeted balance sheet as of June 30.

CHAPTER 9

Flexible Budgets and Performance Analysis

Why Do Companies Need Flexible Budgets?

The difficulty of accurately predicting future financial performance can be readily understood by reading the annual report of any publicly traded company. For example, Nucor Corporation, a steel manufacturer headquartered in Charlotte, North Carolina, cites numerous reasons why its actual results may differ from expectations, including the following: (1) changes in the supply and cost of raw materials; (2) changes in the availability and cost of electricity and natural gas; (3) changes in the market demand for steel products; (4) fluctuations in currency conversion rates; (5) significant changes in laws or government regulations; and (6) the cyclical nature of the steel industry. ■

Source: Nucor Corporation 2011 Annual Report, p. 3.

LEARNING OBJECTIVES

After studying Chapter 9, you should be able to:

LO9–1   Prepare a flexible budget.

LO9–2   Prepare a report showing activity variances.

LO9–3   Prepare a report showing revenue and spending variances.

LO9–4   Prepare a performance report that combines activity variances and revenue and spending variances.

LO9–5   Prepare a flexible budget with more than one cost driver.

LO9–6   Understand common errors made in preparing performance reports based on budgets and actual results.

I n the last chapter we explored how budgets are developed before a period begins. In this chapter, we explain how budgets can be adjusted to help guide actual operations and influence the performance evaluation process. For example, an organization's actual expenses will rarely equal its budgeted expenses as estimated at the beginning of the period. The reason is that the actual level of activity (such as unit sales) will rarely be the same as the budgeted activity; therefore, many actual expenses and revenues will naturally differ from what was budgeted. Should a manager be penalized for spending 10% more than budgeted for a variable expense like direct materials if unit sales are 10% higher than budgeted? Of course not. After studying this chapter, you'll know how to adjust a budget to enable meaningful comparisons to actual results.

The Variance Analysis Cycle

Companies use the *variance analysis cycle,* as illustrated in Exhibit 9–1, to evaluate and improve performance. The cycle begins with the preparation of performance reports in the accounting department. These reports highlight variances, which are the differences between the actual results and what should have occurred according to the budget. The variances raise questions. Why did this variance occur? Why is this variance larger than it was last period? The significant variances are investigated so that their root causes can be either replicated or eliminated. Then, next period's operations are carried out and the cycle begins again with the preparation of a new performance report for the latest period. The emphasis should be on highlighting superior and unsatisfactory results, finding the root causes of these outcomes, and then replicating the sources of superior achievement and eliminating the sources of unsatisfactory performance. The variance analysis cycle should not be used to assign blame for poor performance.

Managers frequently use the concept of *management by exception* in conjunction with the variance analysis cycle. Management by exception is a management system that compares actual results to a budget so that significant deviations can be flagged as exceptions and investigated further. This approach enables managers to focus on the most important variances while bypassing trivial discrepancies between the budget and actual results. For example, a variance of $5 is probably not big enough to warrant attention, whereas a variance of $5,000 might be worth tracking down. Another clue is the size of the variance relative to the amount of spending. A variance that is only 0.1% of spending on an item is probably caused by random factors. On the other hand, a variance of 10% of spending is much more likely to be a signal that something is wrong. In addition to

EXHIBIT 9–1
The Variance Analysis Cycle

watching for unusually large variances, the pattern of the variances should be monitored. For example, a run of steadily mounting variances should trigger an investigation even though none of the variances is large enough by itself to warrant investigation.

Next, we explain how organizations use flexible budgets to compare actual results to what should have occurred according to the budget.

Flexible Budgets

Characteristics of a Flexible Budget

LO9–1
Prepare a flexible budget.

The budgets that we explored in the last chapter were *planning budgets*. A **planning budget** is prepared before the period begins and is valid for only the planned level of activity. A static planning budget is suitable for planning but is inappropriate for evaluating how well costs are controlled. If the actual level of activity differs from what was planned, it would be misleading to compare actual costs to the static, unchanged planning budget. If activity is higher than expected, variable costs should be higher than expected; and if activity is lower than expected, variable costs should be lower than expected.

Flexible budgets take into account how changes in activity affect costs. A **flexible budget** is an estimate of what revenues and costs should have been, given the actual level of activity for the period. When a flexible budget is used in performance evaluation, actual costs are compared to what the costs *should have been for the actual level of activity during the period* rather than to the static planning budget. This is a very important distinction. If adjustments for the level of activity are not made, it is very difficult to interpret discrepancies between budgeted and actual costs.

IN BUSINESS

WINNERS AND LOSERS FROM THE NBA LOCKOUT

A company's actual net operating income can deviate from the budget for numerous and often uncontrollable reasons. For example, when the National Basketball Association (NBA) decided to suspend play because of a dispute between its team owners and players, many small businesses suffered—caterers, sports bars, apparel retailers, and parking lot owners all experienced a drop in revenues. BestSportsApparel.com experienced a substantial drop in NBA apparel sales due to the work stoppage. Rather than hiring 12 extra employees for the NBA season, the company reduced the size of its workforce.

While some companies lost revenues when the NBA shut down, others benefited from the situation. Andrew Zimbalist, professor of economics at Smith College, notes that "local economies are not impacted by sports work stoppages" because people choose to spend their entertainment dollars at other venues such as the theater, the zoo, or the museum.

Source: Emily Maltby and Sarah E. Needleman, "NBA Lockout: Local Firms Lose Big," *The Wall Street Journal*, October 13, 2011, p. B5.

Deficiencies of the Static Planning Budget

To illustrate the difference between a static planning budget and a flexible budget, consider Rick's Hairstyling, an upscale hairstyling salon located in Beverly Hills that is owned and managed by Rick Manzi. Recently Rick has been attempting to get better control of his revenues and costs, and at the urging of his accounting and business adviser, Victoria Kho, he has begun to prepare monthly budgets. Victoria Kho is an accountant in independent practice who specializes in small service-oriented businesses like Rick's Hairstyling.

At the end of February, Rick prepared the March budget that appears in Exhibit 9–2. Rick believes that the number of customers served in a month (also known as the number

Flexible Budgets and Performance Analysis

EXHIBIT 9–2
Planning Budget

Rick's Hairstyling
Planning Budget
For the Month Ended March 31

Budgeted client-visits (q)	1,000
Revenue ($180.00q)	$180,000
Expenses:	
Wages and salaries ($65,000 + $37.00q)	102,000
Hairstyling supplies ($1.50q)	1,500
Client gratuities ($4.10q)	4,100
Electricity ($1,500 + $0.10q)	1,600
Rent ($28,500)	28,500
Liability insurance ($2,800)	2,800
Employee health insurance ($21,300)	21,300
Miscellaneous ($1,200 + $0.20q)	1,400
Total expense	163,200
Net operating income	$ 16,800

of client-visits) is the best way to measure the overall level of activity in his salon. A customer who comes into the salon and has his or her hair styled is counted as one client-visit.

Note that the term *revenue* is used in the planning budget rather than *sales*. We use the term revenue throughout the chapter because some organizations have sources of revenue other than sales. For example, donations, as well as sales, are counted as revenue in nonprofit organizations.

Rick has identified eight major categories of costs—wages and salaries, hairstyling supplies, client gratuities, electricity, rent, liability insurance, employee health insurance, and miscellaneous. Client gratuities consist of flowers, candies, and glasses of champagne that Rick gives to his customers while they are in the salon.

Working with Victoria, Rick estimated a cost formula for each cost. For example, the cost formula for electricity is $1,500 + \$0.10q$, where q equals the number of client-visits. In other words, electricity is a mixed cost with a $1,500 fixed element and a $0.10 per client-visit variable element. Once the budgeted level of activity was set at 1,000 client-visits, Rick computed the budgeted amount for each line item in the budget. For example, using the cost formula, he set the budgeted cost for electricity at $1,600 (= \$1,500 + \$0.10 \times 1,000$). To finalize his budget, Rick computed his expected net operating income for March of $16,800.

At the end of March, Rick prepared the income statement in Exhibit 9–3, which shows that 1,100 clients actually visited his salon in March and that his actual net operating income for the month was $21,230. It is important to realize that the actual results are *not* determined by plugging the actual number of client-visits into the revenue and cost formulas. The formulas are simply estimates of what the revenues and costs should be for a given level of activity. What actually happens usually differs from what is supposed to happen.

The first thing Rick noticed when comparing Exhibits 9–2 and 9–3 is that the actual profit of $21,230 (from Exhibit 9-3) was substantially higher than the budgeted profit of $16,800 (from Exhibit 9-2). This was, of course, good news, but Rick wanted to know more. Business was up by 10%—the salon had 1,100 client-visits instead of the budgeted 1,000 client-visits. Could this alone explain the higher net operating income? The answer is no. An increase in net operating income of 10% would have resulted in net operating income of only $18,480 (= 1.1 \times \$16,800$), not the $21,230 actually earned during the month. What is responsible for this better outcome? Higher prices? Lower costs? Something else? Whatever the cause, Rick would like to know the answer and then hopefully repeat the same performance next month.

In an attempt to analyze what happened in March, Rick prepared the report comparing actual to budgeted costs that appears in Exhibit 9–4. Note that most of the variances

EXHIBIT 9–3
Actual Results—Income
Statement

Rick's Hairstyling
Income Statement
For the Month Ended March 31

Actual client-visits	1,100
Revenue	$194,200
Expenses:	
Wages and salaries	106,900
Hairstyling supplies	1,620
Client gratuities	6,870
Electricity	1,550
Rent	28,500
Liability insurance	2,800
Employee health insurance	22,600
Miscellaneous	2,130
Total expense	172,970
Net operating income	$ 21,230

EXHIBIT 9–4
Comparison of Actual Results
to the Static Planning Budget

Rick's Hairstyling
Comparison of Actual Results to the Planning Budget
For the Month Ended March 31

	Actual Results	Planning Budget	Variances*
Client-visits	1,100	1,000	
Revenue	$194,200	$180,000	$14,200 F
Expenses:			
Wages and salaries	106,900	102,000	4,900 U
Hairstyling supplies	1,620	1,500	120 U
Client gratuities	6,870	4,100	2,770 U
Electricity	1,550	1,600	50 F
Rent	28,500	28,500	0
Liability insurance	2,800	2,800	0
Employee health insurance	22,600	21,300	1,300 U
Miscellaneous	2,130	1,400	730 U
Total expense	172,970	163,200	9,770 U
Net operating income	$ 21,230	$ 16,800	$ 4,430 F

*The revenue variance is labeled favorable (unfavorable) when the actual
revenue is greater than (less than) the planning budget. The expense variances
are labeled favorable (unfavorable) when the actual expense is less than
(greater than) the planning budget.

in this report are labeled unfavorable (U) rather than favorable (F) even though net operating income was actually higher than expected. For example, wages and salaries show
an unfavorable variance of $4,900 because the actual wages and salaries expense was
$106,900, whereas the budget called for wages and salaries of $102,000. The problem
with the report, as Rick immediately realized, is that it compares revenues and costs at
one level of activity (1,000 client-visits) to revenues and costs at a different level of activity (1,100 client-visits). This is like comparing apples to oranges. Because Rick had 100
more client-visits than expected, some of his costs should be higher than budgeted. From
Rick's standpoint, the increase in activity was good; however, it appears to be having a
negative impact on most of the costs in the report. Rick knew that something would have

to be done to make the report more meaningful, but he was unsure of what to do. So he made an appointment to meet with Victoria Kho to discuss the next step.

Victoria: How is the budgeting going?

Rick: Pretty well. I didn't have any trouble putting together the budget for March. I also prepared a report comparing the actual results for March to the budget, but that report isn't giving me what I really want to know.

Victoria: Because your actual level of activity didn't match your budgeted activity?

Rick: Right. I know the level of activity shouldn't affect my fixed costs, but we had more client-visits than I had expected and that had to affect my other costs.

Victoria: So you want to know whether the higher actual costs are justified by the higher level of activity?

Rick: Precisely.

Victoria: If you leave your reports and data with me, I can work on it later today, and by tomorrow I'll have a report to show you.

How a Flexible Budget Works

A flexible budget approach recognizes that a budget can be adjusted to show what costs *should be* for the actual level of activity. To illustrate how flexible budgets work, Victoria prepared the report in Exhibit 9–5 that shows what the *revenues and costs should have been given the actual level of activity* in March. Preparing the report is straightforward. The cost formula for each cost is used to estimate what the cost should have been for 1,100 client-visits—the actual level of activity for March. For example, using the cost formula $1,500 + $0.10q$, the cost of electricity in March *should have been* $1,610 (= $1,500 + $0.10 \times 1,100$). Also, notice that the amounts of rent ($28,500), liability insurance ($2,800), and employee health insurance ($21,300) in the flexible budget equal the corresponding amounts in the planning budget (see Exhibit 9–2). This occurs because fixed costs are not affected by the activity level.

We can see from the flexible budget that the net operating income in March *should have been* $30,510, but recall from Exhibit 9–3 that the net operating income was actually only $21,230. The results are not as good as we thought. Why? We will answer that question shortly.

To summarize to this point, Rick had budgeted for a profit of $16,800. The actual profit was quite a bit higher—$21,230. However, Victoria's analysis shows that given the

Rick's Hairstyling Flexible Budget For the Month Ended March 31	
Actual client-visits *(q)*	1,100
Revenue ($180.00q)	$198,000
Expenses:	
Wages and salaries ($65,000 + $37.00q)	105,700
Hairstyling supplies ($1.50q)	1,650
Client gratuities ($4.10q)	4,510
Electricity ($1,500 + $0.10q)	1,610
Rent ($28,500)	28,500
Liability insurance ($2,800)	2,800
Employee health insurance ($21,300)	21,300
Miscellaneous ($1,200 + $0.20q)	1,420
Total expense	167,490
Net operating income	$ 30,510

EXHIBIT 9–5
Flexible Budget Based on Actual Activity

398   Chapter 9

actual number of client-visits in March, the profit should have been even higher—$30,510. What are the causes of these discrepancies? Rick would certainly like to build on the positive factors, while working to reduce the negative factors. But what are they?

Flexible Budget Variances

To answer Rick's questions concerning the discrepancies between budgeted and actual costs, Victoria broke down the variances shown in Exhibit 9–4 into two types of variances—activity variances and revenue and spending variances. We explain how she did it in the next two sections.

Activity Variances

LO9–2
Prepare a report showing activity variances.

Part of the discrepancy between the budgeted profit and the actual profit is due to the fact that the actual level of activity in March was higher than expected. How much of this discrepancy was due to this single factor? Victoria prepared the report in Exhibit 9–6 to answer this question. In that report, the flexible budget based on the actual level of activity for the period is compared to the planning budget from the beginning of the period. The flexible budget shows what should have happened at the actual level of activity, whereas the planning budget shows what should have happened at the budgeted level of activity. Therefore, the differences between the flexible budget and the planning budget show what should have happened solely because the actual level of activity differed from what had been expected.

For example, the flexible budget based on 1,100 client-visits shows revenue of $198,000 (= $180 per client-visit × 1,100 client-visits). The planning budget based on 1,000 client-visits shows revenue of $180,000 (= $180 per client-visit × 1,000 client-visits). Because the salon had 100 more client-visits than anticipated in the

EXHIBIT 9–6
Activity Variances from Comparing the Flexible Budget Based on Actual Activity to the Planning Budget

Rick's Hairstyling Activity Variances For the Month Ended March 31	Flexible Budget	Planning Budget	Activity Variances*
Client-visits	1,100	1,000	
Revenue ($180.00q)	$198,000	$180,000	$18,000 F
Expenses:			
Wages and salaries ($65,000 + $37.00q)	105,700	102,000	3,700 U
Hairstyling supplies ($1.50q)	1,650	1,500	150 U
Client gratuities ($4.10q)	4,510	4,100	410 U
Electricity ($1,500 + $0.10q)	1,610	1,600	10 U
Rent ($28,500)	28,500	28,500	0
Liability insurance ($2,800)	2,800	2,800	0
Employee health insurance ($21,300)	21,300	21,300	0
Miscellaneous ($1,200 + $0.20q)	1,420	1,400	20 U
Total expense	167,490	163,200	4,290 U
Net operating income	$ 30,510	$ 16,800	$13,710 F

*The revenue variance is labeled favorable (unfavorable) when the revenue in the flexible budget is greater than (less than) the planning budget. The expense variances are labeled favorable (unfavorable) when the expense in the flexible budget is less than (greater than) the planning budget.

budget, actual revenue should have been higher than budgeted revenue by $18,000 (= $198,000 − $180,000). This activity variance is shown on the report as $18,000 F (favorable). Similarly, the flexible budget based on 1,100 client-visits shows electricity costs of $1,610 (= $1,500 + $0.10 per client-visit × 1,100 client-visits). The planning budget based on 1,000 client-visits shows electricity costs of $1,600 (= $1,500 + $0.10 per client-visit × 1,000 client-visits). Because the salon had 100 more client-visits than anticipated in the budget, actual electricity costs should have been higher than budgeted costs by $10 (= $1,610 − $1,600). The activity variance for electricity is shown on the report as $10 U (unfavorable). Note that in this case, the label "unfavorable" may be a little misleading. Costs *should* be $10 higher for electricity simply because business was up by 100 client-visits; therefore, is this variance really unfavorable if it was a necessary cost of serving more customers? For reasons such as this, we would like to caution you against assuming that unfavorable variances always indicate bad performance and favorable variances always indicate good performance.

Because all of the variances on this report are solely due to the difference between the actual level of activity and the level of activity in the planning budget from the beginning of the period, they are called **activity variances**. For example, the activity variance for revenue is $18,000 F, the activity variance for electricity is $10 U, and so on. The most important activity variance appears at the very bottom of the report; namely, the $13,710 F (favorable) variance for net operating income. This variance says that because activity was higher than expected in the planning budget, the net operating income should have been $13,710 higher. We caution against placing too much emphasis on any other single variance in this report. As we have said above, one would expect some costs to be higher as a consequence of more business. It is misleading to think of these unfavorable variances as indicative of poor performance.

On the other hand, the favorable activity variance for net operating income is important. Let's explore this variance a bit more thoroughly. First, as we have already noted, activity was up by 10%, but the flexible budget indicates that net operating income should have increased much more than 10%. A 10% increase in net operating income from the $16,800 in the planning budget would result in net operating income of $18,480 (= 1.1 × $16,800); however, the flexible budget shows much higher net operating income of $30,510. Why? The short answer is: Because of the presence of fixed costs. When we apply the 10% increase to the budgeted net operating income to estimate the profit at the higher level of activity, we implicitly assume that the revenues and *all* of the costs increase by 10%. But they do not. Note that when the activity level increases by 10%, three of the costs—rent, liability insurance, and employee health insurance—do not increase at all. These are all purely fixed costs. So while sales do increase by 10%, these costs do not increase. This results in net operating income increasing by more than 10%. A similar effect occurs with the mixed costs, which contain fixed cost elements—wages and salaries, electricity, and miscellaneous. While sales increase by 10%, these mixed costs increase by less than 10%, resulting in an overall increase in net operating income of more than 10%. Because of the existence of fixed costs, net operating income does not change in proportion to changes in the level of activity. There is a leverage effect. The percentage changes in net operating income are ordinarily larger than the percentage increases in activity.

Revenue and Spending Variances

In the last section we answered the question "What impact did the change in activity have on our revenues, costs, and profit?" In this section we will answer the question "How well did we control our revenues, our costs, and our profit?"

Recall that the flexible budget based on the actual level of activity in Exhibit 9–5 shows what *should have happened given the actual level of activity*. Therefore, Victoria's next step was to compare actual results to the flexible budget—in essence comparing what actually happened to what should have happened. Her work is shown in Exhibit 9–7.

LO9–3
Prepare a report showing revenue and spending variances.

EXHIBIT 9–7
Revenue and Spending
Variances from Comparing
Actual Results to the Flexible
Budget

Rick's Hairstyling
Revenue and Spending Variances
For the Month Ended March 31

	Actual Results	Flexible Budget	Revenue and Spending Variances*
Client-visits	1,100	1,100	
Revenue ($180.00q)	$194,200	$198,000	$3,800 U
Expenses:			
Wages and salaries ($65,000 + $37.00q)	106,900	105,700	1,200 U
Hairstyling supplies ($1.50q)	1,620	1,650	30 F
Client gratuities ($4.10q)	6,870	4,510	2,360 U
Electricity ($1,500 + $0.10q)	1,550	1,610	60 F
Rent ($28,500)	28,500	28,500	0
Liability insurance ($2,800)	2,800	2,800	0
Employee health insurance ($21,300)	22,600	21,300	1,300 U
Miscellaneous ($1,200 + $0.20q)	2,130	1,420	710 U
Total expense	172,970	167,490	5,480 U
Net operating income	$ 21,230	$ 30,510	$9,280 U

*The revenue variance is labeled favorable (unfavorable) when the actual revenue
is greater than (less than) the flexible budget. The expense variances are labeled
favorable (unfavorable) when the actual expense is less than (greater than) the
flexible budget.

Focusing first on revenue, the actual revenue totaled $194,200. However, the flexible budget indicates that, given the actual level of activity, revenue should have been $198,000. Consequently, revenue was $3,800 less than it should have been, given the actual number of client-visits for the month. This discrepancy is labeled as a $3,800 U (unfavorable) variance and is called a *revenue variance*. A **revenue variance** is the difference between the actual total revenue and what the total revenue should have been, given the actual level of activity for the period. If actual revenue exceeds what the revenue should have been, the variance is labeled favorable. If actual revenue is less than

IN BUSINESS

STATE OF THE UNION SPEECH HURTS CORPORATE JET INDUSTRY

In December 2008, Detroit auto executives flew private corporate jets to Washington D.C. to plead for billions of taxpayer dollars to save their companies. The public outcry was loud and clear: How could companies on the verge of bankruptcy afford to transport their executives in private corporate jets? One month later President Obama's State of the Union speech included criticism of CEOs who "disappear on a private jet."

The impact of these events on the corporate jet manufacturing industry was swift and severe. Dassault Aviation had 27 more order cancellations than new orders in the first quarter of 2009. Cessna Aircraft had 92 first-quarter order cancellations and laid off 42% of its workforce. Approximately 3,100 jets flooded the resale market compared to 1,800 jets for resale in the first quarter of the prior year. The CEO of Cessna and the president of Gulfstream Aerospace went to the White House in May 2009 to seek an end to the rhetoric that was destroying their sales.

These facts illustrate how an activity variance can be affected by uncontrollable events. The actual first-quarter sales at these companies were substantially lower than their budgeted sales due to reasons that they could not foresee or control.

Source: Carol Matlack, "Public Flak Grounds Private Jets," *BusinessWeek*, June 8, 2009, p. 13.

what the revenue should have been, the variance is labeled unfavorable. Why would actual revenue be less than or more than it should have been, given the actual level of activity? Basically, the revenue variance is favorable if the average selling price is greater than expected; it is unfavorable if the average selling price is less than expected. This could happen for a variety of reasons including a change in selling price, a different mix of products sold, a change in the amount of discounts given, poor accounting controls, and so on.

Focusing next on costs, the actual electricity cost was $1,550; however, the flexible budget indicates that electricity costs should have been $1,610 for the 1,100 client-visits in March. Because the cost was $60 less than we would have expected for the actual level of activity during the period, it is labeled as a favorable variance, $60 F. This is an example of a *spending variance*. By definition, a **spending variance** is the difference between the actual amount of the cost and how much a cost should have been, given the actual level of activity. If the actual cost is greater than what the cost should have been, the variance is labeled as unfavorable. If the actual cost is less than what the cost should have been, the variance is labeled as favorable. Why would a cost have a favorable or unfavorable variance? There are many possible explanations including paying a higher price for inputs than should have been paid, using too many inputs for the actual level of activity, a change in technology, and so on. In the next chapter we will explore these types of explanations in greater detail.

Note from Exhibit 9–7 that the overall net operating income variance is $9,280 U (unfavorable). This means that given the actual level of activity for the period, the net operating income was $9,280 lower than it should have been. There are a number of reasons for this. The most prominent is the unfavorable revenue variance of $3,800. Next in line is the $2,360 unfavorable variance for client gratuities. Looking at this in another way, client gratuities were more than 50% larger than they should have been according to the flexible budget. This is a variance that Rick would almost certainly want to investigate further. He may find that this unfavorable variance is not necessarily a bad thing. It is possible, for example, that more lavish use of gratuities led to the 10% increase in client-visits.

Exhibit 9–7 also includes a $1,300 unfavorable variance related to employee health insurance, thereby highlighting how a fixed cost can have a spending variance. While fixed costs do not depend on the level of activity, the actual amount of a fixed cost can differ from the estimated amount included in a flexible budget. For example, perhaps Rick's employee health insurance premiums unexpectedly increased by $1,300 during March.

In conclusion, the revenue and spending variances in Exhibit 9–7 will help Rick better understand why his actual net operating income differs from what should have happened given the actual level of activity.

A Performance Report Combining Activity and Revenue and Spending Variances

Exhibit 9–8 displays Victoria's performance report that combines the activity variances (from Exhibit 9–6) with the revenue and spending variances (from Exhibit 9–7). The report brings together information from those two earlier exhibits in a way that makes it easier to interpret what happened during the period. The format of this report is a bit different from the format of the previous reports in that the variances appear between the amounts being compared rather than after them. For example, the activity variances appear between the flexible budget amounts and the planning budget amounts. In Exhibit 9–6, the activity variances appeared after the flexible budget and the planning budget.

Note two numbers in particular in the performance report—the activity variance for net operating income of $13,710 F (favorable) and the overall revenue and spending variance for net operating income of $9,280 U (unfavorable). It is worth repeating what those two numbers mean. The $13,710 favorable activity variance occurred because actual

LO9–4
Prepare a performance report that combines activity variances and revenue and spending variances.

EXHIBIT 9–8
Performance Report Combining Activity Variances with Revenue and Spending Variances

Rick's Hairstyling
Flexible Budget Performance Report
For the Month Ended March 31

	(1) Actual Results	Revenue and Spending Variances (1) – (2)	(2) Flexible Budget	Activity Variances (2) – (3)	(3) Planning Budget
Client-visits	1,100		1,100		1,000
Revenue ($180.00q)	$194,200	$3,800 U	$198,000	$18,000 F	$180,000
Expenses:					
Wages and salaries ($65,000 + $37.00q)	106,900	1,200 U	105,700	3,700 U	102,000
Hairstyling supplies ($1.50q)	1,620	30 F	1,650	150 U	1,500
Client gratuities ($4.10q)	6,870	2,360 U	4,510	410 U	4,100
Electricity ($1,500 + $0.10q)	1,550	60 F	1,610	10 U	1,600
Rent ($28,500)	28,500	0	28,500	0	28,500
Liability insurance ($2,800)	2,800	0	2,800	0	2,800
Employee health insurance ($21,300)	22,600	1,300 U	21,300	0	21,300
Miscellaneous ($1,200 + $0.20q)	2,130	710 U	1,420	20 U	1,400
Total expense	172,970	5,480 U	167,490	4,290 U	163,200
Net operating income	$ 21,230	$9,280 U	$ 30,510	$13,710 F	$ 16,800

activity (1,100 client-visits) was greater than the budgeted level of activity (1,000 client-visits). The $9,280 unfavorable overall revenue and spending variance occurred because the profit was not as large as it should have been for the actual level of activity for the period. These two different variances mean very different things and call for different types of actions. To generate a favorable activity variance for net operating income, managers must take actions to increase client-visits. To generate a favorable overall revenue and spending variance, managers must take actions to protect selling prices, increase operating efficiency, and reduce the prices of inputs.

The performance report in Exhibit 9–8 provides much more useful information to managers than the simple comparison of budgeted to actual results in Exhibit 9–4. In Exhibit 9–4, the effects of changes in activity were jumbled together with the effects of how well prices were controlled and operations were managed. The performance report in Exhibit 9–8 clearly separates these effects, allowing managers to take a much more focused approach in evaluating operations.

To get a better idea of how the performance report accomplishes this task, look at hairstyling supplies in the performance report. The actual cost of hairstyling supplies was $1,620 for the period, whereas in the planning budget, this cost was $1,500. In the comparison of the actual results to the planning budget in Exhibit 9–4, this difference is shown as an unfavorable variance of $120. Exhibit 9–4 uses a static planning budget approach that compares actual costs at one level of activity to budgeted costs at a different level of activity. As we said before, this is like comparing apples to oranges. This variance is actually a mixture of two different effects. This becomes clear in the performance report in Exhibit 9–8. The $120 difference between the actual results and the budgeted amount is composed of two different variances—a favorable spending variance of $30 and an unfavorable activity variance of $150. The favorable spending variance occurred because less was spent on hairstyling supplies than one would have expected, given the actual level of activity for the month. The activity variance occurs because activity was greater than anticipated in the planning budget, which naturally resulted in a higher total cost for this variable cost.

The flexible budget performance report in Exhibit 9–8 provides a more valid assessment of performance than simply comparing actual costs to static planning budget costs because actual costs are compared to what costs should have been at the actual level of activity. In other words, apples are compared to apples. When this is done, we see that the spending variance for hairstyling supplies is $30 F (favorable) rather than $120 U (unfavorable) as it was in the original static planning budget performance report (see Exhibit 9–4). In some cases, as with hairstyling supplies in Rick's report, an unfavorable static planning budget variance may be transformed into a favorable revenue or spending variance when an increase in activity is properly taken into account. The following discussion took place the next day at Rick's salon.

MANAGERIAL ACCOUNTING IN ACTION
THE WRAP-UP

Victoria: Let me show you what I've got. [Victoria shows Rick the flexible budget performance report in Exhibit 9–8.] I simply used the cost formulas to update the budget to reflect the increase in client-visits you experienced in March. That allowed me to come up with a better benchmark for what the costs should have been.

Rick: That's what you labeled the "flexible budget based on 1,100 client-visits"?

Victoria: That's right. Your original budget was based on 1,000 client-visits, so it understated what some of the costs should have been when you actually served 1,100 customers.

Rick: That's clear enough. These spending variances aren't quite as shocking as the variances on my first report.

Victoria: Yes, but you still have an unfavorable variance of $2,360 for client gratuities.

Rick: I know how that happened. In March there was a big political fundraising dinner that I forgot about when I prepared the March budget. To fit all of our regular clients in, we had to push them through here pretty fast. Everyone still got top-rate service, but I felt bad about not being able to spend as much time with each customer. I wanted to give my customers a little extra something to compensate them for the less personal service, so I ordered a lot of flowers, which I gave away by the bunch.

Victoria: With the prices you charge, Rick, I am sure the gesture was appreciated.

Rick: One thing bothers me about the report. When we discussed my costs before, you called rent, liability insurance, and employee health insurance fixed costs. How can I have a variance for a fixed cost? Doesn't fixed mean that it doesn't change?

Victoria: We call these costs *fixed* because they shouldn't be affected by *changes in the level of activity*. However, that doesn't mean that they can't change for other reasons. Also, the use of the term *fixed* also suggests to people that the cost can't be controlled, but that isn't true. It is often easier to control fixed costs than variable costs. For example, it would be fairly easy for you to change your insurance bill by adjusting the amount of insurance you carry. It would be more difficult for you to significantly reduce your spending on hairstyling supplies—a variable cost that is a necessary part of serving customers.

Rick: I think I understand, but it *is* confusing.

Victoria: Just remember that a cost is called variable if it is proportional to activity; it is called fixed if it does not depend on the level of activity. However, fixed costs can change for reasons unrelated to changes in the level of activity. And controllability has little to do with whether a cost is variable or fixed. Fixed costs are often more controllable than variable costs.

IN BUSINESS

HOTELS MANAGE REVENUE AND COST LEVERS AMID RECESSION

When the economy spiraled downward in 2009, it forced hotel chains to make tough decisions in an effort to achieve their profit goals. For example, Wyndham Hotels and Resorts decided to take sewing kits, mouthwash, and showercaps out of its rooms—instead, requiring customers to ask for these amenities at the front desk. Intercontinental Hotels Group stopped delivering newspapers to loyalty-program members' rooms; Marriott International cut back its breakfast offerings; and the Ritz-Carlton reduced operating hours at its restaurants, spas, and retail shops. In addition, many hotel chains reduced their rental rates.

A flexible budget performance report can help hotel managers analyze how the changes described above impact net operating income. It isolates activity, revenue, and spending variances that help identify the underlying reasons for differences between budgeted and actual net operating income.

Source: Sarah Nassauer, "No Showercaps at the Inn," *The Wall Street Journal*, January 22, 2009, pp. D1–D2.

Performance Reports in Nonprofit Organizations

The performance reports in nonprofit organizations are basically the same as the performance reports we have considered so far—with one prominent difference. Nonprofit organizations usually receive a significant amount of funding from sources other than sales. For example, universities receive their funding from sales (i.e., tuition charged to students), from endowment income and donations, and—in the case of public universities—from state appropriations. This means that, like costs, the revenue in governmental and nonprofit organizations may consist of both fixed and variable elements. For example, the Seattle Opera Company's revenue in a recent year consisted of grants and donations of $12,719,000 and ticket sales of $8,125,000 (or about $75.35 per ticket sold). Consequently, the revenue formula for the opera can be written as:

$$\text{Revenue} = \$12,719,000 + \$75.35q$$

where q is the number of tickets sold. In other respects, the performance report for the Seattle Opera and other nonprofit organizations would be similar to the performance report in Exhibit 9–8.

Performance Reports in Cost Centers

Performance reports are often prepared for organizations that do not have any source of outside revenue. In particular, in a large organization a performance report may be prepared for each department—including departments that do not sell anything to outsiders. For example, a performance report is very commonly prepared for production departments in manufacturing companies. Such reports should be prepared using the same principles we have discussed and should look very much like the performance report in Exhibit 9–8—with the exception that revenue, and consequently net operating income, will not appear on the report. Because the managers in these departments are responsible for costs, but not revenues, they are often called *cost centers*.

Flexible Budgets with Multiple Cost Drivers

LO9–5
Prepare a flexible budget with more than one cost driver.

At Rick's Hairstyling, we have thus far assumed that there is only one cost driver—the number of client-visits. However, in the activity-based costing chapter, we found that more than one cost driver might be needed to adequately explain all of the costs in an organization. For example, some of the costs at Rick's Hairstyling probably depend more on the number of

Rick's Hairstyling Flexible Budget For the Month Ended March 31		EXHIBIT 9–9 Flexible Budget Based on More than One Cost Driver
Actual client-visits (q_1)	1,100	
Actual hours of operation (q_2)	190	
Revenue $(\$180.00q_1)$	$198,000	
Expenses:		
Wages and salaries $(\$65,000 + \$220q_2)$	106,800	
Hairstyling supplies $(\$1.50q_1)$	1,650	
Client gratuities $(\$4.10q_1)$	4,510	
Electricity $(\$390 + \$0.10q_1 + \$6.00q_2)$	1,640	
Rent $(\$28,500)$	28,500	
Liability insurance $(\$2,800)$	2,800	
Employee health insurance $(\$21,300)$	21,300	
Miscellaneous $(\$1,200 + \$0.20q_1)$	1,420	
Total expense	168,620	
Net operating income	$ 29,380	

hours that the salon is open for business than the number of client-visits. Specifically, most of Rick's employees are paid salaries, but some are paid on an hourly basis. None of the employees is paid on the basis of the number of customers actually served. Consequently, the cost formula for wages and salaries would be more accurate if it were stated in terms of the hours of operation rather than the number of client-visits. The cost of electricity is even more complex. Some of the cost is fixed—the heat must be kept at some minimum level even at night when the salon is closed. Some of the cost depends on the number of client-visits—the power consumed by hair dryers depends on the number of customers served. Some of the cost depends on the number of hours the salon is open—the costs of lighting the salon and heating it to a comfortable temperature. Consequently, the cost formula for electricity would be more accurate if it were stated in terms of both the number of client-visits and the hours of operation rather than just in terms of the number of client-visits.

   Exhibit 9–9 shows a flexible budget in which these changes have been made. In that flexible budget, two cost drivers are listed—client-visits and hours of operation—where q_1 refers to client-visits and q_2 refers to hours of operation. For example, wages and salaries

HOSPITALS TURN TO FLEXIBLE BUDGETS

Mary Wilkes, a senior managing director with Phase 2 Consulting, says that hospitals may have to pay as much as $300,000 to install a flexible budgeting system, but the investment should readily pay for itself by enabling "more efficient use of hospital resources, particularly when it comes to labor." One of the keys to creating an effective flexible budgeting system is to recognize the existence of multiple cost drivers. Many hospitals frequently use patient volume as a cost driver when preparing flexible budgets; however, other variables can influence revenues and costs. For example, the percentage of patients covered by private insurance, Medicaid, or Medicare, as well as the proportion of uninsured patients all influence revenues and costs. A flexible budgeting system that incorporates patient volume and these other variables will be more accurate than one based solely on patient volume.

Source: Paul Barr, "Flexing Your Budget," *Modern Healthcare*, September 12, 2005, pp. 24–26.

Chapter 9

depend on the hours of operation and its cost formula is $65,000 + $220q_2$. Because the salon actually operated 190 hours, the flexible budget amount for wages and salaries is $106,800 (= $65,000 + 220×190). The electricity cost depends on both client-visits and the hours of operation and its cost formula is $390 + $0.10q_1 + $6.00q_2$. Because the actual number of client-visits was 1,100 and the salon actually operated for 190 hours, the flexible budget amount for electricity is $1,640 (= $390 + $0.10 \times 1,100 + 6.00×190). Notice that the net operating income in the flexible budget based on two cost drivers is $29,380, whereas the net operating income in the flexible budget based on one cost driver (see Exhibit 9–5) is $30,510. These two amounts differ because the flexible budget based on two cost drivers is more accurate than the flexible budget based on one driver.

The revised flexible budget based on both client-visits and hours of operation can be used exactly like we used the earlier flexible budget based on just client-visits to compute activity variances as in Exhibit 9–6, revenue and spending variances as in Exhibit 9–7, and a performance report as in Exhibit 9–8. The difference is that because the cost formulas based on more than one cost driver are more accurate than the cost formulas based on just one cost driver, the variances will also be more accurate.

Some Common Errors

LO9–6

Understand common errors made in preparing performance reports based on budgets and actual results.

We started this chapter by discussing the need for managers to understand the difference between what actually happened and what was expected to happen—formalized by the planning budget. To meet this need, we developed a flexible budget that allowed us to isolate activity variances and revenue and spending variances. Unfortunately, this approach is not always followed in practice—resulting in misleading and difficult-to-interpret reports. The most common errors in preparing performance reports are to implicitly assume that all costs are fixed or to implicitly assume that all costs are variable. These erroneous assumptions lead to inaccurate benchmarks and incorrect variances.

We have already discussed one of these errors—assuming that all costs are fixed. This is the error that is made when static planning budget costs are compared to actual costs without any adjustment for the actual level of activity. Such a comparison appeared in Exhibit 9–4. For convenience, the comparison of actual to budgeted revenues and costs is repeated in Exhibit 9–10. Looking at that exhibit, note that the actual cost of hairstyling supplies of $1,620 is directly compared to the budgeted cost of $1,500, resulting in an unfavorable variance of $120. But this comparison only makes sense if the cost of hairstyling supplies is

EXHIBIT 9–10
Faulty Analysis Comparing Actual Amounts to Budgeted Amounts (Implicitly Assumes All Income Statement Items Are Fixed)

Rick's Hairstyling For the Month Ended March 31			
	Actual Results	Planning Budget	Variances
Client-visits	1,100	1,000	
Revenue	$194,200	$180,000	$14,200 F
Expenses:			
Wages and salaries	106,900	102,000	4,900 U
Hairstyling supplies	1,620	1,500	120 U
Client gratuities	6,870	4,100	2,770 U
Electricity	1,550	1,600	50 F
Rent	28,500	28,500	0
Liability insurance	2,800	2,800	0
Employee health insurance	22,600	21,300	1,300 U
Miscellaneous	2,130	1,400	730 U
Total expense	172,970	163,200	9,770 U
Net operating income	$ 21,230	$ 16,800	$ 4,430 F

Rick's Hairstyling For the Month Ended March 31	(1) Actual Results	(2) Planning Budget × (1,100/1,000)	Variances (1) – (2)
Client-visits	1,100		
Revenue	$194,200	$198,000	$3,800 U
Expenses:			
Wages and salaries	106,900	112,200	5,300 F
Hairstyling supplies	1,620	1,650	30 F
Client gratuities	6,870	4,510	2,360 U
Electricity	1,550	1,760	210 F
Rent	28,500	31,350	2,850 F
Liability insurance	2,800	3,080	280 F
Employee health insurance	22,600	23,430	830 F
Miscellaneous	2,130	1,540	590 U
Total expense	172,970	179,520	6,550 F
Net operating income	$ 21,230	$ 18,480	$2,750 F

EXHIBIT 9–11
Faulty Analysis That Assumes All
Budget Items Are Variable

fixed. If the cost of hairstyling supplies isn't fixed (and indeed it is not), one would *expect* the cost to go up because of the increase in activity over the budget. Comparing actual costs to static planning budget costs only makes sense if the cost is fixed. If the cost isn't fixed, it needs to be adjusted for any change in activity that occurs during the period.

The other common error when comparing budgets to actual results is to assume that all costs are variable. A report that makes this error appears in Exhibit 9–11. The variances in this report are computed by comparing actual results to the amounts in the second numerical column where *all* of the budget items have been inflated by 10%—the percentage by which activity increased. This is a perfectly valid adjustment to make if an item is strictly variable—like sales and hairstyling supplies. It is *not* a valid adjustment if the item contains any fixed element. Take, for example, rent. If the salon serves 10% more customers in a given month, would you expect the rent to increase by 10%? The answer is no. Ordinarily, the rent is fixed in advance and does not depend on the volume of business. Therefore, the amount shown in the second numerical column of $31,350 is incorrect, which leads to the erroneous favorable variance of $2,850. In fact, the actual rent paid was exactly equal to the budgeted rent, so there should be no variance at all on a valid report.

IN BUSINESS

SNOW REMOVAL BUDGETS GET PLOWED UNDER

The District of Columbia budgeted $6.2 million for its annual snow removal needs based on an expectation of 15 inches of snow per year. So, when it received 28 inches of snow in one weekend, its snow removal budget got plowed under. During this same weekend, the Virginia Department of Transportation estimated that 500,000 tons of snow dropped on its northern Virginia roadways, leading to historic cost overruns in its $79 million snow removal budget.

In these types of situations, a flexible budget can help managers assess operational efficiency. For example, a manager could create a cost formula such as "the snow removal cost per inch of snow" to estimate what the total variable snow removal costs should be for the actual inches of snowfall. This "flexed" snow removal cost could be compared to the actual snow removal cost in an effort to identify sources of exceptional performance or opportunities for process improvement.

Source: Sudeep Reddy and Clare Ansberry, "States Face Big Costs to Dig Out From Blizzard," *The Wall Street Journal*, February 9, 2010, p. A6.

Summary

Directly comparing actual revenues and costs to static planning budget revenues and costs can easily lead to erroneous conclusions. Actual revenues and costs differ from budgeted revenues and costs for a variety of reasons, but one of the biggest is a change in the level of activity. One would expect actual revenues and costs to increase or decrease as the activity level increases or decreases. Flexible budgets enable managers to isolate the various causes of the differences between budgeted and actual costs.

A flexible budget is a budget that is adjusted to the actual level of activity. It is the best estimate of what revenues and costs should have been, given the actual level of activity during the period. The flexible budget can be compared to the budget from the beginning of the period or to the actual results.

When the flexible budget is compared to the budget from the beginning of the period, activity variances are the result. An activity variance shows how a revenue or cost should have changed in response to the difference between actual and budgeted activity.

When actual results are compared to the flexible budget, revenue and spending variances are the result. A favorable revenue variance indicates that revenue was larger than should have been expected, given the actual level of activity. An unfavorable revenue variance indicates that revenue was less than it should have been, given the actual level of activity. A favorable spending variance indicates that the cost was less than expected, given the actual level of activity. An unfavorable spending variance indicates that the cost was greater than it should have been, given the actual level of activity.

A flexible budget performance report combines activity variances and revenue and spending variances on one report.

Common errors in comparing actual costs to budgeted costs are to assume all costs are fixed or to assume all costs are variable. If all costs are assumed to be fixed, the variances for variable and mixed costs will be incorrect. If all costs are assumed to be variable, the variances for fixed and mixed costs will be incorrect. The variance for a cost will only be correct if the actual behavior of the cost is used to develop the flexible budget benchmark.

Review Problem: Variance Analysis Using a Flexible Budget

Harrald's Fish House is a family-owned restaurant that specializes in Scandinavian-style seafood. Data concerning the restaurant's monthly revenues and costs appear below (q refers to the number of meals served):

	Formula
Revenue	$16.50q$
Cost of ingredients	$6.25q$
Wages and salaries	$10,400
Utilities	$800 + 0.20q$
Rent	$2,200
Miscellaneous	$600 + 0.80q$

Required:

1. Prepare the restaurant's planning budget for April assuming that 1,800 meals are served.
2. Assume that 1,700 meals were actually served in April. Prepare a flexible budget for this level of activity.
3. The actual results for April appear below. Prepare a flexible budget performance report for the restaurant for April.

Revenue	$27,920
Cost of ingredients	$11,110
Wages and salaries	$10,130
Utilities	$1,080
Rent	$2,200
Miscellaneous	$2,240

Solution to Review Problem

1. The planning budget for April appears below:

Harrald's Fish House Planning Budget For the Month Ended April 30	
Budgeted meals served (q)	1,800
Revenue ($16.50q)	$29,700
Expenses:	
Cost of ingredients ($6.25q)	11,250
Wages and salaries ($10,400)	10,400
Utilities ($800 + $0.20q)	1,160
Rent ($2,200)	2,200
Miscellaneous ($600 + $0.80q)	2,040
Total expense	27,050
Net operating income	$ 2,650

2. The flexible budget for April appears below:

Harrald's Fish House Flexible Budget For the Month Ended April 30	
Actual meals served (q)	1,700
Revenue ($16.50q)	$28,050
Expenses:	
Cost of ingredients ($6.25q)	10,625
Wages and salaries ($10,400)	10,400
Utilities ($800 + $0.20q)	1,140
Rent ($2,200)	2,200
Miscellaneous ($600 + $0.80q)	1,960
Total expense	26,325
Net operating income	$ 1,725

3. The flexible budget performance report for April appears below:

Harrald's Fish House Flexible Budget Performance Report For the Month Ended April 30					
	(1) Actual Results	Revenue and Spending Variances (1) – (2)	(2) Flexible Budget	Activity Variances (2) – (3)	(3) Planning Budget
Meals served	1,700		1,700		1,800
Revenue ($16.50q)	$27,920	$130 U	$28,050	$1,650 U	$29,700
Expenses:					
Cost of ingredients ($6.25q)	11,110	485 U	10,625	625 F	11,250
Wages and salaries ($10,400)	10,130	270 F	10,400	0	10,400
Utilities ($800 + $0.20q)	1,080	60 F	1,140	20 F	1,160
Rent ($2,200)	2,200	0	2,200	0	2,200
Miscellaneous ($600 + $0.80q)	2,240	280 U	1,960	80 F	2,040
Total expense	26,760	435 U	26,325	725 F	27,050
Net operating income	$ 1,160	$565 U	$ 1,725	$ 925 U	$ 2,650

Glossary

Activity variance The difference between a revenue or cost item in the flexible budget and the same item in the static planning budget. An activity variance is due solely to the difference between the actual level of activity used in the flexible budget and the level of activity assumed in the planning budget. (p. 399)

Flexible budget A report showing estimates of what revenues and costs should have been, given the actual level of activity for the period. (p. 394)

Planning budget A budget created at the beginning of the budgeting period that is valid only for the planned level of activity. (p. 394)

Revenue variance The difference between the actual revenue for the period and how much the revenue should have been, given the actual level of activity. A favorable (unfavorable) revenue variance occurs because the revenue is higher (lower) than expected, given the actual level of activity for the period. (p. 400)

Spending variance The difference between the actual amount of the cost and how much the cost should have been, given the actual level of activity. A favorable (unfavorable) spending variance occurs because the cost is lower (higher) than expected, given the actual level of activity for the period. (p. 401)

Questions

9–1 What is a static planning budget?

9–2 What is a flexible budget and how does it differ from a static planning budget?

9–3 What are some of the possible reasons that actual results may differ from what had been budgeted at the beginning of a period?

9–4 Why is it difficult to interpret a difference between how much expense was budgeted and how much was actually spent?

9–5 What is an activity variance and what does it mean?

9–6 What is a revenue variance and what does it mean?

9–7 What is a spending variance and what does it mean?

9–8 What does a flexible budget performance report do that a simple comparison of budgeted to actual results does not do?

9–9 How does a flexible budget based on two cost drivers differ from a flexible budget based on a single cost driver?

9–10 What assumption is implicitly made about cost behavior when actual results are directly compared to a static planning budget? Why is this assumption questionable?

9–11 What assumption is implicitly made about cost behavior when all of the items in a static planning budget are adjusted in proportion to a change in activity? Why is this assumption questionable?

Multiple-choice questions are provided on the text website at www.mhhe.com/garrison15e.

Applying Excel ▤ connect |ACCOUNTING

LO9–1, LO9–2, LO9–3, LO9–4

Available with McGraw-Hill's *Connect® Accounting.*

The Excel worksheet form that appears on the next page is to be used to recreate the Review Problem on pages 408–409. Download the workbook containing this form from the Online Learning Center at www.mhhe.com/garrison15e. *On the website you will also receive instructions about how to use this worksheet form.*

You should proceed to the requirements below only after completing your worksheet.

Required:

1. Check your worksheet by changing the revenue in cell D4 to $16.00; the cost of ingredients in cell D5 to $6.50; and the wages and salaries in cell B6 to $10,000. The activity variance for net operating income should now be $850 U and the spending variance for total expenses

should be $410 U. If you do not get these answers, find the errors in your worksheet and correct them.

   a.   What is the activity variance for revenue? Explain this variance.

   b.   What is the spending variance for the cost of ingredients? Explain this variance.

	A	B	C	D	E	F	G	H
1	Chapter 9: Applying Excel							
2								
3	**Data**							
4	Revenue			$16.50 q				
5	Cost of ingredients			$6.25 q				
6	Wages and salaries	$10,400						
7	Utilities	$800	+	$0.20 q				
8	Rent	$2,200						
9	Miscellaneous	$600	+	$0.80 q				
10								
11	Actual results:							
12	Revenue	$27,920						
13	Cost of ingredients	$11,110						
14	Wages and salaries	$10,130						
15	Utilities	$1,080						
16	Rent	$2,200						
17	Miscellaneous	$2,240						
18								
19	Planning budget activity		1,800	meals served				
20	Actual activity		1,700	meals served				
21								
22	*Enter a formula into each of the cells marked with a ? below*							
23	**Review Problem: Variance Analysis Using a Flexible Budget**							
24								
25	*Construct a flexible budget performance report*							
26			Revenue					
27			and					
28		Actual	Spending		Flexible	Activity		Planning
29		Results	Variances		Budget	Variances		Budget
30	Meals served	?			?			?
31	Revenue	?	?		?	?		?
32	Expenses:							
33	Cost of ingredients	?	?		?	?		?
34	Wages and salaries	?	?		?	?		?
35	Utilities	?	?		?	?		?
36	Rent	?	?		?	?		?
37	Miscellaneous	?	?		?	?		?
38	Total expenses	?	?		?	?		?
39	Net operating income	?	?		?	?		?

H ◀ ▶ H   **Chapter 9 Form**   Filled in Chapter 9 Form   Chapter 9 Form

2.   Revise the data in your worksheet to reflect the results for the following year:

Data

Revenue		$16.50q
Cost of ingredients		$6.25q
Wages and salaries	$10,400	
Utilities	$800 +	$0.20q
Rent	$2,200	
Miscellaneous	$600 +	$0.80q
Actual results:		
Revenue	$28,900	
Cost of ingredients	$11,300	
Wages and salaries	$10,300	
Utilities	$1,120	
Rent	$2,300	
Miscellaneous	$2,020	
Planning budget activity	1,700 meals served	
Actual activity	1,800 meals served	

Using the flexible budget performance report, briefly evaluate the company's performance for the year and indicate where attention should be focused.

The Foundational 15   connect
ACCOUNTING

LO9–1, LO9–2, LO9–3

Available with McGraw-Hill's *Connect® Accounting.*

Adger Corporation is a service company that measures its output based on the number of customers served. The company provided the following fixed and variable cost estimates that it uses for budgeting purposes and the actual results for May as shown below:

	Fixed Element per Month	Variable Element per Customer Served	Actual Total for May
Revenue		$5,000	$160,000
Employee salaries and wages	$50,000	$1,100	$88,000
Travel expenses		$600	$19,000
Other expenses	$36,000		$34,500

When preparing its planning budget the company estimated that it would serve 30 customers per month; however, during May the company actually served 35 customers.

Required:
1. What amount of revenue would be included in Adger's flexible budget for May?
2. What amount of employee salaries and wages would be included in Adger's flexible budget for May?
3. What amount of travel expenses would be included in Adger's flexible budget for May?
4. What amount of other expenses would be included in Adger's flexible budget for May?
5. What net operating income would appear in Adger's flexible budget for May?
6. What is Adger's revenue variance for May?
7. What is Adger's employee salaries and wages spending variance for May?
8. What is Adger's travel expenses spending variance for May?
9. What is Adger's other expenses spending variance for May?
10. What amount of revenue would be included in Adger's planning budget for May?
11. What amount of employee salaries and wages would be included in Adger's planning budget for May?
12. What amount of travel expenses would be included in Adger's planning budget for May?
13. What amount of other expenses would be included in Adger's planning budget for May?
14. What activity variance would Adger report in May with respect to its revenue?
15. What activity variances would Adger report with respect to each of its expenses?

Exercises   connect
ACCOUNTING

All applicable exercises are available with McGraw-Hill's *Connect® Accounting.*

EXERCISE 9–1 Prepare a Flexible Budget [LO9–1]
Puget Sound Divers is a company that provides diving services such as underwater ship repairs to clients in the Puget Sound area. The company's planning budget for May appears below:

Puget Sound Divers Planning Budget For the Month Ended May 31	
Budgeted diving-hours (*q*)	100
Revenue ($365.00*q*)	$36,500
Expenses:	
Wages and salaries ($8,000 + $125.00*q*)	20,500
Supplies ($3.00*q*)	300
Equipment rental ($1,800 + $32.00*q*)	5,000
Insurance ($3,400)	3,400
Miscellaneous ($630 + $1.80*q*)	810
Total expense	30,010
Net operating income	$ 6,490

Required:
During May, the company's activity was actually 105 diving-hours. Prepare a flexible budget for that level of activity.

EXERCISE 9–2 Prepare a Report Showing Activity Variances [LO9–2]

Flight Café is a company that prepares in-flight meals for airlines in its kitchen located next to the local airport. The company's planning budget for July appears below:

Flight Café Planning Budget For the Month Ended July 31	
Budgeted meals (q)	18,000
Revenue ($4.50q)	$81,000
Expenses:	
Raw materials ($2.40q)	43,200
Wages and salaries ($5,200 + $0.30q)	10,600
Utilities ($2,400 + $0.05q)	3,300
Facility rent ($4,300)	4,300
Insurance ($2,300)	2,300
Miscellaneous ($680 + $0.10q)	2,480
Total expense	66,180
Net operating income	$14,820

In July, 17,800 meals were actually served. The company's flexible budget for this level of activity appears below:

Flight Café Flexible Budget For the Month Ended July 31	
Budgeted meals (q)	17,800
Revenue ($4.50q)	$80,100
Expenses:	
Raw materials ($2.40q)	42,720
Wages and salaries ($5,200 + $0.30q)	10,540
Utilities ($2,400 + $0.05q)	3,290
Facility rent ($4,300)	4,300
Insurance ($2,300)	2,300
Miscellaneous ($680 + $0.10q)	2,460
Total expense	65,610
Net operating income	$14,490

Required:

1. Prepare a report showing the company's activity variances for July.
2. Which of the activity variances should be of concern to management? Explain.

EXERCISE 9–3 Prepare a Report Showing Revenue and Spending Variances [LO9–3]

Quilcene Oysteria farms and sells oysters in the Pacific Northwest. The company harvested and sold 8,000 pounds of oysters in August. The company's flexible budget for August appears below:

Quilcene Oysteria Flexible Budget For the Month Ended August 31	
Actual pounds (q)	8,000
Revenue ($4.00q)	$32,000
Expenses:	
Packing supplies ($0.50q)	4,000
Oyster bed maintenance ($3,200)	3,200
Wages and salaries ($2,900 + $0.30q)	5,300
Shipping ($0.80q)	6,400
Utilities ($830)	830
Other ($450 + $0.05q)	850
Total expense	20,580
Net operating income	$11,420

414   Chapter 9

The actual results for August appear below:

	Quilcene Oysteria Income Statement For the Month Ended August 31
Actual pounds	8,000
Revenue	$35,200
Expenses:	
Packing supplies	4,200
Oyster bed maintenance	3,100
Wages and salaries	5,640
Shipping	6,950
Utilities	810
Other	980
Total expense	21,680
Net operating income	$13,520

Required:

Prepare a report showing the company's revenue and spending variances for August.

EXERCISE 9–4 Prepare a Flexible Budget Performance Report [LO9–4]

Vulcan Flyovers offers scenic overflights of Mount St. Helens, the volcano in Washington State that explosively erupted in 1982. Data concerning the company's operations in July appear below:

	Vulcan Flyovers Operating Data For the Month Ended July 31		
	Actual Results	Flexible Budget	Planning Budget
Flights (q)	48	48	50
Revenue ($320.00q)	$13,650	$15,360	$16,000
Expenses:			
Wages and salaries ($4,000 + $82.00q)	8,430	7,936	8,100
Fuel ($23.00q)	1,260	1,104	1,150
Airport fees ($650 + $38.00q)	2,350	2,474	2,550
Aircraft depreciation ($7.00q)	336	336	350
Office expenses ($190 + $2.00q)	460	286	290
Total expense	12,836	12,136	12,440
Net operating income	$ 814	$ 3,224	$ 3,560

The company measures its activity in terms of flights. Customers can buy individual tickets for overflights or hire an entire plane for an overflight at a discount.

Required:

1. Prepare a flexible budget performance report for July.
2. Which of the variances should be of concern to management? Explain.

EXERCISE 9–5 Prepare a Flexible Budget with More Than One Cost Driver [LO9–5]

Alyeski Tours operates day tours of coastal glaciers in Alaska on its tour boat the Blue Glacier. Management has identified two cost drivers—the number of cruises and the number of passengers—that it uses in its budgeting and performance reports. The company publishes a schedule of day cruises that it may supplement with special sailings if there is sufficient demand. Up to 80 passengers can be accommodated on the tour boat. Data concerning the company's cost formulas appear below:

	Fixed Cost per Month	Cost per Cruise	Cost per Passenger
Vessel operating costs	$5,200	$480.00	$2.00
Advertising	$1,700		
Administrative costs	$4,300	$24.00	$1.00
Insurance	$2,900		

Flexible Budgets and Performance Analysis

For example, vessel operating costs should be $5,200 per month plus $480 per cruise plus $2 per passenger. The company's sales should average $25 per passenger. The company's planning budget for July is based on 24 cruises and 1,400 passengers.

Required:
Prepare the company's planning budget for July.

EXERCISE 9–6 Critique a Variance Report [LO9–6]

The Terminator Inc. provides on-site residential pest extermination services. The company has several mobile teams who are dispatched from a central location in company-owned trucks. The company uses the number of jobs to measure activity. At the beginning of April, the company budgeted for 100 jobs, but the actual number of jobs turned out to be 105. A report comparing the budgeted revenues and costs to the actual revenues and costs appears below:

The Terminator Inc.
Variance Report
For the Month Ended April 30

	Actual Results	Planning Budget	Variances
Jobs	105	100	
Revenue	$20,520	$19,500	$1,020 F
Expenses:			
Mobile team operating costs	10,320	10,000	320 U
Exterminating supplies	960	1,800	840 F
Advertising	800	800	0
Dispatching costs	2,340	2,200	140 U
Office rent	1,800	1,800	0
Insurance	2,100	2,100	0
Total expense	18,320	18,700	380 F
Net operating income	$ 2,200	$ 800	$1,400 F

Required:
Is the above variance report useful for evaluating how well revenues and costs were controlled during April? Why, or why not?

EXERCISE 9–7 Critique a Variance Report [LO9–6]

Refer to the data for The Terminator Inc. in Exercise 9–6. A management intern has suggested that the budgeted revenues and costs should be adjusted for the actual level of activity in April before they are compared to the actual revenues and costs. Because the actual level of activity was 5% higher than budgeted, the intern suggested that all budgeted revenues and costs should be adjusted upward by 5%. A report comparing the budgeted revenues and costs, with this adjustment, to the actual revenues and costs appears below.

The Terminator Inc.
Variance Report
For the Month Ended April 30

	Actual Results	Adjusted Planning Budget	Variances
Jobs	105	105	
Revenue	$20,520	$20,475	$ 45 F
Expenses:			
Mobile team operating costs	10,320	10,500	180 F
Exterminating supplies	960	1,890	930 F
Advertising	800	840	40 F
Dispatching costs	2,340	2,310	30 U
Office rent	1,800	1,890	90 F
Insurance	2,100	2,205	105 F
Total expense	18,320	19,635	1,315 F
Net operating income	$ 2,200	$ 840	$1,360 F

416

Chapter 9

Required:
Is the above variance report useful for evaluating how well revenues and costs were controlled during April? Why, or why not?

EXERCISE 9–8 Flexible Budgets and Activity Variances [LO9–1, LO9–2]
Jake's Roof Repair has provided the following data concerning its costs:

	Fixed Cost per Month	Cost per Repair-Hour
Wages and salaries	$23,200	$16.30
Parts and supplies		$8.60
Equipment depreciation	$1,600	$0.40
Truck operating expenses	$6,400	$1.70
Rent	$3,480	
Administrative expenses	$4,500	$0.80

For example, wages and salaries should be $23,200 plus $16.30 per repair-hour. The company expected to work 2,800 repair-hours in May, but actually worked 2,900 repair-hours. The company expects its sales to be $44.50 per repair-hour.

Required:
Prepare a report showing the company's activity variances for May.

EXERCISE 9–9 Flexible Budget [LO9–1]
Wyckam Manufacturing Inc. has provided the following information concerning its manufacturing costs:

	Fixed Cost per Month	Cost per Machine-Hour
Direct materials		$4.25
Direct labor	$36,800	
Supplies		$0.30
Utilities	$1,400	$0.05
Depreciation	$16,700	
Insurance	$12,700	

For example, utilities should be $1,400 per month plus $0.05 per machine-hour. The company expects to work 5,000 machine-hours in June. Note that the company's direct labor is a fixed cost.

Required:
Prepare the company's planning budget for manufacturing costs for June.

EXERCISE 9–10 Flexible Budget [LO9–1]
Lavage Rapide is a Canadian company that owns and operates a large automatic carwash facility near Montreal. The following table provides data concerning the company's costs:

	Fixed Cost per Month	Cost per Car Washed
Cleaning supplies		$0.80
Electricity	$1,200	$0.15
Maintenance		$0.20
Wages and salaries	$5,000	$0.30
Depreciation	$6,000	
Rent	$8,000	
Administrative expenses	$4,000	$0.10

For example, electricity costs are $1,200 per month plus $0.15 per car washed. The company expects to wash 9,000 cars in August and to collect an average of $4.90 per car washed.

Required:
Prepare the company's planning budget for August.

EXERCISE 9–11 Flexible Budget [LO9–1]

Refer to the data for Lavage Rapide in Exercise 9–10. The company actually washed 8,800 cars in August.

Required:

Prepare the company's flexible budget for August.

EXERCISE 9–12 Prepare a Report Showing Activity Variances [LO9–2]

Refer to the data for Lavage Rapide in Exercise 9–10. The actual operating results for August appear below.

Lavage Rapide Income Statement For the Month Ended August 31	
Actual cars washed	8,800
Revenue	$43,080
Expenses:	
Cleaning supplies	7,560
Electricity	2,670
Maintenance	2,260
Wages and salaries	8,500
Depreciation	6,000
Rent	8,000
Administrative expenses	4,950
Total expense	39,940
Net operating income	$ 3,140

Required:

Prepare a report showing the company's activity variances for August.

EXERCISE 9–13 Prepare a Report Showing Revenue and Spending Variances [LO9–3]

Refer to the data for Lavage Rapide in Exercises 9–10 and 9–12.

Required:

Prepare a report showing the company's revenue and spending variances for August.

EXERCISE 9–14 Prepare a Flexible Budget Performance Report [LO9–4]

Refer to the data for Lavage Rapide in Exercises 9–10 and 9–12.

Required:

Prepare a flexible budget performance report that shows the company's revenue and spending variances and activity variances for August.

EXERCISE 9–15 Flexible Budget Performance Report in a Cost Center [LO9–1, LO9–4]

Packaging Solutions Corporation manufactures and sells a wide variety of packaging products. Performance reports are prepared monthly for each department. The planning budget and flexible budget for the Production Department are based on the following formulas, where q is the number of labor-hours worked in a month:

	Cost Formulas
Direct labor	$15.80q$
Indirect labor	$8,200 + $1.60q$
Utilities	$6,400 + $0.80q$
Supplies	$1,100 + $0.40q$
Equipment depreciation	$23,000 + $3.70q$
Factory rent	$8,400
Property taxes	$2,100
Factory administration	$11,700 + $1.90q$

Chapter 9

The actual costs incurred in March in the Production Department are listed below:

	Actual Cost Incurred in March
Direct labor	$134,730
Indirect labor	$19,860
Utilities	$14,570
Supplies	$4,980
Equipment depreciation	$54,080
Factory rent	$8,700
Property taxes	$2,100
Factory administration	$26,470

Required:
1. The company had budgeted for an activity level of 8,000 labor-hours in March. Prepare the Production Department's planning budget for the month.
2. The company actually worked 8,400 labor-hours in March. Prepare the Production Department's flexible budget for the month.
3. Prepare the Production Department's flexible budget performance report for March, including both the spending and activity variances.
4. What aspects of the flexible budget performance report should be brought to management's attention? Explain.

EXERCISE 9–16 Flexible Budgets and Revenue and Spending Variances [LO9–1, LO9–3]
Via Gelato is a popular neighborhood gelato shop. The company has provided the following data concerning its operations:

	Fixed Element per Month	Variable Element per Liter	Actual Total for June
Revenue		$12.00	$71,540
Raw materials		$4.65	$29,230
Wages	$5,600	$1.40	$13,860
Utilities	$1,630	$0.20	$3,270
Rent	$2,600		$2,600
Insurance	$1,350		$1,350
Miscellaneous	$650	$0.35	$2,590

While gelato is sold by the cone or cup, the shop measures its activity in terms of the total number of liters of gelato sold. For example, wages should be $5,600 plus $1.40 per liter of gelato sold and the actual wages for June were $13,860. Via Gelato expected to sell 6,000 liters in June, but actually sold 6,200 liters.

Required:
Prepare a report showing Via Gelato revenue and spending variances for June.

EXERCISE 9–17 Flexible Budget Performance Report [LO9–1, LO9–4]
AirQual Test Corporation provides on-site air quality testing services. The company has provided the following data concerning its operations:

	Fixed Component per Month	Variable Component per Job	Actual Total for February
Revenue		$360	$18,950
Technician wages	$6,400		$6,450
Mobile lab operating expenses	$2,900	$35	$4,530
Office expenses	$2,600	$2	$3,050
Advertising expenses	$970		$995
Insurance	$1,680		$1,680
Miscellaneous expenses	$500	$3	$465

The company uses the number of jobs as its measure of activity. For example, mobile lab operating expenses should be $2,900 plus $35 per job, and the actual mobile lab operating expenses for February were $4,530.

The company expected to work 50 jobs in February, but actually worked 52 jobs.

Required:
Prepare a flexible budget performance report showing AirQual Test Corporation's revenue and spending variances and activity variances for February.

EXERCISE 9–18 Working with More Than One Cost Driver [LO9–4, LO9–5]
The Gourmand Cooking School runs short cooking courses at its small campus. Management has identified two cost drivers that it uses in its budgeting and performance reports—the number of courses and the total number of students. For example, the school might run two courses in a month and have a total of 50 students enrolled in those two courses. Data concerning the company's cost formulas appear below:

	Fixed Cost per Month	Cost per Course	Cost per Student
Instructor wages		$3,080	
Classroom supplies			$260
Utilities	$870	$130	
Campus rent	$4,200		
Insurance	$1,890		
Administrative expenses	$3,270	$15	$4

For example, administrative expenses should be $3,270 per month plus $15 per course plus $4 per student. The company's sales should average $800 per student.

The actual operating results for September appear below:

	Actual
Revenue	$32,400
Instructor wages	$9,080
Classroom supplies	$8,540
Utilities	$1,530
Campus rent	$4,200
Insurance	$1,890
Administrative expenses	$3,790

Required:
1. The Gourmand Cooking School expects to run three courses with a total of 45 students in September. Prepare the company's planning budget for this level of activity.
2. The school actually ran three courses with a total of 42 students in September. Prepare the company's flexible budget for this level of activity.
3. Prepare a flexible budget performance report that shows both revenue and spending variances and activity variances for September.

 Problems

All applicable problems are available with McGraw-Hill's *Connect® Accounting*.

PROBLEM 9–19 Activity and Spending Variances [LO9–1, LO9–2, LO9–3]
You have just been hired by FAB Corporation, the manufacturer of a revolutionary new garage door opening device. The president has asked that you review the company's costing system and "do what you can to help us get better control of our manufacturing overhead costs." You find that the company has never used a flexible budget, and you suggest that preparing such a budget would be an excellent first step in overhead planning and control.

After much effort and analysis, you determined the following cost formulas and gathered the following actual cost data for March:

	Cost Formula	Actual Cost in March
Utilities	$20,600 plus $0.10 per machine-hour	$24,200
Maintenance	$40,000 plus $1.60 per machine-hour	$78,100
Supplies	$0.30 per machine-hour	$8,400
Indirect labor	$130,000 plus $0.70 per machine-hour	$149,600
Depreciation	$70,000	$71,500

During March, the company worked 26,000 machine-hours and produced 15,000 units. The company had originally planned to work 30,000 machine-hours during March.

Required:
1. Prepare a report showing the activity variances for March. Explain what these variances mean.
2. Prepare a report showing the spending variances for March. Explain what these variances mean.

PROBLEM 9–20 More than One Cost Driver [LO9–4, LO9–5]

Milano Pizza is a small neighborhood pizzeria that has a small area for in-store dining as well as offering take-out and free home delivery services. The pizzeria's owner has determined that the shop has two major cost drivers—the number of pizzas sold and the number of deliveries made. Data concerning the pizzeria's costs appear below:

	Fixed Cost per Month	Cost per Pizza	Cost per Delivery
Pizza ingredients		$3.80	
Kitchen staff	$5,220		
Utilities	$630	$0.05	
Delivery person			$3.50
Delivery vehicle	$540		$1.50
Equipment depreciation	$275		
Rent	$1,830		
Miscellaneous	$820	$0.15	

In November, the pizzeria budgeted for 1,200 pizzas at an average selling price of $13.50 per pizza and for 180 deliveries.

Data concerning the pizzeria's operations in November appear below:

	Actual Results
Pizzas	1,240
Deliveries	174
Revenue	$17,420
Pizza ingredients	$4,985
Kitchen staff	$5,281
Utilities	$984
Delivery person	$609
Delivery vehicle	$655
Equipment depreciation	$275
Rent	$1,830
Miscellaneous	$954

Required:

1. Prepare a flexible budget performance report that shows both revenue and spending variances and activity variances for the pizzeria for November.
2. Explain the activity variances.

PROBLEM 9–21 Critique a Report; Prepare a Performance Report [LO9–1, LO9–4, LO9–6]

TipTop Flight School offers flying lessons at a small municipal airport. The school's owner and manager has been attempting to evaluate performance and control costs using a variance report that compares the planning budget to actual results. A recent variance report appears below:

	TipTop Flight School Variance Report For the Month Ended July 31		
	Actual Results	Planning Budget	Variances
Lessons	155	150	
Revenue	$33,900	$33,000	$900 F
Expenses:			
Instructor wages	9,870	9,750	120 U
Aircraft depreciation	5,890	5,700	190 U
Fuel	2,750	2,250	500 U
Maintenance	2,450	2,330	120 U
Ground facility expenses	1,540	1,550	10 F
Administration	3,320	3,390	70 F
Total expense	25,820	24,970	850 U
Net operating income	$ 8,080	$ 8,030	$ 50 F

After several months of using such variance reports, the owner has become frustrated. For example, she is quite confident that instructor wages were very tightly controlled in July, but the report shows an unfavorable variance.

The planning budget was developed using the following formulas, where q is the number of lessons sold:

	Cost Formulas
Revenue	$220q$
Instructor wages	$65q$
Aircraft depreciation	$38q$
Fuel	$15q$
Maintenance	$530 + 12q$
Ground facility expenses	$1,250 + 2q$
Administration	$3,240 + 1q$

Required:
1. Should the owner feel frustrated with the variance reports? Explain.
2. Prepare a flexible budget performance report for the school for July.
3. Evaluate the school's performance for July.

PROBLEM 9–22 Performance Report for a Nonprofit Organization [LO9–1, LO9–4, LO9–6]

The St. Lucia Blood Bank, a private charity partly supported by government grants, is located on the Caribbean island of St. Lucia. The blood bank has just finished its operations for September, which was a particularly busy month due to a powerful hurricane that hit neighboring islands causing many injuries. The hurricane largely bypassed St. Lucia, but residents of St. Lucia willingly donated their blood to help people on other islands. As a consequence, the blood bank collected and processed over 20% more blood than had been originally planned for the month.

A report prepared by a government official comparing actual costs to budgeted costs for the blood bank appears below. Continued support from the government depends on the blood bank's ability to demonstrate control over its costs.

St. Lucia Blood Bank Cost Control Report For the Month Ended September 30			
	Actual Results	Planning Budget	Variances
Liters of blood collected	620	500	
Medical supplies	$ 9,250	$ 7,500	$1,750 U
Lab tests	6,180	6,000	180 U
Equipment depreciation	2,800	2,500	300 U
Rent	1,000	1,000	0
Utilities	570	500	70 U
Administration	11,740	11,250	490 U
Total expense	$31,540	$28,750	$2,790 U

The managing director of the blood bank was very unhappy with this report, claiming that his costs were higher than expected due to the emergency on the neighboring islands. He also pointed out that the additional costs had been fully covered by payments from grateful recipients on the other islands. The government official who prepared the report countered that all of the figures had been submitted by the blood bank to the government; he was just pointing out that actual costs were a lot higher than promised in the budget.

The following cost formulas were used to construct the planning budget:

	Cost Formulas
Medical supplies	$15.00q$
Lab tests	$12.00q$
Equipment depreciation	$2,500
Rent	$1,000
Utilities	$500
Administration	$10,000 + 2.50q$

422

Chapter 9

Required:
1. Prepare a new performance report for September using the flexible budget approach.
2. Do you think any of the variances in the report you prepared should be investigated? Why?

PROBLEM 9–23 Critiquing a Report; Preparing a Performance Budget [LO9–1, LO9–4, LO9–6]

Exchange Corp. is a company that acts as a facilitator in tax-favored real estate swaps. Such swaps, know as 1031 exchanges, permit participants to avoid some or all of the capital gains taxes that would otherwise be due. The bookkeeper for the company has been asked to prepare a report for the company to help its owner/manager analyze performance. The first such report appears below:

	Actual Unit Revenues and Costs	Planning Budget Unit Revenues and Costs	Variances
Exchange Corp			
Analysis of Revenues and Costs			
For the Month Ended May 31			
Exchanges completed	50	40	
Revenue	$385	$395	$10 U
Expenses:			
Legal and search fees	184	165	19 U
Office expenses	112	135	23 F
Equipment depreciation	8	10	2 F
Rent	36	45	9 F
Insurance	4	5	1 F
Total expense	344	360	16 F
Net operating income	$ 41	$ 35	$ 6 F

Note that the revenues and costs in the above report are *unit* revenues and costs. For example, the average office expense is $135 per exchange completed on the planning budget; whereas, the average actual office expense is $112 per exchange completed.

Legal and search fees is a variable cost; office expenses is a mixed cost; and equipment depreciation, rent, and insurance are fixed costs. In the planning budget, the fixed component of office expenses was $5,200.

All of the company's revenues come from fees collected when an exchange is completed.

Required:
1. Evaluate the report prepared by the bookkeeper.
2. Prepare a performance report that would help the owner/manager assess the performance of the company in May.
3. Using the report you created, evaluate the performance of the company in May.

PROBLEM 9–24 Critiquing a Variance Report; Preparing a Performance Report [LO9–1, LO9–4, LO9–6]

Several years ago, Westmont Corporation developed a comprehensive budgeting system for planning and control purposes. While departmental supervisors have been happy with the system, the factory manager has expressed considerable dissatisfaction with the information being generated by the system.

A typical departmental cost report for a recent period follows:

	Actual Results	Planning Budget	Variances
Assembly Department			
Cost Report			
For the Month Ended March 31			
Machine-hours	35,000	40,000	
Variable costs:			
Supplies	$ 29,700	$ 32,000	$ 2,300 F
Scrap	19,500	20,000	500 F
Indirect materials	51,800	56,000	4,200 F
Fixed costs:			
Wages and salaries	79,200	80,000	800 F
Equipment depreciation ...	60,000	60,000	—
Total cost	$240,200	$248,000	$ 7,800 F

After receiving a copy of this cost report, the supervisor of the Assembly Department stated, "These reports are super. It makes me feel really good to see how well things are going in my department. I can't understand why those people upstairs complain so much about the reports."

For the last several years, the company's marketing department has chronically failed to meet the sales goals expressed in the company's monthly budgets.

Required:
1. The company's president is uneasy about the cost reports and would like you to evaluate their usefulness to the company.
2. What changes, if any, should be made in the reports to give better insight into how well departmental supervisors are controlling costs?
3. Prepare a new performance report for the quarter, incorporating any changes you suggested in question (2) above.
4. How well were costs controlled in the Assembly Department in March?

PROBLEM 9–25 Critiquing a Cost Report; Preparing a Performance Report [LO9–1, LO9–4, LO9–6]

Frank Weston, supervisor of the Freemont Corporation's Machining Department, was visibly upset after being reprimanded for his department's poor performance over the prior month. The department's cost control report is given below:

Freemont Corporation–Machining Department Cost Control Report For the Month Ended June 30			
	Actual Results	Planning Budget	Variances
Machine-hours	38,000	35,000	
Direct labor wages	$ 86,100	$ 80,500	$ 5,600 U
Supplies	23,100	21,000	2,100 U
Maintenance	137,300	134,000	3,300 U
Utilities	15,700	15,200	500 U
Supervision	38,000	38,000	0
Depreciation	80,000	80,000	0
Total	$380,200	$368,700	$11,500 U

"I just can't understand all of these unfavorable variances," Weston complained to the supervisor of another department. "When the boss called me in, I thought he was going to give me a pat on the back because I know for a fact that my department worked more efficiently last month than it has ever worked before. Instead, he tore me apart. I thought for a minute that it might be over the supplies that were stolen out of our warehouse last month. But they only amounted to a couple of hundred dollars, and just look at this report. Everything is unfavorable."

Direct labor wages and supplies are variable costs; supervision and depreciation are fixed costs; and maintenance and utilities are mixed costs. The fixed component of the budgeted maintenance cost is $92,000; the fixed component of the budgeted utilities cost is $11,700.

Required:
1. Evaluate the company's cost control report and explain why the variances were all unfavorable.
2. Prepare a performance report that will help Mr. Weston's superiors assess how well costs were controlled in the Machining Department.

Cases

All applicable cases are available with McGraw-Hill's _Connect_® Accounting.

CASE 9–26 Ethics and the Manager [LO9–3]

Tom Kemper is the controller of the Wichita manufacturing facility of Prudhom Enterprises, Inc. The annual cost control report is one of the many reports that must be filed with corporate headquarters and is due at corporate headquarters shortly after the beginning of the New Year. Kemper does not like putting work off to the last minute, so just before Christmas he prepared a preliminary draft of the cost control report. Some adjustments would later be required for transactions that occur between Christmas and New Year's Day. A copy of the preliminary draft report, which Kemper completed on December 21, follows:

Wichita Manufacturing Facility
Cost Control Report
December 21 Preliminary Draft

	Actual Results	Flexible Budget	Spending Variances
Labor-hours	18,000	18,000	
Direct labor	$ 326,000	$ 324,000	$ 2,000 U
Power	19,750	18,000	1,750 U
Supplies	105,000	99,000	6,000 U
Equipment depreciation	343,000	332,000	11,000 U
Supervisory salaries	273,000	275,000	2,000 F
Insurance	37,000	37,000	0
Industrial engineering	189,000	210,000	21,000 F
Factory building lease	60,000	60,000	0
Total expense	$1,352,750	$1,355,000	$ 2,250 F

Melissa Ilianovitch, the general manager at the Wichita facility, asked to see a copy of the preliminary draft report. Kemper carried a copy of the report to her office where the following discussion took place:

Ilianovitch: Ouch! Almost all of the variances on the report are unfavorable. The only favorable variances are for supervisory salaries and industrial engineering. How did we have an unfavorable variance for depreciation?

Kemper: Do you remember that milling machine that broke down because the wrong lubricant was used by the machine operator?

Ilianovitch: Yes.

Kemper: We couldn't fix it. We had to scrap the machine and buy a new one.

Ilianovitch: This report doesn't look good. I was raked over the coals last year when we had just a few unfavorable variances.

Kemper: I'm afraid the final report is going to look even worse.

Ilianovitch: Oh?

Kemper: The line item for industrial engineering on the report is for work we hired Ferguson Engineering to do for us. The original contract was for $210,000, but we asked them to do some additional work that was not in the contract. We have to reimburse Ferguson Engineering for the costs of that additional work. The $189,000 in actual costs that appears on the preliminary draft report reflects only their billings up through December 21. The last bill they had sent us was on November 28, and they completed the project just last week. Yesterday I got a call from Laura Sunder over at Ferguson and she said they would be sending us a final bill for the project before the end of the year. The total bill, including the reimbursements for the additional work, is going to be . . .

Ilianovitch: I am not sure I want to hear this.

Kemper: $225,000

Ilianovitch: Ouch!

Kemper: The additional work added $15,000 to the cost of the project.

Ilianovitch: I can't turn in a report with an overall unfavorable variance! They'll kill me at corporate headquarters. Call up Laura at Ferguson and ask her not to send the bill until after the first of the year. We have to have that $21,000 favorable variance for industrial engineering on the report.

Required:
What should Tom Kemper do? Explain.

CASE 9–27 Critiquing a Report; Preparing Spending Variances [LO9–3, LO9–5, LO9–6]

Boyne University offers an extensive continuing education program in many cities throughout the state. For the convenience of its faculty and administrative staff and to save costs, the university operates a motor pool. The motor pool's monthly planning budget is based on operating 20 vehicles; however, for the month of March the university purchased one additional vehicle. The motor pool furnishes gasoline, oil, and other supplies for its automobiles. A mechanic does routine maintenance and minor repairs. Major repairs are performed at a nearby commercial garage.

The following cost control report shows actual operating costs for March of the current year compared to the planning budget for March.

Boyne University Motor Pool Cost Control Report For the Month Ended March 31			
	March Actual	Planning Budget	(Over) Under Budget
Miles	63,000	50,000	
Autos	21	20	
Gasoline	$ 9,350	$ 7,500	$(1,850)
Oil, minor repairs, parts	2,360	2,000	(360)
Outside repairs	1,420	1,500	80
Insurance	2,120	2,000	(120)
Salaries and benefits	7,540	7,540	0
Vehicle depreciation	5,250	5,000	(250)
Total	$28,040	$25,540	$(2,500)

The planning budget was based on the following assumptions:
a. $0.15 per mile for gasoline.
b. $0.04 per mile for oil, minor repairs, and parts.
c. $75 per automobile per month for outside repairs.
d. $100 per automobile per month for insurance.
e. $7,540 per month for salaries and benefits.
f. $250 per automobile per month for depreciation.
     The supervisor of the motor pool is unhappy with the report, claiming it paints an unfair picture of the motor pool's performance.

Required:
1.   Prepare a new performance report for March based on a flexible budget that shows spending variances.
2.   What are the deficiencies in the original cost control report? How does the report that you prepared in part (1) above overcome these deficiencies?

(CMA, adapted)

CASE 9–28 Performance Report with More than One Cost Driver [LO9–4, LO9–5]
The Little Theatre is a nonprofit organization devoted to staging plays for children. The theater has a very small full-time professional administrative staff. Through a special arrangement with the actors' union, actors and directors rehearse without pay and are paid only for actual performances.
     The costs from the current year's planning budget appear below. The Little Theatre had tentatively planned to put on six different productions with a total of 108 performances. For example, one of the productions was *Peter Rabbit,* which had a six-week run with three performances on each weekend.

The Little Theatre Costs from the Planning Budget For the Year Ended December 31	
Budgeted number of productions	6
Budgeted number of performances	108
Actors' and directors' wages	$216,000
Stagehands' wages	32,400
Ticket booth personnel and ushers' wages	16,200
Scenery, costumes, and props	108,000
Theater hall rent	54,000
Printed programs	27,000
Publicity	12,000
Administrative expenses	43,200
Total	$508,800

Some of the costs vary with the number of productions, some with the number of performances, and some are fixed and depend on neither the number of productions nor the number of performances. The costs of scenery, costumes, props, and publicity vary with the number of productions. It doesn't make any difference how many times *Peter Rabbit* is performed, the cost of the scenery is the same. Likewise, the cost of publicizing a play with posters and radio commercials is the same whether there are 10, 20, or 30 performances of the play. On the other hand, the wages of the actors, directors, stagehands, ticket booth personnel, and ushers vary with the number of performances. The greater the number of performances, the higher the wage costs will be. Similarly, the costs of renting the hall and printing the programs will vary with the number of performances. Administrative expenses are more difficult to pin down, but the best estimate is that approximately 75% of the budgeted costs are fixed, 15% depend on the number of productions staged, and the remaining 10% depend on the number of performances.

After the beginning of the year, the board of directors of the theater authorized expanding the theater's program to seven productions and a total of 168 performances. Not surprisingly, actual costs were considerably higher than the costs from the planning budget. (Grants from donors and ticket sales were also correspondingly higher, but are not shown here.) Data concerning the actual costs appear below:

The Little Theatre Actual Costs For the Year Ended December 31	
Actual number of productions	7
Actual number of performances	168
Actors' and directors' wages	$341,800
Stagehands' wages	49,700
Ticket booth personnel and ushers' wages	25,900
Scenery, costumes, and props	130,600
Theater hall rent	78,000
Printed programs	38,300
Publicity	15,100
Administrative expenses	47,500
Total	$726,900

Required:
1. Prepare a flexible budget for The Little Theatre based on the actual activity of the year.
2. Prepare a flexible budget performance report for the year that shows both spending variances and activity variances.
3. If you were on the board of directors of the theater, would you be pleased with how well costs were controlled during the year? Why, or why not?
4. The cost formulas provide figures for the average cost per production and average cost per performance. How accurate do you think these figures would be for predicting the cost of a new production or of an additional performance of a particular production?

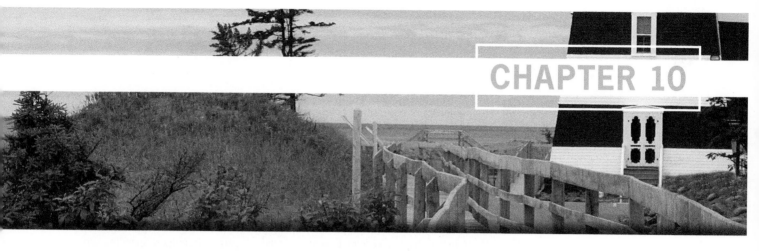

CHAPTER 10

Standard Costs and Variances

Managing Materials and Labor

Schneider Electric's Oxford, Ohio, plant manufactures *busways* that transport electricity from its point of entry into a building to remote locations throughout the building. The plant's managers pay close attention to direct material costs because they are more than half of the plant's total manufacturing costs. To help control scrap rates for direct materials such as copper, steel, and aluminum, the accounting department prepares direct materials quantity variances. These variances compare the amount of direct materials that were actually used to the standard quantity of direct materials that should have been used to make a product (according to computations by the plant's engineers). Keeping a close eye on these differences helps to identify and deal with the causes of excessive scrap, such as an inadequately trained machine operator, poor quality raw material inputs, or a malfunctioning machine.

Because direct labor is also a significant component of the plant's total manufacturing costs, the management team daily monitors the direct labor efficiency variance. This variance compares the actual amount of labor time used to the standard amount of labor time allowed to make a product. When idle workers cause an unfavorable labor efficiency variance, managers temporarily move workers from departments with slack to departments with a backlog of work to be done. ■

Source: Author's conversation with Doug Taylor, plant controller, Schneider Electric's Oxford, Ohio, plant.

LEARNING OBJECTIVES

After studying Chapter 10, you should be able to:

LO10–1 Compute the direct materials price and quantity variances and explain their significance.

LO10–2 Compute the direct labor rate and efficiency variances and explain their significance.

LO10–3 Compute the variable manufacturing overhead rate and efficiency variances and explain their significance.

LO10–4 *(Appendix 10A) Compute and interpret the fixed overhead budget and volume variances.*

LO10–5 *(Appendix 10B) Prepare journal entries to record standard costs and variances.*

In the last chapter, we investigated flexible budget variances. These variances provide feedback concerning how well an organization performed in relation to its budget. The impact on profit of a change in the level of activity is captured in the overall net operating income activity variance. The revenue and spending variances indicate how well revenues and costs were controlled—given the actual level of activity. In the case of many of the spending variances, we can get even more detail about how well costs were controlled. For example, at Rick's Hairstyling, an unfavorable spending variance for hairstyling supplies could be due to paying too much for the supplies or to using too many supplies, or some combination of the two. It would be useful to separate those two different effects, particularly if different people are responsible for purchasing the supplies and for using them. In this chapter, we learn how to use standard costs to decompose spending variances into two parts—a part that measures how well the acquisition prices of resources were controlled and a part that measures how efficiently those resources were used.

Standard Costs—Setting the Stage

A *standard* is a benchmark for measuring performance. Standards are found everywhere. Auto service centers like **Firestone** and **Sears**, for example, often set specific labor time standards for the completion of certain tasks, such as installing a carburetor or doing a valve job, and then measure actual performance against these standards. Fast-food outlets such as **McDonald's** and **Subway** have exacting standards for the quantity of meat going into a sandwich, as well as standards for the cost of the meat. Your doctor evaluates your weight using standards for individuals of your age, height, and gender. The buildings we live in conform to standards set in building codes.

Standards are also widely used in managerial accounting where they relate to the *quantity* and acquisition *price* of inputs used in manufacturing goods or providing services. *Quantity standards* specify how much of an input should be used to make a product or provide a service. *Price standards* specify how much should be paid for each unit of the input. If either the quantity or acquisition price of an input departs significantly from the standard, managers investigate the discrepancy to find the cause of the problem and eliminate it.

Next we'll demonstrate how a company can establish quantity and price standards for direct materials, direct labor, and variable manufacturing overhead and then we'll discuss how those standards can be used to calculate variances and manage operations.

**MANAGERIAL
ACCOUNTING IN ACTION
THE ISSUE**

Colonial Pewter Company

The Colonial Pewter Company makes only one product—an elaborate reproduction of an 18th century pewter statue. The statue is made largely by hand, using traditional metal-working tools. Consequently, the manufacturing process is labor intensive and requires a high level of skill.

Colonial Pewter has recently expanded its workforce to take advantage of unexpected demand for the statue as a gift. The company started with a small cadre of experienced pewter workers but has had to hire less experienced workers as a result of the expansion. The president of the company, J. D. Wriston, has called a meeting to discuss production problems. Attending the meeting are Tom Kuchel, the production manager; Janet Warner, the purchasing manager; and Terry Sherman, the corporate controller.

J. D.:   I've got a feeling that we aren't getting the production we should out of our new people.

Tom: Give us a chance. Some of the new people have been with the company for less than a month.

Janet: Let me add that production seems to be wasting an awful lot of material—particularly pewter. That stuff is very expensive.

Tom: What about the shipment of defective pewter that you bought—the one with the iron contamination? That caused us major problems.

Janet: How was I to know it was off-grade? Besides, it was a great deal.

J. D.:   Calm down everybody. Let's get the facts before we start attacking each other.

Tom: I agree. The more facts the better.

J. D.:   Okay, Terry, it's your turn. Facts are the controller's department.

Terry: I'm afraid I can't provide the answers off the top of my head, but if you give me about a week I can set up a system that can routinely answer questions relating to worker productivity, material waste, and input prices.

J. D.:   Let's mark it on our calendars.

Setting Direct Materials Standards

Terry Sherman's first task was to prepare quantity and price standards for the company's only significant raw material, pewter ingots. The **standard quantity per unit** defines the amount of direct materials that should be used for each unit of finished product, including an allowance for normal inefficiencies, such as scrap and spoilage.[1] After consulting with the production manager, Tom Kuchel, Terry set the quantity standard for pewter at 3.0 pounds per statue.

The **standard price per unit** defines the price that should be paid for each unit of direct materials and it should reflect the final, delivered cost of those materials. After consulting with purchasing manager Janet Warner, Terry set the standard price of pewter at $4.00 per pound.

Once Terry established the quantity and price standards he computed the standard direct materials cost per statue as follows:

$$3.0 \text{ pounds per statue} \times \$4.00 \text{ per pound} = \$12.00 \text{ per statue}$$

IN BUSINESS

MANAGING RAW MATERIAL COSTS IN THE APPAREL INDUSTRY

A company's raw material costs can rise for numerous and often uncontrollable reasons. For example, severe weather in China, which is the world's largest producer of cotton, can influence the cotton prices paid by Abercrombie & Fitch. Rising fuel costs can influence what Maidenform Brands pays for its petroleum-based synthetic fabrics. When farmers stop producing cotton in favor of soybeans, it increases the price Jones Apparel Group pays for a shrinking supply of cotton.

When faced with rising raw material costs, companies can respond three ways. First, they can maintain existing selling prices and consequently operate with lower margins. Second, they can pass the cost increases along to customers in the form of higher prices. Third, they can try to lower their raw material costs. For example, Hanesbrands buys hedging contracts that lock in its cotton prices, thereby insulating the company from future cost increases. J.C. Penney is changing the blend of raw materials used in its garments, whereas Maidenform has started buying some of its raw materials from lower-cost producers in Bangladesh.

Source: Elizabeth Holmes and Rachel Dodes, "Cotton Tale: Apparel Prices Set to Rise," *The Wall Street Journal,* May 19, 2010, p. B8.

---

[1] Although companies often create "practical" rather than "ideal" materials quantity standards that include allowances for normal inefficiencies such as scrap, spoilage, and rejects, this practice is often criticized because it contradicts the zero defects goal that underlies many process improvement programs. If these types of allowances are built into materials quantity standards, they should be periodically reviewed and reduced over time to reflect improved processes, better training, and better equipment.

Setting Direct Labor Standards

Direct labor quantity and price standards are usually expressed in terms of labor-hours or a labor rate. The **standard hours per unit** defines the amount of direct labor-hours that should be used to produce one unit of finished goods. One approach used to determine this standard is for an industrial engineer to do a time and motion study, actually clocking the time required for each task. Throughout the chapter, we'll assume that "tight but attainable" labor standards are used rather than "ideal" standards that can only be attained by the most skilled and efficient employees working at peak effort 100% of the time. Therefore, after consulting with the production manager and considering reasonable allowances for breaks, personal needs of employees, cleanup, and machine downtime, Terry set the standard hours per unit at 0.50 direct labor-hours per statue.

The **standard rate per hour** defines the company's expected direct labor wage rate per hour, including employment taxes and fringe benefits. Using wage records and in consultation with the production manager, Terry Sherman established a standard rate per hour of $22.00. This standard rate reflects the expected "mix" of workers, even though the actual hourly wage rates may vary somewhat from individual to individual due to differing skills or seniority.

Once Terry established the time and rate standards, he computed the standard direct labor cost per statue as follows:

0.50 direct labor-hours per statue × $22.00 per direct labor-hour = $11.00 per statue

Setting Variable Manufacturing Overhead Standards

As with direct labor, the quantity and price standards for variable manufacturing overhead are usually expressed in terms of hours and a rate. The *standard hours per unit* for variable overhead measures the amount of the allocation base from a company's predetermined overhead rate that is required to produce one unit of finished goods. In the case of Colonial Pewter, we will assume that the company uses direct labor-hours as the allocation base in its predetermined overhead rate. Therefore, the standard hours per unit for variable overhead is exactly the same as the standard hours per unit for direct labor—0.50 direct labor-hours per statue.

The *standard rate per unit* that a company expects to pay for variable overhead equals *the variable portion of the predetermined overhead rate*. At Colonial Pewter, the variable portion of the predetermined overhead rate is $6.00 per direct labor-hour. Therefore, Terry computed the standard variable manufacturing overhead cost per statue as follows:

0.50 direct labor-hours per statue × $6.00 per direct-labor hour = $3.00 per statue

This $3.00 per unit cost for variable manufacturing overhead appears along with direct materials ($12 per unit) and direct labor ($11 per unit) on the *standard cost card* in Exhibit 10–1. A **standard cost card** shows the standard quantity (or hours) and standard price (or rate) of the inputs required to produce a unit of a specific product. The **standard**

EXHIBIT 10–1
Standard Cost Card—Variable Manufacturing Costs

Inputs	(1) Standard Quantity or Hours	(2) Standard Price or Rate	Standard Cost (1) × (2)
Direct materials	3.0 pounds	$4.00 per pound	$12.00
Direct labor	0.50 hours	$22.00 per hour	11.00
Variable manufacturing overhead	0.50 hours	$6.00 per hour	3.00
Total standard cost per unit			$26.00

cost per unit for all three variable manufacturing costs is computed the same way. The standard quantity (or hours) per unit is multiplied by the standard price (or rate) per unit to obtain the standard cost per unit.

Using Standards in Flexible Budgets

Once Terry Sherman created the standard cost card shown in Exhibit 10–1, he was ready to use this information to calculate direct materials, direct labor, and variable manufacturing overhead variances. Therefore, he gathered the following data for the month of June:

Originally budgeted output in June	2,100 statues
Actual output in June	2,000 statues
Actual direct materials cost in June*	$24,700
Actual direct labor cost in June	$22,680
Actual variable manufacturing overhead cost in June . . .	$7,140

*There were no beginning or ending inventories of raw materials in June; all materials purchased were used.

Using the above data and the standard cost data from Exhibit 10–1, Terry computed the spending and activity variances shown in Exhibit 10–2. Notice that the actual results and flexible budget columns are each based on the actual output of 2,000 statues. The planning budget column is based on the planned output of 2,100 statues. The standard costs of $12.00 per unit for materials, $11.00 per unit for direct labor, and $3.00 per unit for variable manufacturing overhead are each multiplied by the actual output of 2,000 statues to compute the amounts in the flexible budget column. For example, the standard direct labor cost per unit of $11.00 multiplied by 2,000 statues equals the direct labor flexible budget of $22,000. Similarly, the three standard variable cost figures are multiplied by 2,100 units to compute the amounts in the planning budget column. For example, the direct labor cost for the planning budget is $23,100 (= $11.00 per unit × 2,100 units).

The spending variances shown in Exhibit 10–2 are computed by taking the amounts in the actual results column and subtracting the amounts in the flexible budget column. For all three variable manufacturing costs, this computation results in a positive number because the actual amount of the cost incurred to produce 2,000 statues exceeds the standard cost allowed for 2,000 statues. Because, in all three instances, the actual cost incurred exceeds the standard cost allowed for the actual level of output, the variance is labeled unfavorable (U). Had any of the actual costs incurred been less than the standard cost allowed for the actual level of output, the corresponding variances would have been labeled favorable (F).

The activity variances shown in the exhibit are computed by taking the amounts in the flexible budget column and subtracting the amounts in the planning budget column.

EXHIBIT 10–2
Flexible Budget Performance Report for Variable Manufacturing Costs

Colonial Pewter
Flexible Budget Performance Report—Variable Manufacturing Costs Only
For the Month Ended June 30

	Actual Results	Spending Variances	Flexible Budget	Activity Variances	Planning Budget
Statues produced (q)	2,000		2,000		2,100
Direct materials ($12.00q)	$24,700	$700 U	$24,000	$1,200 F	$25,200
Direct labor ($11.00q)	$22,680	$680 U	$22,000	$1,100 F	$23,100
Variable manufacturing overhead ($3.00q)	$7,140	$1,140 U	$6,000	$300 F	$6,300

For all three variable manufacturing costs, these computations result in negative numbers and what are labeled as favorable (F) variances. The label favorable is used in these instances because the standard cost allowed for the actual output is less than the standard cost allowed for the planned output. Had the actual level of activity been greater than the planned level of activity, all of the computations would have resulted in positive numbers and unfavorable (U) activity variances.

While the performance report in Exhibit 10–2 is useful, it would be even more useful if the spending variances could be broken down into their price-related and quantity-related components. For example, the direct materials spending variance in the report is $700 unfavorable. This means that, given the actual level of production for the period, direct materials costs were too high by $700—at least according to the standard costs. Was this due to higher than expected prices for materials? Or was it due to too much material being used? The standard cost variances we will be discussing in the rest of the chapter are designed to answer these questions.

A General Model for Standard Cost Variance Analysis

Standard cost variance analysis decomposes spending variances from the flexible budget into two elements—one due to the price paid for the input and the other due to the amount of the input that is used. A **price variance** is the difference between the actual amount paid for an input and the standard amount that should have been paid, multiplied by the actual amount of the input purchased. A **quantity variance** is the difference between how much of an input was actually used and how much should have been used and is stated in dollar terms using the standard price of the input.

Why are standards separated into two categories—price and quantity? Price variances and quantity variances usually have different causes. In addition, different managers are usually responsible for buying and using inputs. For example, in the case of a raw material, the purchasing manager is responsible for its price and the production manager is responsible for the amount of the raw material actually used to make products. Therefore, it is important to clearly distinguish between deviations from price standards (the responsibility of the purchasing manager) and deviations from quantity standards (the responsibility of the production manager).

Exhibit 10–3 presents a general model that can be used to decompose the spending variance for a variable cost into a *price variance* and a *quantity variance.*[2] Column (1) in this exhibit corresponds with the Actual Results column in Exhibit 10–2. Column (3) corresponds with the Flexible Budget column in Exhibit 10–2. Column (2) has been inserted into Exhibit 10–3 to enable separating the spending variance into a price variance and a quantity variance.

Three things should be noted from Exhibit 10–3. First, it can be used to compute a price variance and a quantity variance for each of the three variable cost elements—direct materials, direct labor, and variable manufacturing overhead—even though the variances have different names. A price variance is called a *materials price variance* in the case of direct materials, a *labor rate variance* in the case of direct labor, and a *variable overhead rate variance* in the case of variable manufacturing overhead. A quantity variance is called a *materials quantity variance* in the case of direct materials, a *labor efficiency variance* in the case of direct labor, and a *variable overhead efficiency variance* in the case of variable manufacturing overhead.

Second, all three columns in the exhibit are based on the *actual amount of output* produced during the period. Even the flexible budget column depicts the standard cost

---

[2] This general model can always be used to compute direct labor and variable manufacturing overhead variances. However, it can be used to compute direct materials variances only when the actual quantity of materials purchased equals the actual quantity of materials used in production. Later in the chapter, we will explain how to compute direct materials variances when these quantities differ.

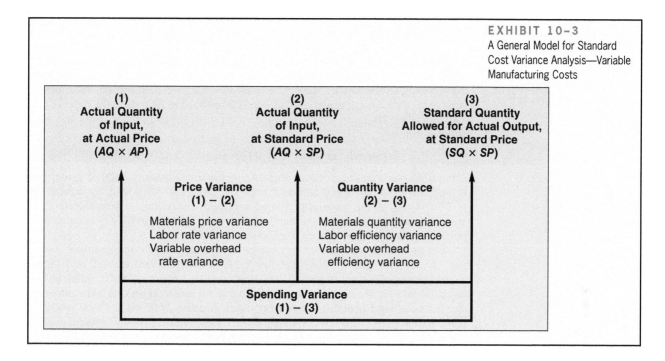

EXHIBIT 10–3
A General Model for Standard Cost Variance Analysis—Variable Manufacturing Costs

allowed for the *actual amount of output* produced during the period. The key to understanding the flexible budget column in Exhibit 10–3 is to grasp the meaning of the term *standard quantity allowed (SQ)*. The **standard quantity allowed** (when computing direct materials variances) or **standard hours allowed** (when computing direct labor and variable manufacturing overhead variances) refers to the amount of an input *that should have been used* to manufacture the actual output of finished goods produced during the period. It is computed by multiplying the actual output by the standard quantity (or hours) per unit. The standard quantity (or hours) allowed is then multiplied by the standard price (or rate) per unit of the input to obtain the total cost according to the flexible budget. For example, if a company actually produced 100 units of finished goods during the period and its standard quantity per unit of finished goods for direct materials is 3 pounds, then its *standard quantity allowed (SQ)* would be 300 pounds (= 100 units × 3 pounds per unit). If the company's standard cost per pound of direct materials is $2.00, then the total direct materials cost in its flexible budget would be $600 (= 300 pounds × $2.00 per pound).

Third, the spending, price, and quantity variances—regardless of what they are called—are computed exactly the same way regardless of whether one is dealing with direct materials, direct labor, or variable manufacturing overhead. The spending variance is computed by taking the total cost in column (1) and subtracting the total cost in column (3). The price variance is computed by taking the total cost in column (1) and subtracting the total cost in column (2). The quantity variance is computed by taking the total cost in column (2) and subtracting the total cost in column (3). In all of these variance calculations, a positive number should be labeled as an unfavorable (U) variance and a negative number should be labeled as a favorable (F) variance. An unfavorable price variance indicates that the actual price (AP) per unit of the input was greater than the standard price (SP) per unit. A favorable price variance indicates that the actual price (AP) of the input was less than the standard price per unit (SP). An unfavorable quantity variance indicates that the actual quantity (AQ) of the input used was greater than the standard quantity allowed (SQ). Conversely, a favorable quantity variance indicates that the actual quantity (AQ) of the input used was less than the standard quantity allowed (SQ).

With this general model as the foundation, we will now calculate Colonial Pewter's price and quantity variances.

Using Standard Costs—Direct Materials Variances

LO10–1

Compute the direct materials price and quantity variances and explain their significance.

After determining Colonial Pewter Company's standard costs for direct materials, direct labor, and variable manufacturing overhead, Terry Sherman's next step was to compute the company's variances for June. As discussed in the preceding section, variances are computed by comparing actual costs to standard costs. Terry referred to the standard cost card in Exhibit 10–1 that shows the standard direct materials cost per statue was computed as follows:

$$3.0 \text{ pounds per statue} \times \$4.00 \text{ per pound} = \$12.00 \text{ per statue}$$

Colonial Pewter's records for June showed that the actual quantity (AQ) of pewter purchased was 6,500 pounds at an actual price (AP) of $3.80 per pound, for a total cost of $24,700. All of the material purchased was used during June to manufacture 2,000 statues.[3] Using these data and the standard costs from Exhibit 10–1, Terry computed the price and quantity variances shown in Exhibit 10–4.

Notice that the variances in this exhibit are based on three different total costs—$24,700, $26,000, and $24,000. The first, $24,700, is the actual amount paid for the actual amount of pewter purchased. The third total cost figure, $24,000, refers to how much should have been spent on pewter to produce the actual output of 2,000 statues. The standards call for 3 pounds of pewter per statue. Because 2,000 statues were produced, 6,000 pounds of pewter should have been used. This is referred to as the *standard quantity allowed* for the actual output and its computation can be stated in formula form as follows:

$$\text{Standard quantity allowed for actual output} = \text{Actual output} \times \text{Standard quantity}$$

If 6,000 pounds of pewter had been purchased at the standard price of $4.00 per pound, the company would have spent $24,000. This is the amount that appears in the company's flexible budget for the month. The difference between the $24,700 actually spent and the $24,000 that should have been spent is the spending variance for the month of $700 U. This variance is unfavorable (denoted by U) because the amount that was actually spent exceeds the amount that should have been spent.

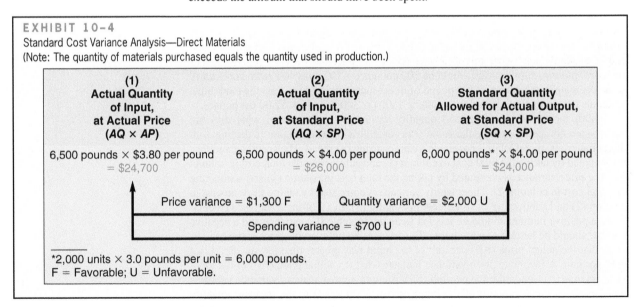

EXHIBIT 10–4
Standard Cost Variance Analysis—Direct Materials
(Note: The quantity of materials purchased equals the quantity used in production.)

(1) Actual Quantity of Input, at Actual Price (AQ × AP)	(2) Actual Quantity of Input, at Standard Price (AQ × SP)	(3) Standard Quantity Allowed for Actual Output, at Standard Price (SQ × SP)
6,500 pounds × $3.80 per pound = $24,700	6,500 pounds × $4.00 per pound = $26,000	6,000 pounds* × $4.00 per pound = $24,000

Price variance = $1,300 F   Quantity variance = $2,000 U

Spending variance = $700 U

*2,000 units × 3.0 pounds per unit = 6,000 pounds.
F = Favorable; U = Unfavorable.

---

[3] Throughout this section, we assume zero beginning and ending inventories of materials and that all materials purchased during the period are used during that period. The more general case in which there are beginning and ending inventories of materials and materials are not necessarily used during the period in which they are purchased is considered later in the chapter.

The second total cost figure in Exhibit 10–4, $26,000, is the key that allows us to decompose the spending variance into two distinct elements—one due to price and one due to quantity. It represents how much the company should have spent if it had purchased the actual amount of input, 6,500 pounds, at the standard price of $4.00 a pound rather than the actual price of $3.80 a pound.

The Materials Price Variance

Using the $26,000 total cost figure in column (2) of Exhibit 10–4, we can make two comparisons—one with the total cost of $24,700 in column (1) and one with the total cost of $24,000 in column (3). The difference between the $24,700 in column (1) and the $26,000 in column (2) is the *materials price variance* of $1,300, which is labeled as favorable (denoted by F). A **materials price variance** measures the difference between an input's actual price and its standard price, multiplied by the actual quantity purchased.

To understand the price variance, note that the actual price of $3.80 per pound of pewter is $0.20 less than the standard price of $4.00 per pound. Because 6,500 pounds were purchased, the total amount of the variance is $1,300 (= $0.20 per pound × 6,500 pounds). This variance is labeled favorable (F) because the actual purchase price per pound is less than the standard purchase price per pound. A price variance is labeled unfavorable (U) if the actual purchase price exceeds the standard purchase price.

Generally speaking, the purchasing manager has control over the price paid for goods and is therefore responsible for the materials price variance. Many factors influence the prices paid for goods including how many units are ordered, how the order is delivered, whether the order is a rush order, and the quality of materials purchased. If any of these factors deviates from what was assumed when the standards were set, a price variance can result. For example, purchasing second-grade materials rather than top-grade materials may result in a favorable price variance because the lower-grade materials may be less costly. However, the lower-grade materials may create production problems. It also bears emphasizing that someone other than the purchasing manager could be responsible for a materials price variance. For example, due to production problems beyond the purchasing manager's control, the purchasing manager may have to use express delivery. In these cases, the production manager should be held responsible for the resulting price variances.

DIRECT MATERIAL PURCHASES: A RISK MANAGEMENT PERSPECTIVE

Shenzhen Hepalink manufactures heparin, a blood-thinning medication that is injected directly into the bloodstream of some surgical patients. The company relies on suppliers to extract its raw material, called crude heparin, from the intestines of slaughtered pigs. The harvesting of crude heparin is susceptible to contamination if the process is improperly managed and monitored. For example, Baxter International recently recalled tainted heparin that some people believe caused illnesses, allergic reactions, and deaths in some patients in the United States and Germany.

Shenzhen Hepalink strives to reduce contamination risks by buying crude heparin only from Chinese government-regulated slaughterhouses instead of rural unregulated slaughterhouses. The company also maintains quality assurance laboratories on each supplier's premises to ensure compliance with applicable rules. These safeguards increase Shenzhen Hepalink's raw materials cost, but they also reduce the risk of contaminated heparin eventually being injected into a patient's bloodstream.

Source: Gordon Fairclough, "How a Heparin Maker in China Tackles Risks," *The Wall Street Journal*, March 10, 2009, pp. B1 and B5.

436

Chapter 10

The Materials Quantity Variance

Referring again to Exhibit 10–4, the difference between the $26,000 in column (2) and the $24,000 in column (3) is the *materials quantity variance* of $2,000, which is labeled as unfavorable (denoted by U). The **materials quantity variance** measures the difference between the actual quantity of materials used in production and the standard quantity of materials allowed for the actual output, multiplied by the standard price per unit of materials. It is labeled as unfavorable (favorable) when the actual quantity of material used in production is greater than (less than) the quantity of material that should have been used according to the standard.

To understand the materials quantity variance, note that the actual amount of pewter used in production was 6,500 pounds. However, the standard amount of pewter allowed for the actual output is 6,000 pounds. Therefore, too much pewter was used to produce the actual output—by a total of 500 pounds. To express this in dollar terms, the 500 pounds is multiplied by the standard price of $4.00 per pound to yield the quantity variance of $2,000 U. Why is the standard price of pewter, rather than the actual price, used in this calculation? The production manager is ordinarily responsible for the quantity variance. If the actual price were used in the calculation of the quantity variance, the production manager's performance evaluation would be unfairly influenced by the efficiency or inefficiency of the purchasing manager.

Excessive materials usage can result from many factors, including faulty machines, inferior materials quality, untrained workers, and poor supervision. Generally speaking, it is the responsibility of the production manager to see that material usage is kept in line with standards. There may be times, however, when the *purchasing* manager is responsible for an unfavorable materials quantity variance. For example, if the purchasing manager buys inferior materials at a lower price, the materials may be unsuitable for use and may result in excessive waste. Thus, the purchasing manager rather than the production manager would be responsible for the quantity variance.

Thus far, we have shown how to compute direct materials variances using the general model depicted in Exhibit 10–4; however, these variances can also be calculated using basic mathematical equations. Exhibit 10–5 shows how Colonial Pewter can compute its direct materials variances using the equations-based approach.

EXHIBIT 10–5 Direct Materials Variances: The Equations-Based Approach	Materials Price Variance: Materials price variance = $(AQ \times AP) - (AQ \times SP)$ Materials price variance = $AQ(AP - SP)$ Materials price variance = 6,500 pounds ($3.80 per pound − $4.00 per pound) Materials price variance = $1,300 F Materials Quantity Variance: Materials quantity variance = $(AQ \times SP) - (SQ \times SP)$ Materials quantity variance = $SP(AQ - SQ)$ Materials quantity variance = $4.00 per pound (6,500 pounds − 6,000 pounds) Materials quantity variance = $2,000 U where: AQ = Actual quantity of pounds purchased and used in production SQ = Standard quantity of pounds allowed for the actual output AP = Actual price per unit of the input SP = Standard price per unit of the input

CUSTOMERS SPEAK LOUD AND CLEAR

When ConAgra Foods raised the price of its Banquet frozen dinners from $1.00 to $1.25, many customers stopped buying the product. The resulting drop in sales contributed to a 40% decline in the company's stock price. It also presented ConAgra with an interesting challenge—lowering its raw material costs so that Banquet frozen dinners could be profitable at the customer-mandated price of $1.00. ConAgra responded by replacing expensive entrees such as barbecued chicken and country-fried pork with less costly choices such as meat patties and rice and beans. It also shrank standard portion sizes and expanded the use of cheaper side items such as mashed potatoes and brownies. However, the company did not sacrifice on variety—it still offers more than 100 Banquet-branded products.

Source: Joseph Weber, "Over a Buck for Dinner? Outrageous," *BusinessWeek*, March 9, 2009, p. 57.

Using Standard Costs—Direct Labor Variances

Terry Sherman's next step in determining Colonial Pewter's variances for June was to compute the direct labor variances for the month. Recall from Exhibit 10–1 that the standard direct labor cost per statue is $11, computed as follows:

LO10–2
Compute the direct labor rate and efficiency variances and explain their significance.

$$0.50 \text{ hours per statue} \times \$22.00 \text{ per hour} = \$11.00 \text{ per statue}$$

In addition, Colonial Pewter's records for June showed that 1,050 direct labor-hours were actually worked. Given that the company paid its direct labor workers a total of $22,680 (including payroll taxes and fringe benefits), the average actual wage rate was $21.60 per hour (= $22,680 ÷ 1,050 hours). Using these data and the standard costs from Exhibit 10–1, Terry computed the direct labor rate and efficiency variances that appear in Exhibit 10–6.

Notice that the column headings in Exhibit 10–6 are the same as those used Exhibits 10–3 and 10–4, except that in Exhibit 10–6 the terms *rate* and *hours* are used in place of the terms *price* and *quantity*.

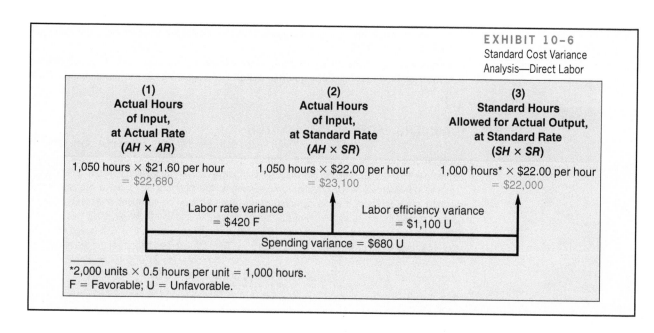

EXHIBIT 10–6
Standard Cost Variance Analysis—Direct Labor

438   Chapter 10

The Labor Rate Variance

Using the $23,100 total cost figure in column (2) of Exhibit 10–6, we can make two comparisons—one with the total cost of $22,680 in column (1) and one with the total cost of $22,000 in column (3). The difference between the 22,680 in column (1) and the $23,100 in column (2) is the *labor rate variance* of $420 F. The **labor rate variance** measures the difference between the actual hourly rate and the standard hourly rate, multiplied by the actual number of hours worked during the period.

To understand the labor rate variance, note that the actual hourly rate of $21.60 is $0.40 less than the standard rate of $22.00 per hour. Because 1,050 hours were actually worked, the total amount of the variance is $420 (= $0.40 per hour × 1,050 hours). The variance is labeled favorable (F) because the actual hourly rate is less than the standard hourly rate. If the actual hourly rate had been greater than the standard hourly rate, the variance would have been labeled unfavorable (U).

In most companies, the wage rates paid to workers are quite predictable. Nevertheless, rate variances can arise based on how production supervisors use their direct labor workers. Skilled workers with high hourly rates of pay may be given duties that require little skill and call for lower hourly rates of pay. This will result in an unfavorable labor rate variance because the actual hourly rate of pay will exceed the standard rate specified for the particular task. In contrast, a favorable rate variance would result when workers who are paid at a rate lower than specified in the standard are assigned to the task. However, the lower-paid workers may not be as efficient. Finally, overtime work at premium rates will result in an unfavorable labor rate variance if the overtime premium is charged to the direct labor account.

The Labor Efficiency Variance

Referring back to Exhibit 10–6, the difference between the $23,100 in column (2) and the $22,000 in column (3) is the *labor efficiency variance* of $1,100 unfavorable (U). The **labor efficiency variance** measures the difference between the actual hours used and the standard hours allowed for the actual output, multiplied by the standard hourly rate.

To understand Colonial Pewter's labor efficiency variance, note that the actual amount of hours used in production was 1,050 hours. However, the standard amount of hours allowed for the actual output is 1,000 hours. Therefore, the company used 50 more hours for the actual output than the standards allow. To express this in dollar terms, the 50 hours are multiplied by the standard rate of $22.00 per hour to yield the efficiency variance of $1,100 U.

Possible causes of an unfavorable labor efficiency variance include poorly trained or motivated workers; poor-quality materials, requiring more labor time; faulty

IN BUSINESS

CASHIERS FACE THE STOPWATCH

Operations Workforce Optimization (OWO) writes software that uses engineered labor standards to determine how long it should take a cashier to check out a customer. The software measures an employee's productivity by continuously comparing actual customer checkout times to pre-established labor efficiency standards. For example, the cashiers at Meijer, a regional retailer located in the Midwest, may be demoted or terminated if they do not meet or exceed labor efficiency standards for at least 95% of customers served. In addition to Meijer, OWO has attracted other clients such as Gap, Limited Brands, Office Depot, Nike, and Toys "R" Us, based on claims that its software can reduce labor costs by 5–15%. The software has also attracted the attention of the United Food and Commercial Workers Union, which represents 27,000 Meijer employees. The union has filed a grievance against Meijer related to its cashier monitoring system.

Source: Vanessa O'Connell, "Stores Count Seconds to Cut Labor Costs," *The Wall Street Journal*, November 17, 2008, pp. A1–A15.

equipment, causing breakdowns and work interruptions; poor supervision of workers; and inaccurate standards. The managers in charge of production would usually be responsible for control of the labor efficiency variance. However, the purchasing manager could be held responsible if the purchase of poor-quality materials resulted in excessive labor processing time.

Another important cause of an unfavorable labor efficiency variance may be insufficient demand for the company's products. Managers in some companies argue that it is difficult, and perhaps unwise, to constantly adjust the workforce in response to changes in the amount of work that needs to be done. In such companies, the direct labor workforce is essentially fixed in the short run. If demand is insufficient to keep everyone busy, workers are not laid off and an unfavorable labor efficiency variance will often be recorded.

If customer orders are insufficient to keep the workers busy, the work center manager has two options—either accept an unfavorable labor efficiency variance or build inventory. A central lesson of Lean Production is that building inventory with no immediate prospect of sale is a bad idea. Excessive inventory—particularly work in process inventory—leads to high defect rates, obsolete goods, and inefficient operations. As a consequence, when the workforce is basically fixed in the short term, managers must be cautious about how labor efficiency variances are used. Some experts advocate eliminating labor efficiency variances in such situations—at least for the purposes of motivating and controlling workers on the shop floor.

Direct labor variances can also be computed using equations instead of the general model depicted in Exhibit 10–6. Exhibit 10–7 shows how Colonial Pewter can compute its direct labor variances using the equations-based approach.

Labor Rate Variance:

Labor rate variance = $(AH \times AR) - (AH \times SR)$
Labor rate variance = $AH(AR - SR)$
Labor rate variance = 1,050 hours ($21.60 per hour − $22.00 per hour)
Labor rate variance = $420 F

Labor Efficiency Variance:

Labor efficiency variance = $(AH \times SR) - (SH \times SR)$
Labor efficiency variance = $SR(AH - SH)$
Labor efficiency variance = $22.00 per hour (1,050 hours − 1,000 hours)
Labor efficiency variance = $1,100 U

where:
AH = Actual quantity of hours used in production
SH = Standard quantity of hours allowed for the actual output
AR = Actual rate per direct labor-hour
SR = Standard rate per direct labor-hour

EXHIBIT 10–7
Direct Labor Variances: The Equations-Based Approach

Using Standard Costs—Variable Manufacturing Overhead Variances

The final step in Terry Sherman's analysis of Colonial Pewter's variances for June was to compute the variable manufacturing overhead variances. The variable portion of manufacturing overhead can be analyzed using the same basic formulas that we used to analyze direct materials and direct labor. Recall from Exhibit 10–1 that the standard variable manufacturing overhead is $3.00 per statue, computed as follows:

0.50 hours per statue $\times$ $6.00 per hour = $3.00 per statue

LO10–3
Compute the variable manufacturing overhead rate and efficiency variances and explain their significance.

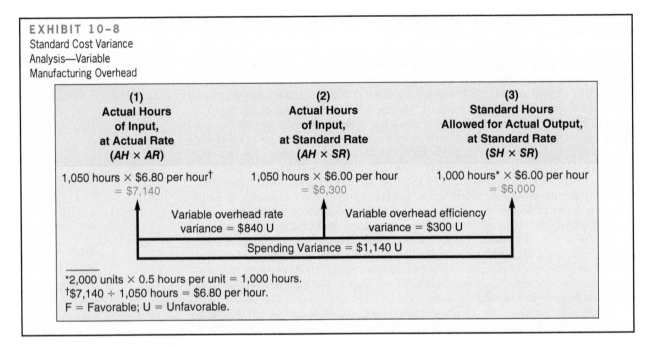

EXHIBIT 10–8
Standard Cost Variance
Analysis—Variable
Manufacturing Overhead

(1) Actual Hours of Input, at Actual Rate (*AH* × *AR*)	(2) Actual Hours of Input, at Standard Rate (*AH* × *SR*)	(3) Standard Hours Allowed for Actual Output, at Standard Rate (*SH* × *SR*)
1,050 hours × $6.80 per hour† = $7,140	1,050 hours × $6.00 per hour = $6,300	1,000 hours* × $6.00 per hour = $6,000

Variable overhead rate variance = $840 U   Variable overhead efficiency variance = $300 U

Spending Variance = $1,140 U

*2,000 units × 0.5 hours per unit = 1,000 hours.
†$7,140 ÷ 1,050 hours = $6.80 per hour.
F = Favorable; U = Unfavorable.

Also recall that Colonial Pewter's cost records showed that the total actual variable manufacturing overhead cost for June was $7,140 and that 1,050 direct labor-hours were worked in June to produce 2,000 statues. Terry's analysis of this overhead data appears in Exhibit 10–8.

Notice the similarities between Exhibits 10–6 and 10–8. These similarities arise from the fact that direct labor-hours are being used as the base for allocating overhead cost to units of product; thus, the same hourly figures appear in Exhibit 10–8 for variable manufacturing overhead as in Exhibit 10–6 for direct labor. The main difference between the two exhibits is in the standard hourly rate being used, which in this company is much lower for variable manufacturing overhead than for direct labor.

The Variable Manufacturing Overhead Rate and Efficiency Variances

Using the $6,300 total cost figure in column (2) of Exhibit 10–8, we can make two comparisons—one with the total cost of $7,140 in column (1) and one with the total cost of $6,000 in column (3). The difference between the $7,140 in column (1) and the $6,300 in column (2) is the *variable overhead rate variance* of $840 U. The **variable overhead rate variance** measures the difference between the actual variable overhead cost incurred during the period and the standard cost that should have been incurred based on the actual activity of the period. The difference between the $6,300 in column (2) and the $6,000 in column (3) is the *variable overhead efficiency variance* of $300 U. The **variable overhead efficiency variance** measures the difference between the actual level of activity and the standard activity allowed for the actual output, multiplied by the variable part of the predetermined overhead rate.

To understand Colonial Pewter's variable overhead efficiency variance, note that the actual amount of hours used in production was 1,050 hours. However, the standard amount of hours allowed for the actual output is 1,000 hours. Therefore, the company used 50 more hours for the actual output than the standards allow. To express this in dollar terms, the 50 hours are multiplied by the variable part of the predetermined overhead rate of $6.00 per hour to yield the variable overhead efficiency variance of $300 U.

The interpretation of the variable overhead variances is not as clear as the direct materials and direct labor variances. In particular, the variable overhead efficiency variance is exactly the same as the direct labor efficiency variance except for one detail—the rate that is used to

Variable Overhead Rate Variance:

Variable overhead rate variance = $(AH \times AR) - (AH \times SR)$
Variable overhead rate variance = $AH(AR - SR)$
Variable overhead rate variance = 1,050 hours ($6.80 - $6.00)
Variable overhead rate variance = $840 U

Variable Overhead Efficiency Variance:

Variable overhead efficiency variance = $(AH \times SR) - (SH \times SR)$
Variable overhead efficiency variance = $SR(AH - SH)$
Variable overhead efficiency variance = $6.00 per hour (1,050 hours - 1,000 hours)
Variable overhead efficiency variance = $300 U

where:
AH = Actual quantity of hours used in production
SH = Standard quantity of hours allowed for the actual output
AR = Actual rate per direct labor-hour
SR = Standard rate per direct labor-hour

EXHIBIT 10–9
Variable Manufacturing Overhead
Variances: The Equations-Based
Approach

translate the variance into dollars. In both cases, the variance is the difference between the actual hours worked and the standard hours allowed for the actual output. In the case of the direct labor efficiency variance, this difference is multiplied by the standard direct labor rate. In the case of the variable overhead efficiency variance, this difference is multiplied by the variable portion of the predetermined overhead rate. So when direct labor is used as the base for overhead, whenever the direct labor efficiency variance is favorable, the variable overhead efficiency variance will also be favorable. And whenever the direct labor efficiency variance is unfavorable, the variable overhead efficiency variance will be unfavorable. Indeed, the variable overhead efficiency variance really doesn't tell us anything about how efficiently overhead resources were used. It depends solely on how efficiently direct labor was used.

Variable manufacturing overhead variances can also be computed using equations instead of the general model depicted in Exhibit 10–8. Exhibit 10–9 shows how Colonial Pewter can compute its variable overhead variances using the equations-based approach.

**MANAGERIAL
ACCOUNTING IN ACTION**
THE WRAP-UP

In preparation for the scheduled meeting to discuss his analysis of Colonial Pewter's standard costs and variances, Terry distributed his computations to the management group of Colonial Pewter. This included J. D. Wriston, the president of the company; Tom Kuchel, the production manager; and Janet Warner, the purchasing manager. J. D. Wriston opened the meeting with the following question:

**Colonial
Pewter
Company**

J. D.: Terry, I think I understand what you have done, but just to make sure, would you mind summarizing the highlights of what you found?

Terry: As you can see, the biggest problems are the unfavorable materials quantity variance of $2,000 and the unfavorable labor efficiency variance of $1,100.

J. D.: Tom, you're the production boss. What do you think is causing the unfavorable labor efficiency variance?

Tom: It has to be the new production workers. Our experienced workers shouldn't have much problem meeting the standard of half an hour per unit. We all knew that there would be some inefficiency for a while as we brought new people on board. My plan for overcoming the problem is to pair up each of the new guys with one of our old-timers and have them work together for a while. It would slow down our older guys a bit, but I'll bet the unfavorable variance disappears and our new workers would learn a lot.

J. D.: Sounds good. Now, what about that $2,000 unfavorable materials quantity variance?

Terry: Tom, are the new workers generating a lot of scrap?

Chapter 10

Tom: Yeah, I guess so.

J. D.: I think that could be part of the problem. Can you do anything about it?

Tom: I can watch the scrap closely for a few days to see where it's being generated. If it is the new workers, I can have the old-timers work with them on the problem when I team them up.

J. D.: Janet, the favorable materials price variance of $1,300 isn't helping us if it is contributing to the unfavorable materials quantity and labor efficiency variances. Let's make sure that our raw material purchases conform to our quality standards.

Janet: Will do.

J. D.: Good. Let's reconvene in a few weeks to see what has happened. Hopefully, we can get those unfavorable variances under control.

An Important Subtlety in the Materials Variances

Most companies use the *quantity of materials purchased* to compute the materials price variance and the *quantity of materials used* in production to compute the materials quantity variance. There are two reasons for this practice. First, delaying the computation of the price variance until the materials are used would result in less timely variance reports. Second, computing the price variance when the materials are purchased allows materials to be carried in the inventory accounts at their standard cost. This greatly simplifies bookkeeping. (See Appendix 10B at the end of the chapter for an explanation of how the bookkeeping works in a standard costing system.)

When we computed materials price and quantity variances for Colonial Pewter in Exhibit 10–4, we assumed that 6,500 pounds of materials were purchased and used in production. However, it is very common for a company's quantity of materials purchased to differ from its quantity used in production. When this happens, the materials price variance is computed using the *quantity of materials purchased,* whereas the materials quantity variance is computed using the *quantity of materials used* in production.

To illustrate, assume that during June Colonial Pewter purchased 7,000 pounds of materials at $3.80 per pound instead of 6,500 pounds as assumed earlier in the chapter. Also assume that the company continued to use 6,500 pounds of materials in production and that the standard price remained at $4.00 per pound.

Given these assumptions, Exhibit 10–10 shows how to compute the materials price variance of $1,400 F and the materials quantity variance of $2,000 U. Note that the price variance is based on the amount of the input purchased whereas the quantity variance is based on the quantity of the input used in production. Column (2) of Exhibit 10–10 contains two different total costs for this reason. When the price variance is computed, the total cost used from column (2) is $28,000—which is the cost of the input *purchased,* evaluated at the standard price. When the quantity variance is computed, the total cost used from column (2) is $26,000—which is the cost of the actual input *used,* evaluated at the standard price.

Exhibit 10–10 shows that the price variance is computed on the entire amount of material purchased (7,000 pounds), whereas the quantity variance is computed only on the amount of materials used in production during the month (6,500 pounds). What about the other 500 pounds of material that were purchased during the period, but that have not yet been used? When those materials are used in future periods, a quantity variance will be computed. However, a price variance will not be computed when the materials are finally used because the price variance was computed when the materials were purchased.

Because the price variance is based on the amount purchased and the quantity variance is based on the amount used, the two variances do not generally sum to the spending variance from the flexible budget, which is wholly based on the amount used. We would also like to emphasize that the variances depicted in Exhibit 10–10 can also be computed using the equations shown in Exhibit 10–11. The approaches shown in *Exhibits 10–10 and 10–11 can always be used to compute direct materials variances.* However, *Exhibits 10–4 and 10–5 can only be used in the special case when the quantity of materials purchased equals the quantity of materials used.*

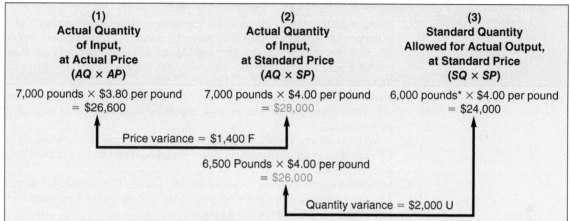

EXHIBIT 10–10
Standard Cost Variance
Analysis—Direct Materials
(Note: The quantity of materials purchased does not equal the quantity used in production.)

(1) **Actual Quantity of Input, at Actual Price (AQ × AP)**	(2) **Actual Quantity of Input, at Standard Price (AQ × SP)**	(3) **Standard Quantity Allowed for Actual Output, at Standard Price (SQ × SP)**
7,000 pounds × $3.80 per pound = $26,600	7,000 pounds × $4.00 per pound = $28,000	6,000 pounds* × $4.00 per pound = $24,000

Price variance = $1,400 F

6,500 Pounds × $4.00 per pound
= $26,000

Quantity variance = $2,000 U

In this case, the price variance and the quantity variance do not sum to the spending variance because the price variance is based on the quantity purchased whereas the quantity variance is based on the quantity used in production, and the two numbers differ.

_____
*2,000 units × 3.0 pounds per unit = 6,000 pounds.
F = Favorable; U = Unfavorable.

Materials Price Variance:

Materials price variance = (AQ × AP) − (AQ × SP)
Materials price variance = AQ(AP − SP)
Materials price variance = 7,000 pounds ($3.80 per pound − $4.00 per pound)
Materials price variance = $1,400 F

where:

AQ = Actual quantity of pounds *purchased*
AP = Actual price per unit of the input
SP = Standard price per unit of the input

Materials Quantity Variance:

Materials quantity variance = (AQ × SP) − (SQ × SP)
Materials quantity variance = SP(AQ − SQ)
Materials quantity variance = $4.00 per pound (6,500 pounds − 6,000 pounds)
Materials quantity variance = $2,000 U

where:

AQ = Actual quantity of pounds *used in production*
SQ = Standard quantity of pounds allowed for the actual output
SP = Standard price per unit of the input

EXHIBIT 10–11
Direct Materials Variances:
The Equations-Based Approach
(when the quantity of materials
purchased does not equal the
quantity used in production)

Standard Costs—Managerial Implications

Advantages of Standard Costs

Standard cost systems have a number of advantages.

1. Standard costs are a key element in a management by exception approach as defined in the previous chapter. If costs conform to the standards, managers can focus on other issues. When costs are significantly outside the standards, managers are alerted that problems may exist that require attention. This approach helps managers focus on important issues.
2. Standards that are viewed as reasonable by employees can promote economy and efficiency. They provide benchmarks that individuals can use to judge their own performance.
3. Standard costs can greatly simplify bookkeeping. Instead of recording actual costs for each job, the standard costs for direct materials, direct labor, and overhead can be charged to jobs.
4. Standard costs fit naturally in an integrated system of "responsibility accounting." The standards establish what costs should be, who should be responsible for them, and whether actual costs are under control.

Potential Problems with Standard Costs

The improper use of standard costs can present a number of potential problems.

1. Standard cost variance reports are usually prepared on a monthly basis and often are released days or even weeks after the end of the month. As a consequence, the information in the reports may be so outdated that it is almost useless. Timely, frequent reports that are approximately correct are better than infrequent reports that are very precise but out of date by the time they are released. Some companies are now reporting variances and other key operating data daily or even more frequently.
2. If managers use variances only to assign blame and punish subordinates, morale may suffer. Furthermore, subordinates may be tempted to cover up unfavorable variances or take actions that are not in the best interests of the company to make sure the variances are favorable.
3. Labor-hour standards and efficiency variances make two important assumptions. First, they assume that the production process is labor-paced; if labor works faster, output will go up. However, output in many companies is not determined by how fast labor works; rather, it is determined by the processing speed of machines. Second, the computations assume that labor is a variable cost. However, direct labor may be essentially fixed. If labor is fixed, then an undue emphasis on labor efficiency variances creates pressure to build excess inventories.
4. In some cases, a "favorable" variance can be worse than an "unfavorable" variance. For example, McDonald's has a standard for the amount of hamburger meat that should be in a Big Mac. A "favorable" variance would mean that less meat was used than the standard specifies. The result is substandard Big Macs and possibly numerous dissatisfied customers.
5. Too much emphasis on meeting the standards may overshadow other important objectives such as maintaining and improving quality, on-time delivery, and customer satisfaction. This tendency can be reduced by using supplemental performance measures that focus on these other objectives.
6. Just meeting standards is not sufficient because companies need to continually improve to remain competitive. For this reason, some companies focus on the trends in the standard cost variances—aiming for continual improvement rather than just

meeting the standards. In other companies, engineered standards are replaced either by a rolling average of actual costs, which is expected to decline, or by very challenging target costs.

In sum, managers should exercise considerable care when using a standard cost system. It is particularly important that managers go out of their way to focus on the positive, rather than just on the negative, and to be aware of possible unintended consequences.

Summary

A standard is a benchmark for measuring performance. Standards are set for both the quantity and the cost of inputs needed to manufacture goods or to provide services. Quantity standards indicate how much of an input, such as labor time or raw materials, should be used to make a product or provide a service. Cost standards indicate what the cost of the input should be.

When standards are compared to actual performance, the difference is referred to as a *variance*. Variances are computed and reported to management on a regular basis for both the quantity and the price elements of direct materials, direct labor, and variable overhead. Price variances are computed by taking the difference between actual and standard prices and multiplying the result by the amount of input purchased. Quantity variances are computed by taking the difference between the actual amount of the input used and the amount of input that is allowed for the actual output, and then multiplying the result by the standard price of the input.

Standard cost systems provide companies with a number of advantages, such as supporting the management by exception approach, simplifying bookkeeping, and providing a benchmark that employees can use to judge their own performance. However, critics of standard cost systems argue that they provide information that is outdated, they can motivate employees to make poor decisions in an effort to generate favorable variances, and they fail to adequately embrace the mindset of continuous process improvement.

Traditional standard cost variance reports are often supplemented with other performance measures to ensure that overemphasis on standard cost variances does not lead to problems in other critical areas such as product quality, inventory levels, and on-time delivery.

Review Problem: Standard Costs

Xavier Company produces a single product. Variable manufacturing overhead is applied to products on the basis of direct labor-hours. The standard costs for one unit of product are as follows:

Direct material: 6 ounces at $0.50 per ounce	$ 3.00
Direct labor: 0.6 hours at $30.00 per hour	18.00
Variable manufacturing overhead: 0.6 hours at $10.00 per hour	6.00
Total standard variable cost per unit	$27.00

During June, 2,000 units were produced. The costs associated with June's operations were as follows:

Material purchased: 18,000 ounces at $0.60 per ounce	$10,800
Material used in production: 14,000 ounces	—
Direct labor: 1,100 hours at $30.50 per hour	$33,550
Variable manufacturing overhead costs incurred	$12,980

Required:

Compute the direct materials, direct labor, and variable manufacturing overhead variances.

446

Chapter 10

Solution to Review Problem

Direct Materials Variances

Actual Quantity of Input, at Actual Price (AQ × AP)	Actual Quantity of Input at Standard Price (AQ × SP)	Standard Quantity Allowed for Actual Output, at Standard Price (SQ × SP)
18,000 ounces × $0.60 per ounce = $10,800	18,000 ounces × $0.50 per ounce = $9,000	12,000 ounces* × $0.50 per ounce = $6,000

Price variance = $1,800 U

14,000 ounces × $0.50 per ounce = $7,000

Quantity variance = $1,000 U

*2,000 units × 6 ounces per unit = 12,000 ounces.

Using the formulas in the chapter, the same variances would be computed as follows:

$$
\begin{aligned}
\text{Materials price variance} &= (AQ \times AP) - (AQ \times SP) \\
&= AQ(AP - SP) \\
&= 18{,}000 \text{ ounces } (\$0.60 \text{ per ounce} - \$0.50 \text{ per ounce}) \\
&= \$1{,}800 \text{ U} \\
\text{Materials quantity variance} &= (AQ \times SP) - (SQ \times SP) \\
&= SP(AQ - SQ) \\
&= \$0.50 \text{ per ounce } (14{,}000 \text{ ounces} - 12{,}000 \text{ ounces}) \\
&= \$1{,}000 \text{ U}
\end{aligned}
$$

Direct Labor Variances

Actual Hours of Input, at Actual Rate (AH × AR)	Actual Hours of Input, at Standard Rate (AH × SR)	Standard Hours Allowed for Actual Output, at Standard Rate (SH × SR)
1,100 hours × $30.50 per hour = $33,550	1,100 hours × $30.00 per hour = $33,000	1,200 hours* × $30.00 per hour = $36,000

Labor rate variance = $550 U   Labor efficiency variance = $3,000 F

Spending variance = $2,450 F

*2,000 units × 0.6 hours per unit = 1,200 hours.
F = Favorable; U = Unfavorable.

Using the formulas in the chapter, the same variances can be computed as follows:

$$
\begin{aligned}
\text{Labor rate variance} &= (AH \times AR) - (AH \times SR) \\
&= AH(AR - SR) \\
&= 1{,}100 \text{ hours } (\$30.50 \text{ per hour} - \$30.00 \text{ per hour}) \\
&= \$550 \text{ U}
\end{aligned}
$$

$$
\begin{aligned}
\text{Labor efficiency variance} &= (AH \times SR) - (SH \times SR) \\
&= SR(AH - SH) \\
&= \$30.00 \text{ per hour } (1{,}100 \text{ hours} - 1{,}200 \text{ hours}) \\
&= \$3{,}000 \text{ F}
\end{aligned}
$$

Variable Manufacturing Overhead Variances

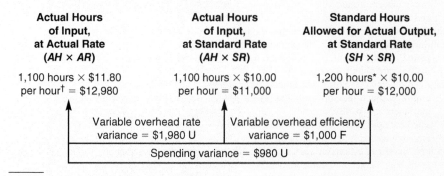

Actual Hours of Input, at Actual Rate (*AH* × *AR*)	Actual Hours of Input, at Standard Rate (*AH* × *SR*)	Standard Hours Allowed for Actual Output, at Standard Rate (*SH* × *SR*)
1,100 hours × \$11.80 per hour† = \$12,980	1,100 hours × \$10.00 per hour = \$11,000	1,200 hours* × \$10.00 per hour = \$12,000

Variable overhead rate variance = \$1,980 U   Variable overhead efficiency variance = \$1,000 F

Spending variance = \$980 U

---

*2,000 units × 0.6 hours per unit = 1,200 hours.
†\$12,980 ÷ 1,100 hours = \$11.80 per hour.
F = Favorable; U = Unfavorable.

Using the formulas in the chapter, the same variances can be computed as follows:

$$\text{Variable overhead rate variance} = (AH \times AR) - (AH \times SR)$$

$$= AH(AR - SR)$$

$$= 1{,}100 \text{ hours } (\$11.80 \text{ per hour} - \$10.00 \text{ per hour})$$

$$= \$1{,}980 \text{ U}$$

$$\text{Variable overhead efficiency variance} = (AH \times SR) - (SH \times SR)$$

$$= SR(AH - SH)$$

$$= \$10.00 \text{ per hour } (1{,}100 \text{ hours} - 1{,}200 \text{ hours})$$

$$= \$1{,}000 \text{ F}$$

Glossary

Labor efficiency variance The difference between the actual hours taken to complete a task and the standard hours allowed for the actual output, multiplied by the standard hourly labor rate. (p. 438)

Labor rate variance The difference between the actual hourly labor rate and the standard rate, multiplied by the number of hours worked during the period. (p. 438)

Materials price variance The difference between the actual unit price paid for an item and the standard price, multiplied by the quantity purchased. (p. 435)

Materials quantity variance The difference between the actual quantity of materials used in production and the standard quantity allowed for the actual output, multiplied by the standard price per unit of materials. (p. 436)

Price variance A variance that is computed by taking the difference between the actual price and the standard price and multiplying the result by the actual quantity of the input. (p. 432)

Quantity variance A variance that is computed by taking the difference between the actual quantity of the input used and the amount of the input that should have been used for the actual level of output and multiplying the result by the standard price of the input. (p. 432)

Standard cost card A detailed listing of the standard amounts of inputs and their costs that are required to produce one unit of a specific product. (p. 430)

Standard cost per unit The standard quantity allowed of an input per unit of a specific product, multiplied by the standard price of the input. (p. 430)

Standard hours allowed The time that should have been taken to complete the period's output. It is computed by multiplying the actual number of units produced by the standard hours per unit. (p. 433)

448 Chapter 10

Standard hours per unit The amount of direct labor time that should be required to complete a single unit of product, including allowances for breaks, machine downtime, cleanup, rejects, and other normal inefficiencies. (p. 430)

Standard price per unit The price that should be paid for an input. (p. 429)

Standard quantity allowed The amount of an input that should have been used to complete the period's actual output. It is computed by multiplying the actual number of units produced by the standard quantity per unit. (p. 433)

Standard quantity per unit The amount of an input that should be required to complete a single unit of product, including allowances for normal waste, spoilage, rejects, and other normal inefficiencies. (p. 429)

Standard rate per hour The labor rate that should be incurred per hour of labor time, including employment taxes and fringe benefits. (p. 430)

Variable overhead efficiency variance The difference between the actual level of activity (direct labor-hours, machine-hours, or some other base) and the standard activity allowed, multiplied by the variable part of the predetermined overhead rate. (p. 440)

Variable overhead rate variance The difference between the actual variable overhead cost incurred during a period and the standard cost that should have been incurred based on the actual activity of the period. (p. 440)

Questions

10–1 What is a quantity standard? What is a price standard?

10–2 Why are separate price and quantity variances computed?

10–3 Who is generally responsible for the materials price variance? The materials quantity variance? The labor efficiency variance?

10–4 The materials price variance can be computed at what two different points in time? Which point is better? Why?

10–5 If the materials price variance is favorable but the materials quantity variance is unfavorable, what might this indicate?

10–6 Should standards be used to identify who to blame for problems?

10–7 "Our workers are all under labor contracts; therefore, our labor rate variance is bound to be zero." Discuss.

10–8 What effect, if any, would you expect poor-quality materials to have on direct labor variances?

10–9 If variable manufacturing overhead is applied to production on the basis of direct labor-hours and the direct labor efficiency variance is unfavorable, will the variable overhead efficiency variance be favorable or unfavorable, or could it be either? Explain.

10–10 Why can undue emphasis on labor efficiency variances lead to excess work in process inventories?

Multiple-choice questions are provided on the text website at www.mhhe.com/garrison15e.

Applying Excel

Available with McGraw-Hill's *Connect*® Accounting.

LO10–1, LO10–2, LO10–3

The Excel worksheet form that appears on the next page is to be used to recreate the main example in the text on pages 428–442. Download the workbook containing this form from the Online Learning Center at www.mhhe.com/garrison15e. *On the website you will also receive instructions about how to use this worksheet form.*

You should proceed to the requirements below only after completing your worksheet.

Required:

1. Check your worksheet by changing the direct materials standard quantity in cell B6 to 2.9 pounds, the direct labor quantity standard quantity in cell B7 to 0.6 hours, and the variable

	A	B	C	D	E	F	G
1	Chapter 10: Applying Excel						
2							
3	Data						
4	*Exhibit 10-1: Standard Cost Card*						
5	Inputs	Standard Quantity		Standard Price			
6	Direct materials	3.0 pounds		$4.00 per pound			
7	Direct labor	0.50 hours		$22.00 per hour			
8	Variable manufacturing overhead	0.50 hours		$6.00 per hour			
9							
10	Actual results:						
11	Actual output	2,000 units					
12	Actual variable manufacturing overhead cost	$7,140					
13		Actual Quantity		Actual price			
14	Actual direct materials cost	6,500 pounds		$3.80 per pound			
15	Actual direct labor cost	1,050 hours		$21.60 per hour			
16							
17	*Enter a formula into each of the cells marked with a ? below*						
18	**Main Example: Chapter 10**						
19							
20	*Exhibit 10-4: Standard Cost Variance Analysis–Direct Materials*						
21	Actual Quantity of Input, at Actual Price		? pounds ×		? per pound =		?
22	Actual Quantity of Input, at Standard Price		? pounds ×		? per pound =		?
23	Standard Quantity Allowed for the Actual Output, at Standard Price		? pounds ×		? per pound =		?
24	Direct materials variances:						
25	Materials price variance	?					
26	Materials quantity variance	?					
27	Materials spending variance	?					
28							
29	*Exhibit 10-6: Standard Cost Variance Analysis–Direct Labor*						
30	Actual Hours of Input, at Actual Rate		? hours ×		? per hour =		?
31	Actual Hours of Input, at Standard Rate		? hours ×		? per hour =		?
32	Standard Hours Allowed for the Actual Output, at Standard Rate		? hours ×		? per hour =		?
33	Direct labor variances:						
34	Labor rate variance	?					
35	Labor efficiency variance	?					
36	Labor spending variance	?					
37							
38	*Exhibit 10-8: Standard Cost Variance Analysis–Variable Manufacturing Overhead*						
39	Actual Hours of Input, at Actual Rate		? hours ×		? per hour =		?
40	Actual Hours of Input, at Standard Rate		? hours ×		? per hour =		?
41	Standard Hours Allowed for the Actual Output, at Standard Rate		? hours ×		? per hour =		?
42	Variable overhead variances:						
43	Variable overhead rate variance	?					
44	Variable overhead efficiency variance	?					
45	Variable overhead spending variance	?					
46							

H ◀ ▶ H   **Chapter 10 Form** / Filled in Chapter 10 Form / Chapter 10 Formulas

manufacturing overhead in cell B8 to 0.6 hours. The materials spending variance should now be $1,500 U, the labor spending variance should now be $3,720 F, and the variable overhead spending variance should now be $60 F. If you do not get these answers, find the errors in your worksheet and correct them.

    a.   What is the materials quantity variance? Explain this variance.

    b.   What is the labor rate variance? Explain this variance.

2.   Revise the data in your worksheet to reflect the results for the subsequent period:

Data

Exhibit 10–1: Standard Cost Card

Inputs	Standard Quantity	Standard Price
Direct materials	3.0 pounds	$4.00 per pound
Direct labor	0.50 hours	$22.00 per hour
Variable manufacturing overhead	0.50 hours	$6.00 per hour

Actual results:

Actual output	2,100 units	
Actual variable manufacturing overhead cost ...	$5,100	

	Actual Quantity	Actual price
Actual direct materials cost	6,350 pounds	$4.10 per pound
Actual direct labor cost	1,020 hours	$22.10 per hour

450 Chapter 10

a. What is the materials quantity variance? What is the materials price variance?
b. What is the labor efficiency variance? What is the labor rate variance?
c. What is the variable overhead efficiency variance? What is the variable overhead rate variance?

The Foundational 15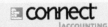

Available with McGraw-Hill's *Connect*® Accounting.

LO10–1, LO10–2, LO10–3

Preble Company manufactures one product. Its variable manufacturing overhead is applied to production based on direct labor-hours and its standard cost card per unit is as follows:

Direct materials: 5 pounds at $8.00 per pound	$40.00
Direct labor: 2 hours at $14 per hour	28.00
Variable overhead: 2 hours at $5 per hour	10.00
Total standard cost per unit	$78.00

The planning budget for March was based on producing and selling 25,000 units. However, during March the company actually produced and sold 30,000 units and incurred the following costs:
a. Purchased 160,000 pounds of raw materials at a cost of $7.50 per pound. All of this material was used in production.
b. Direct laborers worked 55,000 hours at a rate of $15.00 per hour.
c. Total variable manufacturing overhead for the month was $280,500.

Required:
1. What raw materials cost would be included in the company's planning budget for March?
2. What raw materials cost would be included in the company's flexible budget for March?
3. What is the materials price variance for March?
4. What is the materials quantity variance for March?
5. If Preble had purchased 170,000 pounds of materials at $7.50 per pound and used 160,000 pounds in production, what would be the materials price variance for March?
6. If Preble had purchased 170,000 pounds of materials at $7.50 per pound and used 160,000 pounds in production, what would be the materials quantity variance for March?
7. What direct labor cost would be included in the company's planning budget for March?
8. What direct labor cost would be included in the company's flexible budget for March?
9. What is the labor rate variance for March?
10. What is the labor efficiency variance for March?
11. What is the labor spending variance for March?
12. What variable manufacturing overhead cost would be included in the company's planning budget for March?
13. What variable manufacturing overhead cost would be included in the company's flexible budget for March?
14. What is the variable overhead rate variance for March?
15. What is the variable overhead efficiency variance for March?

Exercises

All applicable exercises are available with McGraw-Hill's *Connect*® Accounting.

EXERCISE 10–1 Direct Materials Variances [LO10–1]
Bandar Industries Berhad of Malaysia manufactures sporting equipment. One of the company's products, a football helmet for the North American market, requires a special plastic. During the quarter ending June 30, the company manufactured 35,000 helmets, using 22,500 kilograms of plastic. The plastic cost the company $171,000.

According to the standard cost card, each helmet should require 0.6 kilograms of plastic, at a cost of $8 per kilogram.

Required:

1. According to the standards, what cost for plastic should have been incurred to make 35,000 helmets? How much greater or less is this than the cost that was incurred?
2. Break down the difference computed in (1) above into a materials price variance and a materials quantity variance.

EXERCISE 10–2 Direct Labor Variances [LO10–2]

SkyChefs, Inc., prepares in-flight meals for a number of major airlines. One of the company's products is grilled salmon in dill sauce with baby new potatoes and spring vegetables. During the most recent week, the company prepared 4,000 of these meals using 960 direct labor-hours. The company paid these direct labor workers a total of $9,600 for this work, or $10.00 per hour.

According to the standard cost card for this meal, it should require 0.25 direct labor-hours at a cost of $9.75 per hour.

Required:

1. According to the standards, what direct labor cost should have been incurred to prepare 4,000 meals? How much does this differ from the actual direct labor cost?
2. Break down the difference computed in (1) above into a labor rate variance and a labor efficiency variance.

EXERCISE 10–3 Variable Overhead Variances [LO10–3]

Logistics Solutions provides order fulfillment services for dot.com merchants. The company maintains warehouses that stock items carried by its dot.com clients. When a client receives an order from a customer, the order is forwarded to Logistics Solutions, which pulls the item from storage, packs it, and ships it to the customer. The company uses a predetermined variable overhead rate based on direct labor-hours.

In the most recent month, 120,000 items were shipped to customers using 2,300 direct labor-hours. The company incurred a total of $7,360 in variable overhead costs.

According to the company's standards, 0.02 direct labor-hours are required to fulfill an order for one item and the variable overhead rate is $3.25 per direct labor-hour.

Required:

1. According to the standards, what variable overhead cost should have been incurred to fill the orders for the 120,000 items? How much does this differ from the actual variable overhead cost?
2. Break down the difference computed in (1) above into a variable overhead rate variance and a variable overhead efficiency variance.

EXERCISE 10–4 Direct Labor and Variable Manufacturing Overhead Variances [LO10–2, LO10–3]

Erie Company manufactures a small mp3 player called the Jogging Mate. The company uses standards to control its costs. The labor standards that have been set for one Jogging Mate mp3 player are as follows:

Standard Hours	Standard Rate per Hour	Standard Cost
18 minutes	$12.00	$3.60

During August, 5,750 hours of direct labor time were needed to make 20,000 units of the Jogging Mate. The direct labor cost totaled $73,600 for the month.

Required:

1. According to the standards, what direct labor cost should have been incurred to make 20,000 units of the Jogging Mate? By how much does this differ from the cost that was incurred?
2. Break down the difference in cost from (1) above into a labor rate variance and a labor efficiency variance.
3. The budgeted variable manufacturing overhead rate is $4 per direct labor-hour. During August, the company incurred $21,850 in variable manufacturing overhead cost. Compute the variable overhead rate and efficiency variances for the month.

Chapter 10

EXERCISE 10–5 Working Backwards from Labor Variances [LO10–2]

The auto repair shop of Quality Motor Company uses standards to control the labor time and labor cost in the shop. The standard labor cost for a motor tune-up is given below:

Job	Standard Hours	Standard Rate	Standard Cost
Motor tune-up	2.5	$9.00	$22.50

The record showing the time spent in the shop last week on motor tune-ups has been misplaced. However, the shop supervisor recalls that 50 tune-ups were completed during the week, and the controller recalls the following variance data relating to tune-ups:

Labor rate variance	$87 F
Labor spending variance	$93 U

Required:
1. Determine the number of actual labor-hours spent on tune-ups during the week.
2. Determine the actual hourly rate of pay for tune-ups last week.

(*Hint:* A useful way to proceed would be to work from known to unknown data either by using the variance formulas in Exhibit 10–7 or by using the columnar format shown in Exhibit 10–6.)

EXERCISE 10–6 Direct Materials and Direct Labor Variances [LO10–1, LO10–2]

Huron Company produces a commercial cleaning compound known as Zoom. The direct materials and direct labor standards for one unit of Zoom are given below:

	Standard Quantity or Hours	Standard Price or Rate	Standard Cost
Direct materials	4.6 pounds	$2.50 per pound	$11.50
Direct labor	0.2 hours	$12.00 per hour	$2.40

During the most recent month, the following activity was recorded:
a. Twenty thousand pounds of material were purchased at a cost of $2.35 per pound.
b. All of the material purchased was used to produce 4,000 units of Zoom.
c. 750 hours of direct labor time were recorded at a total labor cost of $10,425.

Required:
1. Compute the materials price and quantity variances for the month.
2. Compute the labor rate and efficiency variances for the month.

EXERCISE 10–7 Direct Materials Variances [LO10–1]

Refer to the data in Exercise 10–6. Assume that instead of producing 4,000 units during the month, the company produced only 3,000 units, using 14,750 pounds of material. (The rest of the material purchased remained in raw materials inventory.)

Required:
Compute the materials price and quantity variances for the month.

EXERCISE 10–8 Direct Materials and Direct Labor Variances [LO10–1, LO10–2]

Dawson Toys, Ltd., produces a toy called the Maze. The company has recently established a standard cost system to help control costs and has established the following standards for the Maze toy:

Direct materials: 6 microns per toy at $0.50 per micron	
Direct labor: 1.3 hours per toy at $8 per hour	

During July, the company produced 3,000 Maze toys. Production data for the month on the toy follow:

Direct materials: 25,000 microns were purchased at a cost of $0.48 per micron. 5,000 of these microns were still in inventory at the end of the month.
Direct labor: 4,000 direct labor-hours were worked at a cost of $36,000.

Standard Costs and Variances   **453**

Required:

1. Compute the following variances for July:
   a. The materials price and quantity variances.
   b. The labor rate and efficiency variances.
2. Prepare a brief explanation of the possible causes of each variance.

 Problems

All applicable problems are available with McGraw-Hill's Connect® Accounting.

PROBLEM 10–9 Comprehensive Variance Analysis [LO10–1, LO10–2, LO10–3]
Marvel Parts, Inc., manufactures auto accessories. One of the company's products is a set of seat covers that can be adjusted to fit nearly any small car. The company has a standard cost system in use for all of its products. According to the standards that have been set for the seat covers, the factory should work 2,850 hours each month to produce 1,900 sets of covers. The standard costs associated with this level of production are:

	Total	Per Set of Covers
Direct materials	$42,560	$22.40
Direct labor	$17,100	9.00
Variable manufacturing overhead		
(based on direct labor-hours)	$6,840	3.60
		$35.00

During August, the factory worked only 2,800 direct labor-hours and produced 2,000 sets of covers. The following actual costs were recorded during the month:

	Total	Per Set of Covers
Direct materials (12,000 yards)	$45,600	$22.80
Direct labor	$18,200	9.10
Variable manufacturing overhead	$7,000	3.50
		$35.40

At standard, each set of covers should require 5.6 yards of material. All of the materials purchased during the month were used in production.

Required:
Compute the following variances for August:
1. The materials price and quantity variances.
2. The labor rate and efficiency variances.
3. The variable overhead rate and efficiency variances.

PROBLEM 10–10 Multiple Products, Materials, and Processes [LO10–1, LO10–2]
Mickley Corporation produces two products, Alpha6s and Zeta7s, which pass through two operations, Sintering and Finishing. Each of the products uses two raw materials, X442 and Y661. The company uses a standard cost system, with the following standards for each product (on a per unit basis):

Product	Raw Material		Standard Labor Time	
	X442	Y661	Sintering	Finishing
Alpha6	1.8 kilos	2.0 liters	0.20 hours	0.80 hours
Zeta7	3.0 kilos	4.5 liters	0.35 hours	0.90 hours

Chapter 10

Information relating to materials purchased and materials used in production during May follows:

Material	Purchases	Purchase Cost	Standard Price	Used in Production
X442	14,500 kilos	$52,200	$3.50 per kilo	8,500 kilos
Y661	15,500 liters	$20,925	$1.40 per liter	13,000 liters

The following additional information is available:
a. The company recognizes price variances when materials are purchased.
b. The standard labor rate is $19.80 per hour in Sintering and $19.20 per hour in Finishing.
c. During May, 1,200 direct labor-hours were worked in Sintering at a total labor cost of $27,000, and 2,850 direct labor-hours were worked in Finishing at a total labor cost of $59,850.
d. Production during May was 1,500 Alpha6s and 2,000 Zeta7s.

Required:
1. Prepare a standard cost card for each product, showing the standard cost of direct materials and direct labor.
2. Compute the materials price and quantity variances for each material.
3. Compute the labor rate and efficiency variances for each operation.

PROBLEM 10–11 Direct Materials and Direct Labor Variances; Computations from Incomplete Data [LO10–1, LO10–2]
Sharp Company manufactures a product for which the following standards have been set:

	Standard Quantity or Hours	Standard Price or Rate	Standard Cost
Direct materials	3 feet	$5 per foot	$15
Direct labor	? hours	? per hour	?

During March, the company purchased direct materials at a cost of $55,650, all of which were used in the production of 3,200 units of product. In addition, 4,900 hours of direct labor time were worked on the product during the month. The cost of this labor time was $36,750. The following variances have been computed for the month:

Materials quantity variance	$4,500 U
Labor spending variance	$1,650 F
Labor efficiency variance	$800 U

Required:
1. For direct materials:
    a. Compute the actual cost per foot for materials for March.
    b. Compute the price variance and the spending variance.
2. For direct labor:
    a. Compute the standard direct labor rate per hour.
    b. Compute the standard hours allowed for the month's production.
    c. Compute the standard hours allowed per unit of product.
(*Hint:* In completing the problem, it may be helpful to move from known to unknown data either by using the columnar format shown in Exhibits 10–4 and 10–6 or by using the variance formulas in Exhibits 10–5 and 10–7.)

PROBLEM 10–12 Variance Analysis in a Hospital [LO10–1, LO10–2, LO10–3]
John Fleming, chief administrator for Valley View Hospital, is concerned about the costs for tests in the hospital's lab. Charges for lab tests are consistently higher at Valley View than at other hospitals and have resulted in many complaints. Also, because of strict regulations on amounts reimbursed for lab tests, payments received from insurance companies and governmental units have not been high enough to cover lab costs.

Mr. Fleming has asked you to evaluate costs in the hospital's lab for the past month. The following information is available:
a. Two types of tests are performed in the lab—blood tests and smears. During the past month, 1,800 blood tests and 2,400 smears were performed in the lab.

b. Small glass plates are used in both types of tests. During the past month, the hospital purchased 12,000 plates at a cost of $28,200. 1,500 of these plates were unused at the end of the month; no plates were on hand at the beginning of the month.
c. During the past month, 1,150 hours of labor time were recorded in the lab at a cost of $13,800.
d. The lab's variable overhead cost last month totaled $7,820.

Valley View Hospital has never used standard costs. By searching industry literature, however, you have determined the following nationwide averages for hospital labs:

Plates: Two plates are required per lab test. These plates cost $2.50 each and are disposed of after the test is completed.
Labor: Each blood test should require 0.3 hours to complete, and each smear should require 0.15 hours to complete. The average cost of this lab time is $14 per hour.
Overhead: Overhead cost is based on direct labor-hours. The average rate for variable overhead is $6 per hour.

Required:
1. Compute a materials price variance for the plates purchased last month and a materials quantity variance for the plates used last month.
2. For labor cost in the lab:
    a. Compute a labor rate variance and a labor efficiency variance.
    b. In most hospitals, one-half of the workers in the lab are senior technicians and one-half are assistants. In an effort to reduce costs, Valley View Hospital employs only one-fourth senior technicians and three-fourths assistants. Would you recommend that this policy be continued? Explain.
3. Compute the variable overhead rate and efficiency variances. Is there any relation between the variable overhead efficiency variance and the labor efficiency variance? Explain.

PROBLEM 10–13 Basic Variance Analysis; the Impact of Variances on Unit Costs [LO10–1, LO10–2, LO10–3]

Koontz Company manufactures a number of products. The standards relating to one of these products are shown below, along with actual cost data for May.

	Standard Cost per Unit	Actual Cost per Unit
Direct materials:		
Standard: 1.80 feet at $3.00 per foot	$ 5.40	
Actual: 1.80 feet at $3.30 per foot		$5.94
Direct labor:		
Standard: 0.90 hours at $18.00 per hour	16.20	
Actual: 0.92 hours at $17.50 per hour		16.10
Variable overhead:		
Standard: 0.90 hours at $5.00 per hour	4.50	
Actual: 0.92 hours at $4.50 per hour		4.14
Total cost per unit	$26.10	$26.18
Excess of actual cost over standard cost per unit	$0.08	

The production superintendent was pleased when he saw this report and commented: "This $0.08 excess cost is well within the 2 percent limit management has set for acceptable variances. It's obvious that there's not much to worry about with this product."

Actual production for the month was 12,000 units. Variable overhead cost is assigned to products on the basis of direct labor-hours. There were no beginning or ending inventories of materials.

Required:
1. Compute the following variances for May:
    a. Materials price and quantity variances.
    b. Labor rate and efficiency variances.
    c. Variable overhead rate and efficiency variances.
2. How much of the $0.08 excess unit cost is traceable to each of the variances computed in (1) above.
3. How much of the $0.08 excess unit cost is traceable to apparent inefficient use of labor time?
4. Do you agree that the excess unit cost is not of concern?

Chapter 10

PROBLEM 10–14 Basic Variance Analysis [LO10–1, LO10–2, LO10–3]
Becton Labs, Inc., produces various chemical compounds for industrial use. One compound, called Fludex, is prepared using an elaborate distilling process. The company has developed standard costs for one unit of Fludex, as follows:

	Standard Quantity	Standard Price or Rate	Standard Cost
Direct materials	2.5 ounces	$20.00 per ounce	$50.00
Direct labor	1.4 hours	$12.50 per hour	17.50
Variable manufacturing overhead	1.4 hours	$3.50 per hour	4.90
			$72.40

During November, the following activity was recorded related to the production of Fludex:
a. Materials purchased, 12,000 ounces at a cost of $225,000.
b. There was no beginning inventory of materials; however, at the end of the month, 2,500 ounces of material remained in ending inventory.
c. The company employs 35 lab technicians to work on the production of Fludex. During November, they worked an average of 160 hours at an average rate of $12 per hour.
d. Variable manufacturing overhead is assigned to Fludex on the basis of direct labor-hours. Variable manufacturing overhead costs during November totaled $18,200.
e. During November, 3,750 good units of Fludex were produced.

Required:
1. For direct materials:
    a. Compute the price and quantity variances.
    b. The materials were purchased from a new supplier who is anxious to enter into a long-term purchase contract. Would you recommend that the company sign the contract? Explain.
2. For direct labor:
    a. Compute the rate and efficiency variances.
    b. In the past, the 35 technicians employed in the production of Fludex consisted of 20 senior technicians and 15 assistants. During November, the company experimented with fewer senior technicians and more assistants in order to save costs. Would you recommend that the new labor mix be continued? Explain.
3. Compute the variable overhead rate and efficiency variances. What relation can you see between this efficiency variance and the labor efficiency variance?

PROBLEM 10–15 Comprehensive Variance Analysis [LO10–1, LO10–2, LO10–3]
Miller Toy Company manufactures a plastic swimming pool at its Westwood Plant. The plant has been experiencing problems as shown by its June contribution format income statement below:

	Budgeted	Actual
Sales (15,000 pools)	$450,000	$450,000
Variable expenses:		
Variable cost of goods sold*	180,000	196,290
Variable selling expenses	20,000	20,000
Total variable expenses	200,000	216,290
Contribution margin	250,000	233,710
Fixed expenses:		
Manufacturing overhead	130,000	130,000
Selling and administrative	84,000	84,000
Total fixed expenses	214,000	214,000
Net operating income	$ 36,000	$ 19,710

*Contains direct materials, direct labor, and variable manufacturing overhead.

Janet Dunn, who has just been appointed general manager of the Westwood Plant, has been given instructions to "get things under control." Upon reviewing the plant's income statement, Ms. Dunn has concluded that the major problem lies in the variable cost of goods sold. She has been provided with the following standard cost per swimming pool:

	Standard Quantity or Hours	Standard Price or Rate	Standard Cost
Direct materials	3.0 pounds	$2.00 per pound	$ 6.00
Direct labor	0.8 hours	$6.00 per hour	4.80
Variable manufacturing overhead	0.4 hours*	$3.00 per hour	1.20
Total standard cost			$12.00

*Based on machine-hours.

During June the plant produced 15,000 pools and incurred the following costs:
a. Purchased 60,000 pounds of materials at a cost of $1.95 per pound.
b. Used 49,200 pounds of materials in production. (Finished goods and work in process inventories are insignificant and can be ignored.)
c. Worked 11,800 direct labor-hours at a cost of $7.00 per hour.
d. Incurred variable manufacturing overhead cost totaling $18,290 for the month. A total of 5,900 machine-hours was recorded.
   It is the company's policy to close all variances to cost of goods sold on a monthly basis.

Required:
1. Compute the following variances for June:
   a. Materials price and quantity variances.
   b. Labor rate and efficiency variances.
   c. Variable overhead rate and efficiency variances.
2. Summarize the variances that you computed in (1) above by showing the net overall favorable or unfavorable variance for the month. What impact did this figure have on the company's income statement? Show computations.
3. Pick out the two most significant variances that you computed in (1) above. Explain to Ms. Dunn possible causes of these variances.

PROBLEM 10–16 Comprehensive Variance Analysis [LO10–1, LO10–2, LO10–3]
Highland Company produces a lightweight backpack that is popular with college students. Standard variable costs relating to a single backpack are given below:

	Standard Quantity or Hours	Standard Price or Rate	Standard Cost
Direct materials	?	$6 per yard	$?
Direct labor	?	?	?
Variable manufacturing overhead	?	$3 per direct labor-hour	?
Total standard cost			$?

Overhead is applied to production on the basis of direct labor-hours. During March, 1,000 backpacks were manufactured and sold. Selected information relating to the month's production is given below:

	Materials Used	Direct Labor	Variable Manufacturing Overhead
Total standard cost allowed*	$16,800	$10,500	$4,200
Actual costs incurred	$15,000	?	$3,600
Materials price variance	?		
Materials quantity variance	$1,200 U		
Labor rate variance		?	
Labor efficiency variance		?	
Variable overhead rate variance			?
Variable overhead efficiency variance			?

*For the month's production.

Chapter 10

The following additional information is available for March's production:

Actual direct labor-hours	1,500
Standard overhead rate per direct labor-hour	$3.00
Difference between standard and actual cost per backpack produced during March	$0.15 F

Required:
1. What is the standard cost of a single backpack?
2. What was the actual cost per backpack produced during March?
3. How many yards of material are required at standard per backpack?
4. What was the materials price variance for March if there were no beginning or ending inventories of materials?
5. What is the standard direct labor rate per hour?
6. What was the labor rate variance for March? The labor efficiency variance?
7. What was the variable overhead rate variance for March? The variable overhead efficiency variance?
8. Prepare a standard cost card for one backpack.

Case

Available with McGraw-Hill's *Connect*® Accounting.

CASE 10–17 Working Backwards from Variance Data [LO10–1, LO10–2, LO10–3]

You have recently accepted a position with Vitex, Inc., the manufacturer of a popular consumer product. During your first week on the job, the vice president has been favorably impressed with your work. She has been so impressed, in fact, that yesterday she called you into her office and asked you to attend the executive committee meeting this morning for the purpose of leading a discussion on the variances reported for last period. Anxious to favorably impress the executive committee, you took the variances and supporting data home last night to study.

On your way to work this morning, the papers were laying on the seat of your new, red convertible. As you were crossing a bridge on the highway, a sudden gust of wind caught the papers and blew them over the edge of the bridge and into the stream below. You managed to retrieve only one page, which contains the following information:

STANDARD COST CARD

Direct materials, 6 pounds at $3 per pound	$18.00
Direct labor, 0.8 direct labor-hours at $15 per direct labor-hour	$12.00
Variable manufacturing overhead, 0.8 direct labor-hours at $3 per direct labor-hour	$2.40

	Total Standard Cost*	Variances Reported	
		Price or Rate	Quantity or Efficiency
Direct materials	$405,000	$6,900 F	$9,000 U
Direct labor	$270,000	$14,550 U	$21,000 U
Variable manufacturing overhead	$54,000	$1,300 F	$?† U

---
*Applied to Work in Process during the period.
†Entry obliterated.

You recall that manufacturing overhead cost is applied to production on the basis of direct labor-hours and that all of the materials purchased during the period were used in production. Work in process inventories are insignificant and can be ignored.

It is now 8:30 A.M. The executive committee meeting starts in just one hour; you realize that to avoid looking like a bungling fool you must somehow generate the necessary "backup" data for the variances before the meeting begins. Without backup data it will be impossible to lead the discussion or answer any questions.

Required:
1. How many units were produced last period?
2. How many pounds of direct material were purchased and used in production?
3. What was the actual cost per pound of material?
4. How many actual direct labor-hours were worked during the period?
5. What was the actual rate paid per direct labor-hour?
6. How much actual variable manufacturing overhead cost was incurred during the period?

Appendix 10A: Predetermined Overhead Rates and Overhead Analysis in a Standard Costing System

In this appendix, we will investigate how the predetermined overhead rates that we discussed in the job-order costing chapter earlier in the book can be used in a standard costing system. Throughout this appendix, we assume that an absorption costing system is used in which *all* manufacturing costs—both fixed and variable—are included in product costs.

LO10–4
Compute and interpret the fixed overhead budget and volume variances.

Predetermined Overhead Rates

The data in Exhibit 10A–1 pertain to MicroDrive Corporation, a company that produces miniature electric motors. Note that the company budgeted for 50,000 machine-hours based on production of 25,000 motors. At this level of activity, the budgeted variable manufacturing overhead was $75,000 and the budgeted fixed manufacturing overhead was $300,000.

Recall from the job-order costing chapter that the following formula is used to set the predetermined overhead rate at the beginning of the period:

$$\frac{\text{Predetermined}}{\text{overhead rate}} = \frac{\text{Estimated total manufacturing overhead cost}}{\text{Estimated total amount of the allocation base}}$$

The estimated total amount of the allocation base in the formula for the predetermined overhead rate is called the **denominator activity.**

As discussed in the job-order costing chapter, once the predetermined overhead rate has been determined, it remains unchanged throughout the period, even if the actual level

		EXHIBIT 10A–1
Budgeted production	25,000 motors	MicroDrive Corporation Data
Standard machine-hours per motor	2 machine-hours per motor	
Budgeted machine-hours (2 machine-hours per motor × 25,000 motors)	50,000 machine-hours	
Actual production	20,000 motors	
Standard machine-hours allowed for the actual production (2 machine-hours per motor × 20,000 motors)	40,000 machine-hours	
Actual machine-hours	42,000 machine-hours	
Budgeted variable manufacturing overhead ...	$75,000	
Budgeted fixed manufacturing overhead	$300,000	
Total budgeted manufacturing overhead	$375,000	
Actual variable manufacturing overhead	$71,400	
Actual fixed manufacturing overhead	$308,000	
Total actual manufacturing overhead	$379,400	

Chapter 10

of activity differs from what was estimated. Consequently, the amount of overhead applied to each unit of product is the same regardless of when it is produced during the period.

MicroDrive Corporation uses budgeted machine-hours as its denominator activity in the predetermined overhead rate. Consequently, the company's predetermined overhead rate would be computed as follows:

$$\frac{\text{Predetermined}}{\text{overhead rate}} = \frac{\$375,000}{50,000 \text{ MHs}} = \$7.50 \text{ per MH}$$

This predetermined overhead rate can be broken down into its variable and fixed components as follows:

$$\frac{\text{Variable componenet of the}}{\text{predetermined overhead rate}} = \frac{\$75,000}{50,000 \text{ MHs}} = \$1.50 \text{ per MH}$$

$$\frac{\text{Fixed component of the}}{\text{predetermined overhead rate}} = \frac{\$300,000}{50,000 \text{ MHs}} = \$6.00 \text{ per MH}$$

For every standard machine-hour recorded, work in process is charged with $7.50 of manufacturing overhead, of which $1.50 represents variable manufacturing overhead and $6.00 represents fixed manufacturing overhead. In total, MicroDrive Corporation would apply $300,000 of overhead to work in process as shown below:

$$\text{Overhead applied} = \frac{\text{Predetermined}}{\text{overhead rate}} \times \frac{\text{Standard hours allowed}}{\text{for the actual output}}$$

$$= \$7.50 \text{ per machine-hour} \times 40,000 \text{ machine-hours}$$

$$= \$300,000$$

Overhead Application in a Standard Cost System

To understand fixed overhead variances, we first have to understand how overhead is applied to work in process in a standard cost system. Recall that in the job-order costing chapter we applied overhead to work in process on the basis of the actual level of activity. This procedure was correct because at the time we were dealing with a normal cost system.[1] However, we are now dealing with a standard cost system. In such a system, overhead is applied to work in process on the basis of the *standard hours allowed for the actual output of the period* rather than on the basis of the actual number of hours worked. Exhibit 10A–2 illustrates this point. In a standard cost system, every unit of a particular product is charged with the same amount of overhead cost, regardless of how much time the unit actually requires for processing.

EXHIBIT 10A–2
Applied Overhead Costs: Normal Cost System versus Standard Cost System

Normal Cost System		Standard Cost System	
Manufacturing Overhead		Manufacturing Overhead	
Actual overhead costs incurred.	Applied overhead costs: Actual hours × Pre-determined overhead rate.	Actual overhead costs incurred.	Applied overhead costs: Standard hours allowed for actual output × Pre-determined overhead rate.
Underapplied or overapplied overhead		Underapplied or overapplied overhead	

[1] Normal cost systems are discussed on page 90 in the job-order costing chapter.

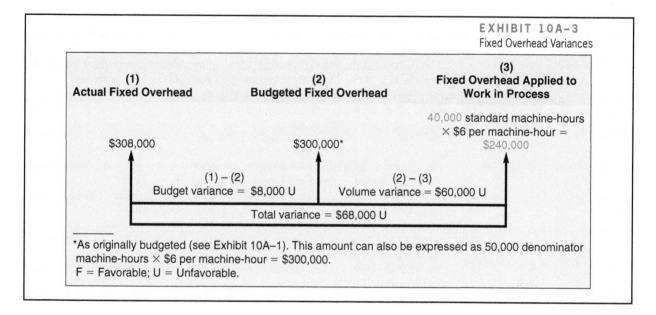

EXHIBIT 10A–3
Fixed Overhead Variances

(1) Actual Fixed Overhead	(2) Budgeted Fixed Overhead	(3) Fixed Overhead Applied to Work in Process
		40,000 standard machine-hours × $6 per machine-hour = $240,000
$308,000	$300,000*	

(1) – (2)
Budget variance = $8,000 U

(2) – (3)
Volume variance = $60,000 U

Total variance = $68,000 U

*As originally budgeted (see Exhibit 10A–1). This amount can also be expressed as 50,000 denominator machine-hours × $6 per machine-hour = $300,000.
F = Favorable; U = Unfavorable.

Budget Variance

Two fixed manufacturing overhead variances are computed in a standard costing system—a *budget variance* and a *volume variance*. These variances are computed in Exhibit 10A–3. The **budget variance** is simply the difference between the actual fixed manufacturing overhead and the budgeted fixed manufacturing overhead for the period. The formula is:

$$\text{Budget variance} = \text{Actual fixed overhead} - \text{Budgeted fixed overhead}$$

If the actual fixed overhead cost exceeds the budgeted fixed overhead cost, the budget variance is labeled unfavorable. If the actual fixed overhead cost is less than the budgeted fixed overhead cost, the budget variance is labeled favorable.

Applying the formula to the MicroDrive Corporation data, the budget variance is computed as follows:

$$\text{Budget variance} = \$308,000 - \$300,000 = \$8,000 \text{ U}$$

According to the budget, the fixed manufacturing overhead should have been $300,000, but it was actually $308,000. Because the actual cost exceeds the budget by $8,000, the variance is labeled as unfavorable; however, this label does not automatically signal ineffective managerial performance. For example, this variance may be the result of waste and inefficiency, or it may be due to an unforeseen yet prudent investment in fixed overhead resources that improves product quality or manufacturing cycle efficiency.

Volume Variance

The **volume variance** is defined by the following formula:

$$\text{Volume variance} = \text{Budgeted fixed overhead} - \text{Fixed overhead applied to work in process}$$

When the budgeted fixed manufacturing overhead exceeds the fixed manufacturing overhead applied to work in process, the volume variance is labeled as unfavorable. When the budgeted fixed manufacturing overhead is less than the fixed manufacturing overhead applied to work in process, the volume variance is labeled as favorable. As we shall see, caution is advised when interpreting this variance.

To understand the volume variance, we need to understand how fixed manufacturing overhead is applied to work in process in a standard costing system. As discussed earlier, fixed manufacturing overhead is applied to work in process on the basis of the standard hours allowed for the actual output of the period. In the case of MicroDrive Corporation, the company produced 20,000 motors and the standard for each motor is 2 machine-hours. Therefore, the standard hours allowed for the actual output is 40,000 machine-hours (= 20,000 motors × 2 machine-hours). As shown in Exhibit 10A–3, the predetermined fixed manufacturing overhead rate of $6.00 per machine-hour is multiplied by the 40,000 standard machine-hours allowed for the actual output to arrive at $240,000 of fixed manufacturing overhead applied to work in process. Another way to think of this is that the standard for each motor is 2 machine-hours. Because the predetermined fixed manufacturing overhead rate is $6.00 per machine-hour, each motor is assigned $12.00 (= 2 machine-hours × $6.00 per machine-hour) of fixed manufacturing overhead. Consequently, a total of $240,000 of fixed manufacturing overhead is applied to the 20,000 motors that are actually produced. Under either explanation, the volume variance according to the formula is:

$$\text{Volume variance} = \$300,000 - \$240,000 = \$60,000 \text{ U}$$

The key to interpreting the volume variance is to understand that it depends on the difference between the hours used in the denominator to compute the predetermined overhead rate and the standard hours allowed for the actual output of the period. While it is not obvious, the volume variance can also be computed using the following formula:

$$\frac{\text{Volume}}{\text{variance}} = \frac{\text{Fixed component of the}}{\text{predetermined overhead rate}} \times \left(\frac{\text{Denominator}}{\text{hours}} - \frac{\text{Standard hours allowed}}{\text{for the actual output}} \right)$$

In the case of MicroDrive Corporation, the volume variance can be computed using this formula as follows:

$$\text{Volume variance} = \frac{\$6.00 \text{ per}}{\text{machine-hour}} \times \left(\frac{50,000}{\text{machine-hours}} - \frac{40,000}{\text{machine-hours}} \right)$$

$$= \$6.00 \text{ per machine-hour} \times (10,000 \text{ machine-hours})$$

$$= \$60,000 \text{ U}$$

Note that this agrees with the volume variance computed using the earlier formula.

Focusing on this new formula, if the denominator hours exceed the standard hours allowed for the actual output, the volume variance is unfavorable. If the denominator hours are less than the standard hours allowed for the actual output, the volume variance is favorable. Stated differently, the volume variance is unfavorable if the actual level of activity is less than expected. The volume variance is favorable if the actual level of activity is greater than expected. It is important to note that the volume variance does not measure overspending or underspending. A company should incur the same dollar amount of fixed overhead cost regardless of whether the period's activity was above or below the planned (denominator) level.

The volume variance is often viewed as a measure of the utilization of facilities. If the standard hours allowed for the actual output are greater than (less than) the denominator hours, it signals efficient (inefficient) usage of facilities. However, other measures of utilization—such as the percentage of capacity utilized—are easier to compute and understand. Perhaps a better interpretation of the volume variance is that it is the error that occurs when the level of activity is incorrectly estimated and the costing system assumes fixed costs behave as if they are variable. This interpretation may be clearer in the next section that graphically analyzes the fixed manufacturing overhead variances.

Graphic Analysis of Fixed Overhead Variances

Exhibit 10A–4 shows a graphic analysis that offers insights into the fixed overhead budget and volume variances. As shown in the graph, fixed overhead cost is applied to work in process at the predetermined rate of $6.00 for each standard hour of activity. (The applied-cost line is the upward-sloping line on the graph.) Because a denominator level of 50,000 machine-hours was used in computing the $6.00 rate, the applied-cost line crosses the budget-cost line at exactly 50,000 machine-hours. If the denominator hours and the standard hours allowed for the actual output are the same, there is no volume variance. It is only when the standard hours differ from the denominator hours that a volume variance arises.

In MicroDrive's case, the standard hours allowed for the actual output (40,000 hours) are less than the denominator hours (50,000 hours). The result is an unfavorable volume variance because less cost was applied to production than was originally budgeted. If the situation had been reversed and the standard hours allowed for the actual output had exceeded the denominator hours, then the volume variance on the graph would have been favorable.

Cautions in Fixed Overhead Analysis

A volume variance for fixed overhead arises because when applying the costs to work in process, we act *as if* the fixed costs are variable. The graph in Exhibit 10A–4 illustrates this point. Notice from the graph that fixed overhead costs are applied to work in process at a rate of $6 per hour *as if* they are variable. Treating these costs as if they are variable is necessary for product costing purposes, but some real dangers lurk here. Managers can easily be misled into thinking that fixed costs are *in fact* variable.

Keep clearly in mind that fixed overhead costs come in large chunks. Expressing fixed costs on a unit or per hour basis, though necessary for product costing for external reports, is artificial. Increases or decreases in activity in fact have no effect on total fixed costs within the relevant range of activity. Even though fixed costs are expressed on a unit or

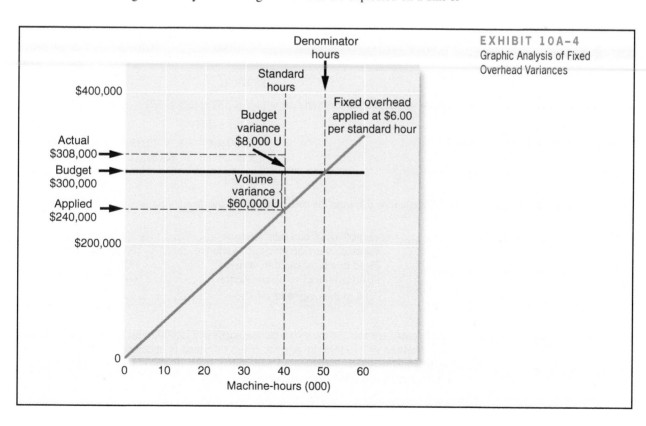

EXHIBIT 10A–4
Graphic Analysis of Fixed Overhead Variances

per hour basis, they are *not* proportional to activity. In a sense, the volume variance is the error that occurs as a result of treating fixed costs as variable costs in the costing system.

Reconciling Overhead Variances and Underapplied or Overapplied Overhead

In a standard cost system, the underapplied or overapplied overhead for a period equals the sum of the overhead variances. To see this, we will return to the MicroDrive Corporation example.

As discussed earlier, in a standard cost system, overhead is applied to work in process on the basis of the standard hours allowed for the actual output of the period. The following table shows how the underapplied or overapplied overhead for MicroDrive is computed.

Predetermined overhead rate (a)	$7.50 per machine-hour
Standard hours allowed for the actual output [Exhibit 10A–1] (b)	40,000 machine-hours
Manufacturing overhead applied (a) × (b)	$300,000
Total actual manufacturing overhead [Exhibit 10A–1]	$379,400
Manufacturing overhead underapplied or overapplied	$79,400 underapplied

We have already computed the budget variance and the volume variance for this company. We will also need to compute the variable manufacturing overhead variances. The data for these computations are contained in Exhibit 10A–1. Recalling the formulas for the variable manufacturing overhead variances from Exhibit 10–9, we can compute the variable overhead rate and efficiency variances as follows:

$$\text{Variable overhead rate variance} = (AH \times AR) - (AH \times SR)$$

$$= AH(AR - SR)$$

$$= \frac{42,000}{\text{machine-hours}} - \left(\frac{\$1.70 \text{ per}}{\text{machine-hour}^1} - \frac{\$1.50 \text{ per}}{\text{machine-hour}} \right)$$

$$= \$8,400 \text{ U}$$

$$\text{Variable overhead efficiency variance} = (AH \times SR) - (SH \times SR)$$

$$= SR(AH - SH)$$

$$= \frac{\$1.50 \text{ per}}{\text{machine-hour}} - \left(\frac{42,000}{\text{machine-hours}} - \frac{40,000 \text{ per}}{\text{machine-hours}} \right)$$

$$= \$3,000 \text{ U}$$

We can now compute the sum of all of the overhead variances as follows:

Variable overhead rate variance	$ 8,400 U
Variable overhead efficiency variance	3,000 U
Fixed overhead budget variance	8,000 U
Fixed overhead volume variance	60,000 U
Total of the overhead variances	$79,400 U

Note that the total of the overhead variances is $79,000, which equals the underapplied overhead of $79,000. In general, if the overhead is underapplied, the total of the standard cost overhead variances is unfavorable. If the overhead is overapplied, the total of the standard cost overhead variances is favorable.

[1] AR = $70,400 ÷ 42,000 machine-hours = $1.70 per machine-hour.

Glossary

Budget variance The difference between the actual fixed overhead costs and the budgeted fixed overhead costs for the period. (p. 459)

Denominator activity The level of activity used to compute the predetermined overhead rate. (p. 461)

Volume variance The variance that arises whenever the standard hours allowed for the actual output of a period are different from the denominator activity level that was used to compute the predetermined overhead rate. It is computed by multiplying the fixed component of the predetermined overhead rate by the difference between the denominator hours and the standard hours allowed for the actual output. (p. 461)

 Appendix 10A Exercises and Problems

All applicable exercises and problems are available with McGraw-Hill's Connect® Accounting.

EXERCISE 10A–1 Fixed Overhead Variances [LO10–4]

Primara Corporation has a standard cost system in which it applies overhead to products based on the standard direct labor-hours allowed for the actual output of the period. Data concerning the most recent year appear below:

Total budgeted fixed overhead cost for the year	$250,000
Actual fixed overhead cost for the year	$254,000
Budgeted standard direct labor-hours (denominator level of activity)	25,000
Actual direct labor-hours	27,000
Standard direct labor-hours allowed for the actual output	26,000

Required:

1. Compute the fixed portion of the predetermined overhead rate for the year.
2. Compute the fixed overhead budget variance and volume variance.

EXERCISE 10A–2 Predetermined Overhead Rate; Overhead Variances [LO10–3, LO10–4]

Norwall Company's variable manufacturing overhead should be $3.00 per standard machine-hour and its fixed manufacturing overhead should be $300,000 per month.

The following information is available for a recent month:

a. The denominator activity of 60,000 machine-hours is used to compute the predetermined overhead rate.

b. At the 60,000 standard machine-hours level of activity, the company should produce 40,000 units of product.

c. The company's actual operating results were:

Number of units produced	42,000
Actual machine-hours	64,000
Actual variable manufacturing overhead cost	$185,600
Actual fixed manufacturing overhead cost	$302,400

Required:

1. Compute the predetermined overhead rate and break it down into variable and fixed cost elements.
2. Compute the standard hours allowed for the actual production.
3. Compute the variable overhead rate and efficiency variances and the fixed overhead budget and volume variances.

EXERCISE 10A–3 Applying Overhead in a Standard Costing System [LO10–4]

Privack Corporation has a standard cost system in which it applies overhead to products based on the standard direct labor-hours allowed for the actual output of the period. Data concerning the most recent year appear below:

Variable overhead cost per direct labor-hour	$2.00
Total fixed overhead cost per year	$250,000
Budgeted standard direct labor-hours (denominator level of activity)	40,000
Actual direct labor-hours	39,000
Standard direct labor-hours allowed for the actual output	38,000

Required:
1. Compute the predetermined overhead rate for the year.
2. Determine the amount of overhead that would be applied to the output of the period.

EXERCISE 10A–4 Fixed Overhead Variances [LO10–4]

Selected operating information on three different companies for a recent year is given below:

	Company		
	A	B	C
Full-capacity machine-hours	10,000	18,000	20,000
Budgeted machine-hours*	9,000	17,000	20,000
Actual machine-hours	9,000	17,800	19,000
Standard machine-hours allowed for actual production	9,500	16,000	20,000

*Denominator activity for computing the predetermined overhead rate.

Required:
For each company, state whether the company would have a favorable or unfavorable volume variance and why.

EXERCISE 10A–5 Using Fixed Overhead Variances [LO10–4]

The standard cost card for the single product manufactured by Cutter, Inc., is given below:

Standard Cost Card—per Unit	
Direct materials, 3 yards at $6.00 per yard	$ 18
Direct labor, 4 hours at $15.50 per hour	62
Variable overhead, 4 hours at $1.50 per hour	6
Fixed overhead, 4 hours at $5.00 per hour	20
Total standard cost per unit	$106

Manufacturing overhead is applied to production on the basis of standard direct labor-hours. During the year, the company worked 37,000 hours and manufactured 9,500 units of product. Selected data relating to the company's fixed manufacturing overhead cost for the year are shown below:

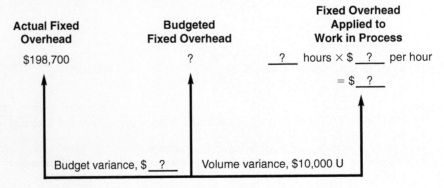

Actual Fixed Overhead	Budgeted Fixed Overhead	Fixed Overhead Applied to Work in Process
$198,700	?	__?__ hours × $ _?_ per hour = $ _?_

Budget variance, $ _?_   Volume variance, $10,000 U

Required:
1. What were the standard hours allowed for the year's production?
2. What was the amount of budgeted fixed overhead cost for the year?
3. What was the fixed overhead budget variance for the year?
4. What denominator activity level did the company use in setting the predetermined overhead rate for the year?

EXERCISE 10A–6 Predetermined Overhead Rate [LO10–4]
Operating at a normal level of 30,000 direct labor-hours, Lasser Company produces 10,000 units of product each year. The direct labor wage rate is $12 per hour. Two and one-half yards of direct materials go into each unit of product; the material costs $8.60 per yard. Variable manufacturing overhead should be $1.90 per standard direct labor-hour. Fixed manufacturing overhead should be $168,000 per period.

Required:
1. Using 30,000 direct labor-hours as the denominator activity, compute the predetermined overhead rate and break it down into variable and fixed elements.
2. Complete the standard cost card below for one unit of product:

Direct materials, 2.5 yards at $8.60 per yard	$21.50
Direct labor, ?	?
Variable manufacturing overhead, ?	?
Fixed manufacturing overhead, ?	?
Total standard cost per unit	$?

EXERCISE 10A–7 Relations Among Fixed Overhead Variances [LO10–4]
Selected information relating to Yost Company's operations for the most recent year is given below:

Activity:	
Denominator activity (machine-hours)	45,000
Standard hours allowed per unit	3
Number of units produced	14,000
Costs:	
Actual fixed overhead costs incurred	$267,000
Fixed overhead budget variance	$3,000 F

The company applies overhead cost to products on the basis of standard machine-hours.

Required:
1. What were the standard machine-hours allowed for the actual production?
2. What was the fixed portion of the predetermined overhead rate?
3. What was the volume variance?

PROBLEM 10A–8 Applying Overhead; Overhead Variances [LO10–3, LO10–4]

Lane Company manufactures a single product that requires a great deal of hand labor. Overhead cost is applied on the basis of standard direct labor-hours. Variable manufacturing overhead should be $2 per standard direct labor-hour and fixed manufacturing overhead should be $480,000 per year.

The company's product requires 3 pounds of material that has a standard cost of $7 per pound and 1.5 hours of direct labor time that has a standard rate of $12 per hour.

The company planned to operate at a denominator activity level of 60,000 direct labor-hours and to produce 40,000 units of product during the most recent year. Actual activity and costs for the year were as follows:

Number of units produced	42,000
Actual direct labor-hours worked	65,000
Actual variable manufacturing overhead cost incurred	$123,500
Actual fixed manufacturing overhead cost incurred	$483,000

Chapter 10

Required:

1. Compute the predetermined overhead rate for the year. Break the rate down into variable and fixed elements.
2. Prepare a standard cost card for the company's product; show the details for all manufacturing costs on your standard cost card.
3. Do the following:
    a. Compute the standard direct labor-hours allowed for the year's production.
    b. Complete the following Manufacturing Overhead T-account for the year:

Manufacturing Overhead

?	?
?	?

4. Determine the reason for any underapplied or overapplied overhead for the year by computing the variable overhead rate and efficiency variances and the fixed overhead budget and volume variances.
5. Suppose the company had chosen 65,000 direct labor-hours as the denominator activity rather than 60,000 hours. State which, if any, of the variances computed in (4) above would have changed, and explain how the variance(s) would have changed. No computations are necessary.

PROBLEM 10A–9 Applying Overhead; Overhead Variances [LO10–3, LO10–4]
Chilczuk, S.A., of Gdansk, Poland, is a major producer of classic Polish sausage. The company uses a standard cost system to help control costs. Manufacturing overhead is applied to production on the basis of standard direct labor-hours. According to the company's flexible budget, the following manufacturing overhead costs should be incurred at an activity level of 35,000 labor-hours (the denominator activity level):

Variable manufacturing overhead cost	$ 87,500
Fixed manufacturing overhead cost	210,000
Total manufacturing overhead cost	$297,500

During the most recent year, the following operating results were recorded:

Activity:	
Actual labor-hours worked	30,000
Standard labor-hours allowed for output	32,000
Cost:	
Actual variable manufacturing overhead cost incurred	$78,000
Actual fixed manufacturing overhead cost incurred	$209,400

At the end of the year, the company's Manufacturing Overhead account contained the following data:

Manufacturing Overhead

Actual	287,400	Applied	272,000
	15,400		

Management would like to determine the cause of the $15,400 underapplied overhead.

Required:

1. Compute the predetermined overhead rate. Break the rate down into variable and fixed cost elements.
2. Show how the $272,000 Applied figure in the Manufacturing Overhead account was computed.
3. Analyze the $15,400 underapplied overhead figure in terms of the variable overhead rate and efficiency variances and the fixed overhead budget and volume variances.
4. Explain the meaning of each variance that you computed in (3) above.

PROBLEM 10A–10 Comprehensive Standard Cost Variances [LO10–1, LO10–2, LO10–3, LO10–4]
"Wonderful! Not only did our salespeople do a good job in meeting the sales budget this year, but our production people did a good job in controlling costs as well," said Kim Clark, president of Martell Company. "Our $18,300 overall manufacturing cost variance is only 1.2% of the $1,536,000 standard cost of products made during the year. That's well within the 3% parameter set by management for acceptable variances. It looks like everyone will be in line for a bonus this year."

The company produces and sells a single product. The standard cost card for the product follows:

Standard Cost Card—per Unit	
Direct materials, 2 feet at $8.45 per foot	$16.90
Direct labor, 1.4 direct labor-hours at $16 per direct labor-hour	22.40
Variable overhead, 1.4 direct labor-hours at $2.50 per direct labor-hour	3.50
Fixed overhead, 1.4 direct labor-hours at $6 per direct labor-hour	8.40
Standard cost per unit	$51.20

The following additional information is available for the year just completed:

a. The company manufactured 30,000 units of product during the year.
b. A total of 64,000 feet of material was purchased during the year at a cost of $8.55 per foot. All of this material was used to manufacture the 30,000 units. There were no beginning or ending inventories for the year.
c. The company worked 43,500 direct labor-hours during the year at a direct labor cost of $15.80 per hour.
d. Overhead is applied to products on the basis of standard direct labor-hours. Data relating to manufacturing overhead costs follow:

Denominator activity level (direct labor-hours)	35,000
Budgeted fixed overhead costs	$210,000
Actual variable overhead costs incurred	$108,000
Actual fixed overhead costs incurred	$211,800

Required:

1. Compute the materials price and quantity variances for the year.
2. Compute the labor rate and efficiency variances for the year.
3. For manufacturing overhead compute:
   a. The variable overhead rate and efficiency variances for the year.
   b. The fixed overhead budget and volume variances for the year.
4. Total the variances you have computed, and compare the net amount with the $18,300 mentioned by the president. Do you agree that bonuses should be given to everyone for good cost control during the year? Explain.

PROBLEM 10A–11 Comprehensive Standard Cost Variances [LO10–1, LO10–2, LO10–3, LO10–4]
Flandro Company uses a standard cost system and sets predetermined overhead rates on the basis of direct labor-hours. The following data are taken from the company's budget for the current year:

Denominator activity (direct labor-hours)	5,000
Variable manufacturing overhead cost	$25,000
Fixed manufacturing overhead cost	$59,000

The standard cost card for the company's only product is given below:

Direct materials, 3 yards at $4.40 per yard	$13.20
Direct labor, 1 hour at $12 per hour	12.00
Manufacturing overhead, 140% of direct labor cost	16.80
Standard cost per unit	$42.00

470

Chapter 10

During the year, the company produced 6,000 units of product and incurred the following costs:

Materials purchased, 24,000 yards at $4.80 per yard	$115,200
Materials used in production (in yards)	18,500
Direct labor cost incurred, 5,800 hours at $13 per hour . . .	$75,400
Variable manufacturing overhead cost incurred	$29,580
Fixed manufacturing overhead cost incurred	$60,400

Required:
1. Redo the standard cost card in a clearer, more usable format by detailing the variable and fixed overhead cost elements.
2. Prepare an analysis of the variances for direct materials and direct labor for the year.
3. Prepare an analysis of the variances for variable and fixed overhead for the year.
4. What effect, if any, does the choice of a denominator activity level have on unit standard costs? Is the volume variance a controllable variance from a spending point of view? Explain.

PROBLEM 10A–12 Selection of a Denominator; Overhead Analysis; Standard Cost Card [LO10–3, LO10–4]
Morton Company's variable manufacturing overhead should be $4.50 per standard direct labor-hour and fixed manufacturing should be $270,000 per year.

The company manufactures a single product that requires two direct labor-hours to complete. The direct labor wage rate is $15 per hour. Four feet of raw material are required for each unit of product; the standard cost of the material is $8.75 per foot.

Although normal activity is 30,000 direct labor-hours each year, the company expects to operate at a 40,000-hour level of activity this year.

Required:
1. Assume that the company chooses 30,000 direct labor-hours as the denominator level of activity. Compute the predetermined overhead rate, breaking it down into variable and fixed cost elements.
2. Assume that the company chooses 40,000 direct labor-hours as the denominator level of activity. Repeat the computations in (1) above.
3. Complete two standard cost cards as outlined below.

Denominator Activity: 30,000 Direct Labor-Hours	
Direct materials, 4 feet at $8.75 per foot	$35.00
Direct labor, ?	?
Variable manufacturing overhead, ?	?
Fixed manufacturing overhead, ?	?
Standard cost per unit	$?

Denominator Activity: 40,000 Direct Labor-Hours	
Direct materials, $4 feet at $8.75 per foot	$35.00
Direct labor, ?	?
Variable manufacturing overhead, ?	?
Fixed manufacturing overhead, ?	?
Standard cost per unit	$?

4. Assume that the company actually produces 18,000 units and works 38,000 direct labor-hours during the year. Actual manufacturing overhead costs for the year are:

Variable manufacturing overhead cost	$174,800
Fixed manufacturing overhead cost	271,600
Total manufacturing overhead cost	$446,400

Do the following:
a. Compute the standard direct labor-hours allowed for this year's production.
b. Complete the Manufacturing Overhead account below. Assume that the company uses 30,000 direct labor-hours (normal activity) as the denominator activity figure in computing predetermined overhead rates, as you have done in (1) above.

Manufacturing Overhead

Actual costs	446,400	Applied costs	?
	?		?

c. Determine the cause of the underapplied or overapplied overhead for the year by computing the variable overhead rate and efficiency variances and the fixed overhead budget and volume variances.
5. Looking at the variances you have computed, what appears to be the major disadvantage of using normal activity rather than expected actual activity as a denominator in computing the predetermined overhead rate? What advantages can you see to offset this disadvantage?

Appendix 10B: Journal Entries to Record Variances

Although standard costs and variances can be computed and used by management without being formally entered into the accounting records, many organizations prefer to make formal journal entries. Formal entries tend to give variances a greater emphasis than informal, off-the-record computations. This emphasis signals management's desire to keep costs within the limits that have been set. In addition, formal use of standard costs simplifies the bookkeeping process enormously. Inventories and cost of goods sold can be valued at their standard costs—eliminating the need to keep track of the actual cost of each unit.

LO10–5
Prepare journal entries to record standard costs and variances.

Direct Materials Variances

To illustrate the journal entries needed to record standard cost variances, we will return to the data contained in the review problem at the end of the chapter. The entry to record the purchase of direct materials would be as follows:

Raw Materials (18,000 ounces at $0.50 per ounce)	9,000	
Materials Price Variance (18,000 ounces at $0.10 per ounce U)	1,800	
Accounts Payable (18,000 ounces at $0.60 per ounce		10,800

Notice that the price variance is recognized when purchases are made, rather than when materials are actually used in production and that the materials are carried in the inventory account at standard cost. As direct materials are later drawn from inventory and used in production, the quantity variance is isolated as follows:

Work in Process (12,000 ounces at $0.50 per ounce)	6,000	
Materials Quantity Variance (2,000 ounces U at $0.50 per ounce) . . .	1,000	
Raw Materials (14,000 ounces at $0.50 per ounce)		7,000

Thus, direct materials are added to the Work in Process account at the standard cost of the materials that should have been used to produce the actual output.

Notice that both the price variance and the quantity variance above are unfavorable and are debit entries. If either of these variances had been favorable, it would have appeared as a credit entry.

472   Chapter 10

Direct Labor Variances

Referring again to the cost data in the review problem at the end of the chapter, the journal entry to record the incurrence of direct labor cost would be:

Work in Process (1,200 hours at $30.00 per hour)	36,000	
Labor Rate Variance (1,100 hours at $0.50 U)	550	
Labor Efficiency Variance (100 hours F at $30.00 per hour)		3,000
Wages Payable (1,100 hours at $30.50 per hour)		33,550

Thus, as with direct materials, direct labor costs enter into the Work in Process account at standard, both in terms of the rate and in terms of the hours allowed for the actual production of the period. Note that the unfavorable labor efficiency variance is a debit entry whereas the favorable labor rate variance is a credit entry.

Cost Flows in a Standard Cost System

The flow of costs through the company's accounts are illustrated in Exhibit 10B–1. Note that entries into the various inventory accounts are made at standard cost—not actual cost. The differences between actual and standard costs are entered into special accounts that accumulate the various standard cost variances. Ordinarily, these standard cost variance accounts are closed out to Cost of Goods Sold at the end of the period. Unfavorable variances increase Cost of Goods Sold, and favorable variances decrease Cost of Goods Sold.

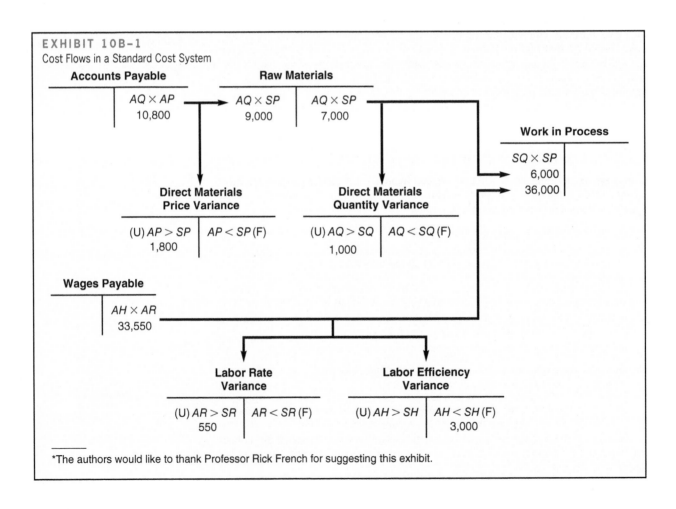

EXHIBIT 10B–1
Cost Flows in a Standard Cost System

*The authors would like to thank Professor Rick French for suggesting this exhibit.

Appendix 10B Exercises and Problems

All applicable exercises and problems are available with McGraw-Hill's Connect® Accounting.

EXERCISE 10B–1 Recording Variances in the General Ledger [LO10–5]
Bliny Corporation makes a product with the following standard costs for direct material and direct labor:

Direct material: 2.00 meters at $3.25 per meter	$6.50
Direct labor: 0.40 hours at $12.00 per hour	$4.80

During the most recent month, 5,000 units were produced. The costs associated with the month's production of this product were as follows:

Material purchased: 12,000 meters at $3.15 per meter	$37,800
Material used in production: 10,500 meters	—
Direct labor: 1,975 hours at $12.20 per hour	$24,095

The standard cost variances for direct material and direct labor are:

Materials price variance: 12,000 meters at $0.10 per meter F	$1,200 F
Materials quantity variance: 500 meters at $3.25 per meter U	$1,625 U
Labor rate variance: 1,975 hours at $0.20 per hour U	$395 U
Labor efficiency variance: 25 hours at $12.00 per hour F	$300 F

Required:
1. Prepare the journal entry to record the purchase of materials on account for the month.
2. Prepare the journal entry to record the use of materials for the month.
3. Prepare the journal entry to record the incurrence of direct labor cost for the month.

EXERCISE 10B–2 Direct Materials and Direct Labor Variances; Journal Entries [LO10–1, LO10–2, LO10–5]
Genola Fashions began production of a new product on June 1. The company uses a standard cost system and has established the following standards for one unit of the new product:

	Standard Quantity or Hours	Standard Price or Rate	Standard Cost
Direct materials	2.5 yards	$14 per yard	$35.00
Direct labor	1.6 hours	$8 per hour	$12.80

During June, the following activity was recorded for the new product:
a. Purchasing acquired 10,000 yards of material at a cost of $13.80 per yard.
b. Production used 8,000 yards of the material to manufacture 3,000 units of the new product.
c. Production reported that 5,000 direct labor-hours were worked on the new product at a cost of $43,000.

Required:
1. For direct materials:
   a. Compute the materials price and quantity variances.
   b. Prepare journal entries to record the purchase of materials and the use of materials in production.
2. For direct labor:
   a. Compute the labor rate and efficiency variances.
   b. Prepare a journal entry to record the incurrence of direct labor cost for the month.

Chapter 10

3. Post the entries you have prepared to the following T-accounts:

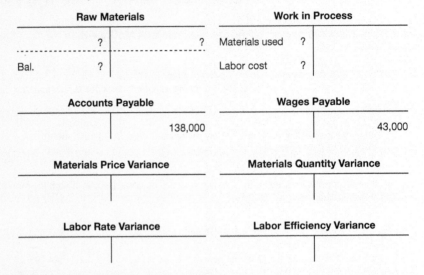

Raw Materials		Work in Process	
?	?	Materials used ?	
Bal. ?		Labor cost ?	

Accounts Payable		Wages Payable	
	138,000		43,000

Materials Price Variance	Materials Quantity Variance

Labor Rate Variance	Labor Efficiency Variance

PROBLEM 10B–3 Comprehensive Variance Analysis; Journal Entries [LO10–1, LO10–2, LO10–3, LO10–5]

Trueform Products, Inc., produces a broad line of sports equipment and uses a standard cost system for control purposes. Last year the company produced 8,000 varsity footballs. The standard costs associated with this football, along with the actual costs incurred last year, are given below (per football):

	Standard Cost	Actual Cost
Direct materials:		
Standard: 3.7 feet at $5.00 per foot	$18.50	
Actual: 4.0 feet at $4.80 per foot		$19.20
Direct labor:		
Standard: 0.9 hours at $7.50 per hour	6.75	
Actual: 0.8 hours at $8.00 per hour		6.40
Variable manufacturing overhead:		
Standard: 0.9 hours at $2.50 per hour	2.25	
Actual: 0.8 hours at $2.75 per hour		2.20
Total cost per football	$27.50	$27.80

The president was elated when he saw that actual costs exceeded standard costs by only $0.30 per football. He stated, "I was afraid that our unit cost might get out of hand when we gave out those raises last year in order to stimulate output. But it's obvious our costs are well under control."

There was no inventory of materials on hand to start the year. During the year, 32,000 feet of materials were purchased and used in production.

Required:
1. For direct materials:
   a. Compute the price and quantity variances for the year.
   b. Prepare journal entries to record all activity relating to direct materials for the year.
2. For direct labor:
   a. Compute the rate and efficiency variances.
   b. Prepare a journal entry to record the incurrence of direct labor cost for the year.
3. Compute the variable overhead rate and efficiency variances.
4. Was the president correct in his statement that "our costs are well under control"? Explain.
5. State possible causes of each variance that you have computed.

PROBLEM 10B–4 Comprehensive Variance Analysis with Incomplete Data; Journal Entries [LO10–1, LO10–2, LO10–3, LO10–5]

Maple Products, Ltd., manufactures a super-strong hockey stick. The standard cost of one hockey stick is:

	Standard Quantity or Hours	Standard Price or Rate	Standard Cost
Direct materials	? feet	$3.00 per foot	$?
Direct labor	2 hours	? per hour	?
Variable manufacturing overhead	? hours	$1.30 per hour	?
Total standard cost			$27.00

Last year, 8,000 hockey sticks were produced and sold. Selected cost data relating to last year's operations follow:

	Dr.	Cr.
Accounts payable—direct materials purchased (60,000 feet)		$174,000
Wages payable (? hours)		$79,200*
Work in process—direct materials	$115,200	
Labor rate variance		$3,300
Variable overhead efficiency variance	$650	

*Relates to the actual direct labor cost for the year.

The following additional information is available for last year's operations:
a. No materials were on hand at the start of last year. Some of the materials purchased during the year were still on hand in the warehouse at the end of the year.
b. The variable manufacturing overhead rate is based on direct labor-hours. Total actual variable manufacturing overhead cost for last year was $19,800.
c. Actual direct materials usage for last year exceeded the standard by 0.2 feet per stick.

Required:
1. For direct materials:
    a. Compute the price and quantity variances for last year.
    b. Prepare journal entries to record all activities relating to direct materials for last year.
2. For direct labor:
    a. Using the rate variance given above, calculate the standard hourly wage rate and compute the efficiency variance for last year.
    b. Prepare a journal entry to record activity relating to direct labor for last year.
3. Compute the variable overhead rate variance for last year and verify the variable overhead efficiency variance given above.
4. State possible causes of each variance that you have computed.
5. Prepare a standard cost card for one hockey stick.

CASE 10B–5 Ethics and the Manager; Rigging Standards [LO10–5]

Stacy Cummins, the newly hired controller at Merced Home Products, Inc., was disturbed by what she had discovered about the standard costs at the Home Security Division. In looking over the past several years of quarterly income statements at the Home Security Division, she noticed that the first-quarter profits were always poor, the second-quarter profits were slightly better, the third-quarter profits were again slightly better, and the fourth quarter always ended with a spectacular performance in which the Home Security Division managed to meet or exceed its target profit for the year. She also was concerned to find letters from the company's external auditors to top management warning about an unusual use of standard costs at the Home Security Division.

When Ms. Cummins ran across these letters, she asked the assistant controller, Gary Farber, if he knew what was going on at the Home Security Division. Gary said that it was common knowledge in the company that the vice president in charge of the Home Security Division, Preston Lansing, had rigged the standards at his division in order to produce the same quarterly income pattern every year. According to company policy, variances are taken directly to the income statement as an adjustment to cost of goods sold.

Favorable variances have the effect of increasing net operating income, and unfavorable variances have the effect of decreasing net operating income. Lansing had rigged the standards so that there were always large favorable variances. Company policy was a little vague about when these variances have to be reported on the divisional income statements. While the intent was clearly to recognize variances on the income statement in the period in which they arise, nothing in the company's accounting manuals actually explicitly required this. So for many years Lansing had followed a practice of saving up the favorable variances and using them to create a nice smooth pattern of growing profits in the first three quarters, followed by a big "Christmas present" of an extremely good fourth quarter. (Financial reporting regulations forbid carrying variances forward from one year to the next on the annual audited financial statements, so all of the variances must appear on the divisional income statement by the end of the year.)

Ms. Cummins was concerned about these revelations and attempted to bring up the subject with the president of Merced Home Products but was told that "we all know what Lansing's doing, but as long as he continues to turn in such good reports, don't bother him." When Ms. Cummins asked if the board of directors was aware of the situation, the president somewhat testily replied, "Of course they are aware."

Required:
1. How did Preston Lansing probably "rig" the standard costs—are the standards set too high or too low? Explain.
2. Should Preston Lansing be permitted to continue his practice of managing reported profits?
3. What should Stacy Cummins do in this situation?

CHAPTER 11

Performance Measurement in Decentralized Organizations

Performance Measures That Drive Financial Results

BUSINESS FOCUS

Companies that wish to achieve strong financial results need to be responsive to employee and customer needs. For example, **Papa John's** uses mystery shoppers and a 10-point scale to measure the quality of 10,000 pizzas per month. The mystery shopper scores, which are tied to executive bonuses, help Papa John's meet the customers' need for high-quality pizza. **American Express** asked its 26,000 call-center employees what they needed to achieve higher job satisfaction—then it responded by delivering flexible schedules, more career development, and higher pay. Collectively, these changes increased the company's service margins by 10%.

This chapter discusses financial measures that companies use to track performance. It also introduces some nonfinancial performance measures, related to customers, employees, and business processes, that companies use to drive financial results. ■

Sources: Scott Cendrowski, "Papa John's John Schnatter," Fortune, September 28, 2009, p. 34; Christopher Tkaczyk, "No. 73: American Express," Fortune, August 16, 2010, p. 14.

LEARNING OBJECTIVES

After studying Chapter 11, you should be able to:

LO11–1   Compute return on investment (ROI) and show how changes in sales, expenses, and assets affect ROI.

LO11–2   Compute residual income and understand its strengths and weaknesses.

LO11–3   Compute delivery cycle time, throughput time, and manufacturing cycle efficiency (MCE).

LO11–4   Understand how to construct and use a balanced scorecard.

LO11–5   *(Appendix 11A) Determine the range, if any, within which a negotiated transfer price should fall.*

LO11–6   *(Appendix 11B) Charge operating departments for services provided by service departments.*

Except in very small organizations, top managers must delegate some decisions. For example, the CEO of the Hyatt Hotel chain cannot be expected to decide whether a particular hotel guest at the Hyatt Hotel on Maui should be allowed to check out later than the normal checkout time. Instead, employees at Maui are authorized to make this decision. As in this example, managers in large organizations have to delegate some decisions to those who are at lower levels in the organization.

Decentralization in Organizations

In a **decentralized organization**, decision-making authority is spread throughout the organization rather than being confined to a few top executives. As noted above, out of necessity all large organizations are decentralized to some extent. Organizations do differ, however, in the extent to which they are decentralized. In strongly centralized organizations, decision-making authority is reluctantly delegated to lower-level managers who have little freedom to make decisions. In strongly decentralized organizations, even the lowest-level managers are empowered to make as many decisions as possible. Most organizations fall somewhere between these two extremes.

Advantages and Disadvantages of Decentralization

The major advantages of decentralization include:

1. By delegating day-to-day problem solving to lower-level managers, top management can concentrate on bigger issues, such as overall strategy.
2. Empowering lower-level managers to make decisions puts the decision-making authority in the hands of those who tend to have the most detailed and up-to-date information about day-to-day operations.
3. By eliminating layers of decision making and approvals, organizations can respond more quickly to customers and to changes in the operating environment.
4. Granting decision-making authority helps train lower-level managers for higher-level positions.
5. Empowering lower-level managers to make decisions can increase their motivation and job satisfaction.

The major disadvantages of decentralization include:

1. Lower-level managers may make decisions without fully understanding the company's overall strategy.
2. If lower-level managers make their own decisions independently of each other, coordination may be lacking.
3. Lower-level managers may have objectives that clash with the objectives of the entire organization.[1] For example, a manager may be more interested in increasing the size of his or her department, leading to more power and prestige, than in increasing the department's effectiveness.

---

[1] Similar problems exist with top-level managers as well. The shareholders of the company delegate their decision-making authority to the top managers. Unfortunately, top managers may abuse that trust by rewarding themselves and their friends too generously, spending too much company money on palatial offices, and so on. The issue of how to ensure that top managers act in the best interests of the company's owners continues to challenge experts. To a large extent, the owners rely on performance evaluation using return on investment and residual income measures, as discussed later in the chapter, and on bonuses and stock options. The stock market is also an important disciplining mechanism. If top managers squander the company's resources, the price of the company's stock will almost surely fall—possibly resulting in a loss of prestige, bonuses, and a job. And, of course, particularly outrageous self-dealing may land a CEO in court.

4. Spreading innovative ideas may be difficult in a decentralized organization. Someone in one part of the organization may have a terrific idea that would benefit other parts of the organization, but without strong central direction the idea may not be shared with, and adopted by, other parts of the organization.

Responsibility Accounting

Decentralized organizations need *responsibility accounting systems* that link lower-level managers' decision-making authority with accountability for the outcomes of those decisions. The term **responsibility center** is used for any part of an organization whose manager has control over and is accountable for cost, profit, or investments. The three primary types of responsibility centers are *cost centers, profit centers,* and *investment centers.*

Cost, Profit, and Investment Centers

Cost Center   The manager of a **cost center** has control over costs, but not over revenue or the use of investment funds. Service departments such as accounting, finance, general administration, legal, and personnel are usually classified as cost centers. In addition, manufacturing facilities are often considered to be cost centers. The managers of cost centers are expected to minimize costs while providing the level of products and services demanded by other parts of the organization. For example, the manager of a manufacturing facility would be evaluated at least in part by comparing actual costs to how much costs should have been for the actual level of output during the period. Standard cost variances and flexible budget variances, such as those discussed in earlier chapters, are often used to evaluate cost center performance.

Profit Center   The manager of a **profit center** has control over both costs and revenue, but not over the use of investment funds. For example, the manager in charge of a Six Flags amusement park would be responsible for both the revenues and costs, and hence the profits, of the amusement park, but may not have control over major investments in the park. Profit center managers are often evaluated by comparing actual profit to targeted or budgeted profit.

Investment Center   The manager of an **investment center** has control over cost, revenue, and investments in operating assets. For example, General Motors' vice president of manufacturing in North America would have a great deal of discretion over investments in manufacturing—such as investing in equipment to produce more fuel-efficient engines. Once General Motors' top-level managers and board of directors approve the vice president's investment proposals, he is held responsible for making them pay off. As discussed in the next section, investment center managers are often evaluated using return on investment (ROI) or residual income measures.

Evaluating Investment Center Performance—Return on Investment

An investment center is responsible for earning an adequate return on investment. The following two sections present two methods for evaluating this aspect of an investment center's performance. The first method, covered in this section, is called *return on investment* (ROI). The second method, covered in the next section, is called *residual income.*

LO11–1
Compute return on investment (ROI) and show how changes in sales, expenses, and assets affect ROI.

Chapter 11

The Return on Investment (ROI) Formula

Return on investment (ROI) is defined as net operating income divided by average operating assets:

$$\text{ROI} = \frac{\text{Net operating income}}{\text{Average operating assets}}$$

The higher a business segment's return on investment (ROI), the greater the profit earned per dollar invested in the segment's operating assets.

Net Operating Income and Operating Assets Defined

Note that *net operating income,* rather than net income, is used in the ROI formula. **Net operating income** is income before interest and taxes and is sometimes referred to as EBIT (earnings before interest and taxes). Net operating income is used in the formula because the base (i.e., denominator) consists of *operating assets.* To be consistent, we use net operating income in the numerator.

Operating assets include cash, accounts receivable, inventory, plant and equipment, and all other assets held for operating purposes. Examples of assets that are not included in operating assets (i.e., examples of nonoperating assets) include land held for future use, an investment in another company, or a building rented to someone else. These assets are not held for operating purposes and therefore are excluded from operating assets. The operating assets base used in the formula is typically computed as the average of the operating assets between the beginning and the end of the year.

Most companies use the net book value (i.e., acquisition cost less accumulated depreciation) of depreciable assets to calculate average operating assets. This approach has drawbacks. An asset's net book value decreases over time as the accumulated depreciation increases. This decreases the denominator in the ROI calculation, thus increasing ROI. Consequently, ROI mechanically increases over time. Moreover, replacing old depreciated equipment with new equipment increases the book value of depreciable assets and decreases ROI. Hence, using net book value in the calculation of average operating assets results in a predictable pattern of increasing ROI over time as accumulated depreciation grows and discourages replacing old equipment with new, updated equipment. An alternative to using net book value is the gross cost of the asset, which ignores accumulated depreciation. Gross cost stays constant over time because depreciation is ignored; therefore, ROI does not grow automatically over time, and replacing a fully depreciated asset with a comparably priced new asset will not adversely affect ROI.

Nevertheless, most companies use the net book value approach to computing average operating assets because it is consistent with their financial reporting practices of recording the net book value of assets on the balance sheet and including depreciation as an operating expense on the income statement. In this text, we will use the net book value approach unless a specific exercise or problem directs otherwise.

Understanding ROI

The equation for ROI, net operating income divided by average operating assets, does not provide much help to managers interested in taking actions to improve their ROI. It only offers two levers for improving performance—net operating income and average operating assets. Fortunately, ROI can also be expressed in terms of **margin** and **turnover** as follows:

$$\text{ROI} = \text{Margin} \times \text{Turnover}$$

where

$$\text{Margin} = \frac{\text{Net operating income}}{\text{Sales}}$$

and

$$\text{Turnover} = \frac{\text{Sales}}{\text{Average operating assets}}$$

Note that the sales terms in the margin and turnover formulas cancel out when they are multiplied together, yielding the original formula for ROI stated in terms of net operating income and average operating assets. So either formula for ROI will give the same answer. However, the margin and turnover formulation provides some additional insights.

Margin and turnover are important concepts in understanding how a manager can affect ROI. All other things the same, margin is ordinarily improved by increasing selling prices, reducing operating expenses, or increasing unit sales. Increasing selling prices and reducing operating expenses both increase net operating income and therefore margin. Increasing unit sales also ordinarily increases the margin because of operating leverage. As discussed in a previous chapter, because of operating leverage, a given percentage increase in unit sales usually leads to an even larger percentage increase in net operating income. Therefore, an increase in unit sales ordinarily has the effect of increasing margin. Some managers tend to focus too much on margin and ignore turnover. However, turnover incorporates a crucial area of a manager's responsibility—the investment in operating assets. Excessive funds tied up in operating assets (e.g., cash, accounts receivable, inventories, plant and equipment, and other assets) depress turnover and lower ROI. In fact, excessive operating assets can be just as much of a drag on ROI as excessive operating expenses, which depress margin.

A STRATEGY OF SCARCITY

Old Rip Van Winkle Distillery employs two people, Julian Van Winkle III and his son Preston. Its annual sales of $2 million pale in comparison to larger competitors such as Makers' Mark and Wild Turkey. Although the company could easily triple its sales volume, it chooses to limit sales to 7,000 cases of bourbon per year. Given that the company's 20-year-old aged whiskey once achieved an unprecedented "99" rating from the Beverage Tasting Institute of Chicago, demand for the company's products far exceeds its supply—thereby enabling regular price increases. For example, a fifth of 20-year-old Pappy Van Winkle bourbon sells for $110. In accounting terms, the Old Rip Van Winkle Distillery purposely foregoes turnover in favor of earning large margins on its award-winning products.

Source: Brian Dumaine, "Creating the Ultimate Cult Brand," *Fortune*, February 28, 2011, pp. 21–24.

Many actions involve combinations of changes in sales, expenses, and operating assets. For example, a manager may make an investment in (i.e., increase) operating assets to reduce operating expenses or increase sales. Whether the net effect is favorable or not is judged in terms of its overall impact on ROI.

For example, suppose that the Montvale Burger Grill expects the following operating results next month:

Sales	$100,000
Operating expenses	$90,000
Net operating income	$10,000
Average operating assets	$50,000

The expected return on investment (ROI) for the month is computed as follows:

$$\text{ROI} = \frac{\text{Net operating income}}{\text{Sales}} \times \frac{\text{Sales}}{\text{Average operating assets}}$$

$$= \frac{\$10,000}{\$100,000} \times \frac{\$100,000}{\$50,000}$$

$$= 10\% \times 2 = 20\%$$

Suppose that the manager of the Montvale Burger Grill is considering investing $2,000 in a state-of-the-art soft-serve ice cream machine that can dispense a number of different flavors. This new machine would boost sales by $4,000, but would require additional operating expenses of $1,000. Thus, net operating income would increase by $3,000, to $13,000. The new ROI would be:

$$\text{ROI} = \frac{\text{Net operating income}}{\text{Sales}} \times \frac{\text{Sales}}{\text{Average operating assets}}$$

$$= \frac{\$13,000}{\$104,000} \times \frac{\$104,000}{\$52,000}$$

$$= 12.5\% \times 2 = 25\% \text{ (as compared to 20\% originally)}$$

In this particular example, the investment increases ROI, but that will not always happen. E.I. du Pont de Nemours and Company (better known as DuPont) pioneered the use of ROI and recognized the importance of looking at both margin and turnover in assessing a manager's performance. ROI is now widely used as the key measure of investment center performance. ROI reflects in a single figure many aspects of the manager's responsibilities. It can be compared to the returns of other investment centers in the organization, the returns of other companies in the industry, and to the past returns of the investment center itself. DuPont also developed the diagram that appears in Exhibit 11–1. This exhibit helps managers understand how they can improve ROI.

IN BUSINESS

MICROSOFT MANAGES IN AN ECONOMIC DOWNTURN

Microsoft responded to tough economic times by lowering its prices, thereby accepting lower margins per unit sold in exchange for higher turnover. For example, Microsoft lowered the price of its Office software from $150 to $100 (after promotional discounts) and realized a 415% increase in unit sales. In China, the company combated huge piracy problems by dropping the price of Office to $29, resulting in an 800% increase in sales. Microsoft established a selling price of $200 for its Windows 7 PC operating system, which was $40 less than the price the company charged for its predecessor Vista PC operating system.

Source: Peter Burrows, "Microsoft's Aggressive New Pricing Strategy," *BusinessWeek*, July 27, 2009, p. 51.

Criticisms of ROI

Although ROI is widely used in evaluating performance, it is subject to the following criticisms:

1. Just telling managers to increase ROI may not be enough. Managers may not know how to increase ROI; they may increase ROI in a way that is inconsistent with the company's strategy; or they may take actions that increase ROI in the short run but harm the company in the long run (such as cutting back on research and development). This is why ROI is best used as part of a balanced scorecard, as discussed later in this chapter. A balanced scorecard can provide concrete guidance to managers,

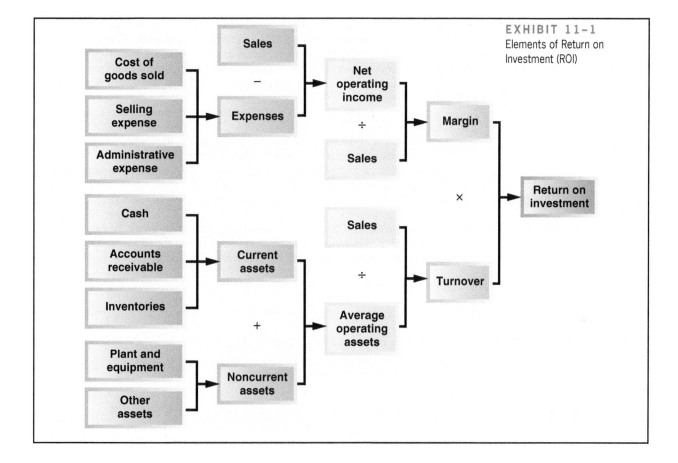

EXHIBIT 11–1
Elements of Return on Investment (ROI)

making it more likely that their actions are consistent with the company's strategy and reducing the likelihood that they will boost short-run performance at the expense of long-term performance.

2. A manager who takes over a business segment typically inherits many committed costs over which the manager has no control. These committed costs may be relevant in assessing the performance of the business segment as an investment but they make it difficult to fairly assess the performance of the manager.

3. As discussed in the next section, a manager who is evaluated based on ROI may reject investment opportunities that are profitable for the whole company but would have a negative impact on the manager's performance evaluation.

Residual Income

LO11–2
Compute residual income and understand its strengths and weaknesses.

Residual income is another approach to measuring an investment center's performance. **Residual income** is the net operating income that an investment center earns above the minimum required return on its operating assets. In equation form, residual income is calculated as follows:

$$\frac{\text{Residual}}{\text{income}} = \frac{\text{Net operating}}{\text{income}} - \left(\frac{\text{Average operating}}{\text{assets}} \times \frac{\text{Minimum required}}{\text{rate of return}} \right)$$

Chapter 11

Economic Value Added (EVA®) is an adaptation of residual income that has been adopted by many companies.[2] Under EVA, companies often modify their accounting principles in various ways. For example, funds used for research and development are often treated as investments rather than as expenses.[3] These complications are best dealt with in a more advanced course; in this text we will not draw any distinction between residual income and EVA.

When residual income or EVA is used to measure performance, the objective is to maximize the total amount of residual income or EVA, not to maximize ROI. This is an important distinction. If the objective were to maximize ROI, then every company should divest all of its products except the single product with the highest ROI.

A wide variety of organizations have embraced some version of residual income or EVA, including Bausch & Lomb, Best Buy, Boise Cascade, Coca-Cola, Dun and Bradstreet, Eli Lilly, Federal Mogul, Georgia-Pacific, Hershey Foods, Husky Injection Molding, J.C. Penney, Kansas City Power & Light, Olin, Quaker Oats, Silicon Valley Bank, Sprint, Toys R Us, Tupperware, and the United States Postal Service.

For purposes of illustration, consider the following data for an investment center—the Ketchikan Division of Alaskan Marine Services Corporation.

Alaskan Marine Services Corporation
Ketchikan Division
Basic Data for Performance Evaluation

Average operating assets	$100,000
Net operating income	$20,000
Minimum required rate of return	15%

Alaskan Marine Services Corporation has long had a policy of using ROI to evaluate its investment center managers, but it is considering switching to residual income. The controller of the company, who is in favor of the change to residual income, has provided the following table that shows how the performance of the division would be evaluated under each of the two methods:

Alaskan Marine Services Corporation
Ketchikan Division

	Alternative Performance Measures	
	ROI	Residual Income
Average operating assets (a)	$100,000	$100,000
Net operating income (b)	$20,000	$20,000
ROI, (b) ÷ (a)	20%	
Minimum required return (15% × $100,000)		15,000
Residual income		$ 5,000

---

[2] The basic idea underlying residual income and economic value added has been around for over 100 years. Economic value added has been popularized and trademarked by the consulting firm Stern, Stewart & Co.

[3] Over 100 different adjustments could be made for deferred taxes, LIFO reserves, provisions for future liabilities, mergers and acquisitions, gains or losses due to changes in accounting rules, operating leases, and other accounts, but most companies make only a few. For further details, see John O'Hanlon and Ken Peasnell, "Wall Street's Contribution to Management Accounting: the Stern Stewart EVA® Financial Management System," *Management Accounting Research* 9, 1998, pp. 421–444.

The reasoning underlying the residual income calculation is straightforward. The company is able to earn a rate of return of at least 15% on its investments. Because the company has invested $100,000 in the Ketchikan Division in the form of operating assets, the company should be able to earn at least $15,000 (15% × $100,000) on this investment. Because the Ketchikan Division's net operating income is $20,000, the residual income above and beyond the minimum required return is $5,000. If residual income is adopted as the performance measure to replace ROI, the manager of the Ketchikan Division would be evaluated based on the growth in residual income from year to year.

Motivation and Residual Income

One of the primary reasons why the controller of Alaskan Marine Services Corporation would like to switch from ROI to residual income relates to how managers view new investments under the two performance measurement methods. The residual income approach encourages managers to make investments that are profitable for the entire company but that would be rejected by managers who are evaluated using the ROI formula.

To illustrate this problem with ROI, suppose that the manager of the Ketchikan Division is considering purchasing a computerized diagnostic machine to aid in servicing marine diesel engines. The machine would cost $25,000 and is expected to generate additional operating income of $4,500 a year. From the standpoint of the company, this would be a good investment because it promises a rate of return of 18% ($4,500 ÷ $25,000), which exceeds the company's minimum required rate of return of 15%.

If the manager of the Ketchikan Division is evaluated based on residual income, she would be in favor of the investment in the diagnostic machine as shown below:

	Alaskan Marine Services Corporation Ketchikan Division Performance Evaluated Using Residual Income		
	Present	New Project	Overall
Average operating assets	$100,000	$25,000	$125,000
Net operating income	$20,000	$4,500	$24,500
Minimum required return	15,000	3,750*	18,750
Residual income	$ 5,000	$ 750	$ 5,750

*$25,000 × 15% = $3,750.

Because the project would increase the residual income of the Ketchikan Division by $750, the manager would choose to invest in the new diagnostic machine.

Now suppose that the manager of the Ketchikan Division is evaluated based on ROI. The effect of the diagnostic machine on the division's ROI is computed below:

	Alaskan Marine Services Corporation Ketchikan Division Performance Evaluated Using ROI		
	Present	New Project	Overall
Average operating assets (a)	$100,000	$25,000	$125,000
Net operating income (b)	$20,000	$4,500	$24,500
ROI, (b) ÷ (a)	20%	18%	19.6%

The new project reduces the division's ROI from 20% to 19.6%. This happens because the 18% rate of return on the new diagnostic machine, while above the company's 15% minimum required rate of return, is below the division's current ROI of 20%. Therefore, the new diagnostic machine would decrease the division's ROI even though it would be a good investment from the standpoint of the company as a whole. If the manager of the division is evaluated based on ROI, she will be reluctant to even propose such an investment.

Generally, a manager who is evaluated based on ROI will reject any project whose rate of return is below the division's current ROI even if the rate of return on the project is above the company's minimum required rate of return. In contrast, managers who are evaluated using residual income will pursue any project whose rate of return is above the minimum required rate of return because it will increase their residual income. Because it is in the best interests of the company as a whole to accept any project whose rate of return is above the minimum required rate of return, managers who are evaluated based on residual income will tend to make better decisions concerning investment projects than managers who are evaluated based on ROI.

Divisional Comparison and Residual Income

The residual income approach has one major disadvantage. It can't be used to compare the performance of divisions of different sizes. Larger divisions often have more residual income than smaller divisions, not necessarily because they are better managed but simply because they are bigger.

As an example, consider the following residual income computations for the Wholesale Division and the Retail Division of Sisal Marketing Corporation:

	Wholesale Division	Retail Division
Average operating assets (a)	$1,000,000	$250,000
Net operating income	$120,000	$40,000
Minimum required return: 10% × (a)	100,000	25,000
Residual income	$ 20,000	$15,000

Observe that the Wholesale Division has slightly more residual income than the Retail Division, but that the Wholesale Division has $1,000,000 in operating assets as compared to only $250,000 in operating assets for the Retail Division. Thus, the Wholesale Division's greater residual income is probably due to its larger size rather than the quality of its management. In fact, it appears that the smaller division may be better managed because it has been able to generate nearly as much residual income with only one-fourth as much in operating assets. When comparing investment centers, it is probably better to focus on the percentage change in residual income from year to year rather than on the absolute amount of the residual income.

Operating Performance Measures

LO11–3
Compute delivery cycle time, throughput time, and manufacturing cycle efficiency (MCE).

In addition to financial performance measures, organizations use many nonfinancial performance measures. While financial measures pick up the *results* of what people in the organization do, they do not measure what *drives* organizational performance. For example, activity and revenue variances pick up the results of efforts aimed at increasing sales, but they do not measure the actions that actually drive sales such as improving quality, exposing more potential customers to the product, filling customer orders on time, and so on. Consequently, many organizations use a variety of nonfinancial performance measures in addition to financial measures. In this section we will discuss three examples of such measures that are critical to success in many organizations—delivery cycle time, throughput time, and manufacturing cycle efficiency (MCE). Note that while these examples focus on manufacturers, very similar measures can be used by any service organization that experiences a delay between receiving a customer request and responding to that request.

Delivery Cycle Time

The amount of time from when a customer order is received to when the completed order is shipped is called **delivery cycle time**. This time is an important concern to many customers, who would like the delivery cycle time to be as short as possible. Cutting the delivery cycle time may give a company a key competitive advantage—and may be necessary for survival. The formula for computing delivery cycle time is as follows:

$$\text{Delivery cycle time} = \text{Wait time} + \text{Throughput time}$$

Throughput (Manufacturing Cycle) Time

The amount of time required to turn raw materials into completed products is called **throughput time**, or *manufacturing cycle time*. The relation between the delivery cycle time and the throughput (manufacturing cycle) time is illustrated in Exhibit 11–2.

As shown in Exhibit 11–2, the throughput time, or manufacturing cycle time, is made up of process time, inspection time, move time, and queue time. *Process time* is the amount of time work is actually done on the product. *Inspection time* is the amount of time spent ensuring that the product is not defective. *Move time* is the time required to move materials or partially completed products from workstation to workstation. *Queue time* is the amount of time a product spends waiting to be worked on, to be moved, to be inspected, or to be shipped.

As shown at the bottom of Exhibit 11–2, only one of these four activities adds value to the product—process time. The other three activities—inspecting, moving, and

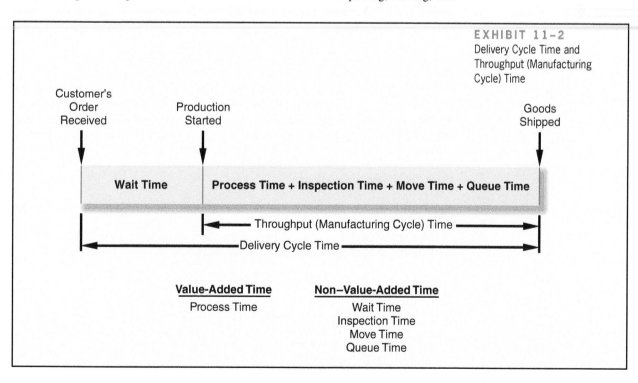

EXHIBIT 11–2
Delivery Cycle Time and Throughput (Manufacturing Cycle) Time

Chapter 11

queuing—add no value and should be eliminated as much as possible. The formula for computing throughput (manufacturing cycle) time is as follows:

$$\text{Throughput (manufacturing cycle) time} =$$
$$\text{Process time} + \text{Inspection time} + \text{Move time} + \text{Queue time}$$

THE DOCTOR WILL SEE YOU . . . LATER

When medical care reimbursement rates drop, doctors often respond by packing more patients into each day, thereby increasing patient wait times. Press Ganey Associates surveyed 2.4 million patients at more than 10,000 locations and determined an average wait time to see a doctor of 22 minutes. While these delays inconvenience patients, they also have financial implications for doctors. For example, Laurie Green, an obstetrician-gynecologist in San Francisco, prides herself on running an efficient medical practice because "she needs to bring in $75 every 15 minutes just to meet her office overhead."

If your doctor's office is overrun with delays, consider getting the first appointment of the day because the "early bird" not only gets the worm, but it also avoids wait time at the doctor's office!

Source: Melinda Beck, "The Doctor Will See You Eventually," *The Wall Street Journal*, October 19, 2010, pp. D1 and D4.

Manufacturing Cycle Efficiency (MCE)

Through concerted efforts to eliminate the *non–value-added* activities of inspecting, moving, and queuing, some companies have reduced their throughput time to only a fraction of previous levels. In turn, this has helped to reduce the delivery cycle time from months to only weeks or hours. Throughput time, which is a key measure in delivery performance, can be put into better perspective by computing the **manufacturing cycle efficiency (MCE)**. The MCE is computed by relating the value-added time to the throughput time. The formula is:

$$\text{MCE} = \frac{\text{Value-added time (Process time)}}{\text{Throughput (manufacturing cycle) time}}$$

Any non–value-added time results in an MCE of less than 1. An MCE of 0.5, for example, would mean that half of the total production time consists of inspection, moving, and similar non–value-added activities. In many manufacturing companies, the MCE is less than 0.1 (10%), which means that 90% of the time a unit is in process is spent on activities that do not add value to the product. Monitoring the MCE helps companies to reduce non–value-added activities and thus get products into the hands of customers more quickly and at a lower cost.

Example To provide an example of these measures, consider the following data for Novex Company:

Novex Company keeps careful track of the time to complete customer orders. During the most recent quarter, the following average times were recorded per order:

	Days
Wait time	17.0
Inspection time	0.4
Process time	2.0
Move time	0.6
Queue time	5.0

Goods are shipped as soon as production is completed.

Required:

1. Compute the throughput time.
2. Compute the manufacturing cycle efficiency (MCE).
3. What percentage of the production time is spent in non–value-added activities?
4. Compute the delivery cycle time.

Solution

1. Throughput time = Process time + Inspection time + Move time + Queue time

$$= 2.0 \text{ days} + 0.4 \text{ days} + 0.6 \text{ days} + 5.0 \text{ days}$$
$$= 8.0 \text{ days}$$

2. Only process time represents value-added time; therefore, MCE would be computed as follows:

$$\text{MCE} = \frac{\text{Value-added time}}{\text{Throughput time}} = \frac{2.0 \text{ days}}{8.0 \text{ days}}$$
$$= 0.25$$

Thus, once put into production, a typical order is actually being worked on only 25% of the time.

3. Because the MCE is 25%, 75% (100% − 25%) of total production time is spent in non–value-added activities.

4. Delivery cycle time = Wait time + Throughput time

$$= 17.0 \text{ days} + 8.0 \text{ days}$$
$$= 25.0 \text{ days}$$

IN BUSINESS

LEAN OPERATING PERFORMANCE MEASURES

Watlow Electric Manufacturing Company implemented *lean accounting* to support its lean manufacturing methods. The company stopped providing standard cost variance reports to operating managers because the information was generated too late (at the end of each month) and it could not be understood by frontline employees. Instead, the company began reporting daily and hourly process-oriented measures that helped frontline workers improve performance.

Examples of lean operating performance measures are shown in the table below:

Measure	Description of Measure
On-time delivery percentage	Measures the percentage of orders that customers would define as being delivered on time.
Day-by-the-hour	Measures the quantity of production on an hourly basis to ensure that it is synchronized with customer demand.
First time through percentage	Measures the percentage of completed units that are free of defects.
Number of accidents and injuries	Measures the number of accidents and injuries on the manufacturing floor.
5S audit	Measures the cell workers' ability to keep their work area organized and clean.

Note: 5S stands for Sort, Straighten, Shine, Standardize, and Sustain.

Sources: Jan Brosnahan, "Unleash the Power of Lean Accounting," *Journal of Accountancy*, July 2008, pp. 60–66; and Brian Maskell and Frances Kennedy, "Why Do We Need Lean Accounting and How Does It Work?" *Journal of Corporate Accounting and Finance*, March/April 2007, pp. 59–73.

Balanced Scorecard

LO11–4
Understand how to construct
and use a balanced scorecard.

Financial measures, such as ROI and residual income, and operating measures, such as those discussed in the previous section, may be included in a *balanced scorecard*. A **balanced scorecard** consists of an integrated set of performance measures that are derived from and support a company's strategy. A strategy is essentially a theory about how to achieve the organization's goals. For example, Southwest Airlines' strategy is to offer an *operational excellence* customer value proposition that has three key components—low ticket prices, convenience, and reliability. The company operates only one type of aircraft, the Boeing 737, to reduce maintenance and training costs and simplify scheduling. It further reduces costs by not offering meals, seat assignments, or baggage transfers and by booking a large portion of its passenger revenue over the Internet. Southwest also uses point-to-point flights rather than the hub-and-spoke approach of its larger competitors, thereby providing customers convenient, nonstop service to their final destination. Because Southwest serves many less-congested airports such as Chicago Midway, Burbank, Manchester, Oakland, and Providence, it offers quicker passenger check-ins and reliable departures, while maintaining high asset utilization (i.e., the company's average gate turnaround time of 25 minutes enables it to function with fewer planes and gates). Overall, the company's strategy has worked. At a time when Southwest Airlines' larger competitors are struggling, it continues to earn substantial profits.

Under the balanced scorecard approach, top management translates its strategy into performance measures that employees can understand and influence. For example, the amount of time passengers have to wait in line to have their baggage checked might be a performance measure for the supervisor in charge of the Southwest Airlines check-in counter at the Burbank airport. This performance measure is easily understood by the supervisor, and can be improved by the supervisor's actions.

Common Characteristics of Balanced Scorecards

Performance measures used in balanced scorecards tend to fall into the four groups illustrated in Exhibit 11–3: financial, customer, internal business processes, and learning and growth. Internal business processes are what the company does in an attempt to satisfy customers. For example, in a manufacturing company, assembling a product is an internal business process. In an airline, handling baggage is an internal business process. The idea underlying these groupings (as indicated by the vertical arrows in Exhibit 11–3) is that learning is necessary to improve internal business processes; improving business processes is necessary to improve customer satisfaction; and improving customer satisfaction is necessary to improve financial results.

Note that the emphasis in Exhibit 11–3 is on *improvement*—not on just attaining some specific objective such as profits of $10 million. In the balanced scorecard approach, continual improvement is encouraged. If an organization does not continually improve, it will eventually lose out to competitors that do.

Financial performance measures appear at the top of Exhibit 11–3. Ultimately, most companies exist to provide financial rewards to owners. There are exceptions. Some companies—for example, The Body Shop—may have loftier goals such as providing environmentally friendly products to consumers. However, even nonprofit organizations must generate enough financial resources to stay in operation.

For several reasons, financial performance measures are not sufficient in themselves—they should be integrated with nonfinancial measures in a well-designed balanced scorecard. First, financial measures are lag indicators that report on the results of past actions. In contrast, nonfinancial measures of key success drivers such as customer satisfaction are leading indicators of future financial performance. Second, top managers are ordinarily responsible for the financial performance measures—not lower-level managers. The supervisor in charge of checking in passengers can be held responsible for how

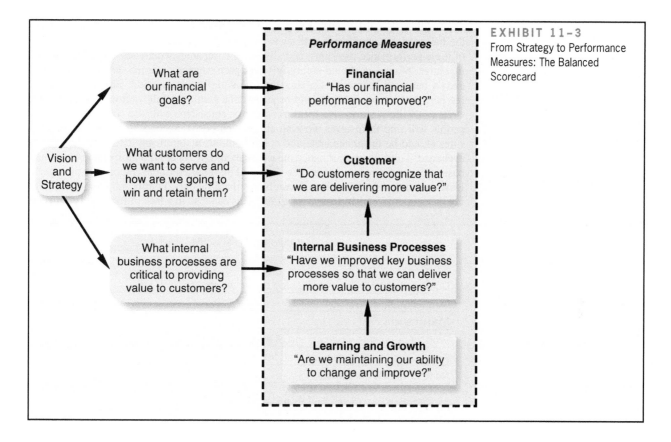

EXHIBIT 11–3
From Strategy to Performance Measures: The Balanced Scorecard

---

WHY DO COMPANIES FAIL TO EXECUTE THEIR STRATEGIES?

Robert Paladino served as the vice president and global leader of the Telecommunications and Utility Practice for the Balanced Scorecard Collaborative—a consulting organization that works with companies to implement balanced scorecards. He offers four reasons why nine out of ten organizations fail to execute their business strategies.

First, only 5% of a company's workforce understands their organization's strategy. Paladino commented "if employees don't understand the strategic objectives, then they could be focused on closing the wrong performance gaps." Second, 85% of management teams spend less than one hour per month discussing strategy. Managers cannot effectively implement strategies if they do not spend enough time talking about them. Third, 60% of organizations do not link their budgets to strategy. The inevitable result is that companies pursue "financial strategies that differ from or, worse, may be in conflict with their business and customer quality strategies." Finally, only 25% of managers have their incentives linked to strategy. Thus, most managers are working to maximize their compensation by improving strategically misguided metrics.

Paladino says the balanced scorecard overcomes these four barriers because it helps employees focus their actions on executing organizational strategies.

Source: Robert E. Paladino, "Balanced Forecasts Drive Value," *Strategic Finance*, January 2005, pp. 37–42.

---

long passengers have to wait in line. However, this supervisor cannot reasonably be held responsible for the entire company's profit. That is the responsibility of the airline's top managers.

Exhibit 11–4 lists some examples of performance measures that can be found on the balanced scorecards of companies. However, few companies, if any, would use all of these performance measures, and almost all companies would add other performance measures. Managers should carefully select performance measures for their own company's balanced scorecard, keeping the following points in mind. First and foremost, the performance measures should be consistent with, and follow from, the company's strategy. If the performance measures are not consistent with the company's strategy, people will find themselves working at cross-purposes. Second, the performance measures should be understandable and controllable to a significant extent by those being evaluated. Third, the performance measures should be reported on a frequent and timely basis. For example, data about defects should be reported to the responsible manager at least once a day so that problems can be resolved quickly. Fourth, the scorecard should not have too many performance measures. This can lead to a lack of focus and confusion.

EXHIBIT 11–4
Examples of Performance Measures for Balanced Scorecards

Customer Perspective	
Performance Measure	Desired Change
Customer satisfaction as measured by survey results	+
Number of customer complaints	−
Market share	+
Product returns as a percentage of sales	−
Percentage of customers retained from last period	+
Number of new customers	+

Internal Business Processes Perspective	
Performance Measure	Desired Change
Percentage of sales from new products	+
Time to introduce new products to market	−
Percentage of customer calls answered within 20 seconds	+
On-time deliveries as a percentage of all deliveries	+
Work in process inventory as a percentage of sales	−
Unfavorable standard cost variances	−
Defect-free units as a percentage of completed units	+
Delivery cycle time	−
Throughput time	−
Manufacturing cycle efficiency	+
Quality costs	−
Setup time	−
Time from call by customer to repair of product	−
Percent of customer complaints settled on first contact	+
Time to settle a customer claim	−

Learning and Growth Perspective	
Performance Measure	Desired Change
Suggestions per employee	+
Employee turnover	−
Hours of in-house training per employee	+

While the entire organization will have an overall balanced scorecard, each responsible individual will have his or her own personal scorecard as well. This scorecard should consist of items the individual can personally influence that relate directly to the performance measures on the overall balanced scorecard. The performance measures on this personal scorecard should not be overly influenced by actions taken by others in the company or by events that are outside of the individual's control. And, focusing on the performance measure should not lead an individual to take actions that are counter to the organization's objectives.

With those broad principles in mind, we will now take a look at how a company's strategy affects its balanced scorecard.

IN BUSINESS

MEASURING CUSTOMER LOYALTY

Bain & Company consultant Fred Reichheld recommends measuring customer loyalty with one question—"On a scale of 0 to 10, how likely is it that you would recommend us to your friends and colleagues?" Customers who choose a score of 9 or 10 are labeled promoters. Those who choose a score of 0 to 6 are categorized as detractors, while those who select 7 or 8 are deemed passively satisfied. The net promoter score measures the difference between the percentages of customers who are promoters and detractors. Reichheld's research suggests that changes in a company's net promoter score correlate with (or move in tandem with) changes in its sales.

General Electric's Healthcare Division used net promoter scores to determine 20% of its managers' bonuses. The metric was eventually rolled out to all General Electric divisions. Other adopters of the net promoter score include American Express, consulting firm BearingPoint, and software maker Intuit.

Source: Jean McGregor, "Would You Recommend Us?" *BusinessWeek*, January 30, 2006, p. 94.

A Company's Strategy and the Balanced Scorecard

Returning to the performance measures in Exhibit 11–3, each company must decide which customers to target and what internal business processes are crucial to attracting and retaining those customers. Different companies, having different strategies, will target different customers with different kinds of products and services. Take the automobile industry as an example. BMW stresses engineering and handling; Volvo, safety; Jaguar, luxury detailing; and Honda, reliability. Because of these differences in emphasis, a one-size-fits-all approach to performance measurement won't work even within this one industry. Performance measures must be tailored to the specific strategy of each company.

Suppose, for example, that Jaguar's strategy is to offer distinctive, richly finished luxury automobiles to wealthy individuals who prize handcrafted, individualized products. To deliver this customer intimacy value proposition to its wealthy target customers, Jaguar might create such a large number of options for details, such as leather seats, interior and exterior color combinations, and wooden dashboards, that each car becomes virtually one of a kind. For example, instead of just offering tan or blue leather seats in standard cowhide, the company may offer customers the choice of an almost infinite palette of colors in any of a number of different exotic leathers. For such a system to work effectively, Jaguar would have to be able to deliver a completely customized car within a reasonable amount of time—and without incurring more cost for this customization than the customer is willing to pay. Exhibit 11–5 suggests how Jaguar might reflect this strategy in its balanced scorecard.

If the balanced scorecard is correctly constructed, the performance measures should be linked together on a cause-and-effect basis. Each link can then be read as a hypothesis in the form "If we improve this performance measure, then this other performance measure should also improve." Starting from the bottom of Exhibit 11–5, we can read the links between performance measures as follows. If employees acquire the skills to install new options more effectively, then the company can offer more options and the options can be installed in less time. If more options are available and they are installed in less time, then customer surveys should show greater satisfaction

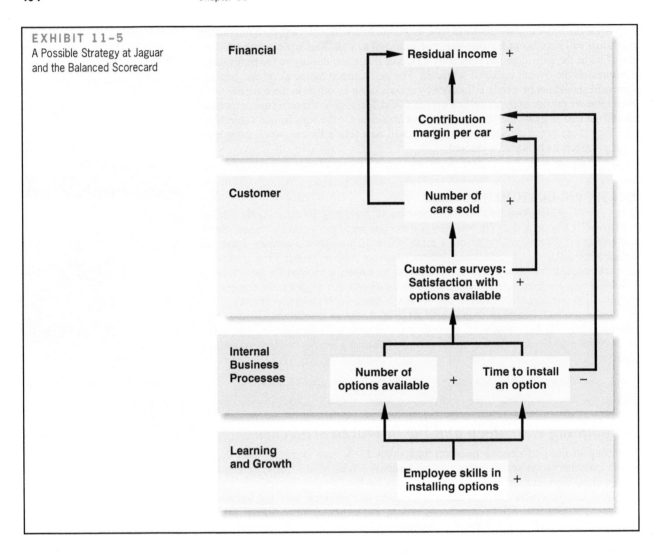

EXHIBIT 11-5
A Possible Strategy at Jaguar
and the Balanced Scorecard

with the range of options available. If customer satisfaction improves, then the number of cars sold should increase. In addition, if customer satisfaction improves, the company should be able to maintain or increase its selling prices, and if the time to install options decreases, the costs of installing the options should decrease. Together, this should result in an increase in the contribution margin per car. If the contribution margin per car increases and more cars are sold, the result should be an increase in residual income.

In essence, the balanced scorecard lays out a theory of how the company can take concrete actions to attain its desired outcomes (financial, in this case). The strategy laid out in Exhibit 11-5 seems plausible, but it should be regarded as only a theory. For example, if the company succeeds in increasing the number of options available and in decreasing the time required to install options and yet there is no increase in customer satisfaction, the number of cars sold, the contribution margin per car, or residual income, the strategy would have to be reconsidered. One of the advantages of the balanced scorecard is that it continually tests the theories underlying management's strategy. If a strategy is not working, it should become evident when some of the predicted effects (i.e., more car sales) don't occur. Without this feedback, the organization may drift on indefinitely with an ineffective strategy based on faulty assumptions.

THE WELLNESS SCORECARD

Towers Watson estimates that America's average annual health care spending per employee now exceeds $10,000, up from $5,386 in 2002. However, companies that have implemented high-performing corporate wellness programs have annual health care costs that are $1,800 per employee less than other organizations. These high-performing companies create and track wellness performance measures as an important part of managing their programs.

The wellness scorecard is one framework for measuring corporate wellness performance. It has four categories of measures—attitudes, participation, physical results, and financial results—that are connected on a cause-and-effect basis. If employee attitudes toward the company's wellness program improve, then it should increase the rate of employee participation in wellness activities. If employees increase their participation rates, then it should produce physical results, such as lower obesity rates, lower incidents of diabetes, and increased smoking cessation rates. These physical improvements should produce positive financial results for the company, such as lower medical, pharmaceutical, and disability disbursements.

Sources: Towers Perrin, "2010 Health Care Cost Survey," www.towerswatson.com; and Peter C. Brewer, Angela Gallo, and Melanie R. Smith, "Getting Fit with Corporate Wellness Programs," *Strategic Finance*, May 2010, pp. 27–33.

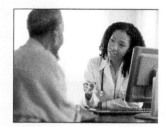

Tying Compensation to the Balanced Scorecard

Incentive compensation for employees, such as bonuses, can, and probably should, be tied to balanced scorecard performance measures. However, this should be done only after the organization has been successfully managed with the scorecard for some time—perhaps a year or more. Managers must be confident that the performance measures are reliable, sensible, understood by those who are being evaluated, and not easily manipulated. As Robert Kaplan and David Norton, the originators of the balanced scorecard concept point out, "compensation is such a powerful lever that you have to be pretty confident that you have the right measures and have good data for the measures before making the link."[4]

SUSTAINABILITY AND THE BALANCED SCORECARD

The Sustainable Investment Research Analyst Network (SIRAN) studied changes in the sustainability reporting practices of the Standard & Poor's (S&P) 100 companies from 2005 to 2007. Eighty-six of the S&P 100 companies had corporate sustainability websites as of 2007, an increase of 48% since 2005. Forty-nine of the S&P 100 companies published sustainability reports in 2007, up 26% from 2005.

Graham Hubbard, a professor at the University of Adelaide, recommends incorporating sustainability reporting into the balanced scorecard by adding two categories of measures related to social performance and environmental performance. Social performance measures focus on a company's philanthropic investments, community service, and employee safety and satisfaction. Environmental measures focus on a company's energy and water use per unit of output and its waste generation and disposal performance.

Sources: Ghostwriter, "Rise in Sustainability Reporting by S&P 100 Companies," *Business and the Environment with ISO14000 Updates*, October 2008, pp. 5–6; and Graham Hubbard, "Measuring Organizational Performance: Beyond the Triple Bottom Line," *Business Strategy and the Environment*, March 2009, pp. 177–191.

---

[4] Lori Calabro, "On Balance: A CFO Interview," *CFO*, February 2001, pp. 73–78.

Summary

For purposes of evaluating performance, business units are classified as cost centers, profit centers, and investment centers. Cost and profit centers are commonly evaluated using standard cost and flexible budget variances as discussed in prior chapters. Investment centers are evaluated using the techniques discussed in this chapter.

Return on investment (ROI) and residual income and its cousin EVA are widely used to evaluate the performance of investment centers. ROI suffers from the underinvestment problem—managers are reluctant to invest in projects that would decrease their ROI but whose returns exceed the company's required rate of return. The residual income and EVA approaches solve this problem by giving managers full credit for any returns in excess of the company's required rate of return.

A balanced scorecard is an integrated system of performance measures designed to support an organization's strategy. The various measures in a balanced scorecard should be linked on a plausible cause-and-effect basis from the very lowest level up through the organization's ultimate objectives. The balanced scorecard is essentially a theory about how specific actions taken by various people in the organization will further the organization's objectives. The theory should be viewed as tentative and subject to change if the actions do not in fact result in improvements in the organization's financial and other goals. If the theory changes, then the performance measures on the balanced scorecard should also change. The balanced scorecard is a dynamic measurement system that evolves as an organization learns more about what works and what doesn't work and refines its strategy accordingly.

Review Problem: Return on Investment (ROI) and Residual Income

The Magnetic Imaging Division of Medical Diagnostics, Inc., has reported the following results for last year's operations:

Sales	$25 million
Net operating income	$3 million
Average operating assets . . .	$10 million

Required:
1. Compute the Magnetic Imaging Division's margin, turnover, and ROI.
2. Top management of Medical Diagnostics, Inc., has set a minimum required rate of return on average operating assets of 25%. What is the Magnetic Imaging Division's residual income for the year?

Solution to Review Problem
1. The required calculations follow:

$$\text{Margin} = \frac{\text{Net operating income}}{\text{Sales}}$$

$$= \frac{\$3,000,000}{\$25,000,000}$$

$$= 12\%$$

$$\text{Turnover} = \frac{\text{Sales}}{\text{Average operating assets}}$$

$$= \frac{\$25,000,000}{\$10,000,000}$$

$$= 2.5$$

$$\text{ROI} = \text{Margin} \times \text{Turnover}$$

$$= 12\% \times 2.5$$

$$= 30\%$$

2. The Magnetic Imaging Division's residual income is computed as follows:

Average operating assets	$10,000,000
Net operating income	$3,000,000
Minimum required return (25% × $10,000,000)	2,500,000
Residual income	$ 500,000

Glossary

Balanced scorecard An integrated set of performance measures that are derived from and support the organization's strategy. (p. 490)

Cost center A business segment whose manager has control over cost but has no control over revenue or investments in operating assets. (p. 479)

Decentralized organization An organization in which decision-making authority is not confined to a few top executives but rather is spread throughout the organization. (p. 478)

Delivery cycle time The elapsed time from receipt of a customer order to when the completed goods are shipped to the customer. (p. 487)

Economic Value Added (EVA) A concept similar to residual income in which a variety of adjustments may be made to GAAP financial statements for performance evaluation purposes. (p. 484)

Investment center A business segment whose manager has control over cost, revenue, and investments in operating assets. (p. 479)

Manufacturing cycle efficiency (MCE) Process (value-added) time as a percentage of throughput time. (p. 488)

Margin Net operating income divided by sales. (p. 480)

Net operating income Income before interest and income taxes have been deducted. (p. 480)

Operating assets Cash, accounts receivable, inventory, plant and equipment, and all other assets held for operating purposes. (p. 480)

Profit center A business segment whose manager has control over cost and revenue but has no control over investments in operating assets. (p. 479)

Residual income The net operating income that an investment center earns above the minimum required return on its operating assets. (p. 483)

Responsibility center Any business segment whose manager has control over costs, revenues, or investments in operating assets. (p. 479)

Return on investment (ROI) Net operating income divided by average operating assets. It also equals margin multiplied by turnover. (p. 480)

Throughput time The amount of time required to turn raw materials into completed products. (p. 487)

Turnover Sales divided by average operating assets. (p. 480)

Questions

11–1 What is meant by the term *decentralization?*

11–2 What benefits result from decentralization?

11–3 Distinguish between a cost center, a profit center, and an investment center.

11–4 What is meant by the terms *margin* and *turnover* in ROI calculations?

11–5 What is meant by residual income?

11–6 In what way can the use of ROI as a performance measure for investment centers lead to bad decisions? How does the residual income approach overcome this problem?

11–7 What is the difference between delivery cycle time and throughput time? What four elements make up throughput time? What elements of throughput time are value-added and what elements are non–value-added?

11–8 What does a manufacturing cycle efficiency (MCE) of less than 1 mean? How would you interpret an MCE of 0.40?

11–9 Why do the measures used in a balanced scorecard differ from company to company?

11–10 Why does the balanced scorecard include financial performance measures as well as measures of how well internal business processes are doing?

Multiple-choice questions are provided on the text website at www.mhhe.com/garrison15e.

498   Chapter 11

Applying Excel   connect

LO11-1, LO11-2

Available with McGraw-Hill's *Connect*® Accounting.

The Excel worksheet form that appears below is to be used to recreate the Review Problem in the text on pages 496–497. Download the workbook containing this form from the Online Learning Center at www.mhhe.com/garrison15e. *On the website you will also receive instructions about how to use this worksheet form.*

	A	B	C	D	E
1	Chapter 11: Applying Excel				
2					
3	Data				
4	Sales	$25,000,000			
5	Net operating income	$3,000,000			
6	Average operating assets	$10,000,000			
7	Minimum required rate of return	25%			
8					
9	*Enter a formula into each of the cells marked with a ? below*				
10	Review Problem: Return on Investment (ROI) and Residual Income				
11					
12	*Compute the ROI*				
13	Margin	?			
14	Turnover	?			
15	ROI	?			
16					
17	*Compute the residual income*				
18	Average operating assets	?			
19	Net operating income	?			
20	Minimum required return	?			
21	Residual income	?			
22					

Chapter 11 Form   Filled in Chapter 11 Form

You should proceed to the requirements below only after completing your worksheet.

Required:

1. Check your worksheet by changing the average operating assets in cell B6 to $8,000,000. The ROI should now be 38% and the residual income should now be $1,000,000. If you do not get these answers, find the errors in your worksheet and correct them.

    Explain why the ROI and the residual income both increase when the average operating assets decrease.

2. Revise the data in your worksheet as follows:

    Data

Sales	$1,200
Net operating income	$72
Average operating assets	$500
Minimum required rate of return	15%

    a. What is the ROI?
    b. What is the residual income?
    c. Explain the relationship between the ROI and the residual income?

The Foundational 15

Available with McGraw-Hill's *Connect®* Accounting.

Westerville Company reported the following results from last year's operations: **LO11–1, LO11–2**

Sales	$1,000,000
Variable expenses	300,000
Contribution margin	700,000
Fixed expenses	500,000
Net operating income	$ 200,000
Average operating assets	$625,000

This year, the company has a $120,000 investment opportunity with the following cost and revenue characteristics:

Sales	$200,000
Contribution margin ratio	60% of sales
Fixed expenses	$90,000

The company's minimum required rate of return is 15%.

Required:

1. What is last year's margin?
2. What is last year's turnover?
3. What is last year's return on investment (ROI)?
4. What is the margin related to this year's investment opportunity?
5. What is the turnover related to this year's investment opportunity?
6. What is the ROI related to this year's investment opportunity?
7. If the company pursues the investment opportunity and otherwise performs the same as last year, what margin will it earn this year?
8. If the company pursues the investment opportunity and otherwise performs the same as last year, what turnover will it earn this year?
9. If the company pursues the investment opportunity and otherwise performs the same as last year, what ROI will it earn this year?
10. If Westerville's chief executive officer will earn a bonus only if her ROI from this year exceeds her ROI from last year, would she pursue the investment opportunity? Would the owners of the company want her to pursue the investment opportunity?
11. What is last year's residual income?
12. What is the residual income of this year's investment opportunity?
13. If the company pursues the investment opportunity and otherwise performs the same as last year, what residual income will it earn this year?
14. If Westerville's chief executive officer will earn a bonus only if her residual income from this year exceeds her residual income from last year, would she pursue the investment opportunity?
15. Assume that the contribution margin ratio of the investment opportunity was 50% instead of 60%. If Westerville's chief executive officer will earn a bonus only if her residual income from this year exceeds her residual income from last year, would she pursue the investment opportunity? Would the owners of the company want her to pursue the investment opportunity?

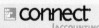 **Exercises**

All applicable exercises are available with McGraw-Hill's *Connect®* Accounting.

EXERCISE 11–1 Compute the Return on Investment (ROI) [LO11–1]

Alyeska Services Company, a division of a major oil company, provides various services to the operators of the North Slope oil field in Alaska. Data concerning the most recent year appear below:

Sales	$7,500,000
Net operating income	$600,000
Average operating assets	$5,000,000

500   Chapter 11

Required:
1. Compute the margin for Alyeska Services Company.
2. Compute the turnover for Alyeska Services Company.
3. Compute the return on investment (ROI) for Alyeska Services Company.

EXERCISE 11–2 Residual Income [LO11–2]
Juniper Design Ltd. of Manchester, England, is a company specializing in providing design services to residential developers. Last year the company had net operating income of $600,000 on sales of $3,000,000. The company's average operating assets for the year were $2,800,000 and its minimum required rate of return was 18%.

Required:
Compute the company's residual income for the year.

EXERCISE 11–3 Measures of Internal Business Process Performance [LO11–3]
Management of Mittel Rhein AG of Köln, Germany, would like to reduce the amount of time between when a customer places an order and when the order is shipped. For the first quarter of operations during the current year the following data were reported:

Inspection time	0.3 days
Wait time (from order to start of production)	14.0 days
Process time	2.7 days
Move time	1.0 days
Queue time	5.0 days

Required:
1. Compute the throughput time.
2. Compute the manufacturing cycle efficiency (MCE) for the quarter.
3. What percentage of the throughput time was spent in non–value-added activities?
4. Compute the delivery cycle time.
5. If by using Lean Production all queue time during production is eliminated, what will be the new MCE?

EXERCISE 11–4 Building a Balanced Scorecard [LO11–4]
Lost Peak ski resort was for many years a small, family-owned resort serving day skiers from nearby towns. Lost Peak was recently acquired by Western Resorts, a major ski resort operator. The new owners have plans to upgrade the resort into a destination resort for vacationers. As part of this plan, the new owners would like to make major improvements in the Powder 8 Lodge, the resort's on-the-hill cafeteria. The menu at the lodge is very limited—hamburgers, hot dogs, chili, tuna fish sandwiches, pizzas, french fries, and packaged snacks. With little competition, the previous owners of the resort had felt no urgency to upgrade the food service at the lodge. If skiers want lunch on the mountain, the only alternatives are the Powder 8 Lodge or a brown bag lunch brought from home.

As part of the deal when acquiring Lost Peak, Western Resorts agreed to retain all of the current employees of the resort. The manager of the lodge, while hardworking and enthusiastic, has very little experience in the restaurant business. The manager is responsible for selecting the menu, finding and training employees, and overseeing daily operations. The kitchen staff prepare food and wash dishes. The dining room staff take orders, serve as cashiers, and clean the dining room area.

Shortly after taking over Lost Peak, management of Western Resorts held a day-long meeting with all of the employees of the Powder 8 Lodge to discuss the future of the ski resort and the new management's plans for the lodge. At the end of this meeting, management and lodge employees created a balanced scorecard for the lodge that would help guide operations for the coming ski season. Almost everyone who participated in the meeting seemed to be enthusiastic about the scorecard and management's plans for the lodge.

The following performance measures were included on the balanced scorecard for the Powder 8 Lodge:
a. Weekly Powder 8 Lodge sales
b. Weekly Powder 8 Lodge profit
c. Number of menu items

Performance Measurement in Decentralized Organizations

d.   Dining area cleanliness as rated by a representative from Western Resorts management
e.   Customer satisfaction with menu choices as measured by customer surveys
f.   Customer satisfaction with service as measured by customer surveys
g.   Average time to take an order
h.   Average time to prepare an order
i.   Percentage of kitchen staff completing basic cooking course at the local community college
j.   Percentage of dining room staff completing basic hospitality course at the local community college

Western Resorts will pay for the costs of staff attending courses at the local community college.

Required:

1.   Using the above performance measures, construct a balanced scorecard for the Powder 8 Lodge. Use Exhibit 11–5 as a guide. Use arrows to show causal links and indicate with a + or − whether the performance measure should increase or decrease.
2.   What hypotheses are built into the balanced scorecard for the Powder 8 Lodge? Which of these hypotheses do you believe are most questionable? Why?
3.   How will management know if one of the hypotheses underlying the balanced scorecard is false?

EXERCISE 11–5 Return on Investment (ROI) [LO11–1]
Provide the missing data in the following table for a distributor of martial arts products:

	Division		
	Alpha	Bravo	Charlie
Sales	$?	$11,500,000	$?
Net operating income	$?	$ 920,000	$210,000
Average operating assets	$800,000	$?	$?
Margin	4%	?	7%
Turnover	5	?	?
Return on investment (ROI)	?	20%	14%

EXERCISE 11–6 Contrasting Return on Investment (ROI) and Residual Income [LO11–1, LO11–2]
Meiji Isetan Corp. of Japan has two regional divisions with headquarters in Osaka and Yokohama. Selected data on the two divisions follow:

	Division	
	Osaka	Yokohama
Sales	$3,000,000	$9,000,000
Net operating income	$210,000	$720,000
Average operating assets	$1,000,000	$4,000,000

Required:

1.   For each division, compute the return on investment (ROI) in terms of margin and turnover. Where necessary, carry computations to two decimal places.
2.   Assume that the company evaluates performance using residual income and that the minimum required rate of return for any division is 15%. Compute the residual income for each division.
3.   Is Yokohama's greater amount of residual income an indication that it is better managed? Explain.

EXERCISE 11–7 Creating a Balanced Scorecard [LO11–4]
Ariel Tax Services prepares tax returns for individual and corporate clients. As the company has gradually expanded to 10 offices, the founder Max Jacobs has begun to feel as though he is losing control of operations. In response to this concern, he has decided to implement a performance

502

Chapter 11

measurement system that will help control current operations and facilitate his plans of expanding to 20 offices.

Jacobs describes the keys to the success of his business as follows:

"Our only real asset is our people. We must keep our employees highly motivated and we must hire the 'cream of the crop.' Interestingly, employee morale and recruiting success are both driven by the same two factors—compensation and career advancement. In other words, providing superior compensation relative to the industry average coupled with fast-track career advancement opportunities keeps morale high and makes us a very attractive place to work. It drives a high rate of job offer acceptances relative to job offers tendered."

"Hiring highly qualified people and keeping them energized ensures operational success, which in our business is a function of productivity, efficiency, and effectiveness. Productivity boils down to employees being billable rather than idle. Efficiency relates to the time required to complete a tax return. Finally, effectiveness is critical to our business in the sense that we cannot tolerate errors. Completing a tax return quickly is meaningless if the return contains errors."

"Our growth depends on acquiring new customers through word-of-mouth from satisfied repeat customers. We believe that our customers come back year after year because they value error-free, timely, and courteous tax return preparation. Common courtesy is an important aspect of our business! We call it service quality, and it all ties back to employee morale in the sense that happy employees treat their clients with care and concern."

"While sales growth is obviously important to our future plans, growth without a corresponding increase in profitability is useless. Therefore, we understand that increasing our profit margin is a function of cost-efficiency as well as sales growth. Given that payroll is our biggest expense, we must maintain an optimal balance between staffing levels and the revenue being generated. As I alluded to earlier, the key to maintaining this balance is employee productivity. If we can achieve cost-efficient sales growth, we should eventually have 20 profitable offices!"

Required:

1. Create a balanced scorecard for Ariel Tax Services. Link your scorecard measures using the framework from Exhibit 11–5. Indicate whether each measure is expected to increase or decrease. Feel free to create measures that may not be specifically mentioned in the chapter, but make sense given the strategic goals of the company.
2. What hypotheses are built into the balanced scorecard for Ariel Tax Services? Which of these hypotheses do you believe are most questionable and why?
3. Discuss the potential advantages and disadvantages of implementing an internal business process measure called *total dollar amount of tax refunds generated*. Would you recommend using this measure in Ariel's balanced scorecard?
4. Would it be beneficial to attempt to measure each office's individual performance with respect to the scorecard measures that you created? Why or why not?

EXERCISE 11–8 Computing and Interpreting Return on Investment (ROI) [LO11–1]
Selected operating data for two divisions of Outback Brewing, Ltd., of Australia are given below:

	Division	
	Queensland	New South Wales
Sales	$4,000,000	$7,000,000
Average operating assets	$2,000,000	$2,000,000
Net operating income	$360,000	$420,000
Property, plant, and equipment (net)	$950,000	$800,000

Required:

1. Compute the rate of return for each division using the return on investment (ROI) formula stated in terms of margin and turnover.
2. Which divisional manager seems to be doing the better job? Why?

EXERCISE 11–9 Return on Investment (ROI) and Residual Income Relations [LO11–1, LO11–2]
A family friend has asked your help in analyzing the operations of three anonymous companies operating in the same service sector industry. Supply the missing data in the table below:

	Company		
	A	B	C
Sales	$9,000,000	$7,000,000	$4,500,000
Net operating income	$?	$ 280,000	$?
Average operating assets	$3,000,000	$?	$1,800,000
Return on investment (ROI)	18%	14%	?
Minimum required rate of return:			
Percentage	16%	?	15%
Dollar amount	$?	$ 320,000	$?
Residual income	$?	$?	$ 90,000

EXERCISE 11–10 Cost-Volume-Profit Analysis and Return on Investment (ROI) [LO11–1]
Posters.com is a small Internet retailer of high-quality posters. The company has $1,000,000 in operating assets and fixed expenses of $150,000 per year. With this level of operating assets and fixed expenses, the company can support sales of up to $3,000,000 per year. The company's contribution margin ratio is 25%, which means that an additional dollar of sales results in additional contribution margin, and net operating income, of 25 cents.

Required:
1. Complete the following table showing the relation between sales and return on investment (ROI).

Sales	Net Operating Income	Average Operating Assets	ROI
$2,500,000	$475,000	$1,000,000	?
$2,600,000	$?	$1,000,000	?
$2,700,000	$?	$1,000,000	?
$2,800,000	$?	$1,000,000	?
$2,900,000	$?	$1,000,000	?
$3,000,000	$?	$1,000,000	?

2. What happens to the company's return on investment (ROI) as sales increase? Explain.

EXERCISE 11–11 Effects of Changes in Profits and Assets on Return on Investment (ROI) [LO11–1]
Fitness Fanatics is a regional chain of health clubs. The managers of the clubs, who have authority to make investments as needed, are evaluated based largely on return on investment (ROI). The company's Springfield Club reported the following results for the past year:

Sales	$1,400,000
Net operating income	$70,000
Average operating assets	$350,000

Required:
The following questions are to be considered independently. Carry out all computations to two decimal places.
1. Compute the Springfield club's return on investment (ROI).
2. Assume that the manager of the club is able to increase sales by $70,000 and that, as a result, net operating income increases by $18,200. Further assume that this is possible without any increase in operating assets. What would be the club's return on investment (ROI)?
3. Assume that the manager of the club is able to reduce expenses by $14,000 without any change in sales or operating assets. What would be the club's return on investment (ROI)?
4. Assume that the manager of the club is able to reduce operating assets by $70,000 without any change in sales or net operating income. What would be the club's return on investment (ROI)?

Chapter 11

EXERCISE 11–12 Evaluating New Investments Using Return on Investment (ROI) and Residual Income [LO11–1, LO11–2]

Selected sales and operating data for three divisions of different structural engineering firms are given as follows:

	Division A	Division B	Division C
Sales	$12,000,000	$14,000,000	$25,000,000
Average operating assets	$3,000,000	$7,000,000	$5,000,000
Net operating income	$600,000	$560,000	$800,000
Minimum required rate of return	14%	10%	16%

Required:
1. Compute the return on investment (ROI) for each division using the formula stated in terms of margin and turnover.
2. Compute the residual income for each division.
3. Assume that each division is presented with an investment opportunity that would yield a 15% rate of return.
   a. If performance is being measured by ROI, which division or divisions will probably accept the opportunity? Reject? Why?
   b. If performance is being measured by residual income, which division or divisions will probably accept the opportunity? Reject? Why?

EXERCISE 11–13 Effects of Changes in Sales, Expenses, and Assets on ROI [LO11–1]

CommercialServices.com Corporation provides business-to-business services on the Internet. Data concerning the most recent year appear below:

Sales	$3,000,000
Net operating income	$150,000
Average operating assets	$750,000

Required:
Consider each question below independently. Carry out all computations to two decimal places.
1. Compute the company's return on investment (ROI).
2. The entrepreneur who founded the company is convinced that sales will increase next year by 50% and that net operating income will increase by 200%, with no increase in average operating assets. What would be the company's ROI?
3. The chief financial officer of the company believes a more realistic scenario would be a $1,000,000 increase in sales, requiring a $250,000 increase in average operating assets, with a resulting $200,000 increase in net operating income. What would be the company's ROI in this scenario?

Problems   **connect** ACCOUNTING

All applicable problems are available with McGraw-Hill's Connect® Accounting.

PROBLEM 11–14 Measures of Internal Business Process Performance [LO11–3]

DataSpan, Inc., automated its plant at the start of the current year and installed a flexible manufacturing system. The company is also evaluating its suppliers and moving toward Lean Production. Many adjustment problems have been encountered, including problems relating to performance measurement. After much study, the company has decided to use the performance measures below, and it has gathered data relating to these measures for the first four months of operations.

	Month			
	1	2	3	4
Throughput time (days)	?	?	?	?
Delivery cycle time (days)	?	?	?	?
Manufacturing cycle efficiency (MCE)	?	?	?	?
Percentage of on-time deliveries	91%	86%	83%	79%
Total sales (units)	3,210	3,072	2,915	2,806

Management has asked for your help in computing throughput time, delivery cycle time, and MCE. The following average times have been logged over the last four months:

	Average per Month (in days)			
	1	2	3	4
Move time per unit	0.4	0.3	0.4	0.4
Process time per unit	2.1	2.0	1.9	1.8
Wait time per order before start				
of production	16.0	17.5	19.0	20.5
Queue time per unit	4.3	5.0	5.8	6.7
Inspection time per unit	0.6	0.7	0.7	0.6

Required:
1. For each month, compute the following:
    a. The throughput time.
    b. The MCE.
    c. The delivery cycle time.
2. Evaluate the company's performance over the last four months.
3. Refer to the move time, process time, and so forth, given above for month 4.
    a. Assume that in month 5 the move time, process time, and so forth, are the same as in month 4, except that through the use of Lean Production the company is able to completely eliminate the queue time during production. Compute the new throughput time and MCE.
    b. Assume in month 6 that the move time, process time, and so forth, are again the same as in month 4, except that the company is able to completely eliminate both the queue time during production and the inspection time. Compute the new throughput time and MCE.

PROBLEM 11–15 Return on Investment (ROI) and Residual Income [LO11–1, LO11–2]
Financial data for Joel de Paris, Inc., for last year follow:

Joel de Paris, Inc. Balance Sheet	Beginning Balance	Ending Balance
Assets		
Cash	$ 140,000	$ 120,000
Accounts receivable	450,000	530,000
Inventory	320,000	380,000
Plant and equipment, net	680,000	620,000
Investment in Buisson, S.A.	250,000	280,000
Land (undeveloped)	180,000	170,000
Total assets	$2,020,000	$2,100,000
Liabilities and Stockholders' Equity		
Accounts payable	$ 360,000	$ 310,000
Long-term debt	1,500,000	1,500,000
Stockholders' equity	160,000	290,000
Total liabilities and stockholders' equity	$2,020,000	$2,100,000

Joel de Paris, Inc. Income Statement		
Sales		$4,050,000
Operating expenses		3,645,000
Net operating income		405,000
Interest and taxes:		
Interest expense	$150,000	
Tax expense	110,000	260,000
Net income		$ 145,000

The company paid dividends of $15,000 last year. The "Investment in Buisson, S.A.," on the balance sheet represents an investment in the stock of another company.

Required:
1. Compute the company's margin, turnover, and return on investment (ROI) for last year.
2. The board of directors of Joel de Paris, Inc., has set a minimum required rate of return of 15%. What was the company's residual income last year?

PROBLEM 11–16 Creating a Balanced Scorecard [LO11–4]
Mason Paper Company (MPC) manufactures commodity grade papers for use in computer printers and photocopiers. MPC has reported net operating losses for the last two years due to intense price pressure from much larger competitors. The MPC management team—including Kristen Townsend (CEO), Mike Martinez (vice president of Manufacturing), Tom Andrews (vice president of Marketing), and Wendy Chen (CFO)—is contemplating a change in strategy to save the company from impending bankruptcy. Excerpts from a recent management team meeting are shown below:

> **Townsend:** As we all know, the commodity paper manufacturing business is all about economies of scale. The largest competitors with the lowest cost per unit win. The limited capacity of our older machines prohibits us from competing in the high-volume commodity paper grades. Furthermore, expanding our capacity by acquiring a new paper-making machine is out of the question given the extraordinarily high price tag. Therefore, I propose that we abandon cost reduction as a strategic goal and instead pursue manufacturing flexibility as the key to our future success.
>
> **Chen:** Manufacturing flexibility? What does that mean?
>
> **Martinez:** It means we have to abandon our "crank out as many tons of paper as possible" mentality. Instead, we need to pursue the low-volume business opportunities that exist in the nonstandard, specialized paper grades. To succeed in this regard, we'll need to improve our flexibility in three ways. First, we must improve our ability to switch between paper grades. Right now, we require an average of four hours to change over to another paper grade. Timely customer deliveries are a function of changeover performance. Second, we need to expand the range of paper grades that we can manufacture. Currently, we can only manufacture three paper grades. Our customers must perceive that we are a "one-stop shop" that can meet all of their paper grade needs. Third, we will need to improve our yields (e.g., tons of acceptable output relative to total tons processed) in the nonstandard paper grades. Our percentage of waste within these grades will be unacceptably high unless we do something to improve our processes. Our variable costs will go through the roof if we cannot increase our yields!
>
> **Chen:** Wait just a minute! These changes are going to destroy our equipment utilization numbers!
>
> **Andrews:** You're right Wendy; however, equipment utilization is not the name of the game when it comes to competing in terms of flexibility. Our customers don't care about our equipment utilization. Instead, as Mike just alluded to, they want just-in-time delivery of smaller quantities of a full range of paper grades. If we can shrink the elapsed time from order placement to order delivery and expand our product offerings, it will increase sales from current customers and bring in new customers. Furthermore, we will be able to charge a premium price because of the limited competition within this niche from our cost-focused larger competitors. Our contribution margin per ton should drastically improve!
>
> **Martinez:** Of course, executing the change in strategy will not be easy. We'll need to make a substantial investment in training because ultimately it is our people who create our flexible manufacturing capabilities.
>
> **Chen:** If we adopt this new strategy, it is definitely going to impact how we measure performance. We'll need to create measures that motivate our employees to make decisions that support our flexibility goals.
>
> **Townsend:** Wendy, you hit the nail right on the head. For our next meeting, could you pull together some potential measures that support our new strategy?

Required:
1. Contrast MPC's previous manufacturing strategy with its new manufacturing strategy.
2. Generally speaking, why would a company that changes its strategic goals need to change its performance measurement system as well? What are some examples of measures that would have been appropriate for MPC prior to its change in strategy? Why would those measures fail to support MPC's new strategy?

Performance Measurement in Decentralized Organizations

3. Construct a balanced scorecard that would support MPC's new manufacturing strategy. Use arrows to show the causal links between the performance measures and show whether the performance measure should increase or decrease over time. Feel free to create measures that may not be specifically mentioned in the chapter, but nonetheless make sense given the strategic goals of the company.
4. What hypotheses are built into MPC's balanced scorecard? Which of these hypotheses do you believe are most questionable and why?

PROBLEM 11–17 Comparison of Performance Using Return on Investment (ROI) [LO11–1]
Comparative data on three companies in the same service industry are given below:

	Company		
	A	B	C
Sales	$600,000	$500,000	$?
Net operating income	$ 84,000	$ 70,000	$?
Average operating assets	$300,000	$?	$1,000,000
Margin	?	?	3.5%
Turnover	?	?	2
ROI	?	7%	?

Required:
1. What advantages are there to breaking down the ROI computation into two separate elements, margin and turnover?
2. Fill in the missing information above, and comment on the relative performance of the three companies in as much detail as the data permit. Make *specific recommendations* about how to improve the ROI.

(Adapted from National Association of Accountants,
Research Report No. 35, p. 34)

PROBLEM 11–18 Return on Investment (ROI) and Residual Income [LO11–1, LO11–2]
"I know headquarters wants us to add that new product line," said Dell Havasi, manager of Billings Company's Office Products Division. "But I want to see the numbers before I make any move. Our division's return on investment (ROI) has led the company for three years, and I don't want any letdown."

Billings Company is a decentralized wholesaler with five autonomous divisions. The divisions are evaluated on the basis of ROI, with year-end bonuses given to the divisional managers who have the highest ROIs. Operating results for the company's Office Products Division for the most recent year are given below:

Sales	$10,000,000
Variable expenses	6,000,000
Contribution margin	4,000,000
Fixed expenses	3,200,000
Net operating income	$ 800,000
Divisional operating assets	$ 4,000,000

The company had an overall return on investment (ROI) of 15% last year (considering all divisions). The Office Products Division has an opportunity to add a new product line that would require an additional investment in operating assets of $1,000,000. The cost and revenue characteristics of the new product line per year would be:

Sales	$2,000,000
Variable expenses	60% of sales
Fixed expenses	$640,000

508

Chapter 11

Required:
1. Compute the Office Products Division's ROI for the most recent year; also compute the ROI as it would appear if the new product line is added.
2. If you were in Dell Havasi's position, would you accept or reject the new product line? Explain.
3. Why do you suppose headquarters is anxious for the Office Products Division to add the new product line?
4. Suppose that the company's minimum required rate of return on operating assets is 12% and that performance is evaluated using residual income.
    a. Compute the Office Products Division's residual income for the most recent year; also compute the residual income as it would appear if the new product line is added.
    b. Under these circumstances, if you were in Dell Havasi's position, would you accept or reject the new product line? Explain.

PROBLEM 11-19 Internal Business Process Performance Measures [LO11-3]
Tombro Industries is in the process of automating one of its plants and developing a flexible manufacturing system. The company is finding it necessary to make many changes in operating procedures. Progress has been slow, particularly in trying to develop new performance measures for the factory.

In an effort to evaluate performance and determine where improvements can be made, management has gathered the following data relating to activities over the last four months:

	Month			
	1	2	3	4
Quality control measures:				
Number of defects	185	163	124	91
Number of warranty claims	46	39	30	27
Number of customer complaints	102	96	79	58
Material control measures:				
Purchase order lead time	8 days	7 days	5 days	4 days
Scrap as a percent of total cost	1%	1%	2%	3%
Machine performance measures:				
Machine downtime as a percentage of availability	3%	4%	4%	6%
Use as a percentage of availability	95%	92%	89%	85%
Setup time (hours)	8	10	11	12
Delivery performance measures:				
Throughput time	?	?	?	?
Manufacturing cycle efficiency (MCE)	?	?	?	?
Delivery cycle time	?	?	?	?
Percentage of on-time deliveries	96%	95%	92%	89%

The president has read in industry journals that throughput time, MCE, and delivery cycle time are important measures of performance, but no one is sure how they are computed. You have been asked to assist the company, and you have gathered the following data relating to these measures:

	Average per Month (in days)			
	1	2	3	4
Wait time per order before start of production	9.0	11.5	12.0	14.0
Inspection time per unit	0.8	0.7	0.7	0.7
Process time per unit	2.1	2.0	1.9	1.8
Queue time per unit	2.8	4.4	6.0	7.0
Move time per unit	0.3	0.4	0.4	0.5

Required:
1. For each month, compute the following performance measures:
    a. Throughput time.
    b. MCE.
    c. Delivery cycle time.

2. Using the performance measures given in the main body of the problem and the performance measures computed in (1) above, do the following:
   a. Identify areas where the company seems to be improving.
   b. Identify areas where the company seems to be deteriorating.
3. Refer to the inspection time, process time, and so forth, given for month 4.
   a. Assume that in month 5 the inspection time, process time, and so forth, are the same as for month 4, except that the company is able to completely eliminate the queue time during production using Lean Production. Compute the new throughput time and MCE.
   b. Assume that in month 6 the inspection time, process time, and so forth, are the same as in month 4, except that the company is able to eliminate both the queue time during production and the inspection time using Lean Production. Compute the new throughput time and MCE.

PROBLEM 11–20 Return on Investment (ROI) Analysis [LO11–1]

The contribution format income statement for Huerra Company for last year is given below:

	Total	Unit
Sales	$4,000,000	$80.00
Variable expenses	2,800,000	56.00
Contribution margin	1,200,000	24.00
Fixed expenses	840,000	16.80
Net operating income	360,000	7.20
Income taxes @ 30%	108,000	2.16
Net operating income	$ 252,000	$ 5.04

The company had average operating assets of $2,000,000 during the year.

Required:

1. Compute the company's return on investment (ROI) for the period using the ROI formula stated in terms of margin and turnover.

    For each of the following questions, indicate whether the margin and turnover will increase, decrease, or remain unchanged as a result of the events described, and then compute the new ROI figure. Consider each question separately, starting in each case from the data used to compute the original ROI in (1) above.
2. Using Lean Production, the company is able to reduce the average level of inventory by $400,000. (The released funds are used to pay off short-term creditors.)
3. The company achieves a cost savings of $32,000 per year by using less costly materials.
4. The company issues bonds and uses the proceeds to purchase $500,000 in machinery and equipment at the beginning of the period. Interest on the bonds is $60,000 per year. Sales remain unchanged. The new, more efficient equipment reduces production costs by $20,000 per year.
5. As a result of a more intense effort by salespeople, sales are increased by 20%; operating assets remain unchanged.
6. Obsolete inventory carried on the books at a cost of $40,000 is scrapped and written off as a loss.
7. The company uses $200,000 of cash (received on accounts receivable) to repurchase and retire some of its common stock.

PROBLEM 11–21 Creating Balanced Scorecards that Support Different Strategies [LO11–4]

The Midwest Consulting Group (MCG) helps companies build balanced scorecards. As part of its marketing efforts, MCG conducts an annual balanced scorecard workshop for prospective clients. As MCG's newest employee, your boss has asked you to participate in this year's workshop by explaining to attendees how a company's strategy determines the measures that are appropriate for its balanced scorecard. Your boss has provided you with the excerpts below from the annual reports of two current MCG clients. She has asked you to use these excerpts in your portion of the workshop.

Excerpt from Applied Pharmaceuticals' annual report:

The keys to our business are consistent and timely new product introductions and manufacturing process integrity. The new product introduction side of the equation is a function of research and development (R&D) yield (e.g., the number of marketable drug compounds created relative to the total number of potential compounds pursued). We seek to optimize our R&D yield and first-to-market capability by investing in state-of-the-art technology, hiring the highest possible percentage of the "best and the brightest" engineers that we pursue, and providing world-class training to those engineers. Manufacturing process integrity is all about establishing world-class quality specifications and then relentlessly engaging in prevention and appraisal activities to minimize defect rates. Our customers must have an awareness of and respect for our brand image of being "first to market and first in quality." If we deliver on this pledge to our customers, then our financial goal of increasing our return on stockholders' equity should take care of itself.

Excerpt from Destination Resorts International's annual report:

Our business succeeds or fails based on the quality of the service that our front-line employees provide to customers. Therefore, it is imperative that we strive to maintain high employee morale and minimize employee turnover. In addition, it is critical that we train our employees to use technology to create one seamless worldwide experience for our repeat customers. Once an employee enters a customer preference (e.g., provide two extra pillows in the room, deliver fresh brewed coffee to the room at 8:00 A.M., etc.) into our database, our worldwide workforce strives to ensure that a customer will never need to repeat it at any of our destination resorts. If we properly train and retain a motivated workforce, we should see continuous improvement in our percentage of error-free repeat customer check-ins, the time taken to resolve customer complaints, and our independently assessed room cleanliness. This in turn should drive improvement in our customer retention, which is the key to meeting our revenue growth goals.

Required:

1. Based on the excerpts above, compare and contrast the strategies of Applied Pharmaceuticals and Destination Resorts International.
2. Select balanced scorecard measures for each company and link the scorecard measures using the framework from Exhibit 11–5. Use arrows to show the causal links between the performance measures and show whether the performance measure should increase or decrease over time. Feel free to create measures that may not be specifically mentioned in the chapter, but nonetheless make sense given the strategic goals of each company.
3. What hypotheses are built into each balanced scorecard? Why do the hypotheses differ between the two companies?

PROBLEM 11–22 Perverse Effects of Some Performance Measures [LO11–4]

There is often more than one way to improve a performance measure. Unfortunately, some of the actions taken by managers to make their performance look better may actually harm the organization. For example, suppose the marketing department is held responsible only for increasing the performance measure "total revenues." Increases in total revenues may be achieved by working harder and smarter, but they can also usually be achieved by simply cutting prices. The increase in volume from cutting prices almost always results in greater total revenues; however, it does not always lead to greater total profits. Those who design performance measurement systems need to keep in mind that managers who are under pressure to perform may take actions to improve performance measures that have negative consequences elsewhere.

Required:

For each of the following situations, describe actions that managers might take to show improvement in the performance measure but which do not actually lead to improvement in the organization's overall performance.

1. Concerned with the slow rate at which new products are brought to market, top management of a consumer electronics company introduces a new performance measure—speed-to-market. The research and development department is given responsibility for this performance measure, which measures the average amount of time a product is in development before it is released to the market for sale.
2. The CEO of an airline company is dissatisfied with the amount of time that her ground crews are taking to unload luggage from airplanes. To solve the problem, she decides to measure the average elapsed time from when an airplane parks at the gate to when all pieces of luggage are unloaded from the airplane. For each month that an airport's ground crew can lower its

"average elapsed time" relative to the prior month, the CEO pays a lump-sum bonus to be split equally among members of the crew.

3. A manufacturing company has been plagued by the chronic failure to ship orders to customers by the promised date. To solve this problem, the production manager has been given the responsibility of increasing the percentage of orders shipped on time. When a customer calls in an order, the production manager and the customer agree to a delivery date. If the order is not completed by that date, it is counted as a late shipment.

4. Concerned with the productivity of employees, the board of directors of a large multinational corporation has dictated that the manager of each subsidiary will be held responsible for increasing the revenue per employee of his or her subsidiary.

  Cases

All applicable cases are available with McGraw-Hill's *Connect® Accounting*.

CASE 11–23 Balanced Scorecard [LO11–4]

Haglund Department Store is located in the downtown area of a small city. While the store had been profitable for many years, it is facing increasing competition from large national chains that have set up stores on the outskirts of the city. Recently the downtown area has been undergoing revitalization, and the owners of Haglund Department Store are somewhat optimistic that profitability can be restored.

In an attempt to accelerate the return to profitability, management of Haglund Department Store is in the process of designing a balanced scorecard for the company. Management believes the company should focus on two key problems. First, customers are taking longer and longer to pay the bills they incur using the department store's charge card, and the company has far more bad debts than are normal for the industry. If this problem were solved, the company would have more cash to make much needed renovations. Investigation has revealed that much of the problem with late payments and unpaid bills results from customers disputing incorrect charges on their bills. These incorrect charges usually occur because salesclerks incorrectly enter data on the charge account slip. Second, the company has been incurring large losses on unsold seasonal apparel. Such items are ordinarily resold at a loss to discount stores that specialize in such distress items.

The meeting in which the balanced scorecard approach was discussed was disorganized and ineffectively led—possibly because no one other than one of the vice presidents had read anything about how to build a balanced scorecard. Nevertheless, a number of potential performance measures were suggested by various managers. These potential performance measures are:

a. Percentage of charge account bills containing errors.
b. Percentage of salesclerks trained to correctly enter data on charge account slips.
c. Average age of accounts receivables.
d. Profit per employee.
e. Customer satisfaction with accuracy of charge account bills from monthly customer survey.
f. Total sales revenue.
g. Sales per employee.
h. Travel expenses for buyers for trips to fashion shows.
i. Unsold inventory at the end of the season as a percentage of total cost of sales.
j. Courtesy shown by junior staff members to senior staff members based on surveys of senior staff.
k. Percentage of suppliers making just-in-time deliveries.
l. Sales per square foot of floor space.
m. Written-off accounts receivable (bad debts) as a percentage of sales.
n. Quality of food in the staff cafeteria based on staff surveys.
o. Percentage of employees who have attended the city's cultural diversity workshop.
p. Total profit.

Required:

1. As someone with more knowledge of the balanced scorecard than almost anyone else in the company, you have been asked to build an integrated balanced scorecard. In your scorecard, use only performance measures listed previously. You do not have to use all of the performance measures suggested by the managers, but you should build a balanced scorecard that reveals a strategy for dealing with the problems with accounts receivable and with unsold merchandise. Construct the balanced scorecard following the format used in Exhibit 11–5. Do not be concerned with whether a specific performance measure falls within the learning and

512 Chapter 11

growth, internal business process, customer, or financial perspective. However, use arrows to show the causal links between performance measures within your balanced scorecard and explain whether the performance measures should show increases or decreases.

2. Assume that the company adopts your balanced scorecard. After operating for a year, some performance measures show improvements, but not others. What should management do next?

3. a. Suppose that customers express greater satisfaction with the accuracy of their charge account bills but the performance measures for the average age of accounts receivable and for bad debts do not improve. Explain why this might happen.

   b. Suppose that the performance measures for the average age of accounts receivable, bad debts, and unsold inventory improve, but total profits do not. Explain why this might happen. Assume in your answer that the explanation lies within the company.

Appendix 11A: Transfer Pricing

Divisions in a company often supply goods and services to other divisions within the same company. For example, the truck division of Toyota supplies trucks to other Toyota divisions to use in their operations. When the divisions are evaluated based on their profit, ROI, or residual income, a price must be established for such a transfer—otherwise, the division that produces the good or service will receive no credit. The price in such a situation is called a *transfer price*. A **transfer price** is the price charged when one segment of a company provides goods or services to another segment of the same company. For example, most companies in the oil industry, such as Shell, have petroleum refining and retail sales divisions that are evaluated on the basis of ROI or residual income. The petroleum refining division processes crude oil into gasoline, kerosene, lubricants, and other end products. The retail sales division takes gasoline and other products from the refining division and sells them through the company's chain of service stations. Each product has a price for transfers within the company. Suppose the transfer price for gasoline is $0.80 a gallon. Then the refining division gets credit for $0.80 a gallon of revenue on its segment report and the retailing division must deduct $0.80 a gallon as an expense on its segment report. Clearly, the refining division would like the transfer price to be as high as possible, whereas the retailing division would like the transfer price to be as low as possible. However, the transaction has no direct effect on the entire company's reported profit. It is like taking money out of one pocket and putting it into the other.

Managers are intensely interested in how transfer prices are set because they can have a dramatic effect on the reported profitability of their divisions. Three common approaches are used to set transfer prices:

1. Allow the managers involved in the transfer to negotiate the transfer price.
2. Set transfer prices at cost using either variable cost or full (absorption) cost.
3. Set transfer prices at the market price.

We will consider each of these transfer pricing methods in turn, beginning with negotiated transfer prices. Throughout the discussion, keep in mind that *the fundamental objective in setting transfer prices is to motivate the managers to act in the best interests of the overall company.* In contrast, **suboptimization** occurs when managers do not act in the best interests of the overall company or even in the best interests of their own division.

Negotiated Transfer Prices

LO11–5
Determine the range, if any, within which a negotiated transfer price should fall.

A **negotiated transfer price** results from discussions between the selling and buying divisions. Negotiated transfer prices have several important advantages. First, this approach preserves the autonomy of the divisions and is consistent with the spirit of decentralization. Second, the managers of the divisions are likely to have much better information about the potential costs and benefits of the transfer than others in the company.

When negotiated transfer prices are used, the managers who are involved in a proposed transfer within the company meet to discuss the terms and conditions of the transfer. They may decide not to go through with the transfer, but if they do, they must agree to a transfer price. Generally speaking, we cannot predict what transfer price they will agree to. However, we can confidently predict two things: (1) the selling division will agree to the transfer only if its profits increase as a result of the transfer, and (2) the buying division will agree to the transfer only if its profits also increase as a result of the transfer. This may seem obvious, but it is an important point.

Clearly, if the transfer price is below the selling division's cost, the selling division will incur a loss on the transaction and it will refuse to agree to the transfer. Likewise, if the transfer price is set too high, it will be impossible for the buying division to make any profit on the transferred item. For any given proposed transfer, the transfer price has both a lower limit (determined by the situation of the selling division) and an upper limit (determined by the situation of the buying division). The actual transfer price agreed to by the two division managers can fall anywhere between those two limits. These limits determine the **range of acceptable transfer prices**—the range of transfer prices within which the profits of both divisions participating in a transfer would increase.

An example will help us to understand negotiated transfer prices. Harris & Louder, Ltd., owns fast-food restaurants and snack food and beverage manufacturers in the United Kingdom. One of the restaurants, Pizza Maven, serves a variety of beverages along with pizzas. One of the beverages is ginger beer, which is served on tap. Harris & Louder has just purchased a new division, Imperial Beverages, that produces ginger beer. The managing director of Imperial Beverages has approached the managing director of Pizza Maven about purchasing Imperial Beverages' ginger beer to sell at Pizza Maven restaurants rather than its usual brand of ginger beer. Managers at Pizza Maven agree that the quality of Imperial Beverages' ginger beer is comparable to the quality of their regular brand. It is just a question of price. The basic facts are as follows:

Imperial Beverages:

Ginger beer production capacity per month	10,000 barrels
Variable cost per barrel of ginger beer	$8 per barrel
Fixed costs per month	$70,000
Selling price of Imperial Beverages ginger beer on the outside market	$20 per barrel

Pizza Maven:

Purchase price of regular brand of ginger beer	$18 per barrel
Monthly consumption of ginger beer	2,000 barrels

The Selling Division's Lowest Acceptable Transfer Price

The selling division, Imperial Beverages, will be interested in a proposed transfer only if its profit increases. Clearly, the transfer price must not fall below the variable cost per barrel of $8. In addition, if Imperial Beverages does not have sufficient capacity to fill the Pizza Maven order while supplying its regular customers, then it would have to sacrifice some of its regular sales. Imperial Beverages would expect to be compensated for the contribution margin on any lost sales. In sum, if the transfer has no effect on fixed costs, then from the selling division's standpoint, the transfer price must cover both the variable costs of producing the transferred units and any opportunity costs from lost sales.

Seller's perspective:

$$\frac{\text{Transfer}}{\text{price}} \geq \frac{\text{Variable cost}}{\text{per unit}} + \frac{\text{Total contribution margin on lost sales}}{\text{Number of units transferred}}$$

Chapter 11

The Buying Division's Highest Acceptable Transfer Price

The buying division, Pizza Maven, will be interested in a transfer only if its profit increases. In cases like this where a buying division has an outside supplier, the buying division's decision is simple. Buy from the inside supplier if the price is less than the price offered by the outside supplier.

Purchaser's perspective:

$$\text{Transfer price} \leq \text{Cost of buying from outside supplier}$$

Or, if an outside supplier does not exist:

$$\text{Transfer price} \leq \text{Profit to be earned per unit sold (not including the transfer price)}$$

We will consider several different hypothetical situations and see what the range of acceptable transfer prices would be in each situation.

Selling Division with Idle Capacity

Suppose that Imperial Beverages has sufficient idle capacity to satisfy Pizza Maven's demand for ginger beer without sacrificing sales of ginger beer to its regular customers. To be specific, let's suppose that Imperial Beverages is selling only 7,000 barrels of ginger beer a month on the outside market. That leaves unused capacity of 3,000 barrels a month—more than enough to satisfy Pizza Maven's requirement of 2,000 barrels a month. What range of transfer prices, if any, would make both divisions better off with the transfer of 2,000 barrels a month?

1. The selling division, Imperial Beverages, will be interested in the transfer only if:

$$\frac{\text{Transfer}}{\text{price}} \geq \frac{\text{Variable cost}}{\text{per unit}} + \frac{\text{Total contribution margin on lost sales}}{\text{Number of units transferred}}$$

Because Imperial Beverages has enough idle capacity, there are no lost outside sales. And because the variable cost per unit is $8, the lowest acceptable transfer price for the selling division is $8.

$$\text{Transfer price} \geq \$8 + \frac{\$0}{2,000} = \$8$$

2. The buying division, Pizza Maven, can buy similar ginger beer from an outside vendor for $18. Therefore, Pizza Maven would be unwilling to pay more than $18 per barrel for Imperial Beverages' ginger beer.

$$\text{Transfer price} \leq \text{Cost of buying from outside supplier} = \$18$$

3. Combining the requirements of both the selling division and the buying division, the acceptable range of transfer prices in this situation is:

$$\$8 \leq \text{Transfer price} \leq \$18$$

Assuming that the managers understand their own businesses and that they are cooperative, they should be able to agree on a transfer price within this range.

Selling Division with No Idle Capacity

Suppose that Imperial Beverages has *no* idle capacity; it is selling 10,000 barrels of ginger beer a month on the outside market at $20 per barrel. To fill the order from Pizza Maven, Imperial Beverages would have to divert 2,000 barrels from its regular customers. What range of transfer prices, if any, would make both divisions better off transferring the 2,000 barrels within the company?

1. The selling division, Imperial Beverages, will be interested in the transfer only if:

$$\text{Transfer price} \geq \frac{\text{Variable cost}}{\text{per unit}} + \frac{\text{Total contribution margin on lost sales}}{\text{Number of units transferred}}$$

Because Imperial Beverages has no idle capacity, there *are* lost outside sales. The contribution margin per barrel on these outside sales is $12 ($20 − $8).

$$\text{Transfer price} \geq \$8 + \frac{(\$20 - \$8) \times 2{,}000}{2{,}000} = \$8 + (\$20 - \$8) = \$20$$

Thus, as far as the selling division is concerned, the transfer price must at least cover the revenue on the lost sales, which is $20 per barrel. This makes sense because the cost of producing the 2,000 barrels is the same whether they are sold on the inside market or on the outside. The only difference is that the selling division loses the revenue of $20 per barrel if it transfers the barrels to Pizza Maven.

2. As before, the buying division, Pizza Maven, would be unwilling to pay more than the $18 per barrel it is already paying for similar ginger beer from its regular supplier.

$$\text{Transfer price} \leq \text{Cost of buying from outside supplier} = \$18$$

3. Therefore, the selling division would insist on a transfer price of at least $20. But the buying division would refuse any transfer price above $18. It is impossible to satisfy both division managers simultaneously; there can be no agreement on a transfer price and no transfer will take place. Is this good? The answer is yes. From the standpoint of the entire company, the transfer doesn't make sense. Why give up sales of $20 to save costs of $18?

Basically, the transfer price is a mechanism for dividing between the two divisions any profit the entire company earns as a result of the transfer. If the company as a whole loses money on the transfer, there will be no profit to divide up, and it will be impossible for the two divisions to come to an agreement. On the other hand, if the company as a whole makes money on the transfer, there will be a profit to share, and it will always be possible for the two divisions to find a mutually agreeable transfer price that increases the profits of both divisions. If the pie is bigger, it is always possible to divide it up in such a way that everyone has a bigger piece.

Selling Division Has Some Idle Capacity

Suppose now that Imperial Beverages is selling 9,000 barrels of ginger beer a month on the outside market. Pizza Maven can only sell one kind of ginger on tap. It cannot buy 1,000 barrels from Imperial Beverages and 1,000 barrels from its regular supplier; it must buy all of its ginger beer from one source.

To fill the entire 2,000-barrel a month order from Pizza Maven, Imperial Beverages would have to divert 1,000 barrels from its regular customers who are paying $20 per barrel. The other 1,000 barrels can be made using idle capacity. What range of transfer prices, if any, would make both divisions better off transferring the 2,000 barrels within the company?

1. As before, the selling division, Imperial Beverages, will insist on a transfer price that at least covers its variable cost and opportunity cost:

$$\text{Transfer price} \geq \frac{\text{Variable cost}}{\text{per unit}} + \frac{\text{Total contribution margin on lost sales}}{\text{Number of units transferred}}$$

Because Imperial Beverages does not have enough idle capacity to fill the entire order for 2,000 barrels, there *are* lost outside sales. The contribution margin per barrel on the 1,000 barrels of lost outside sales is $12 ($20 − $8).

$$\text{Transfer price} \geq \$8 + \frac{(\$20 - \$8) \times 1{,}000}{2{,}000} = \$8 + \$6 = \$14$$

Thus, as far as the selling division is concerned, the transfer price must cover the variable cost of $8 plus the average opportunity cost of lost sales of $6.

2. As before, the buying division, Pizza Maven, would be unwilling to pay more than the $18 per barrel it pays its regular supplier.

$$\text{Transfer price} \leq \text{Cost of buying from outside suppliers} = \$18$$

3. Combining the requirements for both the selling and buying divisions, the range of acceptable transfer prices is:

$$\$14 \leq \text{Transfer price} \leq \$18$$

Again, assuming that the managers understand their own businesses and that they are cooperative, they should be able to agree on a transfer price within this range.

No Outside Supplier

If Pizza Maven has no outside supplier for the ginger beer, the highest price the buying division would be willing to pay depends on how much the buying division expects to make on the transferred units—excluding the transfer price. If, for example, Pizza Maven expects to earn $30 per barrel of ginger beer after paying its own expenses, then it should be willing to pay up to $30 per barrel to Imperial Beverages. Remember, however, that this assumes Pizza Maven cannot buy ginger beer from other sources.

Evaluation of Negotiated Transfer Prices

As discussed earlier, if a transfer within the company would result in higher overall profits for the company, there is always a range of transfer prices within which both the selling and buying division would also have higher profits if they agree to the transfer. Therefore, if the managers understand their own businesses and are cooperative, then they should always be able to agree on a transfer price if it is in the best interests of the company that they do so.

Unfortunately, not all managers understand their own businesses and not all managers are cooperative. As a result, negotiations often break down even when it would be in the managers' own best interests to come to an agreement. Sometimes that is the fault of the way managers are evaluated. If managers are pitted against each other rather than against their own past performance or reasonable benchmarks, a noncooperative atmosphere is almost guaranteed. Nevertheless, even with the best performance evaluation system, some people by nature are not cooperative.

Given the disputes that often accompany the negotiation process, many companies rely on some other means of setting transfer prices. Unfortunately, as we will see below, all of the alternatives to negotiated transfer prices have their own serious drawbacks.

Transfers at the Cost to the Selling Division

Many companies set transfer prices at either the variable cost or full (absorption) cost incurred by the selling division. Although the cost approach to setting transfer prices is relatively simple to apply, it has some major defects.

First, the use of cost—particularly full cost—as a transfer price can lead to bad decisions and thus suboptimization. Return to the example involving the ginger beer. The full cost of ginger beer can never be less than $15 per barrel ($8 per barrel variable cost + $7 per barrel fixed cost at capacity). What if the cost of buying the ginger beer from an outside supplier is less than $15—for example, $14 per barrel? If the transfer price were set at full cost, then Pizza Maven would never want to buy ginger beer from Imperial Beverages because it could buy its ginger beer from an outside supplier at a lower price. However, from the standpoint of the company as a whole, ginger beer should be transferred from Imperial Beverages to Pizza Maven whenever Imperial Beverages has idle capacity. Why? Because when Imperial Beverages has idle capacity, it only costs the company $8 in variable cost to produce a barrel of ginger beer, but it costs $14 per barrel to buy from outside suppliers.

Second, if cost is used as the transfer price, the selling division will never show a profit on any internal transfer. The only division that shows a profit is the division that makes the final sale to an outside party.

Third, cost-based prices do not provide incentives to control costs. If the actual costs of one division are simply passed on to the next, there is little incentive for anyone to work to reduce costs. This problem can be overcome by using standard costs rather than actual costs for transfer prices.

Despite these shortcomings, cost-based transfer prices are often used in practice. Advocates argue that they are easily understood and convenient to use.

Transfers at Market Price

Some form of competitive **market price** (i.e., the price charged for an item on the open market) is sometimes advocated as the best approach to the transfer pricing problem—particularly if transfer price negotiations routinely become bogged down.

The market price approach is designed for situations in which there is an *outside market* for the transferred product or service; the product or service is sold in its present form to outside customers. If the selling division has no idle capacity, the market price is the correct choice for the transfer price. This is because, from the company's perspective, the real cost of the transfer is the opportunity cost of the lost revenue on the outside sale. Whether the item is transferred internally or sold on the outside market, the production costs are exactly the same. If the market price is used as the transfer price, the selling division manager will not lose anything by making the transfer, and the buying division manager will get the correct signal about how much it really costs the company for the transfer to take place.

While the market price works well when the selling division has no idle capacity, difficulties occur when the selling division has idle capacity. Recalling once again the ginger beer example, the outside market price for the ginger beer produced by Imperial Beverages is $20 per barrel. However, Pizza Maven can purchase all of the ginger beer it wants from outside suppliers for $18 per barrel. Why would Pizza Maven ever buy from Imperial Beverages if Pizza Maven is forced to pay Imperial Beverages' market price? In some market price-based transfer pricing schemes, the transfer price would be lowered to $18, the outside vendor's market price, and Pizza Maven would be directed to buy from Imperial Beverages as long as Imperial Beverages is willing to sell. This scheme can work reasonably well, but a drawback is that managers at Pizza Maven will regard the cost of ginger beer as $18 rather than the $8, which is the real cost to the company when the selling division has idle capacity. Consequently, the managers of Pizza Maven will make pricing and other decisions based on an incorrect cost.

Unfortunately, none of the possible solutions to the transfer pricing problem are perfect—not even market-based transfer prices.

Divisional Autonomy and Suboptimization

The principles of decentralization suggest that companies should grant managers autonomy to set transfer prices and to decide whether to sell internally or externally. It may be very difficult for top managers to accept this principle when their subordinate managers are about to make a suboptimal decision. However, if top management intervenes, the purposes of decentralization are defeated. Furthermore, to impose the correct transfer price, top managers would have to know details about the buying and selling divisions' outside market, variable costs, and capacity utilization. The whole premise of decentralization is that local managers have access to better information for operational decisions than top managers at corporate headquarters.

Of course, if a division manager consistently makes suboptimal decisions, the performance of the division will suffer. The offending manager's compensation will be adversely affected and promotion will become less likely. Thus, a performance evaluation system based on divisional profits, ROI, or residual income provides some built-in checks and balances. Nevertheless, if top managers wish to create a culture of autonomy and independent profit responsibility, they must allow their subordinate managers to control their own destiny—even to the extent of granting their managers the right to make mistakes.

Chapter 11

International Aspects of Transfer Pricing

The objectives of transfer pricing change when a multinational corporation is involved and the goods and services being transferred cross international borders. In this context, the objectives of international transfer pricing focus on minimizing taxes, duties, and foreign exchange risks, along with enhancing a company's competitive position and improving its relations with foreign governments. Although domestic objectives such as managerial motivation and divisional autonomy are always important, they often become secondary when international transfers are involved. Companies will focus instead on charging a transfer price that reduces its total tax bill or that strengthens a foreign subsidiary.

For example, charging a low transfer price for parts shipped to a foreign subsidiary may reduce customs duty payments as the parts cross international borders, or it may help the subsidiary to compete in foreign markets by keeping the subsidiary's costs low. On the other hand, charging a high transfer price may help a multinational corporation draw profits out of a country that has stringent controls on foreign remittances, or it may allow a multinational corporation to shift income from a country that has high income tax rates to a country that has low rates.

Review Problem: Transfer Pricing

Situation A

Collyer Products, Inc., has a Valve Division that manufactures and sells a standard valve:

Capacity in units	100,000
Selling price to outside customers	$30
Variable costs per unit	$16
Fixed costs per unit (based on capacity)	$9

The company has a Pump Division that could use this valve in one of its pumps. The Pump Division is currently purchasing 10,000 valves per year from an overseas supplier at a cost of $29 per valve.

Required:

1. Assume that the Valve Division has enough idle capacity to handle all of the Pump Division's needs. What is the acceptable range, if any, for the transfer price between the two divisions?
2. Assume that the Valve Division is selling all of the valves that it can produce to outside customers. What is the acceptable range, if any, for the transfer price between the two divisions?
3. Assume again that the Valve Division is selling all of the valves that it can produce to outside customers. Also assume that $3 in variable expenses can be avoided on transfers within the company, due to reduced selling costs. What is the acceptable range, if any, for the transfer price between the two divisions?

Solution to Situation A

1. Because the Valve Division has idle capacity, it does not have to give up any outside sales to take on the Pump Division's business. Applying the formula for the lowest acceptable transfer price from the viewpoint of the selling division, we get:

$$\text{Transfer price} \geq \frac{\text{Variable cost}}{\text{per unit}} + \frac{\text{Total contribution margin on lost sales}}{\text{Number of units transferred}}$$

$$\text{Transfer price} \geq \$16 + \frac{\$0}{10,000} = \$16$$

The Pump Division would be unwilling to pay more than $29, the price it is currently paying an outside supplier for its valves. Therefore, the transfer price must fall within the range:

$$\$16 \leq \text{Transfer price} \leq \$29$$

2. Because the Valve Division is selling all of the valves that it can produce on the outside market, it would have to give up some of these outside sales to take on the Pump Division's business. Thus, the Valve Division has an opportunity cost, which is the total contribution margin on lost sales:

$$\text{Transfer price} \geq \frac{\text{Variable cost}}{\text{per unit}} + \frac{\text{Total contribution margin on lost sales}}{\text{Number of units transferred}}$$

$$\text{Transfer price} \geq \$16 + \frac{(\$30 - \$16) \times 10{,}000}{10{,}000} = \$16 + \$14 = \$30$$

Because the Pump Division can purchase valves from an outside supplier at only $29 per unit, no transfers will be made between the two divisions.

3. Applying the formula for the lowest acceptable transfer price from the viewpoint of the selling division, we get:

$$\text{Transfer price} \geq \frac{\text{Variable cost}}{\text{per unit}} + \frac{\text{Total contribution margin on lost sales}}{\text{Number of units transferred}}$$

$$\text{Transfer price} \geq (\$16 - \$3) + \frac{(\$30 - \$16) \times 10{,}000}{10{,}000} = \$13 + \$14 = \$27$$

In this case, the transfer price must fall within the range:

$$\$27 \leq \text{Transfer price} \leq \$29$$

Situation B

Refer to the original data in situation A above. Assume that the Pump Division needs 20,000 special high-pressure valves per year. The Valve Division's variable costs to manufacture and ship the special valve would be $20 per unit. To produce these special valves, the Valve Division would have to reduce its production and sales of regular valves from 100,000 units per year to 70,000 units per year.

Required:

As far as the Valve Division is concerned, what is the lowest acceptable transfer price?

Solution to Situation B

To produce the 20,000 special valves, the Valve Division will have to give up sales of 30,000 regular valves to outside customers. Applying the formula for the lowest acceptable transfer price from the viewpoint of the selling division, we get:

$$\text{Transfer price} \geq \frac{\text{Variable cost}}{\text{per unit}} + \frac{\text{Total contribution margin on lost sales}}{\text{Number of units transferred}}$$

$$\text{Transfer price} \geq \$20 + \frac{(\$30 - \$16) \times 30{,}000}{20{,}000} = \$20 + \$21 = \$41$$

Glossary (Appendix 11A)

Market price The price charged for an item on the open market. (p. 517)

Negotiated transfer price A transfer price agreed on between buying and selling divisions. (p. 512)

Range of acceptable transfer prices The range of transfer prices within which the profits of both the selling division and the buying division would increase as a result of a transfer. (p. 513)

Suboptimization An overall level of profits that is less than a segment or a company is capable of earning. (p. 512)

Transfer price The price charged when one division or segment provides goods or services to another division or segment of an organization. (p. 512)

Appendix 11A Exercises and Problems

All applicable exercises and problems are available with McGraw-Hill's Connect® Accounting.

EXERCISE 11A–1 Transfer Pricing Basics [LO11–5]
Sako Company's Audio Division produces a speaker that is used by manufacturers of various audio products. Sales and cost data on the speaker follow:

Selling price per unit on the intermediate market	$60
Variable costs per unit	$42
Fixed costs per unit (based on capacity)	$8
Capacity in units	25,000

Sako Company has a Hi-Fi Division that could use this speaker in one of its products. The Hi-Fi Division will need 5,000 speakers per year. It has received a quote of $57 per speaker from another manufacturer. Sako Company evaluates division managers on the basis of divisional profits.

Required:
1. Assume that the Audio Division is now selling only 20,000 speakers per year to outside customers.
   a. From the standpoint of the Audio Division, what is the lowest acceptable transfer price for speakers sold to the Hi-Fi Division?
   b. From the standpoint of the Hi-Fi Division, what is the highest acceptable transfer price for speakers acquired from the Audio Division?
   c. If left free to negotiate without interference, would you expect the division managers to voluntarily agree to the transfer of 5,000 speakers from the Audio Division to the Hi-Fi Division? Why or why not?
   d. From the standpoint of the entire company, should the transfer take place? Why or why not?
2. Assume that the Audio Division is selling all of the speakers it can produce to outside customers.
   a. From the standpoint of the Audio Division, what is the lowest acceptable transfer price for speakers sold to the Hi-Fi Division?
   b. From the standpoint of the Hi-Fi Division, what is the highest acceptable transfer price for speakers acquired from the Audio Division?
   c. If left free to negotiate without interference, would you expect the division managers to voluntarily agree to the transfer of 5,000 speakers from the Audio Division to the Hi-Fi Division? Why or why not?
   d. From the standpoint of the entire company, should the transfer take place? Why or why not?

EXERCISE 11A–2 Transfer Pricing from the Viewpoint of the Entire Company [LO11–5]
Division A manufactures electronic circuit boards. The boards can be sold either to Division B of the same company or to outside customers. Last year, the following activity occurred in Division A:

Selling price per circuit board	$125
Variable cost per circuit board	$90
Number of circuit boards:	
Produced during the year	20,000
Sold to outside customers	16,000
Sold to Division B	4,000

Sales to Division B were at the same price as sales to outside customers. The circuit boards purchased by Division B were used in an electronic instrument manufactured by that division (one board per instrument). Division B incurred $100 in additional variable cost per instrument and then sold the instruments for $300 each.

Required:

1. Prepare income statements for Division A, Division B, and the company as a whole.
2. Assume that Division A's manufacturing capacity is 20,000 circuit boards. Next year, Division B wants to purchase 5,000 circuit boards from Division A rather than 4,000. (Circuit boards of this type are not available from outside sources.) From the standpoint of the company as a whole, should Division A sell the 1,000 additional circuit boards to Division B or continue to sell them to outside customers? Explain.

EXERCISE 11A–3 Transfer Pricing Situations [LO11–5]

In each of the cases below, assume that Division X has a product that can be sold either to outside customers or to Division Y of the same company for use in its production process. The managers of the divisions are evaluated based on their divisional profits.

	Case	
	A	B
Division X:		
Capacity in units	200,000	200,000
Number of units being sold to outside customers	200,000	160,000
Selling price per unit to outside customers	$90	$75
Variable costs per unit	$70	$60
Fixed costs per unit (based on capacity)	$13	$8
Division Y:		
Number of units needed for production	40,000	40,000
Purchase price per unit now being paid		
to an outside supplier	$86	$74

Required:

1. Refer to the data in case A above. Assume in this case that $3 per unit in variable selling costs can be avoided on intracompany sales. If the managers are free to negotiate and make decisions on their own, will a transfer take place? If so, within what range will the transfer price fall? Explain.
2. Refer to the data in case B above. In this case, there will be no savings in variable selling costs on intracompany sales. If the managers are free to negotiate and make decisions on their own, will a transfer take place? If so, within what range will the transfer price fall? Explain.

PROBLEM 11A–4 Transfer Price with an Outside Market [LO11–5]

Hrubec Products, Inc., operates a Pulp Division that manufactures wood pulp for use in the production of various paper goods. Revenue and costs associated with a ton of pulp follow:

Selling price		$70
Expenses:		
Variable	$42	
Fixed (based on a capacity of		
50,000 tons per year)	18	60
Net operating income		$10

Hrubec Products has just acquired a small company that manufactures paper cartons. This company will be treated as a division of Hrubec with full profit responsibility. The newly formed Carton Division is currently purchasing 5,000 tons of pulp per year from a supplier at a cost of $70 per ton, less a 10% purchase discount. Hrubec's president is anxious for the Carton Division to begin purchasing its pulp from the Pulp Division if an acceptable transfer price can be worked out.

Required:

For (1) and (2) below, assume that the Pulp Division can sell all of its pulp to outside customers for $70 per ton.

1. Are the managers of the Carton and Pulp Divisions likely to voluntarily agree to a transfer price for 5,000 tons of pulp next year? Why or why not?
2. If the Pulp Division meets the price that the Carton Division is currently paying to its supplier and sells 5,000 tons of pulp to the Carton Division each year, what will be the effect on the profits of the Pulp Division, the Carton Division, and the company as a whole?

522   Chapter 11

For (3)–(6) below, assume that the Pulp Division is currently selling only 30,000 tons of pulp each year to outside customers at the stated $70 price.

3. Are the managers of the Carton and Pulp Divisions likely to voluntarily agree to a transfer price for 5,000 tons of pulp next year? Why or why not?
4. Suppose that the Carton Division's outside supplier drops its price (net of the purchase discount) to only $59 per ton. Should the Pulp Division meet this price? Explain. If the Pulp Division does *not* meet the $59 price, what will be the effect on the profits of the company as a whole?
5. Refer to (4) above. If the Pulp Division refuses to meet the $59 price, should the Carton Division be required to purchase from the Pulp Division at a higher price for the good of the company as a whole?
6. Refer to (4) above. Assume that due to inflexible management policies, the Carton Division is required to purchase 5,000 tons of pulp each year from the Pulp Division at $70 per ton. What will be the effect on the profits of the company as a whole?

PROBLEM 11A–5 Market-Based Transfer Price [LO11–5]

Stavos Company's Screen Division manufactures a standard screen for high-definition televisions (HDTVs). The cost per screen is:

Variable cost per screen	$ 70
Fixed cost per screen	30*
Total cost per screen	$100

*Based on a capacity of 10,000 screens per year.

Part of the Screen Division's output is sold to outside manufacturers of HDTVs and part is sold to Stavos Company's Quark Division, which produces an HDTV under its own name. The Screen Division charges $140 per screen for all sales.

The costs, revenue, and net operating income associated with the Quark Division's HDTV are given below:

Selling price per unit		$480
Variable cost per unit:		
Cost of the screen	$140	
Variable cost of electronic parts	210	
Total variable cost		350
Contribution margin		130
Fixed costs per unit		80*
Net operating income per unit		$ 50

*Based on a capacity of 3,000 units per year.

The Quark Division has an order from an overseas source for 1,000 HDTVs. The overseas source wants to pay only $340 per unit.

Required:

1. Assume that the Quark Division has enough idle capacity to fill the 1,000-unit order. Is the division likely to accept the $340 price or to reject it? Explain.
2. Assume that both the Screen Division and the Quark Division have idle capacity. Under these conditions, would it be advantageous for the company as a whole if the Quark Division rejects the $340 price? Show computations to support your answer.
3. Assume that the Quark Division has idle capacity but that the Screen Division is operating at capacity and could sell all of its screens to outside manufacturers. Compute the profit impact to the Quark Division of accepting the 1,000-unit order at the $340 unit price.
4. What conclusions do you draw concerning the use of market price as a transfer price in intra-company transactions?

PROBLEM 11A–6 Basic Transfer Pricing [LO11–5]

Alpha and Beta are divisions within the same company. The managers of both divisions are evaluated based on their own division's return on investment (ROI). Assume the following information relative to the two divisions:

	Case			
	1	2	3	4
Alpha Division:				
Capacity in units	80,000	400,000	150,000	300,000
Number of units now being sold to outside customers	80,000	400,000	100,000	300,000
Selling price per unit to outside customers	$30	$90	$75	$50
Variable costs per unit	$18	$65	$40	$26
Fixed costs per unit (based on capacity)	$6	$15	$20	$9
Beta Division:				
Number of units needed annually	5,000	30,000	20,000	120,000
Purchase price now being paid to an outside supplier..............................	$27	$89	$75*	—

*Before any purchase discount.

Managers are free to decide if they will participate in any internal transfers. All transfer prices are negotiated.

Required:

1. Refer to case 1 shown above. Alpha Division can avoid $2 per unit in commissions on any sales to Beta Division. Will the managers agree to a transfer, and if so, within what range will the transfer price be? Explain.

2. Refer to case 2 shown above. A study indicates that Alpha Division can avoid $5 per unit in shipping costs on any sales to Beta Division.
   a. Would you expect any disagreement between the two divisional managers over what the transfer price should be? Explain.
   b. Assume that Alpha Division offers to sell 30,000 units to Beta Division for $88 per unit and that Beta Division refuses this price. What will be the loss in potential profits for the company as a whole?

3. Refer to case 3 shown above. Assume that Beta Division is now receiving an 8% price discount from the outside supplier.
   a. Will the managers agree to a transfer? If so, what is the range within which the transfer price would be?
   b. Assume that Beta Division offers to purchase 20,000 units from Alpha Division at $60 per unit. If Alpha Division accepts this price, would you expect its ROI to increase, decrease, or remain unchanged? Why?

4. Refer to case 4 shown above. Assume that Beta Division wants Alpha Division to provide it with 120,000 units of a *different* product from the one that Alpha Division is now producing. The new product would require $21 per unit in variable costs and would require that Alpha Division cut back production of its present product by 45,000 units annually. What is the lowest acceptable transfer price from Alpha Division's perspective?

CASE 11A–7 Transfer Pricing; Divisional Performance [LO11–5]

Weller Industries is a decentralized organization with six divisions. The company's Electrical Division produces a variety of electrical items, including an X52 electrical fitting. The Electrical Division (which is operating at capacity) sells this fitting to its regular customers for $7.50 each; the fitting has a variable manufacturing cost of $4.25.

The company's Brake Division has asked the Electrical Division to supply it with a large quantity of X52 fittings for only $5 each. The Brake Division, which is operating at 50% of capacity, will put the fitting into a brake unit that it will produce and sell to a large commercial airline manufacturer. The cost of the brake unit being built by the Brake Division follows:

Purchased parts (from outside vendors)	$22.50
Electrical fitting X52	5.00
Other variable costs	14.00
Fixed overhead and administration	8.00
Total cost per brake unit	$49.50

524

Chapter 11

Although the $5 price for the X52 fitting represents a substantial discount from the regular $7.50 price, the manager of the Brake Division believes that the price concession is necessary if his division is to get the contract for the airplane brake units. He has heard "through the grapevine" that the airplane manufacturer plans to reject his bid if it is more than $50 per brake unit. Thus, if the Brake Division is forced to pay the regular $7.50 price for the X52 fitting, it will either not get the contract or it will suffer a substantial loss at a time when it is already operating at only 50% of capacity. The manager of the Brake Division argues that the price concession is imperative to the well-being of both his division and the company as a whole.

Weller Industries uses return on investment (ROI) to measure divisional performance.

Required:
1. Assume that you are the manager of the Electrical Division. Would you recommend that your division supply the X52 fitting to the Brake Division for $5 each as requested? Why or why not? Show all computations.
2. Would it be profitable for the company as a whole for the Electrical Division to supply the fittings to the Brake Division if the airplane brakes can be sold for $50? Show all computations, and explain your answer.
3. In principle, should it be possible for the two managers to agree to a transfer price in this particular situation? If so, within what range would that transfer price lie?
4. Discuss the organizational behavior problems, if any, inherent in this situation. What would you advise the company's president to do in this situation?

(CMA, adapted)

Appendix 11B: Service Department Charges

LO11–6
Charge operating departments for services provided by service departments.

Most large organizations have both *operating departments* and *service departments*. The central purposes of the organization are carried out in the **operating departments**. In contrast, **service departments** do not directly engage in operating activities. Instead, they provide services or assistance to the operating departments. Examples of service departments include Cafeteria, Internal Auditing, Human Resources, Cost Accounting, and Purchasing.

Service department costs are charged to operating departments for a variety of reasons, including:

- To encourage operating departments to make wise use of service department resources. If the services were provided for free, operating managers would be inclined to waste these resources.
- To provide operating departments with more complete cost data for making decisions. Actions taken by operating departments have impacts on service department costs. For example, hiring another employee will increase costs in the human resources department. Such service department costs should be charged to the operating departments, otherwise the operating departments will not take them into account when making decisions.
- To help measure the profitability of operating departments. Charging service department costs to operating departments provides a more complete accounting of the costs incurred as a consequence of activities in the operating departments.
- To create an incentive for service departments to operate efficiently. Charging service department costs to operating departments provides a system of checks and balances in the sense that cost-conscious operating departments will take an active interest in keeping service department costs low.

In Appendix 11A, we discussed *transfer prices* that are charged within an organization when one part of an organization provides a product to another part of the organization. The service department charges considered in this appendix can be viewed as transfer prices that are charged for services provided by service departments to operating departments.

Charging Costs by Behavior

Whenever possible, variable and fixed service department costs should be charged to operating departments separately to provide more useful data for planning and control of departmental operations.

Variable Costs

Variable costs vary in total in proportion to changes in the level of service provided. For example, the cost of food in a cafeteria is a variable cost that varies in proportion to the number of persons using the cafeteria or the number of meals served.

A variable cost should be charged to consuming departments according to whatever activity causes the incurrence of the cost. For example, variable costs of a maintenance department that are caused by the number of machine-hours worked in the operating departments should be charged to the operating departments on the basis of machine-hours. This will ensure that these costs are properly traced to departments, products, and customers.

Fixed Costs

The fixed costs of service departments represent the costs of making capacity available for use. These costs should be charged to consuming departments in *predetermined lump-sum amounts* that are determined in advance and do not change. The lump-sum amount charged to a department can be based either on the department's peak-period or long-run average servicing needs.

The logic behind lump-sum charges of this type is as follows: When a service department is first established, its capacity will be determined by the needs of the departments that it will serve. This capacity may reflect the peak-period needs of the other departments, or it may reflect their long-run average or "normal" servicing needs. Depending on how much servicing capacity is provided for, it will be necessary to make a commitment of resources, which will be reflected in the service department's fixed costs. These fixed costs should be borne by the consuming departments in proportion to the amount of capacity each consuming department requires. That is, if available capacity in the service department has been provided to meet the peak-period needs of consuming departments, then the fixed costs of the service department should be charged in predetermined lump-sum amounts to consuming departments on that basis. If available capacity has been provided only to meet "normal" or long-run average needs, then the fixed costs should be charged on that basis.

Once set, charges should not vary from period to period, because they represent the cost of having a certain level of service capacity available for each operating department. The fact that an operating department does not need the peak level or even the "normal" level of service every period is immaterial; the capacity to deliver this level of service must be available. The operating departments should bear the cost of that availability.

Should Actual or Budgeted Costs Be Charged?

The *budgeted,* rather than actual, costs of a service department should be charged to operating departments. This ensures that service departments remain solely responsible for explaining any differences between their actual and budgeted costs. If service departments could base their charges on actual costs, then operating departments would be unfairly held accountable for cost overruns in the service departments.

Guidelines for Service Department Charges

The following summarizes how service department costs should be charged to operating departments:

- Variable and fixed service department costs should be charged separately.
- Variable service department costs should be charged using a predetermined rate applied to the actual quantity of services consumed.

- Fixed costs represent the costs of having service capacity available. These costs should be charged in lump sums to each operating department in proportion to their peak-period needs or long-run average needs. The lump-sum amounts should be based on budgeted fixed costs, not actual fixed costs.

Example

Seaboard Airlines has two operating divisions: a Freight Division and a Passenger Division. The company has a Maintenance Department that services both divisions. Variable servicing costs are budgeted at $10 per flight-hour. The department's fixed costs are budgeted at $750,000 for the year. The fixed costs of the Maintenance Department are budgeted based on the peak-period demand, which occurs during the Thanksgiving to New Year's holiday period. The airline wants to make sure that none of its aircraft are grounded during this key period due to unavailability of maintenance facilities. Approximately 40% of the maintenance during this period is performed on the Freight Division's equipment, and 60% is performed on the Passenger Division's equipment. These figures and the budgeted flight-hours for the coming year are as follows:

	Percent of Peak Period Capacity Required	Budgeted Flight-Hours
Freight Division	40%	9,000
Passenger Division	60	15,000
Total	100%	24,000

Year-end records show that actual variable and fixed costs in the aircraft Maintenance Department for the year were $260,000 and $780,000, respectively. One division logged more flight-hours during the year than planned, and the other division logged fewer flight-hours than planned, as shown below:

	Flight-Hours	
	Budgeted	Actual
Freight Division	9,000	8,000
Passenger Division	15,000	17,000
Total flight-hours	24,000	25,000

The amount of Maintenance Department cost charged to each division for the year would be as follows:

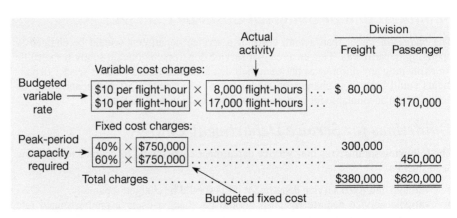

Notice that variable servicing costs are charged to the operating divisions based on the budgeted rate ($10 per hour) and the *actual activity* for the year. In contrast, the charges for fixed costs are based entirely on budgeted data. Also note that the two operating divisions are *not* charged for the actual costs of the service department, which are influenced by how well the service department is managed. Instead, the service department is held responsible for the actual costs not charged to other departments as shown below:

	Variable	Fixed
Total actual costs incurred	$260,000	$780,000
Total charges to operating departments . . .	250,000*	750,000
Spending variance—responsibility of the Maintenance Department	$ 10,000	$ 30,000

*$10 per flight-hour × 25,000 actual flight-hours = $250,000.

Some Cautions in Allocating Service Department Costs

Pitfalls in Allocating Fixed Costs

Rather than charge fixed costs to operating departments in predetermined lump-sum amounts, some companies allocate them using a *variable* allocation base that fluctuates from period to period. This practice can distort decisions and create serious inequities between departments. The inequities arise from the fact that the fixed costs allocated to one department are heavily influenced by what happens in *other* departments.

Sales dollars is an example of a variable allocation base that is often used to allocate fixed costs from service departments to operating departments. Using sales dollars as a base is simple, straightforward, and easy to work with. Furthermore, people tend to view sales dollars as a measure of ability to pay, and, hence, as a measure of how readily costs can be absorbed from other parts of the organization.

Unfortunately, sales dollars are often a very poor base for allocating or charging costs because sales dollars vary from period to period, whereas the costs are often largely *fixed*. Therefore, a letup in sales effort in one department will shift allocated costs from that department to other, more successful departments. In effect, the departments putting forth the best sales efforts are penalized in the form of higher allocations. The result is often bitterness and resentment on the part of the managers of the better departments.

For example, let's assume that a large men's clothing store has one service department and three sales departments—Suits, Shoes, and Accessories. The service department's costs total $60,000 per period and are allocated to the three sales departments according to sales dollars. A recent period showed the following allocation:

	Departments			
	Suits	Shoes	Accessories	Total
Sales by department	$260,000	$40,000	$100,000	$400,000
Percentage of total sales	65%	10%	25%	100%
Allocation of service department costs, based on percentage of total sales	$39,000	$6,000	$15,000	$60,000

In the following period, let's assume the manager of the Suits Department launched a successful program to expand sales in his department by $100,000. Furthermore, let's assume that sales in the other two departments remained unchanged, total service department costs remained unchanged, and the sales departments' expected usage of service

528 Chapter 11

department resources remained unchanged. Given these assumptions, the service department cost allocations to the sales departments would change as shown below:

	Departments			
	Suits	Shoes	Accessories	Total
Sales by department	$360,000	$40,000	$100,000	$500,000
Percentage of total sales	72%	8%	20%	100%
Allocation of service department costs, based on percentage of total sales	$43,200	$4,800	$12,000	$60,000
Increase (or decrease) from prior allocation	$4,200	$(1,200)	$(3,000)	$0

After seeing these allocations, the manager of the Suits Department is likely to complain, because by growing sales in his department, he is being forced to carry a larger share of the service department costs. In essence, this manager is being punished for his outstanding performance by being saddled with a greater proportion of service department costs. On the other hand, the managers of the departments that showed no sales growth are being relieved of a portion of the costs they had been carrying. Yet, there was no change in the amount of services provided for any department across the two periods.

This example shows why a variable allocation base such as sales dollars should only be used as a base for allocating or charging costs in those cases where service department costs actually vary with the chosen allocation base. When service department costs are fixed, they should be charged to operating departments according to the guidelines mentioned earlier.

Glossary (Appendix 11B)

Operating department A department in which the central purposes of the organization are carried out. (p. 524)

Service department A department that does not directly engage in operating activities; rather, it provides services or assistance to the operating departments. (p. 524)

Appendix 11B Exercises and Problems

All applicable exercises and problems are available with McGraw-Hill's *Connect®* Accounting.

EXERCISE 11B–1 Service Department Charges [LO11–6]
Hannibal Steel Company has a Transport Services Department that provides trucks to haul ore from the company's mine to its two steel mills—the Northern Plant and the Southern Plant. Budgeted costs for the Transport Services Department total $350,000 per year, consisting of $0.25 per ton variable cost and $300,000 fixed cost. The level of fixed cost is determined by peak-period requirements. During the peak period, the Northern Plant requires 70% of the Transport Services Department's capacity and the Southern Plant requires 30%.

During the year, the Transport Services Department actually hauled the following amounts of ore for the two plants: Northern Plant, 130,000 tons; Southern Plant, 50,000 tons. The Transport Services Department incurred $364,000 in cost during the year, of which $54,000 was variable cost and $310,000 was fixed cost.

Required:
1. Determine how much of the $54,000 in variable cost should be charged to each plant.
2. Determine how much of the $310,000 in fixed cost should be charged to each plant.
3. Should any of the $364,000 in the Transport Services Department cost not be charged to the plants? Explain.

EXERCISE 11B–2 Sales Dollars as an Allocation Base for Fixed Costs [LO11–6]

Konig Enterprises, Ltd., owns and operates three restaurants in Vancouver, B.C. The company allocates its fixed administrative expenses to the three restaurants on the basis of sales dollars. During 2013, the fixed administrative expenses totaled $2,000,000. These expenses were allocated as follows:

	Restaurants			
	Rick's Harborside	Imperial Garden	Ginger Wok	Total
Total sales—2013	$16,000,000	$15,000,000	$9,000,000	$40,000,000
Percentage of total sales ...	40%	37.5%	22.5%	100%
Allocation (based on the above percentages)	$800,000	$750,000	$450,000	$2,000,000

During 2014, the following year, the Imperial Garden restaurant increased its sales by $10 million. The sales levels in the other two restaurants remained unchanged. The company's 2014 sales data were as follows:

	Restaurants			
	Rick's Harborside	Imperial Garden	Ginger Wok	Total
Total sales—2014	$16,000,000	$25,000,000	$9,000,000	$50,000,000
Percentage of total sales ...	32%	50%	18%	100%

Fixed administrative expenses remained unchanged at $2,000,000 during 2014.

Required:
1. Using sales dollars as an allocation base, show the allocation of the fixed administrative expenses among the three restaurants for 2014.
2. Compare your allocation from (1) above to the allocation for 2013. As the manager of the Imperial Garden, how would you feel about the amount that has been charged to you for 2014?
3. Comment on the usefulness of sales dollars as an allocation base.

EXERCISE 11B–3 Service Department Charges [LO11–6]

Korvanis Corporation operates a Medical Services Department for its employees. Charges to the company's operating departments for the variable costs of the Medical Services Department are based on the actual number of employees in each department. Charges for the fixed costs of the Medical Services Department are based on the long-run average number of employees in each operating department.

Variable Medical Services Department costs are budgeted at $80 per employee. Fixed Medical Services Department costs are budgeted at $400,000 per year. Actual Medical Services Department costs for the most recent year were $41,000 for variable costs and $408,000 for fixed costs. Data concerning employees in the three operating departments follow:

	Cutting	Milling	Assembly
Budgeted number of employees	170	100	280
Actual number of employees for the most recent year	150	80	270
Long-run average number of employees	180	120	300

Required:
1. Determine the Medical Services Department charges for the year to each of the operating departments—Cutting, Milling, and Assembly.
2. How much, if any, of the actual Medical Services Department costs for the year should not be charged to the operating departments?

Chapter 11

PROBLEM 11B–4 Service Department Charges [LO11–6]
Sharp Motor Company has two operating divisions—an Auto Division and a Truck Division. The company has a cafeteria that serves the employees of both divisions. The costs of operating the cafeteria are budgeted at $40,000 per month plus $3 per meal served. The company pays all the cost of the meals.

The fixed costs of the cafeteria are determined by peak-period requirements. The Auto Division is responsible for 65% of the peak-period requirements, and the Truck Division is responsible for the other 35%.

For June, the Auto Division estimated that it would need 35,000 meals served, and the Truck Division estimated that it would need 20,000 meals served. However, due to unexpected layoffs of employees during the month, only 20,000 meals were served to the Auto Division. Another 20,000 meals were served to the Truck Division as planned.

Cost records in the cafeteria show that actual fixed costs for June totaled $42,000 and that actual meal costs totaled $128,000.

Required:
1. How much cafeteria cost should be charged to each division for June?
2. Assume that the company follows the practice of allocating *all* cafeteria costs incurred each month to the divisions in proportion to the number of meals served to each division during the month. On this basis, how much cost would be allocated to each division for June?
3. What criticisms can you make of the allocation method used in part (2) above?
4. If managers of operating departments know that fixed service costs are going to be allocated on the basis of peak-period requirements, what will be their probable strategy as they report their estimate of peak-period requirements to the company's budget committee? As a member of top management, what would you do to neutralize such strategies?

PROBLEM 11B–5 Service Department Charges [LO11–6]
Tasman Products, Ltd., of Australia has a Maintenance Department that services the equipment in the company's Forming Department and Assembly Department. The cost of this servicing is charged to the operating departments on the basis of machine-hours. Cost and other data relating to the Maintenance Department and to the other two departments for the most recent year are presented below.

Data for the Maintenance Department follow:

	Budget	Actual
Variable costs for lubricants	$96,000*	$110,000
Fixed costs for salaries and other	$150,000	$153,000

*Budgeted at $0.40 per machine-hour.

Data for the Forming and Assembly departments follow:

	Percentage of Peak-Period Capacity Required	Machine-Hours	
		Budget	Actual
Forming Department	70%	160,000	190,000
Assembly Department	30%	80,000	70,000
Total	100%	240,000	260,000

The level of fixed costs in the Maintenance Department is determined by peak-period requirements.

Required:
Management would like data to assist in comparing actual performance to planned performance in the Maintenance Department and in the other departments.
1. How much Maintenance Department cost should be charged to the Forming Department and to the Assembly Department? Show all computations.
2. Should any portion of the actual Maintenance Department costs not be charged to the other departments? If all costs should be charged, explain why; if a portion should not be charged, compute the amount and explain why it should not be charged.

CHAPTER 12

Differential Analysis: The Key to Decision Making

Moving Manufacturing Operations Overseas

A survey from **Ventoro Institute LLC** found that many companies expect to realize an 80% cost savings when moving manufacturing operations overseas. However, in this same survey, companies reported an average actual cost savings of less than 10%. Some of the problems encountered by these companies included miscommunications with offshore manufacturers, shipping delays, intellectual property infringement, and substandard product quality. William Botts, vice chairman of **Vegas Valley Angels** (an angel-investing group), suggests that companies with labor-intensive manufacturing processes are most likely to benefit from sending manufacturing operations overseas because the bulk of potential cost savings relate to labor costs. ■

Source: Small Talk, "Kelly Spors Answers Questions on Protecting Ideas, Cutting Off Junk Mail, and Overseas Manufacturing," The Wall Street Journal, March 17, 2008, p. R2.

LEARNING OBJECTIVES

After studying Chapter 12, you should be able to:

LO12–1 Identify relevant and irrelevant costs and benefits in a decision.

LO12–2 Prepare an analysis showing whether a product line or other business segment should be added or dropped.

LO12–3 Prepare a make or buy analysis.

LO12–4 Prepare an analysis showing whether a special order should be accepted.

LO12–5 Determine the most profitable use of a constrained resource.

LO12–6 Determine the value of obtaining more of the constrained resource.

LO12–7 Prepare an analysis showing whether joint products should be sold at the split-off point or processed further.

Managers must decide what products to sell, whether to make or buy component parts, what prices to charge, what channels of distribution to use, whether to accept special orders at special prices, and so forth. Making such decisions is often a difficult task that is complicated by numerous alternatives and massive amounts of data, only some of which may be relevant.

Every decision involves choosing from among at least two alternatives. In making a decision, the costs and benefits of one alternative must be compared to the costs and benefits of other alternatives. The key to making such comparisons is *differential analysis*—focusing on the costs and benefits that *differ* between the alternatives. A difference in cost between any two alternatives is known as a **differential cost**. A difference in revenue between any two alternatives is known as **differential revenue**. Differential costs and revenues are relevant to decision making, whereas costs and revenues that do not differ between alternatives are irrelevant to decision making. Because differential costs and differential revenues are the only inputs that are relevant to decision making, they are also often referred to as **relevant costs** and **relevant benefits**.

Distinguishing between relevant and irrelevant costs and benefits is critical for two reasons. First, irrelevant data can be ignored—saving decision makers tremendous amounts of time and effort. Second, bad decisions can easily result from erroneously including irrelevant costs and benefits when analyzing alternatives. To be successful in decision making, managers must be able to tell the difference between relevant and irrelevant data and must be able to correctly use the relevant data in analyzing alternatives. The purpose of this chapter is to develop these skills by illustrating their use in a wide range of decision-making situations. These decision-making skills are as important in your personal life as they are to managers. After completing your study of this chapter, you should be able to think more clearly about decisions in many facets of your life.

Cost Concepts for Decision Making

Identifying Relevant Costs and Benefits

LO12–1

Identify relevant and irrelevant costs and benefits in a decision.

Only those costs and benefits that differ in total between alternatives are relevant in a decision. If the total amount of a cost will be the same regardless of the alternative selected, then the decision has no effect on the cost, so the cost can be ignored. To elaborate on this point, we'd like to define the terms *avoidable cost, sunk cost,* and *opportunity cost,* and illustrate the concept of *future costs that do not differ between alternatives.*

Assume you are trying to decide whether to go to a movie or rent a DVD for the evening. The rent on your apartment is irrelevant. Whether you go to a movie or rent a DVD, the rent on your apartment will be exactly the same and is therefore irrelevant to the decision. On the other hand, the cost of the movie ticket and the cost of renting the DVD would be relevant in the decision because they are *avoidable costs.*

An **avoidable cost** is a cost that can be eliminated by choosing one alternative over another. By choosing the alternative of going to the movie, the cost of renting the DVD can be avoided. By choosing the alternative of renting the DVD, the cost of the movie ticket can be avoided. Therefore, the cost of the movie ticket and the cost of renting the DVD are both avoidable costs. On the other hand, the rent on your apartment is not an avoidable cost of either alternative. You would continue to rent your apartment under either alternative. Avoidable costs are relevant costs. Unavoidable costs are irrelevant costs.

To refine the notion of relevant costs a little further, two broad categories of costs are never relevant in decisions—sunk costs and future costs that do not differ between the alternatives. As we learned in Chapter 2, a **sunk cost** is a cost that has already been incurred and cannot be avoided regardless of what a manager decides to do. For example, suppose a company purchased a five-year-old truck for $12,000. The amount paid for the truck is a sunk cost because it has already been incurred and the transaction cannot be undone. Even though it is perhaps counterintuitive, the amount the company paid for the truck is irrelevant in making decisions such as whether to keep, sell, or replace the truck. Furthermore, any depreciation expense related to the truck is *irrelevant in making decisions*. This is true because depreciation is a noncash expense that simply spreads the cost of the truck over its useful life.[1] Sunk costs are always the same no matter what alternatives are being considered; therefore, they are irrelevant and should be ignored when making decisions.

Future costs that do not differ between alternatives should also be ignored. Continuing with the example discussed earlier, suppose you plan to order a pizza after you go to the movie theater or you rent a DVD. If you are going to buy the same pizza regardless of your choice of entertainment, the cost of the pizza is irrelevant to the choice of whether you go to the movie theater or rent a DVD. Notice, the cost of the pizza is not a sunk cost because it has not yet been incurred. Nonetheless, the cost of the pizza is irrelevant to the entertainment decision because it is a future cost that does not differ between the alternatives.

Opportunity costs also need to be considered when making decisions. An **opportunity cost** is the potential benefit that is given up when one alternative is selected over another. For example, if you were considering giving up a high-paying summer job to travel overseas, the forgone wages would be an opportunity cost of traveling abroad. Opportunity costs are not usually found in accounting records, but they are costs that must be explicitly considered in every decision a manager makes.

To summarize, only those costs and benefits that differ between alternatives are relevant in a decision. Differential costs are also referred to as relevant costs or avoidable costs. The key to successful decision making is to focus on relevant costs and benefits as well as opportunity costs while ignoring everything else—including sunk costs and future costs and benefits that do not differ between the alternatives.

IN BUSINESS

INDUSTRIAL MOTION HEADS EAST

Eric Kozlowski and Brian Pfeifer founded Industrial Motion Inc. in Rancho Santa Margarita, California; however, after 10 years in California, they decided to cut costs by relocating the company to Mooresville, North Carolina. In Mooresville, the company's 42 employees are paid salaries of $35,000–$45,000 instead of the $60,000 paid to employees in California; furthermore, worker's compensation insurance is one-tenth of the amount paid in California. Property taxes and the cost of real estate are 50% less in Mooresville compared to Rancho Santa Margarita. Even the company's security system in Mooresville costs only $25 per month instead of $280 per month in California.

Source: Simona Covel, "Moving Across the Country to Cut Costs," *The Wall Street Journal*, January 10, 2008, p. B4.

Different Costs for Different Purposes

We need to recognize a fundamental concept from the outset of our discussion—costs that are relevant in one decision situation are not necessarily relevant in another. This means that *managers need different costs for different purposes*. For one purpose, a particular group of costs may be relevant; for another purpose, an entirely different group of costs may be relevant. Thus, *each* decision situation must be carefully analyzed to isolate the relevant costs. Otherwise, irrelevant data may cloud the situation and lead to a bad decision.

The concept of "different costs for different purposes" is basic to managerial accounting; we shall frequently see its application in the pages that follow.

---

[1] See Appendix 13C for a discussion of how depreciation expense impacts decisions when tax implications are considered.

Chapter 12

An Example of Identifying Relevant Costs and Benefits

Cynthia is currently a student in an MBA program in Boston and would like to visit a friend in New York City over the weekend. She is trying to decide whether to drive or take the train. Because she is on a tight budget, she wants to carefully consider the costs of the two alternatives. If one alternative is far less expensive than the other, that may be decisive in her choice. By car, the distance between her apartment in Boston and her friend's apartment in New York City is 230 miles. Cynthia has compiled the following list of items to consider:

	Automobile Costs		
	Item	Annual Cost of Fixed Items	Cost per Mile (based on 10,000 miles per year)
(a)	Annual straight-line depreciation on car [($24,000 original cost − $10,000 estimated resale value in 5 years)/5 years]	$2,800	$0.280
(b)	Cost of gasoline ($3.30 per gallon ÷ 33 miles per gallon)		0.100
(c)	Annual cost of auto insurance and license	$1,380	0.138
(d)	Maintenance and repairs		0.065
(e)	Parking fees at school ($45 per month × 8 months)	$360	0.036
(f)	Total average cost per mile		$0.619

	Additional Data	
	Item	
(g)	Reduction in the resale value of car due solely to wear and tear	$0.026 per mile
(h)	Cost of round-trip train ticket from Boston to New York City	$104
(i)	Benefit of relaxing and being able to study during the train ride rather than having to drive	?
(j)	Cost of putting the dog in a kennel while gone	$40
(k)	Benefit of having a car available in New York City	?
(l)	Hassle of parking the car in New York City	?
(m)	Cost of parking the car in New York City	$25 per day

Which costs and benefits are relevant in this decision? Remember, only those costs and benefits that differ between alternatives are relevant. Everything else is irrelevant and can be ignored.

Start at the top of the list with item (a): the original cost of the car is a sunk cost. This cost has already been incurred and therefore can never differ between alternatives. Consequently, it is irrelevant and should be ignored. The same is true of the accounting depreciation of $2,800 per year, which simply spreads the sunk cost across five years.

Item (b), the cost of gasoline consumed by driving to New York City, is a relevant cost. If Cynthia takes the train, this cost would not be incurred. Hence, the cost differs between alternatives and is therefore relevant.

Item (c), the annual cost of auto insurance and license, is not relevant. Whether Cynthia takes the train or drives on this particular trip, her annual auto insurance premium and her auto license fee will remain the same.[2]

---

[2] If Cynthia has an accident while driving to New York City or back, this might affect her insurance premium when the policy is renewed. The increase in the insurance premium would be a relevant cost of this particular trip, but the normal amount of the insurance premium is not relevant in any case.

Item (d), the cost of maintenance and repairs, is relevant. While maintenance and repair costs have a large random component, over the long run they should be more or less proportional to the number of miles the car is driven. Thus, the average cost of $0.065 per mile is a reasonable estimate to use.

Item (e), the monthly fee that Cynthia pays to park at her school during the academic year is not relevant. Regardless of which alternative she selects—driving or taking the train—she will still need to pay for parking at school.

Item (f) is the total average cost of $0.619 per mile. As discussed above, some elements of this total are relevant, but some are not relevant. Because it contains some irrelevant costs, it would be incorrect to estimate the cost of driving to New York City and back by simply multiplying the $0.619 by 460 miles (230 miles each way × 2). This erroneous approach would yield a cost of driving of $284.74. Unfortunately, such mistakes are often made in both personal life and in business. Because the total cost is stated on a per-mile basis, people are easily misled. Often people think that if the cost is stated as $0.619 per mile, the cost of driving 100 miles is $61.90. But it is not. Many of the costs included in the $0.619 cost per mile are sunk and/or fixed and will not increase if the car is driven another 100 miles. The $0.619 is an average cost, not an incremental cost. Beware of such unitized costs (i.e., costs stated in terms of a dollar amount per unit, per mile, per direct labor-hour, per machine-hour, and so on)—they are often misleading.

Item (g), the decline in the resale value of the car that occurs as a consequence of driving more miles, is relevant in the decision. Because she uses the car, its resale value declines, which is a real cost of using the car that should be taken into account. Cynthia estimated this cost by accessing the *Kelly Blue Book* website at www.kbb.com. The reduction in resale value of an asset through use or over time is often called *real* or *economic depreciation*. This is different from accounting depreciation, which attempts to match the sunk cost of an asset with the periods that benefit from that cost.

Item (h), the $104 cost of a round-trip ticket on the train, is relevant in this decision. If she drives, she would not have to buy the ticket.

Item (i) is relevant to the decision, even if it is difficult to put a dollar value on relaxing and being able to study while on the train. It is relevant because it is a benefit that is available under one alternative but not under the other.

Item (j), the cost of putting Cynthia's dog in the kennel while she is gone, is irrelevant in this decision. Whether she takes the train or drives to New York City, she will still need to put her dog in a kennel.

Like item (i), items (k) and (l) are relevant to the decision even if it is difficult to measure their dollar impacts.

Item (m), the cost of parking in New York City, is relevant to the decision.

Bringing together all of the relevant data, Cynthia would estimate the relevant costs of driving and taking the train as follows:

Relevant financial cost of driving to New York City:

Gasoline (460 miles × $0.100 per mile)	$ 46.00
Maintenance and repairs (460 miles × $0.065 per mile)	29.90
Reduction in the resale value of car due solely to wear and tear (460 miles × $0.026 per mile)	11.96
Cost of parking the car in New York City (2 days × $25 per day)	50.00
Total	$137.86

Relevant financial cost of taking the train to New York City:

Cost of round-trip train ticket from Boston to New York City	$104.00

What should Cynthia do? From a purely financial standpoint, it would be cheaper by $33.86 ($137.86 − $104.00) to take the train than to drive. Cynthia has to decide if the convenience of having a car in New York City outweighs the additional cost and the disadvantages of being unable to relax and study on the train and the hassle of finding parking in the city.

In this example, we focused on identifying the relevant costs and benefits—everything else was ignored. In the next example, we include all of the costs and benefits—relevant or not. Nonetheless, we'll still get the correct answer because the irrelevant costs and benefits will cancel out when we compare the alternatives.

IN BUSINESS

UNDERSTANDING THE IMPORTANCE OF QUALITATIVE FACTORS

SAS is a privately held $2.26 billion company located on a 200-acre campus in Cary, North Carolina. The company has an on-site medical facility (including a lab for blood tests) that is staffed by doctors, nurse practitioners, physical therapists, and a nutritionist. The company also has an infant day care, a Montessori school, a hair salon, a dry cleaning shop, a fitness center, and jogging and biking trails on campus. Employees that use the day care pay $360 per month per child for the service and SAS covers the remaining $720 per month per child that it costs to retain 120 teachers and staffers.

Although it may be difficult to quantify the benefits of these investments, SAS firmly believes that retaining happy and healthy employees is instrumental to its success. Mary Simmons, a SAS software developer says, "At lunch I will go out and bike 20 miles. Then I'll get back and all of a sudden a thought comes to my brain, and I solve something I was struggling with."

Source: Christopher Tkaczyk, "Offer Affordable (Awesome) Day Care," *Fortune*, August 17, 2009, p. 26.

Reconciling the Total and Differential Approaches

Oak Harbor Woodworks is considering a new labor-saving machine that rents for $3,000 per year. The machine will be used on the company's butcher block production line. Data concerning the company's annual sales and costs of butcher blocks with and without the new machine are shown below:

	Current Situation	Situation with the New Machine
Units produced and sold	5,000	5,000
Selling price per unit	$40	$40
Direct materials cost per unit	$14	$14
Direct labor cost per unit	$8	$5
Variable overhead cost per unit	$2	$2
Fixed expenses, other	$62,000	$62,000
Fixed expenses, rental of new machine	—	$3,000

Given the data above, the net operating income for the product under the two alternatives can be computed as shown in Exhibit 12–1.

Note that the net operating income is $12,000 higher with the new machine, so that is the better alternative. Note also that the $12,000 advantage for the new machine can be obtained in two different ways. It is the difference between the $30,000 net operating income with the new machine and the $18,000 net operating income for the current situation. It is also the sum of the differential costs and benefits as shown in the last column of Exhibit 12–1($15,000 + $(3,000) = $12,000). A positive number in the Differential Costs and Benefits column indicates that the difference between the alternatives favors the new machine; a negative number indicates that the difference favors the current situation. A zero in that column simply means that the total amount for the item is exactly the same for both alternatives. Thus, because the difference in the net operating incomes equals the sum of the differences for the individual items, any cost or benefit that is the same for both

	Current Situation	Situation with New Machine	Differential Costs and Benefits
Sales (5,000 units × $40 per unit)	$200,000	$200,000	$ 0
Variable expenses:			
Direct materials (5,000 units × $14 per unit)	70,000	70,000	0
Direct labor (5,000 units × $8 per unit; 5,000 units × $5 per unit)	40,000	25,000	15,000
Variable overhead (5,000 units × $2 per unit)	10,000	10,000	0
Total variable expenses	120,000	105,000	
Contribution margin	80,000	95,000	
Fixed expenses:			
Other	62,000	62,000	0
Rental of new machine	0	3,000	(3,000)
Total fixed expenses	62,000	65,000	
Net operating income	$ 18,000	$ 30,000	$12,000

EXHIBIT 12–1
Total and Differential Costs

alternatives will have no impact on which alternative is preferred. This is the reason that costs and benefits that do not differ between alternatives are irrelevant and can be ignored. If we properly account for them, they will cancel out when we compare the alternatives.

We could have arrived at the same solution much more quickly by completely ignoring the irrelevant costs and benefits.

- The selling price per unit and the number of units sold do not differ between the alternatives. Therefore, the total sales revenues are exactly the same for the two alternatives as shown in Exhibit 12–1. Because the sales revenues are exactly the same, they have no effect on the difference in net operating income between the two alternatives. That is shown in the last column in Exhibit 12–1, which shows a $0 differential benefit.
- The direct materials cost per unit, the variable overhead cost per unit, and the number of units produced and sold do not differ between the alternatives. Consequently, the total direct materials cost and the total variable overhead cost are the same for the two alternatives and can be ignored.
- The "other" fixed expenses do not differ between the alternatives, so they can be ignored as well.

Indeed, the only costs that do differ between the alternatives are direct labor costs and the fixed rental cost of the new machine. Hence, the two alternatives can be compared based only on these relevant costs:

Net Advantage of Renting the New Machine	
Decrease in direct labor costs (5,000 units at a cost savings of $3 per unit)	$15,000
Increase in fixed expenses	(3,000)
Net annual cost savings from renting the new machine	$12,000

If we focus on just the relevant costs and benefits, we get exactly the same answer as when we listed all of the costs and benefits—including those that do not differ between the alternatives and, hence, are irrelevant. We get the same answer because the only costs and benefits that matter in the final comparison of the net operating incomes are those that differ between the two alternatives and, hence, are not zero in the last column of Exhibit 12–1. Those two relevant costs are both included in the above analysis that quantifies the net advantage of renting the new machine.

Why Isolate Relevant Costs?

In the preceding example, we used two different approaches to analyze the alternatives. First, we considered all costs, both those that were relevant and those that were not; and second, we considered only the relevant costs. We obtained the same answer under both approaches. It would be natural to ask, "Why bother to isolate relevant costs when total costs will do the job just as well?" Isolating relevant costs is desirable for at least two reasons.

First, only rarely will enough information be available to prepare a detailed income statement for both alternatives. Assume, for example, that you are called on to make a decision relating to a portion of a single business process in a multidepartmental, multiproduct company. Under these circumstances, it would be virtually impossible to prepare an income statement of any type. You would have to rely on your ability to recognize which costs are relevant and which are not in order to assemble the data necessary to make a decision.

Second, mingling irrelevant costs with relevant costs may cause confusion and distract attention from the information that is really critical. Furthermore, the danger always exists that an irrelevant piece of data may be used improperly, resulting in an incorrect decision. The best approach is to ignore irrelevant data and base the decision entirely on relevant data.

Relevant cost analysis, combined with the contribution approach to the income statement, provides a powerful tool for making decisions. We will investigate various uses of this tool in the remaining sections of this chapter.

Adding and Dropping Product Lines and Other Segments

LO12–2
Prepare an analysis showing whether a product line or other business segment should be added or dropped.

Decisions relating to whether product lines or other segments of a company should be dropped and new ones added are among the most difficult that a manager has to make. In such decisions, many qualitative and quantitative factors must be considered. Ultimately, however, any final decision to drop a business segment or to add a new one hinges primarily on the impact the decision will have on net operating income. To assess this impact, costs must be carefully analyzed.

An Illustration of Cost Analysis

Exhibit 12–2 provides sales and cost information for the preceding month for the Discount Drug Company and its three major product lines—drugs, cosmetics, and housewares. A quick review of this exhibit suggests that dropping the housewares segment would increase the company's overall net operating income by $8,000. However, this would be a flawed conclusion because the data in Exhibit 12–2 do not distinguish between fixed expenses that can be avoided if a product line is dropped and common fixed expenses that cannot be avoided by dropping any particular product line.

In this scenario, the two alternatives under consideration are keeping the housewares product line and dropping the housewares product line. Therefore, only those costs that differ between these two alternatives (i.e., that can be avoided by dropping the housewares product line) are relevant. In deciding whether to drop housewares, it is crucial to identify which costs can be avoided, and hence are relevant to the decision, and which costs cannot be avoided, and hence are irrelevant. The decision should be analyzed as follows.

	Total	Product Line		
		Drugs	Cosmetics	House-wares
Sales	$250,000	$125,000	$75,000	$50,000
Variable expenses	105,000	50,000	25,000	30,000
Contribution margin	145,000	75,000	50,000	20,000
Fixed expenses:				
Salaries	50,000	29,500	12,500	8,000
Advertising	15,000	1,000	7,500	6,500
Utilities	2,000	500	500	1,000
Depreciation—fixtures	5,000	1,000	2,000	2,000
Rent	20,000	10,000	6,000	4,000
Insurance	3,000	2,000	500	500
General administrative	30,000	15,000	9,000	6,000
Total fixed expenses	125,000	59,000	38,000	28,000
Net operating income (loss)	$ 20,000	$ 16,000	$12,000	$ (8,000)

EXHIBIT 12–2
Discount Drug Company
Product Lines

If the housewares line is dropped, then the company will lose $20,000 per month in contribution margin, but by dropping the line it may be possible to avoid some fixed costs such as salaries or advertising costs. If dropping the housewares line enables the company to avoid more in fixed costs than it loses in contribution margin, then its overall net operating income will improve by eliminating the product line. On the other hand, if the company is not able to avoid as much in fixed costs as it loses in contribution margin, then the housewares line should be kept. In short, the manager should ask, "What costs can I avoid if I drop this product line?"

As we have seen from our earlier discussion, not all costs are avoidable. For example, some of the costs associated with a product line may be sunk costs. Other costs may be allocated fixed costs that will not differ in total regardless of whether the product line is dropped or retained.

To show how to proceed in a product-line analysis, suppose that Discount Drug Company has analyzed the fixed costs being charged to the three product lines and determined the following:

1. The salaries expense represents salaries paid to employees working directly on the product. All of the employees working in housewares would be discharged if the product line is dropped.
2. The advertising expense represents advertisements that are specific to each product line and are avoidable if the line is dropped.
3. The utilities expense represents utilities costs for the entire company. The amount charged to each product line is an allocation based on space occupied and is not avoidable if the product line is dropped.
4. The depreciation expense represents depreciation on fixtures used to display the various product lines. Although the fixtures are nearly new, they are custom-built and will have no resale value if the housewares line is dropped.
5. The rent expense represents rent on the entire building housing the company; it is allocated to the product lines on the basis of sales dollars. The monthly rent of $20,000 is fixed under a long-term lease agreement.
6. The insurance expense is for insurance carried on inventories within each of the three product lines. If housewares is dropped, the related inventories will be liquidated and the insurance premiums will decrease proportionately.
7. The general administrative expense represents the costs of accounting, purchasing, and general management, which are allocated to the product lines on the basis of sales dollars. These costs will not change if the housewares line is dropped.

With this information, management can determine that $15,000 of the fixed expenses associated with the housewares product line are avoidable and $13,000 are not:

Fixed Expenses	Total Cost Assigned to Housewares	Not Avoidable*	Avoidable
Salaries	$ 8,000		$ 8,000
Advertising	6,500		6,500
Utilities	1,000	$ 1,000	
Depreciation—fixtures	2,000	2,000	
Rent	4,000	4,000	
Insurance	500		500
General administrative	6,000	6,000	
Total	$28,000	$13,000	$15,000

*These fixed costs represent either sunk costs or future costs that will not change whether the housewares line is retained or discontinued.

As stated earlier, if the housewares product line were dropped, the company would lose the product's contribution margin of $20,000, but would save its associated avoidable fixed expenses. We now know that those avoidable fixed expenses total $15,000. Therefore, dropping the housewares product line would result in a $5,000 *reduction* in net operating income as shown below:

Contribution margin lost if the housewares line is discontinued (see Exhibit 12–2)	$(20,000)
Fixed expenses that can be avoided if the housewares line is discontinued (see above)	15,000
Decrease in overall company net operating income	$ (5,000)

In this case, the fixed costs that can be avoided by dropping the housewares product line ($15,000) are less than the contribution margin that will be lost ($20,000). Therefore, based on the data given, the housewares line should not be discontinued unless a more profitable use can be found for the floor and counter space that it is occupying.

A Comparative Format

This decision can also be approached by preparing comparative income statements showing the effects of either keeping or dropping the product line. Exhibit 12–3 contains such an analysis for the Discount Drug Company. As shown in the last column of the exhibit, if the housewares line is dropped, then overall company net operating income will decrease by $5,000 each period. This is the same answer, of course, as we obtained when we focused just on the lost contribution margin and avoidable fixed costs.

Beware of Allocated Fixed Costs

Go back to Exhibit 12–2. Does this exhibit suggest that the housewares product line should be kept—as we have just concluded? No, it does not. Exhibit 12–2 suggests that the housewares product line is losing money. Why keep a product line that is showing a loss? The explanation for this apparent inconsistency lies in part with the common fixed costs that are being allocated to the product lines. One of the great dangers in allocating common fixed costs is that such allocations can make a product line (or other business segment) look less profitable than it really is. In this instance, allocating the common fixed costs among all product lines makes the housewares product line appear to be unprofitable. However, as we have just shown, dropping the product line would

	Keep Housewares	Drop Housewares	Difference: Net Operating Income Increase (or Decrease)
Sales	$50,000	$ 0	$(50,000)
Variable expenses	30,000	0	30,000
Contribution margin	20,000	0	(20,000)
Fixed expenses:			
Salaries	8,000	0	8,000
Advertising	6,500	0	6,500
Utilities	1,000	1,000	0
Depreciation—fixtures	2,000	2,000	0
Rent	4,000	4,000	0
Insurance	500	0	500
General administrative	6,000	6,000	0
Total fixed expenses	28,000	13,000	15,000
Net operating loss	$ (8,000)	$(13,000)	$ (5,000)

result in a decrease in the company's overall net operating income. This point can be seen clearly if we redo Exhibit 12–2 by eliminating the allocation of the common fixed costs. Exhibit 12–4 uses the segmented approach from Chapter 6 to estimate the profitability of the product lines.

Exhibit 12–4 gives us a much different perspective of the housewares line than does Exhibit 12–2. As shown in Exhibit 12–4, the housewares line is covering all of its own traceable fixed costs and generating a $3,000 segment margin toward covering the common fixed costs of the company. Unless another product line can be found that will generate a segment margin greater than $3,000, the company would be better off keeping the housewares line. By keeping the product line, the company's overall net operating income will be higher than if the product line were dropped.

Additionally, managers may choose to retain an unprofitable product line if the line helps sell other products, or if it serves as a "magnet" to attract customers. Bread, for example, may not be an especially profitable line in some food stores, but customers expect it to be available, and many of them would undoubtedly shift their buying elsewhere if a particular store decided to stop carrying it.

IN BUSINESS

POOR ECONOMY LEADS TO SEGMENT DISCONTINUATIONS

When the economy declines, many companies must decide whether to retain or discontinue struggling products and services. For example, Condé Nast Publications reacted to a steep drop in advertising revenues by cutting 180 jobs and discontinuing four magazines—*Gourmet, Modern Bride, Elegant Bride,* and *Cookie.* It also cut the budgets of its remaining magazines by 20–25%. Pioneer Corp.'s annual plasma television sales dropped from 460,000 units to 290,000 units. The company responded to its shrinking customer demand by cutting thousands of jobs and withdrawing from the plasma television business.

Sources: Russell Adams, "Ax Falls on Four Condé Nast Titles," *The Wall Street Journal,* October 6, 2009, p. B1; and Daisuke Wakabayashi, "Pioneer Unplugs Its TV Business," *The Wall Street Journal,* February 13, 2009, p. B1.

EXHIBIT 12-4
Discount Drug Company Product Lines—Recast in Contribution Format (from Exhibit 12-2)

		Product Line		
	Total	Drugs	Cosmetics	House-wares
Sales	$250,000	$125,000	$75,000	$50,000
Variable expenses	105,000	50,000	25,000	30,000
Contribution margin	145,000	75,000	50,000	20,000
Traceable fixed expenses:				
Salaries	50,000	29,500	12,500	8,000
Advertising	15,000	1,000	7,500	6,500
Depreciation—fixtures	5,000	1,000	2,000	2,000
Insurance	3,000	2,000	500	500
Total traceable fixed expenses ...	73,000	33,500	22,500	17,000
Product-line segment margin	72,000	$ 41,500	$27,500	$ 3,000*
Common fixed expenses:				
Utilities	2,000			
Rent	20,000			
General administrative	30,000			
Total common fixed expenses	52,000			
Net operating income	$ 20,000			

*If the housewares line is dropped, the company will lose the $3,000 segment margin generated by this product line. In addition, we have seen that the $2,000 depreciation on the fixtures is a sunk cost that cannot be avoided. The sum of these two figures ($3,000 + $2,000 = $5,000) would be the decrease in the company's overall profits if the housewares line were discontinued. Of course, the company may later choose to drop the product if circumstances change—such as a pending decision to replace the fixtures.

The Make or Buy Decision

LO12-3
Prepare a make or buy analysis.

Providing a product or service to a customer involves many steps. For example, consider all of the steps that are necessary to develop and sell a product such as tax preparation software in retail stores. First the software must be developed, which involves highly skilled software engineers and a great deal of project management effort. Then the product must be put into a form that can be delivered to customers. This involves burning the application onto a blank CD or DVD, applying a label, and packaging the result in an attractive box. Then the product must be distributed to retail stores. Then the product must be sold. And finally, help lines and other forms of after-sale service may have to be provided. And we should not forget that the blank CD or DVD, the label, and the box must of course be made by someone before any of this can happen. All of these activities, from development, to production, to after-sales service are called a *value chain*.

Separate companies may carry out each of the activities in the value chain or a single company may carry out several. When a company is involved in more than one activity in the entire value chain, it is **vertically integrated**. Some companies control all of the activities in the value chain from producing basic raw materials right up to the final distribution of finished goods and provision of after-sales service. Other companies are content to integrate on a smaller scale by purchasing many of the parts and materials that go into their finished products. A decision to carry out one of the activities in the value chain internally, rather than to buy externally from a supplier, is called a **make or buy decision**. Quite often these decisions involve whether to buy a particular part or to make it internally. Make or buy decisions also involve decisions concerning whether to out-source development tasks, after-sales service, or other activities.

Strategic Aspects of the Make or Buy Decision

Vertical integration provides certain advantages. An integrated company is less dependent on its suppliers and may be able to ensure a smoother flow of parts and materials for pro-duction than a nonintegrated company. For example, a strike against a major parts sup-plier can interrupt the operations of a nonintegrated company for many months, whereas an integrated company that is producing its own parts would be able to continue opera-tions. Also, some companies feel that they can control quality better by producing their own parts and materials, rather than by relying on the quality control standards of outside suppliers. In addition, an integrated company realizes profits from the parts and materi-als that it is "making" rather than "buying," as well as profits from its regular operations.

The advantages of vertical integration are counterbalanced by the advantages of using external suppliers. By pooling demand from a number of companies, a supplier may be able to enjoy economies of scale. These economies of scale can result in higher quality and lower costs than would be possible if the company were to attempt to make the parts or provide the service on its own. A company must be careful, however, to retain control over activities that are essential to maintaining its competitive position. For example, **Hewlett-Packard** controls the software for laser printers that it makes in coop-eration with **Canon Inc.** of Japan. The present trend appears to be toward less vertical integration, with companies like **Oracle** and Hewlett-Packard concentrating on hardware and software design and relying on outside suppliers for almost everything else in the value chain.

An Example of Make or Buy

To provide an illustration of a make or buy decision, consider Mountain Goat Cycles. The company is now producing the heavy-duty gear shifters used in its most popular line of mountain bikes. The company's Accounting Department reports the following costs of producing 8,000 units of the shifter internally each year:

	Per Unit	8,000 Units
Direct materials	$ 6	$ 48,000
Direct labor	4	32,000
Variable overhead	1	8,000
Supervisor's salary	3	24,000
Depreciation of special equipment	2	16,000
Allocated general overhead	5	40,000
Total cost	$21	$168,000

An outside supplier has offered to sell 8,000 shifters a year to Mountain Goat Cycles for a price of only $19 each, or a total of $152,000 (= 8,000 shifters × $19 each). Should the company stop producing the shifters internally and buy them from the outside sup-plier? As always, the focus should be on the relevant costs—those that differ between the alternatives. And the costs that differ between the alternatives consist of the costs that could be avoided by purchasing the shifters from the outside supplier. If the costs that can be avoided by purchasing the shifters from the outside supplier total less than $152,000, then the company should continue to manufacture its own shifters and reject the outside supplier's offer. On the other hand, if the costs that can be avoided by purchasing the shifters from the outside supplier total more than $152,000 the outside supplier's offer should be accepted.

IN BUSINESS

OUTSOURCING TASKS RATHER THAN JOBS

Pfizer saved 4,000 of its managers 66,500 hours of work by enabling them to outsource their tedious, time-consuming tasks to companies in India. With the click of a mouse the managers go to a website called PfizerWorks to prepare online work orders for services such as Powerpoint slide preparation, spreadsheet preparation, or basic market research. The requests are sent overseas and completed by a services-outsourcing firm. This outsourcing enables Pfizer's managers to spend their time on higher value work such as motivating teams, creating new products, and strategy formulation.

Source: Jena McGregor, "The Chore Goes Offshore," *BusinessWeek*, March 23 & 30, 2009, p. 50–51.

Note that depreciation of special equipment is listed as one of the costs of producing the shifters internally. Because the equipment has already been purchased, this depreciation is a sunk cost and is therefore irrelevant. If the equipment could be sold, its salvage value would be relevant. Or if the machine could be used to make other products, this could be relevant as well. However, we will assume that the equipment has no salvage value and that it has no other use except making the heavy-duty gear shifters.

Also note that the company is allocating a portion of its general overhead costs to the shifters. Any portion of this general overhead cost that would actually be eliminated if the gear shifters were purchased rather than made would be relevant in the analysis. However, it is likely that the general overhead costs allocated to the gear shifters are in fact common to all items produced in the factory and would continue unchanged even if the shifters were purchased from the outside. Such allocated common costs are not relevant costs (because they do not differ between the make or buy alternatives) and should be eliminated from the analysis along with the sunk costs.

The variable costs of producing the shifters can be avoided by buying the shifters from the outside supplier so they are relevant costs. We will assume in this case that the variable costs include direct materials, direct labor, and variable overhead. The supervisor's salary is also relevant if it could be avoided by buying the shifters. Exhibit 12–5 contains the relevant cost analysis of the make or buy decision assuming that the supervisor's salary can indeed be avoided.

Because the avoidable costs related to making the shifters is $40,000 less than the total amount that would be paid to buy them from the outside supplier, Mountain Goat Cycles should reject the outside supplier's offer. However, the company may wish to consider one additional factor before coming to a final decision—the opportunity cost of the space now being used to produce the shifters.

EXHIBIT 12–5
Mountain Goat Cycles Make or Buy Analysis

	Total Relevant Costs—8,000 units	
	Make	Buy
Direct materials (8,000 units × $6 per unit)	$ 48,000	
Direct labor (8,000 units × $4 per unit)	32,000	
Variable overhead (8,000 units × $1 per unit)	8,000	
Supervisor's salary	24,000	
Depreciation of special equipment (not relevant)		
Allocated general overhead (not relevant)		
Outside purchase price		$152,000
Total cost	$112,000	$152,000
Difference in favor of continuing to make	$40,000	

Opportunity Cost

If the space now being used to produce the shifters *would otherwise be idle*, then Mountain Goat Cycles should continue to produce its own shifters and the supplier's offer should be rejected, as stated above. Idle space that has no alternative use has an opportunity cost of zero.

But what if the space now being used to produce shifters could be used for some other purpose? In that case, the space would have an opportunity cost equal to the segment margin that could be derived from the best alternative use of the space.

To illustrate, assume that the space now being used to produce shifters could be used to produce a new cross-country bike that would generate a segment margin of $60,000 per year. Under these conditions, Mountain Goat Cycles should accept the supplier's offer and use the available space to produce the new product line:

	Make	Buy
Total annual cost (see Exhibit 12–5)	$112,000	$152,000
Opportunity cost—segment margin forgone on a potential new product line	60,000	
Total cost	$172,000	$152,000
Difference in favor of purchasing from the outside supplier		$20,000

Opportunity costs are not recorded in the organization's general ledger because they do not represent actual dollar outlays. Rather, they represent economic benefits that are *forgone* as a result of pursuing some course of action. The opportunity cost for Mountain Goat Cycles is sufficiently large in this case to change the decision.

IS THERE SUCH A THING AS A $1 BUS TICKET?

When Megabus and Greyhound's Bolt Bus sell tickets for $1 it begs the question—how can that be profitable? The answer lies in understanding the concept of opportunity costs. The bus companies use computer algorithms to determine how many empty seats ordinarily exist on a given bus route. Since the incremental cost of allowing a customer to occupy a seat that would otherwise be empty is zero, the $1 price provides bus companies with additional contribution margin. Of course, only a few $1 tickets are available for each trip on a given bus route. Furthermore, these deeply discounted tickets must be purchased well in advance of the travel date. All other customers pay a higher fare that enables the bus company to earn a profit on its routes.

Source: Anne VanderMey, "What's Up With $1 Bus Tickets?" *Fortune*, November 7, 2011, p. 27.

Special Orders

LO12–4
Prepare an analysis showing whether a special order should be accepted.

Managers must often evaluate whether a *special order* should be accepted, and if the order is accepted, the price that should be charged. A **special order** is a one-time order that is not considered part of the company's normal ongoing business. To illustrate, Mountain Goat Cycles has just received a request from the Seattle Police Department to produce 100 specially modified mountain bikes at a price of $558 each. The bikes would

Chapter 12

be used to patrol some of the more densely populated residential sections of the city. Mountain Goat Cycles can easily modify its City Cruiser model to fit the specifications of the Seattle Police. The normal selling price of the City Cruiser bike is $698, and its unit product cost is $564 as shown below:

Direct materials	$372
Direct labor	90
Manufacturing overhead	102
Unit product cost	$564

The variable portion of the above manufacturing overhead is $12 per unit. The order would have no effect on the company's total fixed manufacturing overhead costs.

The modifications requested by the Seattle Police Department consist of welded brackets to hold radios, nightsticks, and other gear. These modifications would require $34 in incremental variable costs. In addition, the company would have to pay a graphics design studio $2,400 to design and cut stencils that would be used for spray painting the Seattle Police Department's logo and other identifying marks on the bikes.

This order should have no effect on the company's other sales. The production manager says that she can handle the special order without disrupting any of the company's regular scheduled production.

What effect would accepting this order have on the company's net operating income?

Only the incremental costs and benefits are relevant. Because the existing fixed manufacturing overhead costs would not be affected by the order, they are not relevant. The incremental net operating income can be computed as follows:

	Per Unit	Total 100 Bikes
Incremental revenue	$558	$55,800
Less incremental costs:		
Variable costs:		
Direct materials	372	37,200
Direct labor	90	9,000
Variable manufacturing overhead	12	1,200
Special modifications	34	3,400
Total variable cost	$508	50,800
Fixed cost:		
Purchase of stencils		2,400
Total incremental cost		53,200
Incremental net operating income		$ 2,600

Therefore, even though the $558 price on the special order is below the normal $564 unit product cost and the order would require additional costs, the order would increase net operating income. In general, a special order is profitable if the incremental revenue from the special order exceeds the incremental costs of the order. However, it is important to make sure that there is indeed idle capacity and that the special order does not cut into normal unit sales or undercut prices on normal sales. For example, if the company was operating at capacity, opportunity costs would have to be taken into account, as well as the incremental costs that have already been detailed above.

Utilization of a Constrained Resource

What Is a Constraint?

A **constraint** is anything that prevents you from getting more of what you want. Every individual and every organization faces at least one constraint, so it is not difficult to find examples of constraints. You may not have enough time to study thoroughly for every subject *and* to go out with your friends on the weekend, so time is your constraint. United Airlines has only a limited number of loading gates available at its busy Chicago O'Hare hub, so its constraint is loading gates. Vail Resorts has only a limited amount of land to develop as homesites and commercial lots at its ski areas, so its constraint is land.

As an example, long waiting periods for surgery are a chronic problem in the National Health Service (NHS), the government-funded provider of health care in the United Kingdom. The diagram in Exhibit 12–6 illustrates a simplified version of the steps followed by a surgery patient. The number of patients who can be processed through each step in a day is indicated in the exhibit. For example, appointments for outpatient visits can be made for as many as 100 referrals from general practitioners in a day.

The constraint, or **bottleneck**, in the system is determined by the step that limits total output because it has the smallest capacity—in this case surgery. The total number of patients processed through the entire system cannot exceed 15 per day—the maximum number of patients who can be treated in surgery. No matter how hard managers, doctors, and nurses try to improve the processing rate elsewhere in the system, they will never succeed in driving down wait lists until the capacity of surgery is increased. In fact, improvements elsewhere in the system—particularly before the constraint—are likely to result in even longer waiting times and more frustrated patients and health care providers. Thus, to be effective, improvement efforts must be focused on the constraint. A business process, such as the process for serving surgery patients, is like a chain. If you want to increase the strength of a chain, what is the most effective way to do this? Should you concentrate your efforts on strengthening the strongest link, all the links, or the weakest link? Clearly, focusing your effort on the weakest link will bring the biggest benefit.

The procedure to follow to strengthen the chain is clear. First, identify the weakest link, which is the constraint. In the case of the NHS, the constraint is surgery. Second, do not place a greater strain on the system than the weakest link can handle—if you do, the chain will break. In the case of the NHS, more referrals than surgery can accommodate lead to unacceptably long waiting lists. Third, concentrate improvement efforts on strengthening the weakest link. In the case of the NHS, this means finding ways to increase the number of surgeries that can be performed in a day. Fourth, if the improvement efforts are successful, eventually the weakest link will improve to the point where it is no longer the weakest link. At that point, the new weakest link (i.e., the new constraint) must be identified, and improvement efforts must be shifted over to that link. This simple sequential process provides a powerful strategy for optimizing business processes.

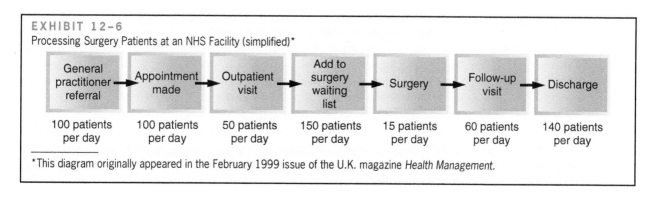

EXHIBIT 12–6
Processing Surgery Patients at an NHS Facility (simplified)*

General practitioner referral	Appointment made	Outpatient visit	Add to surgery waiting list	Surgery	Follow-up visit	Discharge
100 patients per day	100 patients per day	50 patients per day	150 patients per day	15 patients per day	60 patients per day	140 patients per day

*This diagram originally appeared in the February 1999 issue of the U.K. magazine *Health Management*.

548

Chapter 12

Contribution Margin per Unit of the Constrained Resource

Managers routinely face the problem of deciding how constrained resources are going to be used. A department store, for example, has a limited amount of floor space and therefore cannot stock every product that may be available. A manufacturer has a limited number of machine-hours and a limited number of direct labor-hours at its disposal. Because the company cannot fully satisfy demand, managers must decide which products or services should be cut back. In other words, managers must decide which products or services make the best use of the constrained resource. Fixed costs are usually unaffected by such choices, so the course of action that will maximize the company's total contribution margin should ordinarily be selected.

If some products must be cut back because of a constraint, the key to maximizing the total contribution margin may seem obvious—favor the products with the highest unit contribution margins. Unfortunately, that is not quite correct. Rather, the correct solution is to favor the products that provide the highest *contribution margin per unit of the constrained resource*. To illustrate, in addition to its other products, Mountain Goat Cycles makes saddlebags for bicycles called *panniers*. These panniers come in two models—a touring model and a mountain model. Cost and revenue data for the two models of panniers follow:

	Mountain Pannier	Touring Pannier
Selling price per unit	$25	$30
Variable cost per unit	10	18
Contribution margin per unit	$15	$12
Contribution margin (CM) ratio	60%	40%

The mountain pannier appears to be much more profitable than the touring pannier. It has a $15 per unit contribution margin as compared to only $12 per unit for the touring model, and it has a 60% CM ratio as compared to only 40% for the touring model.

But now let us add one more piece of information—the plant that makes the panniers is operating at capacity. This does not mean that every machine and every person in the plant is working at the maximum possible rate. Because machines have different capacities, some machines will be operating at less than 100% of capacity. However, if the plant as a whole cannot produce any more units, some machine or process must be operating at capacity. The machine or process that is limiting overall output is called the bottleneck—it is the constraint.

At Mountain Goat Cycles, the bottleneck (i.e., constraint) is a stitching machine. The mountain pannier requires two minutes of stitching time per unit, and the touring pannier requires one minute of stitching time per unit. The stitching machine is available for 12,000 minutes per month, and the company can sell up to 4,000 mountain panniers and 7,000 touring panniers per month. Producing up to this demand for both products would require 15,000 minutes, as shown below:

	Mountain Pannier	Touring Pannier	Total
Monthly demand (a)	4,000 units	7,000 units	
Stitching machine time required to produce one unit (b)	2 minutes	1 minute	
Total stitching time required (a) × (b)	8,000 minutes	7,000 minutes	15,000 minutes

Producing up to demand would require 15,000 minutes, but only 12,000 minutes are available. This simply confirms that the stitching machine is the bottleneck. By definition, because the stitching machine is a bottleneck, the stitching machine does not have enough capacity to satisfy the existing demand for mountain panniers and touring panniers Therefore, some orders for the products will have to be turned down. Naturally, managers will want to know which product is less profitable. To answer this question, they should focus on the contribution margin per unit of the constrained resource. This figure is computed by dividing a product's contribution margin per unit by the amount of the constrained resource required to make a unit of that product. These calculations are carried out below for the mountain and touring panniers:

	Mountain Pannier	Touring Pannier
Contribution margin per unit (a)	$15.00	$12.00
Stitching machine time required to produce one unit (b)	2 minutes	1 minute
Contribution margin per unit of the constrained resource, (a) ÷ (b)	$7.50 per minute	$12.00 per minute

It is now easy to decide which product is less profitable and should be deemphasized. Each minute on the stitching machine that is devoted to the touring pannier results in an increase of $12.00 in contribution margin and profits. The comparable figure for the mountain pannier is only $7.50 per minute. Therefore, the touring model should be emphasized. Even though the mountain model has the larger contribution margin per unit and the larger CM ratio, the touring model provides the larger contribution margin in relation to the constrained resource.

To verify that the touring model is indeed the more profitable product, suppose an hour of additional stitching time is available and that unfilled orders exist for both products. The additional hour on the stitching machine could be used to make either 30 mountain panniers (60 minutes ÷ 2 minutes per mountain pannier) or 60 touring panniers (60 minutes ÷ 1 minute per touring pannier), with the following profit implications:

	Mountain Pannier	Touring Pannier
Contribution margin per unit	$ 15	$ 12
Additional units that can be processed in one hour	× 30	× 60
Additional contribution margin	$450	$720

Because the additional contribution margin would be $720 for the touring panniers and only $450 for the mountain panniers, the touring panniers make the most profitable use of the company's constrained resource—the stitching machine.

The stitching machine is available for 12,000 minutes per month, and producing the touring panniers is the most profitable use of the stitching machine. Therefore, to maximize profits, the company should produce all of the touring panniers the market will demand (7,000 units) and use any remaining capacity to produce mountain panniers. The computations to determine how many mountain panniers can be produced are as follows:

Monthly demand for touring panniers (a)	7,000 units
Stitching machine time required to produce one touring pannier (b)	1 minute
Total stitching time required to produce touring panniers (a) × (b)	7,000 minutes
Remaining stitching time available (12,000 minutes − 7,000 minutes) (c)	5,000 minutes
Stitching machine time required to produce one mountain pannier (d)	2 minutes
Production of mountain panniers (c) ÷ (d)	2,500 units

Therefore, profit would be maximized by producing 7,000 touring panniers and then using the remaining capacity to produce 2,500 mountain panniers.

This example clearly shows that looking at each product's unit contribution margin alone is not enough; the contribution margin must be viewed in relation to the amount of the constrained resource each product requires.

BOEING IS CONSTRAINED BY A SUPPLIER

Boeing Co. had to delay delivery of its model 777 airplanes to Emirates airline because the German supplier Sell GmbH could not provide the equipment for cooking galleys to Boeing on time. The production bottleneck forced Emirates to repeatedly postpone its planned expansion into the U.S. west coast. It also forced Boeing to accept payment delays for airplanes that sell for more than $200 million apiece. In response, Sell GmbH hired 250 more employees and invested millions of euros in new machine tools and factory space to expand its production capacity.

Source: Daniel Michaels and J. Lynn Lunsford, "Lack of Seats, Galleys Stalls Boeing, Airbus," *The Wall Street Journal*, August 8, 2008, pp. B1 and B4.

LO12–6

Determine the value of obtaining more of the constrained resource.

Managing Constraints

Effectively managing an organization's constraints is a key to increased profits. As discussed above, when a constraint exists in the production process, managers can increase profits by producing the products with the highest contribution margin per unit of the constrained resource. However, they can also increase profits by increasing the capacity of the bottleneck operation.

When a manager increases the capacity of the bottleneck, it is called **relaxing (or elevating) the constraint**. In the case of Mountain Goat Cycles, the company is currently working one eight-hour shift. To relax the constraint, the stitching machine operator could be asked to work overtime. No one else would have to work overtime. Because all of the other operations involved in producing panniers have excess capacity, up to a point, the additional panniers processed through the stitching machine during overtime could be finished during normal working hours in the other operations.

The benefits from relaxing the constraint are often enormous and can be easily quantified—the key is the contribution margin per unit of the constrained resource that we have already computed. This number, which was originally stated in terms of minutes in the Mountain Goat Cycles example, is restated below in terms of hours for easier interpretation:

	Mountain Pannier	Touring Pannier
Contribution margin per unit of the constrained resource (in minutes) . . .	$7.50 per minute × 60 minutes per hour	$12.00 per minute × 60 minutes per hour
Contribution margin per unit of the constrained resource (in hours) . . .	= $450 per hour	= $720 per hour

So what is the value of relaxing the constraint—the time on the stitching machine? The manager should first ask, "What would I do with additional capacity at the bottleneck if it were available?" If the time were to be used to make additional mountain panniers, it would be worth $450 per hour. If the time were to be used to make additional touring panniers, it would be worth $720 per hour. In this latter case, the company should be willing to pay an overtime *premium* to the stitching machine operator of up to $720 per hour! Suppose, for example, that the stitching machine operator is paid $20 per hour during normal working hours and time-and-a-half, or $30 per hour, for overtime. In this case, the premium for overtime is only $10 per hour, whereas in principle, the company should be willing to pay a premium of up to $720 per hour. The difference between what the company should be willing to pay as a premium, $720 per hour, and what it would actually have to pay, $10 per hour, is pure profit of $710 per hour.

To reinforce this concept, suppose that there are only unfilled orders for the mountain pannier. How much would it be worth to the company to run the stitching machine overtime in this situation? Because the additional capacity would be used to make the mountain pannier, the value of that additional capacity would drop to $7.50 per minute or $450 per hour. Nevertheless, the value of relaxing the constraint would still be quite high and the company should be willing to pay an overtime premium of up to $450 per hour.

These calculations indicate that managers should pay great attention to the bottleneck operation. If a bottleneck machine breaks down or is ineffectively utilized, the losses to the company can be quite large. In our example, for every minute the stitching machine is down due to breakdowns or setups, the company loses between $7.50 and $12.00.[3] The losses on an hourly basis are between $450 and $720! In contrast, there is no such loss of contribution margin if time is lost on a machine that is not a bottleneck—such machines have excess capacity anyway.

The implications are clear. Managers should focus much of their attention on managing the bottleneck. As we have discussed, managers should emphasize products that most profitably utilize the constrained resource. They should also make sure that products are processed smoothly through the bottleneck, with minimal lost time due to breakdowns and setups. And they should try to find ways to increase the capacity at the bottleneck.

The capacity of a bottleneck can be effectively increased in a number of ways, including:

- Working overtime on the bottleneck.
- Subcontracting some of the processing that would be done at the bottleneck.
- Investing in additional machines at the bottleneck.
- Shifting workers from processes that are not bottlenecks to the process that is the bottleneck.
- Focusing business process improvement efforts on the bottleneck.
- Reducing defective units. Each defective unit that is processed through the bottleneck and subsequently scrapped takes the place of a good unit that could have been sold.

The last three methods of increasing the capacity of the bottleneck are particularly attractive because they are essentially free and may even yield additional cost savings.

The Problem of Multiple Constraints

What does a company do if it has more than one potential constraint? For example, a company may have limited raw materials, limited direct labor-hours available, limited floor space, and limited advertising dollars to spend on product promotion. How would it determine the right combination of products to produce? The proper combination or "mix" of products can be found by use of a quantitative method known as *linear programming,* which is covered in quantitative methods and operations management courses.

---

[3] Setups are required when production switches from one product to another. For example, consider a company that makes automobile side panels. The panels are painted before shipping them to an automobile manufacturer for final assembly. The customer might require 100 blue panels, 50 black panels, and 20 yellow panels. Each time the color is changed, the painting equipment must be purged of the old paint color, cleaned with solvents, and refilled with the new paint color. This takes time. In fact, some equipment may require such lengthy and frequent setups that it is unavailable for actual production more often than not.

Joint Product Costs and the Contribution Approach

LO12–7
Prepare an analysis showing whether joint products should be sold at the split-off point or processed further.

In some industries, a number of end products are produced from a single raw material input. For example, in the petroleum refining industry a large number of products are extracted from crude oil, including gasoline, jet fuel, home heating oil, lubricants, asphalt, and various organic chemicals. Another example is provided by the Santa Maria Wool Cooperative of New Mexico. The company buys raw wool from local sheepherders, separates the wool into three grades—coarse, fine, and superfine—and then dyes the wool using traditional methods that rely on pigments from local materials. Exhibit 12–7 contains a diagram of the production process.

EXHIBIT 12–7
Santa Maria Wool Cooperative

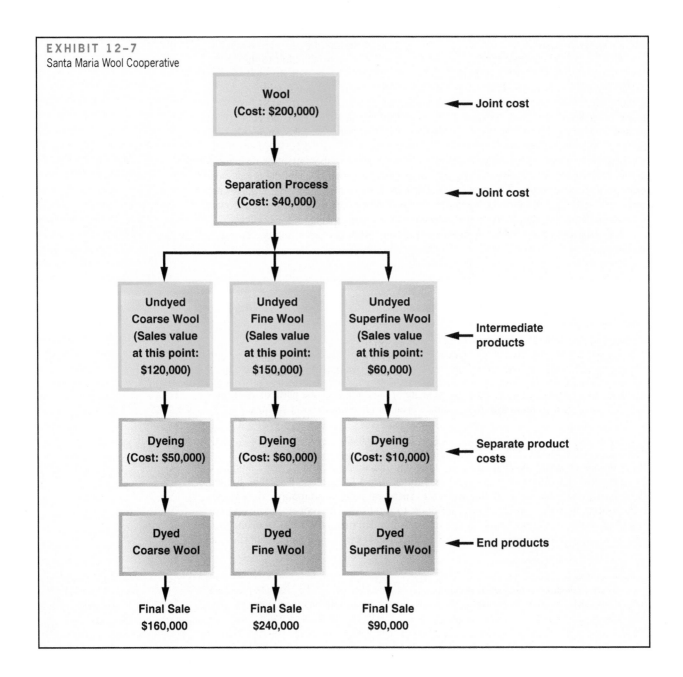

At Santa Maria Wool Cooperative, coarse wool, fine wool, and superfine wool are produced from one input—raw wool. Two or more products that are produced from a common input are known as **joint products**. The **split-off point** is the point in the manufacturing process at which the joint products can be recognized as separate products. This does not occur at Santa Maria Wool Cooperative until the raw wool has gone through the separating process. The term **joint cost** is used to describe the costs incurred up to the split-off point. At Santa Maria Wool Cooperative, the joint costs are the $200,000 cost of the raw wool and the $40,000 cost of separating the wool. The undyed wool is called an *intermediate product* because it is not finished at this point. Nevertheless, a market does exist for undyed wool—although at a significantly lower price than finished, dyed wool.

The Pitfalls of Allocation

Joint costs are common costs that are incurred to simultaneously produce a variety of end products. These joint costs are often allocated among the different products at the split-off point. A typical approach is to allocate the joint costs according to the relative sales value of the end products.

Although allocation of joint product costs is needed for some purposes, such as balance sheet inventory valuation, allocations of this kind are extremely misleading for decision making. The In Business box "Getting It All Wrong" (see below) illustrates an incorrect decision that resulted from using such an allocated joint cost. You should stop now and read that box before proceeding further.

GETTING IT ALL WRONG

A company located on the Gulf of Mexico produces soap products. Its six main soap product lines are produced from common inputs. Joint product costs up to the split-off point constitute the bulk of the production costs for all six product lines. These joint product costs are allocated to the six product lines on the basis of the relative sales value of each line at the split-off point.

A waste product results from the production of the six main product lines. The company loaded the waste onto barges and dumped it into the Gulf of Mexico because the waste was thought to have no commercial value. The dumping was stopped, however, when the company's research division discovered that with some further processing the waste could be sold as a fertilizer ingredient. The further processing costs $175,000 per year. The waste was then sold to fertilizer manufacturers for $300,000.

The accountants responsible for allocating manufacturing costs included the sales value of the waste product along with the sales value of the six main product lines in their allocation of the joint product costs at the split-off point. This allocation resulted in the waste product being allocated $150,000 in joint product cost. This $150,000 allocation, when added to the further processing costs of $175,000 for the waste, made it appear that the waste product was unprofitable—as shown in the table below. When presented with this analysis, the company's management decided that further processing of the waste should be stopped. The company went back to dumping the waste in the Gulf.

Sales value of the waste product after further processing	$300,000
Less costs assigned to the waste product	325,000
Net loss	$ (25,000)

Chapter 12

Sell or Process Further Decisions

Joint costs are irrelevant in decisions regarding what to do with a product from the split-off point forward. Once the split-off point is reached, the joint costs have already been incurred and nothing can be done to avoid them. Furthermore, even if the product were disposed of in a landfill without any further processing, all of the joint costs must be incurred to obtain the other products that come out of the joint process. None of the joint costs are avoidable by disposing of any one of the products that emerge from the split-off point. Therefore, none of the joint costs are economically attributable to any one of the intermediate or end products. The joint costs are a common cost of all of the intermediate and end products and should not be allocated to them for purposes of making decisions about the individual products. In the case of the soap company in the accompanying In Business box "Getting It All Wrong," the $150,000 in allocated joint costs should not have influenced what was done with the waste product from the split-off point forward. Even ignoring the negative environmental impact of dumping the waste in the Gulf of Mexico, a correct analysis would have shown that the company was making money by further processing the waste into a fertilizer ingredient. The analysis should have been done as follows:

	Dump in Gulf	Process Further
Sales value of fertilizer ingredient	0	$300,000
Additional processing costs	0	175,000
Contribution margin	0	$125,000
Advantage of processing further		$125,000

Decisions of this type are known as **sell or process further decisions**. It is profitable to continue processing a joint product after the split-off point *so long as the incremental revenue from such processing exceeds the incremental processing cost incurred after the split-off point.* Joint costs that have already been incurred up to the split-off point are always irrelevant in decisions concerning what to do from the split-off point forward.

To provide a detailed example of the sell or process further decision, return to the data for Santa Maria Wool Cooperative in Exhibit 12–7. We can answer several important questions using this data. First, is the company making money if it runs the entire process from beginning to end? Assuming there are no costs other than those displayed in Exhibit 12–7, the company is indeed making money as follows:

Analysis of the profitability of the overall operation:

Combined final sales value		
($160,000 + $240,000 + $90,000)		$490,000
Less costs of producing the end products:		
Cost of wool	$200,000	
Cost of separating wool	40,000	
Combined costs of dyeing		
($50,000 + $60,000 + $10,000)	120,000	360,000
Profit		$130,000

Note that the joint costs of buying the wool and separating the wool *are* relevant when considering the profitability of the entire operation. This is because these joint costs *could* be avoided if the entire operation were shut down. However, these joint costs are *not* relevant when considering the profitability of any one product. As long as the process is being run to make the other products, no additional joint costs are incurred to make the specific product in question.

Even though the company is making money overall, it may be losing money on one or more of the products. If the company buys wool and runs the separation process, it will get all three intermediate products. Nothing can be done about that. However, each of these products can be sold *as is* without further processing. It may be that the company would be better off selling one or more of the products prior to dyeing to avoid the dyeing costs. The appropriate way to make this choice is to compare the incremental revenues to the incremental costs from further processing as follows:

Analysis of sell or process further:

	Coarse Wool	Fine Wool	Superfine Wool
Final sales value after further processing	$160,000	$240,000	$90,000
Less sales value at the split-off point	120,000	150,000	60,000
Incremental revenue from further processing ...	40,000	90,000	30,000
Less cost of further processing (dyeing)	50,000	60,000	10,000
Profit (loss) from further processing	$ (10,000)	$ 30,000	$20,000

As this analysis shows, the company would be better off selling the undyed coarse wool as is rather than processing it further. The other two products should be processed further and dyed before selling them.

Note that the joint costs of the wool ($200,000) and of the wool separation process ($40,000) play no role in the decision to sell or further process the intermediate products. These joint costs are relevant in a decision of whether to buy wool and to run the wool separation process, but they are not relevant in decisions about what to do with the intermediate products once they have been separated.

Activity-Based Costing and Relevant Costs

As discussed in an earlier chapter, activity-based costing can be used to help identify potentially relevant costs for decision-making purposes. Activity-based costing improves the traceability of costs by focusing on the activities caused by a product or other segment. However, managers should exercise caution against reading more into this "traceability" than really exists. People have a tendency to assume that if a cost is traceable to a segment, then the cost is automatically an avoidable cost. That is not true because the costs provided by a well-designed activity-based costing system are only *potentially* relevant. Before making a decision, managers must still decide which of the potentially relevant costs are actually avoidable. Only those costs that are avoidable are relevant and the others should be ignored.

To illustrate, refer again to the data relating to the housewares line in Exhibit 12–4. The $2,000 fixtures depreciation is a traceable cost of the housewares lines because it directly relates to activities in that department. We found, however, that the $2,000 is not avoidable if the housewares line is dropped. The key lesson here is that the method used to assign a cost to a product or other segment does not change the basic nature of the cost. A sunk cost such as depreciation of old equipment is still a sunk cost regardless of whether it is traced directly to a particular segment on an activity basis, allocated to all segments on the basis of labor-hours, or treated in some other way in the costing process. Regardless of the method used to assign costs to products or other segments, the principles discussed in this chapter must be applied to determine the costs that are avoidable in each situation.

Summary

Everything in this chapter consists of applications of one simple but powerful idea—only those costs and benefits that differ between alternatives are relevant in a decision. All other costs and benefits are irrelevant and should be ignored. In particular, sunk costs are irrelevant as are future costs that do not differ between alternatives.

This simple idea was applied in a variety of situations including decisions that involve adding or dropping a product line, making or buying a component, accepting or rejecting a special order, using a constrained resource, and processing a joint product further. This list includes only a small sample of the possible applications of the relevant cost concept. Indeed, any decision involving costs hinges on the proper identification and analysis of the costs that are relevant. We will continue to focus on the concept of relevant costs in the following chapter where long-term investment decisions are considered.

Review Problem: Relevant Costs

Charter Sports Equipment manufactures round, rectangular, and octagonal trampolines. Sales and expense data for the past month follow:

	Total	Trampoline		
		Round	Rectangular	Octagonal
Sales	$1,000,000	$140,000	$500,000	$360,000
Variable expenses	410,000	60,000	200,000	150,000
Contribution margin	590,000	80,000	300,000	210,000
Fixed expenses:				
Advertising—traceable	216,000	41,000	110,000	65,000
Depreciation of special equipment	95,000	20,000	40,000	35,000
Line supervisors' salaries	19,000	6,000	7,000	6,000
General factory overhead*	200,000	28,000	100,000	72,000
Total fixed expenses	530,000	95,000	257,000	178,000
Net operating income (loss)	$ 60,000	$ (15,000)	$ 43,000	$ 32,000

*A common fixed cost that is allocated on the basis of sales dollars.

Management is concerned about the continued losses shown by the round trampolines and wants a recommendation as to whether or not the line should be discontinued. The special equipment used to produce the trampolines has no resale value. If the round trampoline model is dropped, the two line supervisors assigned to the model would be discharged.

Required:
1. Should production and sale of the round trampolines be discontinued? The company has no other use for the capacity now being used to produce the round trampolines. Show computations to support your answer.
2. Recast the above data in a format that would be more useful to management in assessing the profitability of the various product lines.

Solution to Review Problem

1. No, production and sale of the round trampolines should not be discontinued. Computations to support this answer follow:

Differential Analysis: The Key to Decision Making   **557**

Contribution margin lost if the round trampolines are discontinued . . .	$(80,000)
Less fixed expenses that can be avoided:	
Advertising—traceable	$41,000
Line supervisors' salaries	6,000 47,000
Decrease in net operating income for the company as a whole	$(33,000)

The depreciation of the special equipment is a sunk cost, and therefore, it is not relevant to the decision. The general factory overhead is allocated and will presumably continue regardless of whether or not the round trampolines are discontinued; thus, it is not relevant.

2. If management wants a clearer picture of the profitability of the segments, the general factory overhead should not be allocated. It is a common cost and, therefore, should be deducted from the total product-line segment margin. A more useful income statement format would be as follows:

		Trampoline		
	Total	Round	Rectangular	Octagonal
Sales	$1,000,000	$140,000	$500,000	$360,000
Variable expenses	410,000	60,000	200,000	150,000
Contribution margin	590,000	80,000	300,000	210,000
Traceable fixed expenses:				
Advertising—traceable	216,000	41,000	110,000	65,000
Depreciation of special equipment . . .	95,000	20,000	40,000	35,000
Line supervisors' salaries	19,000	6,000	7,000	6,000
Total traceable fixed expenses	330,000	67,000	157,000	106,000
Product-line segment margin	260,000	$ 13,000	$143,000	$104,000
Common fixed expenses	200,000			
Net operating income	$ 60,000			

Glossary

Avoidable cost A cost that can be eliminated by choosing one alternative over another in a decision. This term is synonymous with *differential cost* and *relevant cost*. (p. 532)

Bottleneck A machine or some other part of a process that limits the total output of the entire system. (p. 548)

Constraint A limitation under which a company must operate, such as limited available machine time or raw materials, that restricts the company's ability to satisfy demand. (p. 547)

Differential cost A difference in cost between any two alternatives. (p. 532)

Differential revenue A difference in revenue between any two alternatives. (p. 532)

Joint costs Costs that are incurred up to the split-off point in a process that produces joint products. (p. 553)

Joint products Two or more products that are produced from a common input. (p. 553)

Make or buy decision A decision concerning whether an item should be produced internally or purchased from an outside supplier. (p. 542)

Opportunity cost The potential benefit that is given up when one alternative is selected over another. (p. 533)

Relaxing (or elevating) the constraint An action that increases the amount of a constrained resource. Equivalently, an action that increases the capacity of the bottleneck. (p. 550)

558   Chapter 12

Relevant benefit A benefit that differs between alternatives in a decision. *Differential revenue* is a *relevant benefit*. (p. 532)

Relevant cost A difference in cost between any two alternatives. Synonyms are *avoidable cost, differential cost,* and *incremental cost.* (p. 532)

Sell or process further decision A decision as to whether a joint product should be sold at the split-off point or sold after further processing. (p. 554)

Special order A one-time order that is not considered part of the company's normal ongoing business. (p. 545)

Split-off point That point in the manufacturing process where some or all of the joint products can be recognized as individual products. (p. 556)

Sunk cost Any cost that has already been incurred and that cannot be changed by any decision made now or in the future. (p. 532)

Vertical integration The involvement by a company in more than one of the activities in the entire value chain from development through production, distribution, sales, and after-sales service. (p. 542)

Questions

12–1 What is a *relevant cost?*

12–2 Define the following terms: *incremental cost, opportunity cost,* and *sunk cost.*

12–3 Are variable costs always relevant costs? Explain.

12–4 "Sunk costs are easy to spot—they're the fixed costs associated with a decision." Do you agree? Explain.

12–5 "Variable costs and differential costs mean the same thing." Do you agree? Explain.

12–6 "All future costs are relevant in decision making." Do you agree? Why?

12–7 Prentice Company is considering dropping one of its product lines. What costs of the product line would be relevant to this decision? What costs would be irrelevant?

12–8 "If a product is generating a loss, then it should be discontinued." Do you agree? Explain.

12–9 What is the danger in allocating common fixed costs among products or other segments of an organization?

12–10 How does opportunity cost enter into a make or buy decision?

12–11 Give at least four examples of possible constraints.

12–12 How will relating product contribution margins to the amount of the constrained resource they consume help a company maximize its profits?

12–13 Define the following terms: *joint products, joint costs,* and *split-off point.*

12–14 From a decision-making point of view, should joint costs be allocated among joint products?

12–15 What guideline should be used in determining whether a joint product should be sold at the split-off point or processed further?

12–16 Airlines sometimes offer reduced rates during certain times of the week to members of a businessperson's family if they accompany him or her on trips. How does the concept of relevant costs enter into the decision by the airline to offer reduced rates of this type?

Multiple-choice questions are provided on the text website at www.mhhe.com/garrison15e.

Applying Excel

Available with McGraw-Hill's *Connect® Accounting*.

LO12–7

The Excel worksheet form that appears on the next page is to be used to recreate the example in the text on pages 552–555. Download the workbook containing this form from the Online Learning Center at www.mhhe.com/garrison15e. *On the website you will also receive instructions about how to use this worksheet form.*

	A	B	C	D	E
1	Chapter 12: Applying Excel				
2					
3	Data				
4	Exhibit 12-7 Santa Maria Wool Cooperative				
5	Cost of wool	$200,000			
6	Cost of separation process	$40,000			
7	Sales value of intermediate products at split-off point:				
8	Undyed coarse wool	$120,000			
9	Undyed fine wool	$150,000			
10	Undyed superfine wool	$60,000			
11	Costs of further processing (dyeing) intermediate products:				
12	Undyed coarse wool	$50,000			
13	Undyed fine wool	$60,000			
14	Undyed superfine wool	$10,000			
15	Sales value of end products:				
16	Dyed coarse wool	$160,000			
17	Dyed fine wool	$240,000			
18	Dyed superfine wool	$90,000			
19					
20	*Enter a formula into each of the cells marked with a ? below*				
21	**Example: Joint Product Costs and the Contribution Approach**				
22					
23	*Analysis of the profitability of the overall operation:*				
24	Combined final sales value		?		
25	Less costs of producing the end products:				
26	Cost of wool	?			
27	Cost of separation process	?			
28	Combined costs of dyeing	?	?		
29	Profit		?		
30					
31	*Analysis of sell or process further:*				
32		Coarse	Fine	Superfine	
33		Wool	Wool	Wool	
34	Final sales value after further processing	?	?	?	
35	Less sales value at the split-off point	?	?	?	
36	Incremental revenue from further processing	?	?	?	
37	Less cost of further processing (dyeing)	?	?	?	
38	Profit (loss) from further processing	?	?	?	
39					

H ◀ ▶ H   Chapter 12 Form / Filled in Chapter 12 Form / Chapter ◀

You should proceed to the requirements below only after completing your worksheet.

Required:

1. Check your worksheet by changing the cost of further processing undyed coarse wool in cell B12 to $30,000. The overall profit from processing all intermediate products into final products should now be $150,000 and the profit from further processing coarse wool should now be $10,000. If you do not get these answers, find the errors in your worksheet and correct them.

    How should operations change in response to this change in cost?

560   Chapter 12

2. In industries that process joint products, the costs of the raw materials inputs and the sales values of intermediate and final products are often volatile. Change the data area of your worksheet to match the following:

Data	
Exhibit 12–7 Santa Maria Wool Cooperative	
Cost of wool	$290,000
Cost of separation process	$40,000
Sales value of intermediate products at split-off point:	
Undyed coarse wool	$100,000
Undyed fine wool	$110,000
Undyed superfine wool	$90,000
Costs of further processing (dyeing) intermediate products:	
Undyed coarse wool	$50,000
Undyed fine wool	$60,000
Undyed superfine wool	$10,000
Sales value of end products:	
Dyed coarse wool	$180,000
Dyed fine wool	$210,000
Dyed superfine wool	$90,000

a. What is the overall profit if all intermediate products are processed into final products?
b. What is the profit from further processing each of the intermediate products?
c. With these new costs and selling prices, what recommendations would you make concerning the company's operations? If your recommendation is followed, what should be the overall profit of the company?

The Foundational 15   connect
|ACCOUNTING

Available with McGraw-Hill's *Connect*® Accounting.

LO12–2, LO12–3, LO12–4, LO12–5, LO12–6

Cane Company manufactures two products called Alpha and Beta that sell for $120 and $80, respectively. Each product uses only one type of raw material that costs $6 per pound. The company has the capacity to annually produce 100,000 units of each product. Its unit costs for each product at this level of activity are given below:

	Alpha	Beta
Direct materials	$ 30	$12
Direct labor	20	15
Variable manufacturing overhead	7	5
Traceable fixed manufacturing overhead	16	18
Variable selling expenses	12	8
Common fixed expenses	15	10
Total cost per unit	$100	$68

The company considers its traceable fixed manufacturing overhead to be avoidable, whereas its common fixed expenses are deemed unavoidable and have been allocated to products based on sales dollars.

Required:
(Answer each question independently unless instructed otherwise.)
1. What is the total amount of traceable fixed manufacturing overhead for the Alpha product line and for the Beta product line?
2. What is the company's total amount of common fixed expenses?
3. Assume that Cane expects to produce and sell 80,000 Alphas during the current year. One of Cane's sales representatives has found a new customer that is willing to buy 10,000 additional Alphas for a price of $80 per unit. If Cane accepts the customer's offer, how much will its profits increase or decrease?

4. Assume that Cane expects to produce and sell 90,000 Betas during the current year. One of Cane's sales representatives has found a new customer that is willing to buy 5,000 additional Betas for a price of $39 per unit. If Cane accepts the customer's offer, how much will its profits increase or decrease?

5. Assume that Cane expects to produce and sell 95,000 Alphas during the current year. One of Cane's sales representatives has found a new customer that is willing to buy 10,000 additional Alphas for a price of $80 per unit. If Cane accepts the customer's offer, it will decrease Alpha sales to regular customers by 5,000 units. Should Cane accept this special order?

6. Assume that Cane normally produces and sells 90,000 Betas per year. If Cane discontinues the Beta product line, how much will profits increase or decrease?

7. Assume that Cane normally produces and sells 40,000 Betas per year. If Cane discontinues the Beta product line, how much will profits increase or decrease?

8. Assume that Cane normally produces and sells 60,000 Betas and 80,000 Alphas per year. If Cane discontinues the Beta product line, its sales representatives could increase sales of Alpha by 15,000 units. If Cane discontinues the Beta product line, how much would profits increase or decrease?

9. Assume that Cane expects to produce and sell 80,000 Alphas during the current year. A supplier has offered to manufacture and deliver 80,000 Alphas to Cane for a price of $80 per unit. If Cane buys 80,000 units from the supplier instead of making those units, how much will profits increase or decrease?

10. Assume that Cane expects to produce and sell 50,000 Alphas during the current year. A supplier has offered to manufacture and deliver 50,000 Alphas to Cane for a price of $80 per unit. If Cane buys 50,000 units from the supplier instead of making those units, how much will profits increase or decrease?

11. How many pounds of raw material are needed to make one unit of Alpha and one unit of Beta?

12. What contribution margin per pound of raw material is earned by Alpha and Beta?

13. Assume that Cane's customers would buy a maximum of 80,000 units of Alpha and 60,000 units of Beta. Also assume that the company's raw material available for production is limited to 160,000 pounds. How many units of each product should Cane produce to maximize its profits?

14. If Cane follows your recommendation in requirement 13, what total contribution margin will it earn?

15. If Cane uses its 160,000 pounds of raw materials as you recommended in requirement 13, up to how much should it be willing to pay per pound for additional raw materials?

 Exercises

All applicable exercises are available with McGraw-Hill's *Connect®* Accounting.

EXERCISE 12–1 Identifying Relevant Costs [LO12–1]
A number of costs are listed below that may be relevant in decisions faced by the management of Svahn, AB, a Swedish manufacturer of sailing yachts:

	Case 1		Case 2	
Item	Relevant	Not Relevant	Relevant	Not Relevant
a. Sales revenue				
b. Direct materials				
c. Direct labor				
d. Variable manufacturing overhead				
e. Depreciation—Model B100 machine				
f. Book value—Model B100 machine				
g. Disposal value—Model B100 machine				
h. Market value—Model B300 machine (cost) ...				
i. Fixed manufacturing overhead (general)				
j. Variable selling expense				
k. Fixed selling expense				
l. General administrative overhead				

Required:

Copy the information above onto your answer sheet and place an X in the appropriate column to indicate whether each item is relevant or not relevant in the following situations. Requirement 1 relates to Case 1 above, and requirement 2 relates to Case 2.

1.   The company chronically has no idle capacity and the old Model B100 machine is the company's constraint. Management is considering purchasing a Model B300 machine to use in addition to the company's present Model B100 machine. The old Model B100 machine will continue to be used to capacity as before, with the new Model B300 machine being used to expand production. This will increase the company's production and sales. The increase in volume will be large enough to require increases in fixed selling expenses and in general administrative overhead, but not in the fixed manufacturing overhead.

2.   The old Model B100 machine is not the company's constraint, but management is considering replacing it with a new Model B300 machine because of the potential savings in direct materials with the new machine. The Model B100 machine would be sold. This change will have no effect on production or sales, other than some savings in direct materials costs due to less waste.

EXERCISE 12–2 Dropping or Retaining a Segment [LO12–2]

The Regal Cycle Company manufactures three types of bicycles—a dirt bike, a mountain bike, and a racing bike. Data on sales and expenses for the past quarter follow:

	Total	Dirt Bikes	Mountain Bikes	Racing Bikes
Sales	$300,000	$90,000	$150,000	$60,000
Variable manufacturing and selling expenses	120,000	27,000	60,000	33,000
Contribution margin	180,000	63,000	90,000	27,000
Fixed expenses:				
Advertising, traceable	30,000	10,000	14,000	6,000
Depreciation of special equipment	23,000	6,000	9,000	8,000
Salaries of product-line managers	35,000	12,000	13,000	10,000
Allocated common fixed expenses*	60,000	18,000	30,000	12,000
Total fixed expenses	148,000	46,000	66,000	36,000
Net operating income (loss)	$ 32,000	$17,000	$ 24,000	$ (9,000)

*Allocated on the basis of sales dollars.

Management is concerned about the continued losses shown by the racing bikes and wants a recommendation as to whether or not the line should be discontinued. The special equipment used to produce racing bikes has no resale value and does not wear out.

Required:

1.   Should production and sale of the racing bikes be discontinued? Explain. Show computations to support your answer.

2.   Recast the above data in a format that would be more usable to management in assessing the long-run profitability of the various product lines.

EXERCISE 12–3 Make or Buy a Component [LO12–3]

Troy Engines, Ltd., manufactures a variety of engines for use in heavy equipment. The company has always produced all of the necessary parts for its engines, including all of the carburetors. An outside supplier has offered to sell one type of carburetor to Troy Engines, Ltd., for a cost of $35 per unit. To evaluate this offer, Troy Engines, Ltd., has gathered the following information relating to its own cost of producing the carburetor internally:

Differential Analysis: The Key to Decision Making **563**

	Per Unit	15,000 Units per Year
Direct materials	$14	$210,000
Direct labor	10	150,000
Variable manufacturing overhead	3	45,000
Fixed manufacturing overhead, traceable	6*	90,000
Fixed manufacturing overhead, allocated	9	135,000
Total cost	$42	$630,000

*One-third supervisory salaries; two-thirds depreciation of special equipment (no resale value).

Required:

1. Assuming that the company has no alternative use for the facilities that are now being used to produce the carburetors, should the outside supplier's offer be accepted? Show all computations.
2. Suppose that if the carburetors were purchased, Troy Engines, Ltd., could use the freed capacity to launch a new product. The segment margin of the new product would be $150,000 per year. Should Troy Engines, Ltd., accept the offer to buy the carburetors for $35 per unit? Show all computations.

EXERCISE 12–4 Evaluating a Special Order [LO12–4]

Imperial Jewelers is considering a special order for 20 handcrafted gold bracelets to be given as gifts to members of a wedding party. The normal selling price of a gold bracelet is $189.95 and its unit product cost is $149.00 as shown below:

Direct materials	$ 84.00
Direct labor	45.00
Manufacturing overhead	20.00
Unit product cost	$149.00

Most of the manufacturing overhead is fixed and unaffected by variations in how much jewelry is produced in any given period. However, $4.00 of the overhead is variable with respect to the number of bracelets produced. The customer who is interested in the special bracelet order would like special filigree applied to the bracelets. This filigree would require additional materials costing $2.00 per bracelet and would also require acquisition of a special tool costing $250 that would have no other use once the special order is completed. This order would have no effect on the company's regular sales and the order could be fulfilled using the company's existing capacity without affecting any other order.

Required:

What effect would accepting this order have on the company's net operating income if a special price of $169.95 per bracelet is offered for this order? Should the special order be accepted at this price?

EXERCISE 12–5 Utilizing a Constrained Resource [LO12–5]

Outdoor Luggage Inc. makes high-end hard-sided luggage for sports equipment. Data concerning three of the company's most popular models appear below.

	Ski Guard	Golf Guard	Fishing Guard
Selling price per unit	$200	$300	$255
Variable cost per unit	$60	$140	$55
Plastic injection molding machine processing time required to produce one unit	2 minutes	5 minutes	4 minutes
Pounds of plastic pellets per unit	7 pounds	4 pounds	8 pounds

Required:

1. The total time available on the plastic injection molding machine is the constraint in the production process. Which product would be the most profitable use of this constraint? Which product would be the least profitable use of this constraint?
2. A severe shortage of plastic pellets has required the company to cut back its production so much that the plastic injection molding machine is no longer the bottleneck. Instead, the constraint is the total available pounds of plastic pellets. Which product would be the most profitable use of this constraint? Which product would be the least profitable use of this constraint?
3. Which product has the largest unit contribution margin? Why wouldn't this product be the most profitable use of the constrained resource in either case?

EXERCISE 12–6 Managing a Constrained Resource [LO12–6]

Portsmouth Company makes fine colonial reproduction furniture. Upholstered furniture is one of its major product lines and the bottleneck on this production line is time in the upholstery shop. Upholstering is a craft that takes years of experience to master and the demand for upholstered furniture far exceeds the company's capacity in the upholstering shop. Information concerning three of the company's upholstered chairs appears below:

	Recliner	Sofa	Love Seat
Selling price per unit	$1,400	$1,800	$1,500
Variable cost per unit	$800	$1,200	$1,000
Upholstery shop time required to produce one unit	8 hours	10 hours	5 hours

Required:

1. More time could be made available in the upholstery shop by asking the employees who work in this shop to work overtime. Assuming that this extra time would be used to produce sofas, up to how much of a premium should the company be willing to pay per hour to keep the upholstery shop open after normal working hours?
2. A small nearby upholstering company has offered to upholster furniture for Portsmouth at a fixed charge of $45 per hour. The management of Portsmouth is confident that this upholstering company's work is high quality and their craftsmen should be able to work about as quickly as Portsmouth's own craftsmen on the simpler upholstering jobs such as the love seat. Should management accept this offer? Explain.

EXERCISE 12–7 Sell or Process Further [LO12–7]

Dorsey Company manufactures three products from a common input in a joint processing operation. Joint processing costs up to the split-off point total $350,000 per quarter. The company allocates these costs to the joint products on the basis of their relative sales value at the split-off point. Unit selling prices and total output at the split-off point are as follows:

Product	Selling Price	Quarterly Output
A	$16 per pound	15,000 pounds
B	$8 per pound	20,000 pounds
C	$25 per gallon	4,000 gallons

Each product can be processed further after the split-off point. Additional processing requires no special facilities. The additional processing costs (per quarter) and unit selling prices after further processing are given below:

Product	Additional Processing Costs	Selling Price
A	$63,000	$20 per pound
B	$80,000	$13 per pound
C	$36,000	$32 per gallon

Differential Analysis: The Key to Decision Making   **565**

Required:
Which product or products should be sold at the split-off point and which product or products should be processed further? Show computations.

EXERCISE 12–8 Utilization of a Constrained Resource [LO12–5, LO12–6]
Barlow Company manufactures three products: A, B, and C. The selling price, variable costs, and contribution margin for one unit of each product follow:

	Product		
	A	B	C
Selling price	$180	$270	$240
Variable expenses:			
Direct materials	24	72	32
Other variable expenses	102	90	148
Total variable expenses	126	162	180
Contribution margin	$ 54	$108	$ 60
Contribution margin ratio	30%	40%	25%

The same raw material is used in all three products. Barlow Company has only 5,000 pounds of raw material on hand and will not be able to obtain any more of it for several weeks due to a strike in its supplier's plant. Management is trying to decide which product(s) to concentrate on next week in filling its backlog of orders. The material costs $8 per pound.

Required:
1. Compute the amount of contribution margin that will be obtained per pound of material used in each product.
2. Which orders would you recommend that the company work on next week—the orders for product A, product B, or product C? Show computations.
3. A foreign supplier could furnish Barlow with additional stocks of the raw material at a substantial premium over the usual price. If there is unfilled demand for all three products, what is the highest price that Barlow Company should be willing to pay for an additional pound of materials? Explain.

EXERCISE 12–9 Special Order [LO12–4]
Delta Company produces a single product. The cost of producing and selling a single unit of this product at the company's normal activity level of 60,000 units per year is:

Direct materials	$5.10
Direct labor	$3.80
Variable manufacturing overhead	$1.00
Fixed manufacturing overhead	$4.20
Variable selling and administrative expense	$1.50
Fixed selling and administrative expense	$2.40

The normal selling price is $21 per unit. The company's capacity is 75,000 units per year. An order has been received from a mail-order house for 15,000 units at a special price of $14.00 per unit. This order would not affect regular sales.

Required:
1. If the order is accepted, by how much will annual profits be increased or decreased? (The order will not change the company's total fixed costs.)
2. Assume the company has 1,000 units of this product left over from last year that are inferior to the current model. The units must be sold through regular channels at reduced prices. What unit cost is relevant for establishing a minimum selling price for these units? Explain.

EXERCISE 12–10 Make or Buy a Component [LO12–3]
For many years Futura Company has purchased the starters that it installs in its standard line of farm tractors. Due to a reduction in output, the company has idle capacity that could be used to

produce the starters. The chief engineer has recommended against this move, however, pointing out that the cost to produce the starters would be greater than the current $8.40 per unit purchase price:

	Per Unit	Total
Direct materials	$3.10	
Direct labor	2.70	
Supervision	1.50	$60,000
Depreciation	1.00	$40,000
Variable manufacturing overhead	0.60	
Rent	0.30	$12,000
Total production cost	$9.20	

A supervisor would have to be hired to oversee production of the starters. However, the company has sufficient idle tools and machinery that no new equipment would have to be purchased. The rent charge above is based on space utilized in the plant. The total rent on the plant is $80,000 per period. Depreciation is due to obsolescence rather than wear and tear.

Required:
Prepare computations showing how much profits will increase or decrease as a result of making the starters.

EXERCISE 12–11 Make or Buy a Component [LO12–3]
Han Products manufactures 30,000 units of part S-6 each year for use on its production line. At this level of activity, the cost per unit for part S-6 is:

Direct materials	$ 3.60
Direct labor	10.00
Variable manufacturing overhead	2.40
Fixed manufacturing overhead	9.00
Total cost per part	$25.00

An outside supplier has offered to sell 30,000 units of part S-6 each year to Han Products for $21 per part. If Han Products accepts this offer, the facilities now being used to manufacture part S-6 could be rented to another company at an annual rental of $80,000. However, Han Products has determined that two-thirds of the fixed manufacturing overhead being applied to part S-6 would continue even if part S-6 were purchased from the outside supplier.

Required:
Prepare computations showing how much profits will increase or decrease if the outside supplier's offer is accepted.

EXERCISE 12–12 Utilization of a Constrained Resource [LO12–5]
Benoit Company produces three products, A, B, and C. Data concerning the three products follow (per unit):

	Product		
	A	B	C
Selling price	$80	$56	$70
Variable expenses:			
Direct materials	24	15	9
Other variable expenses	24	27	40
Total variable expenses	48	42	49
Contribution margin	$32	$14	$21
Contribution margin ratio	40%	25%	30%

Demand for the company's products is very strong, with far more orders each month than the company can produce with the available raw materials. The same material is used in each product. The material costs $3 per pound with a maximum of 5,000 pounds available each month.

Required:
Which orders would you advise the company to accept first, those for A, for B, or for C? Which orders second? Third?

EXERCISE 12–13 Sell or Process Further [LO12–7]

Wexpro, Inc., produces several products from processing 1 ton of clypton, a rare mineral. Material and processing costs total $60,000 per ton, one-fourth of which is allocated to product X15. Seven thousand units of product X15 are produced from each ton of clypton. The units can either be sold at the split-off point for $9 each, or processed further at a total cost of $9,500 and then sold for $12 each.

Required:

Should product X15 be processed further or sold at the split-off point?

EXERCISE 12–14 Identification of Relevant Costs [LO12–1]

Kristen Lu purchased a used automobile for $8,000 at the beginning of last year and incurred the following operating costs:

Depreciation ($8,000 ÷ 5 years)	$1,600
Insurance	$1,200
Garage rent	$360
Automobile tax and license	$40
Variable operating cost	$0.14 per mile

The variable operating cost consists of gasoline, oil, tires, maintenance, and repairs. Kristen estimates that, at her current rate of usage, the car will have zero resale value in five years, so the annual straight-line depreciation is $1,600. The car is kept in a garage for a monthly fee.

Required:

1. Kristen drove the car 10,000 miles last year. Compute the average cost per mile of owning and operating the car.
2   Kristen is unsure about whether she should use her own car or rent a car to go on an extended cross-country trip for two weeks during spring break. What costs above are relevant in this decision? Explain.
3. Kristen is thinking about buying an expensive sports car to replace the car she bought last year. She would drive the same number of miles regardless of which car she owns and would rent the same parking space. The sports car's variable operating costs would be roughly the same as the variable operating costs of her old car. However, her insurance and automobile tax and license costs would go up. What costs are relevant in estimating the incremental cost of owning the more expensive car? Explain.

EXERCISE 12–15 Dropping or Retaining a Segment [LO12–2]

Thalassines Kataskeves, S.A., of Greece makes marine equipment. The company has been experiencing losses on its bilge pump product line for several years. The most recent quarterly contribution format income statement for the bilge pump product line follows:

Thalassines Kataskeves, S.A.
Income Statement—Bilge Pump
For the Quarter Ended March 31

Sales		$850,000
Variable expenses:		
Variable manufacturing expenses	$330,000	
Sales commissions	42,000	
Shipping	18,000	
Total variable expenses		390,000
Contribution margin		460,000
Fixed expenses:		
Advertising	270,000	
Depreciation of equipment (no resale value)	80,000	
General factory overhead	105,000*	
Salary of product-line manager	32,000	
Insurance on inventories	8,000	
Purchasing department	45,000†	
Total fixed expenses		540,000
Net operating loss		$ (80,000)

*Common costs allocated on the basis of machine-hours.
†Common costs allocated on the basis of sales dollars.

Chapter 12

Discontinuing the bilge pump product line would not affect sales of other product lines and would have no effect on the company's total general factory overhead or total Purchasing Department expenses.

Required:

Would you recommend that the bilge pump product line be discontinued? Support your answer with appropriate computations.

EXERCISE 12–16 Identification of Relevant Costs [LO12–1]

Bill has just returned from a duck hunting trip. He has brought home eight ducks. Bill's friend, John, disapproves of duck hunting, and to discourage Bill from further hunting, John has presented him with the following cost estimate per duck:

Camper and equipment:	
Cost, $12,000; usable for eight seasons; 10 hunting trips per season...........	$150
Travel expense (pickup truck):	
100 miles at $0.31 per mile (gas, oil, and tires—$0.21 per mile; depreciation	
and insurance—$0.10 per mile)	31
Shotgun shells (two boxes)	20
Boat:	
Cost, $2,320, usable for eight seasons; 10 hunting trips per season	29
Hunting license:	
Cost, $30 for the season; 10 hunting trips per season	3
Money lost playing poker:	
Loss, $24 (Bill plays poker every weekend)	24
Bottle of whiskey:	
Cost, $15 (used to ward off the cold)	15
Total cost	$272
Cost per duck ($272 ÷ 8 ducks)	$ 34

Required:

1. Assuming that the duck hunting trip Bill has just completed is typical, what costs are relevant to a decision as to whether Bill should go duck hunting again this season?
2. Suppose that Bill gets lucky on his next hunting trip and shoots 10 ducks in the amount of time it took him to shoot 8 ducks on his last trip. How much would it have cost him to shoot the last two ducks? Explain.
3. Which costs are relevant in a decision of whether Bill should give up hunting? Explain.

EXERCISE 12–17 Dropping or Retaining a Segment [LO12–2]

Bed & Bath, a retailing company, has two departments, Hardware and Linens. The company's most recent monthly contribution format income statement follows:

		Department	
	Total	Hardware	Linens
Sales	$4,000,000	$3,000,000	$1,000,000
Variable expenses	1,300,000	900,000	400,000
Contribution margin	2,700,000	2,100,000	600,000
Fixed expenses	2,200,000	1,400,000	800,000
Net operating income (loss)	$ 500,000	$ 700,000	$ (200,000)

A study indicates that $340,000 of the fixed expenses being charged to Linens are sunk costs or allocated costs that will continue even if the Linens Department is dropped. In addition, the elimination of the Linens Department will result in a 10% decrease in the sales of the Hardware Department.

Required:

If the Linens Department is dropped, what will be the effect on the net operating income of the company as a whole?

Problems

All applicable problems are available with McGraw-Hill's *Connect® Accounting*.

PROBLEM 12–18 Relevant Cost Analysis in a Variety of Situations [LO12–2, LO12–3, LO12–4]
Andretti Company has a single product called a Dak. The company normally produces and sells
60,000 Daks each year at a selling price of $32 per unit. The company's unit costs at this level of
activity are given below:

Direct materials	$10.00	
Direct labor	4.50	
Variable manufacturing overhead	2.30	
Fixed manufacturing overhead	5.00	($300,000 total)
Variable selling expenses	1.20	
Fixed selling expenses	3.50	($210,000 total)
Total cost per unit	$26.50	

A number of questions relating to the production and sale of Daks follow. Each question is
independent.

Required:
1. Assume that Andretti Company has sufficient capacity to produce 90,000 Daks each year
without any increase in fixed manufacturing overhead costs. The company could increase
its sales by 25% above the present 60,000 units each year if it were willing to increase
the fixed selling expenses by $80,000. Would the increased fixed selling expenses be
justified?
2. Assume again that Andretti Company has sufficient capacity to produce 90,000 Daks each
year. A customer in a foreign market wants to purchase 20,000 Daks. Import duties on the
Daks would be $1.70 per unit, and costs for permits and licenses would be $9,000. The only
selling costs that would be associated with the order would be $3.20 per unit shipping cost.
Compute the per unit break-even price on this order.
3. The company has 1,000 Daks on hand that have some irregularities and are therefore considered to be "seconds." Due to the irregularities, it will be impossible to sell these units at the
normal price through regular distribution channels. What unit cost figure is relevant for setting
a minimum selling price? Explain.
4. Due to a strike in its supplier's plant, Andretti Company is unable to purchase more material for the production of Daks. The strike is expected to last for two months. Andretti
Company has enough material on hand to operate at 30% of normal levels for the two-
month period. As an alternative, Andretti could close its plant down entirely for the two
months. If the plant were closed, fixed manufacturing overhead costs would continue at
60% of their normal level during the two-month period and the fixed selling expenses
would be reduced by 20%. What would be the impact on profits of closing the plant for the
two-month period?
5. An outside manufacturer has offered to produce Daks and ship them directly to Andretti's customers. If Andretti Company accepts this offer, the facilities that it uses to produce Daks would
be idle; however, fixed manufacturing overhead costs would be reduced by 75%. Because the
outside manufacturer would pay for all shipping costs, the variable selling expenses would be
only two-thirds of their present amount. Compute the unit cost that is relevant for comparison
to the price quoted by the outside manufacturer.

PROBLEM 12–19 Dropping or Retaining a Segment [LO12–2]
Jackson County Senior Services is a nonprofit organization devoted to providing essential services to seniors who live in their own homes within the Jackson County area. Three services are

Chapter 12

provided for seniors—home nursing, Meals On Wheels, and housekeeping. Data on revenue and expenses for the past year follow:

	Total	Home Nursing	Meals On Wheels	House-keeping
Revenues	$900,000	$260,000	$400,000	$240,000
Variable expenses	490,000	120,000	210,000	160,000
Contribution margin	410,000	140,000	190,000	80,000
Fixed expenses:				
Depreciation	68,000	8,000	40,000	20,000
Liability insurance	42,000	20,000	7,000	15,000
Program administrators' salaries	115,000	40,000	38,000	37,000
General administrative overhead*	180,000	52,000	80,000	48,000
Total fixed expenses	405,000	120,000	165,000	120,000
Net operating income (loss)	$ 5,000	$ 20,000	$ 25,000	$ (40,000)

*Allocated on the basis of program revenues.

The head administrator of Jackson County Senior Services, Judith Miyama, is concerned about the organization's finances and considers the net operating income of $5,000 last year to be razor-thin. (Last year's results were very similar to the results for previous years and are representative of what would be expected in the future.) She feels that the organization should be building its financial reserves at a more rapid rate in order to prepare for the next inevitable recession. After seeing the above report, Ms. Miyama asked for more information about the financial advisability of perhaps discontinuing the housekeeping program.

The depreciation in housekeeping is for a small van that is used to carry the housekeepers and their equipment from job to job. If the program were discontinued, the van would be donated to a charitable organization. None of the general administrative overhead would be avoided if the housekeeping program were dropped, but the liability insurance and the salary of the program administrator would be avoided.

Required:
1. Should the Housekeeping program be discontinued? Explain. Show computations to support your answer.
2. Recast the above data in a format that would be more useful to management in assessing the long-run financial viability of the various services.

PROBLEM 12-20 Sell or Process Further [LO12-7]
(Prepared from a situation suggested by Professor John W. Hardy.) Lone Star Meat Packers is a major processor of beef and other meat products. The company has a large amount of T-bone steak on hand, and it is trying to decide whether to sell the T-bone steaks as they are initially cut or to process them further into filet mignon and the New York cut.

If the T-bone steaks are sold as initially cut, the company figures that a 1-pound T-bone steak would yield the following profit:

Selling price ($2.25 per pound)	$2.25
Less joint costs incurred up to the split-off point where T-bone steak can be identified as a separate product	1.80
Profit per pound	$0.45

As mentioned above, instead of being sold as initially cut, the T-bone steaks could be further processed into filet mignon and New York cut steaks. Cutting one side of a T-bone steak provides the filet mignon, and cutting the other side provides the New York cut. One 16-ounce T-bone steak cut in this way will yield one 6-ounce filet mignon and one 8-ounce New York cut; the remaining ounces are waste. The cost of processing the T-bone steaks into these cuts is $0.25 per pound. The filet mignon can be sold for $4.00 per pound, and the New York cut can be sold for $2.80 per pound.

Required:

1. Determine the profit per pound from processing the T-bone steaks into filet mignon and New York cut steaks.
2. Would you recommend that the T-bone steaks be sold as initially cut or processed further? Why?

PROBLEM 12–21 Dropping or Retaining a Flight [LO12–2]

Profits have been decreasing for several years at Pegasus Airlines. In an effort to improve the company's performance, consideration is being given to dropping several flights that appear to be unprofitable.

A typical income statement for one round-trip of one such flight (flight 482) is as follows:

Ticket revenue (175 seats × 40% occupancy × $200 ticket price)	$14,000	100.0%
Variable expenses ($15 per person)	1,050	7.5
Contribution margin	12,950	92.5%
Flight expenses:		
Salaries, flight crew	1,800	
Flight promotion	750	
Depreciation of aircraft	1,550	
Fuel for aircraft	5,800	
Liability insurance	4,200	
Salaries, flight assistants	1,500	
Baggage loading and flight preparation	1,700	
Overnight costs for flight crew and		
assistants at destination	300	
Total flight expenses	17,600	
Net operating loss	$ (4,650)	

The following additional information is available about flight 482:

a. Members of the flight crew are paid fixed annual salaries, whereas the flight assistants are paid based on the number of round trips they complete.

b. One-third of the liability insurance is a special charge assessed against flight 482 because in the opinion of the insurance company, the destination of the flight is in a "high-risk" area. The remaining two-thirds would be unaffected by a decision to drop flight 482.

c. The baggage loading and flight preparation expense is an allocation of ground crews' salaries and depreciation of ground equipment. Dropping flight 482 would have no effect on the company's total baggage loading and flight preparation expenses.

d. If flight 482 is dropped, Pegasus Airlines has no authorization at present to replace it with another flight.

e. Aircraft depreciation is due entirely to obsolescence. Depreciation due to wear and tear is negligible.

f. Dropping flight 482 would not allow Pegasus Airlines to reduce the number of aircraft in its fleet or the number of flight crew on its payroll.

Required:

1. Prepare an analysis showing what impact dropping flight 482 would have on the airline's profits.
2. The airline's scheduling officer has been criticized because only about 50% of the seats on Pegasus' flights are being filled compared to an industry average of 60%. The scheduling officer has explained that Pegasus' average seat occupancy could be improved considerably by eliminating about 10% of its flights, but that doing so would reduce profits. Explain how this could happen.

PROBLEM 12–22 Accept or Reject a Special Order [LO12–4]

Polaski Company manufactures and sells a single product called a Ret. Operating at capacity, the company can produce and sell 30,000 Rets per year. Costs associated with this level of production and sales are given below:

	Unit	Total
Direct materials	$15	$ 450,000
Direct labor	8	240,000
Variable manufacturing overhead . . .	3	90,000
Fixed manufacturing overhead	9	270,000
Variable selling expense	4	120,000
Fixed selling expense	6	180,000
Total cost	$45	$1,350,000

The Rets normally sell for $50 each. Fixed manufacturing overhead is constant at $270,000 per year within the range of 25,000 through 30,000 Rets per year.

Required:

1. Assume that due to a recession, Polaski Company expects to sell only 25,000 Rets through regular channels next year. A large retail chain has offered to purchase 5,000 Rets if Polaski is willing to accept a 16% discount off the regular price. There would be no sales commissions on this order; thus, variable selling expenses would be slashed by 75%. However, Polaski Company would have to purchase a special machine to engrave the retail chain's name on the 5,000 units. This machine would cost $10,000. Polaski Company has no assurance that the retail chain will purchase additional units in the future. Determine the impact on profits next year if this special order is accepted.
2. Refer to the original data. Assume again that Polaski Company expects to sell only 25,000 Rets through regular channels next year. The U.S. Army would like to make a one-time-only purchase of 5,000 Rets. The Army would pay a fixed fee of $1.80 per Ret, and it would reimburse Polaski Company for all costs of production (variable and fixed) associated with the units. Because the army would pick up the Rets with its own trucks, there would be no variable selling expenses associated with this order. If Polaski Company accepts the order, by how much will profits increase or decrease for the year?
3. Assume the same situation as that described in (2) above, except that the company expects to sell 30,000 Rets through regular channels next year. Thus, accepting the U.S. Army's order would require giving up regular sales of 5,000 Rets. If the Army's order is accepted, by how much will profits increase or decrease from what they would be if the 5,000 Rets were sold through regular channels?

PROBLEM 12–23 Make or Buy Decision [LO12–3]

Silven Industries, which manufactures and sells a highly successful line of summer lotions and insect repellents, has decided to diversify in order to stabilize sales throughout the year. A natural area for the company to consider is the production of winter lotions and creams to prevent dry and chapped skin.

After considerable research, a winter products line has been developed. However, Silven's president has decided to introduce only one of the new products for this coming winter. If the product is a success, further expansion in future years will be initiated.

The product selected (called Chap-Off) is a lip balm that will be sold in a lipstick-type tube. The product will be sold to wholesalers in boxes of 24 tubes for $8 per box. Because of excess capacity, no additional fixed manufacturing overhead costs will be incurred to produce the product. However, a $90,000 charge for fixed manufacturing overhead will be absorbed by the product under the company's absorption costing system.

Using the estimated sales and production of 100,000 boxes of Chap-Off, the Accounting Department has developed the following cost per box:

Direct material	$3.60
Direct labor	2.00
Manufacturing overhead	1.40
Total cost	$7.00

Differential Analysis: The Key to Decision Making

The costs above include costs for producing both the lip balm and the tube that contains it. As an alternative to making the tubes, Silven has approached a supplier to discuss the possibility of purchasing the tubes for Chap-Off. The purchase price of the empty tubes from the supplier would be $1.35 per box of 24 tubes. If Silven Industries accepts the purchase proposal, direct labor and variable manufacturing overhead costs per box of Chap-Off would be reduced by 10% and direct materials costs would be reduced by 25%.

Required:

1. Should Silven Industries make or buy the tubes? Show calculations to support your answer.
2. What would be the maximum purchase price acceptable to Silven Industries? Explain.
3. Instead of sales of 100,000 boxes, revised estimates show a sales volume of 120,000 boxes. At this new volume, additional equipment must be acquired to manufacture the tubes at an annual rental of $40,000. Assuming that the outside supplier will not accept an order for less than 120,000 boxes, should Silven Industries make or buy the tubes? Show computations to support your answer.
4. Refer to the data in (3) above. Assume that the outside supplier will accept an order of any size for the tubes at $1.35 per box. How, if at all, would this change your answer? Show computations.
5. What qualitative factors should Silven Industries consider in determining whether they should make or buy the tubes?

(CMA, adapted)

PROBLEM 12–24 Shutting Down or Continuing to Operate a Plant [LO12–2]

(Note: This type of decision is similar to keeping or dropping a product line.)

Birch Company normally produces and sells 30,000 units of RG-6 each month. RG-6 is a small electrical relay used as a component part in the automotive industry. The selling price is $22 per unit, variable costs are $14 per unit, fixed manufacturing overhead costs total $150,000 per month, and fixed selling costs total $30,000 per month.

Employment-contract strikes in the companies that purchase the bulk of the RG-6 units have caused Birch Company's sales to temporarily drop to only 8,000 units per month. Birch Company estimates that the strikes will last for two months, after which time sales of RG-6 should return to normal. Due to the current low level of sales, Birch Company is thinking about closing down its own plant during the strike, which would reduce its fixed manufacturing overhead costs by $45,000 per month and its fixed selling costs by 10%. Start-up costs at the end of the shutdown period would total $8,000. Because Birch Company uses Lean Production methods, no inventories are on hand.

Required:

1. Assuming that the strikes continue for two months, would you recommend that Birch Company close its own plant? Explain. Show computations.
2. At what level of sales (in units) for the two-month period should Birch Company be indifferent between closing the plant or keeping it open? Show computations. (Hint: This is a type of break-even analysis, except that the fixed cost portion of your break-even computation should include only those fixed costs that are relevant [i.e., avoidable] over the two-month period.)

PROBLEM 12–25 Utilization of a Constrained Resource [LO12–5, LO12–6]

The Walton Toy Company manufactures a line of dolls and a doll dress sewing kit. Demand for the dolls is increasing, and management requests assistance from you in determining an economical sales and production mix for the coming year. The company has provided the following data:

Product	Demand Next Year (units)	Selling Price per Unit	Direct Materials	Direct Labor
Debbie	50,000	$13.50	$4.30	$3.20
Trish	42,000	$5.50	$1.10	$2.00
Sarah	35,000	$21.00	$6.44	$5.60
Mike	40,000	$10.00	$2.00	$4.00
Sewing kit	325,000	$8.00	$3.20	$1.60

The following additional information is available:

a. The company's plant has a capacity of 130,000 direct labor-hours per year on a single-shift basis. The company's present employees and equipment can produce all five products.
b. The direct labor rate of $8 per hour is expected to remain unchanged during the coming year.

574

Chapter 12

c.   Fixed costs total $520,000 per year. Variable overhead costs are $2 per direct labor-hour.
d.   All of the company's nonmanufacturing costs are fixed.
e.   The company's finished goods inventory is negligible and can be ignored.

Required:
1.   Determine the contribution margin per direct labor-hour expended on each product.
2.   Prepare a schedule showing the total direct labor-hours that will be required to produce the units estimated to be sold during the coming year.
3.   Examine the data you have computed in (1) and (2) above. How would you allocate the 130,000 direct labor-hours of capacity to Walton Toy Company's various products?
4.   What is the highest total contribution margin that the company can earn if it makes optimal use of its constrained resource?
5.   What is the highest price, in terms of a rate per hour, that Walton Toy Company would be willing to pay for additional capacity (that is, for added direct labor time)?
6.   Assume again that the company does not want to reduce sales of any product. Identify ways in which the company could obtain the additional output.

(CMA, adapted)

PROBLEM 12–26 Close or Retain a Store [LO12–2]
Superior Markets, Inc., operates three stores in a large metropolitan area. A segmented absorption costing income statement for the company for the last quarter is given below:

Superior Markets, Inc. Income Statement For the Quarter Ended September 30				
	Total	North Store	South Store	East Store
Sales	$3,000,000	$720,000	$1,200,000	$1,080,000
Cost of goods sold	1,657,200	403,200	660,000	594,000
Gross margin	1,342,800	316,800	540,000	486,000
Selling and administrative expenses:				
Selling expenses	817,000	231,400	315,000	270,600
Administrative expenses	383,000	106,000	150,900	126,100
Total expenses	1,200,000	337,400	465,900	396,700
Net operating income (loss)	$ 142,800	$ (20,600)	$ 74,100	$ 89,300

The North Store has consistently shown losses over the past two years. For this reason, management is giving consideration to closing the store. The company has asked you to make a recommendation as to whether the store should be closed or kept open. The following additional information is available for your use:
a.   The breakdown of the selling and administrative expenses is as follows:

	Total	North Store	South Store	East Store
Selling expenses:				
Sales salaries	$239,000	$ 70,000	$ 89,000	$ 80,000
Direct advertising	187,000	51,000	72,000	64,000
General advertising*	45,000	10,800	18,000	16,200
Store rent	300,000	85,000	120,000	95,000
Depreciation of store fixtures	16,000	4,600	6,000	5,400
Delivery salaries	21,000	7,000	7,000	7,000
Depreciation of delivery equipment	9,000	3,000	3,000	3,000
Total selling expenses	$817,000	$231,400	$315,000	$270,600

*Allocated on the basis of sales dollars.

Differential Analysis: The Key to Decision Making

	Total	North Store	South Store	East Store
Administrative expenses:				
Store management salaries	$ 70,000	$ 21,000	$ 30,000	$ 19,000
General office salaries*	50,000	12,000	20,000	18,000
Insurance on fixtures and inventory	25,000	7,500	9,000	8,500
Utilities	106,000	31,000	40,000	35,000
Employment taxes	57,000	16,500	21,900	18,600
General office—other*	75,000	18,000	30,000	27,000
Total administrative expenses	$383,000	$106,000	$150,900	$126,100

*Allocated on the basis of sales dollars.

b. The lease on the building housing the North Store can be broken with no penalty.
c. The fixtures being used in the North Store would be transferred to the other two stores if the North Store were closed.
d. The general manager of the North Store would be retained and transferred to another position in the company if the North Store were closed. She would be filling a position that would otherwise be filled by hiring a new employee at a salary of $11,000 per quarter. The general manager of the North Store would be retained at her normal salary of $12,000 per quarter. All other employees in the store would be discharged.
e. The company has one delivery crew that serves all three stores. One delivery person could be discharged if the North Store were closed. This person's salary is $4,000 per quarter. The delivery equipment would be distributed to the other stores. The equipment does not wear out through use, but does eventually become obsolete.
f. The company's employment taxes are 15% of salaries.
g. One-third of the insurance in the North Store is on the store's fixtures.
h. The "General office salaries" and "General office—other" relate to the overall management of Superior Markets, Inc. If the North Store were closed, one person in the general office could be discharged because of the decrease in overall workload. This person's compensation is $6,000 per quarter.

Required:
1. Prepare a schedule showing the change in revenues and expenses and the impact on the company's overall net operating income that would result if the North Store were closed.
2. Assuming that the store space can't be subleased, what recommendation would you make to the management of Superior Markets, Inc.?
3. Disregard requirement 2. Assume that if the North Store were closed, at least one-fourth of its sales would transfer to the East Store, due to strong customer loyalty to Superior Markets. The East Store has enough capacity to handle the increased sales. You may assume that the increased sales in the East Store would yield the same gross margin as a percentage of sales as present sales in that store. What effect would these factors have on your recommendation concerning the North Store? Show all computations to support your answer.

PROBLEM 12–27 Sell or Process Further [LO12–7]

Come-Clean Corporation produces a variety of cleaning compounds and solutions for both industrial and household use. While most of its products are processed independently, a few are related, such as the company's Grit 337 and its Sparkle silver polish.

Grit 337 is a coarse cleaning powder with many industrial uses. It costs $1.60 a pound to make, and it has a selling price of $2.00 a pound. A small portion of the annual production of Grit 337 is retained in the factory for further processing. It is combined with several other ingredients to form a paste that is marketed as Sparkle silver polish. The silver polish sells for $4.00 per jar.

This further processing requires one-fourth pound of Grit 337 per jar of silver polish. The additional direct costs involved in the processing of a jar of silver polish are:

Other ingredients	$0.65
Direct labor	1.48
Total direct cost	$2.13

576 Chapter 12

Overhead costs associated with processing the silver polish are:

Variable manufacturing overhead cost	25% of direct labor cost
Fixed manufacturing overhead cost (per month):	
Production supervisor	$3,000
Depreciation of mixing equipment	$1,400

The production supervisor has no duties other than to oversee production of the silver polish. The mixing equipment is special-purpose equipment acquired specifically to produce the silver polish. Its resale value is negligible and it does not wear out through use.

Direct labor is a variable cost at Come-Clean Corporation.

Advertising costs for the silver polish total $4,000 per month. Variable selling costs associated with the silver polish are 7.5% of sales.

Due to a recent decline in the demand for silver polish, the company is wondering whether its continued production is advisable. The sales manager feels that it would be more profitable to sell all of the Grit 337 as a cleaning powder.

Required:
1. What is the incremental contribution margin per jar from further processing of Grit 337 into silver polish?
2. What is the minimum number of jars of silver polish that must be sold each month to justify the continued processing of Grit 337 into silver polish? Explain. Show all computations.

(CMA, adapted)

PROBLEM 12–28 Make or Buy Analysis [LO12–3]
"In my opinion, we ought to stop making our own drums and accept that outside supplier's offer," said Wim Niewindt, managing director of Antilles Refining, N.V., of Aruba. "At a price of $18 per drum, we would be paying $5 less than it costs us to manufacture the drums in our own plant. Since we use 60,000 drums a year, that would be an annual cost savings of $300,000." Antilles Refining's current cost to manufacture one drum is given below (based on 60,000 drums per year):

Direct materials	$10.35
Direct labor	6.00
Variable overhead	1.50
Fixed overhead ($2.80 general company	
overhead, $1.60 depreciation	
and, $0.75 supervision)	5.15
Total cost per drum	$23.00

A decision about whether to make or buy the drums is especially important at this time because the equipment being used to make the drums is completely worn out and must be replaced. The choices facing the company are:

Alternative 1: Rent new equipment and continue to make the drums. The equipment would be rented for $135,000 per year.
Alternative 2: Purchase the drums from an outside supplier at $18 per drum.

The new equipment would be more efficient than the equipment that Antilles Refining has been using and, according to the manufacturer, would reduce direct labor and variable overhead costs by 30%. The old equipment has no resale value. Supervision cost ($45,000 per year) and direct materials cost per drum would not be affected by the new equipment. The new equipment's capacity would be 90,000 drums per year.

The company's total general company overhead would be unaffected by this decision.

Required:
1. To assist the managing director in making a decision, prepare an analysis showing the total cost and the cost per drum for each of the two alternatives given above. Assume that 60,000 drums are needed each year. Which course of action would you recommend to the managing director?
2. Would your recommendation in (1) above be the same if the company's needs were: (a) 75,000 drums per year or (b) 90,000 drums per year? Show computations to support your answer, with costs presented on both a total and a per unit basis.
3. What other factors would you recommend that the company consider before making a decision?

Cases

Available with McGraw-Hill's *Connect® Accounting.*

CASE 12–29 Sell or Process Further Decision [LO12–7]

The Scottie Sweater Company produces sweaters under the "Scottie" label. The company buys raw wool and processes it into wool yarn from which the sweaters are woven. One spindle of wool yarn is required to produce one sweater. The costs and revenues associated with the sweaters are given below:

		Per Sweater
Selling price		$30.00
Cost to manufacture:		
Raw materials:		
Buttons, thread, lining	$ 2.00	
Wool yarn	16.00	
Total raw materials	18.00	
Direct labor	5.80	
Manufacturing overhead	8.70	32.50
Manufacturing profit (loss)		$ (2.50)

Originally, all of the wool yarn was used to produce sweaters, but in recent years a market has developed for the wool yarn itself. The yarn is purchased by other companies for use in production of wool blankets and other wool products. Since the development of the market for the wool yarn, a continuing dispute has existed in the Scottie Sweater Company as to whether the yarn should be sold simply as yarn or processed into sweaters. Current cost and revenue data on the yarn are given below:

		Per Spindle of Yarn
Selling price		$20.00
Cost to manufacture:		
Raw materials (raw wool)	$7.00	
Direct labor	3.60	
Manufacturing overhead	5.40	16.00
Manufacturing profit		$ 4.00

The market for sweaters is temporarily depressed, due to unusually warm weather in the western states where the sweaters are sold. This has made it necessary for the company to discount the selling price of the sweaters to $30 from the normal $40 price. Since the market for wool yarn has remained strong, the dispute has again surfaced over whether the yarn should be sold outright rather than processed into sweaters. The sales manager thinks that the production of sweaters should be discontinued; she is upset about having to sell sweaters at a $2.50 loss when the yarn could be sold for a $4.00 profit. However, the production superintendent does not want to close down a large portion of the factory. He argues that the company is in the sweater business, not the yarn business, and that the company should focus on its core strength.

All of the manufacturing overhead costs are fixed and would not be affected even if sweaters were discontinued. Manufacturing overhead is assigned to products on the basis of 150% of direct labor cost. Materials and direct labor costs are variable.

Required:

1. Would you recommend that the wool yarn be sold outright or processed into sweaters? Support your answer with appropriate computations and explain your reasoning.
2. What is the lowest price that the company should accept for a sweater? Support your answer with appropriate computations and explain your reasoning.

CASE 12–30 Ethics and the Manager; Shut Down or Continue Operations [LO12–2]

Haley Romeros had just been appointed vice president of the Rocky Mountain Region of the Bank Services Corporation (BSC). The company provides check processing services for small banks. The banks send checks presented for deposit or payment to BSC, which records the data on each check in a computerized database. BSC then sends the data electronically to the nearest Federal Reserve Bank check-clearing center where the appropriate transfers of funds are made between banks. The Rocky Mountain Region has three check processing centers, which are located in Billings, Montana; Great Falls, Montana; and Clayton, Idaho. Prior to her promotion to vice president, Ms. Romeros had been the manager of a check processing center in New Jersey.

Immediately after assuming her new position, Ms. Romeros requested a complete financial report for the just-ended fiscal year from the region's controller, John Littlebear. Ms. Romeros specified that the financial report should follow the standardized format required by corporate headquarters for all regional performance reports. That report follows:

Bank Services Corporation (BSC)
Rocky Mountain Region
Financial Performance

	Total	Check Processing Centers		
		Billings	Great Falls	Clayton
Sales	$50,000,000	$20,000,000	$18,000,000	$12,000,000
Operating expenses:				
Direct labor	32,000,000	12,500,000	11,000,000	8,500,000
Variable overhead	850,000	350,000	310,000	190,000
Equipment depreciation	3,900,000	1,300,000	1,400,000	1,200,000
Facility expense	2,800,000	900,000	800,000	1,100,000
Local administrative expense*	450,000	140,000	160,000	150,000
Regional administrative expense†	1,500,000	600,000	540,000	360,000
Corporate administrative expense‡	4,750,000	1,900,000	1,710,000	1,140,000
Total operating expense	46,250,000	17,690,000	15,920,000	12,640,000
Net operating income (loss)	$ 3,750,000	$ 2,310,000	$ 2,080,000	$ (640,000)

*Local administrative expenses are the administrative expenses incurred at the check processing centers.

†Regional administrative expenses are allocated to the check processing centers based on sales.

‡Corporate administrative expenses are charged to segments of the company such as the Rocky Mountain Region and the check processing centers at the rate of 9.5% of their sales.

Upon seeing this report, Ms. Romeros summoned John Littlebear for an explanation.

Romeros: What's the story on Clayton? It didn't have a loss the previous year did it?

Littlebear: No, the Clayton facility has had a nice profit every year since it was opened six years ago, but Clayton lost a big contract this year.

Romeros: Why?

Littlebear: One of our national competitors entered the local market and bid very aggressively on the contract. We couldn't afford to meet the bid. Clayton's costs—particularly their facility expenses—are just too high. When Clayton lost the contract, we had to lay off a lot of employees, but we could not reduce the fixed costs of the Clayton facility.

Romeros: Why is Clayton's facility expense so high? It's a smaller facility than either Billings or Great Falls and yet its facility expense is higher.

Littlebear: The problem is that we are able to rent suitable facilities very cheaply at Billings and Great Falls. No such facilities were available at Clayton; we had them built. Unfortunately, there were big cost overruns. The contractor we hired was inexperienced at this kind of work and in fact went bankrupt before the project was completed. After hiring another contractor to finish the work, we were way over budget. The large depreciation charges on the facility didn't matter at first because we didn't have much competition at the time and could charge premium prices.

Romeros: Well we can't do that anymore. The Clayton facility will obviously have to be shut down. Its business can be shifted to the other two check processing centers in the region.

Littlebear: I would advise against that. The $1,200,000 in depreciation at the Clayton facility is misleading. That facility should last indefinitely with proper maintenance. And it has no resale value; there is no other commercial activity around Clayton.

Romeros: What about the other costs at Clayton?

Differential Analysis: The Key to Decision Making   **579**

Littlebear: If we shifted Clayton's business over to the other two processing centers in the region, we wouldn't save anything on direct labor or variable overhead costs. We might save $90,000 or so in local administrative expense, but we would not save any regional administrative expense and corporate headquarters would still charge us 9.5% of our sales as corporate administrative expense.

In addition, we would have to rent more space in Billings and Great Falls in order to handle the work transferred from Clayton; that would probably cost us at least $600,000 a year. And don't forget that it will cost us something to move the equipment from Clayton to Billings and Great Falls. And the move will disrupt service to customers.

Romeros: I understand all of that, but a money-losing processing center on my performance report is completely unacceptable.

Littlebear: And if you shut down Clayton, you are going to throw some loyal employees out of work.

Romeros: That's unfortunate, but we have to face hard business realities.

Littlebear: And you would have to write off the investment in the facilities at Clayton.

Romeros: I can explain a write-off to corporate headquarters; hiring an inexperienced contractor to build the Clayton facility was my predecessor's mistake. But they'll have my head at headquarters if I show operating losses every year at one of my processing centers. Clayton has to go. At the next corporate board meeting, I am going to recommend that the Clayton facility be closed.

Required:

1. From the standpoint of the company as a whole, should the Clayton processing center be shut down and its work redistributed to other processing centers in the region? Explain.
2. Do you think Haley Romeros's decision to shut down the Clayton facility is ethical? Explain.
3. What influence should the depreciation on the facilities at Clayton have on prices charged by Clayton for its services?

CASE 12–31 Integrative Case: Relevant Costs; Pricing [LO12–1, LO12–4]

Wesco Incorporated's only product is a combination fertilizer/weedkiller called GrowNWeed. GrowNWeed is sold nationwide to retail nurseries and garden stores.

Zwinger Nursery plans to sell a similar fertilizer/weedkiller compound through its regional nursery chain under its own private label. Zwinger does not have manufacturing facilities of its own, so it has asked Wesco (and several other companies) to submit a bid for manufacturing and delivering a 20,000-pound order of the private brand compound to Zwinger. While the chemical composition of the Zwinger compound differs from that of GrowNWeed, the manufacturing processes are very similar.

The Zwinger compound would be produced in 1,000-pound lots. Each lot would require 25 direct labor-hours and the following chemicals:

Chemicals	Quantity in Pounds
AG-5	300
KL-2	200
CW-7	150
DF-6	175

The first three chemicals (AG-5, KL-2, and CW-7) are all used in the production of GrowNWeed. DF-6 was used in another compound that Wesco discontinued several months ago. The supply of DF-6 that Wesco had on hand when the other compound was discontinued was not discarded. Wesco could sell its supply of DF-6 at the prevailing market price less $0.10 per pound selling and handling expenses.

Wesco also has on hand a chemical called BH-3, which was manufactured for use in another product that is no longer produced. BH-3, which cannot be used in GrowNWeed, can be substituted for AG-5 on a one-for-one basis without affecting the quality of the Zwinger compound. The BH-3 in inventory has a salvage value of $600.

Inventory and cost data for the chemicals that can be used to produce the Zwinger compound are shown below:

Raw Material	Pounds in Inventory	Actual Price per Pound When Purchased	Current Market Price per Pound
AG-5	18,000	$1.15	$1.20
KL-2	6,000	$1.10	$1.05
CW-7	7,000	$1.35	$1.35
DF-6	3,000	$0.80	$0.70
BH-3	3,500	$0.90	(Salvage)

The current direct labor wage rate is $14 per hour. The predetermined overhead rate is based on direct labor-hours (DLH). The predetermined overhead rate for the current year, based on a two-shift capacity with no overtime, is as follows:

Variable manufacturing overhead	$ 3.00 per DLH
Fixed manufacturing overhead	10.50 per DLH
Combined predetermined overhead rate	$13.50 per DLH

Wesco's production manager reports that the present equipment and facilities are adequate to manufacture the Zwinger compound. Therefore, the order would have no effect on total fixed manufacturing overhead costs. However, Wesco is within 400 hours of its two-shift capacity this month. Any additional hours beyond the 400 hours must be done in overtime. If need be, the Zwinger compound could be produced on regular time by shifting a portion of GrowNWeed production to overtime. Wesco's direct labor wage rate for overtime is $21 per hour. There is no allowance for any overtime premium in the predetermined overhead rate.

Required:
1. Wesco has decided to submit a bid for the 20,000 pound order of Zwinger's new compound. The order must be delivered by the end of the current month. Zwinger has indicated that this is a one-time order that will not be repeated. Calculate the lowest price that Wesco could bid for the order without reducing its net operating income.
2. Refer to the original data. Assume that Zwinger Nursery plans to place regular orders for 20,000-pound lots of the new compound. Wesco expects the demand for GrowNWeed to remain strong. Therefore, the recurring orders from Zwinger would put Wesco over its two-shift capacity. However, production could be scheduled so that 90% of each Zwinger order could be completed during regular hours. As another option, some GrowNWeed production could be shifted temporarily to overtime so that the Zwinger orders could be produced on regular time. Current market prices are the best available estimates of future market prices.

    Wesco's standard markup policy for new products is 40% of the full manufacturing cost, including fixed manufacturing overhead. Calculate the price that Wesco, Inc., would quote Zwinger Nursery for each 20,000 pound lot of the new compound, assuming that it is to be treated as a new product and this pricing policy is followed.

(CMA, adapted)

CASE 12–32 Make or Buy; Utilization of a Constrained Resource [LO12–1, LO12–3, LO12–5]
TufStuff, Inc., sells a wide range of drums, bins, boxes, and other containers that are used in the chemical industry. One of the company's products is a heavy-duty corrosion-resistant metal drum, called the WVD drum, used to store toxic wastes. Production is constrained by the capacity of an automated welding machine that is used to make precision welds. A total of 2,000 hours of welding time is available annually on the machine. Because each drum requires 0.4 hours of welding machine time, annual production is limited to 5,000 drums. At present, the welding machine is used exclusively to make the WVD drums. The accounting department has provided the following financial data concerning the WVD drums:

WVD Drums		
Selling price per drum		$149.00
Cost per drum:		
Direct materials	$52.10	
Direct labor ($18 per hour)	3.60	
Manufacturing overhead	4.50	
Selling and administrative expense ..	29.80	90.00
Margin per drum		$ 59.00

Management believes 6,000 WVD drums could be sold each year if the company had sufficient manufacturing capacity. As an alternative to adding another welding machine, management has considered buying additional drums from an outside supplier. Harcor Industries, Inc., a supplier of quality products, would be able to provide up to 4,000 WVD-type drums per year at a price of $138 per drum, which TufStuff would resell to its customers at its normal selling price after appropriate relabeling.

Megan Flores, TufStuff's production manager, has suggested that the company could make better use of the welding machine by manufacturing bike frames, which would require only 0.5 hours of welding machine time per frame and yet sell for far more than the drums. Megan believes that TufStuff could sell up to 1,600 bike frames per year to bike manufacturers at a price of $239 each. The accounting department has provided the following data concerning the proposed new product:

	Bike Frames	
Selling price per frame		$239.00
Cost per frame:		
Direct materials	$99.40	
Direct labor ($18 per hour)	28.80	
Manufacturing overhead	36.00	
Selling and administrative expense . .	47.80	212.00
Margin per frame		$ 27.00

The bike frames could be produced with existing equipment and personnel. Manufacturing overhead is allocated to products on the basis of direct labor-hours. Most of the manufacturing overhead consists of fixed common costs such as rent on the factory building, but some of it is variable. The variable manufacturing overhead has been estimated at $1.35 per WVD drum and $1.90 per bike frame. The variable manufacturing overhead cost would not be incurred on drums acquired from the outside supplier.

Selling and administrative expenses are allocated to products on the basis of revenues. Almost all of the selling and administrative expenses are fixed common costs, but it has been estimated that variable selling and administrative expenses amount to $0.75 per WVD drum whether made or purchased and would be $1.30 per bike frame.

All of the company's employees—direct and indirect—are paid for full 40-hour workweeks and the company has a policy of laying off workers only in major recessions.

Required:

1. Would you be comfortable relying on the financial data provided by the accounting department for making decisions related to the WVD drums and bike frames? Why?
2. Compute the contribution margin per unit for:
   a. Purchased WVD drums.
   b. Manufactured WVD drums.
   c. Manufactured bike frames.
3. Determine the number of WVD drums (if any) that should be purchased and the number of WVD drums and/or bike frames (if any) that should be manufactured. What is the increase in net operating income that would result from this plan over current operations?

   As soon as your analysis was shown to the top management team at TufStuff, several managers got into an argument concerning how direct labor costs should be treated when making this decision. One manager argued that direct labor is always treated as a variable cost in textbooks and in practice and has always been considered a variable cost at TufStuff. After all, "direct" means you can directly trace the cost to products. "If direct labor is not a variable cost, what is?" Another manager argued just as strenuously that direct labor should be considered a fixed cost at TufStuff. No one had been laid off in over a decade, and for all practical purposes, everyone at the plant is on a monthly salary. Everyone classified as direct labor works a regular 40-hour workweek and overtime has not been necessary since the company adopted Lean Production techniques. Whether the welding machine is used to make drums or frames, the total payroll would be exactly the same. There is enough slack, in the form of idle time, to accommodate any increase in total direct labor time that the bike frames would require.

4. Redo requirements (2) and (3) making the opposite assumption about direct labor from the one you originally made. In other words, if you treated direct labor as a variable cost, redo the analysis treating it as a fixed cost. If you treated direct labor as a fixed cost, redo the analysis treating it as a variable cost.
5. What do you think is the correct way to treat direct labor cost in this situation—as variable or as fixed? Explain.

CASE 12–33 Plant Closing Decision [LO12–1, LO12–2]

QualSupport Corporation manufactures seats for automobiles, vans, trucks, and various recreational vehicles. The company has a number of plants around the world, including the Denver Cover Plant, which makes seat covers.

Ted Vosilo is the plant manager of the Denver Cover Plant but also serves as the regional production manager for the company. His budget as the regional manager is charged to the Denver Cover Plant.

Vosilo has just heard that QualSupport has received a bid from an outside vendor to supply the equivalent of the entire annual output of the Denver Cover Plant for $35 million. Vosilo was astonished at the low outside bid because the budget for the Denver Cover Plant's operating costs for the upcoming year was set at $52 million. If this bid is accepted, the Denver Cover Plant will be closed down.

The budget for Denver Cover's operating costs for the coming year is presented below.

Denver Cover Plant
Annual Budget for Operating Costs

Materials		$14,000,000
Labor:		
Direct	$13,100,000	
Supervision	900,000	
Indirect plant	4,000,000	18,000,000
Overhead:		
Depreciation—equipment	3,200,000	
Depreciation—building	7,000,000	
Pension expense	5,000,000	
Plant manager and staff	800,000	
Corporate expenses*	4,000,000	20,000,000
Total budgeted costs		$52,000,000

*Fixed corporate expenses allocated to plants and other operating units based on total budgeted wage and salary costs.

Additional facts regarding the plant's operations are as follows:

a. Due to Denver Cover's commitment to use high-quality fabrics in all of its products, the Purchasing Department was instructed to place blanket purchase orders with major suppliers to ensure the receipt of sufficient materials for the coming year. If these orders are canceled as a consequence of the plant closing, termination charges would amount to 20% of the cost of direct materials.

b. Approximately 400 plant employees will lose their jobs if the plant is closed. This includes all of the direct laborers and supervisors as well as the plumbers, electricians, and other skilled workers classified as indirect plant workers. Some would be able to find new jobs while many others would have difficulty. All employees would have difficulty matching Denver Cover's base pay of $18.80 per hour, which is the highest in the area. A clause in Denver Cover's contract with the union may help some employees; the company must provide employment assistance to its former employees for 12 months after a plant closing. The estimated cost to administer this service would be $1.5 million for the year.

c. Some employees would probably choose early retirement because QualSupport has an excellent pension plan. In fact, $3 million of the annual pension expense would continue whether Denver Cover is open or not.

d. Vosilo and his staff would not be affected by the closing of Denver Cover. They would still be responsible for administering three other area plants.

e. If the Denver Cover Plant were closed, the company would realize about $3.2 million salvage value for the equipment and building. If the plant remains open, there are no plans to make any significant investments in new equipment or buildings. The old equipment is adequate and should last indefinitely.

Required:

1. Without regard to costs, identify the advantages to QualSupport Corporation of continuing to obtain covers from its own Denver Cover Plant.

2. QualSupport Corporation plans to prepare a financial analysis that will be used in deciding whether or not to close the Denver Cover Plant. Management has asked you to identify:
    a. The annual budgeted costs that are relevant to the decision regarding closing the plant (show the dollar amounts).
    b. The annual budgeted costs that are *not* relevant to the decision regarding closing the plant and explain why they are not relevant (again show the dollar amounts).
    c. Any nonrecurring costs that would arise due to the closing of the plant, and explain how they would affect the decision (again show any dollar amounts).

3. Looking at the data you have prepared in (2) above, should the plant be closed? Show computations and explain your answer.

4. Identify any revenues or costs not specifically mentioned in the problem that QualSupport should consider before making a decision.

(CMA, adapted)

Pricing Products and Services

LEARNING OBJECTIVES

After studying this appendix, you should be able to:

LOA–1   Compute the profit-maximizing price of a product or service using the price elasticity of demand and variable cost.

LOA–2   Compute the selling price of a product using the absorption costing approach.

LOA–3   Compute the target cost for a new product or service.

714   Appendix A

Introduction

Some products have an established market price. Consumers will not pay more than this price and there is no reason for a supplier to charge less—the supplier can sell all that it produces at this price. Under these circumstances, the supplier simply charges the prevailing market price for the product. Markets for basic raw materials such as farm products and minerals follow this pattern.

In this appendix, we are concerned with the more common situation in which a business is faced with the problem of setting its own prices. Clearly, the pricing decision can be critical. If the price is set too high, customers won't buy the company's products. If the price is set too low, the company's costs won't be covered.

The usual approach in pricing is to *mark up* cost.[1] A product's **markup** is the difference between its selling price and its cost and is usually expressed as a percentage of cost.

$$\text{Selling price} = (1 + \text{Markup percentage}) \times \text{Cost}$$

For example, a company that uses a markup of 50% adds 50% to the costs of its products to determine selling prices. If a product costs $10, then the company would charge $15 for the product. This approach is called **cost-plus pricing** because a predetermined markup percentage is applied to a cost base to determine the selling price.

Two key issues must be addressed with the cost-plus approach to pricing. First, what cost should be used? Second, how should the markup be determined? Several alternative approaches are considered in this appendix, starting with the approach generally favored by economists.

IN BUSINESS

THE BUSINESS OF ART SCULPTURE

Shidoni Foundry, located in Tesuque, New Mexico, is a fine art casting and fabrication facility. The process of creating a bronze or other metal sculpture is complex. The artist creates the sculpture using modeling clay and then hires a foundry such as Shidoni to produce the actual metal sculpture. Shidoni craftspeople make a rubber mold from the clay model then use that mold to make a wax version of the original. The wax is in turn used to make a ceramic casting mold, and finally the bronze version is cast. Both the wax and the ceramic casting mold are destroyed in the process of making the metal casting, but the rubber mold is not and can be reused to make additional castings.

The surface of the metal sculpture can be treated with various patinas. One of the accompanying photos shows Harry Gold, the shop's patina artist, applying a patina to a metal sculpture with brush and blowtorch. The other photo shows a finished sculpture with patinas applied.

The artist is faced with a difficult business decision. The rubber mold for a small figure such as the seated Indian in the accompanying photo costs roughly $500; the mold for a life-size figure such as the cowboy costs $3,800 to $5,000. This is just for the mold! Fortunately, as discussed above, a number of metal castings can be made from each mold. However, each life-size casting costs $8,500 to $11,000. In contrast, a casting of the much smaller Indian sculpture would cost about $750. Given the fixed costs of the mold and variable costs of the casting, finish treatments, and bases, the artist must decide how many castings to produce and how to price them. The fewer the castings, the greater the rarity factor, and hence the higher the price that can be charged to art lovers. However, in that case, the fixed costs of making the mold must be spread across fewer items. The artist must make sure not to price the sculptures so high that the investment in molds and in the castings cannot be recovered.

Source: Conversations with Shidoni personnel, including Bill Rogers and Harry Gold, and Shidoni literature. See www.shidoni.com for more information concerning the company.

---

[1]   There are some legal restrictions on prices. Antitrust laws prohibit "predatory" prices, which are generally interpreted by the courts to mean a price below average variable cost. "Price discrimination"—charging different prices to customers in the same market for the same product or service—is also prohibited by the law.

The Economists' Approach to Pricing

If a company raises the price of a product, unit sales ordinarily fall. Because of this, pricing is a delicate balancing act in which the benefits of higher revenues per unit are traded off against the lower volume that results from charging a higher price. The sensitivity of unit sales to changes in price is called the *price elasticity of demand*.

LO1–1
Compute the profit-maximizing price of a product or service using the price elasticity of demand and variable cost.

Elasticity of Demand

A product's price elasticity should be a key element in setting its price. The **price elasticity of demand** measures the degree to which a change in price affects the unit sales of a product or service. Demand for a product is said to be *inelastic* if a change in price has little effect on the number of units sold. The demand for designer perfumes sold by trained personnel at cosmetic counters in department stores is relatively inelastic. Raising or lowering prices on these luxury goods has little effect on unit sales. On the other hand, demand for a product is *elastic* if a change in price has a substantial effect on the volume of units sold. An example of a product whose demand is elastic is gasoline. If a gas station raises its price for gasoline, unit sales will drop as customers seek lower prices elsewhere.

Price elasticity is very important in determining prices. Managers should set higher markups over cost when customers are relatively insensitive to price (i.e., demand is inelastic) and lower markups when customers are relatively sensitive to price (i.e., demand is elastic). This principle is followed in department stores. Merchandise sold in the bargain basement has a much lower markup than merchandise sold elsewhere in the store because customers who shop in the bargain basement are much more sensitive to price (i.e., demand is elastic).

The price elasticity of demand for a product or service, ϵ_d, can be estimated using the following formula.[2,3]

$$\epsilon_d = \frac{\ln(1 + \% \text{ change in quantity sold})}{\ln(1 + \% \text{ change in price})}$$

For example, suppose that the managers of Nature's Garden believe that a 10% increase in the selling price of their apple-almond shampoo would result in a 15% decrease in the number of bottles of shampoo sold.[4] The price elasticity of demand for this product would be computed as follows:

$$\epsilon_d = \frac{\ln[1 + (-0.15)]}{\ln[1 + (0.10)]} = \frac{\ln(0.85)}{\ln(1.10)} = -1.71$$

For comparison purposes, the managers of Nature's Garden believe that another product, strawberry glycerin soap, would experience a 20% drop in unit sales if its price is increased by 10%. (Purchasers of this product are more sensitive to price than the purchasers of the apple-almond shampoo.) The price elasticity of demand for the strawberry glycerin soap is:

$$\epsilon_d = \frac{\ln[1 + (-0.20)]}{\ln[1 + (0.10)]} = \frac{\ln(0.80)}{\ln(1.10)} = -2.34$$

Both of these products, like other normal products, have a price elasticity that is less than -1.

---

[2] The term "ln( )" is the natural log function. You can compute the natural log of any number using the LN or lnx key on your calculator. For example, $\ln(0.85) = -0.1625$.

[3] This formula assumes that the price elasticity of demand is constant. This occurs when the relation between the selling price, p, and the unit sales, q, can be expressed in the following form: $\ln(q) = a + \epsilon_d \ln(p)$. Even if this is not precisely true, the formula provides a useful way to estimate a product's price elasticity.

[4] The estimated change in unit sales should take into account competitors' responses to a price change.

Note that the price elasticity of demand for the strawberry glycerin soap is larger (in absolute value) than the price elasticity of demand for the apple-almond shampoo. This indicates that the demand for strawberry glycerin soap is more elastic than the demand for apple-almond shampoo.

In the next subsection, the price elasticity of demand will be used to compute the selling price that maximizes the profits of the company.

The Profit-Maximizing Price

Under certain conditions, the profit-maximizing price can be determined by marking up *variable cost* using the following formula:[5]

$$\text{Profit-maximizing markup on variable cost} = \frac{-1}{1 + \epsilon_d}$$

Using the above markup, the selling price would be set using the formula:

$$\text{Profit-maximizing price} = (1 + \text{Profit-maximizing markup on variable cost}) \times \text{Variable cost per unit}$$

The profit-maximizing prices for the two Nature's Garden products are computed below using these formulas:

Apple-Almond Shampoo

$$\text{Profit-maximizing markup on variable cost} = \left|\frac{-1}{1 + (-1.71)}\right| = 1.41$$

$$\text{Profit-maximizing price} = (1 + 1.41)\$2.00 = \$4.82$$

Strawberry Glycerin Soap

$$\text{Profit-maximizing markup on variable cost} = \left|\frac{-1}{1 + (-2.34)}\right| = 0.75$$

$$\text{Profit-maximizing price} = (1 + 0.75)\$0.40 = \$0.70$$

Note that the 75% markup for the strawberry glycerin soap is lower than the 141% markup for the apple-almond shampoo. The reason for this is that the purchasers of strawberry glycerin soap are more sensitive to price than the purchasers of apple-almond shampoo. Strawberry glycerin soap is a relatively common product with close substitutes available in nearly every grocery store.

Exhibit A–1 shows how the profit-maximizing markup is generally affected by how sensitive unit sales are to price. For example, if a 10% increase in price leads to a 20% decrease in unit sales, then the optimal markup on variable cost according to the exhibit is 75%—the figure computed above for the strawberry glycerin soap. Note that the optimal markup drops as unit sales become more sensitive to price.

Caution is advised when using these formulas to establish a selling price. The formulas rely on simplifying assumptions and the estimate of the percentage change in unit sales that would result from a given percentage change in price is likely to be inexact. Nevertheless, the formulas can provide valuable clues regarding whether prices should be increased or decreased. Suppose, for example, that the strawberry glycerin soap is currently being sold for $0.60 per bar. The formula indicates that the profit-maximizing

---

[5] The formula assumes that (a) the price elasticity of demand is constant; (b) Total cost = Total fixed cost + Variable cost per unit × Quantity sold; and (c) the price of the product has no effect on the sales or costs of any other product. The formula can be derived using calculus.

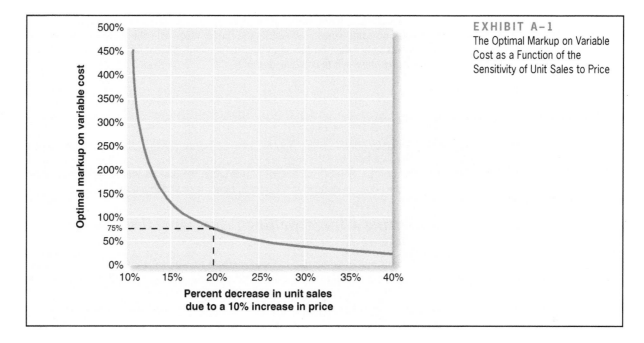

EXHIBIT A–1
The Optimal Markup on Variable Cost as a Function of the Sensitivity of Unit Sales to Price

price is $0.70 per bar. Rather than increasing the price by $0.10, it would be prudent to increase the price by a more modest amount to observe what happens to unit sales and to profits.

The formula for the profit-maximizing price conveys a very important lesson. If the total fixed costs are the same whether the company charges $0.60 or $0.70, they cannot be relevant in the decision of which price to charge for the soap. The optimal selling price should depend on two factors—the variable cost per unit and how sensitive unit sales are to changes in price. Fixed costs play no role in setting the optimal price. Fixed costs are relevant when deciding whether to offer a product but are not relevant when deciding how much to charge for the product.

We can directly verify that an increase in selling price for the strawberry glycerin soap from the current price of $0.60 per bar is warranted, based just on the forecast that a 10% increase in selling price would lead to a 20% decrease in unit sales. Suppose, for example, that Nature's Garden is currently selling 200,000 bars of the soap per year at the price of $0.60 a bar. If the change in price has no effect on the company's fixed costs or on other products, the effect on profits of increasing the price by 10% can be computed as follows:

	Present Price	Higher Price
Selling price (a)	$0.60	$0.60 + (0.10 × $0.60) = $0.66
Unit sales (b)	200,000	200,000 − (0.20 × 200,000) = 160,000
Sales (a) × (b)	$120,000	$105,600
Variable cost ($0.40 per unit)	80,000	64,000
Contribution margin	$ 40,000	$ 41,600

Despite the apparent optimality of prices based on marking up variable costs according to the price elasticity of demand, surveys consistently reveal that most managers approach the pricing problem from a completely different perspective. They prefer to mark up some version of full, not variable, costs, and the markup is based on desired profits rather than on factors related to demand. This approach is called the *absorption costing approach to cost-plus pricing.*

The Absorption Costing Approach to Cost-Plus Pricing

LOA–2

Compute the selling price of a product using the absorption costing approach.

The absorption costing approach to cost-plus pricing differs from the economists' approach both in what costs are marked up and in how the markup is determined. Under the absorption approach to cost-plus pricing, the cost base is the absorption costing unit product cost, as defined in Chapter 3, rather than variable cost.

Setting a Target Selling Price Using the Absorption Costing Approach

To illustrate, assume that the management of Ritter Company wants to set the selling price on a product that has just undergone some design modifications. The accounting department has provided cost estimates for the redesigned product as shown below:

	Per Unit	Total
Direct materials	$6	
Direct labor	$4	
Variable manufacturing overhead	$3	
Fixed manufacturing overhead		$70,000
Variable selling and administrative expenses	$2	
Fixed selling and administrative expenses		$60,000

The first step in the absorption costing approach to cost-plus pricing is to compute the unit product cost. For Ritter Company, this amounts to $20 per unit at a volume of 10,000 units, as computed below:

Direct materials	$ 6
Direct labor	4
Variable manufacturing overhead	3
Fixed manufacturing overhead ($70,000 ÷ 10,000 units)	7
Unit product cost	$20

Ritter Company has a general policy of marking up unit product costs by 50%. A price quotation sheet for the company prepared using the absorption approach is presented in Exhibit A–2. Note that selling and administrative expenses are not included in the cost base. Instead, the markup is supposed to cover these expenses.

EXHIBIT A–2
Price Quotation Sheet—
Absorption Basis (10,000 Units)

Direct materials	$ 6
Direct labor	4
Variable manufacturing overhead	3
Fixed manufacturing overhead (based on 10,000 units)	7
Unit product cost	20
Markup to cover selling and administrative expenses and desired profit—50% of unit manufacturing cost	10
Target selling price	$30

Determining the Markup Percentage

Ritter Company's markup percentage of 50% could be a widely used rule of thumb in the industry or just a company tradition that seems to work. The markup percentage may also be the result of an explicit computation. As we have discussed, the markup over cost should be largely determined by market conditions. However, many companies base their markup on cost and desired profit. The reasoning goes like this. The markup must be large enough to cover selling and administrative expenses and provide an adequate return on investment (ROI). Given the forecasted unit sales, the markup can be computed as follows:

$$\text{Markup percentage on absorption cost} = \frac{(\text{Required ROI} \times \text{Investment}) + \text{Selling and administrative expenses}}{\text{Unit product cost} \times \text{Unit sales}}$$

To show how this formula is applied, assume Ritter Company invests $100,000 in operating assets such as equipment to produce and market 10,000 units of the product each year. If Ritter Company requires a 20% ROI, then the markup for the product would be determined as follows:

$$\text{Markup percentage on absorption cost} = \frac{(20\% \times \$100{,}000) + (\$2 \text{ per unit} \times 10{,}000 \text{ units} + \$60{,}000)}{\$20 \text{ per unit} \times 10{,}000 \text{ units}}$$

$$= \frac{(\$20{,}000) + (\$80{,}000)}{\$200{,}000} = 50\%$$

As shown earlier, this markup of 50% leads to a target selling price of $30 for Ritter Company. *If the company actually sells 10,000 units* of the product at this price, the company's ROI on this product will indeed be 20%. This is verified in Exhibit A–3. However,

Direct materials	$ 6
Direct labor.	4
Variable manufacturing overhead	3
Fixed manufacturing overhead ($70,000 ÷ 10,000 units)	_7_
Unit product cost	$20

EXHIBIT A–3
Income Statement and ROI Analysis—Ritter Company Actual Unit Sales = 10,000 Units; Selling Price = $30

Ritter Company
Absorption Costing Income Statement

Sales ($30 per unit × 10,000 units)	$300,000
Cost of goods sold ($20 per unit × 10,000 units)	200,000
Gross margin	100,000
Selling and administrative expenses ($2 per unit × 10,000 units + $60,000)	80,000
Net operating income	$ 20,000

ROI

$$\text{ROI} = \frac{\text{Net operating income}}{\text{Average operating assets}}$$

$$= \frac{\$20{,}000}{\$100{,}000}$$

$$= 20\%$$

720 Appendix A

if it turns out that more than 10,000 units are sold at this price, the ROI will be greater than 20%. If less than 10,000 units are sold, the ROI will be less than 20%. *The required ROI will be attained only if the forecasted unit sales volume is attained.*

Problems with the Absorption Costing Approach

The absorption costing approach makes pricing decisions look deceptively simple. All a company needs to do is compute its unit product cost, decide how much profit it wants, and then set its price. It appears that a company can ignore demand and arrive at a price that will safely yield whatever profit it wants. However, as noted above, the absorption costing approach relies on a forecast of unit sales. Neither the markup nor the unit product cost can be computed without such a forecast.

The absorption costing approach essentially assumes that customers *need* the forecasted unit sales and will pay whatever price the company decides to charge. However, customers have a choice. If the price is too high, they can buy from a competitor or they may choose not to buy at all. Suppose, for example, that when Ritter Company sets its price at $30, it sells only 7,000 units rather than the 10,000 units forecasted. As shown in Exhibit A–4, the company would then have a loss of $25,000 on the product instead of a profit of $20,000.[6] Some managers believe that the absorption costing approach to pricing is safe. This is an illusion. The absorption costing approach is safe only if customers choose to buy at least as many units as managers forecasted they would buy.

EXHIBIT A–4
Income Statement and ROI Analysis—Ritter Company Actual Unit Sales = 7,000 Units; Selling Price = $30

Direct materials	$ 6
Direct labor	4
Variable manufacturing overhead	3
Fixed manufacturing overhead ($70,000 ÷ 7,000 units)	10
Unit product cost	$23

Ritter Company
Absorption Costing Income Statement

Sales ($30 per unit × 7,000 units)	$210,000
Cost of goods sold ($23 per unit × 7,000 units)	161,000
Gross margin	49,000
Selling and administrative expenses ($2 per unit × 7,000 units + $60,000)	74,000
Net operating loss	$ (25,000)

ROI

$$\text{ROI} = \frac{\text{Net operating income}}{\text{Average operating assets}}$$

$$= \frac{-\$25,000}{\$100,000}$$

$$= -25\%$$

---

[6] It may be *impossible* to break even using an absorption costing approach when the company has more than one product—even when it would be possible to make substantial profits using the economists' approach to pricing. For details, see Eric Noreen and David Burgstahler, "Full Cost Pricing and the Illusion of Satisficing," *Journal of Management Accounting Research* 9 (1997).

Target Costing

LOA–3
Compute the target cost for a new product or service.

Our discussion thus far has presumed that a product has already been developed, has been costed, and is ready to be marketed as soon as a price is set. In many cases, the sequence of events is just the reverse. That is, the company already *knows* what price should be charged, and the problem is to *develop* a product that can be marketed profitably at the desired price. Even in this situation, where the normal sequence of events is reversed, cost is still a crucial factor. The company can use an approach called *target costing*. **Target costing** is the process of determining the maximum allowable cost for a new product and then developing a prototype that can be profitably made for that maximum target cost figure. A number of companies have used target costing, including Compaq, Culp, Cummins Engine, Daihatsu Motors, Chrysler, Ford, Isuzu Motors, ITT Automotive, Komatsu, Matsushita Electric, Mitsubishi Kasei, NEC, Nippodenso, Nissan, Olympus, Sharp, Texas Instruments, and Toyota.

The target cost for a product is computed by starting with the product's anticipated selling price and then deducting the desired profit, as follows:

$$\text{Target cost} = \text{Anticipated selling price} - \text{Desired profit}$$

The product development team is then given the responsibility of designing the product so that it can be made for no more than the target cost.

Reasons for Using Target Costing

The target costing approach was developed in recognition of two important characteristics of markets and costs. The first is that many companies have less control over price than they would like to think. The market (i.e., supply and demand) really determines price, and a company that attempts to ignore this does so at its peril. Therefore, the anticipated market price is taken as a given in target costing. The second observation is that most of a product's cost is determined in the design stage. Once a product has been designed and has gone into production, not much can be done to significantly reduce its cost. Most of the opportunities to reduce cost come from designing the product so that it is simple to make, uses inexpensive parts, and is robust and reliable. If the company has little control over market price and little control over cost once the product has gone into production, then it follows that the major opportunities for affecting profit come in the design stage where valuable features that customers are willing to pay for can be added and where most of the costs are really determined. So that is where the effort is concentrated—in designing and developing the product. The difference between target costing and other approaches to product development is profound. Instead of designing the product and then finding out how much it costs, the target cost is set first and then the product is designed so that the target cost is attained.

An Example of Target Costing

To provide a simple example of target costing, assume the following situation: Handy Company wishes to invest $2,000,000 to design, develop, and produce a new hand mixer. The company's Marketing Department surveyed the features and prices of competing products and determined that a price of $30 would enable Handy to sell an estimated 40,000 hand mixers per year. Because the company desires a 15% ROI, the target cost to manufacture, sell, distribute, and service one mixer is $22.50 as computed below:

Projected sales (40,000 mixers × $30 per mixer)	$1,200,000
Less desired profit (15% × $2,000,000)	300,000
Target cost for 40,000 mixers	$ 900,000
Target cost per mixer ($900,000 ÷ 40,000 mixers)	$22.50

This $22.50 target cost would be broken down into target costs for the various functions: manufacturing, marketing, distribution, after-sales service, and so on. Each functional area would be responsible for keeping its actual costs within target.

Summary

Pricing involves a delicate balancing act. Higher prices result in more revenue per unit but drive down unit sales. Exactly where to set prices to maximize profit is a difficult problem, but, in general, the markup over cost should be highest for those products where customers are least sensitive to price. The demand for such products is said to be price inelastic.

Managers often rely on cost-plus formulas to set target prices. From the economists' point of view, the cost base for the markup should be variable cost. In contrast, in the absorption costing approach the cost base is the absorption costing unit product cost and the markup is computed to cover both nonmanufacturing costs and to provide an adequate return on investment. With the absorption approach, costs will not be covered and return on investment will not be adequate unless the unit sales forecast used in the cost-plus formula is accurate. If applying the cost-plus formula results in a price that is too high, the unit sales forecast will not be attained.

Some companies take a different approach to pricing. Instead of starting with costs and then determining prices, they start with prices and then determine allowable costs. Companies that use target costing estimate what a new product's market price is likely to be based on its anticipated features and prices of products already on the market. They subtract desired profit from the estimated market price to arrive at the product's target cost. The design and development team is then given the responsibility of ensuring that the actual cost of the new product does not exceed the target cost.

Glossary

Cost-plus pricing A pricing method in which a predetermined markup is applied to a cost base to determine the target selling price. (p. 714)

Markup The difference between the selling price of a product or service and its cost. The markup is usually expressed as a percentage of cost. (p. 714)

Price elasticity of demand A measure of the degree to which a change in price affects the unit sales of a product or service. (p. 715)

Target costing The process of determining the maximum allowable cost for a new product and then developing a prototype that can be profitably made for that maximum target cost figure. (p. 721)

Questions

A–1 What is cost-plus pricing?

A–2 What does the price elasticity of demand measure? What is inelastic demand? What is elastic demand?

A–3 According to the economists' approach to setting prices, the profit-maximizing price should depend on what two factors?

A–4 Which product should have a larger markup over variable cost, a product whose demand is elastic or a product whose demand is inelastic?

A–5 When the absorption costing approach to cost-plus pricing is used, what is the markup supposed to cover?

A–6 What assumption does the absorption costing approach make about how consumers react to prices?

A–7 Discuss the following statement: "Full cost can be viewed as a floor of protection. If a company always sets its prices above full cost, it will never have to worry about operating at a loss."

A–8 What is target costing? How do target costs enter into the pricing decision?

Multiple-choice questions are provided on the text website at www.mhhe.com/garrison15e.

Exercises

All applicable exercises are available with McGraw-Hill's *Connect® Accounting.*

EXERCISE A–1 The Economists' Approach to Pricing [LOA–1]

Maria Lorenzi owns an ice cream stand that she operates during the summer months in West Yellowstone, Montana. Her store caters primarily to tourists passing through town on their way to Yellowstone National Park.

Maria is unsure of how she should price her ice cream cones and has experimented with two prices in successive weeks during the busy August season. The number of people who entered the store was roughly the same each week. During the first week, she priced the cones at $1.89 and 1,500 cones were sold. During the second week, she priced the cones at $1.49 and 2,340 cones were sold. The variable cost of a cone is $0.43 and consists solely of the costs of the ice cream and of the cone itself. The fixed expenses of the ice cream stand are $675 per week.

Required:
1. Did Maria make more money selling the cones for $1.89 or for $1.49?
2. Estimate the price elasticity of demand for the ice cream cones.
3. Estimate the profit-maximizing price for ice cream cones.

EXERCISE A–2 Absorption Costing Approach to Setting a Selling Price [LOA–2]

Martin Company is considering the introduction of a new product. To determine a selling price, the company has gathered the following information:

Number of units to be produced and sold each year	14,000
Unit product cost	$25
Projected annual selling and administrative expenses	$50,000
Estimated investment required by the company	$750,000
Desired return on investment (ROI)	12%

Required:
The company uses the absorption costing approach to cost-plus pricing.
1. Compute the markup required to achieve the desired ROI.
2. Compute the selling price per unit.

EXERCISE A–3 Target Costing [LOA–3]

Shimada Products Corporation of Japan is anxious to enter the electronic calculator market. Management believes that in order to be competitive in world markets, the price of the electronic calculator that the company is developing cannot exceed $15. Shimada's required rate of return is 12% on all investments. An investment of $5,000,000 would be required to purchase the equipment needed to produce the 300,000 calculators that management believes can be sold each year at the $15 price.

Required:
Compute the target cost of one calculator.

PROBLEM A–4 The Economists' Approach to Pricing [LOA–1]

The postal service of St. Vincent, an island in the West Indies, obtains a significant portion of its revenues from sales of special souvenir sheets to stamp collectors. The souvenir sheets usually contain several high-value St. Vincent stamps depicting a common theme, such as the life of Princess Diana. The souvenir sheets are designed and printed for the postal service by Imperial Printing, a stamp agency service company in the United Kingdom. The souvenir sheets cost the postal service $0.80 each. St. Vincent has been selling these souvenir sheets for $7.00 each and ordinarily sells about 100,000 units. To test the market, the postal service recently priced a new souvenir sheet at $8.00 and sales dropped to 85,000 units.

Required:
1. Does the postal service of St. Vincent make more money selling souvenir sheets for $7.00 each or $8.00 each?
2. Estimate the price elasticity of demand for the souvenir sheets.
3. Estimate the profit-maximizing price for souvenir sheets.
4. If Imperial Printing increases the price it charges to the St. Vincent postal service for souvenir sheets to $1.00 each, how much should the St. Vincent postal service charge its customers for the souvenir sheets?

Problems   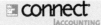 ACCOUNTING

All applicable problems are available with McGraw-Hill's *Connect*® Accounting.

PROBLEM A–5 Standard Costs; Absorption Costing Approach to Setting Prices [LOA–2]

Wilderness Products, Inc., has designed a self-inflating sleeping pad for use by backpackers and campers. The following information is available about the new product:

a.   An investment of $1,350,000 will be necessary to carry inventories and accounts receivable and to purchase some new equipment needed in the manufacturing process. The company's required rate of return is 24% on all investments.

b.   A standard cost card has been prepared for the sleeping pad, as shown below:

	Standard Quantity or Hours	Standard Price or Rate	Standard Cost
Direct materials	4.0 yards	$2.70 per yard	$10.80
Direct labor	2.4 hours	$8.00 per hour	19.20
Manufacturing overhead (⅕ variable)	2.4 hours	$12.50 per hour	30.00
Total standard cost per pad			$60.00

c.   The only variable selling and administrative expense will be a sales commission of $9 per pad. Fixed selling and administrative expenses will be (per year):

Salaries	$ 82,000
Warehouse rent	50,000
Advertising and other	600,000
Total	$732,000

d.   Because the company manufactures many products, no more than 38,400 direct labor-hours per year can be devoted to production of the new sleeping pads.

e.   Manufacturing overhead costs are allocated to products on the basis of direct labor-hours.

Required:

1.   Assume that the company uses the absorption approach to cost-plus pricing.
    a.   Compute the markup that the company needs on the pads to achieve a 24% return on investment (ROI) if it sells all of the pads it can produce.
    b.   Using the markup you have computed, prepare a price quotation sheet for a single sleeping pad.
    c.   Assume that the company is able to sell all of the pads that it can produce. Prepare an income statement for the first year of activity and compute the company's ROI for the year on the pads, using the ROI formula from Chapter 11.

2.   After marketing the sleeping pads for several years, the company is experiencing a falloff in demand due to an economic recession. A large retail outlet will make a bulk purchase of pads if its label is sewn in and if an acceptable price can be worked out. What is the minimum acceptable price for this special order?

PROBLEM A–6 Missing Data; Markup Computations: Return on Investment (ROI); Pricing [LOA–2]

South Seas Products, Inc., has designed a new surfboard to replace its old surfboard line. Because of the unique design of the new surfboard, the company anticipates that it will be able to sell all the boards that it can produce. On this basis, the following incomplete budgeted income statement for the first year of activity is available:

Sales (? boards at ? per board)	$?
Cost of goods sold (? boards at ? per board)	1,600,000
Gross margin	?
Selling and administrative expenses	1,130,000
Net operating income	$?

Additional information on the new surfboard follows:

a. An investment of $1,500,000 will be necessary to carry inventories and accounts receivable and to purchase some new equipment. The company's required rate of return is 18% on all investments.

b. A partially completed standard cost card for the new surfboard follows:

	Standard Quantity or Hours	Standard Price or Rate	Standard Cost
Direct materials	6 feet	$4.50 per foot	$27
Direct labor	2 hours	? per hour	?
Manufacturing overhead	? hours	? per hour	?
Total standard cost per surfboard			$?

c. The company will employ 20 workers to make the new surfboards. Each will work a 40-hour week, 50 weeks a year.

d. Other information relating to production and costs follows:

Variable manufacturing overhead cost (per board)	$5
Variable selling expense (per board)	$10
Fixed manufacturing overhead cost (total)	$600,000
Fixed selling and administrative expense (total)	$?
Number of boards produced and sold (per year)	?

e. Overhead costs are allocated to production on the basis of direct labor-hours.

Required:

1. Complete the standard cost card for a single surfboard.
2. Assume that the company uses the absorption costing approach to cost-plus pricing.
    a. Compute the markup that the company needs on the surfboards to achieve an 18% return on investment (ROI).
    b. Using the markup you have computed, prepare a price quotation sheet for a single surfboard.
    c. Assume, as stated, that the company is able to sell all of the surfboards that it can produce. Complete the income statement for the first year of activity, and then compute the company's ROI for the year.
3. Assuming that direct labor is a variable cost, how many units would the company have to sell at the price you computed in (2) above to achieve the 18% ROI? How many units would have to be sold to just break even?

PROBLEM A–7 The Economists' Approach to Pricing; Absorption Costing Approach to Cost-Plus Pricing [LOA–1, LOA–2]

Software Solutions, Inc., was started by two young software engineers to market SpamBlocker, a software application they had written that screens incoming e-mail messages and eliminates unsolicited mass mailings. Sales of the software have been good at 50,000 units a month, but the company has been losing money as shown below:

Sales (50,000 units × $25 per unit)	$1,250,000
Variable cost (50,000 units × $6 per unit)	300,000
Contribution margin	950,000
Fixed expenses	960,000
Net operating loss	$ (10,000)

The company's only variable cost is the $6 fee it pays to another company to reproduce the software on CDs, print manuals, and package the result in an attractive box for sale to consumers. Monthly fixed selling and administrative expenses are $960,000.

The company's marketing manager has been arguing for some time that the software is priced too high. She estimates that every 5% decrease in price will yield an 8% increase in unit sales. The marketing manager would like your help in preparing a presentation to the company's owners concerning the pricing issue.

726   Appendix A

Required:

1. To help the marketing manager prepare for her presentation, she has asked you to fill in the blanks in the following table. The selling prices in the table were computed by successively decreasing the selling price by 5%. The estimated unit sales were computed by successively increasing the unit sales by 8%. For example, $23.75 is 5% less than $25.00 and 54,000 units is 8% more than 50,000 units.

Selling Price	Estimated Unit Sales	Sales	Variable Cost	Fixed Expenses	Net Operating Income
$25.00	50,000	$1,250,000	$300,000	$960,000	$(10,000)
$23.75	54,000	$1,282,500	$324,000	$960,000	$ (1,500)
$22.56	58,320	?	?	?	?
$21.43	62,986	?	?	?	?
$20.36	68,025	?	?	?	?
$19.34	73,467	?	?	?	?
$18.37	79,344	?	?	?	?
$17.45	85,692	?	?	?	?
$16.58	92,547	?	?	?	?
$15.75	99,951	?	?	?	?

2. Using the data from the table, construct a chart that shows the net operating income as a function of the selling price. Put the selling price on the *X*-axis and the net operating income on the *Y*-axis. Using the chart, determine the approximate selling price at which net operating income is maximized.
3. Compute the price elasticity of demand for the SpamBlocker software. Based on this calculation, what is the profit-maximizing price?
4. The owners have invested $2,000,000 in the company and feel that they should be earning at least 2% per month on these funds. If the absorption costing approach to pricing were used, what would be the target selling price based on the current sales of 50,000 units? What do you think would happen to the net operating income of the company if this price were charged?
5. If the owners of the company are dissatisfied with the net operating income and return on investment at the selling price you computed in (3) above, should they increase the selling price? Explain.

PROBLEM A–8 Target Costing [LOA–3]

National Restaurant Supply, Inc., sells restaurant equipment and supplies throughout most of the United States. Management is considering adding a machine that makes sorbet to its line of ice cream making machines. Management will negotiate the price of the sorbet machine with its Swedish manufacturer.

Management of National Restaurant Supply believes the sorbet machine can be sold to its customers in the United States for $4,950. At that price, annual sales of the sorbet machine should be 100 units. If the sorbet machine is added to National Restaurant Supply's product lines, the company will have to invest $600,000 in inventories and special warehouse fixtures. The variable cost of selling the sorbet machines would be $650 per machine.

Required:

1. If National Restaurant Supply requires a 15% return on investment (ROI), what is the maximum amount the company would be willing to pay the Swedish manufacturer for the sorbet machines?
2. The manager who is flying to Sweden to negotiate the purchase price of the machines would like to know how the purchase price of the machines would affect National Restaurant Supply's ROI. Construct a chart that shows National Restaurant Supply's ROI as a function of the purchase price of the sorbet machine. Put the purchase price on the *X*-axis and the resulting ROI on the *Y*-axis. Plot the ROI for purchase prices between $3,000 and $4,000 per machine.
3. After many hours of negotiations, management has concluded that the Swedish manufacturer is unwilling to sell the sorbet machine at a low enough price so that National Restaurant Supply is able to earn its 15% required ROI. Apart from simply giving up on the idea of adding the sorbet machine to National Restaurant Supply's product lines, what could management do?

Online Supplements

Connect Accounting with LearnSmart One-Semester Online Access for Managerial Accounting, 15th Edition

McGraw-Hill Connect is a digital teaching and learning environment that improves performance over a variety of critical outcomes. With Connect, instructors can deliver assignments, quizzes and tests easily online. Students can practice important skills at their own pace and on their own schedule.

HOW TO REGISTER

Using a <u>Print Book</u>?
To register and activate your Connect account, simply follow these easy steps:
1. **Go to the Connect course web address provided by your instructor or visit the Connect link set up on your instructor's course within your campus learning management system.**
2. **Click on the link to register.**
3. **When prompted, enter the Connect code found on the inside back cover of your book and click Submit. Complete the brief registration form that follows to begin using Connect.**

Using an <u>eBook</u>?
To register and activate your Connect account, simply follow these easy steps:
1. **Upon purchase of your eBook, you will be granted automatic access to Connect.**
2. **Go to the Connect course web address provided by your instructor or visit the Connect link set up on your instructor's course within your campus learning management system.**
3. **Sign in using the same email address and password you used to register on the eBookstore. Complete your registration and begin using Connect.**

Note: Access Code is for one use only. If you did not purchase this book new, the access code included in this book is no longer valid.

Need help? Visit mhhe.com/support